"In *Freethinker*, Andrée Lévesque unveils a fascinating woman: an uncompromising mind, a skilful and prolific writer, and a pioneer of Montreal's public libraries. From this insightful portrait and rich analysis, Éva Circé-Côté emerges as a woman with deep convictions, but also with the self-contradictions of a woman with an open mind. Simultaneously a patriot, a feminist, a liberal, and a progressive, she is an essential figure to study in order to better understand the ideas and culture of early twentieth-century Quebec."

— CAROLINE DURAND, associate professor, History Department, Trent University

"This book is another tour de force for Andrée Lévesque. Éva Circé-Côté comes alive as a poet, writer, journalist, playwright, and musician. Lévesque provides the reader with a thorough contextualization of Circé-Côté's life in Montreal and its cultural scene from the early 1900s to the interwar years. This must-read will delight and inform all those who want to know more about Éva Circé-Côté's contributions to Quebec history and its ideas."

— CHERYL GOSSELIN, professor, Sociology Department, Bishop's University

"How did we ever make sense of the early years of feminism in Canada without understanding the crucial complexities of life in Montreal? In an extraordinary work of biographical research, Lévesque opens up to us a crucial period in Canadian history through the life of a feminist, liberal, Quebec writer of amazing resilience. This is a truly splendid work."

— LORNA MARSDEN, feminist, professor, and formal Liberal senator

FREETHINKER

The Life and Works of
ÉVA CIRCÉ-CÔTÉ

ANDRÉE LÉVESQUE

Translated by Lazer Lederhendler

Between the Lines
Toronto

Freethinker

Originally published in French as Éva Circé-Côté, libre penseuse, 1871–1949
© Les Éditions du remue-ménage, Montreal, 2010
www.editions-rm.ca

English translation
© 2017 Lazer Lederhendler

First published in English translation in 2017 by
Between the Lines
401 Richmond Street West, Studio 281
Toronto, Ontario M5V 3A8 Canada
1-800-718-7201
www.btlbooks.com

All rights reserved. No part of this publication may be photocopied, reproduced, stored in a retrieval system, or transmitted in any form or by any means, electronic, mechanical, recording, or otherwise, without the written permission of Between the Lines, or (for photocopying in Canada only) Access Copyright, 320 – 56 Wellesley Street West, Toronto, Ontario, M5S 2S3.

Every reasonable effort has been made to identify copyright holders.
Between the Lines would be pleased to have any errors or omissions brought to its attention.

Library and Archives Canada Cataloguing in Publication

Lévesque, Andrée
[Éva Circé-Côté, libre-penseuse, 1871-1949. English]
Freethinker : the life and works of Éva Circé Côté / Andrée Lévesque ;
translated by Lazer Lederhendler.

Translation of: Éva Circé-Côté, libre penseuse, 1871-1949.
Includes bibliographical references and index.
Issued in print and electronic formats.
ISBN 978-1-77113-331-9 (softcover).—ISBN 978-1-77113-332-6 (EPUB).
ISBN 978-1-77113-333-3 (PDF)

1. Circé-Côté, Ève, 1871-1949. 2. Authors, Canadian (French)—Québec (Province)—Biography.
3. Freethinkers—Québec (Province)—Biography. I. Lederhendler, Lazer, 1950–, translator
II. Title. III. Title: Éva Circé-Côté, libre-penseuse, 1871-1949. English

PS8455.O58Z7613 2017   C848'.52   C2017-903010-8
                          C2017-903011-6

Cover design by Gordon Robertson
Printed in Canada

We acknowledge for their financial support of our publishing activities: the Government of Canada; the Canada Council for the Arts, which last year invested $153 million to bring the arts to Canadians throughout the country; and the Government of Ontario through the Ontario Arts Council, the Ontario Book Publishers Tax Credit program, and the Ontario Media Development Corporation.

We acknowledge the financial support of the Government of Canada through the National Translation Program for Book Publishing, an initiative of the *Roadmap for Canada's Official Languages 2013-2018: Education, Immigration, Communities*, for our translation activities.

This book has been published with the help of a grant from the Federation for the Humanities and Social Sciences, through the Awards to Scholarly Publications Program, using funds provided by the Social Sciences and Humanities Research Council of Canada.

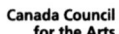   

For Alexandra, Jeanne, and Julia

CONTENTS

Acknowledgements ix
Foreword xiii

Part One

1 Woman of Letters on the Cusp of the Century   3
2 Woe to That Woman By Whom the Offence Cometh   37
3 Socially Committed City-Dweller in a Country at War   75
4 Enlightened Citizen   113
5 To Live Is to Fight   155

Part Two

6 Liberalism   175
7 Religion   197
8 Patriotism, French Canadians, and Others   221
9 Feminisms   249
10 The Right to Work and Women's Work   285
   Conclusion   305

Notes   309
Appendices   377
Bibliography   381
Index   395

ACKNOWLEDGEMENTS

ACKNOWLEDGEMENTS are in order, and it has become almost a formality to list everyone who contributed to the research for a book. I might feel uncomfortable about trotting out the usual tired clichés and phrases, but there are only a limited number of ways to say thank you. To appreciate the importance of the assistance I received from many people, one should keep in mind that Éva Circé-Côté left no personal documents, diaries, correspondence, memoires, or autobiography. True, she had amassed an impressive number of papers, two unpublished manuscripts—a novel and a collection of biographies of historical figures—but after her death, her daughter, accompanied by a friend, decided, in the face of "such a jumble," to throw everything out. I therefore had to reconstruct her life from her 1,798 columns, her two published books—*Bleu, Blanc, Rouge* and *Papineau*—and a few portraits reproduced in publications at the turn of the twentieth century.

There are two people who helped to enrich this book with extremely valuable biographical information. The first is Danaé Michaud-Mastoras, Éva Circé-Côté's great-great-niece. She approached me after deciding to write her master's dissertation on her great-great-aunt's writings for the stage. Danaé Michaud-Mastoras found the script of *Maisonneuve*, staged in 1921, and successfully defended her dissertation under the direction of Micheline Cambron at the Université de Montréal. Thanks to Danaé, I met two of Éva Circé-Côté's great-nieces, the daughters of her sister Maria. Andrée Michaud and Marie Michaud, Danaé's mother, contributed some unpublished photos. Andrée Michaud's husband, Jean-Charles Labbé, traced the family tree of the Circés and Côtés back to the first immigration from Europe. Anne Michaud allowed me to photograph the three paintings by Éva Circé-Côté in her possession. Without the generosity of the Michaud family, a whole area of Éva Circé-Côté's personal life would have eluded me.

For a long time, my quest for correspondence between Éva Circé-Côté and her intimates went nowhere, until Gustave Labbé, a professor of literature, a poet, and an authority on the poet Marcel Dugas, shared with me the fruits of his research on Dugas, an intimate of Circé-Côté despite being twelve years her junior. She was his mentor, his friend, and his colleague at the Municipal Library. Gustave and Marie Labbé received me more than once at their home and in their garden in the Notre-Dame-de-Grâce neighbourhood. Mr. Labbé was glad to share with me five long letters that Éva Circé-Côté had written to Marcel Dugas, as well as the notes from interviews he had conducted over many years with friends and relations of Dugas and Circé-Côté. It was Danaé Michaud-Mastoras and Gustave Labbé who enabled us to become more closely acquainted with Éva Circé.

For many years I was not aware that hidden behind the pseudonym Julien Saint-Michel was a literary woman. In 1991, Lisette Girouard and Nicole Brossard published *Anthologie de la poésie des femmes du Québec: des origines à nos jours* (Éditions du remue-ménage), an anthology of women's poetry in Quebec, which included a poem by Colombine and identified nearly all the pseudonyms used by Éva Circé-Côté. This was vital for the pursuit of my research.

Several historians and colleagues directed me to relevant archives or answered baffling questions. Michelle Dagenais, whose work at the Municipal Library is well known, put me on the trail to Éva Circé-Côté's employment file. Micheline Dumont, a walking encyclopaedia, whom I too often bothered with my queries, displayed great generosity and never discouraged my questions about education and feminism. Among other things, she led me to the letters held in the archives of the Congrégation de Notre-Dame concerning the Lycée des jeunes filles.

The historian Marcel Bellavance, himself a descendant of the Côtés of Rimouski, provided me with information on the family of Éva Circé's husband, Pierre-Salomon Côté.

Circé-Côté was a musician as well as a literary woman, and Marie-Thérèse Lefebvre, a historian of music in Quebec, shared her findings with me a number of times.

Other friends and colleagues read chapters of the manuscript and made suggestions. Ian McKay, an expert on the Left and on the Canadian liberal state, offered advice on various aspects of Circé-Côté's liberalism.

Sean Mills was highly supportive, and I am indebted to him for comments that have made it easier to grasp Circé-Côté's patriotism.

On several occasions I turned to Gregory Baum to help me locate and understand the papal encyclicals that had left their mark on Circé-Côté's epoch. He consistently supported me, and I am thankful for his observations on the chapters dealing with religion and patriotism.

Others who read chapters, provided references, and endured my endless queries include: Brian Young, Maïe Fortin, Patrick Tillard, Jeanne Maranda, and Paul Gradvohl. They have my wholehearted gratitude.

The demographer Hubert Charbonneau untangled the skein of biographical information, the dates and places of births and marriages, of the Circé and Côté families. I could not have wished for a better guide.

One episode illustrates the labyrinth of historical research and the importance of collaboration among friends and colleagues. While sifting through the correspondence between Louis Dantin and Alfred Desrochers, the Belgian historian Cécile Vanderpelen stumbled on an allusion to an article by Éva Circé-Côté in the *Jewish Daily Eagle* (Kanader Adler). My own research at the Montreal Jewish Public Library had been fruitless, as I was told that this newspaper had been published only in Yiddish. Later, Pierre Anctil informed me that for its twenty-fifth anniversary in 1932, the paper had invited French-speaking and English-speaking personalities to contribute to a special issue. The archivist Shannon Hodge found this edition shortly before I was to submit the manuscript to my publisher. Thus, I have a three-fold debt for this piece of detective work.

I am very grateful to Jean-Louis Lalonde of the United Church for having directed me to the Francophone protestant newspaper *L'Aurore*, archived at the Evangelical Theological College. I will not forget Eric Reiter's generosity in sharing his research on Circé-Côté's court case against the *Standard* just in time for me to include this significant episode in this English edition.

It behoves me to mention as well Lyse Nantais Picher, the daughter of Isaïe Nantais; unable to find the correspondence between her parents and Éva Circé-Côté, she sent me a lovely silver bonbonnière that Circé-Côte had given them for their wedding in 1914. "It was our only wedding gift," they had said.

Like any historian, I had to rely on the help of archivists in numerous archival repositories. It was essential to go back to Éva Circé-Côté's early education, given all the emphasis she placed on instruction and reading. The research carried out by Hélène Élément, the archivist of the Sisters of Saint Anne, was crucial for my efforts to reconstruct the formative years of the future poet. Thanks also to Catherine Bouillez of the Collège de l'Assomption's archives, the archivists of the Centre de recherche en civilisation française, and those of the City of Montreal.

Finally, what would we do without our research assistants? Élise Detellier, Sean Mills, Dahlia Smolash, and Catherine Brathwaite, among others, spent long, tedious hours photocopying innumerable columns, freeing me up to devote myself to more creative work, which their help made possible.

I must also mention the students in Denyse Baillargeon's history seminar, who gave me the decisive nudge that prompted me to undertake this biography.

In addition, my heartfelt appreciation goes to the members of the Groupe d'histoire de Montréal, my scientific family, for their encouragement. I imagine that they are relieved to know that henceforth I can talk to them about other subjects.

Lastly, I must thank my publisher, Élise Bergeron, for her invaluable work to find pictures and illustrations, and Rachel Bédard, for her unflagging support and encouragement over the years.

For this translation, I was fortunate to have Lazer Lederhendler as translator; I couldn't have wished for anyone better. I owe a great debt to Between the Lines and especially to Cameron Duder whose meticulous copy-editing helped me correct ambiguities, imprecisions, and incomplete footnotes. And my thanks to Bettina Bradbury for having introduced me to Amanda Crocker, the managing editor of Between the Lines.

To all these people, and to those I may have forgotten: many thanks.

And, as is the custom, I affirm that any factual errors or misinterpretations are mine alone.

FOREWORD

Beginnings

FOR A LONG TIME the journalist Julien Saint-Michel remained an enigma. Twenty-odd years ago I read his columns in *Le Monde ouvrier* when I was looking for a discourse at variance with the religious and intellectual norms prevailing in Quebec during the interwar period, especially on the subject of women. What I found was an outlook uncommon in Quebec at the time, one supporting women's employment, wage parity, women's suffrage, and—a rarity in North America—the toleration and regulation of prostitution. Who was it that had dared to express such ideas between 1916 and 1936? I spoke to Geoffrey Ewen, who was drafting a master's thesis on Gustave Francq, the editor-in-chief of *Le Monde ouvrier*. He, too, had read Saint-Michel's columns but, like me, did not know who this journalist was. I also consulted André LeBlanc, who had written his doctoral dissertation on *Le Monde ouvrier*. He was as intrigued as I was. He had tried to discover the identity of this mysterious person and had even discussed the matter with Francq's nephew, his successor at *Le Monde ouvrier*, who could not recall having met this colleague in the newsroom. A hypothesis was formulated: I believed that for the journalist behind the name Saint-Michel to articulate such opinions he must have been European. Possibly Belgian, LeBlanc added, because Francq hailed from Belgium. Or was it Francq himself who had put forward his boldest ideas under that pseudonym? I therefore cited the writings of the avant-gardist Saint-Michel in *La Norme et les Déviantes*, a book about the discourses on women's sexuality during the interwar period.

A few years later, Rachel Bédard of Les Éditions du remue-ménage, the publisher of the work in which I had quoted Saint-Michel, called to tell me she knew who was hiding behind the pen name: a poet named Colombine, whom I had come across in my literary history textbook by Camille Roy when I was in secondary school. How had she made the connection between the poet of the turn of the twentieth century and the columnist for a trade union periodical? The *Anthologie de la poésie des femmes au Québec* (Anthology of women's poetry in Quebec), edited by Nicole Brossard and Lisette Girouard and published by Remue–ménage, included poems by Colombine together with a biographical note listing most of Éva Circé-Côté's pseudonyms: Colombine, Musette, Jean Nay, Paul S. Bédard, Arthur Maheu, and Julien Saint-Michel, all found in *Pseudonymes canadiens* by Francis-J. Audet and Gérard Malchelosse. Neither a Belgian nor a trade unionist, but a Québécoise, a lifelong resident of Montreal educated by the Sisters of Saint Anne, turned out to be the author of numerous columns in a dozen publications.

Andrée Michaud, the granddaughter of Maria Circé-Michaud, showed me the family albums and shared the precious photographs reproduced here. Her husband, Charles-Eugène Labbé, presented me with the family tree he had established of the Circé and Côté families, including both the maternal and paternal forebears. Another great-niece of Éva Circé-Côté, the artist Anne Michaud, allowed me to photograph the three pictures (one oil and two pastels) by her great-aunt that were in her possession. I was soon informed of the pseudonym's origin: Julien Saint-Michel was Éva Circé's grandfather.

Throughout the research work, I was constantly evaluating my sources. This is true for all historians, but the multiple pen names and the varied nature of the texts and subjects covered by Éva Circé-Côté demanded that I be especially attentive. Consequently, I generally take the statements of Arthur Maheu—made in a comical vein—less seriously than those of Jean Nay or Fantasio. And I attribute more weight to letters addressed to a close friend, more specifically the poet Marcel Dugas, than to some of the columns.

I am well aware that I my exploration of certain aspects of her writing is insufficient. I leave it up to postcolonial studies specialists to interpret the articles on the First Nations, just as I leave it up to literary scholars to analyze Éva Circé-Côté's stories and poems.

Biography

While the grand narratives have gone out of fashion, biography continues to serve as a vehicle for depicting an era. The material is all the richer if the biography's subject was an illustrious writer for more than forty years. Éva Circé-Côté's wrote in a range of genres, including poetry, drama, journalism, history, and fiction, but she left very little in the way of personal texts; her columns in various weeklies were the main source.

To quote Pierre Bourdieu: "writing is the product of a practice subjected in part to a social rationale." For the biographer, the columns that Éva Circé-Côté left us are not at first glance significant for aesthetic reasons—though one day literary scholars will study them from that perspective—but rather because of their value as documents enabling one to paint the portrait of an era, a portrait both social and cultural, with its palimpsests, its chiaroscuro, its metaphorical trompe l'oeils, and its protean representations. Like any work of art, such a portrait constructs and subverts. And what's more, it is bound up with a particular context: it tells a Montreal story. Montreal in all its urbanity, with its factory chimneys, its streetcars, its kaleidoscopic crowds, its pungent marketplaces, and its street scenes. The Montreal that Éva Circé-Côté loved and knew how to describe, the city she represented and sought to reform. This writer is part of the collective imaginary of an entire historical period, of its Zeitgeist and Weltanschauung, as the German philosophers would say, and, through her writings, she allows us to better understand the culture of the first four decades of the twentieth century.

Given the lack of a personal diary, the scarcity of letters, and the virtually inexistent interviews or contemporary accounts after 1903, the columns, which comprise nearly all of Éva Circé-Côté's corpus, provide the key to her thinking. Accordingly, I have made liberal—but not, I hope, excessive—use of quotations. It is through them that one can more fully grasp her anger and joy, her sarcasm and gentleness.

Her Montreal stood in contrast to a rural- and religious-minded Quebec. The city let her breathe and to some degree distance herself from the Church authorities, but a woman, deprived of the right to vote and access to the priesthood, could not aspire to enter the ruling circles. Her criticisms were formulated all the more freely for being made outside those circles. Going further than her contemporaries in her observations on politics and religion, denouncing the injustices visited on women and for that matter on all the minority groups inhabiting the city, she positioned herself as a nonconformist in a society that still bowed to the dictates of its elites.

It takes more than a hermeneutical reading of a columnist's texts, however eloquent they may be, to reconstitute a life, which is the biographer's first duty. I have never claimed to completely comprehend Éva Circé-Côté. Every biographer could make the same confession, but in this case there was no ready solution to the problem of discerning some cohesion in a long life. She was undeniably a prolific writer, but the absence of personal or autobiographical documents, in addition to her many pseudonyms, hamper any effort to fully apprehend the subject. That said, there are a few exceptions to this autobiographical lacuna: the five long letters to Marcel Dugas, given to me by the poet and academic Gustave Labbé, have proved invaluable. The letters, in which Circé-Côté opens up unreservedly and pours out her feelings, confirm the positions framed in her columns on topics as crucial as her faith, or, rather, her irreligion, her criticism of Quebec society, and her appreciation of contemporary literature. Three dramatic moments of her life are mentioned in this correspondence: her husband's funeral, her mother's death, and Circé-Côté's dismissal from the Municipal Library. In light of these few letters, we feel even more keenly the lack of all those buried among the papers of her correspondents, which their descendants probably destroyed more often than not. So we are left with the view of others: her close relations, intimates, and critics. Even taking into account the element of complacency or self-interest in the praise she received, what emerges is the picture of a generous woman with strong convictions and a highly cultured iconoclast.

A biography follows a specific chronology: the beginning and end belong to the public domain, the facts known to demographers and genealogists. The evolution of ideas, however, has its own chronology, one that coincides with the other to varying degrees. To do justice to Éva Circé-Côté's ideas, this book is divided into two parts: her biography as such and her involvement in the key debates of her time, followed by a more in-depth study of the core themes that were the wellspring of her thought and writing.

PART ONE

CHAPTER 1

WOMAN OF LETTERS ON THE CUSP OF THE CENTURY

*The period of 1890 to 1905 is distant not only in time
but above all with regard to the form of things,
people's appearance, ideas, and feelings.*
— ROBERT DE ROQUEBRUNE, *Testament de mon enfance*, 1951

THE YEAR 1903 brought Éva Circé a triple crown: her first book, *Bleu, Blanc, Rouge: Paysages, Causeries*, a collection of columns, poems, and lectures, was published in April and was well received by the critics; in May, her drama *Hildelang et De Lorimier* was acclaimed at the Théâtre National Français; in August, she was appointed as librarian at the Bibliothèque technique de Montréal (Montreal technical library), the city's first free, public library. At the age of thirty-two, Éva Circé was a well-known figure of the cultural community, first as a musician and poet and, from 1900 on, as a regular columnist in Montreal's progressive newspapers. She was and would remain a committed Montrealer, commenting on social and political issues throughout the first four decades of the twentieth century.

* * *

Marie Arzélie Éva Circé was born on January 31, 1871, the year that Louis-Joseph Papineau, who would become her great hero, died. She was the fifth child of Julie-Ézilda (or Exilda) Décarie (1846–1926) and Narcisse Circé (1842–1911), who had married in the Notre-Dame de Montréal church six years earlier.¹ When Éva was born, only the eldest child, Marie-Thérèse, was still alive, the other three having died soon after birth; their mother was twenty-five years old. Ézilda's ancestor, Jean Descarries, had arrived from France around 1650 and settled in Montreal, where his descendants would continue to reside. Jean Descarries—the spelling of the family name changed several times over the course of five generations—(circa 1620–87), known as Le Houx, was an illiterate coalman; his wife, Michelle Artus was a native of Anjou. Over four generations, the Décaries commingled with the Picards, the Lécuyers, and the Waldans. Éva Circé's maternal grandmother, Marie-Louis Lanthier (1814–1901), wife of Jean-Baptiste Décarie, is said to have been a writer, painter, and sculptor. With thirteen children, including Éva's mother Ézilda, it is hard to imagine how this talented woman could find the time for such creative pursuits, but in a brief biography of Éva Circé that appeared in *La Patrie* in 1903, the journalist Anne-Marie Gleason Huguenin (Madeleine), states her appreciation of "the Canadian-style statuettes fashioned by the grandmother."²*

The Circé family, too, arrived in New France during the seventeenth century. François Sircé de Saint-Michel (1650–1714), who hailed from the Paris area, was a soldier and surgeon at the Quebec City garrison when, in 1680, he married Marie-Madeleine Berthelot, a seventeen-year-old native of Saintonge, France, who lived with her mother in Neuville. After staying for a while in Batiscan and then Sorel, the family finally settled in Saint-Philippe-de-La Prairie.³

The former *seigneurie* of La Prairie-de-la-Magdeleine was an agricultural region regarded in 1839 as less subject to the influence of the clergy than any other Catholic region.⁴ The Circés had inhabited the area for five generations when Éva's father, Narcisse Circé, left his hometown, La Prairie, and moved to Montreal. Over the years the Circés witnessed the War of 1812 and the insubordination of the militiamen, the inauguration of the first Canadian railroad between La Prairie and Saint-Jean-sur-Richelieu in 1836, and the devastating fires that followed the Rebellions. Throughout her life, Éva Circé-Côté would draw on a legacy of resistance and revolt. The Troubles of 1837–38 left their mark and inspired Jules Verne's novel *Famille Sans-Nom*, a story set near La Prairie.⁵ The families of this county gained a reputation for being unbowed and even anti-clerical; for many years they kept alive the memory of the Rebellions.

Through marriage, the Circés were joined with the Babeus, the Réaumes, the Lefebres, the Perras, and the Dupuis. Narcisse dropped the name Saint-

* This and all other quotations from French-language sources are rendered in our translation unless otherwise noted.—Trans.

Michel used by his father, Julien Circé aka Saint-Michel. At the time Éva was born her father was a train engineer for the Grand Trunk Railway. A man of the countryside, in 1865 he married into the cultured and urban milieu to which his children would belong. The couple took up residence on Saint-Bonaventure Street—now Saint-Jacques West—a short distance from his workplace at Grand Trunk Station, in the part of the Notre-Dame parish that was home to a petite bourgeoisie made up of artisans, merchants, and Grand Trunk employees.

Among the many children born in the Circé home, few survived. Éva was brought to the baptismal font in Notre-Dame church on February 2. The godmother was her aunt, Marie-Philomène Descarries, and the godfather, her uncle Louis Kingsley.[6] A whole host of relatives lived nearby. Her godfather, though incapable of signing the baptismal certificate, ran the grocery store at 79 St-Félix Street, on the corner of Saint-Bonaventure. There were Descarries and Lanthiers a few doors down. No other Circés lived there, however, because Narcisse's family had stayed in La Prairie.

During Éva's early childhood, an event took place that affected the entire Circé family. Four years after Éva's birth, her father, a freight train engineer since 1870, took up a new occupation and, in partnership with Jos Dumouchel, opened a men's clothing store in their neighbourhood on Saint-Joseph Street. In 1877—Éva was six—the family's social status improved markedly when the Circé Dumouchel store became the Narcisse Circé store, still located on Saint-Joseph Street a stone's throw from the family home. In 1883 or 1884, the family moved farther west to a somewhat larger house on Notre-Dame Street, one block south of Saint-Bonaventure. The shop, now situated at 2009 Notre-Dame, stood adjacent to the family residence, at number 2007.[7] Moving from the Saint-Jacques neighbourhood to that of Saint-Antoine also meant going from the old Notre-Dame parish to that of Sainte-Cunégonde, whose lovely church was inaugurated in 1885.[8]

Montreal was already a metropolis, with its neighbourhoods in the process of differentiation, its linguistic divides, its factories, and its commercial thoroughfares. The 1870s saw a shift in the city's linguistic makeup: for the first time in decades, the majority of the population was of French descent. Its political institutions became increasingly Francophone, while the banks and major businesses remained Anglophone. Until the middle of the twentieth century, the socioeconomic pyramid coincided with the ethnolinguistic hierarchy, dominated by people of British extraction and resting on a base of Francophones and immigrants. Catholic institutions—churches, convents, seminaries—the vast majority of which were Francophone, held sway over the urban landscape; in 1876, the Quebec City establishment Université Laval opened a branch in

Julien Saint-Michel and Catherine Dupuis, Éva Circé's paternal grandparents. From the collection of Marie Michaud.

what would become the Quartier Latin (Latin Quarter), with buildings scattered along Notre-Dame, Saint-Denis and Sherbrooke Streets. Notre-Dame Street, where the faculties of law and medicine were located, was a beehive of activity at all hours of the day. Among the throng crowding the often muddy roadway one could come across professors, such as the lawyer—and future

Premier—Joseph-Adolphe Chapleau, or students like Lomer Gouin or René Detertoc, who would write under the name René de Cotret.

In the vicinity of the port, Montreal was a dirty place full of damp alleyways, where the proliferation of rats gave rise to extermination contests among the neighbourhood boys.[9] Epidemics frequently spread through homes, leaving many families decimated. Between 1865 and 1885, Ézilda and Narcisse Circé had twelve children, of whom only three would reach adulthood. By her twelfth birthday, Éva had lost six brothers and sisters, four of them between April 1881 and September 1882. That year, after the death of Thérèse at the age of seventeen, Éva became the eldest child. Such tragedies were not uncommon among nineteenth-century families living in the city, but Éva would never forget them, and in her columns she often returned to the subject of infant mortality and the little white coffins that regularly went up to the Côte-des-Neiges cemetery.

The town of Sainte-Cunégonde, where Éva, her younger sister Maria, and her little brother Arthur grew up, had a population of ten thousand and a cultural life rivalling that of the Quartier Latin to the east. In the late nineteenth century, owing to the literary cafés, bookshops, theatres, and venues for public lectures clustered around Vinet Street, this was a "trendy" area associated with public figures such as the printer and bookseller Victor Grenier, the librarian and archivist Édouard Zotique Massicotte, and the poet and entomologist Germain Beaulieu. It was an independent municipality with its own identity and would not be incorporated into the City of Montreal until 1905.

From age five to ten, Éva spent part of her vacations at the convent with her Carmelite godmother, Sister Marie de Saint-Pierre,[10] a woman not entirely cut off from the outside world. Because of her knowledge of English, she was the extern and served as intermediary between "the world" and the congregation. In the summer of 1876, little Éva wore a frock and wimple sewn by her godmother: "I saw myself as a real nun, attended the chapel services and the readings; *The City of God* interested me like a novel." She would later attribute her rejection of "vulgar antichristianism"[11] to her affection for her godmother. She would also recall holidays spent on a farm with her grandmother and surrounded by "little cousins."[12] The few early memories that she set down in writing suggest a happy childhood in a united and warm family environment.

Éva was thirteen years old when her parents, most likely influenced by the solid reputation of the Sisters of Saint Anne, enrolled her in the Villa Anna boarding school in Lachine. Since 1861, the convent had been offering a comprehensive curriculum that was ahead of its time. Its library held more than

Éva and her sister Maria Circé, circa 1884. From the collection of Marie Michaud.

1,400 books. There was a staff of twenty-four nuns, and of the four hundred students more than half were boarders. Éva attended the convent school for the last four years of the French programme, which was limited to a few basic subjects: religious instruction, French, English, vocal and instrumental music, drawing, sewing, and home economics. Éva's report cards include no grades

The Décarie-Circé family. From left to right: Éva, Narcisse, Arthur, Exilda, Maria. From the collection of Marie Michaud.

for mathematics, science, or history, even though the nuns' reports to the Superintendent of Public Education state that those subjects were taught at the school; this may explain why she would later describe herself as self-taught.[13]

Life in a boarding school was not restricted to classes; the students would put on plays, often written by the nuns, on edifying religious or historical topics.[14] The students' behaviour was considered no less important than the subjects taught and was duly graded in their term reports. The assessments were tersely conveyed as "good," "very good," or "excellent," without doing justice to either the quality of instruction or the student's talent.[15] From the very first day, Éva's conduct was exemplary, and she excelled in French and music, but she would never do as well in sewing, a sphere deemed as necessary to a girl's education as arts such as drawing and music. In her final year, Éva Circé won the bronze medal for literature awarded by Lady and Lord Stanley of Preston, the Governor-General of Canada.[16]

Her parents, apparently satisfied with Éva's education, enrolled her ten-year-old sister Maria in the same convent when Éva was in her second year there. But Maria was frequently ill and had to abandon her studies. In fact, very few students managed to complete the programme; when Éva graduated in 1888, she did so with only one classmate, Mélina Hurtubise. She nevertheless befriended a young girl of her age, Georgine Normandin, to whom she would remain loyal for the rest of her life.

Years later, notwithstanding her anticlericalism and harsh appraisal of the education available to girls, Éva Circé would cherish the memory of her convent years and remain deeply grateful to her teachers. In 1903, in her tribute to Sister Marie-Anasthasie of the Sisters of Saint Anne, recently appointed Superior of the convent in Saint-Jérôme, Circé described her as having "a man's head"—a compliment in those days—"and a woman's heart."[17] In 1915, in a publication renowned for its anticlericalism, *Le Pays*, she devoted a column to the reunion of the alumnae of the Lachine convent, where "the nuns are wonders that are a pleasure to behold."[18]

Elsewhere, however, she acknowledged the limitations of her schooling. Responding to a reader in 1910, she wrote:

> You complain, Cyrano, that I am poorly educated. You will be appalled at my confession that I am scarcely educated. The special matter of my brain has remained resistant to moulding. I emerged from that bland and grinding education unscathed, like the children of Israel out of the fiery furnace.[19]

Music, drawing, and sewing were among the arts in which young girls from good families were expected to excel, albeit as amateurs. The nuns enjoyed a strong reputation as musicians, and Éva benefited from their piano and vocal instruction. She even considered turning her passion for music into more than a pastime and took classes with the pianist, composer, and poet Clara Lanctôt.[20] She pursued her vocal training with Charles Labelle, who was well known for his classes at the conservatory of the Société artistique de Montréal and as the choirmaster at the Saint-Louis-de-France church. She gave concerts at the Bonsecours hall,[21] among other venues. She also went in for oil painting, but without the same degree of success.[22] And she would soon arrive on the literary scene as a poet.

Between her graduation from the convent in 1888 and her recognition as a Montreal woman of letters at the turn of the century, nothing is known about her social life among the literati, except that she mixed with the city's cultural and intellectual avant-garde. There is no doubt that these were highly formative years during which she read a great deal. Nearly all her literary and scientific references are from the last decade of the nineteenth century.

According to the census of 1901, Éva, then thirty years old, still lived with her parents at their new address on Sherbrooke between Amherst and

Woman of Letters on the Cusp of the Century / 11

Early artwork by Éva Circé. From the collection of Marie Michaud.

Saint-André, close to Lafontaine Park.²³ By moving up to the new neighbourhoods north of Sherbrooke Street, the Circé family realized the dream of many Montrealers.

One can only speculate as to what may have prompted Éva to send a few poems in 1899 to Louvigny de Montigny, the secretary-archivist of the École littéraire de Montréal and editor of the journal *Les Débats*. It was probably the fame of the circle of exclusively male writers to which he belonged, who, from 1895 on, had been meeting to discuss their work and the literature of Quebec more generally. Her decision turned out to be a wise one; De Montigny would never turn his back on her.

Éva Circé thus joined the young cohort of Montreal writers—Louvigny de Montigny was five years her junior—worthy of the title "bohemian," not because they were indigent, as most of them were scions of the bourgeoisie, but because they refused to compromise on matters of principle and were relatively marginalized. This generation of newcomers to the literary scene was inspired by the Parnassian, Romantic, and Symbolist movements in France, and was "free of the influence—if not the control—of the clergy."[24] Stirred by Verlaine and Baudelaire, these young authors embraced modernity, and their convictions were not confined to aesthetics but spurred them on occasion to speak out on social issues such as education.

The École littéraire de Montréal, described by Charles Gill as a school with neither masters nor doctrine, encouraged mutual criticism and helped authors to attract a readership. The young men were eager to "learn to write," and wreathed in cigarette smoke at their Friday night meetings at the Château Ramezay they read, analyzed, and appraised each other's work.[25] Éva Circé flourished in the company of these not so much revolutionary as rebel writers, and of her forward-looking journalist colleagues. But because she was kept outside their inner circle she was obliged to polish her poems, stories, and essays alone.

During the peak years of the École littéraire, from 1895 to 1905, its members were primarily poets. Yet, though Éva Circé, under the name Colombine, was also known as a poet at the time, she could rub shoulders with the insiders but never belong to their association. As she would remark some years later, "[women] are allowed into the nave, but they cannot gain access to the chancel."[26] Like the École littéraire de Montréal, the Tribu des Casoars, the Six Éponges, and the other small groups existing at the turn of the century remained an exclusively male preserve. The gatherings at L'Arche on Notre Dame Street or Café Ayotte—the "petit Procope" of Sainte-Catherine Street—brought together Éva Circé's friends and colleagues.[27] Marcel Dugas, Honoré Parent, and Isaïe Nantais would meet at L'Arche; Louvigny de Montigny, Germain Beaulieu, Jean Charbonneau, Gonzalve Desaulniers, and Charles Gill gathered at Ayotte's café. These were essentially male lairs from which women, except for the painters' models of the Quartier Latin, were barred.[28] There is no evidence, however, that Colombine actually asked—as Georgina Bélanger (Gaëtane de Montreuil) dared to do—to join the clique of the École littéraire de Montréal.

The homosocial networks, with their favourite meeting places and masculine practices, had a significant effect on the careers of young men; one would be hard put to find an equivalent for their female colleagues, who, already denied access to the *collèges classiques*, an essential prerequisite for admission to a university, were frowned upon in the public places where criticisms were exchanged and reputations built. The women's interactions were confined to sewing circles, eventually supplemented by reading circles, which, however, lacked the camaraderie and freedom of the male circles. The exclusion of Georgina Bélanger, editor of *Pour vous mesdames*, the women's section of the daily *La Presse*; of Anne-Marie Gleason Huguenin (Madeleine), who succeeded Robertine Barry (Françoise) as editor of the women's page of *La Patrie*; and of Éva Circé, deprived these writers of critical appraisal and the privilege of signing their texts, "Member of the École littéraire de Montréal," a source of pride for some, but for others a guarantee of being published. It could be argued that the rules of propriety prevented members of "the fair sex," as women were called in those days, from lingering in the garrets, sheds, and other dens of young men, but the meetings were not always held in such places. It can also be presumed that non-conformist, freethinking women would scoff at the conventions compiled in Madame Sauvalle's handbook of etiquette, which prescribed that a chaperon must be present in most public places.[29] Some members of the School were married, and women could have been accompanied by their husbands or brothers. In short, the flourishing homosociality facilitating the literary and artistic careers of men had no female counterpart, and barring women from the literary societies could only hinder them inasmuch as they, just like their male colleagues, might have benefitted from these discussion forums, while taking advantage of them to attract readers to their work.

In choosing to submit her poems to *Les Débats*, a publication founded by de Montigny and others, Éva Circé was no doubt drawn by its ideological orientation. The journal took an anti-imperialist stance and opposed Britain's intervention in South Africa with the support of troops from various parts of the British Empire, including Canada. As of September 1900, Circé joined the anti-imperialist weekly of Sainte-Catherine Street, which was to become, in Olivar Asselin's opinion, "the paper most widely read by intelligent people."[30] De Montigny, a child of Montreal's legal elite, set the tone. He was an aesthete and a polemicist who in December 1899, together with Paul Le Moyne de Martigny, established a weekly that prided itself on being independent of all political parties. De Martigny became the owner and director, and de Montigny its editor-in-chief. The staff was made up of members of the École littéraire de Montréal such as Beaulieu, Gill, and Charbonneau, and was soon reinforced by Arsène Bessette as well as Olivar Asselin, a journalist from the Lower St. Lawrence, who, at twenty-six years of age, had acquired a store of experience in several New England newspapers. They possessed the spiritedness of youth and the strength of their convictions, and they happily welcomed the collaboration of Éva Circé, then twenty-nine years old.

As part of a diverse team, in which the journalists were poets, the critics were musicians, and the columnists were writers, Éva was soon working in

Front page of *Les Débats*, September 16, 1900. BAnQ.

every genre. Among the forty texts she published in *Les Débats* between September 16, 1900, and September 8, 1901, there were four poems, dozens of columns premised on human-interest stories, and a few remarkable reports, all signed Colombine or Musette.

In Colombine's very first column, squeezed between a tale by Guy de Maupassant and a fashion review on page 8 and titled "Confessions," the author recounts a little love story and shares her thoughts on such affairs. It is a lighthearted piece offering lessons meant for young women: Are they the cause of breakups? How can they hold on to their lovers? This conventional presentation of love relationships also cautions against "the world-weary stomachs of our century that demand corrosive liqueurs" and "human panthers: Agnès Sorel, *Mesdames* Maintenon, Montespan, du Barry, and their queen, Madame du Pompadour!"[31] There was nothing here that might shock the readers, nor any early sign of the politically committed and iconoclastic journalist to come.

Week after week she produced poems, anecdotes, and lyrical, moralizing essays. Her tone began to grow bolder. On the subject of romantic relationships, Éva championed the heart as opposed to the voice of reason. Many of her columns during this period dealt with love and socializing and, though not intending to discuss her personal life, she sometimes dropped revealing hints. On August 11, 1901, for instance, she published a "Une histoire canadienne" (A [French] Canadian story), in which Mariette and Jean court each other while playing cards under the watchful eyes of their parents. After a time, Mariette's mother forces Jean to state his intentions. Jean, who is studying law, plans to take Mariette as his wife once he has graduated. The young man goes away promising to return, but the mother's scepticism has planted the seeds of doubt in his mind. The young woman waits for a few years and then marries someone else. Jean never gets over it and drowns his sorrows in society life and alcohol. According to Éva Circé, there is a lesson to be learned from these two broken lives. Like the preface to some books or an invitation to a waltz, premarital happiness may be the best part: "hence, if marriage is the epilogue of the novel, one ought to put it off for as long as possible." And she appeals to mothers to foster this conjugal prelude: "let her believe in her fiancé as she does in God."[32] Circé tellingly chose to reproduce this story two years later in *Bleu, Blanc, Rouge* under a different title: "Nouvelle vécue. La voix de la raison" (A true-life story: The voice of reason).

In her early texts on Quebec society, written in a more traditional vein, she deplored the encroachment of the city on the countryside, sympathized with the poor, and lauded the mothers of large families. Her columns were punctuated by seasonal themes: "Songeries d'octobre" (October reveries), "la Sainte-Catherine" (St. Catherine's Day), Christmas, Epiphany, Easter, spring. Before long, however, she was tackling more social topics, expressing concern for the plight of single women, and for the first time reflecting on the literary community, with portraits of different types, like the cold

16 / Freethinker

Portrait of Louvigny de Montigny by Basibi. *Les Débats*, September 8, 1901. BAnQ.

Anglophone or the artist's muse. She bolstered her statements with irony, a weapon that she would hone and occasionally abuse. Her initial discussions of feminism presented what amounted to classic caricatures of the nagging woman and the man on a leash.[33] Yet Éva Circé herself did not fit this model. She was independent, earned her living, and, as of 1903, plied not just one but two professions; but she was able to keep her personal situation separate from her writing and revealed very little of the woman behind Colombine and Musette.

She wrote poems and essays, and created pictures of domestic life and urban landscapes. She was able to convey "the incredible delight of going for a stroll . . . of taking one's ennui for a walk" on St-Laurent Boulevard or Sainte-Catherine Street, an essentially male pleasure, for women must not dilly-dally.[34] Her columns, while meant to be didactic, were also amusing or playful, as evidenced by those devoted to the new male vogue of going cleanshaven: "each day sees legions of moustaches, sideburns, pencil moustaches, and goatees felled by the coarse blades of common Figaros."[35]

Her reportage on the environs of Montreal was more earnest. In the summer of 1901, under the byline Musette, she wrote sketches of a series of villages—Boucherville, Saint-Ours, Longue-Pointe, Caughnawaga (Kahnawake),

Napierville, as well as Saint Helen's Island—conjuring up their colours, sounds, and smells. The articles evinced Circé's emotional response to these places, an attachment that was both aesthetic and patriotic. Napierville, "a fraternal landscape of my dreams," with its windmill, its red bridge across the river, its charming abodes, evoked "a cry of liberty and the martyrdom of the Patriotes."[36] After a stay in Quebec City she published a description in *Le Monde illustré* showing "the seventeenth-century faith"[37] of the city. Upon returning home she captured the topography of the Montreal region from season to season.

The weekly *Les Débats*, "a newspaper exercising freedom of thought and expression," which frequently aroused the wrath of church authorities, rose from its ashes and was reborn under a different name. Colombine had been with the paper for no more than a few months when the owner, Alexandre Duclos, accepted the financial offer made by the son of the Liberal organizer Israël Tarte in exchange for editorial support for the Liberal Party. The brothers Louvigny and Gaston de Montigny, true to their non-partisan principles, resigned from the newspaper that they had founded and countered with the short-lived *Vrais Débats*, which was replaced in October 1900 by *L'Avenir*. From October 1900 to January 1901, thirteen texts were published in *L'Avenir* under the name Colombine. Louvigny de Montigny would acknowledge Éva Circé's active role in the paper's history: "*L'Avenir* was founded with Colombine."[38] She found herself among the same stellar group of writers as before. Each of them used one or more pseudonyms, while Gustave Conte and Olivar Asselin, indifferent to individual glory, both adopted the pen name Joseph Saint-Hilaire. Éva Circé worked alongside Eugène Seers (Louis Dantin), Paul Bertin, Ludovic Brunet (Lucette), Joseph Marie Arthur Bussières (Arthur de Bussières), J.-Étienne Gauthier (Paul Hyssons), Émile Nelligan, and Thibaudeau. In spite of the staff's complete devotion to this new Saturday paper, the director was hounded by creditors, and the final issue of *L'Avenir* came out in January 1901. According to Louvigny de Montigny, Colombine was the one who consoled her colleagues. They all returned to *Les Débats*, now "purified, disinfected, and exorcised."[39]

Éva Circé was not the only woman to write under a nom de plume. Most female journalists of that period, not to mention many men, hid behind a borrowed identity, a name that was neither their father's nor their husband's.[40] Who was this Colombine? In answer to a female reader who had called her a dove [*une colombe* in French—Trans.], she wrote: "I am Colombine who laughs a little at everything; at times at Arlequin, at times Pierrot, at other times Léandre."[41] In February 1901, while retaining Colombine, she also adopted the name Musette, and during her first years in journalism she was known under those two aliases. Moreover, as stated by Louvigny de Montigny, "she signs Colombine, she signs Musette, and she leaves a host of articles unsigned"; hence the ongoing problem of attributing numerous articles to her and the attendant difficulty of adding these to the complete corpus of her works.

From the moment she began contributing to *Les Débats* in 1901, and later that same year to *Le Pionnier* and *Le Monde illustré*, Éva Circé's reputation as a literary woman spread throughout Quebec. When the Société de colonisation du lac Saint-Jean (Society for the colonization of Lac Saint-Jean) sought to promote its projects in October 1901, it turned to the three preeminent female journalists of the day, and Éva Circé found herself in the company of her seniors Georgina Bélanger (Gaëtane de Montreuil) of *La Presse* and Anne-Marie Gleason (Madeleine) de *La Patrie*, on a six-day expedition to the headwaters of the Saguenay. Quebec Premier Simon-Napoléon Parent was enthusiastic about settlement; as a disciple of Laurier, who had proclaimed that the twentieth century would belong to Canada, Parent firmly intended to explore and populate the country. The minister in charge of settlement was Lomer Gouin, and his secretary was none other than Olivar Asselin, who had met Éva Circé in the newsrooms. On the strength of his careful attention to language, his broadmindedness, and his non-conformism, he had earned Éva's respect, which he would not lose even when their views sharply diverged in the course of their respective careers.[42] He had read the visionaries, such as Arthur Buies, Edmond de Nevers, and Errol Bouchette, all of whom were advocates of economic nationalism, and, like curé Labelle, Asselin declared that it was necessary "to take possession of the soil" and clear the land.[43]

The expedition of the three women journalists proved to be an excellent propaganda tool in favour of settlement. Together they covered more than 640 kilometres by train and another 240 by buckboard and boat, staying with locals, and paying special attention to the women of the region.[44] From Roberval to Saint-Prime, Saint-Félicien, L'Afrique, Mistassini, and Péribonka, the roads were rough, and the snow came early. The three journalists admirably carried out their task as propagandists, singing the praises of the settler's life so as to persuade confirmed city-dwellers and gain their support, if they had not already given it, to the Liberal government's settlement projects.

Upon completing their tour of the Saguenay, they were invited at the end of October to the Institut canadien de Québec (Canadian institute in Quebec City), where they were greeted by its president, Honoré Chassé, and asked to give lectures. The hall was overflowing, as many notables had

Front page of *Le Monde illustré*, November 30, 1901. BAnQ.

made it a point to come hear the accounts of the women referred to in the daily *Le Soleil*, where their talks were reproduced in full, as "the lionesses of the hour in Quebec City."[45] At the outset, the three intrepid and renowned women standing before the prestigious audience felt it necessary—not so much out of conviction as a concern for proprieties—to apologize. Madeleine asked the audience to forgive her for being unworthy and daring; Colombine apologized for her boldness. The speakers had agreed among themselves to each cover a different aspect of the expedition. Éva Circé's talk was the most lyrical, whereas her companions went into detail about the settlers' experiences, while all three made sure to emphasize their "patriotic" ardour.

Colombine came back from Lac Saint-Jean afflicted by "poetic madness." In the train to Roberval, she had been mesmerized by the vastness of nature, the magical twilight hours, the sun setting on Lac Bouchette, the stone fortresses raised up by the mountains, the lakes, and the rivers. In that idyllic land she found "a people of brothers," happy and peaceful, free of hypocrisy and prejudice, with "simple, patriarchal mores," "the haven of Bethany," no less. The women who had followed their husbands there "are happy, believe me, among their spouses and children, who make up their whole world, and proudly wear the halo of those who have done their duty." The presentation concluded with a tribute to Canada, "the most beautiful and greatest country in the world," and to the language kept alive thanks to "the blood of our forebears."[46] Thus, a rather traditional Colombine reassured her audience as to the value of the colonization policy. The reporter of *L'Événement* wrote that "'Colombine' of *Le Pionnier* speaks with a smooth voice and superb diction. Like her namesake, the correspondent of *Le Pionnier* soars and glides, and she literally captivated her audience."[47] The lectures were each published in the speakers' respective newspapers: Madeleine's in *La Patrie*, Gaëtane de Montreuil's in *La Presse*, and Éva Circé's in *Le Pionnier*. The photo that

The three journalists, Madeleine, Colombine, and Gaëtane de Montreuil, upon returning from their assignment for the Société de colonisation du Lac Saint-Jean, October 1901. *Le Soleil*, October 25, 1901.

appeared in *Le Soleil* upon their return shows the three women looking in the same direction, all wearing the extravagant hats of their era, all attired in the style of what was then termed "new women": emancipated and sensibly clothed, here in a suit and blouse. Standing on the left-hand side, Anne-Marie Gleason (Madeleine) wears a mischievous half-smile; seated on the right, Georgina Bélanger (Gaëtane de Montreuil) has a glazed, tired look in her eyes. Éva Circé (Colombine) stands between them with her shoulders proudly thrown back and a dignified, determined expression on her face; her mouth evinces resolve and the angle of her body suggests a woman of action. The paths of these three explorers would meet again and they would cross swords with each other for years to come.

The brothers Gaston and Louvigny de Montigny wrote the first portrait of Éva Circé in May 1901, on the front page of the review *Le Passe-Temps musical, littéraire, fantaisiste* (The musical, literary, fanciful pastime). In it they praise "the originality of her oh-so French use of language, [...] her rather unfeminine sense of judgment, [...] and, lastly, her erudition, no doubt a surprise in this land of ours (given the circumstances, the prudishness, the prejudices, and the manifold hypocrisy in society, that is, the general context in which the education of our young women takes place)." And, drawing a flattering comparison with a well-known French feminist journalist, they add: "Miss Circé is our Séverine."[48] Continuing in a more personal vein, the de Montigny brothers write: "Kindness is the dominant note of Miss Circé's columns. Her style is the sworn enemy of whatever is commonplace, trite, old-fashioned, hackneyed, worn out; it accepts an idea only after it has made it her own through a personal reworking. . . . She spontaneously hates all that is inauthentic."[49] They also applaud her knowledge of literature, for she is well read and constantly quotes the Bible as well as the classics, from Dante to the Enlightenment authors, from Balzac to Anatole France. The article is accompanied by a photograph of Éva Circé, no doubt taken at her graduation, which shows her with a broad ribbon draped across her chest, and curly, almost frizzy hair tied over her nape, gazing toward a lofty horizon, in what was a conventional pose representing the vision of a hope-filled future for young women.

Meanwhile, the poet Albert Lozeau was moved by a Colombine who "speaks of the humble, the lowly, the forsaken . . . but being an artist, in the folds of the soft fabric of her sentences she inserts original and colourful expressions that strike and assault the mind."[50] A few months later, Louvigny de Montigny was at it again in *Le Monde illustré*. He returns to his portrait of Éva Circé, stressing her originality, her "mathematically Parisian use of language," her "slightly exaggerated emotion," and, once again "her altogether unfeminine sense of judgment."[51] While Parisian mathematics has remained a mystery, his assessment of his colleague's sense of judgment is evidence of the prejudices of that period even among minds as enlightened as de Montigny's, who, as has been seen, is aware of the shortcomings in girls' education. The epithet "feminine" used in an exclusively pejorative sense, and its opposite, "virile" (or "manly"), in an exclusively positive sense, constituted an endlessly repeated cliché, especially with respect to judgment and writing. Consequently, for the writer Robert de Roquebrune, that Éva Circé's judgment was unfeminine could only make it more valid. As for her emotional exaggeration, de Roquebrune confirmed that impression as well, describing her sentiments as "exaggerated."[52]

Following the change of ownership at *Les Débats* and its loss of political independence, the staff migrated to Sherbrooke's Sunday weekly *Le Pionnier*, "the great nationalist newspaper," which described itself as "*Franc et sans dol,*" that is, plain-spoken and honest. *Le Pionnier* and *Le Monde illustré* shared the same office on Saint-Gabriel Street in Montreal, both under the direction of Amédée Denault.[53] In Olivar Asselin's view, the staff of *Le Pionnier* was a "wild clan."[54] In the front page photo of *Le Monde illustré*, the prestigious

Éva Circé. Photo credit: Laprès and Lavergne.

assemblage is arrayed around the editorial board; there, among others, are Louvigny, Gaston, and Marguerite (Margot) de Montigny, Olivar Asselin, Harry Bernard, Gustave Comte, Stanislas Côté, Omer Héroux, Paul Hyssons, Albert Lozeau, Édouard-Zotique Massicotte, Adjutor Rivard, and Éva Circé.[55]

Having gone from *Les Débats* to *Le Pionnier*, Éva arrived at *Le Monde illustré* in September 1901; two months later she became the secretary of the editorial board.⁵⁶ Between September and December 1901, she published some twenty essays and poems in this weekly. Its director Amedée Denault, a sometime poet, had also moved from one publication to another, specifically from *La Minerve* to *La Croix*, but at that point Colombine was apparently not afraid to mix with militant Catholics like Denault, Harry Bernard, and Omer Héroux. Starting in 1903, Colombine also published in *L'Avenir du Nord*, the organ of the Liberal Party in the Terrebonne district. Based in Saint-Jérôme, the weekly, under the direction of Jules-Édouard Prévost, made no secret of its political affiliation: the logo was flanked on the left by a drawing of curé Labelle and by one of the *Patriote* Chenier (killed by British troops) on the right. Among its contributors were Arthur Buies, Gonzalve Desaulniers, J.-J Grignon,⁵⁷ and Charles Gill, whose poem "À Victor Hugo"⁵⁸ was published there. Circé, however, would not renew her collaboration with this paper until January 1903.

Éva Circé did not enter into journalism as a dilettante; this was her profession, and she devoted herself to it wholeheartedly. Henceforward a columnist, she went beyond Arthur Buies' definition of what that meant:

What is a newspaper column, if not the day-to-day account of occurrences witnessed at close range, personal events in which we are directly involved or that happen before our eyes? It is a keen, swift look at the small aspects of the history of our time, which today's historical criticism, if it claims to be serious, cannot do without.⁵⁹

As a columnist—her other vocation for forty years—Circé went beyond "the small aspects of the history of our time" and became an observer of events, an arbiter of taste and progress, and an educator. On February 17, 1901, she responded to an article in *La Presse*, where a journalist named Boch bemoaned the sad fate of female journalists, whose profession, he contended, required "the loss of vital fluid." Éva countered that it was "the sweetest profession," better, she argued, "than chasing after one's fees as a music teacher" or "trying one's patience and nerves to inject French, arithmetic, or harmony into the heavy, indolent blood of badly brought up or nasty kids." Better, especially, than being a stenographer and having to "put up with boorish characters, while being unable to shield one's ears against the degrading language of the people who pay her." The columnist's profession is ultimately the only one "to which an educated *canadienne* [French-Canadian woman—Trans.] can aspire."⁶⁰

In 1901 women represented 5 percent of professional journalists. In Quebec, 325 men and 18 women were categorized as "journalists, editors, and reporters" in the Canadian census. Fifteen of the women were Canadian-born,

The staff of *Le Pionnier*, *Le Monde illustré*, November 23, 1901. BanQ.

and several of them were Anglophones.[61] They knew each other for the most part, engaged in alliances and rivalries among themselves, and banded together to defend their interests. In 1904, a year after Olivar Asselin founded the Association des journalistes canadiens-français (French-Canadian journalists' association), Éva Circé, Robertine Barry, and other women established the Association des femmes journalistes canadiennes-françaises (Association of French-Canadian women journalists), affiliated with the Association Saint-Jean-Baptiste.[62] Circé, well known as a columnist for *Les Débats* and *L'Avenir du Nord*, was actively involved in the new association; at their annual convention, it was she who presented the female journalists' report. Journalism was not a way to bide one's time or amuse oneself while waiting for Prince Charming. It was a demanding career and, above all, an instrument for creating a better world.

At the turn of the century, Éva Circé, like many of her contemporaries, was fully aware of being on the cusp of new era, the threshold of a century full of promise, a time when the grandest hopes could be entertained. She believed the incipient historical period would be one of progress,[63] but in a world still subjected to political and religious interests, she turned her pro-

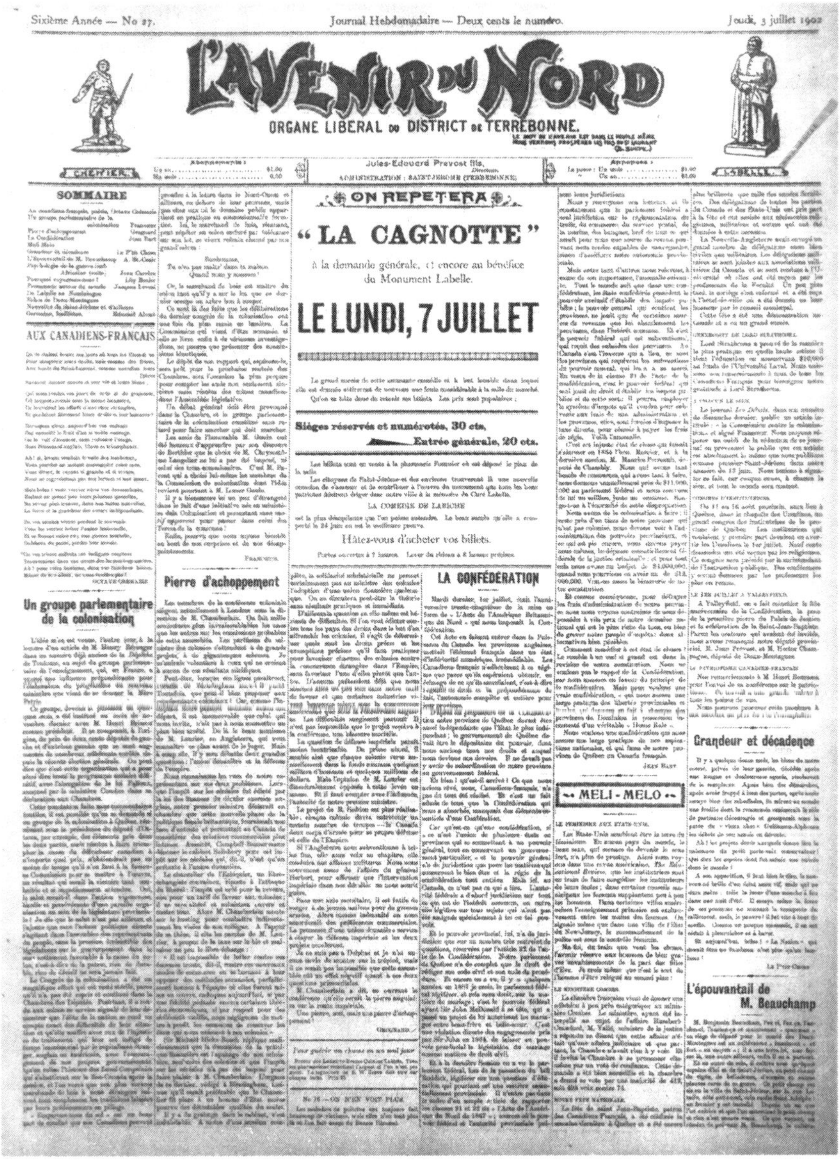
Sixième Année — No 27. Journal Hebdomadaire — Deux cents le numéro. Jeudi, 3 juillet 1902

L'AVENIR DU NORD

ORGANE LIBERAL DU DISTRICT DE TERREBONNE.

Jules-Edouard Prevost fils, Directeur.

ADMINISTRATION : SAINT-JEROME (TERREBONNE)

SOMMAIRE

AUX CANADIENS-FRANCAIS

Un groupe parlementaire de la colonisation

Pierre d'achoppement

ON REPETERA

"LA CAGNOTTE"

à la demande générale, et encore au bénéfice du Monument Labelle.

LE LUNDI, 7 JUILLET

Siéges réservés et numérotés, 30 cts,

Entrée générale, 20 cts.

Hâtez-vous d'acheter vos billets.

LA CONFÉDERATION

MELI-MELO

Grandeur et décadence

L'épouvantail de M. Beauchamp

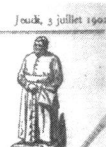

Front page of *L'Avenir du Nord*, July 3, 1902, BAnQ.

fession into a mission and, from the outset, framed a programme of conscious commitment, as encapsulated in this 1903 article:

> Whatever may be said, I will follow my own road, true to the programme I articulated two year ago. To fight for generous and bold ideas; defend

the destitute, because their suffering always wins out against fear; celebrate all that is superb in nature, all that is consoling in art, all the hope that science holds out to humanity; keep a close eye on the jails to hold any injustice at bay; ensure the education of children, the respect due to women; seek repose for one's own people; make of this pen a tool of deliverance; proclaim the song of love; think, admire, live; and all this without fanfare, with no futile vainglorious expectations, but only the wish to be useful, kind, and comforting in the face of misfortune.[64]

In the year 1901, a lucidly committed, strong-willed young woman took the liberty of writing that she lacked "a gift for sensitivity."[65] Her readers were not fooled, for this observer of the social scene, who was praised for her sensitivity and generosity, was more than just a sensitive soul; she was a rational person, one who pulled no punches when it came to the monarchy, religion, and the courts.

Why write for others when Circé could just as well run her own publication? She was ready to take up the challenge, and in December 1902 she launched *L'Étincelle* (the spark) in the capacity of owner and publisher.[66] That year saw a bumper crop of women's publications. Marie Gérin-Lajoie put out her *Traité de droit usuel* (*Treatise on Everyday Law*) to inform women of the constraints and benefits of civil and constitutional law. The same year, Robertine Barry founded *Le Journal de Françoise*, and Anne-Marie Gleason published her collection *Premier Péché* under the name Madeleine. Just as the pseudonym Colombine was fashionable in the nineteenth century in France, Spain, and Italy, various *Étincelle*s shone on behalf of different ideologies. Éva Circé teamed up with Arsène Bessette, a kindred spirit whose indignation and ideas on education she shared, and with the poet and painter Charles Gill, who had just married Georgina Bélanger. *L'Étincelle* opened its pages to the poets: Nelligan published "L'Idiote aux cloches" there, next to Colombine's "Réminescences." Théodore Botrel, a Breton who was very popular in Quebec, contributed the lament of his "Veuve Rousick," and Cazeneuve dedicated an "idyll" to *mademoiselle* Circé: "La Lyre, le Papillon."[67] Under the aliases Colombine and Musette, the publisher produced two or three texts per issue, including stories, poems, and essays. In her review of Madeleine's *Premier Péché* she applauds its author's "charming delicacy and sensitiveness" and patriotism, comparing her to George Sand and—in a reference that was self-evident among female journalists—Séverine. Yet amid the accolades she makes a point of adding, "depth of thought is replaced here by richness of expression and formal elegance."[68] Madeleine's reaction has not come down to us, but it is worth underscoring the courage needed to write a mixed review in such a small literary circle, where the two journalists often bumped into each other. Both women would marry literary-minded doctors and would champion women's rights and the French language, but Madeleine's relatively conventional thinking, her fondness for the housewife and the Catholic religion, would ultimately exhaust Éva's patience.

Among Éva Circé's early journalistic texts, an instructive essay titled "Comment se fait un journal" (How a newspaper is made) stands out. In it she explains the whole production process while cautioning those tempted by this profession that journalists, pressed by tight deadlines and editorial demands, "must shed their illusions, their cult of the ideal, and their generous utopias at the newsroom door." The journalist becomes "a pariah who will never again be permitted to see the sun but will be condemned instead to a vegetative existence lived between heaven and earth, in the fear of falling prey to a big shark." Conditions are daunting, with no allowances made for women; it is a hard, even soul-destroying environment for any idealists undertaking a campaign of moral regeneration.[69] She was so fond of this article that she reproduced it six months later in *L'Avenir du Nord*.[70]

Yet another pseudonym, Jean Ney, appeared as of 1903 in the byline of an article on the stock market, in which readers are encouraged to cultivate a piece of land in the Laurentians north of Montreal or the Lac Saint-Jean region instead of engaging in risky speculation. One can already discern here the germ of an idea she was to develop much later: the stock market is a "gaming house" and "the product of a transitory social state that must disappear one day, when people understand that wealth should be the reward for talent and labour, and not the result of hazardous gambles."[71] It can be assumed that more than one unsigned article in *L'Étincelle* was also penned by Éva. She multiplied herself and filled most of the columns under three different names. Despite her enthusiasm and efforts, however, the newspaper's seventh and last issue came out on February 14, 1903. Of the (at least) fourteen pieces she had written for *L'Étincelle*, the last, published in the final issue, was the text of a lecture titled, "Étude sur les causes de l'infériorité de la femme" (Study of the causes of women's inferiority).[72] This was the first essay of hers that can be classed as feminist.

That *L'Étincelle* faded so soon in no way tarnished its publisher's reputation. The crew at *Les Débats* immediately welcomed back their colleague of the early days. After a one-year hiatus, a new owner was found, the Frenchman Édouard Charlier, and de Montigny once again took the helm of the newspaper, now located on Notre-Dame Street. Between March and September 1903, Colombine published some twenty columns there while pursuing her collaboration with *L'Avenir du Nord*. The bold positions expressed in

Les Débats on the subjects of education and religion shocked the archbishop of Montreal, who was outraged to see "the clergy held in contempt and the observance of Sunday ridiculed." In his pastoral statement, which was read on January 4, 1903 in every parish of the Montreal archdiocese and every religious community, Mgr Paul Bruchési, having sent a "paternal note to the director" of *Les Débats*, warned the faithful that a newspaper he preferred not to name, "is doing evil work. It insults bishops, priests, citizens worthy of respect, the most sacred things. This paper has become the panegyrist of reprehensible literary works, the panegyrist of a recently deceased French writer whose very name cannot be spoken from the Christian pulpit."[73] The archbishop's statement, which forbade church members from selling or buying *Les Débats* or keeping it their possession, was the weekly's death knell.

The editorial board of *Les Débats* did not bid adieu but only au revoir: "Mgr Paul Bruchési is looking for scandal and spoiling for a fight, and we will take him up on his invitation and prepare for battle unflinchingly."[74] The first issue of *Le Combat* was put out on October 11 by the people who had staffed *Les Débats*, including Éva Circé. The articles signed by Colombine were hardly scandalous: a visit to Louis-Joseph Papineau's tomb in Montebello, autumn in the Mount Royal cemetery, a column about panhandlers and the tax on dogs, another about tramway conductors and decent working-class passengers; elsewhere she voiced her preference for nurses as opposed to women doctors.[75] Her colleagues were more outspoken in their defence of mandatory education and freedom of the press. In January 1904, rumours of the archbishop's intention to ban *Le Combat* caused it to change its name.[76] Its successor, *L'Action*, would last no more than a single issue, in which Éva had no part.

She nevertheless maintained her position and confirmed her reputation in the Québécois literary world by virtue of the publication of a collection of her writings. As early as 1901, the Montigny brothers had encouraged Colombine to assemble her columns in a book. She took their advice to heart, and *Bleu, Blanc, Rouge* (blue, white, red) was published in late April 1903 by Déom Frères. The publishing house had not been chosen haphazardly. Déom, a relative newcomer compared to the major booksellers and publishers Beauchemin and Granger, was less subservient to the Church and dared to publish young authors.[77] One of the very first poetry collections put out by a woman in Quebec,[78] *Bleu, Blanc, Rouge* also includes essays and papers presented at lectures. The dedication, written in alexandrines and followed by a halo, is to "a dear friend," "a captive star," presumably Nelligan, the halo being the poet herself.

The book's title, a tribute to the French flag, sets the tone by signalling the unfailing love of France that would run through the author's entire career. It placed the book at the heart of a divisive debate going on among French Canadians: the choice of a national flag for Quebec. At the time, the tricolour flag was flown at least as often as the Union Jack at official ceremonies. Various groups were calling for a truly national flag. Some wanted Quebec's Catholicism to be prominently displayed; others preferred a standard free of religious references. The ultramontanist Jules-Paul Tardivel proposed a white flag, representing the monarchy, with the Sacred Heart of Jesus at the centre. An abbot suggested a compromise, which would be rejected: the Sacred Heart at the centre of the tricolour flag. Lastly, a committee made up of Jesuits and nationalist clerics endorsed what they called the Sacred Heart Carillon (*Carillon Sacré-Cœur*): a white cross on a blue field with a fleur-de-lys in each quarter, and in the centre, the Sacred Heart ringed with a crown of thorns over a pendant half-crown of maple leaves. In this way, there would be something for everyone! A number of Liberals were quick to ridicule this proposal, as were many nationalists, including Louis Fréchette and Laurent-Olivier David, who wished to keep the French tricolour and to that end were willing to add a maple leaf as a distinguishing emblem of French Canadians.[79] Éva Circé took a firm stand alongside those wanting to maintain the reference to republican France, and she showed her colours in the title of her book and that of the opening poem. The three hundred and sixty-nine pages of *Bleu, Blanc, Rouge* include stories and poems that had appeared in the newspapers as well as other texts, most of which are didactic and much concerned with morality. Her descriptions of places recreate not just bygone realities but also a vibrant atmosphere, like that of the Bonsecours market, which she portrays in terms reminiscent of Zola's depiction of les Halles in *Le Ventre de Paris* (*The Belly of Paris*).

In the Quebec City daily *Le Soleil*, Marcelle reported that Colombine's book was all the rage and selling like hot cakes.[80] Her colleague at *La Patrie*, Madeleine, declared her admiration for the book and underscored the quality of the descriptions.[81] *L'Album universel* praised the writer's "powerful imagination, superior judgment, and equally tender and generous heart."[82] Only a Belgian critic, Louis Tytgat of Liège, expressed some reservations in a generally favourable review. A conservative Catholic, Tytgat, in his series of articles on French-Canadian literature, devoted an entire column to Éva Circé, whom he reproached for wishing to be French first of all. How could Colombine want anything to do with Zola's France, with the "Masonic damper," where the home is "deserted, depopulation looms, women are debased"? Tytgat kept his best compliments for Circé's style: "sparkling, studded with inventive turns of phrases, filled with surprises, striking contrasts, a profusion of vivacious wit."[83]

Anonymous, Bonsecours market, Jacques-Cartier Square, Montreal, circa 1910, MP-0000. 817-8 © McCord Museum.

Scarcely a month after the publication of *Bleu, Blanc, Rouge*, Éva Circé was again drawing critical attention, this time for her drama *Hindelang et Delorimier*, which was playing at the Théâtre National Français. The director and artistic director, Paul Cazeneuve, who had just recently moved to Montreal, played Hindelang, who had also come from Paris. This "patriotic drama," to use the playwright's own words, was based on the story of two *Patriotes* executed in 1839. At the turn of the twentieth century, the theme of the Rebellions of 1837–38 was much in vogue. Circé's play was the fourth one to deal with that subject in the space of a year.[84]

Circé had always been fascinated by the events of 1837–38 and revisited them several times; for her, the Rebellions represented the founding moment of Quebec democracy. The Frenchman Charles Hindenlang—and not "Hindelang," as she mistakenly spelled his name—and Chevalier de Lorimier distinguished themselves at Napierville in the autumn of 1838. Éva knew the place—her father was born there—and had written in a column in 1901: "From this village came the first breath of liberty. I like to think that the first calls for the country's independence could very well originate in Napierville, and I know there are old heroes who are tormented to see that Canada is still a colony with no prestige abroad, the vassal of an ignorant lord."[85] Two years later, her play stayed true to this line of thought.

As is the case for the majority of dramatic works of those years, the script of the play has not come down to us; only the newspaper reviews provide a glimpse of its contents. Unlike the dramas by Louis Guyon, Ernest Choquette, and Germain Beaulieu, staged contemporaneously with Circé's play but set in a time long after the Rebellions, the story of *Hindelang et Delorimier* unfolds in the heart of the action. While the struggle of the two rebels serves as the narrative framework, a love affair between Hindelang and Jacqueline Giroux is woven into it. There are also comic scenes, which were appreciated by the audience and, according to the reviews, greeted with peals of laughter.[86] Yet the subject was serious and topical. In Éva Circé's view, Hindenlang and de Lorimier were the embodiment of progress. She revived their memory and brought back to life their last hours in the Pied-du-Courant prison. In keeping with her mission, she pursued her moral objectives and promoted both patriotic feelings and progressive ideas. In *Les Débats*, a fellow columnist makes a point of highlighting the example that Circé holds up to "rouse our people out of its inertia" and sees in her drama "a lesson in tolerance, devotion, and generosity."[87]

Already before opening night, *La Patrie* was reporting that the play "has reached the proportions of a national event."[88] It was put on at the prestigious Théâtre National Français, "le National," on the corner of Sainte-Catherine and Beaudry, which, with its three thousand seats, was Canada's largest theatre. Founded in 1900 by Julien Daoust, who dreamed of turning it into the Comédie française of Montreal, and soon managed by Georges Gauvreau and Paul Cazeneuve, the National was the first venue in Montreal devoted exclusively to theatre. The plays changed from week to week, usually after a run of eleven performances. The artistic director, Cazeneuve, hired famous actors for the lead roles: Henriette Moret, Henri Nangys, Joseph Philias Filion, and even the one whom Louis Fréchette had dubbed the "Canadian Sarah Bernhardt," Blanche de la Sablonnière.[89] As was the custom, the audience was entertained during the intermission by musicians, in this instance, two very popular xylophonists. Éva Circé had every reason to be proud of her first theatrical hit. In the women's section of *Canada*, the columnist known as Fantaisie (Fantasy) called it an apotheosis.[90]

Soon the new playwright was at it again. On May 19, 1904, Circé submitted a manuscript to a contest organized by Georges Gauvreau, the director of the Théâtre National de Montréal. He received thirty-five submissions, including one signed Colombine: *Le Fumeur endiablé* (The rambunctious smoker), a one-act comedy about the tribulations of a good *Canadien* who, to do penitence for Lent, puts aside his pipe. The play tied for first prize with *Un arrêt judicieux* (A judicious stop) by Circé's colleague, the journalist Germain Beaulieu. Other contestants included such notables as Paul Hyssons, Arsène Bessette, Louis Guyon, and Louvigny de Montigny.[91] Like so many other plays, *Le Fumeur* left no trace, but the French section of the Canadian Authors Association (CAA) thought highly enough of it to have it staged again in 1922.

Thus, Éva Circé made her mark not only in the realm of journalism but also on Montreal's cultural scene. In 1903, when the Commission de la bibliothèque de la Ville de Montréal (City of Montreal Library Commission) sought to fill the position of librarian at the Bibliothèque technique (Municipal Library), she applied for the job.

Since the end of the nineteenth century, progressives had been demanding, among other things, the establishment of a library where any citizen could borrow contemporary works of literature. In 1881, the city had the opportunity to acquire the ten thousand volumes of the Institut canadien, which had been banned in 1869 by Mgr Bourget; the city council dared not accept such a nefarious offer. As a result, it was the library of the Fraser Institute, a private body located in the city's west end, that came into possession of the precious collection. Thereafter, each time the project of a public library was discussed, the question of censorship came up: could librarians be exempt from religious authority when it comes to obtaining books meant for the general public? Jules-Paul Tardivel's right-wing paper *La Vérité*, for one, was categorically opposed to such an exemption.[92] Yet the idea of a public library was hardly new; Honoré Mercier had endorsed it when he became Liberal Party leader in 1883. It must be granted, however, that the institution of the library was far more prevalent in Protestant countries than in Latin countries, owing at least in part to the Reformation, the reading of the Bible, and an attitude of tolerance. English-speaking Montrealers had access to the Mechanic's Institute since 1828 and the Fraser Institute's library since 1885; the Catholic parochial libraries paled by comparison. The demand for a library was included in the programme of the new Parti ouvrier (workers' party) in 1899 and soon after in that of the Trades and Labor Congress of Canada. In addition, the Freemasons considered the library an essential component of popular education and actively advocated it to the point where Circé-Côté would later write that the Bibliothèque technique was a "product of the secular spirit."[93] At the turn of the century, the École littéraire de Montréal also deplored the lack of a public library. The project was supported by the liberal press, by literary men like Gonzalve Desaulniers and by the journalist Robertine Barry, who published an article lamenting the city administration's slowness to act: "In Montreal, dubious houses are tolerated . . . [while] prudish minds are appalled by a public library!"[94]

In 1899, the founding of a public library in Westmount rekindled the interest of the city councillors, who then created the Commission de la bib-

"The Municipal Library—for pity's sake, find a place for my books!" *La Patrie*, June 14, 1913.

liothèque publique (Civic Library Commission).[95] But it was the offer made by US philanthropist Andrew Carnegie to endow public libraries in a number of North American cities that gave rise to vigorous debates in the press and the city council. While cities like Ottawa took advantage of the generous proposal, in Montreal, the offer of $150,000 prompted a good deal of wavering. Whereas the progressive mayor Préfontaine wished to accept this boon, which he had previously solicited, the archbishop of Montreal, Mgr Bruchési, with the support of the Catholic press, sensed that this was a road to perdition for his flock.[96] In *La Vérité*, Tardivel not only feared the impossibility of censoring all the books in the public library, but also regarded Carnegie's gesture as another intrusion of the United States in French Canada.[97]

Monetary factors also needed to be taken into consideration. In addition to the $150,000 granted by the donor for the building's construction, an equal sum would be needed to ensure the institution's ongoing operation, yet the City's finances were in poor shape. In November 1902, the city administration voted in favour of the library's construction, while deferring the question of censorship, only to immediately retract its decision.

After the Carnegie Foundation's ambitious project was abandoned, the city's Chamber of Commerce proposed to establish a technical and scientific library that could facilitate vocational training. The powers that be were not easily swayed by the pleas of progressives in favour of giving the population access to French-language cultural and intellectual works, but the social elite's economic arguments calling for a more qualified workforce, one better prepared for the requirements of industrial capitalism and the production needs of a rapidly expanding country, proved more convincing. The idea of a library dedicated to training workers—a stop-gap according to the historian Michèle Dagenais—was endorsed by the City Council, and in May 1903 the members of the Commission de la bibliothèque and the Association Saint-Jean-Baptiste

From *Bleu, Blanc, Rouge*, 1903.

finally agreed to jointly manage a library that would be housed in the Monument-National, owned by the Association.⁹⁸

The library's location was also arrived at through compromise. After agreeing on the importance of locating the library in the French-speaking part of the city, the commissioners examined various sites, all of them equally unsatisfactory. The Marché Saint-Laurent, on St-Laurent Boulevard between Dorchester (today René-Lévesque) and Sainte-Catherine, would have been suitable, and the area's merchants were happy to be rid of

MADEMOISELLE EVA CIRCÉ (Colombine)

La Patrie, May 16, 1903, p. 22. BAnQ.

the fruit and vegetable market, but the City was confronted with the united front of butchers against the project.⁹⁹ On January 30, 1903, *La Patrie*'s front page headline read: "Long live the library... definitely to be built on Place Viger."¹⁰⁰ But this did not take into account the opposition of local residents, who were determined to preserve this oasis of greenery, with its tall trees and pond. Not wanting to ruffle any feathers, the elected officials fell back on lots already belonging to the City. But unable to agree on a specific piece of land and under pressure from the Montreal Chamber of Commerce and the Association Saint-Jean-Baptiste, the Library Commission recommended that the City accept the Association's offer to rent a room in its Monument-National building for the purpose of housing the new library.¹⁰¹

Given that it would be a technical library offering workers books on either their trades or scientific topics, Mgr Bruchési could not withhold his approval of this project. Yet Éva Circé would later write:

> What was the thinking of the library's founders? Well, let's talk about that; I'm familiar with it: they called it technical so that it might quietly evolve within that framework... [one was forced] to play on the word technical, to expand its meaning and give it enough breadth to cover the classics. The word was stretched to enable the library to house philosophy, history, literary criticism.¹⁰²

This first library was quite modest, but it was free and open to the public. Three candidates applied for the position of librarian (*bibliothécaire et conservatrice*), three women, as this was a woman's profession and the library was not yet regarded as very important: Mrs. Tremblay, Idola Saint-Jean, who gave elocution courses at the Monument-National, and Éva Circé, well known as a journalist and an ardent promoter of the library. Supported by ladies who were patrons of the Association Saint-Jean-Baptiste, which had some say in this project, Circé received the endorsement of the Civic Library

Committee members.[103] She was hired with an annual salary of four hundred dollars.[104] It was understood that she would be "replaced by a man when the needs of the service required it."[105]

Choosing Circé was a good decision. She believed in the power of books. She defined herself as self-taught and always recognized how much she owed to her reading. The erudition she achieved was drawn from a heterogeneous, international body of works ranging from the church fathers to Voltaire as well as Canadian writers. Her columns were full of quotations that she had gleaned from her readings and turned over in her mind. It is unlikely that the haberdasher's house on Notre-Dame Street was well stocked with books banned by Rome, and it can be assumed that Eva quenched her thirst for literature, history, and philosophy in the personal libraries of her friends and acquaintances. Books were her passion, and the library became her life's work. The library meant books that were chosen, fingered, borrowed, brought home, read and reread at one's own pace, with the pauses needed for reflection and a pencil handy to annotate and often dialogue with the author. It was also the local and foreign magazines and newspapers that put readers in touch with opinions from abroad, opened their minds to other references, and left the door open to the kind of relativity that Catholic authoritarianism so feared.

The first months were spent acquiring books and periodicals. By October, everything was in place, and the board approved subscriptions to eleven French-language and forty-one English-language periodicals.[106] The groundwork had been laid. Henceforward, Éva Circé pursued two careers in tandem: journalist and librarian.

* * *

Two photographs of Éva Circé taken around 1903 show her in two different poses. In the first, reproduced in *Bleu, Blanc, Rouge*, she stands facing the camera, almost smiling, and wearing a dress—possibly the much-decried bag dress—belted at the waist with a narrow sash. Her hair is tied up in a frizzy chignon, and a small crucifix is suspended from her choker.

When *Bleu, Blanc, Rouge* came out, *La Patrie* published a photo of the author in which the predominant features, as always, are her intense eyes and unruly hair; the portrait is surrounded by the decorative leafage design so common at the turn of the century.

In both pictures, it is the intense gaze that holds our attention. This is the gaze she would fix on her times and her contemporaries, a gaze that could be compassionate or pitiless, ironic or cynical, but always frank and never complacent.

CHAPTER 2

WOE TO THAT WOMAN BY WHOM THE OFFENCE COMETH

Many other works produced by our writers, worthy of a place of honour on our library shelves, have already perished and will perish again, though they attest to the remarkable talents day by day repressed through the indifference of the community, and then forever snuffed out.[1]

LOUVIGNY DE MONTIGNY

On April 29, 1905, having granted a dispensation from the reading of the banns, Magloire Auclair, the priest of the Saint-Jean-Baptiste parish, blessed the marriage of thirty-four-year-old Éva Circé, librarian at the public library, and twenty-nine-year-old Pierre-Salomon Côté, physician.[2] The couple married at the church of the *village* Saint-Jean-Baptiste, a quasi-suburban neighbourhood north of the city centre. The parish had been created in 1874, and the church on Rachel Street served a population made up primarily of small merchants and workers. Even though the "village," just recently incorporated into the City of Montreal, was a working-class district, it contained few large-scale industrial installations. Upon retiring at the age of sixty, Narcisse Circé had given up his men's clothing store and moved with his wife and his children Éva and Arthur to 462 Rachel Street, in the very heart of the "village," between Hôtel-de-Ville and de Bullion, a block away from the church.

Dr. Pierre-Salomon Côté opened his first clinic in 1902 on St-Denis Street just south of Rachel. Whereas Éva's parents only had to cross the street to get to the marriage ceremony, the groom's family were unable to make the long trip from Sainte-Luce in the Lower St. Lawrence district to Montreal. Olivier Asselin, who also hailed from the "Bas-du-Fleuve," published this item in *Le Nationaliste*:

> Yesterday morning at the Saint-Jean-Baptiste church, Rev. Father Auclair blessed the union of Miss Éva Circé, librarian at the Municipal Library, and Dr. Salomon Côté, of Laval Street.
> The bride, who was accompanied by her father, wore a green ensemble with a matching hat. Mr. N. Patenaude was the best man.
> Mrs. Côté is well known as a journalist writing under the pseudonym "Colombine." She is a delightfully intelligent and big-hearted woman. Her husband is also a charming and highly cultured man. I trust they both will accept the best wishes for happiness from a man who knows how much they deserve it.[3]

Intelligence and culture, heart and charm: all the ingredients for a harmonious marriage were brought together, a marriage of love celebrated in a private ceremony. There was no reading of the banns in church during the preceding weeks, no doubt to ensure that, given the reputations of both parties, especially Éva's, the privacy of the event would not be spoiled by prying eyes. The marriage may have been a concession to the families' religious traditions, but it was a far cry from the long white gown and the garland of orange blossoms! A short time before, Asselin apparently had organized a bachelor party for the young doctor, as he had already done for Louvigny de Montigny.[4]

Pierre-Salomon Côté, five years his wife's junior, settled in the Saint-Jean-Baptiste neighbourhood after completing his medical training in 1902. A native of the Lower St. Lawrence region, he was the seventh child of the Liberal Elzéar Côté (1841–1920), a militia captain, an important merchant, and the former mayor of Sainte-Luce de Rimouski, and of Ann Jane Haney (1847–1921), a still quite young woman of Irish extraction.[5] Infant mortality befell the countryside just as it did the city, and of their sixteen children, only seven reached adulthood.[6] Pierre-Salomon was evidently a talented student, and he pursued his education at the Saint-Joseph College in Memramcook, New Brunswick, before going on to the faculty of medicine of Université Laval in Quebec City.

It is not known when and where Éva and Pierre-Salomon first met, but her poem "Erin Go Bragh!" appeared in 1903 and was dedicated to Mrs. Côté, Pierre-Salomon's mother. Nor can the identity of the "dear friend" to whom she dedicated *Bleu, Blanc, Rouge* be ascertained. Colombine and

Musette wrote more than once on the subject of love, and perhaps those texts were not purely fictitious. If the facts presented there were drawn from reality, were they based on observations or personal experience?

The newlyweds took up residence in Pierre-Salomon's apartment on Laval Street for a short time, after which they moved in with Circé's parents on Rachel Street, where the doctor practised as a "specialist in nervous disorders." Thus, Éva, Pierre-Salomon, Ézilda and Narcisse Circé, as well as nineteen-year-old Arthur Circé, all shared the same house. The parish priest in their working-class neighbourhood, Father Magloire Auclair, devoted himself to establishing social services like the Société de protection des malades (Society for the protection of the sick) and the Hospice Auclair for poor children and the needy, located next to the church. However freethinking they may have been, Éva and Pierre maintained good relationships with the priest, whom Éva had previously praised in *Les Débats*, applauding his social work and, because of it, forgiving him for being "anti-Voltairean and hunting down freethinkers and Protestants."[7] Dr. Côté was also socially committed and was soon dubbed "doctor to the poor."[8]

The union of the two freethinkers inevitably drew criticism, so that twenty years later Éva would write: "when I married, every possible dark deed was fabricated about my husband and me. He was accused of all the vices and so was I. Naturally, we couldn't care less. I actually think it increased our love for each other."[9] Ignoring the rumours, husband and wife were happy and mutually supportive. Pierre-Salomon encouraged Éva when a priest threatened to get her dismissed from the newspaper.[10] They moved in the same vanguard circles, where they mixed with those identified as the bohemians of Montreal: atheist journalists, symbolist poets, iconoclastic artists, not to mention young dissenting professionals who gathered at the Freemasons' lodge or the Ligue de l'Enseignement (League of instruction). Though they led secular lives, Éva and Pierre were not averse to acting as godmother and godfather to the son of Éva's sister Maria Circé and J. S. H. Michaud in March 1906.[11] The priest in Sorel, where the baptism took place, must have been unaware of the Freemasonic sympathies of these enlightened Montrealers; otherwise, he necessarily would have denied them the right to hold their nephew over the baptismal font.

The couple would spend their summer vacations at Saint-Luce. This did not involve intellectual exile; one of their neighbours was Arthur Buies, who in 1900 had had a house built on the shores of the river.[12] In 1911 his daughter Yvonne married Pierre-Salomon's younger brother, the jurist Auguste Côté.[13] Buies, even after returning to the Church, remained provocative, liberal, and anticonformist, qualities that endeared him to his neighbour Éva.[14]

This part of the Lower St. Lawrence area was a veritable nest of *Rouges*, where family connections reinforced intellectual affinities. An uncle of Pierre-Salomon was godfather to Sophie Asselin, Olivar Asselin's younger sister, whose family had settled in Sainte-Flavie in the 1880s.[15] Anne-Marie Gleason also hailed from Rimouski. Éva would become attached to this region and would speak highly of its inhabitants, whom she found "cultivated" and whose speech was "peppered with archaic expressions, the last vestiges of a faraway France."[16]

Éva and Pierre-Salomon managed to reconcile their attachment to the Côté family, with its traditional Catholic ways, and their involvement with their radical and Freemason friends in Montreal. Indeed, Freemasonry occupied an important place in their milieu, and the positions defended by the couple, their materialism and secular ideas, cannot be comprehended without some understanding of Freemasonry at the turn of the century.

The roots of Freemasonry in Quebec go back to the beginning of the nineteenth century, when the Grand Lodge of Quebec, which traced its origins to Scotland and England, established lodges in Quebec City and Montreal. The Cœurs-Unis (United hearts), the Montreal section of the Grand Lodge, was found wanting by some of its progressive French-speaking members. In 1896, given "the complete lack of moral influence of English Freemasonry on the French-Canadian population,"[17] the French-speaking Freemasons, led by the journalist Godfroy Langlois, submitted a petition to the Grand Orient de France demanding a symbolic constitution, which they obtained in July 1896. In France, Freemasonry went back to the eighteenth century and was part of the "cultural sociability of the Enlightenment."[18] Whereas the British lodges respected each person's religion and occasionally had ties with some protestant congregations, the Grand Orient de France, imbued with the ideas of the Philosophers, promoted free inquiry, free thought, and made no secret of its anticlericalism. Thus, a lodge was founded in Montreal under the name L'Émancipation and whose motto was "Raison, travail, liberté" (Reason, work, liberty);[19] its offices were located in the Odd Fellows' Hall on Notre-Dame Street. Out of this first lodge came a second one, Force et Courage (Strength and courage), which was established in January 1910 on the initiative of five members. In its ranks were forward-thinking politicians like the former mayor of Montreal Honoré Beaugrand; physicians specializing in public health, such as Alfred Marcil and Adelstan Le Moyne de Martigny, who were behind the Gouttes de lait (Well Baby) clinics; journalists such as Godfroy Langlois and Arsène Bessette; the poet and lawyer Gonzalve Desaulniers; trade unionists, of whom Gustave Francq was the best known; and even a police detective. The same names could be found in the Côtés' social circle. Women in France could be admitted to a mixed-gender order, which became a veritable breeding ground for feminists, but this model was not followed in Quebec.

Masons discussed social issues, education—the key to progress—health, and municipal reforms. Because knowledge was considered of vital importance, in 1909 the lodge L'Émancipation founded the Alpha Omega society for the purpose of organizing lectures and setting up a library. Broad-minded individuals no longer had to go to the Fraser Institute to consult "advanced" works, such as the Institut canadien's collection of books, banned by the Catholic Church. At the Alpha Omega library they now had access to eighteenth-century philosophers like Voltaire and Champfort, the radical politician Aristide Briand, the feminist Maria Deraisme (the first woman in France to join the Freemasons), the scientists James George Frazer, Félix Le Dantec, and Henri Poincaré, and the anarchist Élisée Reclus. Members could also read, albeit with some delay, the French periodicals *Le Quotidien*, *L'Humanité*, *Les Cahiers des Droits de l'Homme*.[20]

A secret society that defied the teachings of Rome and was openly anticlerical and even atheistic could not be tolerated by the Catholic Church. In 1738 Pope Clement XII had condemned Freemasonry for its anti-Catholicism and its secret oath, and nineteenth-century popes had maintained the anathema.[21] In Quebec, from the moment L'Émancipation was founded in 1896, the clergy deemed it a scourge against which their flock must be protected.

What was the doctrine of this association that made the bishops tremble so? It was based on a belief in progress inherited from the Enlightenment and upheld by the liberal thinking of the nineteenth century. Human beings, endowed with the freedom to choose, are perfectible. Knowledge and science guide society toward a progress that is ineluctable but slowed by reaction and religion. People's actions must be informed and not imposed through religious beliefs. Learning therefore becomes a primordial issue, because the transformation of society depends on secularity and education. Ideally, this education must be secular and available to everyone, men and women alike, hence free and compulsory. This battle had been won in France under the Third Republic; the radical left-wing government of Émile Combes (1902–5), which had barred religious congregations from teaching in France and closed their schools, was associated with the mass exodus of priests and nuns, many of whom then sought refuge in Quebec, where they would nurture the fear and loathing of anticlericalism. The demonization of the lodges was propagated by the Catholic press, such as *La Vérité*, *La Croix*, and *L'Action sociale catholique* founded by Mgr Bégin and owned by the archdiocese of Quebec

City; it was opposed by the enlightened elites claiming to act on behalf of a civilizing mission and whose views could be read in Godfroy Langlois's *Le Canada*. In 1908, Omer Héroux, editor of *La Vérité*, took the opportunity offered by an interview with the anti-Semitic Parisian newspaper *La Libre Parole* of Paris to make the (baseless) connection between Freemasonry and Jews in Canada. The interview was reproduced in Olivar Asselin's *Le Nationaliste*.[22] A three-act vaudeville comedy titled *Les Francs-Maçons* (The Freemasons) was staged in October 1909.[23]

The announcement of an International Eucharistic Congress to be held in Montreal in September 1910 stoked the flames of anti-Freemasonry.[24] Albert-J. Lemieux, a young zealot of the Action catholique de la jeunesse canadienne-française (Catholic action of French-Canadian youth) went so far as to spy on the lodge and note down conversations held during its meetings, subsequently unmasking a so-called plot to embarrass certain members of the clergy during the Eucharistic Congress by taking them to brothels in Montreal's red-light district. However bold and ingenious the plan may have been, it had never been seriously considered. Lemieux published a pamphlet revealing the names of all those in attendance at that meeting.[25] It seems the assailants of Freemasons could act with impunity. The artist Ludger Larose, who taught painting and drawing at the École du Plateau and was the lodge's treasurer, was attacked and relieved of his money and the list of members. Soon thereafter he was stripped of his teaching position in Montreal's Catholic public schools.[26] The campaign against Freemasons was at its height. Quebec society was in the midst of a conflict between progressive and reactionary forces, between radical, progressive liberalism and traditional conservatism.

As was the case elsewhere, the Masons provided mutual assistance. Did Lorenzo Prince and Frédéric Villeneuve owe their nominations for the position of chief librarian to the influence of their Masonic brethren? At any rate, there is no doubt that Masons, if only for ideological reasons, supported those running for elected office, as when Langlois ran for a seat in the provincial assembly and Francq for one on the municipal council.

* * *

It was after her marriage that Éva Circé earned the reputation of a freethinking woman. She was already a rebel and an idealist, but her husband's involvement with Freemasonry probably was what led her to adopt increasingly bold and radical positions. A column signed Colombine in the Saint-Jérôme weekly ignited a controversy as intense as the summer heat in 1904. It all began with an essay in *L'Avenir du Nord* in which Circé came out against the death penalty. Addressing her as yet unborn great-great-niece, she hopes for a future when the circumstances that produce criminality would be taken into account: "The error of my epoch," she tells her interlocutor, "is to believe, after four thousand years of experience, that the murderer is responsible for his crime, as if it was always the result of his wish to kill."[27] Flirting with eugenic ideas, she ascribes part of the blame to heredity, "the perennial culprit." And she adds that in the future, thanks to Combes, the crucifix will have disappeared from the courts. It was a clumsy argument, premised on the notion that the French minister could somehow influence Quebec. Moreover, no Canadian courtroom was adorned with a crucifix. While ignoring this inaccuracy, the small right-wing press was outraged; Jean-Paul Tardivel fired the first shot in his newspaper *La Vérité*.

In his article, Tardivel depicted Colombine by turns as hysterical, neuropathic, foolish, perverse, an anarchist and a nihilist who wrote tortuous nonsense amounting to an "indigestible hodgepodge." Once he was done with the personal insults, Tardivel set himself up as the champion of justice, justifying the death penalty in the name of the killers' victims. But what galled this entrenched ultramontanist more than anything was the suggestion that the crucifix should be removed from the courts. Twice, Tardivel—who never had any scruples when it came to censorship—asked why Colombine was allowed to write in newspapers.[28] Immediately the next day, the editor in-chief of *L'Avenir du Nord*, Jules-Édouard Prévost, came to his columnist's defence, quoting the Gospel on forgiveness and presenting Colombine as neither blasphemous nor irreligious, but instead as "a clever columnist," whose aim was not to excuse Combes—still despised in Quebec—but to spare Christ on the Cross the sight of the injustices and perjuries "defiling the courts."[29] With the support of the *La Nation*, run by the conservative Guillaume-Alphonse Nantel of Saint-Jérôme, *La Vérité* pursued the debate, and before long the exchanges between *L'Avenir du Nord* and the two Catholic papers shifted to the crimes—were they substantiated or exaggerated?—of the Inquisition.[30]

Éva Circé waited two months to respond to Tardivel's "lament." Rather than retaliating head-on, she used an anecdote, in which the character of a Craig Street bookseller discredits *La Vérité* and ridicules Tardivel's love for his Christ and his church. She derided Tardivel for unwittingly taking the bait of "the gentle image of Christ being absent from our courtrooms."[31] Concluding on a mystical note, Circé depicted some nuns amid stained-glass windows, fragrances, and melodies, who turn the sacrament, separated from the world by "a wall of peace," into "a sacrament of poetry and love for the rosy-haired Christ," in which all the wretched march past "without respect for the purity of the spotless Lamb." Although Colombine was not religious, she retained the mystical inflections of her early writings.

While the columns that she submitted to *Rouge* newspapers like *L'Avenir du Nord* presented a modern, critical view of society in the early years of the twentieth century, her vision could grow nostalgic, even backward-looking at times, as evidenced in a text published in the popular daily *La Patrie*. Soon after Circé's marriage, on the occasion of the Saint-Jean-Baptiste feast day, *La Patrie* opened its pages to Quebec's women of letters, asking them to write "charming articles." Éva accepted the challenge and wrote what was indeed a "charming" piece, "Impressions de Pierrot sur la ville" (Pierrot's impressions of the city), which in no way threatened to upset its readers. The tenor of the biographical note about Colombine suggests that her popularity was somewhat on the wane. Whereas the other women contributors were entitled to a few lines about their publications, Circé was introduced as "Colombine, Miss Circé, wife of Dr. S. A [sic] Côté, was a columnist for *Les Débats* and a few dailies."[32] That is all. In her "modest Saint-Jean-Baptiste Day salute" Colombine addresses a farmwoman whose husband and son have gone to sell their produce at the Bonsecours market in Montreal. Upon discovering the dirty, noisy city, young Pierrot is quickly disenchanted. It is a conventional piece, rooted in the land, which may as well have been dictated by the ministère de la Colonisation (Ministry in charge of settlements), and it ends with Pierrot sighing, "The city . . . well . . . it makes me feel sick."[33] Could this be an expression of her ambivalence toward city life or an effort to bow to the conventions befitting Quebec's national holiday?

Even though her output as a columnist slowed down as of 1904—just five texts were published in *L'Avenir du Nord*, three in *Le Nationaliste*, and two in the *Bulletin de la Caisse d'économie*—Éva Circé-Côté maintained a continuing presence on the literary scene. Then as now, language in Quebec was as much a political issue as a literary one, and literature and politics overlapped. In February 1904, Éva was deeply affected by a mass meeting of the Ligue nationaliste held at the Théâtre National. That winter evening was to remain a crucial event for the nationalist movement and the opposition against British imperialism. Henri Bourassa's speech on Canadian and provincial autonomy surely moved Éva, and she was enthused by the announcement that Olivar Asselin, the organizer of the event, was founding a Sunday paper. She immediately sent Asselin a letter offering her collaboration in the most exalted terms:

> I am ready to follow you wherever you may go, certain of walking the straight path of loyalty and of the man you are. If you are in need of

unwavering devotion, persevering labour, and a disciple who embraces your cause with the passion of a neophyte prepared for martyrdom, I offer you all this, in the belief that I would be fulfilling a duty of gratitude.[34]

On March 6, Asselin launched *Le Nationaliste*, and on the front page he published a programme that Éva Circé would not have disputed.

1. For Canada, the greatest possible degree of autonomy in its relationship with Great Britain, along with the maintenance of colonial ties;
2. For the Canadian provinces, in their relationship with the federal authorities, the greatest possible degree of autonomy compatible with the maintenance of federal ties;
3. The adoption by the federal and provincial governments of an essentially Canadian policy of economic and intellectual development.[35]

Éva kept her word and sent articles to the new periodical. On March 13, *Le Nationaliste* published a rather didactic column on parent-child relationships,[36] which was signed Éva Circé and not Colombine, as would also be the case for the two texts published in May and July 1904. This apparently low output may have been due to her courtship with Pierre-Salomon Côté as well as her involvement in other projects. Or perhaps there had been disagreements with other members of the crew. Then again, she may have published under another, unknown, pseudonym. In any case, the quality of her contributions to Asselin's weekly fell short of the offer she had made in February.

Though less busy with journalism, Éva Circé had not fallen silent. She was enough of a celebrity for the Association Saint-Jean-Baptiste[37] to ask for her opinion as to what constituted "the most heroic act in the history of the French race in Canada." Her answer: the events of 1837–38,[38] not a surprising response, since she had already made known her feelings on the subject in *Hindelang et Delorimier*.

In 1905, *Le Nationaliste* asked a number of intellectuals to contribute to a series of articles on the future of French Canada. Week after week, writers, scientists, and businessmen expressed their respective visions. In keeping with the prevailing practice of that period, the texts contributed by women of letters were all published together in a single issue, which appeared on November 19. It included six articles, all signed with pseudonyms: "Lisette" (Élisa David-Rainville), "Margot" (Marguerite de Montigny), "Françoise" (Robertine Barry), "Madeleine" (Anne-Marie Gleason), "Colette" (Edouardine Lesage) and "Colombine" (Éva Circé-Côté). Each writer presented her conception of Quebec and French Canada—only rarely differentiating between them—but there was no consensus that might have justified grouping them together in the same issue.

Élisa David-Rainville ("Lisette"), the daughter of L.-O. David, places her hopes in her two sons, brought up to love their country. She refers to the independence of Quebec, and concludes, in a tone of resignation, "the reality of this dream, this desire, is highly problematic, for what can old Quebec do alone in the face of the other provinces?" Finally, she praises England, "which, after all, grants us all our freedoms, all our rights, all the privileges of independent states."[39]

Marguerite de Montigny ("Margot"), the sister of Louvigny and Gaston de Montigny and a contributor to liberal newspapers, demands that French Canadians be the masters in their own country. In a spirit of outright racism, she wishes to shut the door on all immigrants, "who are turning our country into a potpourri of nations instead of a Canadian land, for the Chinese have replaced our laundresses, the Jews lend money against stolen goods, the Italians and Greeks invade our streets selling candies, the Germans, Poles, and Syrians crowd our factories, and all of them loiter in the parks and bring epidemics, strikes, and bad ice cream!"[40]

Robertine Barry ("Françoise") was the most eminent journalist among this group of women: editor from 1891 to 1900 of the "Chronique du lundi" (Monday column) covering issues of interest to women; editor from 1897 to 1900 of "Le Coin de Franchette" (Frankie's corner) in *La Patrie*, whose director during those years was the radical Honoré Beaugrand; founder of her own weekly, *Le Journal de Françoise*; delegate to the Universal Exhibition in Paris in 1900; member of the Société des gens de lettres (Writers' association); officer of the Académie by appointment of the French government.[41] Hers is a generous dream. With Switzerland as her model, she hopes for a Canadian republic for all the country's inhabitants, regardless of language or religion.

For Anne-Marie Gleason ("Madeleine"), editor of the women's page in *La Patrie* and proud of her French and Irish heritage, the future must bring "deliverance from a yoke ... [but] without clashes in an empire too vast for our ambitions" and establish freedom within a republic.[42]

Edouardine Lesage's ("Colette") ties to the liberal press were not as strong as those of her colleagues. She had worked for *Le Pionnier* and *La Patrie* and was now on the staff of the women's page in *La Presse* and the editorial board of *L'Album universel*. Writing in a more traditional vein, she puts her hopes in faith, work, and study.

In introducing "Madame P. S. Côté (née Circé) (Colombine)," the editors emphasized, once again, her big-heartedness: "she is filled with indignation at all the social injustices and takes a passionate interest in every cause. Her writings bear the imprint of this temperament and often are all the more stirring for it." Colombine addresses her text directly to the "impetuous Asselin." She lyrically compares French Canada to a newborn child. The allegory extends from the danger of premature death, to the loss of the mother that had compelled the country to feed on maple syrup, and to the child's education, which must be guided by self-respect and the veneration of honour. French Canada requires an education befitting its nature and its milieu: "it belongs to us women to train the soul, to prepare the ground for the fruitful cultivation of literature and the development of noble sentiments." In 1905 she still held to a traditional view of the separation of domains: civic education remained the prerogative of women. Colombine aims high: by virtue of its moral and intellectual superiority, French-Canada would rise to dominance in Canada and throughout the continent. Reason, not might, would hold sway. Éva Circé-Côté drew her inspiration from the late-nineteenth-century writers who sought to apply the new findings of science to social problems. She concludes with this statement: "I believe that in both the economic and psychological spheres there is a natural selection at work: the inferior races tend to disappear, through the workings of justice, through the law of equilibrium." Meanwhile, Canadians have survived despite being less numerous and "we shall be the masters if we deserve to be. Thanks to reason, will, and nature, but not chance, we shall triumph because the eternal march of progress ultimately strives for the truth, the glorification of the good."[43]

This single column aptly encapsulated Éva Circé's outlook in 1905. Despite her plea for the education of women, she still believed in the essential difference between women's and men's mentalities. Because she was also a strong believer in willpower, she placed all her hopes in enlightened thinking. She was strongly influenced by Darwin's theory and, especially, Herbert Spencer's social Darwinism, but the relative roles played by human intervention and natural selection in ensuring the survival of the French-Canadian "race" remained to be sorted out.

*   *   *

Éva Circé had carved out an enviable reputation in Québécois journalism since 1900. She was also well known as a champion of women's education. It was, therefore, not surprising to find her taking part in the founding convention of the Fédération nationale Saint-Jean-Baptiste in 1907.

It would be apposite here to provide some detail on the different organizations incorporating in their names that of French Canada's patron saint, John the Baptist, whose feast day, June 24, had been celebrated since 1834.

The name of Jesus's forerunner was first used by the Association Saint-Jean-Baptiste, a "charitable society and national society of French Canadians" founded by Ludger Duvernay in 1843.[44] Under the direction of L.-O. David, its chairman from 1888 to 1892, the Association Saint-Jean-Baptiste (ASJB, later to become the Société Saint-Jean-Baptiste, SSJB) built the Monument-National to house its offices and rent halls for various cultural and educational events. But it was a costly project and, as was often the case, the wives and daughters of the board members joined forces to collect funds. Long before their association was founded, the *dames patronnesses* of the Association Saint-Jean-Baptiste held bazaars, fairs, picnics, banquets, and art galas to support the works of the society. Because they were women, they were excluded, but since they, too, had a stake in the Monument-National project, they demanded special status within the society. The board, under the chairmanship of Frédéric-Ligori Béïque, acceded to their demand at the end of 1901. The first general meeting of the *dames patronnesses* was held at the Monument-National in April 1902 with Caroline Béïque as chairwoman. In addition to relatives of the society's members, they granted membership to women making an annual contribution of one dollar, which opened the door to Éva Circé and her fellow female journalists.[45] The board of directors had around forty members, including wives of ASJB members (identified by their husbands' names) such as Mesdames L.-O. David, Raoul Dandurand, Louis Beaubien, L. J. A. Surveyer, G. Langlois, J. B. Rottot, as well as the journalists Robertine Barry, Georgina Bélanger, Anne-Marie Gleason, Édouardine Lesage, and Éva Circé.[46] Aside from providing financial assistance to the SSJB, the *dames patronnesses* made a name for themselves by setting up courses open to the public and, in particular, by establishing the first housekeeping schools.[47] The reason Éva Circé joined the Association des dames patronnesses de l'Association Saint-Jean-Baptiste de Montréal was most likely that she wanted to ensure the creation of a cultural space in the city, a project that was dear to her heart.[48] In 1902, she painted a very positive picture of the Association des dames patronnesses in a text reprinted in *Bleu, Blanc, Rouge*.

Éva Circé and Georgina Bélanger belonged to the literary circle of Marie Gérin-Lajoie, who was active in the Montreal Local Council of Women, an Anglophone body dedicated to defending women's rights.[49] Meetings of the literary circle gave rise to the idea of founding a Francophone organization distinct from the Conseil des femmes de Montréal (Montreal Council of Women). Thus, in 1907, the Fédération nationale Saint-Jean-Baptiste (FNSJB) was born, bringing together several women's groups, including the *dames patronnesses*, with the prior endorsement of Mgr Bruchési, to whom they had presented their goals in the following terms:

We wish to unite French-Canadian women through the bond of charity in an national association, so that they may help one another in life and, by dint of their union, strengthen, heighten and develop women's actions in the family and society, thereby working for the country's prosperity and the glory of God, the end of all things.

We therefore seek your blessing, Mgr, and ask that, as Jesus Christ's representative, you see fit to help us in our enterprise of social restoration.

In the hope that you may grant us our request, we gratefully remain,

Your obedient children,

The request was signed by Lady Lacoste, Mesdames Béïque, Gérin-Lajoie, Thibaudeau, Hamilton, Rottot, Leman, Provencher, Huguenin, Cartier, and Gagnon.[50] Mgr Bruchési could not do otherwise but approve this association of women professing a Christian feminism, "quite different," he remarked, "from that other feminism, which, on the pretext of demanding the unrecognized rights of women, forgets the special role that providence has assigned them in the world."[51]

The Federation's Catholicism, its spirit of submission to the clergy, and the presence of a chaplain in every association did nothing to kindle Éva Circé-Côté's enthusiasm for this organization. Unlike her colleagues Françoise and Madeleine, she did not sit on the organizing committee of the future Fédération.[52] Nevertheless, Marie Gérin-Lajoie invited her to speak at its founding convention at the end of May 1907. She and Camille, her colleague at *La Patrie*, represented the association of women journalists affiliated with the FNSJB and, in that capacity, they addressed an issue of great concern to religious circles: the protection of young girls. Mrs. Côté no doubt shocked some of the delegates when, in her discussion of women's work, she asked, "whether it would be preferable to educate young girls as to all the dangers of life, rather than seeking to spare their innocence for as long as possible the revelation of things that may disturb them." For the paper *Le Canada*, this was a "very questionable" notion. Circé-Côté's speech at the closing session on economic undertakings was along the same lines. Basing herself on her observations at the Miséricorde hospital for unwedded mothers, the reform school, and in prisons, Éva deplored the culpable ignorance and lack of moral direction in the guidance given to young working-class women in those institutions. Far from opposing work for women, she put forward "uplifting work."[53] It was through education and the reading of journals headed by women and books other than sentimental novels that the situation of working-class women could be improved. "Let us work for the emancipation of women through education," she concluded.[54]

Éva Circé-Côté's presence was out of harmony with a meeting where the archbishop asked that the utopia of social equality be left to others, whereas "it was up to them [the members of the FNSJB] to lift up fallen women, to combat unseemly fashions, . . . intemperance, evil literature and theatre" and to be "apostles within the family," and where the chairwoman, Marie Gérin-Lajoie, reassured its members that the Federation was "the propagator of the national faith" and "a place of mutual assistance for women."[55]

Some time after the founding convention, Marie Gérin-Lajoie asked Éva Circé-Côté to write a piece for the Fédération. In her response, Circé-Côté wrote that she had tried at first to resist because she could not betray her principles, but in the end she felt "happy to sacrifice my vanity as a writer to the triumph of a cause that you have taken up."[56] Here one sees the journalist Circé-Côté worrying about her reputation as an author and finding that such an article was not worthy of her writing. She points to the incompatibility of friendship—she calls Gérin-Lajoie her friend—and the latter's cause with what she called her principles, while at the same time saying she was happy to have yielded to what could only be a compromise. For Circé-Côté was already a freethinking woman, who, along with her husband, was associated with the most independent minds of Quebec's intellectual milieu. As to the journalists' association she represented, it was short-lived. According to the founder of the FNSJB, it was the only association in the Fédération that "remained lifeless."[57] There were, however, women writers on the FNSJB's board of directors: Robertine Barry, Joséphine Marchand-Dandurand, Félicité Angers, Louis Marmette Brodeur, and, until her resignation in 1916, Anne-Marie Gleason-Huguenin. Éva Circé-Côté's principles kept her at a distance from an association so tightly corseted by the clergy.

* * *

From Éva's wedding day until 1909, her publications were few and far between, yet she was hardly idle. The birth of her daughter Ève, on August 17, 1906, indubitably restricted her activities, but there is no evidence that she gave up her work at the library.[58] Nor was she the only one among her female colleagues to publish at a slower pace during the first years of marriage. Georgina Bélanger (Gaëtane de Montreuil), after marrying Charles Gill in 1902, and Joséphine Marchand, after her marriage to Senator Raoul Dandurand, also wrote less than before.[59] As for Circé, she published sixty-one columns in 1903 but only twenty-six between May 1904 and the end of

1909.[60] She wrote sporadically for *L'Avenir du Nord*, for example, when she railed against the death penalty or shared a Christmas tale. She was no more inclined to submit articles to the *Journal de Françoise*, launched by Robertine Barry in 1905. Éva's collaboration was announced, but between 1905 and 1908 she would publish just four columns.

Starting in 1905, the tone and tenor of her writings changed. Though still optimistic, she grew more critical and evinced a degree of disappointment. Her bitterness arose in response not to her personal situation but, rather, to the oppressive climate prevailing on the literary scene in Quebec. For, "to be well regarded here, one must say that Voltaire is a second-rate writer, Rousseau a figure of depravity, Zola a pornographer, Michelet a mediocre historian, and make sure to have them all die of shameful causes. To be thought clever and talented, one must carry a *billet de confession* in one's pocket. What a sad mentality is ours!"[61] This was not the only time she would pen this observation.

In the summer of 1909, she adopted the pseudonym Fantasio for two pieces published in *La Vigie*, while still writing under the name Colombine. One was a reprint of an article that had previously appeared in *L'Avenir du Nord*, in which she impugns the bombastic speeches made at the Saint-Jean-Baptiste celebrations. She would return to these topics a number of times on the occasion of Quebec's national holiday: the speakers flatter French Canadians by having them believe in the superiority of their people, which, she contends, is no doubt better than preaching humility and submissiveness. She recalls the heroes of New France and those of 1837–38, as well as French Canadians' Iroquois and Huron roots, and also France, "light of the world, brain of humanity; in its heart the notions of regeneration, of universal solidarity were developed." And she concludes with this appeal: "Therefore let us be optimistic, let us look to the future serenely, and see the dawning of our day of independence: French blood, any more than life or light, cannot die. With it, we possess the certain seed of resurrection!"[62] In this peroration referring to biological essence, the future lies in the blood. The article raises a paradox in the thinking of many progressive reformists of that epoch: the appeal, on the one hand, to science and its proof of heredity, and, on the other, to Enlightenment philosophy, allowing the possibility of transforming the environment and remodelling the human species. Scientists lecture on the soil and the seed; the journalist Circé counts on education to improve the soil, while believing in biological antecedents, which presumably render the people more apt to thrive. Finally, the notion of independence is not made explicit. Some of her contemporaries envisioned a French Canada within the British Empire, others a republic. She herself often referred to the independence project of the *Patriotes*, but without specifying what form this might take in the twentieth century.

52 / Freethinker

BAPTISTE :—Comment voulez-vous que j'suive les autres, avec ce damné mouton qui est toujours à m'barrer les jambes ?

Le Pays, February 15, 1913. BAnQ.

The article did not go unnoticed, and this time its author was attacked not in the right-wing papers, which she easily could have ignored, but in Asselin's *Le Nationaliste* by a reader who signed, "A young seminarian."[63] The letter, oozing sarcasm, quotes Colombine out of context so as to highlight what the letter-writer interprets as a disparagement of French immigrants. In her response to the "young seminarian" she pleaded her case, and neither Asselin nor Prévost stood up for her, in contrast to what happened during the controversy at *L'Avenir du Nord* in 1904.

She begins by refuting the accusation of having offended the French. Being a Francophile, Éva Circé-Côté could account for herself before her French friends. Having addressed the substantive question, she proceeds to deal with the gibes directed at her style, slipping into a very personal defence: "I lack the spare time to smooth out my sentences; each minute represents so many nickels that I must save. I envy those who are at leisure to hammer out their periods." She continues with an unexpected line of argument for a woman used to manoeuvring in a world of men, and plays on her being a woman to embarrass her critic:

> You prefer to sully the white dress of a woman of letters, a mother who, standing beside a cradle, writes things she holds to be true, a feminist, you say—humanist would be closer to the truth—who upholds without

distinction the rights of the oppressed, of the destitute, exalts devotion and heroism, denounces fanaticism, condemns lies, a woman who was persecuted and deprived for having the courage of her ideas.[64]

Her rejoinder may have been surprising coming from someone as strong as Circé-Côté, but the image of a mother torn between the cradle and the writing desk while her husband's health was in decline was nonetheless accurate. She might have added that she was busy with another project in 1908: the inauguration of a *lycée* for girls in Montreal.

Education occupied a fundamental position in Éva Circé-Côté's thinking. She considered it the *sine qua non* of the progress she never stopped believing in, the indispensable key to human perfectibility. In 1902, a group of citizens calling for education, a responsibility of the state, to be made compulsory and free for everyone, founded the Ligue de l'Enseignement (League for instruction). Its vice-president was Godfroy Langlois, and it brought together a variety of well-known citizens, ranging from the financier Louis-Joseph Forget to the socialist Albert Saint-Martin.[65] The ideal of free and compulsory schooling was also shared by the members of the Masonic lodge and by the international labour unions. Éva Circé-Côté embraced it wholeheartedly. Was education not mandatory in most countries as well as Ontario since 1891? She came back to this subject in a number of her columns: schooling would reduce crime—"Opening a school means closing a prison," Victor Hugo had written—stifle the gullibility that enables corruption, give rise to citizens, both male and female—for women have the same right to an education as men—who are informed and able to judge the candidates running in elections, and it would reduce maternal mortality rates, which Circé-Côté ascribed to ignorance, and clear the way to prosperity. Going further than the League, she demanded secular instruction, a demand to which only a few other members subscribed.

Herself a graduate of one of the best educational establishments in Quebec, the convent of the Sisters of Saint Anne in Lachine, a private school, Éva Circé-Côté was aware of the disparities between the programmes available to girls and boys and the predominant place of religion in Catholic teaching. Together with her colleague Georgina Bélanger Gill (Gaëtane de Montreuil), she developed the project of a secular *lycée* where the reforms she was proposing could be put into practice. In April 1908, *La Patrie* announced the September opening of the Lycée des jeunes filles inc. (*Lycée* for girls), which would welcome both boarders and day students. The article was accompanied by a photo of the building at 286 St-Denis, a lovely house surrounded with trees.[66] As Éva and Pierre-Salomon now lived at number 75 St-Denis, just south of Lagauchetière Street, she had only to go up the hill to arrive at the *lycée* and then to continue on to the library.

For the first year, Éva combined her work at the library with that of volunteer principal of the school. She was assisted by Georgina Bélanger Gill and Gonzalve Desaulniers, who acted as president of the establishment. Robertine Barry gave the school excellent publicity in *Le Journal de Françoise*, as did *La Patrie*, lauding the benefits of an education adapted to "the struggle for life" awaiting modern young women. The provincial government was about to open a postsecondary business school for young men, and the *lycée* proposed to give young women access to an equivalent curriculum. In contrast to the education provided to girls in the Catholic schools of Quebec, the programme of the *lycée* was modelled on those available in the United States and France. With its three-year programme, the *lycée*'s aim was to offer a modern, varied curriculum: In addition to French and English courses, the students could choose to study fine arts with the artist Ludger Larose, music, singing, painting, and dance, as well as stenography and commerce.[67] Upon leaving the school, graduates would be able "to find respectable employment, such as, secretary in a governmental body, a commercial establishment or a similar organization, an office, etc., whereas such positions seem to have been reserved until now for our young English-speaking compatriots, who were better equipped for the fight because their training was more practical."[68] Moreover, the shareholders and donors would endeavour to find them jobs. The directors hoped that, with the knowledge and skills acquired at the *lycée*, the students not bound for the labour market would make outstanding homemakers, fully capable of helping their husbands.

The awards handed out in June 1909 attested to the quality of the teaching provided at the school. Through its prizes and bursaries, one can identify the establishment's benefactors: the prize for French sponsored by the Alliance française, the de Martigny prize (probably funded by Paul de Martigny) for history and French diction, the director's prize, the prize sponsored by Mrs. Gonzalve Desaulniers for French and English, the prize sponsored by Dr. Côté for the physical and natural sciences, as well as bursaries ranging from six to fifty dollars.[69] Accomplishments in both the humanities and sciences were rewarded, and the presence of Freemasons among the donors was obvious. According to the report published in *La Patrie* in August 1909, that inaugural year was a success. The establishment gained a good reputation, such that Mayor Louis Payette accepted the position of honorary president. But in September 1909, just before the start of the new school year, Éva Circé-Côté was "forced by unforeseen circumstances beyond her control" to hand over the directorship to Mrs. de la Chaux.[70] Madame Chaux, a music teacher and distinguished educator, had taught for thirteen years at the Sacré-Cœur convent in Rennes (France) before joining the staff of the *lycée* the previous year.

The only testimony left by a student of the Lycée des jeunes filles is that of Albina Sanguinet, who was interviewed at the age of ninety-six for the book *Montréal de vive mémoire, 1900–1939* by Marcelle Brisson and Suzanne Côté-Gauthier:[71]

> That's where I learned that with the nuns I'd learned nothing. We went from nine to five, and it was divided into courses: history, English, French, dance, philosophy, drawing; we learned how to entertain. It was very much about being a socialite. It was an extraordinary school. For dance and drawing, the instructors were men. And a pure Englishwoman taught us English... Children under fifteen weren't admitted. I was a day student... In dance, there was the gavotte... but mainly the waltz."[72]

The founding of the *lycée* acted as a catalyst for giving girls access to higher learning in Quebec. For several years, Marie Gérin-Lajoie, the FNSJB, and the religious teaching congregations had dreamed of a *collège classique* for young women along the lines of those open to young men of the province since the middle of the nineteenth century. The goal was to steer young French-Canadian women wishing to pursue a higher education away from McGill University and the University of Toronto.[73]

Indeed, since 1904, the nuns of the Notre-Dame congregation had petitioned Mgr Bruchési several times for permission to open a *collège classique*, a higher learning institution, for young women. The prelate remained unmoved until news of the forthcoming inauguration of a secular establishment was made public. After the publication on April 25, 1908, of the report in *La Patrie* on the founding of the Lycée des jeunes filles, Mgr Bruchési agreed to receive Mother Sainte-Anne-Marie and Sister Sainte-Sophorine of the Notre-Dame congregation:

> "Today, Your Excellency, we have come to ask your permission to open a higher learning establishment for young women."
> "A school of higher learning! But... where will you put it?"
> "In our new mother house on Sherbrooke Street. Your Excellency, you can not leave the higher education of women in the hands of the Lycée's president and his ilk. And we ourselves are convinced that our venerable Mother Bourgeoys would reproach us for it."
> "Oh! As for the Lycée, it does not frighten me; I shall kill it!"[74]

Circumstance would take it upon itself to bring about the premature death of the Lycée des jeunes filles, so that the bishop's role in that outcome remains unknown. However, he did heartily encourage the nuns: "Found your school, I shall be its father." The state, for its part, was quick to grant a thousand dollars to the new college, which welcomed its first students on October 12, 1908, two weeks after the Lycée des jeunes filles had opened its doors on St-Denis Street.[75]

The bishop waxed enthusiastic in his message to the college's principal, Sister Sainte-Euphrosyne: "Your school of higher learning, it seems to me, fulfils a need in our city," for, after boarding school, young girls, "if they read, do so haphazardly, confining themselves for the most part to light reading and popular novels." In a religious institution, "they will expand the circumference of their knowledge, without leaving the sphere that Providence has allotted them" and they will learn "true Christian science," that which is "harmful to no one." He then quoted the saying, "Men make laws, women make morals."[76] These words of congratulation greeted the opening in the fall of 1908 of Quebec's first *collège classique* for young women, the École d'enseignement supérieur (School of higher learning) of the Sisters of the Congrégation de Notre-Dame.[77]

The secular *lycée*, a veritable provocation for right-minded people, was bound to annoy Catholic groups. After all, had the school not received material support from the Force et Courage Masonic lodge?[78] The board of directors was chaired by Gonzalve Desaulniers, a Freemason and contributor to the *Le Pionnier*; and its vice-chairman, Oscar Normandin, was also on friendly terms with the lodge.[79] The establishment's connections with the freethinkers of Montreal compelled the Sulpician Stanislas Charrier, curé of the Saint-Jacques parish, to have a warning to parents published in *L'Action sociale*, the organ of the Quebec City diocese. Although it was unlikely that the Lycée des jeunes filles would try to recruit students, the priest was upset that the person presiding over the distribution of awards was a Mason. When the lodge undertook to hold a fund-raising event for the Lycée, the newspaper *La Vérité* reminded the faithful that Catholics were no more entitled to support that establishment than to send their children there.[80] For all the polemics that raged at the time, and despite the enrolment of several dozen students over two years, the Lycée des jeunes filles disappeared without a trace.

While devoting herself to all her duties as an educator, in addition to her family responsibilities, Éva Circé-Côté continued to work at the Bibliothèque technique from 10 a.m. to 1 p.m. and 7 p.m. to 10 p.m. on weekdays and from 2 p.m. to 6 p.m. on Sundays.[81] She endeavoured to broaden the library's man-

One of the rooms in the Municipal Library of Montreal. *L'Album universel* 22, no. 1132, pp. 1094-1095, December 30, 1905. BAnQ.

date, ordering classics, books of philosophy and history, and novels, in sum, works she considered essential for a people's cultural growth. "Light literature" could also be found on the shelves, because, like "the gold that guilds the pill of science," novels attracted readers of both sexes, who would then go on to more serious books. One begins with Alexandre Dumas and Jules Verne, she believed, and then moves on to Schopenhauer and Nietzsche.[82] She moreover preferred contemporary works to "old things" that landed in the library, for example, as part of a bequest overflowing with religious books and almanacs. Indeed, pious donations to the library reinforced its prudery. Occasionally, the Commission de la bibliothèque (Library Commission) would reluctantly agree to decline such offers; hence, Circé-Côté the librarian was glad that the Sicotte collection, after lengthy deliberations, was sent to the Saint-Sulpice Library, far better suited for such "old, uninteresting stuff."[83] Her conception of the library was shared not only by *Le Pays* and the Freemasons, but also by Asselin, who gave her his endorsement in *Le Nationaliste*.[84] Circé-Côté's vision always exceeded what was concretely possible and excluded the influence of the Church. She saw big and even envisioned the library as an archival repository.[85]

The religious authorities were not about to accept the library's literary ecumenism. When Mgr Bruchési was apprised of acquisitions not confined to the strictly technical, he intervened, though without much success, to deprive the librarians of their prerogative to select new works. The city's commissioners, who held the purse strings, contended that the books proposed by the librarian lacked literary value, even though they did not balk at purchasing collections of religious volumes.[86] Éva Circé-Côté's stubbornness exasperated the commissioners, but she persevered in her mission to enlighten and educate, while continuing to write weekly columns.

* * *

The Circé-Côté couple belonged to the circle of freethinking Montrealers, and Pierre-Salomon was hoping to be initiated into the Masonic lodge when he was laid low by serious health problems in September 1909. According to Dr. Alfred Marcil, a member of the L'Émancipation lodge and later of the Force et Courage lodge, all that prevented Côté's initiation was his illness.[87] Pierre-Salomon, keenly interested in heredity and the theory of evolution, was working on a "biological history" of French Canadians. He was forced to give up his medical practice and accepted the invitation of his friends at the daily *Le Canada* to contribute to their paper. He suffered from intestinal tuberculosis and had been bed-ridden for three weeks when Éva left for work at the library on the afternoon of Wednesday, December 22. During her absence, Pierre-Salomon's condition took a turn for the worse and the person watching over him had the priest summoned to his bedside. Father Auclair had married Éva and Pierre-Salomon; he was a friend and he did his duty. Asked if he wished to confess, Dr. Côté said no, adding: "If ever I did confess, I'd prefer it be to you rather than anyone else, because I trust you completely."[88] When his wife came home, the sick man felt weak and asked for a doctor. True to his convictions until the very end, Pierre-Salomon told the doctor: "Henceforward, I ask not to be left alone with a priest; I don't want it said that I confessed when I did not wish to." There was no crucifix in the room, but, as she would later write, Éva placed the reproduction of a Flemish painter's Christ, "evoking much gentleness, because I know my husband was Christian in spirit if not the letter."[89] Éva recalled his last moments: "He remained firm in the calm of his conscience; he saw death coming with the clear-sightedness of a man of the arts, with the philosopher's stoicism, like the oak that stands tall before the lightning that will electrocute its heart." He was thirty-three years old. The following day, *Le Canada* paid tribute to "the poor people's doctor."[90] The funeral took place the day after Christmas,

Dr. Pierre-Salomon Côté, obituary notice, *La Presse*, December 23, 1909.

a Sunday, while Montreal was afflicted with a typhoid epidemic. To cover the costs, Éva had to borrow from a cousin. "I am not ashamed of these alms," she would write. "Our poverty is more honourable than ill-gotten wealth."[91]

The funeral service, held on December 26, 1909, triggered a debate that was to last for months. For it was a civil funeral, and there was no cross on the coffin. Furthermore, the remains were incinerated at the Mount Royal cemetery and not the Côte-des-Neiges cemetery, an action punishable by excommunication. The brothers of the lodge came out in force to accompany the cortège from St-Denis Street to Rachel and then up toward the Mountain. Wishing to avoid a scandal, Mgr Bruchési attempted to hush up the event and asked the newspapers to refrain from mentioning it. Senator Dandurand is also said to have tried unavailingly to keep the names of those who had marched in the procession from being published. *La Presse* disregarded the episcopal directives and in its *Carnet mondain* (Society pages) identified a hundred and forty-three notables who had followed the casket.

The list reads like a who's who of the radicals, Masons, and reformers of the day: Senator L.-O. David, Honoré Gervais, Liberal member of parliament for the Saint-Jacques riding, city councillors Dagenais and Prud'homme, a number of physicians, including Doctors Globensky, Laberge, Marcil, and Bourdon, the journalists Jules Helbronner, Godfroy Langlois, Gonzalve Desaulniers, Olivar Asselin, Louvigny de Montigny, and Gustave Comte, the librarian Frédéric Villeneuve, the socialist clerk of the court Albert Saint-Martin, police inspector Grandchamp, the actor-director-playwright Palmieri (aka Joseph Archambault), the writer Albert Laberge (author of *La Scouine*), various musicians, at least three judges, several lawyers, and the editorial staff of *Le Canada*. A few women were named at the very end of the list, among them Mrs. Drolet of the Ligue pour l'instruction.[92] Flowers were sent by, among others, the staff of the Lycée pour jeunes filles and by Dr. Louis Laberge on behalf of the Alliance scientifique universelle (World science alliance). After the funeral, the Alpha Omega circle held a gathering in honour of the deceased at which poems were read.[93] The cortège was followed by many well-known people who had shared desks in the same newsrooms, who had known the École littéraire de Montréal, who had been active in the Ligue de l'Enseignement during its campaign for secular, compulsory schooling, who belonged to Masonic lodges. The number of people present at the funeral could not be ascertained: *La Presse*'s estimate was four hundred, Éva would write six hundred, and *La Vérité*, no doubt wishing to minimize the Masonic peril, put it at one hundred and twenty.[94]

Two days later, the scandal erupted, first in the Quebec City publication *L'Action sociale*, whose headline was "Un affligeant scandale" (A shocking scandal). The paper, outraged by both the civil nature of the event and the cremation, described these as "a macabre masquerade of defiance toward the Church, organized around a decomposing corpse, a coffin transformed into a Masonic pedestal."[95] The scandal, the article continues, also lies in the people who took part in the ceremony. In addition to "a few Masons, a few imports, and a few good brutes who felt honoured to be admitted into the lodge," there were notables as well. "This scandal played out in public amid a Catholic French-Canadian population resides not so much in the folly of a poor wretch drawn in by influences that are well known, but, above all, in those who attended."[96] The major newspapers were far more moderate in their comments. A contributor to the liberal Quebec City daily *Le Soleil* deplored "the brutal sally" and the "lack of charity" of the bishop's publication, which was engaged in a settling of accounts among journalists: "*L'Action sociale* spits on a grave all the venom it has stored up against journalists."[97] *L'Action sociale* fired back with two articles emphasizing the underhanded way in which the funeral was organized and the fact it had taken on the appearance of a freethinkers' rally, and ending with the alarming conclusion: "Evidence of a conspiracy against Catholicism in the province of Quebec is becoming increasingly apparent, and it is about time people opened their eyes."[98] It was *Le Soleil*'s turn to reply, but, undoubtedly yielding to pressure, its editor distanced himself from the paper's initial responses and disavowed the journalist who had written them.[99] In the capital city, it was difficult, even for a liberal newspaper, to stray from the straight and narrow.

As of January 1, 1910, the Catholic right entered into the fray. Its vehicles were small-circulation weeklies, which were read by members of the clergy and distributed in the rectories and educational establishments. An article in the ultramontanist *La Vérité*, whose headline—"Pour mourir en chien" (To die like a dog)—was especially hurtful for the family, inveighed against death without the succour of religion. Citing a supposedly Masonic text exhorting lodge brothers to choose a secular death, the article assures readers that "there is nothing more satanic than this exhortation."[100] *La Vérité* also published anonymous letters, such as the one signed Z. B., who saw in Côté's funeral "an act of revolt against the Church" and sets about unmasking those who "rubbed shoulders with the Montreal's crème de la crème of impiety and Freemasonry." In a comment designed to arouse the readership, the ultramontane paper's correspondent added: "What is most distressing is that some women involved in this affair demonstrated more irreligion than their men." One woman in particular is targeted: the wife, who is said to have removed "the crucifix that had been placed in the hands of the departed." This is followed by a warning against the secular *lycée*: "this female impiety will find nourishment in the training provided here in our neutral *lycée*. . . . The education of girls is where secularization, in the worst sense of the word, begins." Continuing his diatribe, the *La Vérité* journalist affirms that Éva Circé-Côté is said to have acted against the last wishes of her husband, who apparently received a priest shortly before dying. The absence of the deceased's brothers is interpreted as a protest against the civil funeral. Their sister-in-law seems to have ignored their authorization for a Catholic burial.[101] In a similar vein, Pierre Bayard of *La Croix* engaged in personal attacks against Pierre-Salomon Côté, "a casual scribbler, with no ideas or style."[102]

Neither *La Vérité* nor *La Croix* was willing to let the scandal die down.[103] The attitude of the Catholic press, with its assuredly limited readership, was hardly surprising. Far more wounding was the defection of people close to the couple. On December 29, the Honourable L.-O. David, clerk of the City of Montreal, sent the newspapers a letter to exonerate himself for having taken part in the funeral. Once the cortège was underway, he explains, he suddenly noticed it was headed toward the Protestant cemetery and that there was no cross on the hearse. "I then left the procession and returned home." Continuing on behalf of his friends, he writes: "I am authorized by Justices Lafontaine and Choquette to state that they attended the funeral under the same circumstances and as a result of the same error."[104] His letter was published in *L'Action sociale*, and in liberal papers such as *La Patrie* as well as on the front page of *Le Nationaliste*. Éva magnanimously forgave him two months later: "I take into account Mr. L.-O. David's first gesture, which is always the best."[105] Gonzalve Desaulniers, a member of the lodge and one of the couple's intimates, also left the cortège.[106]

On January 2, it was Olivar Asselin's turn, in his paper *Le Nationaliste* (which was about the become the Sunday supplement of *Le Devoir*), to justify himself. Ever the rebel, he opens with a tribute to his old schoolmate and to Éva Circé-Côté, Asselin's fellow journalist. Drawing a portrait of Pierre-Salomon, he explains that they were both "from the lands," the doctor from Sainte-Luce and the journalist from Sainte-Flavie, the neighbouring village, both of them graduates of the *collège* in Rimouski. "He was a passionate boy, even crazy when it came to certain subjects." He goes on to sing the praises of Éva, his former colleague, unjustly attacked in his newspaper, and then explains his presence at the funeral, admitting he had been aware it would be a purely civil ceremony; he had taken part nevertheless, but, realizing the cortège was "composed almost exclusively of Freemasons (*Frères Trois Points*)," he "very visibly" detached himself from it when he passed in front of his house, thereby eschewing participation from any further demonstration, be it religious or irreligious, at the cemetery or elsewhere. He also mentions the desertion of other Masons.[107] The enfant terrible of journalism would go even further. In an article with the rather indelicate title "Au four, les gars! (Into the oven, guys!)," he hailed the "loyalty of frankness" of the man who had owned his convictions until the end.[108]

Then on January 4, the Member of Parliament Honoré Gervais denied having attended the funeral.[109] *Le Nationaliste* and *La Croix* hastened to publish his denial.[110]

Two papers supported the woman henceforth referred to as the widow Côté. The French-language protestant weekly *L'Aurore* ran a front-page article by its editor S. Rondeau relating the funeral of the "poor people's doctor," the insults of the Catholic press, and the statement made by Mgr Bruchési at Mont-Saint-Louis College: "let us build children's characters so that we may never again witness a distressing spectacle like the one seen in recent days, when a christened man who had repudiated the faith of his fathers, was taken in a casket without a cross to the crematorium."[111] The article also cites the ruder words of curé Charrier: "this poor man's body was treated the way the incineration department treats dogs and other animals—it was burned!" The editor of the protestant paper concludes that the crisis of faith experienced by some French Canadians requires that they be introduced to a kind God and "a religion that helps us live."[112] In addition, Éva received providential aid, so to speak, from a new publication, *Le Pays*, established in January 1910 by Godfroy Langlois with the support of the new lodge Force et Courage. On the front page, "Polignac," a pen name, reminds readers that many of those who marched in the procession were the same people who had followed the caskets of Mercier, Lafontaine, Doutre, Fréchette, or Robertine Barry. Polignac deplores all the attention given to the death of a "poor doctor, [who] in this miserable life had tasted nothing more than the intimacy of a good woman to whom he was faithful, like the spouse in the Gospel. But he committed the crime that cannot be forgiven in this province, that of dying at peace with one's conscience."[113] Two weeks later, when Senator Drummond was incinerated, *Le Pays* pointed out that the right-wing press seemed unperturbed by the presence of members of Montreal's elite who had walked in Pierre-Salomon Côté's cortège.[114]

The Côte affair, which had ruffled cassocks and inkwells alike, had consequences for local politics. Municipal elections were imminent. In the Saint-Louis ward, the councillor Dr. Joseph-Pierre Gadbois had no hesitation in using the affair to attack the member of the provincial assembly for the Saint-Louis riding, none other than Godfroy Langlois, founder of the L'Émancipation lodge. Gadbois assailed Freemasonry and its alleged influence on appointments in the municipal administration. To better besmirch his adversary, Gadbois cited the so-called regulations that supposedly encouraged Masons to support their brothers in order to keep priests away when they were at death's door. To round off his damning arguments, he stated that Langlois was "constantly at Dr. Côté's side when he was ill, paid from his pocket and 'fraternally' took care of the funeral."[115] This was too much for Éva Circé-Côté and left her no choice but to make things clear. *Le Devoir*, which had published a summary of Gadbois's speech, also published the letter Éva addressed to him. Defiant and refusing to renounce anything, she clarified her husband's relationship with the Freemasons:

> I regret to admit it, but my husband was not a Freemason, although after reading the Masonic regulations that you were imprudent enough to publish, I would have been honoured to count him among the members of that respectable brotherhood. To misquote the Académie française, I say: "He was missing from its glory . . . it was missing from his."

She goes on to refute the rumour of Langlois' visit to her sick husband's bedside and acknowledges having had to avail herself of a cousin's generosity—not that of Langlois—to pay for the funeral. In reply to the insinuations she had benefited from preferential treatment on the part of the Lodge brothers, she writes, quite openly:

> You will easily recognize your error . . . when you consider that the founder of the Municipal Library, who, after six years of loyal service, according to the testimony of the chairman of the city commission, saw her salary lowered from $600 to $300 and was robbed this year of a bonus of $50, so that her monthly earnings are now $26.19!

As testimony to her husband's conduct, she recalls his friendship for Father Auclair and concludes: "It will be to his great credit in the eyes of everyone, even those who do not share his ideas, that he was above all an honest man."[116]

La Vérité deemed the letter cynical: "the author is a woman and, more disturbingly, a columnist whose prose is spread through many liberal papers."[117]

La Croix also commented on this "blasphemous cry" and warned the public against "this bluestocking Voltairian," adding that, according to Pius VII: "Aiding and hiding Freemasonry are both grounds for excommunication."[118] The journalist André Chauveau excoriated Mrs. Côté in these terms: "Freethought is ridiculous and detestable in all men wherever it is encountered; in a woman it is a monstrosity."[119] For these high-minded people, Éva Circé-Côté's sex added an element of malevolence, or even perversion, which would have been perhaps not excusable but at least more understandable coming from a man. The scandal continued to make news. Two months after Dr. Côté's death, *La Vérité* feared he could become "the new patron saint of French-Canadian freethought."[120]

In the face of so much malice and to dispel any ambiguity as to her husband's final decision, Éva Circé-Côté sent a second letter to the newspapers. In it she explained the dying man's last moments, Father Auclair's visit, the refusal of confession, how on the day of his death he had told two of his friends, "that he persevered in his ideas, which he believed were right, and that in the final hour he would not deny his work and his life." She had also kept two documents confirming his desire to be cremated. In answer to her detractors, she stated: "I did not tear the crucifix from my husband's rigid fingers." She had listened to her conscience:

> You are your husband's executor; do as he wished, without judging whether it was good or bad. Do not listen to the voice of interest but to that of justice. A Catholic funeral will in no way change his fate, which is irrevocably fixed. Rightly or wrongly, this man believed he was doing salutary work. Leave him the benefit of his sincerity.[121]

In this letter, Éva Circé-Côté revealed herself to the public as never before.

One might have thought the affair had run its course, were it not for the deceased's two brothers. The youngest, Elzéar-Auguste, was a law student at Université Laval in Montreal. Goaded by his sister-in-law's second letter, he responded in *La Vérité*. He was convinced his brother had wanted a Catholic burial. The last time Dr. Côté had been to see his family in Sainte-Luce, he visited his father's grave and reportedly said: "My most ardent wish now is to sleep my last sleep in the shade of this mausoleum." A few months before his death he had apparently joked with his friends, "I see that I'll be spending the winter on Côte-des-Neiges."[122] So what could explain Colombine's actions? According to the budding lawyer, they were the actions of a woman:

I know that at the critical moment when a man is in the grips of irremediable agony, when he is wrestling with the vampire of death poised over its victim, it happens that the woman loses her reason and, like Colombine, runs in disarray through the streets more or less aimlessly.

There is no record of Éva's reaction to the twenty-one-year-old fledgling's letter. His mindset was deeply conservative and a few years later, in his doctoral dissertation in law, he would defend some extremely reactionary ideas on paternal power.[123]

Another of Pierre-Salomon's brothers, Jean-Joachim, who, like Auguste, had visited the Côté residence the day after his death, wrote from Sainte-Luce and described their mother's grief. Éva allegedly had not advised them in writing of Pierre-Salomon's death and, even though the brothers held a burial permit for the Catholic cemetery, she apparently had consulted a friend and persisted in her idea of holding a civil funeral followed by incineration, saying, "I will never bend to ecclesiastic authority!"[124] After the death of her mother-in-law some years later, in a letter to her friend, the poet Marcel Dugas, Éva would write how she had loved this woman, who, unlike the other members of the family, had supported her.[126] It is quite possible that Éva had wanted to shut out her brothers-in-law, who were shocked by her beliefs and may have tried to influence her. And she had sought advice from her friends, who were also her husband's—why not? As for the cremation, this was more than a mere innovation (the incinerator at the Mount Royal cemetery was inaugurated in 1905); it signified insubordination to Catholic doctrine. Forbidden by Rome, it represented progress to broad-minded people, and in Europe associations had been established to promote its propagation as a modern rite.

In Quebec, the radical press, such as *L'Avenir* in the early years of the century and *Le Pays* thereafter, came out in support of cremation.[126] For progressives, this funeral rite was profoundly significant, because it was a hygienic way to dispose of human remains and exemplified the most recent scientific advances. A rational method of disposal without reference to an afterlife or the resurrection of the dead at the Last Judgment, cremation was one of the reforms advocated by the Freemasons. It also symbolized the abandonment of old religious beliefs and the affirmation of material values, both of which were of course abhorrent to the religious and civil Catholic authorities.[127] Later on, Éva Circé-Côté would devote at least two of her columns to this topic. In 1915, the wishes of a citizen to be incinerated were overridden by his heirs, who decided instead to have him buried at the Côte-des-Neiges cemetery. Without alluding to her personal experience, Éva commented: "We must respect the voice of the dead and bow to their orders."[128] In 1917, when European newspapers reported that the Germans were using chemical processes to retrieve useful products from corpses—glycerine, oil, fertilizer, etc.—she criticized the pope, who kept silent on the subject, pointing out that in Quebec cremation was forbidden on pain of excommunication. She then argued in favour of "this most hygienic form of obsequies" and mocked "the resurrection of the dead, who will have to run after their tibias and femurs. God's omnipotence enables him to reassemble bodies; to doubt this would supposedly show a lack of faith."[129]

One reason the debate sparked by Dr. Côté's cremation persisted for so long was that it provided grist for an intensive anti-Masonic campaign on the eve of the International Eucharistic Congress in Quebec City in the spring of 1910. Things heated up between the two new Montreal newspapers—Henri Bourassa's Catholic and nationalistic *Le Devoir* (The Duty) was founded in January 1910, at the same time as Godfroy Langlois' liberal and anticlerical *Le Pays*—which exchanged volleys of insults. *Le Devoir* reproduced the 1898 rules of the L'Émancipation lodge and, not entirely without reason, accused Langlois' paper of being Masonic. In a front-page article on the funeral of Pierre-Salomon Côté in the first issue of *Le Pays*, Éva Circé-Côté, writing under the pen name Jean Nay, arraigned *Le Devoir* for being so austere: "Without a doubt, 'Le Devoir' is a macabre newspaper. Its very title seems to have been fashioned out of coffin wood."[130] *Le Pays* would soon be referring to "Le Devoir du crétin" (the cretin's duty).[131]

In the political realm, while a number of Freemasons were close to the seats of power—for example, the journalist Godfroy Langlois, the typographer and trade-unionist Gustave Francq, and the public health specialist Dr. Louis Laberge—their association with the lodge could be used against them at any given moment. Nothing could sully a reputation as easily as the accusation of being "a three points brother," that is, a Mason; it was enough to utterly ruin a career. Thus, early in 1910, Wilfrid Laurier and the Liberal Party jettisoned Godfroy Langlois and had him removed from his position as editor of *Le Canada*.[132]

People suspected of Masonic connections had to defend their reputations in court. Accused by the conservative French-born writer Henri Bernard of belonging to a lodge, the Liberal Member of the Legislative Assembly (MLA) for Saint-Hyacinthe, Télesphore-Damien Bouchard, launched a suit against his slanderer. The court handed down a "verdict of 'No Bill,' meaning there were no grounds for a trial."[133] According to his memoires, Bouchard also sued

"Victor Chartier, who had accused me of being a member of the Montreal lodge."[134] To avoid a scandal, he withdrew his claim in 1910.

The bogeyman of Freemasonry caused casualties. The MLA for Saint-Hyacinthe also wrote that his friend Joseph Huette had never recovered "from the nervous shock and moral distress brought about by those who accused him of being a Freemason."[135] He saw his family tainted, especially his sister, who headed a school where the clientele was drawn to a large extent from an elite close to the clergy.

The publication of the list of so-called lodge members compromised all those mentioned in it. Dr. Louis Laberge, a physician in the employ of the City of Montreal, and Police Inspector Grandchamps, both members of the L'Émancipation lodge, were attacked for allegedly plotting against the Eucharistic Congress of 1910. The City Council of Montreal established a special commission of inquiry, which questioned witnesses on July 26 and 28 and August 1, 1910, but the proceedings were interrupted in November by a Superior Court injunction; eventually, an out-of-court settlement was reached, but not before 1915. The harm done, however, was irreparable, and Dr. Laberge was forced to resign from his position as head of Montreal's Public Health department.[136]

When the Ligue de L'Enseignement submitted a brief to the Dandurand commission on education, demanding "a single school board for the city and its suburbs; the same textbooks across the board; election of board members by taxpayers, owners, and tenants," *Le Devoir* had no trouble discrediting its representatives by identifying them as participants in Dr. Côté's funeral.[137]

* * *

A month before her husband's death, the *Standard*, the widely read weekend supplement of the *Montreal Daily Star*, published an article on spiritualism naming Éva Circé-Côté as a participant in séances on Saint-Hubert Street:

> There are quite a number of spiritualists in town. Dr. Cote, on Saint-Denis Street, is a great believer, and his wife, 'Colombine'—you know who writes in the French papers and who used to be and may be now at the Civic Library—she also was a great spiritualist. Some years ago. I understand that she left the faith recently, and is an unbeliever now.[138]

As someone who had repeatedly denounced charlatans, and who, in 1903, had published a text on "psychic sciences" ridiculing those who summoned the dead, Circé-Côté was particularly vexed. She turned to her lawyer and

Godfroy Langlois driven from *Le Canada*, *Le Nationaliste*, January 16, 1910. BAnQ.

friend Gonzalve Desaulniers who, with his partner Mr. Vallé, brought a civil suit against the owner of the *Standard*, George Murray Publishing, asking $5,000 on the grounds that the above lines were "false, injurious, mendacious, and malicious of a nature to cause considerable injury to [Circé-Côté's] business, to her honour, her sensitivities and her reputation."[139] The case dragged on for three years, during which time Circé-Côté saw her husband die and went through the scandal of the funeral; she also lost her jobs at the library and the lycée, two events she attributed directly to the defamatory article.[140]

When she appeared in court on October 26, 1911, immediately after swearing on the Bible that she would tell the truth, Circé-Côté had to answer Murray's lawyer, who wanted to know if she believed in God and eternal damnation. The questions were ruled out of order, but it gives some idea of her reputation as an atheist. When asked to explain how her reputation had suffered from the allegations, she first answered: "I felt completely isolated." As director of the Lycée de jeunes filles—work that she did without pay "so that the project might live"—she noticed that she no longer had the trust of some of the students; since she was a liability for the school, she had to leave. Moreover, after seven years at the Municipal Library she lost her position as chief librarian with only three days notice and no reason given. She was reinstated a month later as assistant librarian. Recently widowed, she would have to manage on half her salary, that is $25 a month. She would regain her full salary of $50 a month in January 1910, but her demotion to assistant librarian was maintained. She attributed the loss of both jobs to the *Standard*'s article.

When questioned by the defence as to her relationship with the "psychic sciences," Circé-Côté had to explain her article of 1903 in which she denounced the "magnetizers" and others who claimed to communicate with long-dead famous men. She admitted that she had attended a séance out of curiosity, and she stated that she was interested in "scientific experiments" such as those of the French neurologist Charcot.[141]

Éva Circé-Côté could never prove she lost her jobs as a consequence of the libellous article. In his judgment, Justice Bruneau nevertheless considered the article defamatory: Éva Circé-Côté never practised spiritualism, she was a Roman Catholic and had never written against Catholic dogma or the teachings of the Church, she had been humiliated, and her destitution as director of the Lycée was "an attack against her honour." Consequently, she was to receive $200,[142] a paltry sum compared to the $5,000 that she had initially expected from the newspaper. The verdict came three years almost to the day after Pierre-Salomon Côté's death. Nothing in the journalist's work betrays her ordeal at that time: she kept her weekly columns, she wrote her Christmas tale, always under pseudonyms.

Would Éva Circé-Côté ever get over the attacks she underwent at the time? Probably not. The ostracism she endured would have lasting effects. Fifteen years later, she admitted to Marcel Dugas that she was ashamed of herself for having forgotten those "who caused my husband's death and spit on his coffin."[143] As for the *lycée* of which she was the chairwoman, even though its clientele was composed of parents already won over to secular education, her name now hindered efforts to recruit students. She had already handed over the reins to Madame de Chaux, and no trace of the institution can be found after 1910.

When he died, Pierre-Salomon Côté possessed nothing in the way of material wealth; having nothing to bequeath, he had refused to leave a useless will. As a result, Éva owned only their flat on St-Denis Street. She had no other choice but to provide for herself and her three-year-old daughter. Returning to her occupation as a librarian, she was back at work as of December 31, 1909, a few days after the funeral.[144] Consequent to the funeral scandal and the piece in the *Standard*, she became *persona non grata* in some quarters. On June 16, 1909, City Hall passed a resolution that "as of the 19th of the month, Mrs. Côté, as well as her assistant Miss Payment, will no longer be employed by the city." As mentioned earlier, she was reinstated, but as assistant librarian to the new head librarian, the journalist Lorenzo Prince.[145]

Soon after the funeral, the library had to deal with a pressing matter. On January 21, the City Council recommended the acquisition of the Philéas Gagnon collection for $31,000,[146] a bargain, considering it was actually worth upwards of $40,000. But because it had not yet found a proper location to house its library, the city could hardly justify the purchase. For the widow Côté this decision was of the highest importance; in her view, the expense was fully justified. When they eventually took the collection out of storage a few years later, she became the first custodian of those ten thousand precious books.

She would no longer write under the names Colombine and de Musette, which had become too readily identified with her. It was at this point that Godfroy Langlois offered a helping hand. Having been dismissed from *Le Canada*, he had just recently founded *Le Pays* with "a large group of Montreal citizens to fight the good fights."[147] It began as a small, four-page weekly but soon expanded to six, then eight pages. The title alludes to the *Patriotes* of 1837–38, a conflict whose embers refused to be extinguished, and Langlois's crew walked in the footsteps of the *Patriotes* and their followers. Circé-Côté admired Langlois and saw him as "the one who most brilliantly incarnated the ideas of Papineau."[148] *Le Pays* defended the same values as its namesake of the years 1850–60, which had been under the direction of the radical liberals Louis Labrèche-Viger, Louis-Antoine Dessaulles, and Charles Daoust: the belief in progress and the separation of church and state. The paper staked out its position in the very first issue:

> In view of the unhealthy interests and feverish intrigues being played out in the shadow of the old flag, it appears that the concept of the liberal ideal has been lost and that liberalism has transformed into a voracious appetite for civil service positions and honours, into an unbridled exercise of power and the attractions it holds for faltering souls, into a means to gain wealth and mint coins.
>
> To reassure those who have represented *Le Pays* as a radical and anti-Catholic enterprise, this paper hastens to declare that it will scrupulously avoid dealing with any question even remotely related to religion.[149]

Mgr Bruchési was not fooled by this statement of good intentions and quickly responded just as Mgr Bourget had in the 1860s.[150] In a letter to the theatre critic Fernand Rinfret (Paul d'Estrée), who had been named editor-in-chief of the daily *Le Canada*, the archbishop referred to *Le Pays* as "the barkeepers' newspaper."[151] Éva Circé-Côté did not let her grief get the better of her. With the rest of the crew at *Le Pays*, she would endeavour to remedy "the apocalyptic intellectual sterility of the 1910 generation of French Canadians,"[152] as Asselin had described it. As of the very first issue, she resurrected Jean Nay, a pseudonym she had used in her short-lived publication *L'Étincelle*, and began a steadfast collaboration that would produce some 793 columns over a period of twelve years. Her first essay, "Histoire d'une âme" (Story of a soul), appeared on the front page on January 29, 1910. The soul in question here is that of "the Liberal Party ignominiously driven out of the country,"[153] the soul that renews our energy, heralds the credo of love and solidarity, and is reincarnated in *Le Pays*. This set the tone for the newspaper, which considered itself "the voice of all true liberals, those who cherish the ideal."[154]

On June 18, 1910, a new pen name made its entrance: Paul S. Bédard. A few weeks later, it became clear that by writing under two aliases she could publish more than one article in the same issue. In September of the same year, Circé-Côté resuscitated Fantasio, whose name had previously appeared in *Le Monde Illustré* in 1902 and in *La Vigie* in 1909; this was an androgynous character, whose sex she left open to conjecture. The name certainly lends itself to lengthy musings. There was more than one Fantasio during the nineteenth century, de Musset's being the most famous, of course.[155] This pseudonym was added to Circé-Côté's two other bylines and soon dethroned Bédard, who would return occasionally to sign an obituary or an arts review or simply to act as Fantasio's double. One might presume that each heteronym represented a different facet of the journalist, yet Nay, Fantasio, and Bédard were nearly interchangeable and would embody Éva Circé-Côté's various voices until *Le Pays* shut down at the end of 1921.[156]

Nay, Bédard, and Fantasio could not be differentiated according to their subjects and style, nor were they easily distinguishable from the other contributors to *Le Pays*, all of whom were committed to social reform and nationalism. They all wished to educate the readers, as was true of many journalists of that period, especially, perhaps, the female journalists, who, because the women who read them were denied access to higher education, regarded themselves as educators. For Robertine Barry, journalism was a mission and "the women's page [. . .] is our university."[157]

On November 9, 1910, a colourful character named Arthur Maheu appeared in the pages of *Le Pays*, with very few indications as to whom he concealed. Some, like Premier Lomer Gouin, even believed that it was Godfroy Langlois, hiding behind a farmer's identity.[158] Maheu represents a rough-hewn peasant married to a naive woman, Josette, who comes from a family of fifteen children. They have a son and daughter-in-law who live in Montreal, so that their visits to the big city provide ample opportunity for comments on municipal politics and city life. Maheu is almost illiterate, a populist, and full of plain common sense; he voices liberal ideas, denounces corruption, and takes politicians to task. Using a popular idiom, he gives vent to his prejudices, his sexism, and his philistine opinions.[159] Yet the column "Les Idées de M. Maheu" (Mr. Maheu's ideas), is topped by the portrait of a middle-aged man wearing a proper detachable collar and holding a quill pen. Not quite the image of a *habitant*.

From 1912 on, Maheu's column was an integral part of the newspaper. Because the fellow's words were often out of tune with those of Fantasio and Circé-Côté's other identities—Maheu put her more in the camp of the regionalists than the moderns—it is possible that it sometimes functioned as a collective pseudonym used by more than one writer. There is no proof of this, and Circé-Côté may simply have wanted to amuse herself and give free rein to the Rabelaisian, iconoclastic part of her mind; or she may have used this cover whenever it suited her, in order to reach a less earnest public than the readers of her other columns. The fact remains that Maheu's representation of rural Quebec was that of an urban journalist.

Many other writers of that epoch, both men and women, also made use of pseudonyms. They—Robertine Barry (Françoise), for example—saw it as a means to exercise more freedom.[160] For others it was a way to elude censorship or avoid reprisals. Were Colombine and Musette—whom everyone recognized—too discredited by the lingering scandal surrounding Dr. Côté's funeral? Perhaps Éva Circé-Côté disappeared behind all those pen names to ensure that she would get work; her notoriety as of 1910 may explain why even a paper as "advanced" as *Le Pays* would want to keep some distance from an openly freethinking woman. Circé-Côté was surely aware that ideas associated with that name were more vulnerable to being discredited than those presented under an unidentified man's signature. It is also possible that as a politically committed person, she was more concerned with defending her convictions than gaining celebrity for herself. Furthermore, the pseudonyms may have allowed her, in tandem with her job as librarian, to work in a forum where she could express herself freely on any subject at all without being confined to the woman's page and thus be assured of earning some extra income. Moreover, had she written under her own name, it is unlikely she could have kept her position at the library.

Fantasio, Jean Nay, Jean Ney, Arthur Maheu, and, more rarely, Paul Bédard—each in turn painted a critical portrait of Quebec and Québécois society. All of them protested against the corruption of city councillors, argued for public education and education reform, decried the death penalty, and declared their faith in progress. These columns were addressed to metropolitan readers, who were used to the crush in the streetcars and town-planning issues.

There is no way to determine to what extent these writings reflected Éva Circé-Côté's convictions and the degree to which didactic considerations, the temptation to shock readers, or the imperatives of the moment dictated her words. Clearly, her realistic essays and her descriptions gave an accurate rendering of reality as she saw it. Elsewhere, her judgments seem to vary according to the circumstances.

* * *

The year 1910 was a crucial one for Éva Circé-Côté. She was in mourning yet displayed no complacency about this. When not at the library, she wrote and went out at night, constantly occupied with her work. Her daughter Ève was four years old; who took care of her when her mother was working is a matter of speculation: a neighbour or, more likely, her grandparents. Unabashedly modern, Circé-Côté enthusiastically welcomed every sign of the new era. Together with twenty thousand others, she applauded the exploits of Jacques de Lesseps and other aviators and parachutists who spread their wings over the new airfield in the west end of the city.[161] After the electricity fairy, it was the "mechanical bird" that enchanted her and prompted her to exclaim, as though addressing a divinity: "Oh, Man, how great you are and how beautiful are your works!"[162] Moreover, she immediately drew lessons from this brilliant invention: why could not "our people" take part in scientific progress? Hampered by an education system that encourages timidity, they must be given confidence again and "learn to stop doubting themselves, to forge ahead." Her modernity was consonant with a society that was unmooring itself from the nineteenth century, and Éva Circé-Côté embodied the clear-sighted witness of the sea change that many European writers were observing, including Virginia Woolf, who declared, "in or about December 1910 human character changed";[163] in Quebec, Robert de Roquebrune, for one, would write decades hence that "along with the top hat, the frock coat, and gaiters, the nineteenth century died around 1910."[164]

CHAPTER 3

SOCIALLY COMMITTED CITY-DWELLER IN A COUNTRY AT WAR

War, as hideous for morale as it is for physical well-being...
— HENRI BARBUSSE, Le Feu, 1916

IN 1914, this forty-three-year-old woman who left for work each day, who took the streetcar, that "mobile street theatre,"[1] who went shopping on Sainte-Catherine Street, who was not above going to the *café-concert* in Sohmer Park—would she have balked at being described as a *flâneur*? The epithet *flâneuse* would be harder to lay claim to—the feminine form becomes pejorative in French—but the term *flâneur*, in the sense of a person living in symbiosis with the city and observing her own peregrinations, suits her perfectly. Yet "spectator" and "witness" would be more accurate, because, with her job at the library, her writing, and her daughter's upbringing, did she even have the time to take a carefree stroll around the city? Still, while going from her house to the library and then back home again, she had a gift for seeing familiar scenes as if for the first time. She noticed everything: the smells, the sounds, the buildings, the trees, and especially the crowds and the passersby. The little girls jumping rope as soon as the snow melted—because "the sidewalks of Montreal... belong to the little boys and girls of the city"—and the throng packed into the streetcars every morning and evening. Everything was grist for reflection and for drawing lessons, which she would convey to readers with a naturalist touch that easily bears comparison with Zola. On his pedestal in Viger Square "poor Chénier" smells fried food.[2] August 1914 on Bonsecours Street: the "odour of the fish market, rotten vegetables, and the reek of vomit near the bars," overlaid with "sickening fumes."³ And the alleys in 1917:

> When walking past the alleys, one must hold one's nose to avoid choking on the reek of old garbage in full sunlight displaying the whole spectrum of murky greens and dung yellow where rats proliferate. Here the skeleton of a dog, there a crushed cat so crawling with worms it appears to be alive; everywhere our gaze is offended by carrion or some putrid thing.⁴

After the daytime nastiness, there might follow more serious nocturnal aggressions, when thieves and thugs lurked in the streets.⁵ Yet despite the dangers, the effluvia, and the dirt, this was Éva's city; she was fond of Montreal and she celebrated it.

During her excursions to the countryside, she marvelled at the streetcar that took her to Chambly, and she extolled the sweetness of rural life. A true Montrealer, she wanted the city to stay where it was and not spread its "urban dwellings, with bay windows, to the shores of the Richelieu."⁶ Montreal in 1915 was "still Ville-Marie, with a core of naivety, a charming impression of serenity underneath its somewhat licentious appearance. All in all a good girl, open-handed and with much to give."⁷

> If there are days when a worker envies the rich man in pyjamas and slippers sitting in a rocking chair in the hothouse warmth of our modern radiator equipped houses, then they must be the rainy days of December, when he must take the streetcar up to Villeray or to the Annex, unless he is bound for Maisonneuve or Saint-Henri. Picture yourself planted on a street corner, with your feet in a puddle of oily water, clutching an umbrella that makes vain efforts and acts like a parachute wanting to lift you into the air but manages only to flip over and send a stream of water down your neck or to use your hat as a roof tile on which to drip. If you are not in the middle of the roadway, the streetcar driver will take no more notice of you than of the man in the moon. You desperately wave to him but to no avail—the car whizzes by. Even if you are standing at the appointed spot, exposed to the gusting wind and the rascally automobiles, half a dozen streetcars crammed with passengers bunched together on the running board can roll right by you and not deign to stop. But if ever they do see fit to let you in, you must elbow your way along, past the umbrella ribs that poke you, jostle women no more apt to move than a pillar of salt, charge ahead, shake bellies bulging like pallets and offering no resistance, until you

reach a strap that you grasp like a lifebuoy. Then you surrender to the jolts of the car, you sway right and left, and fall on this woman's knees or catch another in your arms before she drops on her backside, and you imagine that you are old garments drying on a clothesline. [. . .] A wet dog odour makes you nauseous. The fogged up windows prevent you from reading the street names. From time to time the driver shouts something unintelligible.[8]

But Éva Circé-Côté did more than just observe the vagaries of daily life; she also surveyed the economic transformations stemming from industrial growth and the city's expansion. The early years of the century saw the development of monopoly capitalism; midsize companies took over smaller ones only to be swallowed up in turn by larger organizations—British, English-Canadian, and, more and more often, American. As a result of mergers in banking, industry, commerce, and finance, family enterprises disappeared. What remained in the hands of French Canadians were the least lucrative sectors, such as clothing and shoe manufacturing and small-scale service and retail businesses. In 1911, Éva Circé-Côté took stock of what French Canadians had lost: the wholesale trade, banks, lumber production, mining, pulp and paper, and hydropower were now controlled by English Canadians or Americans. "The trades have all gotten away from us due to the lack of technical schools, except for barbering: the shorn are now the shearers—it was bound to happen."[9] In short, "We have kept the grocery sector, which is the least profitable."[10] These changes had an impact on the landscape, as the "most salubrious neighbourhoods, the slopes of the mountain, the upstream section of the river, [have gone] to the English." Rather than viewing this as an effect of the massive expansion of an advanced economy, she attributed the situation to the shortcomings of French Canadians, who were unable to protect themselves and "force the English to respect [them]."[11]

The losses were not only material. The fine arts were beggared, owing to the absence of a national conservatory and subsidies for the theatre, and starving artists were forced to work abroad. Literature did not fare much better, because "when brains are squeezed, ideas and works are aborted." As for the French language, it was hurtling toward bankruptcy in North America, a situation that prompted Fantasio to speak of "the agony of a race," just as she had previously lamented that of the Indigenous Peoples. She primarily blamed her fellow citizens, who, being poorly equipped due to inadequate education, were unable to cope with the modern world.

Could the immigration "that enfolds us" bring reinforcements to French Canadians? According to Circé-Côté, to counter the influx of capital from the United States, the example to follow was that of Brazil and Argentina, who were attracting French capital.[12] To raise the population's intellectual level and foster a more qualified workforce, why not encourage immigration from Belgium and France? As a columnist for *Le Pays*, she was not satisfied to simply describe; she could not contain the urge to prescribe. Constantly alive to developments that were changing her city profoundly, she assessed their effects in great detail.

This was a period of industrialization, which the First World War would intensify, of large numbers of immigrants attracted by late nineteenth-century Liberal policies, of migration from the country to the city; city dwellers defined themselves in relation to people living in rural areas. Circé-Côté's depictions of country folk coming to the city were not very flattering. Like all Montrealers, she would see them at the public markets, among the throngs of men and women going to work each morning in the arms industry, and all too often among the unemployed. The farmers she portrayed were at once naive and wily. Out of greed, according to her, some of them had sold the farm to invest in a building in the city or had deserted the land to pay off their debts by turning themselves into factory hands.[13]

Galloping inflation bore down on consumers and workers, and the rising cost of agricultural produce aroused the ire of people in the city. In 1916, Éva Circé-Côté had begun to write for *Le Monde ouvrier*; under the byline Julien Saint-Michel, her paternal grandfather's name, she aimed her columns at a readership of qualified workers and their families, a clientele, in her view, that was being hoodwinked by crafty farmers skilled at taking advantage of people, rigging the scales, and selling spoiled and tainted goods: "ten to a dozen . . . white blood sausage disguised as sausage . . . wool mixed with cotton, cream cheese made with sour milk," "maple syrup watered down beyond reason." And she laid it on, echoing the words of cheated clients: "a leaden quarter, a perforated coin—it was surely a *habitant* who had given it to you. They keep them precisely for the purpose of passing them on to city people," and so they too become "war profiteers."[14]

Women, who dealt with the farmers flocking to the city markets each morning, had their worst prejudices confirmed at the sight of *habitants* who "live high on the hog" thanks to their exorbitant prices. Which led the columnist to conclude:

> We would like to respect [the farmers], because of the valuable work they do and because, together with the working class, they constitute the mainspring of our economic life, but one cannot help wishing they would go to the devil when they steal so brazenly.[15]

Even during the summer holidays, she wrote in 1915, Montrealers should shun the countryside. For decades the urban middle class had been escaping the heat by staying either with relatives in the country or in a summer cottage. For Éva, it was sheer snobbery to spend the vacations looking at "dull country fields or rocks as angular as old maids or pompier-style sunsets." She scoffed at those who went "to immerse themselves again in nature" in order to "return to animal life" during the summer. "The return to the land that we indulge in each year during our vacations brings our intellectual life, our civilization to a halt."[16] Doesn't culture prevail over nature? "Let us be more appreciative of what man has done to enhance our existence."[17]

It should be recalled that she had not always spurned the countryside. In *Bleu, Blanc, Rouge* she extolled the marvels of nature and the twilight on the St. Lawrence. She, who before the war could not understand those who left the land "to trade the babble of the brooks, the birdsongs, the treasure of [nature's] virginity, for the dusty asphalt, the sooty sky, the giraffe-necked chimneys belching smoke,"[18] now blessed the charms of the city and the superiority of urban life.

A city-dweller first and foremost, Éva had no scruples about adopting a populist tone apt to maintain city-country rivalries. In politics, the city was at the mercy of rural legislators who stymied any hope of reform. She proposed that "the first three months of the session be devoted to the education of our ignorant elected members from the Bois-Francs, Gaspésie, or the depths of the North."[19] This sort of contempt was concomitant with her tireless fight for progress, and for public education in particular.

Circé-Côté's discourse was ambiguous, and she could adapt it to the requirements of the cause. A column written in 1916 on the importance of the return to the land provides a good illustration of this double- or even triple-sided discourse. In it, she deplores the desertion of rural areas and calls on men and especially women to sacrifice their life in the city for the pleasures of the countryside, far from the "crude and petty existence in the cities." She is fully aware of what such a sacrifice involves and enumerates the things that make the city interesting for her: "it takes courage to move away, to leave behind the city and its pleasures, the cinemas, the theatres, the perennial enchantment of streets illuminated as if by daylight, that mirage of debauchery and vice."[20] Two years later, she persisted in rhapsodizing over rural life, and, speaking out on behalf of workers, she complained that country-to-city migration was engendering unfair competition for jobs in the arms industry. Writing under the name Saint-Michel, she called on the government to discourage the hiring of farmers in munitions factories. She also demanded that, to curb the depopulation of rural areas and, in so doing, carry out patriotic work, the state legislate against the desertion of farmland, which would lead to famine: "Those who abandon their land and come here to steal other people's jobs should be enlisted at once."[21]

Montreal was the metropolis of Canada at the time, a unique place that had nothing in common with Quebec City, the province's capital and second largest city. Quebec City was the city of *L'Action catholique* and its editor-in-chief, Abbot Joseph-Arthur d'Amours, the nemesis of *Le Pays*.[22] As far as Éva Circé-Côté was concerned Quebec City was guilty of two offences: it rejected progress, and it was hypocritical. For her it was a "city of another age, resistant to life, to pleasure, to gaiety, and which has dug in its heels against progress. Dead to the world, to new ideas, each night, after telling its beads of boxwood, it can go to sleep in its coffin and dream that some succubus wants to violate its modesty."[23] Her reaction to the collapse of the Pont de Québec, the Quebec Bridge, in September 1916 was tinged with cruelty. The capital, she wrote, is "afflicted with plethora. It has been the subject of so much boasting that it is full of itself. Everything it produces is enormous; that, at least, is what it believes." And she mocked Quebec City's conservatives: "In a land that has seen the growing knowledge and wisdom of the likes of Tardivel, Chapais, D'Amours and so many other saintly individuals, the powers above have no choice but to participate in the great work."[24] While the war accelerated the industrialization of Montreal, the capital remained "the city of horse-drawn carriages, where the curfew puts the Haute-Ville (Upper Town) to sleep so the seedy neighbourhoods of the Basse-Ville (Lower Town) may be set ablaze under the ashes."[25] Quebec City, she would write in 1925, was Bruges la Morte (Bruges the dead).[26] Éva Circé-Côté was a diehard Montrealer.

The people that filled the streets and shops each day made the contrast between the two cities even more stark. Quebec City had remained a provincial capital with a largely French-speaking population and a small English-speaking minority whose members were of Anglo-Saxon, Irish, and Jewish descent. Montreal, on the other hand, was a major North American city whose population during the First World War period was three-quarters French-speaking and included a large English-speaking minority and cultural communities whose numbers were increased by immigrants coming mainly from Europe, especially Great Britain, Italy, and Central Europe.[27]

In her columns, Circé-Côté often dealt with the relationship to others, primarily to *les Anglais*, the English. Their economic superiority was inscribed in the topography of Montreal. Between 1914 and 1917 she lived at 524 Sherbrooke Street East, and whenever she found herself in the western half of the city it was impossible for her to ignore the concentration of Anglophones

Henri Julien, "Ice cream vendor in Montreal," M2559 © McCord Museum.

there and their imposing buildings, in particular those of McGill University, which in her eyes incarnated the economic success of the former conquerors. She also remarked on the few "Anglified" French Canadians who, once they had "made their fortune, [moved] to the west end," where they went so far as to "despise their compatriots."[28] If she continued to the southwest, she would come to the large companies and the head offices of banks managed by Anglophones. The Notre-Dame Street of her childhood had been transformed, and the economic domination of the "British" was displayed all across the landscape.[29]

On Saint-Laurent Boulevard she would hear foreign languages and encounter a heterogeneous populace newly settled in the city. Their presence gave rise to colourful scenes: "the Italian and her fortune-telling parrot," the barrel organ player, the Italian ice cream vendor, or the Greek whose shop "sparkles with light and who sells 'Sundae cups,' cream soda, and cones" to the sound of his player piano, or those others, less likeable, "who have taken

Anonymous, Barrel organ, Montreal, circa 1900. MP-1974.2.14P © McCord Museum.

over every street corner and sell ice cream made with imitation milk and sodas made with coloured water."[30]

In the Saint-Louis neighbourhood, her attention was drawn to the Jews in particular. *Le Monde ouvrier* and *Le Pays* provided excellent platforms for combatting anti-Semitism. The owner of *Le Pays*, Godfroy Langlois, owed his election as MLA for the Saint-Louis district to the Jewish constituency there. In the columns signed Arthur Maheu, the Jewish mothers who nurse their children on their doorsteps and take them to play in the parks, on the Mountain or Saint Helen's Island became models for French-Canadian mothers too concerned with housework.[31] She also discovered the places where "Jews, Syrians, and Poles have already learned enough to neutralize the landlords' greed by having two or three families share the same tenement."[32]

At times the "cosmopolitan influx" awakened fears in Circé-Côté that bordered on racism, but there was no question of turning back immigrants. They were here to stay and if employers preferred them to established Canadians, governments were to blame just as much as the inadequate education of French Canadians.

If progress had any chance of one day prevailing in Quebec, it would be in Montreal. Taking the opposite view of the one adopted by traditionalists and regionalists, Éva Circé-Côté enthusiastically welcomed every invention, every modernization of the urban landscape, even to the point of proposing that the Côte-des-Neiges cemetery be relocated because it "impeded the expansion of the metropolis."[33] Following a less provocative, more widely shared line of thought, she marvelled at the "electricity fairy" (*la fée électricité*). "One must see Sainte-Catherine Street brazed at the touch of the electric button," she exclaimed in the summer of 1914,[34] and elsewhere. "the harsh light of a million multi-coloured electric bulbs like rosary beads said around the midriff of our metropolis."[35] On New Year's Day 1916, she was dazzled by the sight of Sainte-Catherine Street and St-Laurent Boulevard lit up with electric lamps while fireworks rang in another year of war.[36] In the summer of that same year, she was fascinated by the machines on display at the exposition of the École technique, and in the pages of *Le Monde ouvrier* she invited workers, mechanics, and electricians to go and admire them.[37]

The city was much more than buildings, electric wires, factories, and streetcars. Strolling around, Circé-Côté took note as well of the river and its piers, which, writing as Musette in *Les Débats*, she had compared to "Rembrandt-like studies," the trading vessels, the stevedores, the ocean liners, and the sounds of the port, Sohmer Park, where the orchestra played music by Suppé, the picnics on Mount Royal or Saint Helen's Island, but also the invasion of automobiles, which changed "the avenues into race tracks."[38]

Nothing was a matter of indifference to this city-dweller. She enjoyed the city with a passion and could hold forth on both its slightest pleasures and its many perils. Hence, her humorous description of a civil servant's fifteen-day, urban vacation: six picnics, three fishing parties, two moonlight excursions, a trip to Carillon, and a field day. The family picnic on Saint Helen's Island was

APRÈS LA FÊTE CHAMPÊTRE, la foule reprenant le bateau passeur. — (Croquis d'un artiste de la PATRIE.)

Île Sainte-Hélène overrun after the Saint-Jean-Baptiste holiday, *La Patire*, June 25, 1909.

entitled to a detailed account of the streetcar ride to the "almost inaccessible shore of the river," then the boat ride to the island, followed by the hunt for a table where one could spread a white cloth, were it not for "the Jews, who had come early and taken the best spots." After searching for a child gone astray, the family missed the boat and had to rent a rowboat to get back to the city.[39] She not only could depict the habits of the civil servant's family revitalizing itself in a natural setting, but she also related the sounds of the city, and she knew the price of a streetcar ticket and was therefore in a position to protest when postwar wages went down while the cost of public transit did not.[40]

She devoted a number of columns to the situation of sales clerks and bore witness to the disappearance of stores, workshops, and the whole host of small businesses wiped out by department stores;[41] she reported on the *Carnaval de février* (February carnival), the tenant families moving en masse on May 1, the Fête Dieu (Corpus Christi) and Saint-Jean-Baptiste parades, as well as on the military parades during the war. She commented on the arrival of foreign visitors, such as the anarchist Emma Goldman, whose presence at the 1906 May Day celebration at the Champ-de-Mars was noted by Colombine, the operatic singer Germaine Manny in 1916, and, in 1917, *maréchal* Joffe, saviour of France and therefore of the world, according to Circé-Côté.[42]

Modern women did not wait until the war of 1914 to take possession of the city and enjoy its diversions. As early as the 1910 years, some of them, at least, were experiencing emancipation. Fantasio commented in *Le Pays* on the transformation of the single woman who was no longer an old maid: "Instead of washing the dishes, wiping kids' noses, or scrubbing floors, she goes to the theatre—alone—goes walking without a chaperon, attends lectures, and leaves the little four o'clock women to their rumour-mongering and malicious gossip!"[43] Elsewhere, she lamented the fate of working women who, at six in the morning, ran to hoist themselves onto a streetcar and squash into the middle of the crowd "in the most abject crush of bodies."[44] She recounted the unforgettable smell of streetcars on rainy days, their steps unsuited for long dresses too tightly wrapped, and their drivers who "twist their mouths out of shape to shout the street names in English . . . St. Andrew, St. Lawrence, St. Deniss."[45]

Keenly aware of fashion, she remarked on the young girls who took advantage of the wind and storms to show off their calves, their legs fleshed out by stuffed stockings, as was the style for a time on St-Laurent. As she neared her fortieth birthday, Circé-Côté admonished her juniors for parading around with "short skirts and stuffed calves" and for taking up "the whole width of the sidewalk, laughing like madwomen, their purses swinging like pendulums to the rhythmic clack of their high heels on the asphalt."[46] Nothing escaped her attention: the feel of slush on the edge of a long dress in April and the difficulty of striding over detritus, the "muslins, sheer stockings, and culottes" of 1912, the turned up hems and truncated skirts (*jupes* "*écourtichées*") during the war.[47] All signs of the times to which one had to adapt. And when the female workers of the Canadian Pacific Railways Angus Shops adopted trousers, she approved, stressing that this would help them avoid work accidents.[48]

Day and night, women could be seen in the public spaces. Labour laws were suspended during the First World War, and the workday, sometimes extended to thirteen or fourteen hours, ended long after sundown. Working the night shift often placed young women in a difficult position, and Éva Circé-Côté, aware of the risks they ran, treated this subject in a number of columns.

At night in Montreal, one might come across people bathing in the pool in the middle of Saint Louis Square[49] or be waylaid by ruffians in spite of the street lamps.[50] And prostitutes, the only women whose night-time presence was thought justifiable, could be seen almost anywhere, from the port to the Monument-National. Circé-Côté scoffed at repression, and in 1916 she humorously exaggerated the situation: "soliciting deep in the alleys, in carriage entranceways, . . . Lafontaine Park is invaded by a throng . . . in the stations, the theatres, heady fragrances, strange smells warn us of the proximity of merchants of love . . . on park benches, behind shutters, under your

Moving day, Montreal, circa 1930. MP-1984.105.21 © McCord Museum.

stairway, everything becomes a surprise package . . . nearly every apartment building harbours one or two."[51]

The May 1st moving day was among the scenes that Montrealers found most amusing and exasperating, and, as an uncompromising observer of city life, Circé-Côté regularly commented on it. Always with a touch of humour, she depicted the unsteady assemblage of furniture and knickknacks in the movers' carts, where "the secrets of private life are brutally put on display and curious passersby examine the ripped armchairs and crooked chairs."[53] These teetering pyramids of "mirrors, barrels of dishes, washing machines, buckets, basins tumbling onto the asphalt, with chesterfields, a gramophone, portraits of staring elderly parents, [where] bread sits next to shoe polish, planters next to chambers pots . . . lumber around every street corner and end up colliding with a bus over here or a truck over there . . . [J]ust picture the fright of the horses and the resigned look of the mares when this sort of cataclysm occurs," not to mention the lost children eventually found at the police station.[54] In 1904, after thirty children were reported missing, this terse comment appeared in *La Presse*: "moving time is the season of lost children."[55] Circé-Côté herself had experienced several moves, having gone from the flat on Saint-Denis Street she had shared with Pierre-Salomon to one on Saint-Louis Square, which she left in 1913 and moved to 673 Hôtel-de-Ville (City

Hall Street), before moving farther east to Plessis Street in 1917. As she put it, she was not "tied down." A pragmatic woman, she was not anchored to any place out of habit or prejudice.

> Each year, moving day gives rise to some more or less comic scenes. Just when the wagon gets underway, a rope snaps and the pyramid of furniture collapses onto the sidewalk. Workmen hauling a crate of dishes foolishly drop it while trying to hoist it atop the wagon, and the whole kit and caboodle smashes into a thousand pieces . . . Your movers may have gotten their hands on the small flask of gin you had planned to treat them to and have polished it off. Well, friends, get out of the way! They pitch chairs from one floor to the next, the sideboard and the dressers weigh nothing in their hands—it's like the movies and it makes your head spin! You get into a state on seeing your framed pictures fly through the air and your furniture dances a devilish jig—it actually seems as though they are the drunk ones. These are "occasional" movers . . . But here is something that does not happen each year: some forty children got lost during the moves and landed up at police stations . . . You will tell me that lost children are not like lost watches—they are always found again.[52]

Wherever she went, Éva Circé-Côté appreciated the spectacles that the city presented her, be it in the street, at the theatre, and more and more in the movie houses. The cinema was the embodiment of modernity. Starting in 1896, filmstrips were shown in the *café-concerts* on St-Laurent Boulevard, in Sohmer Park, and in smaller venues. In 1907, Léo-Ernest Ouimet opened the first palatial movie theatre, which was soon to become the Ouimetoscope, with a seating capacity of one thousand. Its rival was the Nationoscope, which was soon joined by Gymnastoscope, the Readoscope, the Rochonoscope, and the Cinématographe. Montrealers were mad about the cinema, and in 1910 there were about forty halls in the city showing films, most of which came from France and the United States.[56] Éva was unreserved in her enthusiasm for "this marvellous invention, which eternalizes the movement of life and transports us to the most faraway lands at the speed of thought."[57]

For the guardians of public morality in Quebec, the silver screen represented a peril that needed to be scrupulously censored. The Bureau de censure des vues animées (Motion pictures censorship board), created in 1913, brought together religious and secular authorities, who imposed censorship that, in the words of Justice Boyer, was "the strictest in the world."[58] Because many people worked on Saturday, Sunday became the day to go to the "movies." English Canada forbade all public amusements on the Lord's Day, but Quebec never displayed the same zeal for Sunday boredom. When some clerics proposed that the cinemas stay closed on Sunday, Circé-Côté, under the pen name Arthur Maheu, demanded instead to let the people have some enjoyment on this day of rest "to shake off the worries of the past week and give themselves the courage to start another one."[59] In 1918, soon after Lionel Groulx had given a talk at the Monument-National denouncing the cinema, Circé-Côté took issue with those who put "all the depravities of lust down to the cinema."[60] The "marvellous invention" was not at fault; instead, those who misused it were to blame. For "the most beautiful invention of the century ... did not invent the ugly things of life; rather, it has given them a perceptible form, no more. On the other hand, [it] has poeticized the instincts, [it] has made people love the beautiful and the virtuous."[61] For her, the cinema was an art within everyone's reach, a democratic art offering at once wholesome entertainment, enchantments for children, and new knowledge. Circé-Côté was not among those who saw it as a place of perdition, where youth "comes to learn vice, where the heart is perverted by the eyes, where the senses are aroused by suggestive spectacles."[62] It reflected society, was neither better nor worse than it, but the cinema also cultivated taste and intelligence.

Far from being a danger to youth, the cinema dispensed "instruction through the eyes" and made it possible to learn while amusing oneself. Moreover, it was incumbent upon governmental and municipal authorities, according to Circé-Côté, not to decry the cinema and prohibit it for young people but, rather, to provide films meant for them, ideally at Lafontaine Park. She envisaged screenings of "historical episodes ... lessons in natural history, agriculture, elements of the exact sciences, technology, philosophy, sociology, civics, patriotism, philanthropy, etc." After all, parents "would rather ... have [their children] there than exposed to the dangers of the street, to the enticements lurking everywhere." And she added this argument for the benefit of her more down-to-earth readers: "Rather than more and more taxation, this would be a source of revenue that would help to eliminate the deficit."[63]

While Éva Circé-Côté voiced her scepticism as to the moral threat that the cinema was said to represent, she constantly denounced the dangers to which children raised on the sidewalk or in the alleys were exposed. Owing to the lack of hygiene, slum-like dwellings, and contaminated water and milk, as evidenced by the contagious diseases proliferating in crowded, working-class neighbourhoods, too many children ended up in the sad processions of little white coffins going up the road on Mount Royal toward the Côte-des-Neiges cemetery.⁶⁴ Immaculate crepe gave way to the little wreathes of leaves adorned with white ribbons that were hung on the doors of Saint-Denis Street to announce the death of a child.⁶⁵ The many references to infant mortality that appeared under Circé-Côté's various pseudonyms are reminders of her own family's experience, her mother having lost nine of her twelve children. In addition to the victims of contagious diseases, many children died in accidents or due to negligence. In December 1914, Fantasio summed up the previous months' fatalities: "Three infants were scalded to death, six were run over by streetcars, two fell out of windows, seven burned while their parents were out."⁶⁶ In the face of this carnage, Circé-Côté, like other progressives of her epoch, not only reported on the appalling situation but also pleaded for prevention, reforms, and, especially, compulsory education, the key to all social progress. With better instruction, mothers would be more attentive to their offspring. Her feminism did not keep her from holding mothers responsible for the safety of their children, while at the same time contending that the state must ensure sanitary conditions so as to prevent epidemics, contagion, and pollution. This discourse was perfectly in line with the programme of the social reform movement that had spread throughout North America since the beginning of the century, and that would continue in Montreal into the 1920s.

Montreal was growing rapidly and going through both physical and social transformations and dislocations. Suburbs attached themselves to the city; industries sprung up, attracted by the workforce arriving from the countryside and overseas; housing and infrastructures could not keep up with the needs of overcrowded neighbourhoods. These facts provided grist for numerous reports and briefs produced by government bodies as well as men and women demanding that living conditions in the cities be improved. As a progressive journalist who was never confined to the women's pages, Éva Circé-Côté was in a position to scrutinize the municipal administration.

The City of Montreal was governed by councillors whose policies regarding the management of its inhabitants, territory, economy, and development were subject to the critical appraisal of the progressive press. Broken water mains, epidemics, but especially bribery, nepotism, and clientelism provided oppositional columnists with ammunition. Since the end of the nineteenth century Montreal had accumulated an exorbitant debt, and the municipal administration was increasingly plumbing the depths of unpopularity. Under various pen names, Éva Circé-Côté was in the front line of those inveighing against municipal corruption and incompetence. The city's civil servants, in particular, were repeatedly on the receiving end of her sarcasm: department heads, incompetent, even ignorant, pencil pushers who were unemployable outside the city administration and unfit to earn a living if ever they were dismissed.[67] As an employee of the Municipal Council's Library Commission, she was quite familiar with such people.

Arthur Maheu, the voice of rural wisdom, harried Montreal's administration with her jabs. Writing under that byline in April 1914, Circé-Côté placed all her hopes in the newly elected mayor Médéric Martin. He was a man of the people, a former cigar-maker and Liberal Member of Parliament for the Sainte-Marie riding, who was voted into office by the "public sentiment": "all it took to rouse an entire population was a sturdy, bold, and brave man; this is an indictment of submissive and obedient sons, of weak-kneed sheep."[68] The new mayor's mission was clear-cut: clean up the finances, take care of the unemployed, get rid of "the lazy and incompetent people eating up the city's money."[69]

The newspaper of the Conseil des métiers et du travail de Montréal (Montreal Trades and Labour Council), *Le Monde ouvrier*, kept a close eye on municipal politics. Its owner, Gustave Francq, had already been a candidate for the Bureau de contrôle (Control Commission) set up by the reformists in 1909. Under the pen name Julien Saint-Michel, Circé-Côté weighed in on fiscal issues, housing projects for workers, and rent levels; she constantly condemned incompetence and corruption.

After re-electing Médéric Martin as mayor of Montreal, voters were soon disillusioned. In April 1917, seeing that the metropolis had regained its "reputation as a dirty city" and continued to bear a crushing debt, Julien Saint-Michel demanded that the municipal administration be "swept out."[70] Unable to overcome the accumulated financial difficulties of the past twenty years, the city was placed under trusteeship early in 1918. In the pages of *Le Monde ouvrier*, Julien Saint-Michel spoke out on behalf of transparency and democracy in public affairs.[71] Yet despite all the problems regarding the city's management, the war stimulated Montreal's economic development, and Éva Circé-Côté persisted in seeing big: "Montreal is like New York was fifty years ago, on the threshold of an economic movement that will propel vast amounts of assets and capital to our shores."[72]

Librarian

Every workday, Éva Circé-Côté returned to her office at the library on the corner of Sherbrooke and Sainte-Famille and went about cataloguing books. A steady source of income provided a measure of security, for she had learned the hard way that journalism was subject to the discretion of church and political censors. Her colleague at *Les Débats*, Arséne Bessette, gave a fiercely comical description of this environment in his novel *Le Débutant*, which sparked a scandal in 1914 and was banned by the Church. Militant journalism was no meal ticket for those who dared to engage in it. Like *Les Débats* at the beginning of the century, *Le Pays* also incurred the wrath of the archdiocese, and, as a librarian, Circé-Côté was fortunate to receive a regular salary from the City of Montreal.

At the time of her appointment in 1903, Éva Circé had no training as a librarian. When she went from the position of head librarian to that of assistant librarian in 1909, her salary was disproportionately low compared to the head librarian's. It was increased from $650 in 1912 to $700 in 1913, while her supervisor, Frédéric Villeneuve, earned $1500.[73] Encouraged by Villeneuve, who had succeeded Lorenzo Prince in 1909, she took "courses in bibliography" at McGill University in the summer of 1911 and was thus better prepared to continue her work of cataloguing the collection acquired in 1910 from the bibliophile Philéas Gagnon. Her new skills made it possible for Villeneuve to present the municipal authorities with a request that his colleague's annual salary be raised to $900. In consideration of his rank and gender, Villeneuve asked for "at least $2000" for himself.[74] On account of wartime inflation, Circé-Côté, now the director of catalogues, earned $900 in 1916, $1000 in 1918, and $1150 in 1920 for a forty-two-hour workweek. The head librarian's salary, meanwhile, stood at $2000 in 1919.[75] Circé-Côté's salary compared very favourably with what other women were paid at the time; the yearly remuneration of most female teachers, for example, was less than $200.

Frédéric Villeneuve was carried off by disease in April 1915, before he could have the satisfaction of seeing the project for which he had fought so hard completed. His absence was deeply felt by Éva Circé-Côté, his protégée, and she paid tribute to him under the pen name Paul S. Bédard.[76] The sudden death took the municipal commissioners by surprise, and they appointed Circé-Côté as interim librarian.[77] It was out of the question for a woman, and a controversial one at that, to hold such a prestigious position, no matter how qualified she was. Her choice of books was a constant source of exasperation for the commissioners, and the letter she received from Thomas Côté of the Commission de la bibliothèque (Library Commission) in November 1915 made plain how very far apart their views were and perhaps, too, how much weight the Church's word carried: "I persist in my assessment that in the list you forwarded to me there are many books that ought not to have been purchased, especially while our library is still in its infancy ... the question of book purchases will soon be resolved through the appointment of a librarian and of a censorship board."[78]

Éva Circé-Côté occupied the position of librarian for nine months, as she had done from 1903 to 1909. Now, with labour and financial resources mobilized for the war, the Library Commission challenged her proposals for book acquisitions. When the commissioners suggested a reduction in the number of employees, she argued that the library was already understaffed and that she herself, by acting as both librarian and cataloguer, "was saving [her] department $2000."[79] It was urgent to create a catalogue for the new library. The library could no longer even honour its debts, such as the $650 owed to Justice Bruneau for his collection of books. Villeneuve had approved the purchase in 1914, and the bill was still outstanding in 1916.[80] It became even more difficult for the library to benefit from such donations or purchases after the Municipal Library on Sherbrooke Street was incorporated and the censorship board was established.

In addition to the library, the Monument-National was home to many organizations and services: The Association Saint-Jean-Baptiste de Montréal, the Fédération nationale Saint-Jean-Baptiste (FNSJB), a music school, the courses dispensed by the FNSJB, as well as a host of one-time events. It was a cramped and noisy place, where "books lie around in the archways, waiting to be chewed up by rats, unless they are buried in dust in rooms that are far too small."[81] In 1911, the City of Montreal and the École technique (Technical school) signed an agreement whereby the school would house in its building at 70 Sherbrooke West the books of what was known henceforward as the Bibliothèque technique de Montreal (Montreal technical library). But the agreement was only temporary, and the endless moving had to stop. The city had not abandoned the project of a library worthy of the name.[82] Yet the intelligentsia was still divided on this matter, and Éva was displeased with the Société Saint-Jean-Baptiste and the Congrès du parler français (Congress of spoken French), held in June 1912, which were loathe to demand "a public library, compulsory education, the creation of a museum, of a national theatre for local authors and actors."[83]

Her new work environment soon grew vexatious. Relations were strained between the director of the École technique, Mr. De Serres, and the library staff. The city paid only a symbolic annual rent of one dollar, and this had an effect on the prevailing conditions. Heating and electricity were under the school's control, and librarians and users alike suffered the consequences. Climatic "cataclysms" occurred in the summer of 1912, which left the population of Montreal shivering. The exceptionally cold summer continued into September, and the dampness in the library became intolerable; when Villeneuve asked for the heat to be turned on twice a week the school refused on the grounds that it was too early in the year, and an acrimonious exchange of letters ensued.[84] Nerves were frayed in the cramped quarters, and the project of a new, genuine library languished.[85]

After twelve years of waiting, Éva Circé-Côté was exultant when the construction of a municipal library was finally announced in June 1914. "It will be the beneficent ark where those wishing to flee the muddy flow of vice and drunkenness will come to take shelter, a dispensary offering an antidote to all the poisons we are forced to swallow, a serum for every infection." She also praised the mayor, Médéric Martin, who had lit "this triumphant light."[86] Despite the difficulties it presented, the chosen site was located across from Lafontaine Park on Sherbrooke Street, between Beaudry and Montcalm, a stone's thrown from the house where Éva had lived with her parents from 1900 to 1903. The architect was Eugène Payette, who also designed the library of the Sulpicians in 1915.

The Saint-Sulpice Library on Saint-Denis Street would remain the rival of the Bibliothèque municipale for many years. Though it was not intended to serve the same purpose, the Sulpicians' library was endowed with a collection composed of books from a parish reading room, those belonging to the priests of Saint-Sulpice, and others donated by individuals. The works found there were edifying and censored; it was an elitist institution in favour with the archdiocese. Circé-Côté's scorn did not prevent the building on Saint-Denis Street from opening its doors two years before the city library on Sherbrooke Street.[87]

The Library Commission never seriously considered entrusting Éva Circé-Côté with the position of librarian on a permanent basis, regardless of her qualifications. It was a job for men. Villeneuve was a lawyer and neither he nor his predecessor, Lorenzo Prince, had any training in library science. Circé-Côté's appointment was no more than temporary, and in 1916 she had to step aside in favour of Hector Garneau, the grandson of the national historian François-Xavier Garneau. Being a great admirer of F.-X. Garneau, she paid tribute to both the grandfather and the grandson when the latter was inducted into the Royal Society in April 1915.[88] She was delighted with the nomination of a liberal nationalist, a learned man, who shared her belief in progress through books. Their collaboration got off to an auspicious beginning. Hector Garneau also had tried his hand at liberal journalism at *Le Canada* and *Le Soleil*. Their relations would not stay forever harmonious, but both would contribute to the library's development for twenty years and were bound together by a common ideal: to give citizens access to books, a mission too often hindered by the Montreal archdiocese, which was determined to control what its flock could read. The assistant librarian's frustrations would be shared by a young colleague, like her a liberal and even a freethinker, Marcel Dugas.

It was Villeneuve who had hired this thirty-two-year-old man, recently returned from a stay in Paris. Dugas' duties involved preparing the books for the move to the new building, and he worked with Circé-Côté every day, helping her to catalogue the titles.[89] A tortured, complicated person, at times depressed, whose broad-rimmed hat made him easily recognizable, Dugas mixed with the artists at L'Arche on Notre-Dame and had acquired a reputation as a poet and critic. He had contributed under various pseudonyms to Olivar Asselin's *Le Nationaliste* and *L'Action* between 1905 and 1911.[90] In the small world of Québécois letters, where regionalists or *indigénistes* or *terroiristes* ("landists") sparred with the *exotiques*, whom their adversaries dubbed the *francissons* [a playful blend of *français* and *saucissons*, i.e., sausages—Trans.], Dugas stood firmly in the camp of the modernists.[91] In her reviews, Éva Circé-Côté warmly welcomed the young Francophile poets, and, sustained by their literary affinities and their non-conformism, a strong and abiding friendship arose between her and her new colleague. Both positioned themselves on the fringe: Circé-Côté because of her ideas and Dugas because of his deportment. An idealist and an aesthete who was considered effeminate, he was given to extravagant behaviour. There were rumours going around about his personal and social life. He wore a *lavallière*, a floppy necktie, which made him stand out in a crowd, and coped with his headaches by keeping a damp towel wrapped around his head while he worked.[92]

As this was a time when relationships between men and women were bound to spawn rumours, it may be wise to take the testimony of the columnist and musicologist Marcel Valois with a grain of salt. It is unclear whether or not he was joking when he alleged that Circé-Côté and her colleague at the library had married but the marriage had lasted only a week! He added: "it was a strange marriage; she was older than him, she was fifty when he was thirty years old."[93] In fact, the age difference between them was only twelve years, but Valois' error speaks volumes about his perception of the two friends. Be that as it may, despite their affinities they never used the familiar "tu" form when speaking to each other, which was not unusual for close friends in those years.

Were it not for her friendship with Dugas, would she have written this defence of homosexuality under the name Maheu in 1916? "As for these unfortunates, perhaps they are no more responsible for this inversion of affections than they would be for a spinal deviation. It is the result of an undetermined cause, a remnant of animality, some moral, intellectual, or sensory disorder—we do not know. . . . He who came through boarding school or any school unscathed, he who has never sinned, let him cast the first stone!"[94] This kind of tolerance was almost unheard of at a time when men arrested for homosexual activity were liable to be whipped under the prevailing laws.

With the library's continuing expansion, the head librarian was in need of an assistant. In the fall of 1916, the call for applications gave rise to rumours. Éva applied, but in spite of her long association with the institution her appointment was not assured; backed by the Church authorities, Casimir Carreau of the Saint-Sulpice Library stepped forward to vie with Circé-Côté for the position. The newspaper *Le Pays*, faithful to its columnist, contended that the job rightfully belonged to the one who was not just the library's founder but was fully qualified for the position: "Fourteen years of 'good and loyal service' . . . a diploma from McGill University, a store of knowledge gained through study, a rigorous dedication to the fulfilment of her assigned duties, weigh heavily in favour of the current holder of the assistant librarian's position." In addition, J. B., the author of this article, denounced the undue influence of the authorities in support of that "*castor*," Carreau.[95] It just so happened that two weeks earlier Julien Saint-Michel had written a column titled "Undue influence"![96] Given her expertise and her status as founder, it appears astonishing that Éva Circé-Côté should have to submit to the same conditions as the other candidates and could not take her tenure for granted. Nevertheless, her appointment was confirmed and she would never again have to undergo this sort of procedure.

On Sherbrooke Street, the construction of the neoclassical building where the library was to be housed continued. In 1916, in anticipation of the forthcoming expansion, the Library Commission increased the staff. The jobs offered at the library were highly coveted, and around seventy applications were received,[97] some from young men, but for the most part from eminently qualified women. The applicants included the author Henriette Tassé, the *La Presse* journalist Gaëtane de Montreuil, and Marie-Claire Daveluy, known as a writer of children's books. Wishing to remain above suspicion of favouritism, the head librarian, in a letter to the commissioner Joseph Aisney, quoted *Le Monde ouvrier*, which "this morning strongly [insisted]" and demanded that "clientelism be restricted through the requirement that applicants for municipal jobs undergo an impartial examination."[98] Did Garneau suspect that the journalist who, under the byline Julien Saint-Michel, had exposed undue influence on positions in the municipal administration and deplored the lack of examinations in the hiring process, the nepotism, and clientelism, was the same employee whom he met each day? Using that pen name, Circé-Côté proposed that the responsibility for hiring employees be given to the department heads rather than the administrators, who acted like "benevolent or malevolent divinities . . . before whom the courtesans must humiliate themselves to secure a position or a promotion."[99] Even though the applicants' letters of recommendation heavily influenced his decisions, Hector Garneau did subject the applicants to a test of their literary knowledge, going so far as to have them take a dictation.

He put Marie-Claire Daveluy "in charge of the catalogue and the reading room," while Florence Chapman, a Protestant English Canadian, was given another position.[100] Daveluy, who was thirty-seven years old at the time, socialized with the feminists of the Fédération nationale Saint-Jean-Baptiste. She and Éva shared various interests. Like Circé-Côté, Daveluy championed female workers, but in the Catholic publication *La Bonne Parole* (the Good News). While Circé-Côté gave talks in Protestant churches, Daveluy's spoke to participants in the Semaines sociales (Social weeks).[101] Apart from religious issues, everything seemed to indicate the two women would get along well. But relations between them, which were cordial at first, became strained as Circé-Côté grew impatient with Daveluy's Catholicism.

Éva excitedly followed the construction of the Eugène Payette building. From the Amherst Street tramway, one day in June 1916, she caught sight of the edifice and hastened to describe it proudly, even lovingly, in the pages of *Le Monde ouvrier* under the Saint-Michel byline: "The monument ... with its massive weightiness ... seems to have been laid down there like a sea wall to hold back ignorance, whose flood tide, upon crashing against the granite, would disperse in a fine spray." The library, furthermore, would "exert a sort of hypnotic attraction" on people coming to kill time in the "Lafontaine garden."[102] Mindful of the readership of *Le Monde ouvrier*, she underscored the library's advantages for workers, who would benefit from a place that they could enter freely and where they would be able to expand their knowledge while feeling at home. Circé-Côté was attentive to the new building's aesthetics; she was in attendance for the decisions concerning the themes of the stained glass windows, which were to represent literary men, the emblems of the Canadian provinces, and the coats of arms of the French provinces that had been home to the original ancestors of New France.

After more than three years of work, the Bibliothèque de Montréal (Municipal Library of Montreal) was inaugurated in the spring of 1917, a year and a half after the Saint-Sulpice Library. In an enthusiastic account of the visit of General Joffre, the victor of the First Battle of the Marne, invited especially for the occasion, Circé-Côté remarked on the Beauvais tapestry chair and the "magnificent register, fashioned in a single night by [the printer and publisher] Beauchemin for the purpose of receiving the precious signature." And, as the general was leaving, Hector Garneau, "in a gesture that history will retain, had barely enough time to raise his hat above all those heads swaying in the wind of an emotion as deep as the sea and shout, General, long live France! ... than he was already disappearing in the distance."[103]

> If you go by Lafontaine Park, you will see these columns blazing, truly as if a soul were emerging through the very hard pores of the stone ... They are really alive and may appear a fleshy pink in the flaming sunset topped with a Phrygian bonnet, or, if seen at night, they may grow nearly immaterial, such is their brilliance ... the imperative call of these shining pillars, rising up in the aridness of our desert like the fiery pillar of the Hebrew lawgiver, will turn our carefree but good and clever population away from the paths of perdition.[104]

The imposing building must command respect without intimidating visitors, particularly workers. There was no influx of members of the working class in the months following the library's inauguration, and in the union newspaper, Julien Saint-Michel cautioned labour leaders: the library, according to Circé-Côté's conception, must be devoted exclusively to reading; it was certainly not intended to be a venue for society events.[105] She consequently objected to the holding of a formal dinner in honour of a foreign delegation in the entrance hall; it was not a reception hall.[106] But to attract readers, a vast choice of books was needed.

In 1917, the library contained some forty thousand books, a paltry collection when compared to those of other Montreal institutions such as the Saint-Sulpice Library or the Fraser Institute's library.[107] Éva Circé-Côté never forgave the city councillors who, under pressure from the Church, had rejected Carnegie's philanthropic offer and the books of the Institut canadien (Canadian Institute). The unfilled shelves were the result of that refusal.[108] One room was devoted to art exhibitions, and in 1919 an art museum was housed on the second floor, but was not the library's primary goal to provide books? The poverty of the collection did not escape the notice of some eminent visitors.

> It was reported that when the French mission was officially received at the Municipal Library, its members would not have been enthralled had they seen the empty shelves in the book storage area. Indeed, they cast a rather indifferent glance at the authentic signatures of Champlain and Dollard des Ormeaux, at the first French catechism to be printed in Nouvelle France in the eighteenth century. Our riches left them quite unmoved. There is no doubt that those who have been able to admire

the treasures of the Bibliothèque nationale were not bowled over by the exhibition of a few rare papers spread out in front of them and giving off a rancid smell.[109]

As an employee, Circé-Côté answered to the Commission de la bibliothèque (Library Commission), which was appointed by the city administration. In 1917, the board was made up of eminent literary men such as Fernand Rinfret—who signed his theatre reviews in *Les Débats* Paul d'Estrée, alongside the columns of Colombine and Musette—and Victor Morin, whose poetry had earned Fantasio's praise. The councillor Eudore Dubeau was chairman, and the board also included John Boyd, Zotique L'Espérance, and the head librarian Hector Garneau, who acted as secretary.[110] Relations between the librarian, the Library Commission, and the city authorities were strained. The board member Atherton proposed an Anglophone assistant, thereby questioning Hector Garneau's ability to serve the English-speaking public. Circé-Côté boldly defended Garneau and the staff. Garneau does not need an Anglophone assistant, she wrote: "the head librarian is well versed in the English language, just as he is in European and American politics and world history." The staff includes "McGill students, medal-winners of the Alliance française, and literary women."[111] Instead of increasing the number of management positions, it would be wiser, in her opinion, to hire assistant librarians and, especially, to buy more books.

So it was that in November 1918 the head of the Commission, E. R. Décary, wrote to Garneau: "The choice and purchase of the books, publications, periodicals, journals, newspapers, drawings, works of art, and historical objects that must make up the library collection will be left up to your board."[112] Yet it would be wrong to assume that the board enjoyed full latitude regarding acquisitions. Religious influence did not always make itself felt directly; self-censorship arose such that no title on the Catholic Church's "Index" of forbidden books, nor of any other suspect work found its way onto the library shelves.[113]

In *Le Monde ouvrier*, Circé-Côté, the journalist-librarian, would return more than once to the issue of municipal employees' wages, but without ever revealing that she was fully cognizant of the salaries of the thirteen people who made up the library staff: five men—Garneau, Dugas, an accountant, a clerk, and the cloakroom attendant—and eight women, all assigned to the catalogue and the reading room.[114] She, whose salary was half of what the head librarian earned, knew very well that her female colleagues were underpaid and that Dugas, in his capacity as "classifier," earned as much as she did, but in her columns she was not forthcoming about her personal situation.[115]

Journalist

In addition to her forty-two-hour week at the library,[116] which often included weekends and evenings—the library closed at 10 p.m. on weekdays—there was no letup in Éva Circé-Côté's involvement in the world of letters. As a contributor to Godfroy Langlois's *Le Pays*, she, along with all her colleagues, suffered the consequences of Mgr Bruchési's condemnation in 1913. The paper was resurrected, with eight to ten pages coming out every Saturday, and Paul S. Bédard, Fantasio, and Arthur Maheu continued to publish their comments there on political and social issues and, as of August 1914, on the war in Europe and its repercussions for Canada.

In 1916, Gustave Francq, a member of the Émancipation lodge until it was disbanded in 1910, invited Circé-Côté to contribute to his new union paper *Le Monde ouvrier/Labour World*, which was launched in 1916. This bilingual weekly with a circulation of 8,500[117] was the official newspaper of the Conseil des métiers et du travail du Montreal (Montreal Trades and Labour Council) and defended the interests of skilled workers belonging to the international unions, that is, those affiliated with the Trades and Labor Congress of Canada, which in turn was affiliated with the major American union body, the American Federation of Labor. For this new task, Circé-Côté decided to use her grandfather's name, Julien Saint-Michel.[118] The aim was to conceal herself behind the identity of a unionized worker: "we workers," she wrote, adopting what she believed to be a working-class point of view. For over twenty years working men and women would read what they thought was the enlightened opinion of a working-class man; she had no difficulty passing herself off as such to her readers when she depicted their work environment: "the automatic monotony of the movements to which workers are condemned by the machines . . . eating dust all day, enduring the crowded conditions of people robbed of their dignity and the countless humiliations inherent to their situation."[119]

Over the years, she sometimes departed from the Saint-Michel character, defending positions at odds with a working-class perspective. In 1927, for example, she found a host of reasons to have workers deprived of their lunch hour—they would generally eat at home in those days—and to approve the "undivided day" proposed by employers.[120] How many working men and women were willing to follow her advice to have a substantial meal before leaving home and then work steadily until the evening? One could also speculate as to what her readers thought on reading, "When I was in the *collège classique* . . ." Granted, Saint-Michel wrote that "he" was surrounded by scions of affluent families, so that readers might assume he was one of those poor students who had earned a scholarship.[121] Still, the situation was ironic, given that Éva had not been able to attend a *collège* in her youth. But how did her proletarian readers react when she recommended that employers demand of their employees to live up to moral standards?[122] And what about Saint-Julien's style and learned quotations? There is no way of knowing the extent to which the masquerade succeeded; one can only note that despite all of Circé-Côté's efforts to blend in with the newspaper's overall tone, statements like the ones just cited sometimes betrayed her bourgeois background.

Her involvement with the Trades and Labour Council's newspaper in no way impinged on her level of energy. Her output was astonishing. She published numerous articles, as many as four per day. Thus, on July 15, 1916, one could read Julien Saint-Michel inveighing against "Saint-John-Baptism" and the saint's emblem, the sheep, in *Le Monde ouvrier*; Fantasio discussing the presence of women in the life of Jesus in *Le Pays*; Paul S. Bédard, also in *Le Pays*, developing an incisive criticism of Marcel Dugas' latest poetry collection, *Psyché au cinéma*; and Arthur Maheu, on another page of the same paper, reflecting on municipal civil servants. Throughout the following years, three or four columns would appear each week; those in *Le Monde ouvrier* were primarily didactic, while those in *Le Pays* were for the most part social and literary.[123]

All Circé-Côté's columns display a stylist's concern for polishing and refining every line, every sentence. Her critics, de Montigny and Tyard, noticed this very early on. Her writing is clear and energetic, her tone ironic, even sarcastic, though quite often overblown. Every good stylist strives for the *mot juste*, for euphony, and to avoid needless repetitions and hackneyed phrases; Éva Circé-Côté fulfilled the first three criteria very well, but she had trouble abstaining from time-worn analogies and tired metaphors. She would use a human-interest story or an anecdote—"it was reported that . . ."—as her point of departure, either to guarantee authenticity or to refute a rumour or a commonplace. She sometimes had recourse to a colloquial register and first-person narrative: "I have a neighbour . . . " or "I know a man who . . . " To establish good rapport with her readers, she used dialogue, letting a character express her ideas. She was not averse to naturalism to make her descriptions more vivid. Over time, she got rid of the clichés that had peppered her early columns. She always excelled at composing biting portraits of her contemporaries, such as Médéric Martin, Olivar Asselin, Henri Bourassa, or Mgr Bruchési. Her fondness for shocking and provoking led her to contradict herself and to be inconsistent at times.

Would it be fair to point to such contradictions as evidence of cynicism or opportunism? For instance, in 1929 she railed against the smoking craze, that "idiotic tyranny of nicotine-induced intoxication."[124] She tackled the same issue in *Le Monde ouvrier*. "Smoking is not a sin, but a crime against feminism," she wrote, adding, "Everything that weakens the mainspring of the will, paralyzes one's energy, and stiffens the muscles must be banished from our customs."[125] Yet she was well acquainted with the sensation of "the blood urgently demanding the ephemeral exhilaration that the absorption of the magic smoke sends rushing through every limb," because in 1920 she wrote to Dugas, "I read a great deal and I smoke a great deal when I am sad."[126] Was she a reformed smoker? Or did she distance herself from her writing, which, after all, was intended to educate the readers, not the writer of those columns?

She succeeded in vanishing behind her personae. She had been happily married, yet she wrote prolifically on bad marriages, shrewish women, and abusive husbands. She was full-figured yet had no hesitation in making fun of "fat women." Dissimulation became a sign of freedom. In 1923, when the Prince of Wales travelled through Canada under the name Baron Renfrew, a certain "Polémarque" published a vigorous defence of going incognito in *Le Matin*, although it cannot be ascertained whether or not the person behind that Greek name was the woman whose byline elsewhere was Julien Saint Michel.

Éva Circé-Côté's literary reviews, far fewer than her political and social critiques, were always well researched, often enthusiastic, rarely indulgent, and never ingratiating. In 1913, she deemed Jean Charbonneau to be "the Rembrandt of our young [literary] school" while at the same time disapproving of his anachronistic pessimism.[127] In her appraisal of Charbonneau's *Des influences françaises au Canada* (On French influences in Canada), published in 1917, she remarks, "his virile pen produces lines that are accurate, his sense of analysis does not go to the core of beings but encompasses surfaces and is not fooled by appearances," and recommends in particular the chapters on "dream and action in America" and the "influences of French positivism on French-Canadian thinking."[128] This was a topic close to her heart, being herself a positivist who dreamt of the renewal of French America. In the same column she also reviewed the literary output of several young authors: the economist Édouard Montpetit, "a poet imprisoned in his hard shell of economics and who deserves to be counted among the carvers of verse"; Gonzalve Desaulniers, whose "life wholly devoted to the cause of education and the moral regeneration of his fellow citizens is his most beautiful poetry"; Paul Morin, lauded for the "luminous poetry" of his *Paon d'émail* (Enamel peacock); Marcel Dugas, a "symbolist prose-writer, artisan of the sentence, as patient as the goldsmiths of the Middle Ages."[129] When the Alliance française held its fifteenth-anniversary banquet, she analyzed every speech in terms of both style and content: Gonzalve Desaulniers' dream vision in his poem "La fille sauvage" (The wild girl), Édouard Montpetit's sobriety and virtuosity, Raoul Dandurand's good sense.[130] On the occasion of Louvigny de Montigny's induction into the Société royale (Royal Society), she came to the defence of her old colleague, who, after the publication of his book *La Langue française au Canada*, had been ostracized by "inflamed detractors belonging to the clergy and the Orange Order." And when his book was lambasted by *L'Action nationale*, she jumped back into the fray, defending his style and even "the form of his dandyism, his long sentences."[131] Yet it was her friend and co-worker Marcel Dugas who inspired her best critical writing, so it is appropriate to take a closer look.

Dugas was a poet who identified with the exotics and the symbolists. Circé-Côté had no trouble recognizing a true stylist. *Feux de Bengale à Verlaine glorieux* (Bengal lights for glorious Verlaine), a collection published in 1916, put her in mind of a "burst of dazzling words," and she took pleasure in underscoring the similarities between Verlaine and the Québécois poet.[132] Six months later, *Psyché au cinéma* (Psyche at the cinema), "Mr. Dugas' most mature work," was the subject of another of Paul S. Bédard's solid reviews. Bédard/Circé-Côté was moved by this "Prometheus of the sentence," who, she added, gives "new expression to feeling" and "exudes, together with its aphrodisiac virtue, a breath of freshness and inventiveness. He has an ingenuous way of saying daring things."[133]

When Dugas published *Versions*, a study of the poets Louis Le Cardonnel and Charles Péguy, Circé-Côté's comments were frank and even tended toward the intimate. She does not hold back from noting the "mannered modesty," the "preciosity of a marquise," the inconstancy, the paradoxical thinking of the poet she described as a "poet of illusions." The entire column would be worth quoting as an illustration of Éva Circé-Côté's writing at its most incisive. She wonders how "with very pure words he conjures up concupiscent images—that is his secret." She cannot help but point out his "believer's atavism . . . which is hardly more forgiving than hereditary alcoholism." But she also perceives admirable echoes there, for "even in those whose loss of faith is irremediable, mysticism remains like the fragrance in a sachet." She concludes: "We should incorporate in our anthologies the sublimely inspired pages on Jeanne d'Arc, whose formal perfection has not been matched by anyone in Canada."[134] Indeed, this piece by Éva Circé-Côté should also be included in anthologies of literary criticism.

War

The backdrop for all this writing and activity was the conflict in Europe and Canada's military and economic contribution to what would soon be called "the war effort." Between August 1914 and the end of 1919, Éva Circé-Côté wrote more than one hundred and sixty columns for *Le Pays* and *Le Monde ouvrier* on the subject of the war. While the political and military authorities sought to specify Canada's participation, Circé-Côté was among the intellectuals asking, "Why war?" A column in *Le Pays* signed Fantasio was published on August 14, 1914, under the telling headline, "Humanity is moving backward," with the subheading, "The spectre of war has materialized. If only we could hope for a lasting peace to come out of the war." Nothing remained of the beautiful ideal of constant and ineluctable progress, now that nations had begun to "play at doing evil with the inventions of progress." More than a hiatus, for four years the Western world experienced a regression. But Circé-Côté did not shed her optimism so readily: "Who knows," she wonders, "whether or not the premature theories of Jaurès will spring up in this field newly ploughed and watered with the blood of martyrs and whether or not the peace envisioned by the prophet of socialism will appear on this funerary field?"[135] Throughout the war, she would waver between profound despair at humanity's reversion to barbarism and the hope of seeing a better world rise out of the ruins. But at the very start of the hostilities, when "the spectre is a reality" and *La Marseillaise* could be heard in the streets of Montreal and the trains stations overflowed with soldiers departing or returning from battle,[136] she was almost relieved: "Better sooner than later."[137] As a Francophile and a republican, she unhesitatingly supported Canada's participation in the war, because warring France was the land of Jaurès, Voltaire, and the Enlightenment; the Dreyfus affair and those of Drumont and Barrès were left out of account. For her, an entire civilization was in danger of foundering on German barbarism.

In *Le Pays* and, starting in 1916, also in *Le Monde ouvrier*, her columns kept pace with the progress of the war, not on the battlefield but on the home front, where each day women and men dealt with unprecedented economic and social conditions. Her articles followed step by step the Borden government's evolving policies and the reactions of the population in Quebec to the measures adopted.

Circé-Côté's unconditional support for France did not keep her from harshly judging the Canadian government's coercive measures. True to her devotion to individual freedom, she found any such restrictions unacceptable. From the very first, Canadians, especially those born in Great Britain, answered the call for volunteers. The citizen registration programme implemented in 1916 was greeted with sarcasm by her alias Arthur Maheu, who was annoyed by the recruiting agents taking over Viger Square to attract "unemployed workers, vagrants, desperate men," in exchange for "$10 for each recruit."[138] Although she mocked the methods used, she well understood the need to enlist in order to defend France and liberate Belgium, but she preferred to put her trust in individual initiative.[139]

She never succumbed to fanatical patriotism, which ostracized those who did not volunteer and fostered militarism among youths. She opposed, for example, cadet training and military drills in schools. During the gift-giving season at Christmas, she took exception to the military toys displayed in "shop windows decked out like altars." She wrote: "Playing at war and soldiering should not be allowed after what has happened."[140]

In 1915, with no end of the carnage in sight, resistance to the pursuit of hostilities took on various forms: the harshly repressed mutinies in France, the appeal of pacifist feminists gathered in Switzerland, the Vatican's proposal for a negotiated peace. Éva Circé-Côté was vehemently opposed to all these efforts. In her view, any form of surrender would mean condoning the crimes committed against Belgium. She could not forgive President Wilson for keeping the United States out of the conflict. The American republic might have "gone to the aid of butchered France in memory of Rochambeau, La Fayette, and all the French heroes to whom they owe, first, their moral emancipation, and, later, their victorious independence."[141] When Rome maintained its neutrality and refused to condemn Germany, she denounced what she regarded as the hypocrisy of the pope, who, moreover, had been prompt to side with the Catholic Church of Ireland at the expense of French Canadians.[142] This was no time for pacifism: "A people that does not want to fight in the current circumstances does not belong to civilization any more than the orangutans and the buffalos."[143]

Later, however, on seeing the monstrosities of trench warfare and after the millions of deaths, Éva Circé-Côté admitted that the slaughter must not be prolonged. In 1917, when Jeannette Rankin, Montana member of the House of Representatives, voted against the United State's entry into the war, Fantasio praised the congresswoman's courage.[144] She read *Le Feu* (*Under Fire*), Henri Barbusse's great novel based on his personal experience, which describes the horror and absurdity of life at the front. Twice in 1917 she quoted this book, which "will provide excellent material for anthologies."[145] As the conflict became bogged down and civilians learned of the extent of the losses and the horror of trench warfare, her writing showed an unmistakable evolution in her thinking.

Le Monde ouvrier spoke on behalf of the international unions and followed the lead of the headquarters in the United States. Samuel Gompers, president of the American Federation of Labor, continued to oppose American participation until the US declared war in 1917. *Le Pays*, Circé-Côté's other employer, was as favourable as the union paper to criticisms of Ottawa's policy. In January 1917, Fantasio made no secret of her objections to the registration of citizens, which she interpreted as a first step toward conscription and not a mere administrative measure aimed at taking stock of the workforce, regardless of the statements made by the bishops and the cardinal in support of the government's actions.[146] For the duration of the war, Circé-Côté would favour voluntary enlistment over conscription.

As of 1916, as the list of casualties in Europe grew longer, the initial pool of volunteers in Canada was drying up month after month. Starting with the battle of Vimy Ridge in April 1917, losses began to outpace enlistments, such that Prime Minister Borden contemplated the conscription of men fit for service. Quebec was necessarily opposed to this, and Wilfrid Laurier refused to take part in a coalition government that would help persuade French Canadians to accept the draft. Notwithstanding her devotion to the war effort, Éva Circé-Côté felt that "a true liberal cannot be a conscriptionist."[147] Despite Quebec's opposition, the Military Service Act was passed in June 1917. Circé-Côté reacted swiftly.[148] She had made her position clear as early as March: "We liberals must rise up against conscription, because it is a violation of liberty, a display of disregard for justice, for our history, contrary to the country's interests, and especially harmful for the survival of French Canada."[149] Two years later she would add: "The greatness of the cause, the value of the cause we were going to defend, did not justify this betrayal of our past, this neglect of our true interests."[150]

Eva Circé-Côté's writings during the four years of the war chronicled the vicissitudes endured by the civilian population, which, though not directly under military assault, was nevertheless affected by the restrictions and social changes, whose impact was felt by soldiers' families in particular. In Montreal, numerous events were organized to boost civilian keenness for the war effort: exhibitions displaying pieces of German airplanes, parades and marching bands along the major thoroughfares, the "Société des sacs-au-dos" (backpack society) founded in 1915 mainly with the support of the (European) French community, and, in September 1915, a rally in which fifteen thousand people gathered in the streets to celebrate the victory at the Marne.[151] In one report, she described the departure of a regiment: "carrying knapsacks, escorted by wives, children, and friends, the soldiers paraded one last time in Montreal." Some felt "they were being made to sell their flesh to feed their families."[152] However much Circé-Côté wanted to defend France, she was no militarist.

Canada and, very conspicuously, its metropolis, Montreal, were being modernized as a result of the war. Accelerating industrial expansion and migration from the country to the city, and contacts with the outside world owing to the effect of European military politics on many homes—Éva Circé-Côté greeted such changes enthusiastically, so long as they were not based on the exploitation of workers and contributed to women's emancipation. She denounced them when "the people were as always sacrificed."[153] Exploitation, in her view, stemmed as much from the bosses' greed as from the ignorance of working women and men ill-prepared to stand up for their rights.

When Canada declared war in August 1914, the country had been in the grip of a severe economic crisis for a year. Unbridled expansion and overproduction had entailed cutbacks, factory closures, and the attendant loss of jobs. In 1914, Canadians' income plummeted and one out of every six workers was unemployed.[154] Countries investing in Canada or importing its goods cancelled their contracts, thereby aggravating the crisis, which would continue into 1915. Circé-Côté reported on the unemployment, staff reductions, and lay-offs—for which the war served as a pretext—that threw workers, stenographers, clerks, labourers, and servants into the street.[155]

The prosecution of the war and the Allies' needs completely transformed the Canadian economy. After contracts began to flood in, production and exports resumed, workers were hired on, and unemployment receded. Staples grew scarce and costly, rationing was introduced, and prices shot up due to inflation. Wages increased but lagged behind the cost of living, which continued to rise throughout the war years, and Circé-Côté, writing in *Le Monde ouvrier* on behalf of the working class and of the oppressed in general in *Le Pays*, decried the exacerbation of economic injustice.

At the library, she and her colleagues felt the effects of the war effort, which was a drain on budgets and energies. The restrictions slowed down work on the new library building on Sherbrooke Street. On May 30, 1918, the city's administrative board informed the Library Commission that a number of employees would be let go. Hector Garneau had to make a case for his staff to be kept at full strength.[156] Budget cuts affected municipalities and the acquisition of books and periodicals suffered. In his annual report for 1916, the librarian of the Sainte-Cunégonde branch, E. Z. Massicotte, noted that library use had declined because of the enlistment of young men who otherwise would have visited the library.[157] Every activity was affected by the war economy. Even the Saint-Jean-Baptiste parade was pathetic in 1916: the sheep mascot "was grotesque and the butt of jibes and jeers."[158]

Among the sacrifices demanded of the population was support for the Canadian Patriotic Fund, a volunteer organization established to assist families of soldiers at the front whose pay proved to be insufficient. Citizens, businessmen, companies, the City of Montreal, and the Quebec government made generous donations to the annual funding drives, and employers pledged to contribute. One of the sources of money for the Patriotic Fund was a sum that employers deducted directly from their employees' wages. In some companies, employees were asked to voluntarily donate a day's wages each month; those who refused were subject to penalties.[159] As of 1914, under the alias Arthur Maheu, Circé-Côté denounced "the constrained obligation to give away a day's wages."[160] It was a foregone conclusion that the Montreal library would contribute to the Patriotic Fund, and on February 9, 1917, the Bureau des commissaires (Commissioners' bureau) voted in favour of having one day's wages go into the Fund on a quarterly basis.[161] One can easily imagine the reaction of the woman who in 1915 had written: "The people who subscribe to the Patriotic Fund often take from the defenceless the odious war ransom, collecting from all and sundry a hateful booty."[162]

These sacrifices would have been accepted more readily had the country not been shaken by a series of scandals related to war production. Éva Circé-Côté continuously reported on the abuses and brazen profiteering. In 1915, Arthur Maheu was outraged by the fact that "360,000 shells had been rejected by the Canadian government because they could not fit into the barrels."[163] The Minister of the Militia and Defence, Sam Hughes, was not equal to the situation, and the scandal concerning the Ross rifles, made in Canada and liable to jam in mid-combat, was but one example of the prevailing laxness in the awarding of wartime contracts that enriched those supplying the troops with milk, meat, and other staples.

Speaking first and foremost to workers, Julien Saint-Michel presented the "picture of Hell" formed by working conditions in a munitions factory, where "men and women kill themselves to harvest the passing manna," from which the "*trustards*" (the heads of trusts) had the most to gain.[164] Even though a lucky worker could earn up to ten dollars a day in the war industry, unemployment would persist until 1917, and the war contracts would serve the "new caste of multi-millionaires."[165] Circé-Côté called for the conscription of wealth rather than men.[166] It should be remembered that she had railed against the trusts long before the war broke out; as early as 1902, using the pseudonym Jean Ney, she had attacked "the instigators of trusts and schemes"[167] in her short-lived paper *L'Étincelle*. Fifteen years later she saw, on the one hand, the "war profiteers," the trusts, the "insatiable vampires amassing millions stolen from the people," and on the other hand "Baptiste, forever paying for the enrichment of ignoble capitalists."[168]

In *Le Monde ouvrier*, Julien Saint-Michel came to the defence of workers exploited through the demands of the war and subjected to worsening employment conditions; she pointed up the abuses, as in the case of the Carlton Construction company, which, having undertaken to do work for the federal government in La Prairie, reneged on its contract and delayed for three weeks before paying the labourers.[169] Her unceasing condemnation of speculators and the rising cost of living echoed a sentiment shared by both workers and the middle class. The increase in rent in the city, where the rental market was overwhelmed by the influx of people in search of employment, affected the readership of the papers for which she wrote. Early in 1917, when a 10 to 15 percent increase in rents was predicted for Montreal, she came out against a low-rental housing project to be constructed in the Maisonneuve and Parc Amherst districts by companies for their employees, "in order to pen up working people like cattle." Such working-class dwellings "in outlying neighbourhoods" would lead to a deterioration of living conditions for workers used to residing near their workplaces. If pushed out to peripheral areas, they would have to spend more time on streetcars, bring their lunch to work, and eat sandwiches and cakes.[170] Pulling no punches, she stated what her readers were thinking: the landlords, "those bourgeois predators,"[171] were "always on the lookout for ways to relieve their vassals of a few more bucks";[172] "landlords are taking advantage of the war to raise rents."[173]

In denouncing inflation and its consequences for working-class families, Julien Saint-Michel referred to a report by Rosa Henderson, a Montreal social worker and socialist, on infants' health and the extent of anemia and chlorosis resulting from the rise in the price of milk and the "privations imposed on children." As a progressive columnist, Circé-Côté came to consider the ongoing war responsible for "weakening the young generation and holding back our evolution."[174]

There were a number of ways to profit from the war. In addition to material gain, lucrative contracts, and exorbitant profits, there was the recognition of services rendered to one's country. While military service was generally felt to be well deserving of such recognition, the honours bestowed on civilians prompted some sharp reactions. Éva Circé-Côté, for one, had no use for military decorations. *La Presse* noted the absence of French Canadians among those most recently decorated, while in *Le Pays* Éva objected to the "foreign costume jewellery" and titles of nobility; she asked, shouldn't moral and intellectual value outweigh appearances?[175] She came back to this issue again a few months later, when honours were awarded to deserving citizens on May 24, at the King's Birthday celebrations. In wartime, capitalists, arms manufacturers, those who "exploit the slaughter in Europe" are lionized, rather than the soldiers who have risked their lives. The "pomp" must be rejected.[176] Like Asselin and Bourassa before her, Circé-Côté excoriated the "Barons of the Shells," "Lord Bacon," "Lord Blood Pudding," and "that notorious baron in the lard and munitions business"—all those who were selling their country for decorations.[177] "Drugged on nobility" as if it were morphine, she wrote somewhat grandiloquently, they commit "the ultimate folly for a bit of parchment, sacrificing the future of their race, compromising its evolution, burdening their conscience forever with the shame that holds us down in the mire like a ball and chain."[178] This should be understood as a veiled allusion to the industrial tycoon and president of the Imperial Munitions Board, Joseph Flavelle, who had been named baronet and accused of brazen profiteering, accusations of which he would later be absolved.[179]

Though scandals may have been grabbing the headlines, freethinkers like Éva Circé-Côté were also concerned by another, less prominent, issue: censorship. Like any country at war, Canada censored the press. When censorship was stepped up in 1917 Circé-Côté protested against such violations of freedom, which imperilled "our honour as men and, for journalists, the dignity of their calling." She could see how, in light of the indiscretions during the Franco-Prussian war of 1870, censorship was justifiable in France and Germany, but not here. Throughout the war, she argued for support for France and against conscription, excessive profits, and the intrusion of the state, especially by means of censorship.

* * *

Throughout this period the word "upheaval" recurred like a leitmotif, and in tandem with the economic turbulence came a transformation of social mores. The outcry against moral degradation could be heard on all sides. The "malingerers," the "big-legged errand girls," as Circé-Côté called them, were part of the landscape. Their presence was overstated; the number of working women was far greater. Women held jobs in non-traditional sectors, and in Circé-Côté's opinion their wages should have been equal to those of their male colleagues.[180] With the men going off to the war, women became even more visible. They could be seen in the streets taking on unusual tasks, and Arthur Maheu enjoyed poking fun at the ones who sold victory bonds and awarded the buyers "the red badge of the victory loan."[181] Arthur Maheu also complained about the many "war babies who become dependent on the state" and "the widows drawing government pensions," as well as the "legions of damsels who had swooped down here to capture the hearts of our *poilus* and the government pension, and to misappropriate the Patriotic Fund."[182] Another target of Éva Circé-Côté's columns were the "benefactresses" of the Patriotic Fund, who, intent on preventing fraud, meddled in the lives of families and deplored how the beneficiaries used their allowances, claiming that they were buying pianos and luxury items. In the name, once again, of individual freedom, she defended soldiers' families against these women, whom she described as Pharisees, inquisitors, and informers. "People are free to spend as they wish," and to purchase "pianos rather than bread." The war pensions were minimal in comparison with the "sacrifices made by those fighting in France for the rule of law and for civilization."[183]

Feminists contended that women's contribution to the war effort, their sacrifices, and their presence in professions previously regarded as exclusively male should go hand in hand with civil and political rights. Éva Circé-Côté had abandoned her reservations about women's capacity to take part in political life. In the spring of 1917, when the conservative government granted voting rights to soldiers' relatives and to nurses in the armed forces, Circé-Côté denounced this as an electoral ploy because it left aside all the women "who would have been powerful agents of morality, order, and thrift in the management of public affairs."[184] She demanded nothing less than universal suffrage.[185] Her indignation was such that she attacked the very same beneficiaries of the Patriotic Fund she had defended just a few months earlier, women who she now said "had a more than an easy time of it" and "consoled themselves with someone else for the absence of their heroes."[186]

In June 1918 Circé-Côté wrote: "We live in an age of unparalleled ferocity. Bayonets are not the only things that kill. [. . .] Never have the strong oppressed the weak as they do today, to the point where one despairs of civilization."[187] She emerged from the war years disillusioned and anxious about the future of a "civilization" that had sacrificed an entire generation. She continued to define herself as an incorrigible optimist, but her faith in humanity and its inexorable progress was badly shaken. When the carnage had begun she could still justify the "sacrifice for future generations, who will enjoy 'the promised land of the blessings of peace.'"[188] She was not alone in hoping that in the wake of the war would come a land washed by the soldiers' blood, that the war would make way for better, more enlightened times.

Afterward, however, what remained was revulsion, a haunting horror, and the acrimony of the debates. "A kind of stupor in which the desire for silence combined with a paralyzing dread" descended on too many of her fellow citizens, whereas she had lost none of her indignation at the "violations of our freedom, the economic crisis that followed, the flood of misery, tears, grief . . . [which have] darkened our minds forever."[189] After a time, she questioned her early enthusiasm for the Allies. In 1920 she wrote: "The mad ambition and greed of the manufacturers of firearms, munitions, and instruments of war, with the complicity of the stock marketeers, the speculators, were the hidden mainsprings that triggered the great war, in which the peoples, driven by an occult force, were the executioners and the victims."[190] Yet she did not lose hope—life would prevail. The column continues in a realistic vein, with no indulgence for sensitive souls:

> All those brains ejected from their skulls, some still hanging on fences like sparrow nests, all the congealed blood, all the putrefied flesh will be assimilated by the soil, which next year will be carpeted with velvety moss. We should imitate thrifty nature, which lets nothing be lost. There is a moral to be drawn from the events. Now that the savage discord has abated, a new era will shine forth. . . . A new society will be built on the ruins of the one that is collapsing, for life must triumph over death, because that is the reason for our faith—assuming that faith has a reason.[191]

Her faith in progress appears to be indomitable; it is "an artisan of necessary suffering, a remorseless victor."[192]

*   *   *

Among Éva Circé-Côté's contemporaries, the person with whom she could best be compared would not be one of her coworkers at the library, like Marie-Claire Daveluy, or her journalist colleagues, Madeleine or Gaëtane de Montreuil, but the progressive social worker Rose Henderson. She and Circé-Côté were both born in 1871, both were widowed and left alone with a young daughter after only a few years of marriage, both wrote for *Le Monde ouvrier/Labor World* and were in demand as speakers. Henderson was directly involved in social work in her capacity as assistant to Justice Choquet of the Montreal Youth Court. The two women shared the same views. They took similar positions on Irish independence and children's well-being, denouncing the high infant mortality rate, child labour, and the poor health of children. Each of them was concerned about education, condemned the corporal punishment meted out to pupils, and criticized classical education, which did not prepare young people for life. Finally, they opposed the death penalty and were pacifists, though Éva was not at first. Did they know each other? Neither of them left behind personal archives, but Circé-Côté mentioned

Rosa Henderson twice.[193] There were, of course, differences between them. For example, they did not always marshal the same arguments in support of women's suffrage; Henderson saw it as a way for women to extend their maternal influence, whereas for Circé-Côté it was a matter of rights and justice. Henderson was involved in social, and eventually political and union, action, while Circé-Côté was not associated with any organization and defended her causes anonymously.[194] Regardless of the nature of their personal relationship, the parallels between the two women are striking.

Éva Circé-Côté's personal life remains for the most part unknown to us. Her writings show her areas of interest during the war years, but there is little that might shed some light on her feelings or daily doings. We can only imagine the discipline she must have imposed on herself in order to coordinate her family activities, her work at the library, and her abundant and punctual output of copy. There are no sources to confirm whether or not her mother helped take care of her young daughter or if little Ève went to a boarding school, which would have made Circé-Côté's daily life easier to manage. She went to the theatre and the cinema, and she often met with politicians and literary figures, although some continued to shun her company, and she was always hurt by this ostracism.

How did she get over the grief of losing her husband? One Monday morning, November 6, 1916, she very privately had Pierre-Salomon Côté's ashes buried. The urn was removed from the vault and interred in a plot of the Mount Royal cemetery. There is nothing in her writings that might indicate the emotional effect this had on her.[195] The war years temporarily undermined her optimism, but it was not in her nature to succumb to despondency. She pursued her fight for a progressive Quebec throughout the twenties, which would soon come to be known in French as "the crazy years," *les Années folles*.

CHAPTER 4

ENLIGHTENED CITIZEN

Before it turns to dust, let us animate our clay, let us set our nothingness ablaze.[1]
— ÉVA CIRCÉ-CÔTÉ, 1927

We are haunted by doubt, especially since the Great War, which was the collapse of our faith in human perfectibility.[2]
— ÉVA CIRCÉ-CÔTÉ, 1921

ONE DOES NOT go suddenly from years of gloom to euphoria. For a long time after the November 1918 armistice, the brutal impact of the war could be felt in Éva Circé-Côté's writing. She had never accepted Charles Maurras's explanation for the war—that it was punishment for France's sins—endorsed by Henri Bourassa and relayed from the pulpits of Quebec.[3] In 1920, she again lambasted the "preachers of [Catholic] retreats," who proclaimed: "The war was willed, prepared, and prosecuted to punish France and penalize men!"[4] Nor was she among those, such as Henri Bourassa in 1917, who held democracy responsible for the war.[5] In Fantasio's columns, the war was initially seen to be the result of a half-demented Kaiser's thirst for power, so that for France and the Allies it was a matter of legitimate defence. When the hostilities were over, the noble fight had given way to carnage, stubbornness, and human folly. Some of Circé-Côté's writing attested to her disillusionment and the end of her belief in universal progress. "Since the great butchery, we can no longer answer with the certitude of bygone days: Onward to progress!"[6] Quebec appears to her to be in a state of "mortal stagnation."[7] But these moments of despair were brief, and her hope in regeneration was soon revived.

The City in the Postwar Period

At the age of forty-seven, Éva Circé-Côté kept up her peregrinations in the postwar metropolis. In 1918 and 1919, she interrupted her contributions to *Le Pays* and wrote exclusively for *Le Monde ouvrier*. She had moved in 1914 from Hôtel-de-Ville Street to Sherbrooke Street, near the library. She liked to change places, and in 1921 she bought a house a little farther east, at 634 Plessis Street, near the corner of Sherbrooke. She lived there with her now widowed mother—Narcisse Circé had died at the end of March 1911—and her daughter Ève,[8] about whom she confided to Marcel Dugas: "I find her beautiful, because through her I see her father."[9]

There is no information about the education she wished to give Ève, but Circé-Côté's strong interest in education, girls' education in particular, is well known.[10] Having berated the "innocent young things" and decried the education system for being out of step with the realities of the day, she owed it to herself to prepare her daughter for what she called the "struggle for life." Did she agree to send Ève to a Catholic school? Or did she enrol her in a boarding school, perhaps even a Protestant, English-language establishment, like her colleague Georgina Bélanger (Gaëtane de Montreuil), who had sent her son to a school in Grande-Ligne, south of Montreal?[11] There is no way of knowing. If she opted for a boarding school, it would have put a dent in her still modest income. Her salary as catalogue director was raised to $1000 in 1920, with a bonus of $150, and was supplemented by her earnings as a columnist.[12]

In 1920 and 1921, Éva Circé-Côté resumed her collaboration with *Le Pays*, now under the direction of her old friend Arsène Bessette, who had stepped in when Godfroy Langlois left for Brussels in 1914.[13] The weekly would soon be sold to another freethinker and freemason, Dr. Marcil. This was the beginning of the end. Éva became the paper's linchpin, while colleagues such as Gonzalve Desaulniers and Marchant deserted it; Turgeon "has taken a powder," she wrote to Dugas, but she would stay "because I am the captain and I will go down with my ship. Because I am mad, as you have often told me."[14] The paper was foundering, and she was its editor-in-chief, struggling to keep it afloat, while churning out copy almost compulsively. In addition to her columns signed Julien Saint-Michel in *Le Monde ouvrier* she often filled an entire page of *Le Pays*, with Fantasio occupying three columns and Paul S. Bédard two more on the front page of the same edition.[15] She sometimes contributed all told nearly fifteen thousand words to *Le Pays* and another six thousand to *Le Monde ouvrier* in a single week.[16] Another case in point: on July 18, 1921, *Le Pays* published two different articles on disarmament and the League of Nations, both of them by Fantasio and both bearing the headline "Towards Peace."[17]

As of September 1920, Arthur Maheu, who had vanished since January 1919, reappeared on page four of *Le Pays*. At times, Circé-Côté's personae would divide up their subjects: criticism of the city administration and didactic essays by Fantasio; art reviews, denunciation of censorship, and thoughts on education by Bédard; anecdotes about current social mores by Maheu. Often, however, the topics were interchangeable among the different heteronyms and served as pretexts to ferret out injustices and hypocrisy. As eclectic as ever, Circé-Côté could go from a panegyric on Marguerite Bourgeois to a discussion on the economy to a music review with, along the way, a mystical essay on spring. Nothing escaped her attention, neither the death of Laurier in 1919 nor the League of Nations nor the meeting of the International Peace Bureau in Geneva. One might be left wondering what had happened to the poet Colombine, if not for a poem of hers titled "L'érable" (the maple tree), which was published in "the poets' corner" of the July 1920 edition of *Le Passe-Temps*.[18] In both form and content, this poem, written in alexandrines, displays the lyricism of her youth. It is the last one to have come down to us.

Throughout her writing, the constantly changing city is everywhere to be found. With the conclusion of the war came the demobilized soldiers needing to be reintegrated into society, an end to the lucrative contracts, a drop in exports, a lowering of living standards, and unemployment. The country had gone deeply into debt during the war, and it was the municipalities, also heavily indebted, that were in charge of social services. In 1921, one fifth of unionized workers in Canada were jobless; in Quebec, where the rate of unionization was lower, unemployment rose to unprecedented levels. Julien Saint-Michel, who spoke for the workers, identified the causes and consequences of the crisis in the details of everyday life: the price of food, rent, streetcar tickets.[19] In these columns, Circé-Côté denounced the profiteers and the speculators, "those bloodsuckers," while at the same time lamenting the workers' lack of savings.[20] On this point she was in agreement with Quebec nationalists like Bourassa, whom she quoted: "In the churches and public buildings, on the stained glass and marble plaques, one can see the names of fraudsters, of swindlers who are a discredit to our race."[21] And she shared the nationalists' fervour in their struggle with the trusts. She held the trusts responsible not only for the exorbitant prices; in her view these "modern day tyrants" were also behind the corruption of elected officeholders.[22] The accusations against the profiteers and the trusts allowed a number of antagonisms between conservatives and progressives to be smoothed over.

Montreal was home to the head offices of large Canadian insurance companies, banks, and industries; the transformation of the city's landscape attested to a profound mutation. After the wartime building slowdown, there was a boom in both commercial and residential construction starting in 1922.[23] Éva Circé-Côté felt the speculators were disfiguring Montreal:

> To make money, [they] have made it grotesque; these streets of uniform boxes, such as the upper reaches of Saint-Denis and twenty other streets, have turned some parts of Montreal into veritable barracks. With those perch-like staircases, the houses resemble dovecotes—ridiculous and illogical in a land of snow and ice. These deathtraps are eyesores that the municipal authorities should never have tolerated. . . . Those who want to built working-class dwellings using a single model, with no consideration for style and architecture, are committing crimes against the aesthetic.[24]

This statement should not be read as the expression of a nostalgic holdout against urban modernity. Circé-Côte was equally capable of defending modern architecture; in one column, she inveighed against the tall church bell towers that attracted lightning, which sparked off fires and threatened the lives of the workers repainting them. "Fortunately, modern architecture no longer sends those pointed spires skyward, and the aesthetic concept has changed and can be reconciled with 'safety first,'"[25] she asserted, forgetting the skyscrapers that Montreal boasted as of the late 1920s. But the metropolis's transformation amid rapid economic development came with a price: a heavy debt load and glaring social problems.

The debt and municipal corruption continued to disturb the citizens. Montreal, a city of tenants, was not raising sufficient property tax revenues: the numerous religious buildings were exempt, and the owners of buildings and residences resisted tax increases.[26] The city administration, headed by Mayor Médéric Martin through almost the entire decade of the twenties, had lost its reformist impulse and drifted into slackness and favouritism.

The metropolis attracted tourists thirsty for illicit pleasures, especially since other North American jurisdictions were in the grip of prohibition. The supposedly innocent city of the prewar years had given way to a place full of perils and temptations, which Éva's pen did not fail to record. Children were liable to be run over by cars, but the greatest dangers were encountered on the sidewalks: some rascals let themselves be dragged into stealing from a fruit vendor on Ontario Street, a small girl ends up following a "vile character" offering her candies "and who knows what else." A child is found frozen in a barrel, and a six-month-old baby in a rubbish heap. On the street, bands of "little French-Canadians terrorize the passersby."[27] Adults, meanwhile, were experiencing jazz, cabarets, and blind pigs, where gamblers could bet on cards and horse races, but the reputation of Montreal's nightlife was built mainly on the "houses of disorder." Even though owning or frequenting these houses was illegal, enforcement of the bylaws was at the discretion of the authorities. The indulgence of the police, paid for both in kind and with bribes, was a boon for procurers and madams. The scandals exposed in the 1925 report of the Coderre Inquiry breathed new life into Montreal's progressive movement, whose social orientations Circé-Côté shared, though she disagreed with the proposed solutions whenever they trespassed too much for her liking on individual freedom. The most striking example of her moral liberalism was her tolerance of prostitution.[28] She was one of the rare personalities of her epoch, along with Justice Amédée Geoffrion, to call for the toleration and even the regulation of prostitution, as was the case in Paris and other European cities. What she condemned most of all was the hypocrisy of the elites, who tolerated or censured as the fancy took them.

The city's geography was rapidly changing, and its demography, temporarily stabilized by the war, was shifting in tandem with the influx of immigrants. As the country opened up to immigration again, Montreal's cultural diversity was enhanced by waves of newcomers from Central Europe. Circé-Côté was aware of and even concerned about this. She envied France for having been able to assimilate immigrants, including Jews, whereas, "because of our narrow-mindedness, our bigotry, we let them become English subjects. If we had better French schools—that is, free of sectarian thinking—the hundred thousand Jews constituting one fifth of Montreal's population would now be French citizens."[29] In *Le Monde ouvrier* she paid tribute to the Jewish proletariat and their role in the labour movement.[30] As for Poles and other newcomers, she believed they would be more useful farming the land, as unemployed workers were becoming ubiquitous in some neighbourhoods. Circé-Côté's articles took on a Keynesian hue, advocating state-run unemployment insurance as well as borrowing for public works rather than having "soup kitchens on the Champ de Mars."[31]

For her, the core problem remained the unequal distribution of wealth. Injustices gave rise to militancy in the form of mass movements, strikes, and new political parties. Might communism be the answer? Many of Jaurès's disciples thought so at the founding congress of the French Communist Party in Tours. In October 1920, with Mgr Gauthier raging against the reviled doctrine and the Catholic newspapers, such as Quebec City's *L'Action sociale* and Ottawa's *Le Droit*, excoriating Bolshevism, Circé-Côté reminded readers that the "first Christian society was communist."[32] In Canada, a communist party was founded in 1921. A short time later in Montreal, Albert Saint-Martin called to no avail for a Francophone Bolshevist party. As a radical liberal, Éva Circé-Côté remained faithful to Jaurès's brand of socialism, but she was nevertheless well disposed toward the new regime in Russia: "What should it matter that governments crumble and sovereigns are massacred if millions of people conquer their freedom?"[33] A year later, she added: "If communism fails with Lenin, if utopia does not become a reality after the bloody experience of the Russian revolutionary, if Tolstoy's dream does not emerge from abstraction, which political dream will equalize conditions [among different social classes—Trans.]?"[34] She was not afraid to associate with *Le Matin*, the newspaper of Roger Maillet, who, together with Marcel Dugas, was a stalwart of the Casoars. That Maillet openly sympathized with communism did not frighten her, but the same could not be said of Olivar Asselin. When asked to contribute to *Le Matin*, Asselin, pusillanimous and fearing for his reputation, ended his friendship with Maillet and rejected any sort of collaboration, "to protect [his] daily bread."[35]

Éva, however, since her beginnings in journalism at *Les Débats*, had never been afraid to associate with a controversial newspaper, yet she kept away from popular movements and left-wing parties, preferring individual action, which left her freedom of expression intact. It would be a mistake to believe that her fight for justice was confined to philanthropy. Socialist parties would not have disavowed her often anti-capitalist and anti-imperialist discourse, but she rejected the class struggle in her daily actions and fought with her pen. Though an admirer of Jaurès, as were Dugas and Maillet at the time, her Jaurès stayed theoretical and had to tolerate radical liberalism, which was considered much farther to the left in Quebec than in Europe.

Between essays on the international situation or municipal corruption, Circé-Côté dealt with apparently lighter issues, which nevertheless provided her with a way into broader issues. Thus, her comments on fashion gave readers insight into the evolution of hems and trousers, but they were followed by thoughts on women's emancipation or religious censorship. Before the war, she had associated "short skirts and padded calves" with the slackening of social mores,[36] but in the 1920s she observed that bobbed hair proved to be practical and that "the beauty of the devil lasts indefinitely since the advent of short haircuts."[37] Together with cosmetics and more supple fabrics, short haircuts made women look younger. The wearing of trousers also met with her approval; shorter dresses, meanwhile, were more hygienic, and "since women began wearing their dresses above the kneecap, one sees fewer naughty fellows loitering on street corners on rainy days secretly hoping to glimpse a bit of calf."[38] As for the sports that modern young women were practising in growing numbers, Circé-Côté's comments were nothing but positive.[39] When the champion swimmer Annette Kellerman caused a scandal with her swimsuit, Circé-Côté defended the cult of beauty and nudity.[40] Steadfastly inveighing against hypocrisy and prudishness, she denounced the Ligue féminine pour la décence (Women's league for decency), accusing it of opposing women's freedom.[41] Even those whom she still referred to as "old maids" had changed since the war. Now that suitors had grown rare, these women were no longer considered egoists: "instead of the scorn and contempt that had been heaped on them, their value and merit are saluted."[42]

Only one picture of Éva Circé-Côté during that period has come down to us. Reproduced as a medallion accompanying the list of candidates for the 1922 David award, it shows her wearing a heavy hat adorned with a feather. Her features have grown thicker, but she has retained the same expression of self-assurance and composure.[43] She was not one to pamper herself. It can be assumed that she followed the same advice that she would offer others during the flu epidemic of 1928: "It is not a bad thing to go out during a storm and bravely confront the hailstones and the sharp pellets of sleet. These contain elements of strength and vitality, elixirs of longevity that are surely as valuable as costly tonics."[44] She extolled the virtues of walking outdoors, and one can picture her withstanding the gusts of December, making her way to work from her home on Plessis Street along Sherbrooke Street to the library at the corner of Montcalm Street. Braving the elements—what a fitting image to describe the tone of her writings.

Some columns revealed more about her thinking than other more trenchant articles, which were, however, typical of the progressive liberals in Circé-Côté's circles. While her ideological positions could be discerned amid the irony and sarcasm of such pieces, her views were articulated more explicitly in a series of six "epistles to Théodore" (*Épitres à Théodore*), each averaging over eighteen hundred words, which appeared in Le Pays between February 21 and March 27, 1920. These long letters deserve a closer look because they summarize this freethinking woman's outlook on the society in which her interlocutor, young Théodore, has got bogged down. Théodore is a caricature: twenty-seven years old and already a father of seven, a *collège classique* graduate at a loss as to his future. In the first epistle, the advice proffered by Fantasio is reminiscent of Machiavelli and his *Prince*, though they are not alluded to directly. There is the same cynicism—"admire others and despise your own"—but here the tone rises to indignation. Fantasio enumerates the professions available to the young man, pointing out the pros and cons of each one, uses her recommendations as pretexts to articulate her views

Reproduced in Biographies canadiennes-françaises, 1924. BAnQ.

on education, religion, nationalism, and the Indigenous Peoples, and repeatedly insists on the importance of freedom of thought, taking a swipe in passing at *Le Devoir*, *L'Action catholique*, and *La Vérité*. The sixth epistle ends with an exhortation: "Never lose your capacity for critical thinking."[45] This is advice that Circé-Côté consistently followed herself.

Alongside her strictures on platitudes, obliviousness, and unenlightenment, Éva Circé-Côté clung to an ideal: France. She held the Republic so dear—from the publication of *Bleu, Blanc, Rouge* to her calls for the defence of the motherland during the war—that one could only wish she had been able to visit the birthplace of her ancestors. Thanks to the city library's subscriptions, she read literary and political magazines like *Le Mercure de France* and *La Revue des Deux Mondes*. She never had the chance to walk along the boulevards of Paris, visit its museums, meet its writers,[46] notwithstanding the fact that, in March 1920, Fantasio alluded to a trip to France where she had seen "Two Savoyard chimney sweeps in the library reading Ribot's *Revue philosophique*."[47] This seems to have been a bit of journalistic licence to promote a municipal library in Montreal. Although she stopped contributing to *Le Pays* in 1918 and 1919, she published forty-six columns for *Le Monde ouvrier* in 1918 and fifty-one in 1919. Consequently, there was no prolonged absence during that period that might support the hypothesis of a trip to Europe.

Her schedule left her little time for society life. Without letup, Fantasio, Saint-Michel and the others filled their columns between Circé-Côté's shifts at the library, which were often in the evenings and on weekends. For the year 1920, a total of 139 columns have been attributed to her, and she was also busy at the same time polishing her play *Maisonneuve*.[48] This four-act drama presents a new vision of the first contacts between the French colonists and the Iroquois. It was a fashionable subject, as were all those dealing with New France; *Maisonneuve* premiered at His Majesty's on April 3, 1921, two weeks after Laure Conan's *Aux Jours de Maisonneuve* had opened at the Monument-National,[49] but Circé-Côté's hero was very different from

Conan's. The two playwrights based their portraits of the founder of Montreal on quite distinct sources and interpretations. Conan's Maisonneuve is consistent with traditional religious interpretations, whereas Circé-Côté's is rebellious, at loggerheads with the Jesuits, and attracted to a young Indigenous woman.

The first act is set in France, where Maisonneuve decides to leave behind his world of artifice and his beloved, who has been charmed by the king; he is drawn by the dream "of a new world that would know no hatred, a world of liberty and peace where Old Europe would come to renew its blood tainted by twenty centuries of persecution and religious and civil wars."[50] The second act opens with Native Indian dances and unfolds primarily on Iroquois lands. There we meet Chief Atonhieiarho and his daughter Fleur-des-bois (Flower of the woods); in the second scene, Maisonneuve, aboard his ship in the company of Jeanne Mance and a Récollet brother, lands near the Iroquois village of Hochelaga, which they will name Ville-Marie. The French encounter the Iroquois in the third act, first in a skirmish in which Fleur-des-bois saves Maisonneuve's life and then in an exchange between him and the Iroquois chief. The two men discuss God, civilization, and the respective virtues of each. Things come to a head in the fourth act, when, disregarding chronology, Jeanne Mance recounts Dollard's siege at Long-Sault. Fleur-des-bois proves to be intractable when it comes to learning the catechism and puts forward arguments reminiscent of those of Voltaire and Diderot. Smothered in her muslin dress, stifled in the convent where she has been confined, she dies in the arms of Maisonneuve, who avers that his love for her has killed her. In the final scene, betrayed by the Jesuits, he is called back to France, and the play ends with his homage to Ville-Marie, evoking the triumph of eternal France, the France of the Enlightenment and not that of Catholicism.

In her interpretation of these first contacts between the French and the Indigenous Peoples, Circé-Côté's purpose, once again, was educational. There are countless instances of reversed situations and revised historical assumptions. Instead of the austere Maisonneuve, who is said to have taken vows of chastity, her hero falls in love not once but twice; Iroquois thinking appears as valid as that of the colonists, and the French-Iroquois dichotomy is erased; Maisonneuve refuses to fight against the Indigenous Peoples and his heroism resides not in his religious zeal but his humanism; the Jesuits, finally, become the villains, as they are the ones responsible for the governor of Ville-Marie being recalled to France. Civilizing values are relativized, progress proves to be a complex enterprise, and treason threatens the virtuous. This was a long way from the ultramontanist interpretations of Maisonneuve that had prevailed in the nineteenth century.

As had been the case for *Hindelang et Delorimier*, the play's author was identified as Colombine, and the scandals associated with that name on the occasion of her husband's funeral may have been forgotten. Certainly, the journalist at *La Presse* had forgotten *Hindelang et Delorimier*; as far as he was concerned, *Maisonneuve* was the dramatist's first play. The performance was not sold out—not surprising in a city that still preferred productions from France and the US—but the playwright received an ovation, and the next day's reviews in liberal newspapers like *Le Pays*, *Le Canada*, and *La Patrie* were unanimously positive with regard to the drama's content and both its literary and educational value.[51] *La Presse* did not shy away from ranking "'Maisonneuve' [. . .] among the best works in Canadian theatre," even though the critic had reservations about the ideas expressed there. He was likely not the only one upset by the scene between Maisonneuve and Atonhieiarho:

We bitterly regretted, however, that the author had not found better arguments to put in her hero's mouth in response to the Iroquois chief. We are left with an uncomfortable impression and wonder whether or not the author wished to have us admire Iroquois doctrine to the detriment of Christian doctrine.[52]

Circé-Côté eventually revised *Maisonneuve*, as evidenced by an annotated copy found, surprisingly, in the archives of Lionel Groulx.[53] Her additions lend more strength to the text. Thus, the cardinal is no longer just "a shadow" but "a damned shadow." The author also pared down some overlong passages, shortened by half Antonhieiarho's long "plaintive and gloomy song," and deleted several lines from Maisonneuve's final monologue. There is no indication of whether or not these corrections were made for a new staging of the play, in response to criticism, or—less probably—because the dramatist herself was dissatisfied with the first version.

Circé-Cote had always been interested in history, and she venerated the historian François-Xavier Garneau, "one of the secular saints in the calendar of our democracy,"[54] but this appraisal refers to the original Garneau, the one who wrote the first edition of *L'Histoire du Canada*, before he reworked it in reaction to ecclesiastical pressure. She was grateful to Hector Garneau, the grandson, for having reissued the original edition of *L'Histoire du Canada*,[55] including the passages removed from the second edition. In a rare gesture for someone who was not a professional historian, she wrote down for posterity her reflections on historiography: "History, at bottom, is the account of what heroes accomplished for the benefit of the world. Great men, famous women are celebrated because they were the fashioners, the creators of new human types."[56] In other words, a didactic history, a march toward progress in keeping with the liberal interpretation proposed by historians of the Whig school."

While she was drafting her play about Montreal's founder, Circé-Côté also published laudatory portraits of Marguerite Bourgeoys and Jeanne Mance in *Le Pays*. These texts were the fruits of serious research; she had experienced "the mystery of old boxes, shook the dust off forgotten folders, when one has the illusion of feeling them flutter beneath our fingers."[57] She searched in the archives, in the collection of the Hôtel-Dieu hospital, where she was moved on discovering Marguerite Bourgeoys's handwritten letters; she "communed with the immortal thoughts of the women of Ville-Marie." Here she saw the lives of her heroines, so she felt compelled to reproach Laure Conan—in relation to the latter's Maisonneuve—for her pessimistic attitude toward the same parchments, where Conan saw only hands "long ago reduced to ashes."[58]

In the summer of 1921, a long, dark period began for Éva Circé-Côté. The enthusiastic reception, the good reviews must have been a great comfort to her during those difficult times. On June 21, Arsène Bessette died, and his death surely brought to mind that of Pierre-Salomon Côté. Besette had written: "Ignorance, foolishness, and cowardice are the three most formidable enemies of humankind," words that might just as well have been penned by Circé-Côté. The similarities between the two journalists are striking. They both cut their professional teeth at *Les Débats*, and Bessette followed Circé-Côté when she founded *L'Étincelle* in 1903. Their columns were sometimes interchangeable with respect to tone and subject. The world of journalism as described in Bessette's novel *Le Débutant* (The Beginner) calls to mind the barbs that Colombine and Fantasio directed at journalists. Bessette was a member of the Émancipation lodge and was identified with every progressive cause of his epoch. The obituary, written by Arthur Lebel, refers to the final moments of this freethinker's life: "Bessette was honest to the last"; he did not convert at the eleventh hour and was under no pressure from his close relations and friends to do so. In his article, which appeared next to Fantasio's (on the history of the library) on the front page of *Le Pays*, Lebel must surely have had Éva Circé-Côté in mind when he wrote: "In these circumstances, it is the wife, sensitive and seemingly weak, who has my admiration and my respect, for she is the mistress of her husband's corpse and she could have made the funeral arrangements according to her interests. . . . Civil burials have been possible only when the wife was in agreement with her husband." Lebel then paid tribute to Papineau, Boucherville, Dessaulles, Beaugrand, and Pierre-Salomon Côté, "who form an honourable line of people who in the final hour stayed true to themselves."[59]

Circé-Côté did not write about the death of her colleague, possibly because she was preoccupied with her mother's struggle with Bright's disease. Because of the ups and downs of her mother's condition, Éva oscillated between hopefulness and the despair that came with every relapse. While she was worrying about her mother, her mother-in-law Ann Haney Côté, "a most dignified woman," of whom she was very fond, died in December 1921. In 1903, Circé-Côté had dedicated her poem "Erin Go Bragh!" to her mother-in-law; it was an acrostic in honour of Ireland that leaves little doubt as to her support for Irish independence and ends with the words, "Vibrate, ye harps! Sing of O'Connell's proud sons!"[60] Without a doubt, the incineration of her son Pierre-Salomon had pained Ann Haney Côté. For an Irish-born Catholic like her "it anticipated the fires of Hell," Éva wrote to her friend Marcel Dugas.[61] Because of this woman's generosity, Éva always maintained her ties with Sainte-Luce and the Lower St. Lawrence region, which she visited during the summer vacations or at Christmas, shocking her husband's relatives by not attending the local mass.[62] Éva blamed the two ordeals—her mother's illness and her mother-in-law's death—for two fainting fits that occurred between June and December and "a heart condition that puts [her] life at the mercy of any somewhat violent emotion."[63]

She was fifty years old at the time. Despite her best efforts, the weekly *Le Pays* put out its final edition in December 1921, entailing the demise of Fantasio, Jean Nay/Ney, Paul S. Bédard, and Arthur Maheu. The closing of this radical newspaper left a huge void in Circé-Côté's life as a journalist, which her work at *Le Monde ouvrier* could not fill. She would no longer be going to the defunct newspaper's office each Wednesday to deliver copy, and she confessed to Dugas: "I've lost the sense of time, as if I've already entered into my eternity." She feared that her "combative ardour" was waning and admitted that she was sinking into "a morbid melancholy." Her courage seemed worn out.[64]

For ten years, Éva Circé-Côté had concealed herself behind her heteronyms. It was not easy for her now to put aside the characters she had created and identified with, such as Colombine, whom she had abandoned long ago. Yet this persona, her first, came back for a visit in 1920 in *Brèves apologies de nos auteurs féminins*, a series of biographical notes on an august group of Québécoise authors written by the lawyer, journalist, and literary man Georges Bellerive, who included his thoughts on "the moral impact of their works." The note on Colombine was introduced with words of praise: "In the course of her literary career, unfortunately cut short by sad events, Colombine garnered some fine laurels."[65] Nowhere did he mention the name Éva Circé-Côté. After citing the endorsements of Madeleine and

Françoise, he devoted a flattering paragraph to Colombine and then concluded: "How can one not regret, given all this, that certain deplorable circumstances put an end in 1908 to a career that had begun so brilliantly?"[66] In 1908, Éva was suing the *Standard* for defamation, and in December 1909 the scandal surrounding Pierre-Salomon's funeral brought about the disappearance of Colombine and Musette. Bellerive appears to have been oblivious of Éva Circé-Côté's output from that point on. Under the name Fantasio, she subsequently wrote a column on Bellerive's blunder. Rather than regarding it as a simple error in the date, she discerned a ploy designed to allow the inclusion of the controversial Colombine among colleagues who had received the approval of the censors of that period, "so as to place Colombine among other literary women without risking the spite, the ire of the Pharisees who control our unhappy land."[67] She probably was not overstating the pressure exerted on the literary milieu of the 1920s, which too often gave rise to cautious self-censorship.[68]

Aside from her few letters to Marcel Dugas, Éva Circé-Côté did not leave any personal writings. This is what makes Fantasio's article about Colombine worthy of closer attention. In it she explains that Colombine moved away from the literary world because of the constraints imposed on Quebec literature, which was often ephemeral and bound to be forgotten, just as Colombine was: "We live in a country of snow, and our monuments of ice flow down to the river at the spring thaw and nothing is left of what, at the other end of our land, we write on the parquet of frozen waters!" While she is not "asking for immortality from these ephemeral tablets" destined to melt away, writing remains a pleasure for her:

> The pleasure of moving rhythmically on this crystal floor while chiming out bursts of laughter, with a mask covering one's face to better reveal one's soul, the joy of spinning on steel points, of balancing on these bright blades, when so many others have cracked their seats and broken their noses, is surely enough to suit Colombine's fancy.[69]

Readers may have doubts about this degree of self-denial, yet for over ten years Éva Circé-Côté stayed hidden under her pen names, forgoing the recognition that even the most impassive writers would have found flattering. What a contrast with her first years in journalism, when Colombine had been recognized around the Monument-National, when she had been hailed and her poems commented on! But Julien Saint-Michel went unnoticed,[70] and readers were unable to determine the gender of the columnists in *Le Pays*.[71] She is not, however, above self-pity. She states in this article that she chose the hard road, being unwilling to make "sacrifices to false gods." And she makes no secret of her contempt for her colleague Madeleine—for whom Bellerive reserved a place of honour—who came to success along "the broad and sunny path." Circé-Côté concludes: "What does she care about ruination, grief, and death if her work has been accomplished.... Were Colombine still among the living, she must have delighted at the fragrance of that premature funeral wreath."[72]

But Éva Circé-Côté was not as carefree as these lines suggest. Her anonymity as a journalist was without doubt a heavy price to pay for keeping her job at the Municipal Library. The sacrifice was poorly recompensed, and several letters betray the bitterness that continued to gnaw at her. After all, it was Madeleine who was acclaimed; she was the one the eminent professor of literature Brother Camille Roy had called "the undisputed queen of the women's pages," leaving Éva completely in the shade.[73]

Of her exchanges with Marcel Dugas, now an exile in Paris, only five long letters have been preserved, some forty splendid and utterly precious pages, in which Éva bares her soul. These attest to a profound and enduring friendship, for she admits that should it ever fade away, "I would savour that suffering, which still is a way to prolong a feeling and nurture it."[74] Her friendship was requited, but none of Dugas' letters have survived.[75] Their content, however, is suggested by Éva's replies.

In her letters, Éva identifies with Marcel, "a victim of calumny and persecution," and projects onto him her own moods, which seem to match closely those of her exiled friend. For different reasons they each were isolated, disparaged, and both of them feel betrayed. Which of them is she referring to when, by way of consoling him, she writes: "Neither the Catholics nor the freethinkers can like you because you are honest, and honest people are doomed to perpetual isolation"? Or when she observes that he "estranged the egoists, the social climbers, the hypocrites of every stripe that make up our intellectual elite.... In a society of masks you wished to retain your true face."[76]

Unstinting in advice, the letters at times read like lectures, but they contain the sincerest confessions and self-analyses of Circé-Côté that we have. There is no trace of irony here, no abandonment of rigour for the sake of witticisms, only a confidante, a wise woman trying to motivate her correspondent and expressing herself candidly. Their correspondence was truly an exchange; she is attentive to Dugas' torments and she shares her own. She often alludes to her age, takes stock, and revisits her ideals. "But despite all the darkness that may have filled my horizon, I'll have sailed on shining rivers, because I have loved."[77] Love of humanity? Platonic love? Love for Pierre-Salomon?

In Dugas' sensitive and tortured soul, Éva sees "a kinship."[78] Their freethinking offended public morality. His lifestyle was grist for the rumour mill and cost him a fiancée.[79] Dugas always had to hide his homosexuality, which some suspected nevertheless. Éva never mentions it explicitly, but her veiled allusions indicate that she was aware of one of the reasons for the shabby treatment he received. They had in common the persecution they had suffered at the hands of the self-righteous: "You wanted freedom of the flesh, as I wanted freedom of the mind. We are irredeemably condemned in the opinion of our fellow citizens. . . . The difference between us is that I accept the consequences of my acts."[80] In her view, Dugas should own his difference and not believe that he is "moulded from the same clay as others."[81] His difference is no doubt sexual, but intellectual and moral as well: "The proof that you are different from others is that in spite of your constant efforts you could not integrate with those false brothers and you have remained a stranger to them."[82]

In each of her letters, Éva endeavours to lift his spirits, to give him confidence, sometimes by overstating her case: "I would like to know that you are as persuaded of your worth as I am."[83] She strives to convince him that underneath his apparent weakness there is strength: "You are unaware of the luminous wake that the *fugitive meteor* of your passage among us has left behind. It would console you in your despondent hours."[84] Under the name Paul S. Bédard, she sent essays to the newspaper commending his poetry collections; in her letters she sings his praises: "Never has anyone written as you have here," she declares after the publication of *Confins*.[85] Yet the compliment is open to various interpretations. Is she implying that others have written in this way elsewhere? In France, perhaps, but not in Quebec? And for one contributor to the *Mercure de France*, writing "as you have" meant lapsing into convoluted or effeminate prose.[86]

Still, even if she was in a black mood one day in December 1921 when the snow fell unremittingly, she, the optimist "radiantly resigned to her unhappy fate," acknowledged that she had achieved some success because her play *L'Anglomanie* (Anglomania) had just won an award from *L'Action française*."[87] She had submitted the three-act play to the dramatic arts competition launched by *L'Action française* in April 1920, and its theme expressed the prevailing nationalist concerns. This is how the journal articulated the set subject:

> Anglomania [is] not just the deplorable tendency that involves renouncing one's language in favour of the conqueror's, but also a state of mind that by and large takes the form of contempt for one's race and the exclusive admiration of anything English. Anglomania, which it seems

urgent to assail with ridicule and satire, is basically the French Canadian infatuated with Anglo-Saxon superiority and who, out of vanity or self-interest, systematically pushes his family toward national abdication and the melding of the races.[88]

The subject was not new. As early as 1903, R. Lemoine, a colleague at *Le Combat*, described the irksome fashion of denigrating one's compatriots, adopting English manners, tastes, and habits, and even speaking English at home.[89] Twenty years on, with the revival of French Canadian nationalism, the decline in the relative weight of the French-speaking population in Canada, and the fear of assimilation into the Anglophone majority, the issue was still topical. In November 1921, the jury, composed of Olivier Maurault, Édouard Montpetit, Fernand Rinfret, and Léon Lorrain, awarded third prize to the comedy submitted by "Loup de velours" (Velvet Wolf), aka Éva Circé-Côté. The first prize went to the journalist Magali Michelet for *Contre le flot*.[90] The fact that no second prize was awarded raises a question: Did "the judges feel unable to [. . .] award the second prize" to Éva Circé-Côté because they deemed the content of her play inadequate or because they had discovered the identity of this woman who was not afraid of "the melding of the races" and who had so often attacked the Catholic nationalism and the xenophobia of *L'Action française*?[91] The irony of winning a prize awarded by *L'Action française* was not lost on her, and she wrote to Dugas, "[coming from] people who hate me, it's rather flattering."[92]

The text of this play, too, has been lost. We know from the reviews of a staging done several months later that the action is set in a "vigorously characterized"[93] bourgeois environment, according to *La Presse*, and that both Anglophilia and Anglophobia are targeted. Circé-Côté was able to strike a happy medium, as described in the communiqué published in the newspapers: "while not denying Anglo-Saxon superiority, which has become irrefutable dogma, Colombine finds equivalent qualities in French-Canadians."[94] Her heroine, Suzanne Bennington, speaks and thinks in French, whereas Mr. Chénier, the bourgeois, worships all things English. Circé-Côté shows that the Anglophone who adopts the language of the majority displays refinement, whereas the French Canadian who copies the English is portrayed as a wholly inauthentic parvenu.[95] The journalist of *Le Canada* considered this a comedy as much as a play with a message. As in her columns, Circé-Côté marshalled satire and humour to convey her message. She elicited laughter with her use of clichés: the English woman's little dog, the stolid English man, the gentle and conciliatory French-Canadian mother. All the ingredients for success were brought together.

A few months later, Éva Circé-Côté confidently set about presenting her play at the Monument-National. Her project coincided with the establishment of the Merry-Girard theatre troupe, made up of French as well as a few French-Canadian artists, whose aim was to present local works; as a result, this production of *L'Anglomanie* has earned a place in the history of Québécois theatre. The cast included two highly regarded actors: Alfred Daviault and the young Germaine Giroux.[96] The *La Presse* article stated that several actors, motivated by patriotism, "generously contributed their talents toward the success of this work, which adds a gem to our national jewel box while at the same time opening up new possibilities for our playwrights."[97] According to the publicity in the newspapers, it would be an act of patriotism to see and applaud this comedy.[98]

The rehearsal period was altogether inauspicious, and opening night had to be postponed because the actors were not ready. Despite the advance publicity, despite the actors' popularity, on March 21, 1922, theatregoers generally stayed away. A mere three hundred tickets were sold for a hall with a seating capacity of fifteen hundred.[99] Éva Circé-Côté contemplated cancelling the event but pushed on even though she was aware of the oncoming failure. On top of everything, the actors' lack of preparation and memory lapses, magnified by a very audible prompter, undermined the play and undoubtedly annoyed the small audience. During the intermission, the city councillor Léon Trépanier told journalists that he found "inconceivable" the population's indifference toward French-Canadian works, that "the Monument-National should have been sold out," and that he would be asking for the City Council's endorsement of works by intellectuals "who are very much in need of it."[100] The critic of *La Patrie* congratulated the "talented columnist" and decried the public's apathy toward all "home-grown" productions. He insinuated as well that she had not been supported by the French section of the Canadian Authors Association (CAA), but he also remarked on a characteristic specific to Colombine: "confusing the stage with the pulpit of truth or the public speaker's rostrum."[101] There was, however, nothing in the play that might offend the audience. It did not challenge the public's habits, unlike *Le Paquebot ténacité* (The good ship Tenacity), by the French dramatist Charles Vildrac, also presented in March 1922.[102]

One can only speculate about Éva Circé-Côté's reaction to such a flop. Of course, she received flowers after the show, but in addition to the humiliating indifference of the public and amateurism of some of the actors, she suffered a financial loss, as box-office takings covered less than half of her expenses, according to *La Patrie*. For a person leading two careers at once, the theatre was just one of her many activities on the Montreal literary scene.

Éva Circé-Côté was very effective in her role as a literary woman in Montreal's cultural arena. She viewed literature as both an aesthetic and an instrument of liberation: "Literature's part in the people's evolution is providential. The people," she affirmed in a fine article on the place of intellectuals in society, owe a great deal

> to those who grew pale bending over old books to give everyone access to electric lighting, automatic vehicles, inexpensive shows, the music of the great masters recorded on phonographic disks, education available to all![103]

She was actively involved in an event that would have a lasting impact on the literary world. At the initiative of Stephen Leacock, professor of economics at McGill University and renowned humourist, B. K. Sandwell, who also taught at McGill and was the publisher of *Canadian Bookman*, Pelham Edgar, professor in the English Department of the University of Toronto, and the novelist and classicist John Murray Gibbons, the founding convention of the Canadian Authors Association / l'Association des auteurs canadiens was held at McGill University in March 1921. All these men had links with the literary journal the *Canadian Bookman* and were concerned about copyright issues. The Anglophone initiators showed discernment in inviting Francophone authors, critics, and librarians to their meeting. John Murray Gibbons was elected chairman, and a board was named which included Hector Garneau and Louvigny de Montigny, whose legal opinions would be highly appreciated when the group's constitution was drafted.[104]

From the very beginning, the Association recognized the specificity of the world of French literature. In J. M. Gibbons's view, the Association's goal was also to encourage the distribution of French books in English-speaking Canada and English books among French Canadians.[105] A few intellectuals grouped around Louvigny de Montigny and Hector Garneau established a French-Canadian section of the Association,[106] which was autonomous and had its own board of directors. Its aim was to develop French-Canadian literature, defend its members' interests, protect authors' copyrights through appropriate legislation, and maintain cordial ties among Canadian writers and artists.

After the staging of *Maisonneuve*, Circé-Côté was among the thirty founders of the French section, which assembled at the Municipal Library on April 17, 1921. There were ten women present, including the elocution teacher Idola Saint-Jean and the journalist Anne-Marie Gleason (Madeleine), with whom Éva had made the memorable trip to Lac Saint-Jean twenty years earlier, but who later had grown away from her.[107] The process of establishing the French section of the Canadian Authors Association was not free of confrontations. Olivar Asselin, fearing that Francophone literature would be swamped by the more abundant output of English Canadians and recalling "the previous experiences of French Canadians with the federal regime in other areas," proposed the creation of an independent association.[108] Éva Circé-Côté retorted that because of the numbers—five hundred English-language authors, two hundred French-language authors—priority must be given to the quality of first-rate novelists, poets, and dramatists. She also mistrusted an association that could turn nationalistic along the lines of the Association Saint-Jean-Baptiste, now under the influence of the Action Catholique de la jeunesse canadienne-française. This time, Fantasio/Circé-Côté adopted a levelheaded tone in her report on the founders' meeting in *Le Pays*.[109] The first meeting was adjourned on May 1; the majority had voted to create a French section of the Canadian Authors Association and elected Victor Morin as president and Anne-Marie Gleason as vice-president.[110]

The French and English sections of the Association collaborated closely to make Canadian authors known. To that end, they inaugurated Canadian Book Week, and various activities were held from November 21 through 26, 1921 in the three major libraries: the Municipal Library, the Saint-Sulpice Library, and the Fraser Library.[111] Éva Circé-Côté participated in the preparatory discussions, along with Anne-Marie Gleason, Victor Morin, Aegidius Fauteux, as well as other literary personalities and the secretary of the Société Saint-Jean-Baptiste, which also took part in the event. There were exchanges with Toronto, where Émilien Daoust went to give a talk on books in French.[112] A literary competition focusing on Canadian writers was organized in the schools to stimulate young peoples' interest in local authors. Louvigny de Montigny aptly summarized the spirit of Canadian Book Week: "our literature, when one takes the trouble to consider it, does not deserve the look of pity that all too often is cast on it."[113] Throughout the week, bookstores displayed Canadian books, the organizers gave lectures, and writers sent articles to the newspapers; meanwhile, society lunches and dinners brought together critics, authors, and selected members of the public. Despite her active part in founding the Association, Éva Circé-Côté does not appear in any of the photographs of writers and librarians published in the newspapers. While obscurity may be the price to pay for anonymity, her position at the library and her role in the Association should nevertheless have earned her greater public recognition. Under the name Fantasio, she published an excellent article on French-Canadian literature and its origins in storytelling, and on the ingratitude of its reception.[114]

The election of the executive committee of the Association des auteurs canadiens—later to be called the Société des auteurs canadiens—was held in April 1922, with Victor Morin, the law professor and head of the Société Saint-Jean-Baptiste, elected president, Éva Circé-Côté first vice-president and Victor Barbeau, the journalist and critic behind *Les Cahiers de Turc*, second vice-president; the Acadian historian Edmond Montet became the organization's treasurer and P.-Alfred Daviault its secretary.[115] Anne-Marie Gleason was also elected to the executive. Another female colleague, the writer Louise Marmette Brodeur, whose pen name was Louyse de Bienville, as well as Georgine Lemaire, sat on the board of directors. The executive initially met at the Municipal Library and later the Saint-Sulpice Library before finally settling on the offices of *La Revue moderne* as a meeting place, one more appropriate for a freethinking woman. A typical agenda covered the awarding of Association prizes, literary events, and the recruitment of new members. Thus, for instance, an evening of poetry readings was followed by one devoted to writers of prose and titled *Monsieur Jourdain reçoit* (Mr. Jourdain receives guests). The gathering, which took place in the hall of the Saint-Sulpice Library, had an ambitious programme of readings that included the works of sixteen authors, such as Félicité Angers (Laure Conan), Marcel Dugas, Michelle Le Normand (Marie-Antoinette Tardif), and Germain Beaulieu. Victor Morin, Victor Barbeau, Jean-Aubert Loranger, and Éva Circé-Côté read from their own writings.[116]

Delighted by the event's success, the French section of the Association of Canadian Authors announced an evening centred on dramatists, which would present *L'Adieu du poète* (The poet's farewell) by Anne-Marie Gleason, *Le Baiser* (The kiss) by Georgine Lemaire, *L'Orage* (The storm) by Jean-Aubert Loranger, and *Le Fumeur endiablé* (The rambunctious smoker) written by Colombine and to be interpreted by Germaine Giroux and Alfred Daviault. Originally scheduled for May 8, the evening was put off until the 15th and then the fall before it was finally cancelled.[117] While promoting French-language Canadian authors, the Society was not averse to securing France's stamp of approval in order to enhance its prestige. For the Semaine du livre canadien (French-Canadian book week) organized by the Société between October 28 and November 4, 1922, the French actors Cécile Sorel and Albert Lambert were invited to come and contribute to the event's success.[118] Éva Circé-Côté took an active part in the emergence of a group that, for many years, would defend the rights of authors and can be regarded as the forerunner of the Académie canadienne-française— which later became the Académie des lettres du Québec—and of the Union des écrivains et écrivaines québécois (Quebec writers union).

Le Devoir, vol. XIII, no. 252, Saturday, October 28, 1922.

During the years 1922 and 1923 there was a hiatus in Circé-Côté's output as a columnist. *Le Pays* closed down, and she took a leave of absence from *Le Monde ouvrier* from November 1921 to April 1924; this, however, does not mean that she was not publishing elsewhere under different pseudonyms.

She is believed to have contributed to the November 1922 issue of the journal *MusiCanada*, but because only the editors' articles were signed, hers are now shrouded in anonymity.[119] She also published a piece in the Rimouski publication *Saint-Laurent*, in which she sought to discourage the inhabitants of the Lower St. Lawrence from leaving for the United States. The early 1920s witnessed a severe economic crisis. Exports plummeted, urban workers fell prey to unemployment, and debt-ridden farmers were facing bankruptcy. The United States, a traditional way out for French Canadians in times of crisis, exerted a powerful attraction on them, in particular the New England cotton mills. Tens of thousands of people left Quebec each year.[120] Éva Circé-Côté, having considered the factors behind this exodus, warned: "while some may succeed in monetary terms, everyone will lose in terms of health, language, and religion."[121] This article would be reprinted in the cultural journal *Le Passe-Temps*.

She also sent in columns to Roger Maillet's *Le Mâtin*, "a rag, written (just barely!) by a talented idler who does not care if it gets read,"[122] according to Asselin. This time Éva Circé-Côté adopted an unusual pen name, which, however, cannot be identified with absolute certainty. That said, she is probably the author of the "Cahiers de Polémarque" (Polemarchus's notebooks): the style and tone are familiar, one recognizes Fantasio's irony and Arthur Maheu's forthrightness, the topics covered—such as the suffragettes or "old maids" on St. Catherine's Day—are also familiar ones, the references to Mr. Séguin's goat[123] or to St. Augustine, the allusions to compulsory education and the Freemasons, and, finally, the striking or cynical statements, such as this one on marriage: "Why impose eternity on a sentiment more changeable than the mood of the sea?" and "Prosperity is the tomb of talent just as marriage is the tomb of love."[124] She left no clue that would allow us to positively identify her: "polemarchus" refers to a philosopher, a magistrate, or a military man of Ancient Greece. Her collaboration with this publication would end in the summer of 1924. Here is the explanation that Éva gave to Marcel Dugas: "I no longer write for Roger's paper. When I realized the editor of *Le Mâtin* had no principles, not even bad ones, and that his family engaged in blackmail, I left."[125] Yet any journalist who hired Éva Circé-Côté opened himself up to the disapproval of his self-righteous colleagues. The once fiery and now mellow Asselin apparently admonished Maillet for opening his paper to "a revolutionary."[126] The experience was short-lived in any case, since the weekly was shut down in December 1923.

Circé-Côté's many activities demanded a great deal of effort and, starting in 1922, she complained to Marcel Dugas of her health problems. Ever the hardworking employee at the library, she was now putting in thirty-nine hours a week on average. In July 1922 she took a two-week vacation but failed to regain her former level of energy. That fall, she suffered "from dizzy spells, overtiredness, and blackouts."[127] She was in great need of rest but soon returned to the library, where Hector Garneau reappointed her catalogue supervisor, a responsibility to which that of first assistant would be added the following year, at which time her annual salary was raised to $1320,[128] a considerable sum for a woman in those days but still far less than what her male colleagues with the same duties were earning.

In April 1924, having lost none of her fighting spirit, she returned to *Le Monde ouvrier* and published an article titled, "Uniformité de salaire pour les deux sexes" (Wage uniformity for both sexes).[129] This was followed by some essays on the municipal elections, including a flattering portrait of Mayor Médéric Martin, a defence of the secularist policies of the French politician Édouard Hérriot, and contributions on capital punishment and judicial errors. In other pieces, she dealt with social issues, articulated her wish to see the state pay doctors treating poor people in working-class neighbourhoods, and discussed the plight of abandoned, exploited, or delinquent children. In addition, she presented three separate statements to the Coderre inquiry on the police.[130] *Le Monde ouvrier* provided French-speaking readers with a progressive point of view generally quite far from the one found in the daily press.

Her health problems, however, did not go away, as evidenced in her letter to Dugas dated July 1924, where she reported that her condition had improved in recent months thanks to the good care provided by Dr. Trudeau. In spite of bouts of fever, she went to the library every day: "I have tremendous stamina," she boasted.[131] In August she spent a ten-day vacation at Lac-des-Îles in the Upper Laurentians. Her stay in the Laurentian forest was beneficial on various levels: "I breathed easily among these honest people."[132]

In her correspondence with Marcel Dugas, there was one question that concerned her more than her ailments: Dugas was contemplating a return to the Catholic faith. She did not hide her disappointment, but her response to him was one of understanding and consolation:

> The ideal that you embraced and for which you sacrificed everything has been your providence. It kept you from the weaknesses of the soul and the vulgarity of sentiments. . . . I remember that you showed me beauty. Though I could not attain it because I did not possess your means, I am indebted to you for the urge that sought to impel my soul toward other souls.[133]

What a comfort this recognition must have been for Dugas, the misunderstood poet with a persecution complex, who had found refuge in Paris![134] She begs him to make peace with himself when "others take pleasure in casting stones at you to disturb your inner serenity." The letter, continuing in this vein, develops what may be seen as an extremely positive critique of Dugas' oeuvre. She encourages him to write his memoires, a book "that would be as keenly interesting as Gorky's, [and] a way to take revenge on your enemies better than burning their faces with acid, with their shame printed in two thousand copies."[135] For she advises him not to forgive "those who have ruined your existence."

The whole letter reads like a long duet, a dialogue in which she alternates between voicing her benevolent concern for Dugas' moral, psychological, and even physical problems and sharing with him her own anxieties; thus, the persecutions harassing each of them are set side by side. She tells him that she triumphed over discouragement through a supreme effort of the will; she did not listen to herself and recovered her enthusiasm. And she made this effort without ever thinking of "throwing herself into the arms of God" or hastening her death. Marcel's renewed faith created a distance between them, as indicated in the last sentence of this lengthy missive: "I have the impression there is one more ocean between you and me and I look for you on the far side among the stars."[136] This, however, will not put an end to their correspondence. And even if their friendship, which she holds dear, "were to fade, I would not resort to that ultimate subterfuge to make the ordeal more bearable."[137]

Two months later, she felt reassured that his condition was not more serious and predicted, teasingly: "You will get over your attack of religion, which has only affected your sensitive skin."[138] Then, in a more dramatic style, she blamed his humility, his paralyzing weakness, his honour, and his generosity, none of which the "barbarians" who had slandered a civilized man were worthy of, for they were greatly indebted to him: "Those who today devour your heart owe the life of the mind to you."[139] There seems to be a transference going on when she notes that those who had deserted him were precisely the very people he had led out of the shadows; it is hard not to associate this with the readers whom she, too, had always tried to take out of the darkness of irrationality but who had no use for a freethinking woman. The aspersions cast on Dugas had resulted in a broken romantic engagement. But she "refused to believe that deep feelings could be uprooted by the first gust of wind." Love forgives: "it is not in the usual order of things that contradictions, the cruellest ordeals, poverty, illness should thwart love."[140] Hadn't the love between her and Pierre-Salomon survived the basest rumours?

Dugas had apparently asked her to inquire in her circle as to the origin of the slander against him. She declined, adding, "Do I have friends? . . . I am afraid my friends look much like yours," because, like him, she felt betrayed.[141]

She feared the religious "regeneration" that he was now displaying would set off a new round of slander on the part of his former friends. Moreover, she pointed out, "You already resemble your God to a frightening degree, since you do not forgive."[142] By way of consolation, she marshalled numerous arguments, urging him "to rid himself of these horrid memories." And she drew a comparison with the attacks of which she was the target and her response to them: "I am just a weak woman, with no protector, no influence, and I have held some formidable people at bay." As always, she owned her actions. She was not given to regrets and repentance. "If I had to live my life over, I would not change its direction, I would be guided by the same star, I would move through the same stars to arrive at the same goal, and you should do the same because you have been true to yourself."[143] The two letter-writers supported each other to the point of becoming indistinguishable.

She consulted him in her turn. When she was tempted to write a novel, she sought his counsel: "What do you advise me to do now? My friends have asked me for a novel; what do you think?"[144] Later, it was she who encouraged him to publish. In 1926 she would entreat him to bring out the book that he carried within him "for the good of us all." She went on: "I have never been wrong about the quality of your soul. Each time it was touched, it sent out a clear sound evidencing the purity of the metal."[145]

Bouquets and advice were not the only things that Dugas received from her. He was also the preferred recipient of the reviews that Circé-Côté did not submit for publication. Uninhibited by Dugas' friendship for Victor Barbeau, the president of the French Section of the Canadian Authors Association, she described a talk that Barbeau had given on Canadian literature as "stupid." According to Barbeau, French-Canadian literature, with the exception of Marcel Dugas and a few others, was almost non-existent.[146] She reproached Barbeau, who represented an organization established to promote local literature and "books from the land (*terroir*)," for denying its existence. She admitted that this literature might not have been flourishing; books were being published but, regrettably, no one was buying them. Part of the audience shared her indignation and had walked out in protest. Éva, a born polemicist, did not squander this opportunity to paint a trenchant portrait of the speaker:

> Black suit and huge shirtfront heightening his sallow complexion, fingers spread wide in gloves that seemed too long for his hands, a sardonic smile that he forced to the point of grinning, the gesture (?)—Victor Barbeau lacked style. The vulgarity of sentiment came through under the dandified elegance. He is bereft of refinement.[147]

Éva Circé-Côté was not one for compromise.

The two correspondents exchanged not just ideas and advice but books as well. She sent him collections of Québécois poetry, and he, novels that he deemed, with good reason, likely to interest his confidante. Hence, in 1921 she received *Les Feux du couchant*, by Michel Corday, a psychological study that she would read and reread "to drain its bitterness," and a novel by André Thérive (Roger Puthoste), a friend of Dugas, in whom she saw the reflection of her own vision of the good and the true.[148] She soon grew disenchanted with Thérive's work. In 1925, after receiving *La Revanche* from the author himself, she described him in harsh terms in a letter to Dugas: a populist writer and "a shifting mind whose features are as bright and hard as a diamond."[149] Circé-Côté's was an eclectic reader, whose erudition and curiosity were immense. Her writings are full of quotations and references, to the classics especially but also to contemporary authors, such as Anatole France, Henri Barbusse, and Romain Rolland.

As a journalist, Éva Circé-Côté wrote anonymously, but she was nonetheless present on Montreal's cultural scene. In 1924, she found herself in the literary spotlight after the publication of *Papineau. Son influence sur la pensée canadienne. Essai de psychologie historique* (Papineau: His influence on Canadian thought: An essay in historical psychology; no English translation of the biography exists—Trans.). For many years, Éva Circé-Côté had expressed her boundless admiration for Louis-Joseph Papineau. He had died the year Éva was born, and as a little girl she had included him among the fairy-tale heroes; he always remained for her a living model, whose glory never faded.[150] Already in 1911, when Lionel Groulx chose Dollard des Ormeaux to be the hero of Saint-Jean-Baptiste Day, she proposed Papineau instead, because his exploits in 1837–38 "marked our birth as a people, when we threw off the yoke of slavery, under which the Irish still bend."[151] Ten years later, with the declared purpose of "exhuming, of valorizing the liberal pleiad that contributed to the most glorious pages of our history since the conquest," and to "do justice ... to an entire people," to provide an example to the young generation witnessing "our moral depression,"[152] she published her *Papineau*. The work goes beyond the biography of the "ancient hero who has strayed to our shores"[153] and locates the man in his historical context. She corrects contemporary views of Papineau, not the least of which belong to Lionel Groulx, and proceeds to analyze Papineau's liberal nationalism.

Like any good historian, she questions her sources in the light of current issues and her own commitments. She was familiar with the interpretations of her predecessors: Michel Bibaud, the journalist critical of the *Patriotes*; François-Xavier Garneau, the first true French-Canadian historian; the

Francophile J.-G. Barthe; the red Laurent-Olivier David; the Frères des écoles chrétiennes (Brothers of the Christian Schools), who spread the prevailing historical orthodoxy in the educational institutions. Her portrait of society at the time of the 1837–38 Rebellions, of the economy, of the language, and of those forgotten by history—women, Indigenous Peoples, French-speaking protestants—is laden with commentaries on her contemporaries.

The biographer enlists the support of her hero to reiterate the ideas she had been articulating in newspapers for years. Papineau's liberalism, his rationalism, his critique of the relationship between the Church and the English authorities, his secular nationalism all provide grist for Circé-Côté's discourse. Forty-three years after the death of Papineau, lord of the Petite-Nation seigneury, these issues still generated public debate.

There are two more features of this publication that are worth noting. The first is that the book was published at the author's expense. The exact reason is not known, but self-publication was not unusual during this period, as publishers of this kind of work were still rare in Quebec. Few were prepared to invest in a book proffering such controversial ideas about a figure whose anticlericalism and civil funeral had not been forgotten. The second, more perplexing, feature is that the book was signed Ève, not Éva, Circé-Côté. This was not a typographical error, since her letters to Dugas were also signed Ève. Mother and daughter were no doubt very close. Young Ève was following in her mother's footsteps and had decided on a career in library science. Did their personalities overlap to such an extent that the mother might wish to borrow her daughter's given name? That the daughter might wish to lend her name to her mother? When *Papineau* came out, none of the reviews raised any questions about the author's first name.

In her correspondence with Dugas, Circé-Côté defended her hero. Dugas, however, disliked romanticism. Papineau wrote in a style that, a century on, might be called grandiloquent, but, Éva replied, "this great man had enough range to wrap himself in the magnificent phrasing that is considered ridiculous today." Papineau, she contended in his defence, had expressed himself with those grand statements, whose lyricism and grandiosity had not rung false back then but which were considered old-fashioned in 1924. "Had he spoken like everyone else, I would have portrayed him that way. . . . He spoke as he felt: amply. Even if he had the soul of the Cornelian hero, Papineau would have been declamatory and theatrical all the same."[154]

Following the publication of *Papineau*, she fell into a state of depression, a common experience among creative people after the completion of a project. She complained of having "a head like an empty cage," from which her thoughts had flown away.[155] She might have applied to herself what she had

Georgine Boucher-Normandin, standing beside her sculpted bust by J. J. Lacerté, at her home on La Motte-Picquet Street in Paris. From the collection of Gustave Labbé.

Georgine Boucher-Normandin and her daughter Lucienne, in their Paris apartment. From the collection of Gustave Labbé.

written a few years earlier about Marguerite Bourgeoys: "When inspiration no longer breathes through our souls, we are like a lamp whose flame has gone out, poor playthings of the night and of doubt."[156] She was looking for a new passion. But she was so frail in 1925 that her doctor forbade her from doing any work.[157]

However isolated Circé-Côté may have felt, she did have friends. One woman with whom she remained on intimate terms was Georgine Normandin, a former classmate at the Sisters of St. Anne convent.[158] Born the same year, they were, each in her own way, iconoclasts. Georgine had married Urgel-P. Boucher and when the couple separated she took up residence on rue La Motte-Picquet in the 7th arrondissement in Paris, where she held a salon in the company of expatriate French Canadians and devotees of French Canada. She translated, composed music that her daughter Lucienne would play, and was the centre of a small circle of artists and writers.[159] Among those who gathered at these soirées to listen to music and readings were Marcel Dugas, Maurice Guénard-Hodent, author of an essay on Canada,[160] Kodarh, the owner of the *Paris-Canada* magazine, André Thévine, Dugas' friend and winner of the Balzac award, and forward-thinking minds like Abel Léger, who had written an essay about homosexuality, the esoteric poet Victor-Émile Michelet, the actress Suzanne Gionnel, and writers such as Jacques Trèves and Esther van Loo.[161]

In October 1925, one such soirée was centred on Éva Circé-Côté, with a reading of poems from her collection *Bleu, Blanc, Rouge*. There was nothing controversial about this selection of work, nothing indicative of the freethinking woman confined to the periphery of intellectual trends in Quebec. The Aveyronnais poet André Delacour put her "in the top rank of Canada's best literary women."[162] The event was reported on in Montreal, and Éva's pride was palpable when she quoted to a friend the letter from Georgine Boucher-Normandin in which the guests were listed.[163] Yet judging from Circé-Côté's remarks a few years earlier about Georges Bellerives' book,[164] she must have regretted that what she called her saccharine writings (oeuvres à l'eau de rose) had been read at the soirée rather than works that better conveyed her critical and militant thinking. Apparently, her *Papineau* was the focus of another salon, according to a report in the Latin-American journal *Universitario* presenting a summary of Boucher-Normandin's literary gatherings. The report's author considered Circé-Côté "one of the preeminent Canadian women writers of the current generation."[165] But the gratification that Éva derived from this international recognition was marred by an ordeal.

On August 21, 1926, when she came home from work, she found her mother, Ézilda Décarries, lying dead in her chaise longue. Her portrayal of the woman with whom for years she had shared her life was not an indulgent one. Éva described her as someone inclined to pessimism, who "looked at the core of things and saw horror and desperation," read gloomy authors, preferred the shade to the light, and "always refused to accept any principle of justice," especially at the time of her son-in-law's death. Nevertheless, the two women were very close: "She was an integral part of my being.... I expressed her thoughts. She was the soul of the house," Éva Circé-Côté, completely distraught, confided to Marcel Dugas in her first letter to him after her mother's death:[166]

> I find myself at fifty [she was fifty-five years old] at a juncture where I am lost. I had no character other than a pen in my hand to defend my ideas. I poured all my ink and energy into this thankless work because it helped and sustained me. And now I am adrift and I wonder what I shall do with this freedom that has been returned to me and whose cost I am unable to appreciate.

She goes on to liken herself to freed slaves who do not wish to be free. Her mother's death affected her health, leaving her with stomach pains and "tortures that Dante would rue not having invented."[167]

She emerged from this trial "reconciled with existence." She reorganized her daily routine and took on a young couple as tenants, who also looked after the house. Her salary, which stood at over $1,300 since 1924, enabled her to live comfortably.[168] She was able as well to pay for help with the washing and maintenance when she was ordered to take a complete rest for months. Having endured her mother's death and a year of poor health, she accepted this period of forced inactivity.[169]

She wondered what the year 1927 held for her. In a piece for *Le Monde ouvrier*, she reflected on her epoch and perceived it as a transition period with some positive features, not the least of which was greater freedom for women.[170] But to Dugas she confessed her anxieties. The future seemed as bleak and inhospitable as "a voyage on the Gulf of St Lawrence. The farther we sail out toward infinity the sadder and more desolate the shores are. The [?] give way to dark rocks, to mountains dressed in cowls and grimacing under their hoods."[171] France always beckoned her and she was tempted by a trip to Paris, a project contingent on her good health. But this great dream would remain unfulfilled.[172]

Still, she did not lead a life of reclusion. She was invited to speak on the radio,[173] and she appreciated the company of artists and literary people. She dined, for example, with the musician Rudolph Plamondon,[174] who divided his time between Paris, Montreal, and his numerous tours: "His head and his heart are in keeping with his image. What a sane and upright personality! How nice it is to find such simplicity in so great an artist!"[175] She often met with Gonzalvez Desaulniers, appointed judge in 1923, and had nothing but praise for him. A vastly cultured man, both a poet and a Hellenist, Desaulniers looked after Éva's material interests: "What a devoted friend. I owe him my life—which has scarcely any worth—but, more than that, the safety of my home," she wrote, with a measure of pomposity. She worried about his health, feared that he might be ill. She reported to Dugas in 1924 that Desaulniers was indignant at the situation Dugas had been put in: "I am grateful to him for having such a high opinion of your character."[176]

Despite their different views on religion, Circé-Côté maintained an abiding friendship with Augustine Bourassa, Henri's sister and Papineau's granddaughter.[177] She had not as yet broken her ties with her colleague Georgina Bélanger Gill. She wrote to compliment her on her writing and also to give her an account of a soirée at Georgine Boucher-Normandin's salon. She thanked her for her friendship: "I am touched by the interest you have shown in me and I do not know how to thank you . . . Your friendship is precious to me and I wear it proudly like a rare jewel."[178] Notwithstanding her feeling of persecution and isolation, Éva Circé-Côté did not lack for devoted friends.

On reading some of her letters to Dugas, one gets the feeling, nevertheless, that she had lost all those close to her and that the memory of the exiled poet was her one consolation.[179] The people she called her friends, she wrote, were not figments of her imagination, as was the case for Dugas' so-called friends, who were "no more than mannequins."[180] For years, Éva Circé-Côté would continue to feel isolated, even ostracized, and her letters to Dugas bespoke all her bitterness, although she stubbornly persisted in defining herself as an optimist. She wrote that she preferred the company of the old tomes of the Gagnon collection to that of her own "unkind."[181] Cataloguing books, alone, by the light of a banker's lamp, was "altogether dreary, a veritable deathwatch," during which she liked to imagine Dugas easing his headaches with "a damp towel wrapped around your head like a Turkish bey," until her fantasy was dispelled by the beams of light from the newly erected cross on Mount Royal, which, apparently, reached as far as the second-floor windows of the library on Sherbrooke Street.

> So it was that Mr. Morin, who had a few peccadillos requiring the clergy's forgiveness, proposed to that end to erect a luminous cross on the mountain in memory of the wooden cross that Maisonneuve had raised immediately upon setting foot on Canada's southern shore. The project was greeted with enthusiasm and carried out post haste. The consequence is that each night the fateful sign appears to me, no matter where I go to escape it . . . If only it were "the sign of salvation" for me, but, on the contrary, it forms the dagger that many times has stabbed me in the back. It evinces no sense of indulgence, pity, or love. I am filled with dread as I move through its rays, gleaming like steel, like the fulgurations of lethal stars.[182]

In 1927 the Association des auteurs canadiens, of which she was co-director, hosted an event on the novel, which was organized by the publisher Édouard Garant and chaired by Justice Fabre-Surveyer. The journalist Louis Francœur, a staunch Liberal and occasional essayist, gave a lecture titled "Author, Critic, Public," which put literary criticism in Quebec on trial. His verdict was grim: literature was regressing because the critic had almost no influence on the [French-]Canadian public and people were afraid to judge.[183] He was in fact echoing an admonishment that Circé-Côté had been directing at her fellow citizens for years.

Six poets then gave readings: Jean Charbonneau, Hélène Charbonneau, Alice Pépin, Paul Gouin, who recited "Lambert Closse," and Mrs. Buissonneau, who read a poem about the Sainte-Justine Hospital. Toward the end of the long programme two young women, Ève Côté and Henriette Brodeur, read excerpts from the works of their respective mothers, Éva Circé-Côté and Louise Marmette-Brodeur. The timing was unfavourable, as the audience was weary from the lengthy programme and numerous readings. Éva Circé-Côté furthermore added a few pages from a novel in progress. The correspondent of *La Patrie* gave no quarter: the texts were "twice as long as necessary," they were read too quickly and were scarcely heard by those in attendance.[184]

Circé-Côté felt isolated, an unappreciated writer, a misunderstood intellectual; yet her reputation as a literary woman went beyond what was after all the narrow confines of the circle of Québécois writers. On June 24, 1928, on the occasion of Quebec's national holiday, the popular weekly *Le Petit Journal* invited its readers to answer the question, "Which French Canadians do the most for their race?" and added, "It is almost a duty to answer this thrilling question." Every participant submitted a list of twenty people each of whom received points according to his or her ranking. When the results were published, it came as no surprise that political men dominated the honour roll, with Henri Bourassa at the very top. Among the 106 names that followed were those of three women: the journalist Madeleine (Anne Marie Gleason) in 36th position, the feminist Idola Saint-Jean in 69th position, and Éva Circé-Côté in 76th position. Among Circé-Côté's social circle, there were Gonzalve Desaulniers (67th), Lorenzo Prince (68th), and Marcel Dugas (83rd).[185] She derived no solace from seeing herself ranked so far behind her journalist, feminist, and literary colleagues, nor did this do anything to allay her sense of living through a very dark period.

There was one cause that Éva Circé-Côté always held dear, that of keeping alive the memory of Louis-Joseph Papineau. In pursuing this objective she stood alongside the granddaughter of the seigneur of Petite-Nation, Augustine Bourassa, who dreamed of converting her grandfather's erstwhile manor on the shores of the Ottawa River into a museum. Circé-Côté was dismayed by the "unfortunate transformation" of the Montebello manor house: a bar occupied the ground floor, the door of the crypt where he was interred had been staved in, and a number of trees had been felled. The vulgarity, the lack of patriotism, and the primacy of financial interests revolted her.[186] In 1930, she was shocked to learn that Papineau's estate had been sold to some Americans who planned to pursue the profanation of the site by transforming it into a private club, "Lucerne en Québec," which would become the prestigious and exclusive Seigniory Club.[187] Why not, then, try to save the place through a public funding campaign and turn it into a museum of the 1837–38 events? It was a matter of national honour for her. The indifference of elected officials and the general population toward the loss of this heritage reflected the marginal position to which Papineau and those events were relegated for many years by nationalist clerics and Catholic institutions. Banished from the history of Canada, the Rebellions were occulted and even vilified by the rising star of Quebec history, Lionel Groulx, and his followers, as if Circé-Côté's biography of her hero had slid over the French-Canadian consciousness without leaving a trace.

* * *

Nearly every art benefitted from Éva Circé-Côté's talents: she was a musician, a painter, and a poet. And since the turn of the century she was enamoured of the cinema, "that marvellous invention," "the most beautiful invention of human genius," which makes it possible "to travel with one's eyes to fabulous or fictitious lands."[188] In 1927 she devoted no fewer than four columns to the fire at the Laurier Palace, which had claimed the lives of seventy-eight children. This calamity in the working-class district of Hochelaga-Maisonneuve was met with indignation and rekindled the prewar debate on the moral complexion of the cinema. For the bigots, "the dark and unwholesome halls," as Mgr Bruchési called them,[189] were not meant for children, not only because it was almost impossible to get out of them in an emergency, but also because inside them young people were exposed to scandalous scenes. The government established a commission under the chairmanship of Justice Louis Boyer to inquire into the blaze. The commission's report would deal with both physical and moral safety. Justice Boyer refrained from stigmatizing the cinema, the "poor man's entertainment." However, he did recommend safety measures for movie theatres as well as restricting admission to those aged sixteen and over.[190] Considering "the massacre of innocents at the Laurier Palace,"[191] Julien Saint-Michel endorsed Justice Boyer's positions and underscored the lack of safety procedures and the parents' negligence, but without ever blaming the cinema per se.

Just when the higher Catholic clergy and right-wing nationalists were denouncing the supposed domination of the cinema by Jews and Hollywood, Protestant groups were fighting to have commercial forms of recreation banned on Sunday. Circé-Côté, like most Montrealers, had no use for puritanism: "Let our city keep its cheerful appearance. Let's not give it the dour face of the Queen City, which dons a mourner's hat on Sundays."[192] She noted the importance of recreation for workers, hence the need to keep the movie theatres open on Sunday and, displaying more generosity than the commissioner, she proposed to admit children, who were less at risk in the cinemas than on the street.[193] Moreover, for working people, the readers of the *Monde ouvrier*, the cinema provided "a few hours of merriment on Sunday, which compensated for the bleak weekdays that went by in an atmosphere of iron filings and soot that would eventually clog the soul."[194] Addressing herself to the self-righteous, Julien Saint-Michel added: "The same people who tolerate dangerous work forbid children from going to the cinema."[195]

While timid souls were scandalized by the movies, Circé-Côté endeavoured to convince her readers of the importance of the "silent art," that "agent of liberty." As was true of industry, it must "be taken hold of." To appease the religious authorities, she added that, rather than forbidding the movies, they should be employed "to propagate the faith, preach the Gospel, and teach Church history." Better a religious cinema than no cinema at all, for "it is harder to forego the movies than cigarettes, alcohol, and the little white beer."[196] In the wake of the Laurier Palace fire, the Legislative Assembly voted a law barring youths under sixteen from the cinema, even when accompanied by their parents. Circé-Côté could never accept depriving young people of this "healthful enjoyment" and a means to further their education: "A flowering of virtues brought about by the screen's sun has beautified the world. For it is through the cinema that emotions are educated." In her eyes, there was only one possible justification for not taking children to the cinema: the heat inside the movie theatres during the summer. When films came under the threat of censorship, Circé-Côté maintained that "the silent art must be protected like music, sculpture, and painting against the philistines bent on destroying it."[197]

However much she was fascinated by moving pictures, Circé-Côté did not abandon the theatre. On February 8, 1932, the Veillées du bon vieux temps (Good old-time evening get-togethers), directed by Conrad Gauthier, hosted an evening at the Monument-National under the title "Les Jours Gras" (Fat Days). The annual event was appreciated by many French Canadians, especially those who had migrated to the city from the countryside. To get the evening underway, Gauthier had pulled *Le Fumeur endiablé*, written "by a local author," out of oblivion. The one-act play was followed by rigadoons, farandoles, and stories, accordionists and fiddlers, and a Fat Tuesday personified by Ernest Loiselle. The cast of *Le Fumeur* was composed of highly regarded actors: Lorenzo Bariteau, Hector Charland, Louise Clermont, and

Albertine Martin.[198] The choice of this comedy was a timely one just before Lent, as it revolves around a smoker who puts aside his pipe for the forty days of penitence. In promoting the event, both *Le Petit Journal* and *La Patrie* reminded readers of Colombine's past successes and described *Le Fumeur* as "a little gem of a comedy."[199] Éva Circé-Côté, a modern woman, was not averse to being associated with an event described as "dyed-in-the-wool" by *La Patrie*.[200] But times had changed, and although the public was won over and the theatre was overflowing, the next day's reviews showed no mercy. The critic of *La Presse* saw *Le Fumeur* as an "attempt at *marivaudage* (sophisticated banter)" to which the actors' talents had been able "to lend some life."[201] The writing style of 1904 was passé in 1932, and, while the theme of the play was still relevant, the style only accentuated the anachronism of this "Veillée du bon vieux temps." Circé-Côté's success as a playwright had not withstood the test of time. None of her columns betrayed the disappointment—perhaps even bitterness—that she must have felt, and although she poured her heart out in letters to her intimates, it remained a well-kept secret.

The Economic Crisis

After a few years of prosperity, the economy collapsed. The reverberations of the collapse could be heard in the columns of Julien Saint-Michel, who hastened to distinguish between false and true unemployment, between the improvident and the genuine victims of the Depression. Indeed, the tenor of this column was inching closer and closer to the mainstream political discourse.[202] In 1931 Circé-Côté reflected on why France had been sheltered from the crisis up to that point, and her Francophilia led her to praise the wisdom of French business leaders as well as their "sense of moderation and providence" and "the French people's spirit of hard work and saving."[203] These qualities placed the onus on the shoulders of employers and workers, regardless of the economic environment or the policies carried out by political leaders. She appeared over time to have distanced herself from the situation of the working class. When waiting lines in the shelters and soup kitchens grew longer, she contended that "certainly, many of those who living off soup kitchens have come to this through their own fault" because they had not saved when they "were earning between five and ten dollars a day."[204] Yet prior to the Depression only a relatively small number of highly qualified workers could have boasted such wages.

To alleviate the effects of the economic disaster, both political leaders and intellectuals put forward various proposals. All of them involved palliative measures rather than true reforms. When the Minister of Labour Charles-Joseph Arcand proposed to raise men's wages so that women would withdraw from the labour market, Circé-Côté was sceptical. She would continue to protest against the attempts by the clergy and conservative nationalists to restrict women's employment outside the home. It was simply a matter of equality. "One does not bring birds back to the nest once they have taken wing. [. . .] The question of a person's sex does not exist where work is concerned"; and further, "the home to which women are expected to return exists only in the imagination of dreamers."[205] Politicians and clerics persisted in calling on female workers to return home to make room for their brothers, fiancés, and, more rarely, husbands; Circé-Côté opposed the efforts of some politicians to proscribe the employment of married women. In January 1935, the member of the Legislative Assembly J.-A. Francœur, submitted a bill for the second time in two years that would have prohibited the employment of women "who don't need it."[206]

Francœur's discourse represented a point of view that was widespread among Catholics and trade-unionists: women's work was responsible for men's unemployment. This was an enduring myth even though in Quebec only 15 percent of women over the age of ten were gainfully employed in 1932. A minority of these women, most of them unmarried, worked in factories, while 25 percent were in the service sector and one out of five was a domestic, hence, not in competition with men.

The Depression dragged on well into the thirties and cast a pall over daily life. Skilled workers became labourers; Circé-Côté cited the cases of an electrician who sawed lumber, another who shovelled snow and household repair work, and "servants worked to death by inhuman housekeepers." In 1933 Labour Day was a cheerless one.[207]

While members of the bourgeoisie were forced to curtail their spending, they nevertheless were less affected by the economic crisis. "If ordinary people are languishing, it's a sure sign that others are growing fat at their expense." "Is it right that, in order to maintain a social balance, some are awash in comfort and others are starving?"[208] This analysis was to be expected from a trade-union journalist: employers, who benefitted from unemployment and the abundance of available manpower, imposed wage reductions and heavier workloads.

While Julien Saint-Michel documented and discussed the long years of economic stagnation in *Le Monde ouvrier*, Éva Circé-Côté, the librarian, was dealing with budget restrictions and constraints on books purchases and the hiring of personnel. Was the library destined to remain a "book widow," as she had already lamented in 1921?[209] Relations among staff members had not been harmonious for a long time at the Sherbrooke Street institution. Ever since her companion Marcel Dugas had moved to Paris she spent her days with colleagues who did not share her ideas: "I feel the mute hostility pressing down on me like a lead weight."[210] She felt ostracized and wrote about "the solitude that was my friend."[211]

When Marie-Claire Daveluy arrived at the library, Éva Circé-Côté was ready to offer her friendship. In 1920 she wrote to Dugas: "Miss Daveluy and I are still on good terms; this is a friendship of reason and convenience, perhaps the most solid kind."[212] Ideological differences, however, were to get the best of these fine sentiments. Daveluy, the author of utterly exemplary children's books, by no means endorsed her colleague's secularism; a few years later, Éva pictured her saying, with a pretence of affability, "It is not her that I hate, but freethought." She added: "She will torture me, destroy me with magnificent intentions, this tormenter in the shape of an angel—what a reversal of personalities!"[213]

She continued to object to the book acquisition system and Mr. Bausset, "who goes to get books haphazardly" at Déom's. The Library Commission favoured the purchase of collections "from an old college friend" who had gone broke or some gentleman with connections in City Hall. Run-of-the-mill or conventional acquisitions gave rise to numerous duplications, such as multiple copies of *Origines de la France contemporaine* by Hyppolite Taine, the works of Jules Verne and the *Dictionnaire généalogique des familles canadiennes* by Father Cyprien Tanguay. In sum, "we have become a parochial reading room," she complained in 1924. With more than a hint of irony, she included in her inventory of collections the several hundred books of pornography stowed away the Head Librarian's office.[214]

Hector Garneau ran the library with an iron hand. He sent staff members a letter warning them that "any act of disrespect or insubordination toward the head librarian will be reported to the executive committee ... Conversations between employees or with outside people are strictly forbidden during work hours ... Any violation of these orders will be reported to the municipal authorities."[215] To escape the often tense atmosphere at work Circé-Côté found refuge in compiling the catalogue of the Gagnon collection: "I have grown to like these old papers the colour of dead leaves ... I have the sensation of being dead in this cold monument."[216] In early July 1924 she wrote to Dugas that she was glad to get away for a few days of vacation from those "tyrants."[217]

In 1930, Félix Desrochers, a conservative politician, took over from Hector Garneau as head of the library. Now under the orders of an ambitious man, one less cultured than his predecessor, Éva Circé-Côté was no doubt sorry that Garneau had left. The new chief librarian had an entirely different notion of his role. As he would put it a few years later: "the librarian must be a scholar and a gentleman; what's more, he must be a business man."[218] Until then, no librarian had claimed to be a "business man." Desrochers' efforts as of 1931 to have the ruling conservatives in Ottawa appoint him as chief parliamentary librarian did nothing to improve the work environment on Sherbrooke Street.

When Aegidius Fauteux left the Saint-Sulpice Library to succeed Desrochers in May 1932, he initiated a new era at the Municipal Library. Although his intellectual stature contrasted with that of his predecessor, his conception of the library was at odds with all the reasons that Éva Circé-Côté and Hector Garneau had made it their mission. When the establishment of a public library was under consideration in the early years of the century, Fauteux was in favour of an institution available to "scholars and people of the educated class [. . .] [because] the country expected its intellectual advancement to come from them."[219] This view was far removed from Circé-Côté's project of a democratic library open to working people. In a letter to Marcel Dugas, Olivar Asselin, who occasionally spent "an hour or two at St. Sulpice in Fauteux's company," painted this scathing portrait: "He is an educated, loyal, humble fellow, full of wit. But he lacks the ability to understand any intelligence that is not of a bourgeois bent. I am almost certain that he has no taste for Verlaine and is appalled by Rimbaud."[220] In keeping with his conservatism, Fauteux was also opposed to women's suffrage.[221]

In his capacity as guardian of morality, Fauteux wished to put an end to what he regarded as the incompetence of the staff, although he confessed to never having set foot in the Municipal Library before his appointment![222] When he finally did, he found "a library that was seriously ill, one suffering from a little inanition but especially from a sort of interior anarchy." The initial report that he submitted to the Library Commission was sixty-five pages long and was followed by a second "re-organization report (*Rapport de réaménagement*)," which proposed to do away with what he described as the staff's laxity and incompetence.

One episode aptly illustrates the man's character. Fauteux complained that his predecessors had long tolerated the presence of children, often barefoot, who would come in from Lafontaine Park and take refuge in the library. He counted as many as thirty-five of them in the reading room, which had a capacity of eighty people. "This constantly jiggling brood," which had to be sent to the washrooms to wash up, was disturbing the work of the readers. Even more shocking was the fact that some had been caught consulting the anatomy pages in medical journals![223] Now, for years, though for very different reasons, Éva Circé-Côté had been criticizing the Saint-Sulpice Library for not having a children's room—"one of the primary raisons d'être of libraries"—and she nourished the project of opening a reading room suitable for children.[224]

Fauteux set about cleaning house. The staff was hit with terminations; eight women were fired—in one instance because "her duties were more appropriate for a man"[225]—with tragic consequences for those who were breadwinners, whose husband was sick or whose son wanted to pursue his education.[226] Circé-Côté, "Assistant to the head librarian, director of the Gagnon Collection, co-director of the catalogue and co-director of classification," was not exempt from the major "reorganization." She could not count on any sympathy toward her on the part of the new boss. As a journalist, she had come down hard on the *messieurs* of Saint-Sulpice and on more than one occasion had scorned religious libraries that shunned the Enlightenment and rejected books listed on the Catholic Church's Index. Yet she had not expected the terse note dated September 15, 1932 that she received from the city clerk: "Madame, I regret to inform you that your services will no longer be required by the City as of today. The Executive Committee has nevertheless decided to pay you two weeks of salary in lieu of notice."[227] Challenging her competence with regard to the cataloguing of the Gagnon collection, which had been dragging on for ages, and finding her too old at sixty-one to keep up, Fauteux dismissed her. Marie-Claire Daveluy would take over as co-director of the catalogue, "the library's most important technical department," as the new head librarian acknowledged.[228]

Thanks to the intercession of Honoré Parent, a close friend of Dugas from the days of the Casoars de L'Arche and currently director of municipal services, the Pension Commission of the City of Montreal, in accordance with By-Law no. 1149, granted Éva Circé-Côté an annual pension of $809.10 starting October 1, 1932. In an emotional letter to Alderman Parent, she expressed her anxieties and thanked him for interceding on her behalf. The pension was welcome to the widow Côté, but she was obliged nevertheless to sell her already mortgaged house in Westmount.[229] That month, one of her columns dealt with dismissals during the Crisis.

Having so often depicted the madness of moving, she was not a mere spectator for all that. Like so many Montrealers, she moved frequently, from one end of the Plateau Mont-Royal to the other and then much farther west in the 1930s. When she was let go from the Municipal Library she was living on Westmount Boulevard, a prestigious address; now, however, being deprived of a salary, she sold her house and moved east again to Saint-Joseph Boulevard, before returning to the western part of the city in 1933. Until 1948 she lived at 4291 Western, today Maisonneuve Boulevard, in Westmount. It is worth noting that these bourgeois addresses were not indications of great wealth, as she had to rent out rooms to make ends meet.[230]

The plump Mrs. Circé-Côté no longer crossed the city as easily as she had at the start of her career at the library, when she hurried to work along with thousands of young working women. The sidewalks of the Saint-Jean-Baptiste and the Plateau Mont-Royal neighbourhoods were superseded by those of Notre-Dame-de-Grâce—an area she had referred to as "Anglified" twenty years earlier. Montreal had changed. While some merchants—milkmen, bakers, ice vendors, and movers—still drove horse-drawn vehicles, automobiles were ubiquitous and traffic lights began to adorn the intersections. Women no longer had to lift their skirts to stride over mud and detritus, as hemlines had risen even above the knees. It was generally agreed that the city was far cleaner than before.

Éva's visits to Sohmer park were less frequent, and when she went to the cinema she now could choose from a number of French- and English-language talking pictures. The Municipal Library still looked out on Lafontaine Park and, since 1924, sat adjacent to Notre-Dame Hospital, but the former librarian could not be found there anymore. Montreal's nightclubs and jazz scene were the envy of other Canadian cities, yet Éva Circé-Côté never mentioned them in her columns; she still preferred classical music.

CHAPTER 5

TO LIVE IS TO FIGHT

Owing to an inexplicable incoherence, we desperately cling to life.[1]
— ÉVA CIRCÉ-CÔTÉ, 1900

Those who loved deeply and who dedicated themselves... No matter if their names are forgotten, their noble actions remain. You are dead when your heart ceases to beat in the face of human woes and you are powerless to console those who weep.[2]
— ÉVA CIRCÉ-CÔTÉ, 1928

While Éva Circé-Côté had no other choice but to retire from her position at the library, she did not abandon her other pursuits. She was certainly less active in the Association des auteurs canadiens, an organization that began to fall apart in 1929 only to be newly incorporated in 1936 under the name Société des auteurs canadiens, although the titles were at times used interchangeably; however, she did give talks on the radio. In September 1933, station CKAC broadcasted a show organized jointly by the Ordre des Canadiens de naissance (Native Sons of Canada) and the Ligue des filles canadiennes (Canadian Daughters League), of which Circé-Côté was the spokeswoman. She was introduced as "a distinguished journalist, vice-chair of the Assemblée Papineau de la Ligues des filles natives canadiennes (Papineau assembly of the League of Native Daughters of Canada)." Titled, "To succeed in making Canada an exceptional country, it is necessary to elevate the mentality of the Canadian woman," her talk was far more feminist than nationalist in tone and concluded with an appeal to the government to appoint women to honorific positions, such as the Senate or the Civil Service Commission.[3]

Very little information is available about this nationalist league other than the fact it had been founded by Georgina Bélanger Gill (Gaëtane de Montreuil) and, under the name Les Filles natives du Canada (Native Daughters of Canada), was the female and French-language counterpart to the Native Sons of Canada.[4] The latter was founded in British Columbia in 1925 with a twofold objective: the adoption of properly Canadian symbols, such as a flag, and restrictions on immigration. However, in light of the Georgina Bélanger's extremely chauvinistic views, the Native Sons refused to recognize her organization. Bélanger therefore proceeded to create other leagues, assemblies, or Native Daughters committees, such as the Assemblée Rosalie-Papineau, named after Louis-Joseph Papineau's sister.[5] During the Depression, Bélanger pushed the Assembly toward a "back to the land" policy and one of providing assistance to settlers in the Gaspésie and Abitibi regions.

Georgina Bélanger, Éva's friend, with whom she had travelled to the Lac Saint-Jean area in 1901 on behalf of the Société de la colonisation and together founded the secular *lycée* in 1908, the one who shared Circé-Côté's ideas on women's rights and had sustained her in her darkest hours, enlisted Éva's support for this "mission of national uplift," whose xenophobia Circé-Côté—a journalist for *Le Monde ouvrier*, after all—must have found nonetheless repellent.[6] In 1931, aware that her readers were hard hit by the economic crisis and liable to feel threatened by immigrants, she published an article highly critical of immigration. She demanded that the money "used to promote a disastrous immigration could be employed for a more practical purpose," that is, aid to settlers.[7] Her column did not attack immigrants themselves, but government policies that, instead of distributing public assistance, should have directed unemployed workers toward the development of natural resources.

Like many city-dwellers, Éva Circé-Côté had never broken her ties with the countryside, even though she continued to inveigh against rural narrow-mindedness. In 1903 she mentioned that she owned "a charming little lakeside house not far from a small village."[8] As evidenced by her columns, she also vacationed in the Lower Saint Lawrence district or in the Laurentian Mountains. Following in the footsteps of curé Labelle and Arthur Buies, Circé-Côté was captivated by "the North," its virgin lands waiting to be cultivated, its trees waiting to be felled, and its potential pastureland. Always a believer in the intrinsic worth of labour, she saw the development of the Laurentians as the answer to the problem of jobless workers wandering the streets of Montreal. She cited for her readers the example of the pioneer of Saint-Aimé-du-Lac-des-Îles, Mr. Papineau, a baker by profession won over to country life and henceforth happy with his herd of cows and his chicken coop.[9] The stuff of dreams. Eventually, the acidic soil of the North would prove to be less than fertile and the former urban unemployed would end up as the rural poor. Because Circé-Côté's positions coincided with government plans to establish settlers in such areas, she found herself advocating the same solutions as the nationalists and conservatives, who saw the return to the land as the antidote to communism. Writing again under the Julien Saint-Michel byline in 1934, she went so far as to endorse Lionel Groulx's observation: "In less than one generation, farmers and farmers' sons have come to believe that they exist for the proletariat."[10] But unlike the historian-priest, she ascribed the desertion of the countryside to an education ill suited to rural circumstances and to a value system that belittled manual labour and favoured the liberal professions.

Still, it is surprising to find Éva Circé-Côté in the Assemblée Rosalie-Papineau, a nationalist, even nativist, group close to the Société Saint-Jean-Baptiste. In 1934, the Ordre des Canadiens de naissance (Native Sons of Canada) was one of the associations that instigated the resignation of Dr. Samuel Rabinovitch, a Jewish resident doctor at the Hôpital Notre-Dame.[11] For many years, Circé-Côté had condemned anti-Semitism, and, indignant at the treatment meted out to Dr. Rabinovitch, she devoted a column, titled "Question de race," to his case.[12]

Georgina Bélanger was a difficult person, and Éva Circé-Côté had a strong personality. A dispute eventually erupted, apparently over the position of the Filles natives concerning assistance to settlers and the use of the association's funds. Éva, along with other members, tendered her resignation on March 5, 1934; in response, Georgina Bélanger wrote her a scathing letter assuring her that her resignation "was accepted unanimously and without hesitation."[13] Thus, their longstanding friendship came to an end.

Éva was at an age when those close to her were slipping away. Gonzalve Desaulniers was felled by an attack of angina in April 1934. This journalist, poet, and lawyer had been present at every stage of Circé-Côté's life: member of the Émancipation lodge, chairman of the secular *lycée*, colleague at the radical liberal newspapers, adversary of the anti-Semites, early proponent of a public library, Francophone and president of the Alliance française, where he regularly met the journalist-librarian Circé-Côté.[14] Despite his withdrawal from Pierre-Salomon's funeral procession, Éva had continued to trust him implicitly and had lauded him in her columns.[15] In 1924 she had dedicated *Papineau* to him.

Her daughter Ève stayed by her side, following in her mother's footsteps as she pursued her studies in library science. Being bilingual, Ève worked as assistant librarian at the Fraser Institute's library in the west end of Montreal.[16] The two women lived together in a relationship that Circé-Côté's close friends disapproved of because they felt her adored daughter was exploiting her.[17] One mystery has remained unsolved: as of the 1920s, Éva signed her articles Ève.

"There will be some sunshine in my dreary sky," Éva wrote. Her childhood friend Georgine Boucher-Normandin was coming to Montreal for a visit. In April 1937, Éva replied to her in these terms:

> I have begun to feel hopeful about life again. My poor heart has started to beat again, almost jazz-like. How good it is for someone who no longer expected anything to examine the calendar to see which day you are arriving and, in my mind, to strike through one by one the days separating me from you! My spacious house is less empty, for already I hear your melodious voice. I see your silhouette outlined in all the rooms. I say with Shakespeare, "Future events cast their shadow before . . ." The difference is that, here, the shadow is my light. You will stay in the large room in the front, the sunniest, most cheerful room. There, one can breathe in the flowers of Westmount, and you know how abundant they are! You come as my dear sister, from whom I have been kept apart for too long. You will take the room that has always been kept for you. I will come to meet you when the ship or the train arrives, and I will take you here straightaway. Ève is also delighted at the thought of seeing you again and forever, I believe. Your roots are here. It is hard to transplant oneself in another place. Friends are made only in youth. Some friendships can be grafted onto one's life in other seasons, but they are artificial, and disappointing, and do not survive.
>
> I am grateful to you for bringing beauty and harmony into my deliberately isolated existence. You tell me that together we grieve a shared misfortune—granted. But we shall try, if not to forget—the dead would not forgive us for it—then at least to find a palliative for our sorrows, to put a little greenery and coolness in our desert. *And the two great ruins found solace in each other.*"[18]

Georgine did not impose upon her friend's hospitality, and a few months later she sent news to Marcel Dugas, still living in Paris:

> Madame Côté's health is improving daily . . . our poor friend is overworked with a house full of people—tenants, boarders, with no one to help her, and a daughter, her Ève, who is selfishness personified and

lets herself be supported, fed, without giving anything of herself. My Sunday evening visit to our gentle friend is her only ray of sunlight in a week of toil and trouble. Pity her as I do, and let us love her well.[19]

Although the letter-writer's solicitude for Éva is plain to see, as are her impressions of Éva's beloved only daughter, the lack of corroborating evidence makes it is difficult to form a judgment about the mother-daughter relationship.

While she reduced her output for the *Monde ouvrier*—21 columns in 1935—Circé-Côté began a series of articles on the cinema for *La Revue moderne*. The journal's director, Anne-Marie Gleason Huguenin (aka Madeleine), seems not to have borne a grudge for the disobliging remarks Éva had made ten years earlier. Ever the cinema aficionada, now Éva could write about it. Yet her approach was pragmatic as well, for she regarded the cinema as not just an art but also as a form of entertainment and a business. Her favourite films are indicative of her attitude. In 1935, she wrote enthusiastically about John Ford's *The Informer*,[20] an expressionist film set in Northern Ireland in the 1920s, when the country was shaken by the rebellions of the Catholic nationalists. It is a story of remorse and betrayal, a recurrent theme in Circé-Côté's writing.

She had developed closer ties with Protestantism and was known in those circles. In October 1937, Alphonse Primeau-Robert, the editor of the Protestant newspaper *L'Aurore*, invited her to sit on the editorial board. She had lost none of her verve and, until 1941, would write columns on subjects that were close to her heart—the Catholic right, progress, the separation of church and state, education, women's suffrage—all under her own name.[21] In addition, she submitted a number of articles to *L'Autorité*, a liberal weekly close to progressive circles.[22] This is where she published a sharp response to Henri Bourassa's lecture on the defeat of the *Patriotes* in 1837–38.

She had never relinquished her desire to try a new genre, the novel. She had already spoken of it to Dugas, and a work of fiction was born. After a long period of gestation, *Les Quatre Demoiselles Lépine* (The Four Damsels Lépine), seemed to be finished. Her daughter Ève had already read excerpts from the novel at the Association des auteurs canadiens in 1927. It was never published, whether or not she ever submitted it a publisher is unknown, and the manuscript has disappeared.[23]

Circé-Côté had long excelled at biography, as evidenced both by the portraits of historical and contemporary figures that she published in newspapers and in her *Papineau*. Her new project was *L.-O. David et les Hommes proéminents de son temps* (L.-O. David and the Preeminent Men of his Time).[24] She had

Front page of *L'Aurore*, January 28, 1938.

known David in his capacity as clerk of the City of Montreal, among other contexts. He was a patriot, a founder of the Monument-National, a Liberal politician and a journalist opposed to Confederation, and his views on education and the role of the clergy coincided with those of Circé-Côté. In 1896, his pamphlet *Le Clergé canadien: sa mission, son oeuvre* was one of three Québécois titles banned by Mgr Bruchési.[25] Open to women's emancipation, he was one of the few men to have contributed to *Le Journal de Françoise* between 1905 and 1909. Circé-Côté of course admired this passionate *Rouge* [i.e., Liberal—Trans.], but her admiration was not blind. In 1914, she described David's report on libraries as "perfidious" because he estimated that Montreal's six major libraries held half a million books all told. This was a gross exaggeration; Circé-Côté tallied up the resources of every library in Montreal and concluded that in total they held around 100,000 books including the 66,000 of the Fraser Library.[26] But she was also able to appreciate L.-O. David's strengths. She quoted him on several occasions by way of endorsing his anti-imperialism, his position on the *collèges classiques*, which taught too much Latin and Greek at the expense of the sciences and technical subjects, and his opposition to conscription.[27]

Since the 1920s, when she had bought the house on Plessis Street, Éva Circé-Côté, who had written more than once about landladies and their tenants, found herself, like many widows, playing the role of property owner.[28] In 1933 she moved to Western Street, where she, too, would have tenants. In a lecture given in 1906 she spoke out against the proliferation of boarding and rooming houses kept by greedy erstwhile country dwellers or by women "who wish to fatigue themselves as little as possible with housework. . . [and are] attracted by indolence, popular novels, and four o'clock strolls down Saint-Denis and Saint-Catherine." She added, however, that "The scarcity of careers open to women wishing to earn a living explains the prodigious number of boarding houses that crop up each year."[29] She advised young women to "have a home of your own. . . Do not follow a fatal fashion, whose outcome is predictable; the soul of the Canadian family will desert you." Five years later, observing the upsurge in the construction of flats, she warned those contemplating the purchase of a triplex: "If you live on the third floor, you will have the privilege of beating your rugs over the heads of others, but heavenly justice will make sure you freeze in the winter and croak in the summer. Your children have no back yard. . ." Furthermore, families will witness their neighbours' alcoholism and quarrels. She firmly believed in the virtues of small-scale ownership for the working class and encouraged people to save money in order to buy their own houses, "safe from pitiless landlords, fearing neither the bailiff nor the tenant."[30]

As a columnist, she did not always have kind words for landlords, who passed their tax increases on to their tenants.[31] During the First World War, Julien Saint-Michel, whose working-class readers were mostly tenants, heaped scorn on those who took advantage of the war to raise rents[32]; she went so far as to call for the establishment of a tenants' league to confront the landlords and, especially, advised people to read their leases carefully and to avoid living in the same building as the owner.[33] Yet, speaking on behalf of the landlords themselves—she apparently owned two properties at the time—Circé-Côté alias Julien Saint-Michel denounced land taxes several times. As of the 1930s, when she herself had tenants, she unequivocally sided with landlords burdened by taxes and at the mercy of demanding and thoughtless tenants.[34]

In her last article on the subject, published in *Le Monde ouvrier* in 1936 and reprinted in *Le Canada* under the title "La joie d'être propriétaire" (The joys of landlordship),[35] she spelled out the drawbacks—untidy tenants who do not pay their rent, high taxes, exorbitant maintenance costs, accidents, insurance—which prompted many owners to get rid of their houses for the price of the mortgage or in exchange for an automobile. It is somewhat surprising to find this article in a trade union newspaper like *Le Monde ouvrier*. Even more surprising is Circé-Côté's opposition to taxes that will be used "to pay for the education of other people's children" or to maintain the city's infrastructures, water supply system, and sewers. This appears to be a classic case of someone adopting bourgeois values and of the triumph of the petite bourgeoisie. Despite all its disadvantages, she remained favourable to small-scale ownership and supported the proposal of the new premier, Maurice Duplessis, "to assist small landlords in order to thwart communism."[36]

Like many of her contemporaries who were revolted by the corruption of the Liberals after decades of their hold on the government, Éva Circé-Côté was banking on the renewal embodied by the Union nationale. In 1934, Paul Gouin and some progressive Liberals broke with the Liberal Party, which had been discredited by scandals, and founded the Action libérale nationale (ALN). The ALN, made up of reformist Liberals, was nationalistic and promised to enact social measures. For Circé-Côté it represented "a new generation" and "a new era" and rekindled her hopes; she wrote that the ALN "reconciled every ideal and fulfilled every aspiration."[37] Ahead of the 1936 elections, the ALN formed a coalition with the Conservative Party, headed by Maurice Duplessis, and together they founded a new party, the Union nationale. Taking a realistic approach, Duplessis endorsed the social regeneration programme of the ALN, and in return Paul Gouin's party benefited from the new party's financial resources. Torn between the ideals of one side and the pragmatism of the other, this tactical alliance was bound to fall apart. In the wake of the split and Gouin's departure on the eve of the August 1936 elections, Circé-Côté made no secret of her bitter disappointment. She even suggested that Gouin may have "let himself be bought off."[38] Faced with a thorny choice, she put her trust in Maurice Duplessis and the Union nationale, the party of change. Following the Unionists' victory on

"Eve Circé-Côté, literary woman," 1936, *National Reference Book on Canadian Men and Women.* BAnQ.

August 17, 1936, she, like the majority of Quebeckers, believed that "Mr. Duplessis does not wish to betray the trust we have placed in him. . . He will make old Quebec shine again. . . Provided he stands firm!"[39]

Taking a populist stance, Circé-Côté supported the Premier, who "was right to change tactics and to reform everything in his government that was contrary to the new mentality. It is by bonding people to the soil, to the land, that one nips strikes and revolutions in the bud."[40] This shift, from radical liberalism to support for the Union national, can be explained. The Liberals had squandered the "red" legacy. In power for thirty-five years, they had sunk into complacency, nepotism, and abuses of power, as was revealed by the Comité des comptes publics (Public accounts committee) in 1935. The Union nationale, especially its reformist wing represented by the Action libérale nationale, promised economic and social reforms that occulted the new party's conservative origins. Éva Circé-Côté was not the only one to be fooled, but she was soon disillusioned by what she called "the Duplessis-Villeneuve regime" and the ever closer connection between the throne and the altar.[41]

It was the international situation that captured her attention in 1936. She condemned the rape of Ethiopia by Mussolini's troops, referring to him as the "anti-Christ,"[42] as well as all forms of militarism. Commenting on the first anniversary of the Spanish Civil War, she wrote, "Violence attracts violence. Today, Spain is paying for the crime of having perpetrated an unimaginable massacre against the Indians after Christopher Columbus discovered America,"[43] but she made no mention of the threat of fascism. Amid the political transformations taking place in Quebec and the fears engendered by the rise of Nazism in Europe, her columns dealt with women's right to work, even in spheres reserved for men such as the civil service. She did not abandon the fight for women's enfranchisement, despite the fact that the eleventh bill on women's suffrage to be submitted to the Legislative Assembly had been voted down.[44] She also wrote two articles about the funeral of George V, which marked the end of an epoch.[45]

The last photo of her that has come down to us, dated 1936, accompanies the biographical entry for "Eve" Circé-Côté in the *National Reference Book on*

Canadian Men and Women. The hat has disappeared but her hair remains curly. And dark-coloured. Her eyelids have grown heavier, but her chin evinces energy and her expression has stayed resolute. The entry informs us that her pastimes are still music, painting, and singing.[46]

The second Congrès de la langue française (Convention of the French language) took place in June 1937, and Circé-Côté followed its deliberations very closely. With 8,000 participants registered and speakers from every corner of the French-speaking world, the convention caused a stir in nationalist circles. Éva Circé-Côté observed the debates more than she actually took part in them. Most of the speakers were associated with the Catholic nationalist movement, of which she had always disapproved. She could not identify with the Catholic state and the Catholic past celebrated in Lionel Groulx's lecture. The presentation on the deplorable situation of public libraries in Quebec was not made by her but by the very conservative librarian of the Library of Parliament in Ottawa, Félix Desrochers, and Georges-Henri Dagneau, a journalist for *L'Action Catholique*.[47] Over the years, Circé-Côté had grown disillusioned: "Patriotism no longer exists, only ambitions and appetites. The words duty, honesty, devotion, sacrifice are frozen, devoid of light, like dead stars," she wrote.[48]

She wrote less and less frequently, and as of 1936 her columns in *Le Monde ouvrier* did not always appear on the front page. She produced seventeen of them in 1937 and only four in 1938. Her last two articles, published in 1938 and 1942, were Christmas tales. Over the course of her career, she published some 1,760 columns, about twenty reviews and thirty stories, as well as four plays, the poems collected in *Bleu, Blanc, Rouge*, and a biography of Louis-Joseph Papineau. Never once had she complained about the difficulty of writing. Her thoughts, her essays had flowed out with enviable ease and vigour. However timely her writings may have been, they did not bring her significant material reward. As she wrote in 1937, "I certainly did not make any money with literature, and it gratifies me to have an empty purse but a clear conscience."[49]

She had written incognito ever since she had published her first poems. A pen name is never chosen haphazardly, but Circé-Côté never explained the reasons for her choices. Colombine, who, together with Pierrot and Harlequin, formed the famous trio created by the Commedia dell'arte, was an impulsive, mischievous, merry character that had inspired the poet Verlaine and the composer Robert Schumann. During the nineteenth century, a number of women writers, and even some men, in France and elsewhere, had used the name Colombine. Musette, meanwhile, brought to mind the bohemian life, one with which Éva Circé had surely identified. Fantasio, a name borrowed from Alfred de Musset, came along in 1910. Circé-Côté made this character androgynous, as she explained in the only recorded reference to her pseudonyms: "You are concerned about my sex, or a person's sex in general. You should know that I am a consciousness, a body of thought. Does it inhabit the creature 'who wears long hair but is short on ideas'? This is an unimportant detail, *monsieur* Cyrano, believe me."[50] Jean Ney, Jean Nay, and Arthur Maheu have kept the secret of their origins. Paul S. Bédard was likely a reference to Pierre-Stanislas Bédard (1792-1829), one of the founders of the newspaper *Le Canadien* and leader of the Parti canadien.[51] As for Julien Saint-Michel, there is nothing mysterious about this alias. As mentioned earlier, it was the name of her grandfather, who had kept the memory of the *Patriotes* alive in the family.[52] It was common practice to conceal one's identity behind more or less fictitious names. The one time that Éva Circé-Côté articulated her opinion of this practice was in an article on anonymous reviews: "When a journalist signs a piece with his own name or a transparent pseudonym not intended as a mask for hypocrisy, such as Loti and France, he endeavours to find the happy medium."[53] In time, the face behind the mask was revealed. In 1924, three years after the publication of the last issue of *Le Pays*, Éva Circé-Côté was identified as Fantasio in the membership list of the Association des auteurs canadiens.[54] The final unmasking came in 1939, when the director of *L'Aurore* enumerated all the periodicals to which she had contributed.

At the age of sixty-eight, Circé-Côté witnessed the outbreak of yet another war in Europe. For years she had feared a repetition of the previous global war. Several times she had spoken out against the inertia of the League of Nations, the rise of militarism, and the popularity of military toys with which another generation of soldiers was being brought up.[55] During the Depression she foresaw a war that would bring back prosperity at the cost of the lives of unemployed workers sent to the front.[56] On the assumption that she and the whole population had been tricked in 1914, she wrote that she now knew how politicians and financiers hatched wars; it was "impossible to recommence the tragedy whose plot and dénouement are known in advance," she declared.[57]

Instead of trench warfare, the new conflict would give rise to the bombardment of civilian populations from London to Dresden, labour camps, and extermination camps. On the home front, the consequences of the war—rationing and the employment of women, including married women this time—were more pronounced than had been the case in the First World War. In the autumn of 1939, Circé-Côté must have applauded the election of Abelard Godbout's Liberal government and his policies, which, decades later, would be called the first "quiet revolution." She was delighted when women won the right to vote in June 1940, "a progressive measure that will change the face of the world, which overnight was turned into a luminous disc," and published a blistering attack against Cardinal Villeneuve and his misplaced outbursts of anger against a portion of the human race."[58] Her lifelong battles were finally bearing fruit.

While the fall of France surely distressed her, it also brought about the return of her friend Georgine Boucher-Normandin.[59] Moreover, Éva herself was directly affected by the war. Her two nephews, Maria's sons, enlisted, and in 1942 her daughter Ève became the first Montreal woman to don the uniform of the Canadian Women's Auxiliary Air Force, soon to become the Royal Canadian Air Force Women's Division. For the first time, women could serve in the armed forces in a capacity other than nurse or member of the Medical Service. However, the seventeen thousand women who, like Ève Côté, enrolled in the air force, were not given combat roles, as indicated by their motto: "We Serve That Men May Fly." Most of the uniformed women continued to practise the professions they had worked at in civilian life.[60]

On a number of occasions Éva had fallen gravely ill from exhaustion, heart problems, or other ailments entailing periods of complete rest. She was growing old, seriously overweight, and letting herself go,[61] but ideas of death did not arise suddenly with aging; she had always thought about it, as evidenced by her numerous writings in which she reflects on death in all its variations. She had lived in an era where death was ubiquitous.[62] At the beginning of the twentieth century, average life expectancy was barely more than forty years. Work accidents were frequent and, in Montreal, one child out of three died within a year of being born. Furthermore, death was visible. Elderly people usually died at home, deathwatches brought together family members and neighbours, funeral processions would follow the casket, sometimes for over an hour, from the deceased's home to the Côte-des-Neiges Cemetery on Mount Royal. This was a common occurrence and it was not unusual for a family to lose more than one of its members in the same year. Cemeteries became preferred locations for Sunday afternoon strolls and picnics: "the favourite outing for family cars full of children and light-coloured dresses."[63] More than a hundred columns written by Éva Circé-Côté, who had lost many loved ones, dealt with death and the rituals surrounding it.

Starting in 1900, the month of November inspired her to reflect on death. In the sentimental prose style that she used during this period, she would address the deceased person directly: a fiancée, a mother, a father coming back into the world to contemplate betrayals and other unhappy episodes. Still a believer in eternal life at the time, she denied that she held a morose view of earthly existence and assailed the "disillusioned, bitter, cadaverous"

Schopenhauers.[64] She reiterated several times that without passion, without ideals, without love, there could be no life. On November 11, 1919 she reported on the two minutes of silence observed in honour of the war dead.[65] Over the following years she would describe deathwatches, ostentatious funerals—which she portrayed as three-day-long pieces of street theatre[66]— various cemeteries and their tombstones, and wrote several obituaries peppered with comments about social injustice. "Caste distinctions persist in this petrified world," she lamented.[67] At the Côte-des-Neiges cemetery, where the wealthy have the best view, she ridiculed "the magnificent mausoleums that immortalize the vanity of the parvenu. While still alive, he acquires a block of granite or wallows, in advance, in the pleasure of seeing his name inscribed in gold letters, with tears chiselled into the stone."[68] Seeing the "fateful cortège of little hearses climbing up Mount Royal each day," she contrasts those arrogant parades with the solitary parents holding the white casket on their knees.

The cemeteries of Boucherville, Saint-Luce, and Montebello perpetuated the inequalities prevailing in the society of the living. The discovery in 1901 of the "cemetery of the damned," where Pierre de Boucherville was interred, prompted Circé-Côté to call for tolerance.[69] A few years later, she denounced as disgraceful the practice of banishing unbaptized children, people who had been hanged, and Protestants to a separate part of the cemetery, and she assailed the mothers who submissively accepted such segregation.[70] When the Protestant cemetery of Mount Royal, which was open to non-Catholics, decided in 1910 to forbid Chinese funerals, Circé-Côté alias Jean Nay fulminated in *Le Pays*:

> Has anyone wondered what would happened to a follower of Confucius, Buddha, or Mohammed should they die in these parts, now that the Mount Royal cemetery has refused its hospitality to "barbarians"? . . . Would we not be ashamed in a country where the ground denies a grave to a dead person?[71]

Equally grotesque in her eyes were the hangings of criminals that made front-page headlines. Each execution prompted her to demand an end to capital punishment. Everything she wrote on the subject would be consistent with Colombine's statement of 1903: "Although I feel no tenderness toward murderers, I still prefer to see them pardoned than to see humankind sated by a punishment."[72]

For Éva Circé-Côté, the greatest injustice done by death was undoubtedly infant mortality. She was aware of the despair of families visited with such tragedies. She felt that what was called "the bad fairy," was not the result of bad luck; the causes were remediable, the problem was a moral and material one, and she wrote about this issue almost once a year.[73] A change in mothers' attitudes toward the death of their children was necessary, some control was needed over the number of births in a family, and this required education. The situation of the working class also had to be improved, because this was where infant mortality was most prevalent.

In one form or another, the Grim Reaper was always on her mind. In her funereal writings, thoughts of Pierre-Salomon were never far away. As she had once confided to Marcel Dugas, "From the depths of the abyss I have cried out to my husband, who at least still lives in me, and it seemed to me I had not cried out in vain. On more than one occasion I felt his presence envelope me and heard the sound of his voice in my ear."[74] She wrote about cremation, harking back to the scandal of 1909, when "this most hygienic type of funeral—with its vestige of paganism—was presented." She asked, "why refuse to pray before an urn rather than before a corpse?"[75] Many readers may have been won over to this means of disposing of the dead by Circé-Côté's description of the mass burials that took place each year in early May. Because the ground was frozen during the winter, the bodies—which numbered 2,487 in 1927—were held in a charnel house until the spring thaw.[76] A notice in the newspapers then asked the families to come bury their loved ones. "Starting in the morning, the mountain was webbed with a black lines" made up of grieving relatives who had come by car or streetcar. In 1916, after detailing this spectacle, Fantasio concluded: "The scene is so grotesque that it leaves no room for emotion."[77] Here, she was describing what she had experienced after her father's death in March 1911.

She wrote about not just the death of others—her mother's death had inspired some admirable lines—but her own as well, as in her letters to Marcel Dugas: "I have no regrets concerning the singular adventure of my arrival in the world, though it will end with my death."[78] Dugas, her soul-mate, would be the first to go, on January 7, 1947, at age sixty-four.[79] She who in 1916 had written, "The idea of ending one's days among the little sisters of the poor or in the care of one's children holds no appeal; it is a source of misery," stayed independent until the very end, with her cat keeping her company. A tenant found her collapsed in her kitchen on May 4, 1949.[80]

Nothing at all is known about the last days of this self-declared freethinking woman. She lost her sister Maria in 1943. At the end of that same year, her daughter Ève left the armed forces and returned to Montreal. She converted her mother's large house into a rooming house. In 1947, Ève Côté became one of the first female real estate brokers and opened an office on St. James Street.[81]

"—A large family, I s'pose?—Well, I'll tell ya, I had seventeen children, but thirteen of them died . . .—Oh, don't fret, Missus Cayeux, those po'r li'l angels are purty happy there!" Le Pays, September 14, 1912. BanQ.

Few Québécois authors stayed true to their youthful materialism throughout their lives. Arthur Buies, the iconoclast, began to slough it off when he was thirty-five.[82] Did Éva Circé-Côté, who in 1920 had written, "It is almost impossible to die here without confessing,"[83] remain Voltarian to the last? Or had she converted to Protestantism? Even though she was very close to the French-speaking Protestant community, it is doubtful that she joined one religion after leaving another. Her funeral service took place in Saint Jean United Church on Sainte-Catherine Street. She was buried in the Montreal Memorial Park secular cemetery in Ville Saint-Laurent.[84]

With the help of Georgine Boucher-Normandin's daughter, Lucienne Boucher-Dumas, Ève Côté cleaned out her mother's apartment. It overflowed with papers, unpublished works, objects accumulated over the years—sixty-eight years worth of baggage. The clutter is such that, as Lucienne Boucher would admit years later, "we had to destroy [all of it]" because "it would have taken two years to sort everything out."[85] The woman that critics had compared to Séverine and George Sand, the one referred to as "our female Balzac,"[86] whom Jean Charbonneau had called "the Canadian madame de Staël," whom Robert de Roquebrune, himself given to excesses, described as "exaggerated," vanished along with her manuscripts. Gone too were the letters and other documents that would have made it possible to do justice to a life of writing. Already, she had passed out of the collective memory and no more than a few brief announcements of her death appeared in the newspapers.

> Better to inhabit a cemetery than this sad society, with these shadows that call themselves men. The immortality of our soul depends on you, if the works that we accomplish outlive the dissolution of our being. There are those who will live forever because the creations of their genius possess an immortal quality. Those who loved deeply and who until the end devoted themselves to the good of their brethren are exempt from the horror of the general law. If their names are forgotten, it matters not, for the fruit of their noble actions will endure. You are dead when your heart no longer throbs before the spectacle of human misery and when you are powerless to console those who weep.[87]

* * *

This book aims to be more than simply a biography; it proposes, somewhat ambitiously, to open a window on the progressive Quebec of the first decades of the twentieth century. For too long, the agent providing access to this minority current, Éva Circé-Côté, has been forgotten, and it behoves us to restore her to her rightful place in the cultural and social history of Quebec. Her effacement cannot be ascribed solely to the negligence of historians or the indifference of the generations that came after her, but also to the deliberate concealment of the writer under numerous pseudonyms.

From the very early days of the twentieth century, Circé-Côté proudly assumed her role as a literary woman. Can she be considered a French intellectual? Based on the criteria enunciated by the historian of French intellectuals, Christophe Charles, she certainly qualifies as one.[88] According to a widely accepted definition, the term refers to a person who, having acquired a reputation or recognition as an authority in a field such as literature, law, or science, speaks out publicly on the strength of her notoriety on other issues. The status of intellectual depends to some extent on one's education, involvement in public affairs, and recognition. In the twentieth century the intellectual is more than a literary person; in keeping with her or his convictions, the intellectual participates in the ongoing political or social debates. No woman of Circé-Côté's generation could avail herself of a higher education, which is the primary condition to achieve the status of intellectual, but some made their convictions known, openly took positions in the agora and the press, and won the appreciation of their contemporaries. The writings of Éva Circé-Côté, solidly anchored in her epoch, aimed to guide society in the direction of progress. In different publications, under different pen names, Circé-Côté made a political commitment; she wished to guide her contemporaries, to draw them out of their apathy, to educate them and enlighten them so as to prepare them for nothing less than liberty. Yet it cannot be said that she used her prestige as a woman of letters to champion just and emancipatory values and causes, since she hid behind pseudonyms.

Though she wrote in various genres on diverse subjects, Circé-Côté had several occupations, being unable to live exclusively by writing. This was true of all intellectuals, who often earned their living through a liberal profession such as law or medicine—the examples of Gonzalve Desaulniers and René de Cotret come to mind—and, like Godfroy Langlois, sometimes attained a political position. But these professions were closed to women. This left journalism, and it was as a columnist that Circé-Côté the librarian pursued her second career unbeknownst to most of her contemporaries. It was there she waged her great battles for liberalism, patriotism, secularism, and feminism, and these are the themes developed in the following chapters.

PART TWO

CHAPTER 6

LIBERALISM

He adored in the temple of Nature, for him Reason was divine, and Progress its prophet.
— ADRIAN DESMOND AND JAMES MOORE, *Darwin: The Life of a Tormented Evolutionist*

Liberalism is no longer a fixed star. It oscillates from one camp to the other, evolves in all directions, it is a shooting star, an ephemeral meteor.
— ÉVA CIRCÉ-CÔTÉ, *Papineau*

ÉVA CIRCÉ-CÔTÉ was first and foremost a liberal. She embraced this ideology born of the Enlightenment and saw herself as an heir to a legacy which both socialists and liberals considered their own. Her career in journalism started on the cusp of a century full of promise: "the Century of Canada," Liberal Prime Minister Wilfrid Laurier promised in 1904. Circé-Côté's liberalism was an entirely conscious choice. She expressed her views on every facet of liberalism, endorsing the ideology as well as the political movement that laid claim to it. While she unreservedly espoused the ideas of Voltaire and Condorcet, she nevertheless exercised her critical faculties when it came to supporting the political parties of Laurier, Bourassa, Gouin, and Taschereau.

To understand the forces underpinning Circé-Côté's intellectual commitment, one needs to go back to the Enlightenment thinkers and their main ideas, to which she constantly alluded.[1] Her frame of reference was critical reason as articulated in eighteenth century France and introduced into Quebec in the following century. Her first model was "France, the source of light and progress that all modern civilization has drawn on."[2] She declared: "To believe in France is to believe in reason,"³ which was the foundation of the philosophy that inspired her. Illuminated by reason, the individual is no longer subject to blind forces, dogmas, or superstitions, and hence refuses to be constrained by religion and the state.

Reason enables progress, which is the keystone of human history. The glow of the Enlightenment endures in the belief in progress that pervades liberal thought. In his *Esquisse d'un tableau historique des progrès de l'esprit humain* (Outlines of an Historical View of the Progress of the Human Mind) de Condorcet proposes to demonstrate

> that no bounds have been fixed to the improvement of the human faculties; that the perfectibility of man is absolutely indefinite; that the progress of this perfectibility, henceforth above the control of every power that would impede it, has no other limit than the duration of the globe upon which nature has placed us. The course of this progress may doubtless be more or less rapid, but it can never be retrograde, at least while the earth retains its situation in the system of the universe.⁴

Progress comes in the shape of scientific advances and economic growth, but it is no less a factor in the social and individual spheres. For liberalism is centred on the individual, and the individual is malleable. Ever since Darwin had demonstrated the evolution of species, disciples like Herbert Spencer claimed that by applying reason to not just material development but to moral evolution as well, social relationships will progress in the great movement toward a better world. Thus, Éva Circé-Côté fully supported what historians call the "Whig" interpretation of history, which sees history marching inexorably toward a more democratic, more prosperous world.⁵

This modern reading of history is a dynamic vision, open to change, one that runs through Circé-Côté's writings, which seem poised on the threshold of an unstoppable transformation: "Those familiar with the psychology of [French] Canadians know that we must react against our harmful tendency to go back, to live in the past, to look at the setting sun rather than watch for its awakening."⁶ Yet this forward-looking conception of human existence does not deny the past, and Circé-Côté tried to maintain a balance between tradition and innovation. The latter could call on a past more progressive than the present, and Circé-Côté drew directly on the legacy handed down by the likes of Papineau, Dessaulles, and Doutre, because "one must descend into the past to discover genuine liberalism."⁷ The spirit of 1837 and 1848, the spirit of *Le Canadien* and *L'Avenir* continued to act as an impetus for progress. "Work is the means, but progress is the goal," Louis-Antoine

Dessaulles, president of the Institut canadien, had declared in 1862.[8] Arthur Buies gave a lecture on progress at that same institute.[9] Progress asserts itself in scientific and technological advances and is embodied in the economic expansion and the modernization of the city inhabited by Éva Circé-Côté.

As a catalyst of change, progress is, on the one hand, an irreversible force that obeys its own laws, yet it is sustained, on the other, by human actions aimed at effecting reforms and shaping the course of history. As Circé-Côté understood it in 1907, progress is blind, demanding, and implacable. Here is what she wrote in *Le Journal de Françoise*: "When it has extracted from us that which will hasten its triumph, it casts us off like a fruit whose pulp has been sucked dry."[10] In commenting on the demise of Roger Valois, the director of *Le Pays*, who died of tuberculosis at the age of twenty-nine, she reiterated: "Life and progress are pitiless; when they have extracted from a person all the sap needed to nourish his work, they break him."[11] Only enlightened reason can judge the meaning of progress, and such judgment is contingent on freedom of thought—thought free of dogmas and diktats, and reason that demands the separation of church and state. It followed, for Circé-Côté, that individuals must be educated and their education must be unfettered from religious beliefs. Cures must stop being attributed to novenas, hallucinations must not be transformed into miracles, and war must not be seen as punishment for sins.[12] "Everything is subject to reason. Everything must be analyzed, both our beliefs and our feelings, if we are to grasp the why of things."[13] Years later, she stressed that "We should never call on the supernatural to provide an immediate solution to problems that science has not yet solved."[14] To arrive at a materialist interpretation of the world, we must detach ourselves from religious or superstitious explanations; in a word, we must educate ourselves.

Thus, the first reform that progress requires is education, which is essential in order to make an informed judgment; hence, like the nineteenth-century *Rouges* [liberals], Circé-Côté insistently called for a compulsory, free, and secular education system, which she regarded as the cornerstone of both individual emancipation and social development. She did not fail to point out that Quebec trailed behind France, Great Britain, the United States, and, at the end of the nineteenth century, the other Canadian provinces; one after the other, they had made school attendance compulsory until the age of twelve, then fourteen, and, eventually, sixteen. Circé-Côté's was not overstating her case, far from it: according to the 1901 report of the Conseil de l'instruction publique (Council on public education), out of the 173,899 pupils enrolled in Catholic primary schools, only 121,290 actually attended classes.[15]

Even though she believed "in the immanent justice of things, in the triumph of light over darkness," reasonable individuals, and not chance or fate, were ultimately responsible for their destinies.[16] The great wheel of progress needs to be pushed. In spite of her allusions to heredity, Circé-Côté maintained her faith in human perfectibility, stating, "if hereditary incapacity existed among [French] Canadians, we would not undertake this campaign of moral regeneration in the 'Land.'"[17] Moreover, it is the duty of all citizens, and not just the elite, to put their shoulders to the wheel.

In Circé-Côté's view, political structures must reflect the foregoing postulates. An advanced human society is an egalitarian community; consequently, privileges must be abolished and a democracy must be established in which all individuals, without distinction, can choose representatives that are answerable to them. Power is thus delegated to elected officials, who, in principle, are enlightened and deserving of the citizens' trust. At every level, from the premiership to the most humble position, merit replaces inheritance and acquired privilege. The monarchy is an anachronism, whereas the republic "throughout the world is the form of government that, for the time being, best fulfils the democratic ideal of modern peoples."[18] For Circé-Côté, as for many liberals before her—John Stuart Mill comes to mind—the exercise of democracy remained contingent on education: "democracy is possible only through compulsory education."[19] In 1924, lamenting the failures of liberal thought, she wrote:

> We believe that democracy itself, rather than parties, must be blamed for the decline of the liberal concept and for the political incoherence over the past half-century. Although it is the child of liberty, it nevertheless impedes the reign of liberty. Universal suffrage, for a young people deprived of the benefits of compulsory education, obstructs its evolution.[20]

A few years later, going even further in her plea for the prior education of electors, she proposed the introduction of a "voter's permit" so as to exclude vagrants, ex-convicts, the illiterate, speculators, and the heads of trusts.[21] No members of these groups deserved to participate in democracy. Nor were ignorant members of parliament any more deserving. She saw certain elected officials from remote regions as obstacles to progress, a rear guard,

> [...] whose watchword is to block any attempt at emancipation on the part of a few distinguished minds lost in this institution and thwarted

by the ignoramuses, primitives, illiterates, incompetents, and pack-saddled donkeys sent to us from the backwoods and the swamps.[22]

A people lacking judgment elects incompetent and, too often, corrupt politicians, who "are our own condemnation."[23] Notwithstanding the smugness of her remarks, she was voicing the frustration of progressives who saw their efforts to bring in reforms foiled in the Legislative Assembly by pious and submissive colleagues unwilling to offend their spiritual leaders.[24] Moreover, the differences between city-dwellers and country folk are not the only ones that would fade with the advancement of education; those between social classes would diminish as well. For Circé-Côté, "common and equal education" would guarantee social harmony, and, ever the optimist, she foresaw the end of the rivalry between the daughters of the bourgeoisie and those of the working class.[25]

In the first decade of the twentieth century, progressive social reformers such as Éva Circé-Côté took part in various reform movements throughout North America: urban reform involving the fight against corruption and to ameliorate physical and moral conditions in the cities; social reforms and the improvement of the living standards and hygiene of working-class communities; moral reforms including the enforcement of the Sunday holiday and the eradication of prostitution and gambling; and, finally, the elimination of the evils concomitant with economic development, industrialization, and urbanization. With indomitable optimism, Circé-Côté never stopped believing that these reforms could be achieved.

Circé-Côté was an artist, and in her eyes there was an aesthetic aspect to progress. Her quest was twofold: Truth—that is, Justice—and Beauty, "one of the thousand forms of progress, one of the thousand stages of democracy."[26] This is a beauty available to the people, one that wants to be taught and popularized, as in the free courses in drawing, sculpture, painting, and decoration that were given at the Monument-National and that ought to have included cinema. "We demand the right of the masses to be initiated to beauty," she wrote in arguing for outdoor film screenings on Mount Royal.[27] It is unfortunate that she, a musician, painter, and poet in her own right, did not discuss more often the aesthetics of her period, other than in her all too rare literary reviews.

Her optimistic view of history endured until the First World War. Yet Circé-Côté's convictions were not shaken by the outbreak of hostilities; on the contrary, amid the enthusiasm of August 1914, the Kaiser personified the enemy of progress, which in itself was enough to justify the declaration of war.[28] If the British "beat Wilhelm today, it is to remove that spanner from the works of progress."[29] But the war continued beyond her worst predictions. "Is this the end of progress?" Fantasio asked, and "the collapse of our fine theories?"[30] She read Henri Barbusse and Romain Rolland, both revolted by the war. In 1917, when conscription was looming, she distanced herself even farther from militarism. In answer to a Protestant minister who prophesied that the war would give rise to a new world, she wrote, "it seems to me there are ways to improve human races without destroying them." The tragedy of the battlefields undermined her linear vision of history. She came to doubt that the war could hasten "peoples' evolution. It is possible that civilization will undergo a regression of several centuries.... The time has passed when we believed that bloodletting brought relief to the sick."[31] The horrors of trench warfare, the suffering of civilian populations, and the extent of the slaughter unsettled progressive certitudes. What if the twentieth century were hardly any better than the nineteenth? "Oh, and to think that people wrung their hands over the poor nineteenth century!"[32] Circé-Côté was forced to reflect on this backslide in human evolution. But these were only accidents in the course of history; as a "voluntarist," she refused to give in to pessimism. Order arises out of chaos and confusion.[33] After the war, she exclaimed: "Nothing can weaken our radiant optimism. All that blood was not shed in vain."[34]

Still, the war represented a reversal in the inexorable course of the great wheel. The economic depression of the 1930s constituted another moment of retreat and doubt. Was progress not supposed to eliminate human misery and ensure unlimited economic growth? Together with many of her contemporaries, Éva Circé-Côté saw technological innovations, such as electricity, the automobile, and radio, as sources of well-being for the population. Industrialization and the intensification of agriculture engendered a rise in living standards, which, though far from constant, was not put in doubt. The crisis that began in 1929 sapped this vision of progress once again. Seeing the rise in unemployment in 1928—the lack of jobs had become apparent well before the Crash in October 1929—and "the failure of efforts to do away with poverty and fight indigence," she wavered and wondered: might society be evolving in a different direction from nature?[35] Her apprehensions coincided with a general crisis of Western capitalism and the Canadian liberal order, which was challenged on the right by Catholics and on the left by the rise of social-democracy in Western Canada and the growing attraction of communism in the industrial cities and mining regions.[36] Galloping impoverishment and social inequalities caused her to question social evolution: "Progress has led to economic anarchy.... [T]he machine is broken and malfunctioning."[37] She expressed doubts, but these only served to strengthen her faith in the enhancement of humanity sooner or later, and her conviction that civilization maintained as its "eternal ideal... the improvement of humanity."[38]

Without enlightened reason, individuals are subject to the influence of prejudice and demagoguery and are unable to assess what they need to do in order to improve their well-being and take part in the advancement of society, for "free inquiry contains the seed of all social demands."[39] Thought unshackled from preconceived ideas, prejudices, and diktats, is grounded in knowledge. If reason is to be unchained from religious beliefs and superstitions in order for the individual to choose well, he must be exposed to a host of opinions, which he must be able to discuss. Hence the importance of freedom of the press and the right of association. Individual freedom—the right to think and act freely—is, after progress, the second foundational pillar of liberalism. This freedom involves the shedding of conventions, and Circé-Côté repeatedly deplored the absence of independent thinking in Quebec.[40]

Freedom implies tolerance. Voltaire, whom Circé-Côté quoted abundantly, refers to "reason, which slowly but unfailingly enlightens men. Such reason is gentle, it is human, and it fosters tolerance."[41] This tolerance, premised on religious toleration, inspired her to produce some beautiful pages on Protestantism. It is a tolerance opposed to censorship—of newspapers by Mgr Bruchési and of library books, for example—and supportive of the right of association, in particular that of the Freemasons' lodges, one that accepts the coexistence of different communities and condemns anti-Semitism. Circé-Côté believed that we must treat others, more specifically, minority groups, "as we would wish to be treated; otherwise we would fearfully await terrible reactions in the future... we would fall on our knees and beg for the freedoms that we deny [others] today."[42] But there was no room for liberal tolerance in the religious mindset of that era.

The extolment of reason and individual freedom and the appeals for tolerance were sure to elicit a response from the religious authorities, for whom liberalism was redolent of hell. Pius IX, in the 1864 encyclical *Quanta Cura*, had spoken out against freedom of worship and conscience as well as the separation of church and state. The encyclical was followed by the *Syllabus errorum*, a summary of the eighty primary errors of that period, the final one being this: "The Roman Pontiff can and must be reconciled and achieve a compromise with progress, liberalism, and modern civilization." The papal catalogue likewise denounced liberalism, rationalism, religious freedom, as well as secret societies, socialism, and communism.[43] For a long time, the encyclical was quoted from the pulpit throughout Quebec, especially during elections. In the twentieth century, after the Liberal Party had cleansed its reputation, Pius IX's *Syllabus* continued to serve as a reference in the struggle against socialism and communism.

What happens when individual freedom comes into conflict not with religious authorities but the state? Can constraints be imposed so that good may triumph? Depending on the circumstances, Circé-Côté put forward either inviolable individual liberty or the equally crucial common good. She thus distanced herself from the classical liberalism associated with unbridled laisser-faire and even further from a libertarian society. The opposition between the state and individual liberty is not intrinsic to liberalism, and Circé-Côté stayed true to the first liberal philosophers, who regarded the state as their representative and ally.[44] In his panegyric on reason, Voltaire states: "it stifles discord, reinforces virtue, makes obedience to laws agreeable, even more than force upholds them."[45] If laws are produced by the reason of the people's representatives, the people cannot do otherwise but follow them. A century later, John Stuart Mill recognized that government action can prevent harm to others.[46] Moreover, liberty needs the state for protection against intolerance and ecclesiastical power.

The tension between individual freedom and the common good runs through all of Circé-Côté's thinking. In the context of Quebec's manifold liberalism, those who welcomed state intervention were labelled radicals. But the collectivist current was, in Circé-Côté's opinion, nothing other than liberalism properly understood. Accordingly, writing under the pseudonym Paul S. Bédard when *Le Pays* was founded in 1910, she explained that those who supported the newspaper's programme "are purely and simply liberals"[47] and not radicals, as they were called in the conservative press. So it should come as no surprise that she identified herself as at once a liberal and an admirer of Jean Jaurès. Her liberalism was closer to the kind espoused at the time by the left wing of Democratic Party in the United States, that is, social-democracy, and to that of John Maynard Keynes, which, in Great Britain and Canada would eventually engender the welfare state.

As a reformer, Circé-Côté naturally supported state intervention, not just to defend property, regulate the monopolies, protect the vulnerable, provide secular education, but also to exercise control over the social sphere: water treatment, public health, vaccination, management of municipal expenditures. In 1919 she proposed the introduction of mandatory social insurance, whose premiums would be levied on wages, but did not consider this an encroachment on freedom because it was meant to ensure the citizens' future happiness.[48] It was also the state's responsibility to prevent abuses of power, and, in the name of justice, Circé-Côté persistently decried the corruption of elected officials. Freedom of choice in private life, she also contended, was not unlimited. Parents should be obliged to send their children to school: "to overcome their selfish resistance, the law must be applied not through supplication but with orders and threats and, if need be, punishment."[49]

This wish to see a strict approach applied can be observed in Circé-Côté's eugenicist tendencies. She was not the first progressive to believe that restricting reproduction to the mentally and physical sound could remedy social ills. In 1929 she devoted a column to choosing a spouse "fit for marriage," that is, free of transmittable "defects" such as dwarfism or tuberculosis.[50] In a more evolved society, where women's education and financial independence would allow them to choose their partner freely—that is, fully aware of the relevant facts—a prenuptial medical examination would verify the spouses' good health, because the goal of marriage is "to give excellent citizens to the homeland and to perpetuate the race's character."[51] Contrary to the English-speaking countries and some European ones, Quebec did not spawn a major eugenicist movement. Progressive physicians, social reformers, and progressives such as Beatrice and Sidney Webb in England or Margaret Sanger in the United States, were seduced by this pseudo-science, which they regarded as one of the solutions to human misery, going so far as to recommend the sterilization of people deemed "unfit" or "defective." During the twenties, the Birth Control League in Ontario and British Columbia campaigned for the limitation of births as well as the sterilization of people with "flaws" considered hereditary.[52] Circé-Côté never endorsed this type of measure; abandoning Spencer, she declared in 1920: "the system put forward by Darwin does not apply to communities."[53] Contrary to some eugenicists who referred to the pseudo-science to support their prejudices, Circé-Côté favoured demographic control without actual coercion but through education. She expressed no racism or lack of compassion toward the underprivileged but rather a desire to improve the human condition through methods based on genetic science as it was understood at the time. In 1929, "freely chosen maternity" did not yet exist in Catholic societies, nor can one speak of free choice for young people who were deprived of an enlightened education and uninformed of the hereditary consequences of their union.

State intervention, however, should be circumscribed, according to Circé-Côté. For example, the movement to prohibit alcoholic beverages and commercial forms of recreation on Sundays infringed on individual freedom,[54] as did outlawing prostitution, when the clients' rights were at issue. But she was in favour of regulating prostitution for public health reasons. When it was a matter of gender equality, as a feminist she did not hesitate to raise the argument of individual freedom, whereby woman are entitled to do paid work hitherto restricted to men.[55] On the other hand, working conditions, especially where women were concerned, should be regulated and even safeguarded by the sate.

How is one to reconcile Éva Circé-Côté's liberal credo, her defence of individual freedom, and her collaboration with a trade union newspaper? As Julien Saint-Michel, she contributed to *Le Monde ouvrier*, the organ of the Montreal Trades and Labour Council, whose editor-in-chief, Gustave Francq, was appointed in 1919 to head the Commission du salaire minimum des femmes (Commission on the minimum wage for women), which directly implied state intervention in labour relations. Francq had gone from being a socialist in his youth to openly embracing liberalism without ever rejecting the role of the state in labour relations. It should be recalled that the labour organization for which he worked was affiliated to the staunchly anti-socialist American Federation of Labor. In a paper meant for workers, Circé-Côté did not have to align herself with a Marxist current, even though socialism positioned itself at the vanguard of the defence of workers' interests: "The eradication of pauperism through state intervention . . . is just socialism at its best, proclaiming that all the ills of humanity can be cured through legislation."[56] She generally endorsed protective measures for workers, women and men alike, but she could also express reservations, for instance, on the issue of a minimum wage for women: "The minimum wage must not destroy all kinds of businesses and companies or, especially, violate individual freedom, even for the most respectable reasons."[57] She dealt head on with the relationship between the state and freedom in a 1934 column on the regulation of employment for youths under eighteen. To those who invoked parental authority in their denunciation of state interference she replied: "political interference in the sanctuary of the family affects natural rights and individual freedom. . . . Since when is one entitled to do harm?"[58] In her ranking of grand principles, the greatest good for the greatest number trumps the freedom of individuals.

Individual liberty leads to democracy and protects property, which democracy guarantees. Indifferent or sceptical toward collective property, Circé-Côté, as we have seen, defended both small landlords and small business-owners. In the same petit bourgeois line of thought, she regarded saving and foresight as valuable virtues.[59] She had no use for the detachment from material things preached by the Catholic Church. Scientific progress, access to property, and even personal enrichment were commendable goals. Unusual phenomena must no longer be attributed to supernatural causes, but could be explained by psychology, geology, or other sciences. She derided Catholic teachings, which disdained money and lauded "the grandness of poverty, the nobility of filth, the glory of rags." On the contrary, "there is nothing abject about gold as a reward for labour, thrift, initiative, and the entrepreneurial spirit," adding, somewhat provocatively, "it was used to line sacred vessels."[60] The freedom to grow wealthy, protected by the state, is as fundamental as freedom of opinion; it is necessary for the success of capitalism, which she nevertheless constantly decried elsewhere.[61]

Among the many facets of liberalism, economic liberalism, so crucial for philosophers, occupied the least amount of space in Circé-Côté's columns. She of course commented on municipal budgets, prices, and wages, but was not very interested in free trade as such. She opposed tariffs, which constituted the cornerstone of the country's economic development ever since the national policy had been adopted in 1873. *Le Monde ouvrier* supported free trade, and the unions repeatedly argued that tariffs did not improve the workers' situation when applied to US commodities. It entailed higher prices in Canada and did nothing to check emigration to the States.[62] Faced with the threat of another global war, Circé-Côté was convinced that the untrammelled circulation of goods fostered harmony in international relations.[63]

Capitalism and liberalism go hand in hand, and Éva Circé-Côté's lived in a period of company mergers and the expansion of conglomerates. Classical liberalism leads to mergers, but radical or progressive liberalism was leery of monopolies—or, as they were called, trusts—which affected workers "like a whale providing little fish with warm and comfortable shelter by swallowing them."[64] In her columns, she scrutinized the effects of free enterprise on citizens' lives, protested against the rising cost of consumer goods, and denounced the consequences of mergers in the food industry.[65] In their struggle to maintain their material well-being, citizens must protect themselves against the power of large corporations. To avoid being crushed by forces they can neither control nor understand, they must stay informed and resist the apathy and docility preached by their spiritual leaders.

Life is a battle, and on countless occasions Circé-Côté used Herbert Spencer's famous expression "struggle for life," which she would quote in English because it was for her so closely associated with the Anglo-Saxon mentality. This struggle was one for which French Canadians, especially women, were singularly ill-prepared. The concept was never defined, but it implied a confrontation, one based on competition, between individuals and social classes, which opened the door to every sort of exploitation. Hence the need to equip oneself through education, in technical school, and at the library. The least prepared for battle were "the docile and obedient sons," "rich kids," children raised in orphanages, those who find themselves too soon on the labour marker, apprentices, young women lacking education, and workers, those "heroes of work," who almost inevitably become victims of the struggle for survival. The best equipped for this battle were the British, "fed on liberty," Americans, "hardy innovators, for whom the word 'impossible' is meaningless," Jews and immigrants aspiring for success (and enrolled in Montreal's English-language schools).[66]

Property, education, and the struggle for life gave rise to economic and social inequalities, which would result in the assertion of collective demands by those who gained the least advantage from free enterprise. But liberalism rejected class struggle and, because it conceived of progress as a gradual process, preferred reforms to social confrontations. On the strength of her faith in human perfectibility, Circé-Côté was wholly on the side of moderation. "Far from wishing to revolutionize the world, I only wish to humanize it by getting individuals to improve themselves," she wrote early on under the pen name Colombine.[67] Though averse to the class struggle, she still identified with the working class, and, as Julien Saint-Michel, she often wrote, "we workers,"[68] and wondered, "[w]hy do we not elect workers to represent us in the legislative bodies? . . . [i]t is in the interests of the workers, and it should be their ambition, to have a large number of working-class members of parliament."[69]

Éva Circé-Côté discussed class relations very early on. The first time the word "capitalist" appeared in one of her columns in June 1901, her portrayal was unsparing: "The capitalist prefers substantial revenues to the appreciation of his peers. He is moved only in the presence of gold; the more he accumulates the more his soul closes up; he draws everything toward himself, oppresses and absorbs everything with no compassion for the suffering of others; he is always inclined toward whatever stays low to the ground. . . ."[70] During the war, the Kaiser was the plaything of the capitalists, while, in Canada, the Borden government was under the control of millionaires, who, she wrote, had turned into profiteers, *trustards*, "insatiable vampires amassing millions stolen from the people."[71] Capitalism was "this octopus that keeps us in its clutches."[72]

For Circé-Côté, supporting Jaurès did not seem at odds with liberalism. The historian Ian Mackay, who specializes in the history of the left, has shown how socialism was then seen as participating in the science of evolution, as a stage—possibly the last—in the march of progress.[73] But her views on Bolshevism are none the less surprising. In March 1917, she declared: "The Russian revolution is the most sensational, the most fabulous thing to have taken place."[74] And in May of the same year she regarded Bolshevism as pointing the way for the peoples wishing to shake off tyranny.[75] At the end of 1919, however, she had curbed her enthusiasm and was expressing reservations about the Bolshevik Revolution:

> We must not wrap Bolshevism and socialism in the same contempt. The former is chaos, while the latter prepares the ground for global brotherhood. One proceeds through violence, the other through persuasion. The first wants the immediate regeneration of the world, the second wishes to achieve this through persuasion . . . we may be witnessing the early dawn of those happy days."[76]

In the years following the Bolshevik revolution, Circé-Côté was careful not to rush to condemn the new regime. Still, her discourse was not cut and dried. Looking back at her earlier reservations, in 1921 she reiterated that progress emerges out of chaos and "[w]hat does it matter that governments collapse and sovereigns are massacred if millions of people have won their freedom."[77] This conception of communism was linked to Tolstoy and the pantheon of thinkers whom she glorified.

That her sympathies leaned heavily toward socialism was clear when she challenged Mgr Gauthier's condemnation of it in accordance with the Church's encyclicals. Under the Julien Saint-Michel byline, she reminded him of the spirit of the first Christians, comparing the writings of the church fathers to the precepts of Tolstoy, Marx, Proudhon, and Jaurès.[78] In light of the successive economic depressions, she scorned charity, banking instead on redistributive justice.[79]

Circé-Côté's liberalism would not remain compatible with the Soviet experience for very long, and over the years her socialist sympathies waned. When the international unions withdrew their support for the Winnipeg strikers, and the police violently crushed their general strike, Julien Saint-Michel followed her newspaper's editorial policy, stating that, while tyranny may have justified the revolution in Russia, here, where the bosses had working-class backgrounds, "there is no reason to attack a man, who, by dint of work, initiative, and energy, has built up a solid business after leaving behind his plebeian origins."[80] As of October 1919, she called for a "powerful party capable of realizing what is called the chimera of socialism, because today Bolshevism is compromising it and loosening its hold on people's souls."[81] Furthermore, in a Catholic province, where major newspapers echoed the Church's prohibitions, socialism would be able to take root only if it makes a concession to the religious affiliation of the majority of citizens. When *L'Action catholique* (which had replaced *L'Action sociale*) enjoined its readers to choose between being "[e]ither socialist or catholic," Julien Saint-Michel replied: "Those who have attempted to reconcile theories of socialism with faith have done more to consolidate peace than the dogmatists, the demagogues, the sowers of discord, who seek only to divide in the hope of ruling." She added this appeal: "Good Quebeckers, be socialists and good Catholics."[82] This was the only realistic approach to establishing oneself in a society steeped in religion.

Éva Circé-Côté, alias Julien Saint-Michel was soon to follow the same path as her editor Gustave Francq, who, starting in 1921, went from socialism to liberalism, from the Parti ouvrier (Workers' Party) to the Parti libéral.[83] The revolution had lost its attraction and workers must be turned away from it with higher wages.[84] When she later opposed the death sentences of Nicola Sacco and Bartolomeo Vanzetti in 1927, it was "less because they are socialists than because they belong to the great family of humanity."[85] Moreover, their execution, their martyrdom, could but foster Bolshevism. Tolstoy's ideal, communism, had become a scourge.

It was not until 1928, ten years after it was first published, that Circé-Côté discovered Mackenzie King's *Industry and Humanity: A Study in the Principles Under-Lying Industrial Reconstruction*, translated into French as *La Question sociale et le Canada: industrie et humanité*.[86] She reproduced a letter from one of her readers—very possibly herself—who was delighted by this tome of nearly six hundred pages on industrial relations and the ways to regulate them while at the same time preventing workers from being exploited: "a gospel of love," "a new Sermon on the Mount," a sign that "liberalism, eclipsed in Quebec by thick clouds for fifty years, is reappearing on the horizon."[87] The anonymous reader underscored the author's appeal—King was the great-grandson of William Lyon Mackenzie, leader of the rebellion in Upper Canada—for justice and compassion, and his confidence that education could bring about social change. The young King, just like Circé-Côté, called for profound social change; they both sometimes saw themselves as revolutionaries, but always within the framework of a "liberal revolution."[88] The fact she attributed such great importance to this liberal treatise on worker-employer relations attests to how far she had come in twenty years.

With the Great Depression stoking the militancy of Canadian communists, Circé-Côté borrowed the language of the deeply anti-communist international unions to denounce the Soviets.[89] Her wish in 1931 was to see the "trade unions grow in number, because the more there are the more impossible Bolshevism becomes."[90] Meanwhile, however, the Crisis and the exploitation of workers nurtured the far left. An admirer of Jaurès, she did not hesitate in her columns to take advantage of the prevailing anticommunism to argue in favour of women's suffrage, because only the influence of women could "stave off the imminent revolution. They are all that humanity can count on now."[91] Her anticommunism led to her support Maurice Duplessis, elected premier for the first time in August 1936.[92] As for the Soviet Union, she was still reserving judgment at that time. In 1937, when invited to write an article on communism, she refused on these grounds: "I never discuss things I know nothing about." Her sage advice was "to wait and let time solve the Russian problem. If communism is not viable it will perish of its own accord, without our having to kill it."[93]

Circé-Côté did not reject the Soviet regime as such, because, despite all its excesses, it was part of the march of progress. "What will emerge from that blood-soaked land, where plans are being made for an action that we cannot condemn without knowing whether or not the painful and troubled stage it is undergoing is a transitional phase that may be resolved for the good of humanity."[94] This, she felt, was the price of progress; her liberal optimism remained unshaken.

As a liberal, she could see nothing in Quebec or Canada that might justify any revolutionary excesses. Over the years, Circé-Côté had come to regard small-scale property, a family residence, as the best bulwark against the revolution. During the Depression, workers had to be drawn away from the sirens of confrontation and encouraged to become homeowners, "so as to prevent them from being duped by subversive theories, from subtly undermining the established order, from dreaming of another form of government that might bring [them] greater enjoyment, greater well-being. The weight of a home will check the flight of [their] imagination toward chimerical lands."[95] This advice seems out of keeping with a city like Montreal, where, following the European model, tenants predominated, but Circé-Côté was attentive to the expansion of the suburbs and observed with interest the expansion of Île-Jésus (now Laval) and L'Abord-à-Plouffe, populated with workers who were homeowners. Despite the working-class "we" that she used in *Le Monde ouvrier*, if there was a social class with which she consistently identified, it was not so much the proletariat as the petite bourgeoisie, of which the small merchants and the corner grocer were a part.[96] And, once again, the model she proposed was France: "It is the petit bourgeois, workers who have prospered, who have made republican France rich and strong."[97]

Liberalism in Politics

Theoretically, the Liberal Party represented liberal ideals in Canada, which, however, were not very different from conservative ideals since the time of John A. Macdonald. For almost Éva Circé-Côté's entire life, the country was governed by the Liberal Party. At the federal level, Wilfrid Laurier was the prime minister from 1896 to 1911; after the First World War, W. L. M. King led the government from 1921 to 1925, then from 1926 to 1930, and again from 1935 to 1948. In Quebec, the Liberals led by Félix-Gabriel Marchand ousted the Conservatives in 1897, inaugurating thirty-eight years of Liberal domination: Simon-Napoléon Parent from 1900 to 1905, Lomer Gouin from 1905 to 1920, Alexandre Taschereau from 1920 to 1935, and, after the Maurice Duplessis interlude, Adélard Godbout from 1939 to 1944. Circé-Côté's relationship with the governing Liberals was far from harmonious and, as a journalist, her stance toward them was critical, even oppositional. The Liberal Party was not monolithic, so that the liberalism expressed in Quebec City's *Le Soleil* was more moderate than that of *La Patrie* and *Le Canada*, especially when Godfroy Langlois was there, before the start of the war in 1914. Most Liberals in the government had drifted away from the genuine liberals of the 1830s and 1840s, and whatever the pseudonym she was using, Circé-Côté never stopped rebuking them for it.

In 1911, during the twofold dispute over free trade and the creation of a Canadian navy, she found "the great Liberal vessel [to be] in poor condition, neglected by its leaders." The crisis prompted even Henri Bourassa to dissociate himself from Laurier at every opportunity, something for which Circé-Côté would not forgive him. She admired Bourassa's rectitude, his integrity, his concern for the French language, and his oratorical skills, but she admonished him for his "*castorisme*," that is, his brand of ultramontane catholicism, which gave the Church a preeminent role in public affairs:

> [. . .] to go from the clan of Chénier, Papineau, Mercier, and Laurier over to the tribe of Trudel, Bégin, Tardivel, et al. seems inexplicable for a man of Mr. Bourassa's calibre, a man with muscles and a firm hand, one who is neither slippery nor cunning, and who might be proud enough to rely on his own merit. . . . The party of the future, and also of the past, is liberalism, not the watered-down liberalism spawned by the egotism or the petty self-interest of a handful of people, but the liberalism that knocks down old prejudices, that broadens our stifling horizons, that gives everyone the right to think, that hunts down ignor-

ance and superstition, and which will elevate our nationality to the rank of a progressive people."[98]

Here, she included the younger Laurier in the clan of the *Patriotes*, but in dozens of columns, she revisited her disappointment at and the betrayals of twentieth-century Liberals, who were too close to financial interests and the Church. "Had the government of Quebec better understood the obligations stemming from its Liberal title, it would have freed itself from the clergy's influence,"[99] she wrote in 1920. During that period of "spinelessness and the cult of indifference" she undertook "an examination of national conscience," which was concretized in her biographical study, *Papineau: Son influence sur la pensée canadienne* (Papineau: His influence on French-Canadian thinking), published in 1924.[100]

For Éva Circé-Côté, the unprincipled behaviour of Liberal politicians was a cruel betrayal. What had they accomplished in the sphere of education? In 1897, F.-G. Marchand submitted a bill aiming to re-establish the Department of Public Education, which had been abolished by the ultramontanists—the *castors* (beavers), as they were called—when they had held power in 1875, but he was pressured by Laurier to withdraw his proposal. Thereafter, no Liberal premier before Adélard Godbout would try this again. As for compulsory, free, and secular education, this was never included in the Liberals' programme when they were in power. From Honoré Mercier in 1881 to Hector Perrier in 1943, there were many champions of compulsory education. Many other politicians, such as Mercier, Gouin, and David, retracted their ideals. Among those who never wavered was Raoul Dandurand, who was married to the journalist Joséphine Marchand, the daughter of Premier Marchand. Quebec's bishops continued to oppose compulsory education long after the pope had deemed it consistent with Roman Catholic principles.[101]

A few progressive Liberals, hardly representative of their party, continued the campaign in the Legislative Assembly originally launched by the Ligue de l'Enseignement (League for teaching) and then relayed by Godfroy Langlois in *La Patrie*, *Le Canada*, and as of 1910 in *Le Pays*, calling for the creation of a department of public education, obligatory schooling, uniformity of textbooks, the establishment of *écoles normales* (teachers' colleges), higher salaries for teaching staff, and increased budget allocations for education.[102]

In 1912, for the first time since 1901, a bill that would make schooling obligatory was submitted to the Legislative Assembly. The MLA for the riding of Montreal-Saint-Laurent, John Thomas Finnie, seconded by Godfroy Langlois, tabled a bill, which, however, had been watered down. Aware that their party would not support them, they demanded mandatory education only for Protestant children. Unsurprisingly, the bill was defeated, but not without first giving rise to passionate debates triggered by the statements of Langlois and T. D. Bouchard. Circé-Côté and Langlois echoed each other, from *Le Pays* to the legislature; to read one was to hear the other.[103] In November 1913, Langlois used the question period in the Legislative Assembly to demand statistics on the number of children attending school; the next morning, these embarrassing figures appeared under the bylines of Fantasio and Paul S. Bédard, whose conclusion, once again, was that a department of education and compulsory schooling were needed.[104]

Circé-Côté was grateful to Premier Lomer Gouin for bringing about numerous changes in the field of education. Perhaps the reformers had not preached in the wilderness after all; though piecemeal, some reforms can be viewed as partial victories for the radical Liberals.[105] The governing Liberals favoured vocational instruction and the training of teachers. For years, the Association nationale Saint-Jean-Baptiste, the Congrès des métiers et du travail (Trades and Labor Congress), and *Le Pays* had demanded the uniformity of textbooks. The Frères des écoles chrétiennes, Frères maristes, Congregation of Notre-Dame, Sisters of Saint Anne, Clercs de Saint-Viateur, Jesuits, and Dominicans—each community imposed its own textbooks, which changed with almost every new season. Given what was at stake, it is understandable that the clergy was strongly opposed to what it considered interference with their teaching methods. But French Canadians were known for moving often; every year, hundreds of children changed schools, and the required books were different from one institution to the next. Starting in 1914, Montreal school commissions began to standardize their textbooks.

In spite of such reforms, Lomer Gouin was admonished by Éva Circé-Côté for allowing the École des Hautes Études (Business School) to affiliate with Université Laval in 1914, thereby withdrawing its secular status. Circé-Côté wondered about the Catholic Church's unseen influence. As for the workers' demand for free education, Gouin responded in these terms: "Workers here are more educated than those in other places," which earned him Circé-Côté's scorn for his "smug satisfaction."[106]

Under successive Liberal governments, the deficiencies of democracy came to light. Half of the citizens, women, could not vote. Lacking education, voters were uninformed and let themselves be taken in by demagogues.[107] Politicians were incompetent and in some cases almost illiterate. Corruption took root in Montreal, while in Quebec City the revelation of the nepotism practised by the Taschereau government confirmed the worst suspicions of chicanery.

Le Pays, November 9, 1912. BAnQ.

Circé-Côté did not forgive Liberal leaders for getting enmeshed in compromises. The abolition of privilege was one of the original Liberal demands, yet French Canadians like Wilfrid Laurier and Lomer Gouin could not resist having their vanity flattered by being dubbed knights of the British Empire.[108] Genuine liberals, she declared, such as Papineau, Bédard, Viger, Dorion, Doutre, Laflamme, and Dessaulles, were not self-interested and were able to preserve their freedom. To maintain our independence, we must not accept "gifts from either the Greeks, or the English or the Roman court," Saint-Michel proclaimed.[109] The "Legion of Honour, academic awards, knighthood" are so many "violations of our national honour"[110] that the Liberals endorse by accepting them because they appeal to their egotism.

The freedom of thought essential to liberalism implies the separation of church and state, but the bishops' influence was undiminished, religion kept its privileges, and church property remained tax-exempt. During the war, the bishops recommended that people submit to the state and to conscription. The clergy were against any reform that might curtail the Church's control of education and social services. When the Liberal government passed the Public Assistance Act (Loi de l'assistance publique) in 1921—a timid, restrictive piece of legislation bearing only on the hospitalization of the destitute—the episcopate's outcry was such that the Liberals resigned themselves a few years later to introducing amendments guaranteeing the bishops' acquired rights over the religious communities in charge of the institutions concerned. Seeing the law watered down because of pressure from the clergy, Circé-Côté was sure to react. Already ten years earlier, she had written: "[the] Conservative Party enacts progressive measures: on marriage, divorce, suffrage at the federal level.... Today's Liberals have confined their horizon to the bell tower of the parish church, while Conservative policy holds sway throughout Canada."[111]

The censorship enforced by Mgr Bruchési had a direct impact on freedom of thought. *Les Débats* and *Le Pays* were targeted by his pastoral letters and denounced from the pulpit. The church demanded to see the Public Library's list of acquisitions and the librarians had to restrict their selection to approved works. Not one Liberal government opposed the Catholic Church's many intrusions into citizens' lives; by moving closer to the Church, the Liberal Party "repudiated its ideal."[112]

As for the economy, the Liberals even reneged on their free trade credo. The tariff policy introduced in 1873 was pursued by the Liberals after 1896, except for goods affected by reciprocity with Great Britain. The free enterprise principle was traditionally at odds with industrial concentration, but the progressive wing of the party, whose central figure was Godfroy Langlois, had been powerless to prevent the Parent government from approving the expansion of the Montreal Light Heat and Power Company in 1904.[113] Thirty years on, another Liberal government, now led by Louis-Alexandre Taschereau, openly worked hand in glove with the trusts. The progressives, those who had remained true to their allegiance, were relegated to the margins of the Party.

The Liberal Party had betrayed the cause of liberalism, and its leaders were compromised. Though disillusioned, Éva Circé-Côté tirelessly waged the struggle of the Enlightenment against Quebec's obscurantism, guided in her effort by the *Patriotes*, whom she mythicized as the perfect incarnation of liberalism. Initially, Wilfrid Laurier had represented the legacy of the *Rouges*; "[he was] the one we had always regarded as the personification of the liberalism that had inspired the Patriotes of 1837–1838," T. D. Bouchard would write in his *Mémoires*.[114] The young Laurier was a member of the Institut canadien until 1868; he insisted on the importance of education and rejected Confederation. In an incisive speech given in 1877, he distanced himself from the liberalism damned by the Catholic Church. His liberalism grew more moderate and was modelled on the ideology of the British Whigs; it was no longer revolutionary or atheist or social but political.[115] Accordingly, he aligned himself with those wielding financial power and had no part in the rise of the progressives within his party.

The moderate Laurier was a disappointment for Circé-Côté; she acknowledged his magnetic appeal among French Canadians but deplored the loss of his early passion. She compared him to Samson, the victim of Delilah, who with "her captivating caresses, put the conquering hero to sleep with words about conciliation, indulgence, and forgiveness; he let go the reins of his warhorse, gave up control, and let himself be carried along by the whims of his mount, until the day he came noisily tumbling down."[116] Sir Wilfrid would remain the giant dispossessed by the Philistines.[117]

In the wake of the Liberals' defeat in the federal elections of 1911, Circé-Côté gave full vent to her bitterness:

Conservative policy and Liberal policy are twin sisters that can be told apart now only by the blue or red ribbons tied around their wrists. Both are protectionist and loyal to England, both are naval and imperialist, both are against compulsory education, a department of public education, free books, and freedom of opinion.[118]

From that point on, the federal Liberal Party was adrift. Driven from power, Laurier was able to redeem himself by mending fences with progressives in 1916, opposing conscription, and refusing to join a unionist government during the war, but the reconciliation was short-lived.[119] At Sir Wilfrid's death—the "Sir" being another unforgiven breach of trust—Circé-Côté reassessed the old lion's role; she ascribed the difficulties and betrayal of the Liberal Party not to Laurier but to the party representatives' inability to take over from him: "When Laurier fell, the temple veil was torn.... The torch that our fathers had so proudly held aloft was dropped."[120]

Because the social reforms that Circé-Côté called for came under provincial jurisdiction, this arena was the focus of most of her writings. Since the late nineteenth century, the *Rouges* and their principles had become foreign to the Liberal politicians who held power in Quebec. The party's radical wing grew weaker; some members had mellowed with age, others had lost their seats in the Legislative Assembly, and Godfroy Langlois was in Brussels at the head of a Quebec mission. In a striking summation of "the incurable weakness of the government [, which] has not brought in a single liberal measure,"[121] she did not pull any punches for Lomer Gouin, who had been associated with the party's progressive wing when he came to power in 1905.

> *Portrait of Gouin, December 18, 1920*
>
> One of the most curious spectacles of our era is that of the absolute master of power flinging himself from the Tarpeian Rock apparently without being forced to do so, either by men or circumstances. Wrestling with himself, possibly snared in the traps of his own subtle, unbound mind rich in expedients, he collapsed under his own weight. . . . The English, with their fondness for roast beef, admired this bull-politician. They always had great respect for this supermale who held Quebec panting under his heel. . . . Mr. Gouin was never a charmer and his hide was rather rough. He was not a brilliant conversationalist and he lacked gallantry with the ladies. He loves no one, and I believe that no one has loved him. . . . This sphinx is impenetrable and disappointing."[122]

In 1920, a new Liberal leader, Louis-Alexandre Taschereau, seemed for a time to answer the hopes of progressives. Some fifteen years later those hopes were dashed once again. The party abandoned its ideals, the Church's influence was on the rise, and freedom of thought was in jeopardy; Taschereau's party has "stayed too old in a world too young. It has been unable to adapt to current needs."[123] Another disappointment came in the aftermath of Maurice Duplessis' election, when the Action libérale nationale and the Union nationale forgot their promises of change, including state intervention in the economic and social spheres to end the crisis, and a war against corruption.

* * *

The radical flame was not extinguished in 1877 or 1896. It was kept alive in the meetings of Freemasons, in periodicals like *Les Débats, L'Avenir, Le Journal de Françoise, L'Avenir du Nord* and *Le Pays*, and in Montreal's prewar progressive movement. The leaders may have rejected the ideals of the early days, but there remained some faithful disciples. In her book *Papineau*, Éva Circé-Côté mentioned three in particular: L.-O. David, Joséphine Marchand Dandurand, and Godfroy Langlois.[124] For some historians, radical liberalism ended with the nineteenth century, for others it was with the Great War.[125] After the armistice, the flame continued to flicker in *Le Pays* and to a certain extent in Gustave Francq's *Le Monde ouvrier*, and it endured in spite of everything in the writings of Éva Circé-Côté at least until 1936. But the movement eventually withered; only a few relatively marginalized individuals would continue to uphold this ideal of freedom, secularity, and equality.

CHAPTER 7

RELIGION

The theological bias under its general form, tending to maintain a dominance of the subordination element of religion over its ethical element—tending, therefore, to measure actions by their formal congruity with a creed rather than by their intrinsic congruity with human welfare, is unfavourable to that estimation of worth in social arrangements which is made by tracing its results.[1]
— HERBERT SPENCER, 1896

I do not aspire to save souls. To ease my conscience it would be enough to have wrested a single soul from the century's corruption, from the lie adorned with pompous nouns that mislead minds; then I could sleep my last sleep. . . .[2]
— ÉVA CIRCÉ-CÔTÉ, 1920

THE LIBERALISM that arose from the Enlightenment—Éva Circé-Côté's liberalism—rests on the foundation of secularism. The evolution of humanity depends on freedom of thought and deliverance from dogma. It follows that religion's hold over thought and expression can only hamper progress. Ideas such as these smacked of heresy and scandal in the clergy-ridden Quebec of the early twentieth century. Yet Circé-Côté dared to voice them in dozens, indeed hundreds of columns, where she heaped abuse on the Catholic religion and its clerics and made known her own convictions. Thus, a distinction must be drawn between her writings about faith and those concerning religion and the Catholic Church. When one examines the development of her thinking as articulated in her writing over a period of forty years, it is clear that the position she adopted was not unitary. One should also take into account her iconoclastic spirit, which prompted her to provoke so as to "draw the people out of its lethargy," to quote an expression she was fond of.

When *Bleu, Blanc, Rouge* was published in 1903, it was considered exemplary. Her patriotism and religious sentiments were sufficiently edifying for Colombine's book to be presented to young schoolgirls as an end-of-year award.[3] Likewise, at the turn of the century, Musette (another pen name), unambiguously identified herself as "I, *canadienne* Catholic."[4] It is surprising to see articles so imbued with spirituality in *Les Débats*, *L'Avenir du Nord*, and *Le Pionnier*—newspapers condemned by the bishop. The mysticism displayed by Éva Circé was similar to that of many young women at the time.[5] Nothing inhibited her from sharing her religious feelings, which revolved around a form of pantheism captured, for example, in "Mysticisme," a poem published in 1901.

Mysticism

God is in nature
Torch-bearer
Jehovah, thine august power,
Chills the timid prayer
Of the mortals trembling before thee.
Crushed under a hard decree,
The sighs on their lips expire.
Like the broken chord of the lyre
Grieving at the song of Ezekiel
Humans far from heaven are exiled.

Thou, great god whom my soul adores,
I ponder thee each morn,
Shedding into the chalice vermillion
The teardrops of thy sun.
Thou singest the strand's lament,
Thou tellest the poet what he's dreamt.
Let him sigh with the waves as they throb
Rocking their eternal sobs.

Oh! I see thee in every thing!
In the heart of a rose, hiding.
The butterfly drinks in thy splendour
Along with the flower's nectar.
Loves, sighs, perfume, and life

> Portions of the infinite soul,
> In adoration I place a kiss
> On the infant's brow so blessed.
>
> The sacred veil is rent
> I inhale thy breath divine,
> When April's blossoming
> Dizzies me with a subtle scent
> God descends into his creature,
> Bedeck thine altar! O, nature!
> For this holy communion
> Cricket and nightingale burst into song.[11]

In Musette's early writings, nothing foreshadowed the nonbeliever she would later become. In 1901, her poem "Resurrexit" celebrated the resurrection of Christ, and one of her columns described how moved she had been by a First Communion.[6] The day after the Saint-Jean parade in 1903, she wrote: "Once again, little child, white Host, immaculate lamb, you have purified the mother's love and freed the heart from hate. Blessed be the tabernacle where you have come to reside."[7] These outbursts of exaltation expressed a faith that she shared with a readership whose education was still profoundly religious.

For her, Jesus represented love and light. He had come "striking down ignorance and fanaticism, which, in his name, oppressed the defenceless innocent, the woman, vulnerable in the face of love . . . the tyranny of kings [was] abolished, the hypocrisy of the Pharisees unmasked, the atrocity of war condemned."[8] He had lost none of his relevance, the publican representing "the sublime internationalist, who drank from every amphora and dressed the stranger's wounds."[9] Precious little was left, however, of Christ's original message after two millennia. As of 1901, Colombine reinterpreted the Passion: the Christians, in misconstruing his gospel, were the ones who had killed Christ. She reappropriated certain important dogmas of the Catholic Church. Believing in the communion of saints, she thus communed with the *Patriotes* when she visited the monument to the heroes of 1837.[10] They spoke to her.

During her early years as a columnist, Éva Circé's professions of faith were accompanied with generous reflections on religions. Had they not "guided the nations in their slow ascension toward progress[?] Because fanatics and hypocrites perverted their spirit, must temples be destroyed and altars profaned?"[12] There was more to the religion that she professed than mysticism; it also involved a temporal, social mission. At the beginning of the century, she believed in the advent of a modern church renewed through its social works: old people's homes, nurseries, orphanages, etc.[13] In a modern world, in which "religion and science should not be adversaries," she called for a "modern Christianity, where persuasion and charity prevail," and which would make "common cause with those trying to stimulate the movement of ideas, energize the masses' emancipatory drive toward education; awaken the feelings that lie dormant in the soul of our people."[14] What emerges here is a desire to remain faithful to a religion as she conceived it: open to its epoch, able to come to terms with materialism, committed to a civilizing mission. This would hold true until about 1904, when her ideas came under the influence of the freethinking circles in which she moved. She was reading banned books and her writings became increasingly critical of religion and the Catholic Church. Moreover, being a confirmed Francophile, she closely followed political developments in France when the radical socialists were secularizing French society.

In 1905, France adopted the law on the separation of church and state, thus putting an end to the concordat signed by Napoleon. France, the land of freedom of conscience, became a secular country where no religion would enjoy privileges or receive subsidies. French religious congregations found refuge in Quebec and brought with them their opposition to all attempts at secularization. In Montreal, the open secularity of the Freemasons that Éva and Pierre-Salomon Côté were close to caused a scandal at a time when the situation was becoming polarized as the conservatism of the recently arrived religious communities strengthened Mgr Bruchési's position.

Even though Circé-Côté's columns grew more and more anticlerical, she did not abandon Christ. She had supplemented the Catholic education of her youth with independent studies of the church fathers, the apocryphal Gospels, and Saint Augustine's *Confessions*,[15] and she subsequently drew this lesson: "Like the great socialists of today, they despised ill-gotten wealth, condemned the hypocrisy of the Pharisees, stood by the poor, the oppressed, and the fallen woman, against the tyranny of prejudice," and opposed the "arrogant bourgeois."[16]

Her readers, no matter how broadminded, had not slipped through the net of an education based on sacred history and catechism. She knew that her multiple religious allusions were understood, as were her quotations from patristic writings and the Gospels, and she grounded her arguments in the canonical texts. She made countless references to the Old and New Testaments and to religious holidays; Christmas, Twelfth Night, Easter, All Souls' Day, Holy Friday, and the Feast of Saint Catherine all served as pretexts for a column, a poem, or a tale replete with spirituality. And her writing was full of expressions such as "whited sepulchres" or "cast the first stone," and many others drawn from the Gospels.

On the eve of the war, she adopted a decidedly secular tone, which she would always retain: "When one snuffs out the secular spirit, one is well on the way to pulling a sheet up over the people's face. Who, then, was it that drew France out of its slumber and in the space of fifty years turned it into a strong, independent, and wealthy race? The secular spirit, the involvement of free and enlightened intelligences,"[17] she declared in 1914. Henceforward, religion, for Éva, belonged to the private sphere, to an intimate relationship between a person and her Maker.

Toward 1910, leaving behind the quasi-mystical writings of Colombine and Musette, Circé-Côté entered a period of materialism, which remained nevertheless ambivalent. The three theological virtues—faith, hope, and charity—as revised by her, became science, optimism, and justice. Yet she could not relinquish her faith, which, she wrote in 1915, was a gift, not "an act of the will." Quoting Paul Bourget's defence of Renan, she added: "One cannot hold a grudge against someone who is unfortunate enough not to have it."[18] Or, as Arthur Maheu put it, "faith is a gift, which is not given to everyone. The Good Lord, who is far cleverer than men, cannot blame a person for not possessing something that He had not granted him."[19]

God is light and progress and cannot permit war. This was her response to those who saw divine intervention in the war of 1914: "The God of Pasteur, Lacordaire, and Lavigerie could not wield the sword of the exterminating angel: his action is not nihilistic but civilizing and luminous."[20] The atrocities of war were bound to engender a questioning of divine action. How could one reconcile the existence of a God who is good with the horrors of the trenches? "After the Verdun massacre, our moral scruples will suffice to keep us from paying homage to the Eternal for these horrific hecatombs."[21]

Éva Circé-Côté remained a deist and acknowledged that "God's breath, which we all carry within us, is a principle whereby we participate of his divine nature." She hastened to add that secularists and believers alike are invested with this principle; "because their clay contains this flame, [they] can animate the void, direct the course of events, read the past, and see into the future."[22] God is everywhere, even in the souls of secularists. He is present not just in great minds but also omnipresent in nature, by virtue of a pantheism that encompasses all of creation, including the forests, which become the "natural temples" of the Creator.[23]

Circé-Côté's optimism led her to maintain certain beliefs, in the resurrection, for example, for "death, nothingness, must not have the final victory."[24]

In the middle of the war, she reinterpreted the sacrifice of Holy Friday. "The Jews have been washed of the stigma of having killed a God; the true deicides are the Germans."[25] In 1917, as her doubts increased and her pacifism took root, the French battlefields evoked the death of Christ. Now it was the fallen soldiers who were showered with gall and vinegar. Christ died—"if you doubt this, go to the battlefields"—without being able to redeem the hates or prevent wars. And "all Christians crucified him."[26]

"Blaspheming against religion and freedom is like beating a woman: to do so one must love them."[27] Notwithstanding the sexism of this quip made by Fantasio in 1917, the question it raises is this: Did Éva Circé-Côté love the Catholic religion? Had she kept her faith? Other writings suggest a negative answer. Four years on, her letters to Marcel Dugas would confirm her religious scepticism; she was making her own gospel.[28] An epistle addressed in 1920 to Theodore, the young man that Fantasio lavished with advice, stated: "one cannot have the blood of a thousand generations of believers running in one's veins with no ill consequences."[29] This held true both for the columnist and her interlocutor. But she would contradict herself in a letter to Dugas in which she excluded herself from this observation.

Her letters to the poet in the 1920s hinted at her agnosticism, but while she rejected the Church and the Catholic religion, she held on to a spirituality that she would never entirely shed. In her perpetual quest for the absolute, she admitted in 1921: "I try to gather everywhere the infinite faith to believe in the good, the truth, justice, the happiness of humanity, the excellence of efforts to liberate the pariahs, and a future in which the eternal victim of the cowardly forces that govern us is not left to rot."[30] In 1924, Dugas's conversion gave his correspondent an opportunity to present her creed:

> I am convinced, on the contrary, that we are not the playthings of hostile or unconscious forces, that there is an immanent justice in things, an intelligent, good principle, perhaps in the laws that govern nature. I believe, furthermore, in the eternity both of matter and of our world, which does not prevent me from asking this stupid question: Who created it?[31]

Summing up, she wrote to Dugas in 1924: "you have Catholic atheists; accept that there are atheist believers."[32] And she confessed to him: "there are three generations behind me who forbid me from entering the garden of hallucinations."[33] This is a surprising admission, because, while her mother and father may have been unbelievers, she still had a Carmelite aunt.

Even more revealing is this column about the saving faith:

The faith needed by man: first, faith in himself, in his star, the one he created for himself from start to finish when destiny forgot to fix one to his firmament, faith in the redeeming love of humanity, faith in the upward march of progress, despite the apparent backward steps, faith in science; one must put something grand into one's life, set oneself a noble goal.

Faith must be preserved, she wrote to Théodore, because

[. . .] it provides support like a blind person's crutches. . . . It is not the freethinkers who will make you lose your faith; they have more respect than you for that flower of the high peaks that does not grow in every soul! It is the Catholics who will disturb these precious things. . . . Their dishonesty, their hypocrisy, their lust will bring scandal into your conscience.[34]

In the six epistles addressed to Théodore in 1920, Fantasio seems to be describing Circé-Côté herself: "You write that you are neither devout, nor clerical, but inclined toward mysticism." Furthermore, "The faith that moves mountains is not from here. If you have it, fine, but that is no reason to boast, for it is a free gift that has not been earned. The most important thing is to believe in yourself."[35]

Believe in yourself, because, she cautioned readers on several occasions, one should be wary of placing all one's trust in religious and spiritual phenomena. Over the years, Circé-Côté repeatedly advised against faith that produces passivity, leads a person to abdicate responsibility, and blocks critical thinking. Faith is not innocuous; "belief in the supernatural and superstitions can turn us into easy prey for cunning people who know how to exploit them. . . . Faith makes us docile, submissive and obedient sons, fatalistic, resigned to every humiliation." Borrowing a metaphor from Marx, she warned: "Opium is not the only thing that puts the noble passions to sleep, extinguishes energy and action."[36] In spite of her deism, her mystical impulses, and her seemingly contradictory writings, it is her response to Dugas' conversion, as articulated in private letters, that no doubt best expresses her convictions and hence deserves closer attention.

We have seen how upset Circé-Côté was when, in 1924, Dugas informed her that he was once again a believer: "this bending of the knees and the soul so dismayed me that I wept."[37] Giving vent to her irony, she began by saying that she was glad about his conversion, "because it's better than emptiness." She herself had never yielded to nihilism. Continuing in an ironic vein, she warned him that he would experience "remorse and the delicious tears of repentance, which will wash away your venial sins, which you have often turned into mortal sins.... This gift of faith is timely, as your ability to suffer seemed diminished and I was beginning to worry."[38] She almost accused Dugas of masochism, being convinced that faith would only heighten the torments and tortures of an oversensitive soul. As a woman who "had been persecuted in the name of religious sentiments," she had seen religion too often invoked to justify wickedness and injustice, and, she added, "The Christians I have known leave me with no desire to meet their master and embrace their doctrine. It pains me to think of you communing with these nasty and unworthy people, you, who have never hurt anyone.... I do not suffer from not believing but from the faith of others." She admitted, moreover, "Were I in France, I might be Catholic to stand on the side of the weak, but I know from experience what the followers of Christ [do] when they are the stronger ones."[39] French Catholicism, separated from the state, was no doubt more acceptable than its counterpart in Quebec.

Like so many believers, Dugas rejected her atheism. He seemed to find it hard to conceive of agnosticism exempt from suffering and counselled his friend to also "throw [herself] into the bosom of God."[40] Believing only in her own gospel, Éva was unfazed and saw in his faith nothing but a figment of the imagination, a "phantasmagoria." She had long inveighed against illusions, miracles, and the hallucinations brought on by the prolonged fasting of Lent.[41] She had no use for such phantasmagorias.

The just doubt, and so do atheists. What did she feel in her moments of solitude, when, at the age of fifty-three, she already envisaged the end of her life? Was she sometimes tempted to seek consolation in the religion that was ubiquitous in her society?

> In my hours of despond and prostration, I envy those who believe because heaven and earth belong to them, but when I get a hold of myself, when my nerves have settled down and my heart beats more regularly, I tell myself that if I had my life to live over again I would be no different from what I have been: there are no regrets when one has been sincere.[42]

When in need of solace, she found it in the enveloping "presence" of Pierre-Salomon. "I admit to being more drawn to this shadow hovering over me than to God, who does not speak to me and that I can neither pray to nor love," yet, she added, "this is a far cry from negating him."[43]

An apostle of a singular faith, Éva Circé-Côté considered herself faithful to goodness, truth, and justice, and she took it upon herself to articulate a secular discourse on the Catholic Church in Quebec. Although faith could be progressive, the Church's conservatism obstructed progress.[44] "If we wish to live, we must free ourselves from the influence of the clergy."[45] This was the condition for achieving modernity.

The Separation of Church and State

In the name of secularism, Éva Circé-Côté, especially from 1910 onward, undertook a long struggle for the separation of church and state. Her epoch, the first half of the twentieth century, was marked by the Catholic Church's omnipresence in the social sphere and by its open interference in the political sphere. She lamented that Quebec had remained "as in the feudal days of the Middle Ages, with our bishops, canons, archpriests, and abbots still enjoying the *droit du seigneur* regarding political issues."[46] Education was confessional; a Catholic school commission and a Protestant school commission controlled the public education system. French-language hospitals were managed by religious congregations. A Catholic trade union, founded in 1921, vied for members with the Trades and Labor Congress of Canada. Religious influence also made itself felt through the censorship of books and, increasingly, of films deemed immoral. Freedom of opinion, a triumph of secularity, chafed at religious hegemony. "The alliance of government and faith has always been detrimental to both," Circé-Côté wrote, adding, by way of summarizing her thinking: "clerical influence is as fatal to those who exercise it as to those who are subjected to it."[47] What was needed, she concluded in 1920, was "a free Church in a free state."[48]

Both in her columns and her book *Papineau*, Circé-Côté took up the secular arguments of the Enlightenment kept alive in French Canada by Louis-Joseph Papineau and the Voltairian *Rouges* of 1837–38, Laurent-Olivier David in his booklet *Le clergé canadien, sa mission, son oeuvre*, the Institut canadien and the newspaper *L'Avenir*, Honoré Beaugrand, Godfroy Langlois, and the Masonic milieu of the L'Émancipation and Force et Courage lodges. Those ideas continued to live in the publications to which she contributed. Secularity was a matter of freedom of thought and of democracy. For Éva Circé-Côté, the ideal model was Gallican France.[49]

Ever since the *Conquête*, the radicals never forgave the Catholic Church its alliance with the British authorities. Starting in the 1830s, the proximity of ecclesiastical power to political power was their primary target. Circé-Côté's judgment was severe and unequivocal: "these shepherds have always driven their flock to be massacred."[50] The ultramontanists had known their hour of glory during the 1870s, but their influence persisted for another thirty or even fifty years. Éva Circé-Côté repeatedly railed against the *castors* of the twentieth century, who were quick to express their conservative Catholicism and to appeal to Rome to support their positions. She granted that members of the clergy, as citizens, were entitled to hold opinions and to fulfil their obligations as voters, but not to "talk politics from the pulpit or mix politics and religion."[51] Given the great prestige and many privileges that clerics enjoyed in Quebec, Circé-Côté maintained that "at the altar, the priest is sacred, but once he ventures into the political arena, he deserves no more solicitude or consideration than anyone else. No one has the right to shirk responsibility for his actions."[52] She supported her arguments with references to a constellation of great minds such as Herbert Spencer and Anatole France, but she mostly preferred to confront the Church on its own terms by drawing on patristic sources, such as this passage from St. Ambrose: "it is not possible to reconcile the priesthood and power."[53]

True to the traditional relationship between Canada and the Catholic Church in Quebec, the upper clergy, represented by the bishop of Montreal, Mgr Bruchési, preached submission to Ottawa. The rise of clerical nationalism, as embodied by Henri Bourassa and Lionel Groulx, challenged that collaborative relationship. Circé-Côté lambasted both the clerical nationalists and the Church allied to federal power. She had always defined herself as a patriot, but her indignation was aroused by the religious nature as well as the narrow-mindedness and anti-Semitism of militant activities like that of the Jesuit-controlled Action catholique de la jeunesse canadienne-française (ACJC), *L'Action sociale catholique*, the organ of Quebec City's Mgr Bégin, and the Semaine sociales, established by the Jesuits' École sociale populaire.[54] The "right-minded" press responded to her attacks. Father J.-A. D'Amours, an editorialist for *L'Action sociale* and a favourite target of *Le Pays*, devoted an editorial to "the radical element, which pours out its hate and its errors in a number of Montreal weeklies, carefully cultivates an old fallacy."[55] The duel between Circé-Côté and D'Amours would continue for years.

The feast of Saint-Jean-Baptiste provided her with a pretext to write about the separation of church and state in her columns. Circé-Côté was passionate about the secularization of the French Canadians' holiday. The holy preacher, whose beheading was "a terrifying symbol for us . . . (might this be a portent of our destiny? Is Salome not imperialism wrapped in a veil[?])," should make way for a secular figure, Maisonneuve, for example, who would attract citizens, whatever their religious affiliation.[56] The intertwinement of, on the one hand, religion and nationalism, and, on the other, the Church and the federal state dominated Quebec politics during the First World War.

The Church and the War of 1914–18

In reaction to Mgr Bruchési's "excessive pastoral letter" of September 1914 supporting participation in the war, the Patriotic Fund, and the sending of a Canadian contingent overseas, Circé-Côté remarked: "on the question of war, bishops have no more authority than the least layperson."[57] Although she was unwavering in her support for the Allies, France first and foremost, she did not go so far as to encourage military enlistment and was opposed to the Church promoting the recruitment of French Canadians.[58] In defending military enlistment, Father D'Amours of *L'Action sociale* was destroying patriotism, she asserted, because he was "separating Canadians from their soil. He [was] eroding past traditions and pushing thousands of his compatriots into the bloodbath." Priests can hold opinions but "their meddling, in the name of religion, in exclusively political matters such as imperialism and nationalism is intolerable."[59]

When military contribution to the war in Europe was at issue, Prime Minister Robert Borden could count on the backing of the Church in Quebec.[60] In 1916, the Canadian government required all citizens to be registered; when the conscription act was passed in June 1917, Mgr Bruchési, having previously asked Borden to reconsider, advised his flock to obey the law.[61] As far as Circé-Côté was concerned, this was a betrayal on the part of the upper clergy.[62]

Moreover, she found that while the Church interfered in Canadian politics, it was silent as to Germany's responsibility. National churches were bound to respect secular power, but as a state unto itself, the Vatican must take a position in the conflict that was tearing Europe apart. Circé-Côté could not accept Rome's neutrality. She was scathing in her judgments about the Vatican's silence and its reluctance to condemn Germany. "How is it that the Church's duty is to stay silent in Rome but to speak out in Canada, to wish for peace in Europe but to push for war on the banks of the St. Lawrence."[63] Even when disenchantment crept in and sapped the enthusiasm she had felt in the early months of the war, she took up the appeal of the churches of France and Belgium for Rome to intervene.[64] As the hostilities persisted, Circé-Côté took a more aggressive stance, to the point where, in 1916, she denounced the "[Vatican's] benign attitude toward the Kaiser."[65] In spite of her opposition to conscription, Circé-Côté remained steadfast in supporting the war effort until 1917. She regarded pacifism as a trap and thought that, in asking for a peace without victory in 1915, Benedict XV was playing into the hand of the "Teutons."[66] There are echoes here of Léon Bloy, whom she had read, and Clemenceau. In 1916, when the Vatican urged the belligerents to make peace, Circé-Côté, not yet a pacifist, wrote: "One would have to be naive to think that Hugo's France, Victor-Emmanuel's Italy, and Henry VIII's England would accept peace from the hands of the Pope."[67] For her, in his capacity both as head of state and spiritual leader, the Pontiff had failed in his mission, and she would always suspect Benedict XV, who had been the Holy See's representative in Vienna as a young man, of sympathizing with Germany.

The Church and French Canada

The war clearly highlighted Éva Circé-Côté's campaign for secularism, but there were also other manifestations of the Church's place in society that fuelled the conflicts between this freethinking woman and the religious authorities. The upper clergy's support for the policies of the federal government was just one of the issues that drove her to assail the Church's role in politics. Another was the situation of French schools in Ontario, which provided her with ample material for columns on the separation of church and state. She berated the Catholic press and called on *Le Devoir* to react. By way of provocation she asked: "Could it be that Mr. Bourassa [founder and editor-in-chief of *Le Devoir*—Trans.] agrees with the Pope when he asks us to learn English better than French?"[68]

Beyond the interference of the Church and its clergy in politics, Circé-Côté deplored the influence of religion on the French-Canadian mentality. Quebec's "lagging" behind the rest of Canada could be ascribed, in her view, to Catholicism's focus on the hereafter rather than on material progress, and to the Church's control of education, which was based on fear—primarily of sin—and fostered a spirit of submission and routine among the population. "It is indeed an effect of this potent narcotic, which are called religions, to put ambitions to sleep and to dull the material appetites.... Faith distracts the mind from tangible realities and draws it toward invisible and eternal goods."[69]

And yet the very same Church that preached spirituality looked after its own material interests. Circé-Côté did not curb her sarcasm with regard to a religious institution that "charges money for a seat in church or a blessing for the dead."[70] She mocked the vanity and ambitions of clergymen looking for a cardinal's hat, like Mgr Bruchési, who owned "everything needed to be a decorative cardinal."⁷¹ Her judgment may have been harsh, perhaps unfair, but she saw the departure from principles as a betrayal. For her, there was "a reversal of values here, a shifting of the ideal, and a falsification of the truth in its very conception."⁷²

> ### Mgr Bruchési
> His mind was not so very deep that if one were to plumb it the bottom could not be reached, but it was of such a subtle quality that it could not be grasped any more than a ray. Thin as a shadow, insinuating, like groundwater, he succeeded through intrigue where others with great intellect and big-heartedness would have failed. Not learned, but deliciously spiritual. . . . Mgr Bruchési was a born orator. . . . He touched, stirred people's hearts but was the first to become intoxicated with his heady words. . . . Among his most remarkable characteristics was a taste for creating a sensation, the art of staging, a talent for performance. Being impulsive, he spent half his life trying to make up for the results of first impressions. Being vindictive, he was unfamiliar with the ability to forgive.⁷³

Circé-Côté was outraged as well by the privileges granted to properties belonging to religious communities. She criticized the "favouritism" practised with regard to the Sulpicians and congregations exempted from taxes while the perpetually indebted City of Montreal went from one financial crisis to the next.⁷⁴ "Civic-mindedness is not a virtue reserved only for laypeople," she noted in 1917.⁷⁵ She praised the "enlightened faith and civic spirit" of the cities of Lévis, Rimouski, and Saint-Hyacinthe, which, in order to eliminate their deficits, were prepared to tax buildings owned by religious communities.⁷⁶ Nor did she shy away from lecturing the clergy: "Temporal power should not exist for the apostles' successors. Their weakness is their strength, and prayer their weapon."⁷⁷

For an idealist like Circé-Côté, enamoured of the absolute, the Catholic religion as it was practised in Quebec was in reality a perversion of the original Catholicism: "Genuine religious feeling is rare in our so very Catholic French Canada, where everyone boasts of being a believer but scarcely is."⁷⁸ "We are pious, but not believers. Our population is subservient only to the outer forms of worship."⁷⁹ In examining the causes behind the drift away from true faith, she at one point reflected on the influence of the Indigenous Peoples, "We are quite fetishist, superstitious, often fatalistic, as were the natives of this land."⁸⁰ But, while contact with Indigenous Peoples may have left its mark, the Catholic Church and clergy, with their Jansenist and ultramontane background, were Circé-Côté's main targets because they held back freedom of thought and imposed blind submission. It was under the byline of the very commonsensical Arthur Maheu that she observed: "Our priests spell out exactly what we must think; no need for discussion—our brains just have to adapt. Our governments set programs, take care of all our business, and all we have to do is pay."⁸¹ Even with the best shepherds, as Circé-Côté stated elsewhere, the very fact of supervising the faithful throughout their whole lives is in itself an affront to the most fundamental principles of liberalism: freedom of thought and freedom of expression.

Circé-Côté's greatest complaint against the Church had to do with the religious control of Catholics' minds. How could people form an enlightened judgment if they were unable to think on their own? Having been continuously subjected to the judgments of the religious authorities, citizens had grown passive, so that the spirit of initiative needed for any progress to take place was undermined. In the seventeenth century, Mgr Laval had reputedly declared that he wished to have submissive and obedient sons. The phrase was taken up again in sermons three centuries on. What the clergy regarded as a virtue—obedience—Circé-Côté saw as nothing but an insult. In her opinion, submission summed up the character of French Canadians as it had been shaped by religious teaching, and she reiterated this observation some forty times in her columns where she railed against the passivity of her fellow citizens. As late as 1938, finally striking a note of optimism, she wrote: "Submissive and obedient sons... are a thing of the past."⁸²

The clergy cared for the souls of its flock by educating them from a very young age and forbidding not just certain behaviours but readings as well. The censorial power exercised by the Church from the late nineteenth to the middle of the twentieth century must not be underestimated. Robert de Roquebrune told of the auto-da-fé that his father had carried out on the orders of Father Dorval, the priest of the village L'Assomption, burning the books that his grandfather had lovingly preserved at his manor house in Saint-Ours.⁸³ In the Quebec of that period, following the prohibition on reading authors such as Voltaire and Diderot—which a few decades earlier could be found on the shelves of the Institut canadien—a veritable bibliophile's treasure trove was in danger of ending up on the pyre just like Jeanne d'Arc. Not everyone had the good fortune enjoyed by bourgeois families of owning a small *enfer*, a collection of banned books under lock and key, which was a roundabout way of holding on to them without opening the door to sin. For decades the vade mecum of censorship was the book by the French abbot Louis Bethléem, *Romans à lire, Romans à proscrire, essai de classification au point de vue moral des principaux romans et romanciers depuis l'an 1500*.[84]

In *Papineau*, Circé-Côté describes the pressure exerted on François-Xavier Garneau to force him to withdraw his *Histoire du Canada*. She reminds readers of the censorship endured by Gonzalve Doutre and L.-A. Dessaulles in the 1880s, and she devotes an entire chapter to the Institut canadien, whose *Annuaire* (yearbook) was placed on the Index Librorum Prohibitorum.[85] She found herself at the centre of Mgr Bruchési's condemnations when, one after the other, *Les Débats*, *Le Pionnier*, and *Le Pays* were prohibited by means of episcopal letters. In 1903, Mgr Bruchési obliged Napoléon Brisebois, a member of the Ligue de l'Enseignement, to resign his teaching position at the École normale Jacques-Cartier; the archbishop furthermore used his influence to have the Ligue dissolved.[86] In 1913, he forbade the freethinker Gonzalve Desaulniers from participating in the June 24 event organized by Olivar Asselin.[87] In addition to such manoeuvres affecting the people around her, as a librarian Circé-Côté had to deal every day with the clergy's influence on the library's choice of books.[88]

The Church and Society

The issue of secular, compulsory, and free education is so important in Circé-Côté's writing that it would warrant a chapter of its own. The Catholic Church controlled not only the primary and secondary school system but also Université Laval, which held a charter from Rome. In 1919, she devoted a column to the appointment of Mgr Chartier as the university's secretary. Why had a layperson not been chosen?

The fact that the only French-language university in Quebec was Catholic was, in her view, the reason French-Canadian students were migrating to McGill University:[89]

> The preferred road leads to McGill—this shift has already begun—where the teaching is exempt from prejudice, is not tied down, and is not given by Jesuits in short robes or by hypocrites who always overdo things and make an ample display of narrow-mindedness so as not to arouse suspicion. One does not breathe in McGill's atmosphere in vain. Those who come away with an admiration for English institutions feel somewhat disdainful of the others, which, because they were afraid

of drafts, have stayed still, chained to outdated methods, bundled up in yesterday's castoffs, hostile to new things, suspicious of everything that might undermine dogma or alter morality, as chilly as old people, whose blood has frozen in their veins and who, perpetually dreading a congestion of the lungs, fear nothing more than a breath of spring air.[90]

While one should not exaggerate the extent of migration, the fact is that each year a number of French-speaking students graduated from McGill University.

Aside from educational institutions, Catholic organizations like the Action catholique de la jeunesse canadienne-française (ACJC), established in 1904, recruited young people into a school of nationalism that was Catholic above all. The guidance of souls was so restrictive that Circé-Côté accused the ACJC of emasculating its members, of preventing them from thinking independently, and even of reducing them to a vegetative existence.[91] But higher learning and the youth movement were still inaccessible to the working class. Not before the thirties did Quebec witness a blossoming of youth associations, among them the Jeunesse ouvrière catholique, which made its presence felt among the working class and, moreover, accepted girls, who until then had been excluded from student organizations.

To counter the religious neutrality of the unions belonging to the Trades and Labor Congress of Canada, which represented only a small percentage of workers, members of the clergy created Catholic labour unions. The first Catholic union, the Fédération ouvrière catholique de Montréal, was established in 1914. It would be followed in 1921 by the Confédération des travailleurs catholiques du Canada (CTCC). Writing in *Le Monde ouvrier*, the organ of the international unions, Circé-Côté, alias Julien Saint-Michel, naturally strived to free workers from the influence of the Church and the Catholic unions.[92]

The Roman Catholic Church felt threatened even though the vast majority of citizens adhered to it. To combat the effects of modernity and freedom of thought, the clergy, by way of prevention, relied primarily on education, which shaped the personalities of Catholics from a very early age. The parish exercised control over families, which were kept in line from day to day throughout the religious calendar. Priests and religious congregations held retreats, especially during Lent, to win over souls, remind them of their duties as Catholics, and bring those who may have let themselves be seduced by "the century" back to the straight and narrow path. In tandem with parish retreats, extended retreats, lasting between a day and a week, were offered in religious institutions where souls looking for spiritual nourishment were lodged and fed, for a fee. In 1915, Circé-Côté spoke out against such retreats, those "hunts for the shadowy and elusive sinner," those "artificial incubators that warm up the religious sentiment of people of the twentieth century." She denounced, first, the elitism of these meetings, with their "showmen-preachers," since they were meant mainly for the bourgeoisie, whereas parishioners in working-class districts generally attended the evening retreats held in their church. She underscored the variable language used by the preachers, depending on whether their audience was made up of "the educated class or proletarians." No matter the public, however, the goal was the same:

> [. . .] to capture these informed minds, which have been awakened by the century's scepticism through imprudent readings and daily contact with liberalized people, whose subversive theories have sometimes profoundly shaken up long-held beliefs. . . . Our rebellious sons must be shown that they are still in thrall, and to this end they are again made to bend to the rule and to discipline. They must be brought back to uniform thinking, inoculated at least every seven years, if not annually, with the serum of passivity so they may be docile instruments in the hands of Providence, the better to spread wholesome ideas.[93]

The sexes were separated in these retreats, and the women's retreats were better attended than the men's. Women were seen as guardians of Christian values, pillars of the family, and first educators, and therefore received special attention from the Church.

Éva Circé took issue with the Church's teachings on women's traditional role in society. The Church, she wrote, "fought until the very last to stymie measures intended to speed up women's evolution" and "did nothing but delay women's emancipation through the advent of feminism."[94] Starting in the 1910s, in reaction to the development of a feminist movement and campaigns in favour of women's suffrage, the Church mobilized large numbers of Quebec clergymen, who responded to the suffragists' actions with petitions against women's right to vote. The Catholic press, spearheaded by *Le Devoir*, attacked the feminists; *L'Action sociale catholique* declared that women's suffrage was "anti-social and contrary to the divine plan of Creation."[95] This continued until Benedict XV, seeing the benefits of a conservative female vote, did an about-face in July 1919.[96] Éva Circé-Côté believed for a time that the bishops of Quebec and Henri Bourassa would come around to the Vatican's new position, but when Mgr Bégin issued a statement strongly condemning feminism she wrote a column about what she called their "false doctrine."[97] As Marie Gérin-Lajoie would learn to her great chagrin at the International Congress of Catholic Women's Leagues, held in Rome in 1922, the apostolic delegate Mgr Merry del Val (who just happened to be in Rome during the Congress), very probably influenced by Henri Bourassa, had a stipulation inserted in the final report of the International Union of Catholic Women's League, whose effect was to sabotage all progress that Québécoise feminists might have hoped for, to wit, "That any new initiative in the area of women's suffrage be previously submitted *in each country* to the approval of the episcopate."[98] Clearly, however, it was inconceivable that Quebec's bishops would all endorse women's suffrage.

Quebec's Catholic character was inscribed in the Civil Code, which enshrined the legal subordination of women, especially married women, and excluded civil marriage. All couples were obliged to have their union blessed in a Catholic, Protestant, or Jewish place of worship by a priest, minister, or rabbi. Freethinkers saw this obligation as a violation of individual freedom; they usually got married in a Unitarian church. In Quebec, furthermore, it was up to the Church to determine the legitimacy of a marriage. Circé-Côté made a point of reporting on the annulment of a marriage between blood relations on the grounds that the couple apparently had not paid for the requisite dispensation. Not only was this practice a petty one that "abased religion," but marriage, moreover, ought to be "a civil contract independent of all religions."[99]

Divorce, too, was prohibited in Quebec, although, as Canadian citizens, residents of Quebec could apply to the Senate for a divorce, a long and costly procedure. Such a divorce, however, was not recognized by the Catholic authorities, who regarded the bonds of a Catholic marriage as indissoluble. This contradiction gave rise to imbroglios, which Circé-Côté addressed from the very beginning of her career in journalism. In what can be considered her first feminist article, published in *Les Débats* in 1901 under the pseudonym Musette, she covered what was known as the "Delpit affair." It involved a French freethinker whose marriage to a sixteen-year-old French Canadian was celebrated by a Unitarian minister. He later came back to Catholicism and thought he could leave his wife because the marriage was not acknowledged by the Church. Illustrating the clash between civil law and canon law, the dispute was brought before the courts, which upheld the marriage.[100]

Twenty years on, a much more confident Éva Circé-Côté would devote a number of columns to a similar case, the Despatie-Tremblay affair, and, under the Fantasio byline, would use it as a pretext to argue for the separation of church and state and to demand a uniform Canadian marriage law.

The case of the Despatie-Tremblay couple, who wished to have their marriage performed by a Protestant minister, eventually came before the Privy Council, which ruled in their favour. Circé-Côté was delighted by what she interpreted as the priority of the state over the Church.[101] She must have been particularly aware of the difficulty of having a marriage dissolved ever since her friend Georgine Boucher-Normandin had left her husband and taken up residence in Paris, where her situation prompted fewer disparaging remarks than in Quebec, where separated or divorced women were still rare.

Few aspects of private life were immune to religious supervision. At the time, religious opposition to birth control went both without saying and hand in hand with an insistent promotion of large families. But the Church was not alone in encouraging a high birthrate, a notion deeply embedded in nationalist discourse. While not confronting opponents to contraception head-on, Circé-Côté often lamented prolificacy, which she linked to poverty and infant mortality.

Attentive shepherds watched over the souls of their flock from cradle to grave. Secular citizens were outraged by religion's hold on Catholics' final hours. For priests, this moment was an occasion to call on those who had abandoned religious practice to repent. It was not uncommon for confessors to exert their powers of persuasion on Freemasons who were at death's door. Conversions of celebrities were reported in the newspapers. When, for example, Adelstan de Martigny, a well-known Freemason, eminent physician, and founder of the École littéraire de Montréal, died on November 15, 1917, at the age of fifty, the newspapers were quick to report that he had received "the succour of religion" from the hands of Mgr Bruchési himself.[102] Éva Circé-Côté, for whom this event surely brought to mind Pierre-Salomon Côté's death, published a scathing column in *Le Pays* where she vented her indignation at the archbishop's "hunt for souls" and his haste to visit a notable who had fought the Church rather than the deathbeds of humble believers. "One dies as best one can, but in this land where there is no freedom of thought, how can one have the freedom to die?" she asked.[103]

By intruding in both private life and the public space, the Church, in Circé-Côté's view, was disavowing its primary mission. The separation of church and state remained an ideal that she would never abandon. Yet despite the vitriol of her discourse, Circé-Côté always acknowledged the Church's role in the survival of French Canada. "The [Catholic] religion is entwined with the history of our land and has left its imprint on the people's character. . . . [W]e owe the preservation of our language to it, and we are grateful to the simple country clergy for having fought to maintain our most cherished rights."[104] Thus, her secularism did not descend into sectarianism. She stayed loyal to the Sisters of Saint Anne, whom, as she wrote to Dugas, Circé-Côté had always loved. And she composed luminous portraits of Jeanne d'Arc, Jeanne Mance, and Marguerite Bourgeoys, "that admirable androgyne in whom there blossomed a twin ideal, at once religious and secular," founder of the Congrégation de Notre-Dame, which "teaches [us] to live well rather than to die."[105] She wrote this in 1920, when too many religious institutions in Quebec endeavoured to detach Catholics from earthly existence in order to prepare them for the hereafter, whereas Éva Circé-Côté's disposition was toward life, joy, and optimism, and she never was able to accept the austere side of Catholicism and its obsession with death.

Similarly, in her personal relationships, the religious convictions of her intimates were not necessarily an obstacle to friendship. She remained loyal to Dugas after he became a believer. Nor did Augustine Bourassa's faith spoil the friendship between the two women.[106] And nothing seems to have weakened the bond between Circé-Côté and Georgine Boucher-Normandin, whose piety came to light in 1933 when she wrote to Dugas from El Escorial monastery in Spain that she attended high mass each morning at nine and prayed for him.[107]

Notwithstanding the anticlericalism of her writing, Circé-Côté maintained that she did not hate priests. She even excused them for opposing her, as "it is fair to take a blow after dealing one out. . . . But let them attack me face to face and not go behind my back."[108] She respected Father Auclair, of "Saint-Jean-Baptiste village," who had celebrated her marriage and earned her trust and gratitude for not having pressured Pierre-Salomon for a deathbed confession in keeping with her husband's last wishes.[109]

When a Protestant minister denigrated Catholicism, Circé-Côté did her best to set the record straight by pointing to the open-mindedness of progressive Catholics.[110] Knowing who her allies were and giving them due credit, Circé-Côté refrained from lambasting the priests she considered exceptional: Curotte, Perrier, Desrosiers, Dubois, and Blanchard.[111]

While she often assailed the papacy, the dogma of papal infallibility, and the pontiff's attitude during the war, Circé-Côté was also able to recognize the qualities of the Catholic Church. That said, however, her articles favourable to the Church were all written before 1905. In 1901, for instance, she cited the "lessons in tolerance given by Leo XIII" at the death of Ernest Renan, the French philosopher and writer who had refused to convert before dying, about whom the Pope reputedly said: "This is proof of his sincerity and God will forgive him."[112] When Leo XIII died, she lauded him as the "pope of light."[113]

Protestantism

There is no proof of Éva Circé-Côté's conversion to Protestantism.[114] According to the *National Reference Book* of 1936, her religion was Roman Catholic; a year later she was contributing to the Protestant paper *L'Aurore*. Before then, her writing for some years had attested to a deep respect for Protestantism, and *Papineau* includes many fine pages about the contribution of Protestants to the Canadian nation, in particular to the spirit of tolerance in Quebec. Circé's family was from Napierville, where Catholic and Protestants lived side by side and where the Protestant paper *Le Semeur* (The Sower) was published from 1851 to 1861. Circé-Côté devotes an entire chapter of *Papineau* to the "breath of the Reformation," in which she makes this observation:

> If we realized how much of the social, political and moral order we owe to the Protestants, the freedoms they gave us, sometimes against our will, we would not harbour against them the mistrust and hostility that paralyzes their good will and deprives us of their moral support.[115]

Of course, she objected to the Puritan strains of Protestantism, but she admired the religion of the Reformation, the one that respected freedom of conscience and valued material progress. Many of her columns were about the Protestants. In 1920, she rebuked Father Levé, a Lenten preacher, for his "warnings against two imaginary foes, Protestantism and materialism.[116] Materialism, she added, was a sign of progress and should not be thought reprehensible, while the values of Protestantism, its temporal message, deserved to be tolerated and even emulated. Writing in *Le Pays*, she did not omit to acknowledge Luther's fifth centenary in 1921 and used the opportunity to salute the Reformation.[117] Her nationalism was not religious, and her Quebec included all religions as well as freethought. She was furious when Bourassa and the Société Saint-Jean-Baptiste refused to accept Protestants: "By denying non-Catholics the right to call themselves French Canadians and to join our national association, Bourassa and his circle have departed from the tradition of the old-time nationalists, whose legacy they nevertheless lay claim to."[118] At a time when Catholics were forbidden from entering a Protestant house of worship and when associating with the disciples of Luther and Calvin was frowned upon, Circé-Côté's statements verged on heresy.

Protestantism was for Circé-Côté the religion of tolerance and respect for freedom of thought, the religion that advocated the separation of church and state, accepted civil marriage and divorce, worked for social reform and, in predominantly Protestant countries, treated women better by granting them greater equality and tolerating contraception.[119] She articulated her point of view in her preface to the published version of Alphonse Primeau-Roberts's lecture titled *La Place des protestants dans la nationalité canadienne-française*:

> Protestantism has always brought progress, independence, wealth, and freedom to the countries that have embraced it; not the narrow Protestantism that confines itself to the sanctuary, but that of Luther, Calvin, Huss, and Mélancton, the one that regenerates societies and injects movement and life into them.[120]

For *Le Monde ouvrier*, Protestantism was the religion that did not get involved in union affairs, whereas the Catholic clergy established a confessional union central.[121] In all the comparisons between Protestantism and Catholicism, it was the former that served as a model.

The Protestantism admired by Circé-Côté was not the austere, puritanical killjoy that was quick to forbid recreation and preach prohibition. In response to Reverend Straton's condemnation of dancing, she spoke out against puritanism and hypocrisy: "No mind is as skilful in uncovering evil as that of an ecclesiastic."[122] When the Liberal government tried to restrict commercial leisure activities on Sunday, Circé-Côté, ever the champion of Sunday cinema, described this policy as "immoral and anti-Catholic" and in accord with the puritans and the *castors*. "In the absence of wholesome recreations, workers will turn to unwholesome ones. They will fall prey to houses of prostitution, gambling, and other illicit pleasures, or they will shut themselves inside their houses with the blinds drawn and get drunk.... What will become of children conceived in drunkenness ... ?"[123] The issue of Sunday movies persisted for several years. When, in the wake of the Laurier Palace fire of 1927, the authorities considered requiring movie theatres to stay closed on Sundays, she noted in column that not all Protestants were so strict: "Protestantism cannot be against the light over darkness," because "everything that tends toward the spreading of ideas and the march of progress ought to be on its programme."[124] Attacking arts like film, theatre, or dance, forbidding them on Sunday, she maintained, attested to an unenlightened mentality foreign to the spirit of the Reformation.

Circé-Côté's writings on the religion of Calvin and Luther may give the impression that she was strongly inclined toward Protestantism. Yet in 1917 she stated in *Le Pays*: "Protestantism ... is not suited to our temperament.... I believe it would have detached us too quickly from the French ideal.... [To] enjoy a greater amount of freedom and to live and think, the past and future of our race would have to be sacrificed—too high a price to pay for those benefits!"[125] A year after singing the praises of Protestantism in her preface to Primeau-Robert's lecture, she declared outright in a letter to Marcel Dugas: "I do not like Protestantism."[126]

She was in close contact with members of Montreal's French-speaking Protestant community, and in the summer of 1924, while vacationing at Saint-Aimé-du-Lac-des-Îles in the Upper Laurentians, she was surprised to find a tiny congregation there. A neighbour of hers belonged to a group of nine families "as different from the French-Canadian farmers as night from day."[127] She recounted to Dugas how, on a starry night, she had visited the little wooden church, where she heard the impassioned pastor and the congregation singing wonderful hymns off-key and was charmed by the simplicity of the service. She remarked on "[this community's] good influence on the character and mentality of our people," and wondered what Quebec might have become "had the winds of the Reformation swept over it."[128] Yet this was the same letter in which she averred that she did not like Protestantism.

Circé-Côté thought that the union of the Christian churches, Catholic and Protestant, would strengthen French Canada. In 1920, commenting in *Le Pays* on an article about just such a union that had appeared in the Ottawa newspaper *Le Droit*, she wrote:

> The union of religions, like the union of Ireland and England, is discussed as though it were a peace treaty between dogs and cats or an alliance between fire and water.... With a modicum of good will, it seems to me that if the Roman religion made a few concessions, the trust [In the sense of "conglomerate"—Trans.] of beliefs could be achieved.[129]

Protestantism was thought to be in decline, and Catholicism was therefore in a good position to refuse its advances.[130] Three years on, her proposal for an ecumenical approach fell on deaf ears in the Catholic Church. Like Primeau-Robert, she deplored the assimilation of French-speaking Protestants into the English-speaking community and dreamed of seeing all Francophones, whatever their religion, "work shoulder to shoulder for the country's prosperity and greatness."[131]

The Protestants responded in kind to the esteem that she had expressed toward them. Following a number of articles in which she defended the Protestant position in favour of recognizing mixed marriages, the synod of Protestant bishops paid tribute to her as "the greatest writer in Canada."

She, for her part, wrote to Dugas that she was not fooled, adding: "As I shall never be praised by my priest, the preachers' compliments will have to do."[132]

Whether in the Gospels, patristic writings, or the commentaries of the *philosophes*, Éva Circé-Côté never gave up her quest for spirituality, but she dismissed the possibility of returning to her childhood religion. In 1949, on the eve of her death, had she forgotten what she had written on December 23, 1900, about the search for the truth?

> The Truth. . . . When in the course of your quest you will have questioned Moses, Zoroaster, Pythagoras, Socrates, Confucius, Buddha, and Muhammad, and ripped the veil of myth, then you will understand the eternal youth of Christ, symbolized by the child in the nativity scene: you will return to Him, vanquished by the love whose star will shine forever above the manger to illuminate the world.[133]

Nothing in her writings suggests that she had returned to Catholicism. And the mystery of her relationship with Protestantism has remained unsolved.

CHAPTER 8

PATRIOTISM, FRENCH CANADIANS, AND OTHERS

The unsubdued are the true liberators.
— ÉVA CIRCÉ-CÔTÉ, March 20, 1920

In the name of our patron, St. John the Baptist, who is a Jew, let us not cast stones at Israel.
— ÉVA CIRCÉ-CÔTÉ, June 25, 1927

There are virtues, such as humility, passive obedience, and lack of self-confidence, that should be replaced by flaws, namely pride, attention to personal appearance, fear of others' opinion, esteem for oneself and one's nationality.
— ÉVA CIRCÉ-CÔTÉ, August 4, 1928

IN JUNE 1904, on the occasion of its seventieth anniversary, the Association Saint-Jean-Baptiste (ASJB) of Montreal asked a number of "distinguished writers": "What is the most patriotic act in the history of the French race in Canada?" The ASJB's new publication, *Le Bulletin de la Caisse nationale d'économie*, published the brief answers in its first edition. The men and women invited to participate were not chosen haphazardly. Their standing among the turn-of-the-century intellectual elite was such that their opinions were worth publishing. The doyen of this select group, L.-O. David, whose interest in education was well known, regarded the establishment of the first eight educational institutions as an eminently patriotic act. Louvigny de

Montigny, being a literary man, held that the bust of Octave Crémazie, created by the sculptor Louis-Philippe Hébert, symbolized the advent of a new era: that of arts and letters.[1] Meanwhile, the journalist for *La Patrie*, Madeleine (Anne-Marie Gleason-Huguenin), paid tribute to the pioneer of agriculture, Louis Hébert. The poet-lawyer Gonzalve Desaulniers, for his part, had no hesitation in ranking the insurrections of 1837–38 in the top position. The member of parliament Frédérick Debartzch Monk considered the decision made by French Canadians in 1775 to remain loyal to England rather than join the independence movement of the American colonies as the founding act of French Canada—as one would expect from the leader of the Conservative Party in Quebec. For the trailblazer of women's journalism, Joséphine Marchand-Dandurand, the honour of embodying French-Canadian patriotism went to "Josephte," the symbolic figure of the French-Canadian mother. As for Colombine, after enumerating the heroes of New France, from Jeanne Mance to Marguerite Bougeoys, she chose the events of 1837–38, "the purest symbol of freedom and patriotism."[2]

The ASJB's selection of viewpoints offered a cross-section of the intelligentsia's ideological tendencies at the beginning of the century. The female journalists Anne-Marie Gleason-Huguenin and Joséphine Dandurand stayed close to the traditional outlook by giving the patriotism prize to Louis Hébert and the French-Canadian mother. Only Éva Circé and Gonzalve Desaulniers looked beyond the seventeenth and eighteenth centuries and awarded the laurels to a relatively recent historical episode, one that was, moreover, controversial, emancipatory, and modern. The great moment of the *Patriotes* would remain the landmark event for Éva Circé-Côté, who never gave up on nineteenth-century *rougisme*.

Circé-Côté was heir to the liberalism that, during the nineteenth century, demanded freedom for nations as well as individuals. In Quebec, this principle, which had been articulated by Papineau, was still part of the liberal creed. Yet Circé-Cote never identified herself as nationalist; she was a patriot, just like her idol, Papineau, and all the others she had extolled—Hindenlang, De Lorimier et al. Papineau, that "hero of antiquity gone astray on our shores,"[3] a liberal and a democrat, incarnated patriotism as she understood it: an ideology or, rather, a passion dedicated to the affirmation of a French-Canadian nation, with its language and institutions, but a secular, inclusive nation founded on progress, without exclusions based on race and religion.[4] For "heroes belong to all races and all religions."[5]

> Papineau was a messiah for us, a redeemer. He saved both the Church and the nation. We are indebted to him for the fact that we speak

French and for not being treated as conquered people. He was the honour of our race. His worth has shone forth over us. We have drawn on his glory. Papineau's head, on which a price was put so many times, was the nightmare of loathsome tyrants. For nearly a century it travelled like a star through our sky, all eyes were on it, it nourished the illusions of independence and emancipation of an entire people. It had its legend and songs and has remained a symbol.[6]

Circé-Côté recognized that Papineau, seigneur of Montebello, embraced the liberal nationalism of his epoch. She conferred the epithet "nationalist" on him, but she herself, at the beginning of the twentieth century, absolutely refused to identify with the same ideology as the young Catholics under the sway of Lionel Groulx, who was "blinded by his vainglorious ambitions,"[7] or of Henri Bourassa, who, she insisted, took counsel directly from Rome.

The ebb had begun with the implacable repression of the *Patriotes*, and the ideals of 1837–38 Rebellion were again repudiated by the clerical nationalism that continued its rise in the early years of the twentieth century. When, in a lecture on "Papineau and the Martyrs of 1837–1838," Bourassa bemoaned Papineau's loss of faith, and when Lionel Groulx described the 1837 revolt as "a blunder, mad recklessness, a lack of foresight" and proposed Dollard Des Ormeaux and Madeleine de Verchères as national paragons,[8] Circé-Côté stayed true to her heroes and kept her distance from the rising ethnic and Catholic nationalism of her epoch. To her mind, the Rebellions were neither a failure nor a mistake; the visionary *Patriotes* had not fought in vain, because "our birth as a society dates from that moment."[9]

Circé-Côté—who, it is worth recalling, wrote the *Essai de psychologie historique* about Papineau—presented herself as a patriot, one whose allegiance was twofold: to her homeland, French Canada, and her motherland, France. Her homeland was that of the French-Canadian people, a people that had made its home on part of Canada's territory and spoke French. The notion of racial purity is nowhere to be found in her writings. The people of French Canada had a twin heritage: a personality on the one hand bequeathed by France of the Ancien Régime and on the other hand acquired through contact with the Indigenous Peoples. Circé-Côté, who was firmly convinced of the role of heredity and atavism, saw this two-sided legacy as the source of French Canadians' original qualities: a jovial, Rabelaisian temperament, hospitality, pacifism, resourcefulness when it came to work, as well as, admittedly, fickleness, the "congenital need to move," laziness, and lack of foresight.[10] But because she did not espouse biological determinism, she included circumstantial causes in her analysis: the effect of the *Conquête* was grafted onto the original trunk, and, more importantly, the influence of the Catholic Church, which perverted the basic qualities of French Canadians.

That the Church inculcated in its followers a spirit of submissiveness and defeatism was something Circé-Côté often repeated. She was pitiless toward this people that had become "inert, meek, indolent," fatalistic, cowardly, craven, impressionable, and superstitious.[11] At almost every celebration of Quebec's national holiday she berated John the Baptist's sheep, an apt symbol for French Canadians' submissiveness and lack of initiative. In 1911 she expressed the wish to see "the legendary sheep transformed into a ram, the animal symbolizing obstinacy. . . . We have bleated enough; now it is time to hit, to use our hard head to strike a blow against ignorance."[12] Equally inimical were the public men who, every June 24, encouraged docility and acclaimed and flattered the French-Canadian character. Smug praise and complacency were features of the prewar movement that radical critics liked to call *saint-jean-baptisme*,[13] and which Godfroy Langlois described in the Legislative Assembly as "the old doctrine with which our race for the past forty years has been kept in a state of torpor that is difficult to shake off today."[14] In the face of such self-satisfied mediocrity, Éva Circé-Côté was utterly unsympathetic.

The "Anglais"

Like any social group, French Canadians defined themselves in relation to the Other. The first group they set themselves against they called the "*Anglais*," the English, a generic term for English-speaking people whose origins were in the British Isles. Circé-Côté's portrayals sometimes descended into crude caricature. The English "eat beefsteak and have a ruddy complexion," whereas the French have "a subtle mind, as effervescent as the froth of their champagne."[15] The French-Canadian woman has "the shapely leg and slender foot characteristic of the Latin nations, while the long, flat foot of the English woman strikes the asphalt like the tail of a codfish."[16] Mentalities are also depicted in clichéd terms. The English have a gift for business, are inclined to be progressive, and equipped for the "struggle for life."[17] They experienced the Reformation, and their values are more centred on material achievements than the values of Catholics.

A political action or an overly harsh censure could also prompt Circé-Côté to make categorical judgments about the "Anglo-Saxon mentality." When an English-language newspaper criticized the caricature of George V in *Baptiste en voyage*, a revue by Rad and Sal presented at the Théâtres des

—— : Y a d'quoi fortiller d'la queue ! Pensez donc, on a décidé de m'laisser mon plat favori !

"—Thar's good reason t' wag my tail! Just think: They decided t' leave me my fav'rite dish!"
Le Pays, December 14, 1912, BAnQ.

Nouveautés, which some English-Canadian groups threatened to sue for lese-majesty, Fantasio came to the defence of the play maligned by a "prudish paper." She took the opportunity to hold forth on the Anglo-Saxon character: "What a sad type the Saxon is and what a millstone that the Norman-born English, who can sparkle with humour, drags around at the end of an unfortunate hyphen."[18] Like other columnists before her, Éva Circé-Côté, with her facile contrast between the morose Saxon and the merry Gaul from whom the French Canadians inherited their cheerfulness and joie de vivre, helped to make this depiction proverbial.

More serious, in her view, were the effects of Anglo-Saxon assurance, the sense of superiority of the *Anglais* in the face of the timidity and insecurity of a people taught to obey. It was an unequal contest: "The English, less talented than us, Saxons, essentially, on the strength of their wonderful assurance, need only show up to overcome the same obstacles that thwart us."[19]

The allusion here is to the rivalry in the economic sphere, an area where British superiority was commonly acknowledged.

In response to Great Britain's entry into the war alongside France, Éva Circé-Côté lavished praise on the genius, in the sense of "spirit," of the English and their sense of fair play. The nation that declared war on Germany possessed "prophetic statesmen"; it was a country that granted "the right of asylum to all opinions" and allowed "all inhabitants of the British Empire the right to fill their lungs with the air of liberty."[20] Following these general remarks, she compared the predominantly English west side of Montreal to its predominantly French east side, underscored the dominance of the English in Quebec's economy, particularly in the wholesale business, and invited her compatriots not to resent them for their domination. French Canadians, who gravitated toward spirituality, had left the field open to them, while they, the English

> [...] harvested the fruits that were already dropping from the branches. They did not spurn the worldly goods that we hold in contempt.... They improved the lands that we had let go to waste.... We might have protected ourselves through compulsory education; owing to our lack of pride, our gaze turned toward the past, we were unable to command respect.[21]

The English mentality, according to Éva Circé-Côté, explained in part why philanthropy flourished in Montreal's English-speaking community, a corollary factor being the significant proportion within that community of successful businessmen, financiers, merchants, and self-made men, such as she devoutly wished to see emerge among French Canadians.[22] Didn't the English, thanks to their philanthropists, endow themselves with a university whose praises she was constantly singing, McGill University, "a sort of Bethany, a refuge of silence conducive to meditation and study," whose libraries Circé-Côté, the head librarian of the Municipal Library, so envied.[23] As a liberal, freethinking woman, she admired England's "cult of liberty and initiative, which it was able to inculcate in its lowest subjects," and which assured its superiority: "That is the secret source of their strength, their dignity, and that country's ascendancy over the weaker races."[24]

It was by way of her Francophilia that Circé-Côté expressed her loyalty to England, Albion now absolved of its treachery, fighting since August 1914 shoulder to shoulder with France, "the fount of light and progress."[25] Yet this loyalty was not unconditional and not akin to that of Mgr Bruchési, which she considered extreme.[26] When Circé-Côté came out against conscription in 1917, she nevertheless remained faithful to Great Britain.²⁷ After the war her admiration for English values remained intact, so that when the former Labour Prime Minister Ramsay MacDonald—whom she portrayed as the embodiment of liberalism and modernity—visited Canada in 1928, Julien Saint-Michel pointed to the thinkers, economists, and sociologists who were the flower of British culture, and she urged her readers to "live on the best possible terms with England."²⁸

Contact with the English could prove to be rewarding for French Canadians, who could only benefit from imitating their entrepreneurial spirit and adopting their freedom of thought. But this required mutual understanding. Circé-Côté did not demand that the English learn the language of Molière, but whenever she advocated educational reforms she included the teaching of English in French-speaking schools. Far from seeing the English language as a threat, she felt that mastering it would contribute to material advancement and signify openness to modernity. She was realistic in acknowledging that people in the other provinces would never learn French and that English would remain the language of communication in Canada. However, she did demand that French do the same in Quebec, while showing respect for English: "The principle of nationalities tells us to appreciate ways of thinking, as well as their respective languages, which are different from ours."²⁹

Yet it would be wrong to conclude that Circé-Côté blindly admired everything originating on the banks of the Thames, such as English imperialism in Ireland, which she denounced. The Irish people, enslaved and exploited by the large English landowners, burned with the desire for emancipation. Still, while she wrote in defence of Robert Casement, an independentist executed for treason in 1916, she felt that the decision to rise up right in the middle of the war was very ill-advised on the part of the Irish.³⁰

Her sympathy for emerald Erin did not extend to Canadians of Irish extraction: "Former slaves now in the master's position, the Irish proletarians oppress as they were oppressed. Protestantism does not change the Celtic character; they have remained combative, aggressive, passionate, vindictive, intolerant."³¹ Nor was she any more indulgent toward Irish Catholic immigrants. Her infrequent comments about them came in response to the actions of the Irish Catholic higher clergy, who vied with the French-Canadian clergy for control of the Catholic Church in Canada particularly with regard to the appointment of a cardinal or the rights of Franco-Ontarians. They were, in her words, "fanatics" under the leadership of the bishop of London, Ontario, Michael Francis Fallon, whom she accused of siding with the "persecutors of Ireland" and, in Canada, "with the conquerors when it comes to crushing us."³² Indeed, Fallon openly opposed a bilingual education system in Ontario, a stance for which Circé-Côté, ever a champion of the French language, could not forgive him.

Despite her respect for various Anglo-Saxon values, Éva Circé-Côté constantly ridiculed those who aped Anglo-Saxon ways, as evidenced by her comedy *L'Anglomanie*. The French language and those who speak it must never give way: the "French ideal is a beacon . . . by preserving this beautiful language we share in its spirit."[33] Sharing in the spirit of this civilization is an honour and a privilege, is it not? Her statement sounds very much like the messianic message of her nationalist contemporaries.

In the end, it was her fear of the separatism preached by Lionel Groulx that led Circé-Côté to repudiate any inclination toward independence and to rely on England to safeguard secular values and liberate "its French-Canadian subjects from an oppression that impedes their evolution."[34] It was Groulx who drove her to clarify her position on the future of Quebec in 1937.

> Far from being a separatist, I dream of a closer union with England. I would ask it to treat us, the French-Canadians, like the other peoples of the Dominion, to not make exceptions of us, to grant us the same rights as English subjects, to not impose on us an obsolete code that will never change as it did in France, instead of throwing us to the priests.[35]

The French Language

With the advent of French talkies in 1928, cinema's role as a vehicle of French rather than American culture became a tangible reality. Under the pen name Fantasio, Circé-Côté discussed the 1935 Congrès du film parlant français (Congress of French talkies) in *La Revue moderne*. French film, she wrote, is "an instrument of survival," one that helps to preserve our language and to resist "our idiotic admiration of English-speaking gentlemen";[36] furthermore, "what is at stake is nothing less than our life as a nation."[37]

As for the quality of the French spoken in Quebec, Éva Circé-Côté had no illusions. "We speak seventeenth-century French, with half the vocabulary of our brothers in the motherland; it is high time we renewed ourselves."[38] She herself showed the way with her polished and refined writing style.

In 1937 the French-Canadian participants in the celebration of the twenty-fifth anniversary of the Congrès de la langue française (Congress of the French language) fell far short of Circé-Côté's expectations. Unsurprisingly, she was less than enthusiastic about this gathering of the French-speaking world, organized by Camille Roy, where orators railed against materialism and jazz, and Cardinal Rodrigue Villeneuve, the Sulpician Olivier Maurault, and Father Lionel Groulx enjoyed celebrity status.[39] Among the representatives of Quebec she observed "bad speakers lacking vocabulary and unable to express their ideas," whose language was "contaminated by various ethnic influences." She ascribed the sorry state of French to the education system, which favoured dead languages to the detriment of French, a language that, in Quebec, demanded patient study and constant attention.[40] She derided "our mannered, precious poetesses, who came to recite their verses like sibyls on pedestals consisting of ginger ale cases and cracker crates."[41] It was a nasty remark, but Circé-Côté's concern for a strong command of the French language never waned.

Nationalism

An anti-imperialist from the very start—her career in journalism began at *Les Débats*, which was openly opposed to the Boer War—for a long time Circé-Côté endorsed Henri Bourassa's nationalist opposition to the British Empire. In 1904, she was conspicuously present at the creation of the Ligue nationaliste, led by Olivar Asselin and Jules Fournier, with Henri Bourassa as the éminence grise, and she embraced the autonomist current that was sweeping the province on the strength of its call for Canadian autonomy vis-à-vis the British Empire and provincial autonomy vis-à-vis Ottawa. But she soon dissociated herself from the two young men mesmerized by Bourassa; she could appreciate the latter's strong personality, powerful eloquence, and honest approach, but the religious nature of his movement precluded her adhesion. Laurier had called Bourassa a "red beaver" (*castor rouge*) and, indeed, Papineau's grandson had achieved the improbable feat of combining ultramontanism and liberalism. This achievement earned him, as well as the "opportunistic jingoists" of *Le Devoir*, Circé-Côté's anathema:[42]

> When you see these beavers, these secularized rodents who have obstructed the stream with the dam of their traditionalism, their provincialism in order to divert the course of natural, progressive life to their benefit . . . stop your ears to their speeches, which will lead you back to primitive life.[43]

From the founding of *Le Devoir*—which in its very first editions attacked Éva Circé-Côté because of Pierre-Salomon Côté's civil funeral—until 1937, she mentioned Bourassa in eighty-odd columns, some of which were almost exclusively about him. Unable to suppress her admiration for the courage of this journalist-politician who defended the interests of French Canada, she nonetheless spoke out against the religious content of his work and his exclusive conception of the nation. As far as Bourassa was concerned, "a freethinker or a protestant is not a French Canadian."[44] Yet, as soon as Bourassa was criticized by the *bon-ententiste* Church, Fantasio was quick to emphasize his honesty and "moral beauty."[45]

That said, Circé-Côté, who participated in the "moral regeneration campaign" of *Le Pays*,[46] could very well have espoused Bourassa's ideal, as framed in his first editorial as editor-in-chief of *Le Devoir*: "There is only one way to ensure the triumph of ideas over appetites, of the public good over political partisanship: arouse in the people, and especially in the governing classes, the sense of public duty in all its forms."[47] Circé-Côté and Bourassa often found themselves on the same side of the barricade, be it on the issue of anti-imperialism, Canadian autonomy, the rights of Franco-Ontarians, the conscription crisis, the fight against the trusts, or the importance of the French language. She recognized the quality of *Le Devoir* and never put it in the same category as *L'Action sociale*. Nevertheless, she crossed swords with Bourassa a number of times: at the declaration of war in 1914,[48] when Bourassa came out against feminism and women's suffrage, and each time he behaved more like a *castor* than a *rouge* and yielded to pressure from the Vatican. She could not accept his submission to the Church any more than his statements about immigrants, particularly Jews.[49]

Circé-Côté had greater affinities with Asselin and Fournier, whose open-mindedness was closer to the spirit of Papineau. There were many features that attracted her to Asselin, whom she called a "singular musketeer":[50] his integrity, his passion, his irreverence, his love of language. They fought side by side to defend the rights of Franco-Ontarians or to call for the separation of church and state. But Asselin's time at *Le Devoir*, his cooperation with journalists like Omer Héroux, who also wrote in right-wing papers like *La Vérité*, his intransigent nationalism, and, of course, his opposition to women's suffrage got in the way of any true collaboration between them. Still, it was when Asselin served, in her words, as "the dashing president of the Saint-Jean-Baptiste" in 1913 and 1914 that Circé-Côté's ties with French-Canadian nationalist organizations were strongest.[51]

The year 1913 witnessed the struggle for the maintenance of French schools in Ontario. Olivar Asselin, then president of the Société Saint-Jean-Baptiste (SSJB), with the backing of the Fédération nationale Saint-Jean-Baptiste (FNSJB) and Action catholique de la jeunesse canadienne-française (ACJC), launched *Le Sou de la pensée française* (The cent of French thought), a vast funding drive to support French schools in Ontario by way of financial aid for the newspaper *Le Droit*, the advocate for the language rights of Ontario's French-speaking minority. The FNSJB mobilized thousands of volunteers to ask for donations on June 24. Madeleine publicized their cause in *La Patrie*. *Le Pays* followed suit and endorsed the Sou salvateur (the cent of salvation), "the symbol of the touching communion that should exist among Canadians,"[52] French Canadians, that is.

Asselin made a bold move within the SSJB when he cancelled the big Saint-Jean parade of 1913 and scorned the presence of the sheep. Not to be outdone, Fantasio devoted a column to this question, fulminating against the parade in language rivalling Asselin's: "We are Christians, and we repudiate these vestiges of paganism, these processions reminiscent of the feasts of the Apis bull and the sacred cow of India, or the mass celebrations in Egypt glorifying the crocodiles and cats deified by ignorance."[53]

Her opposition to Father Lionel Groulx was altogether different. In 1910, Groulx founded the ACJC, eliciting a strong reaction from Éva Circé-Côté, who was outraged at the mobilization of youths around a religious ideal tinged with racism. She began to berate and deride the members of the ACJC for their sectarianism, anti-Semitism, and fanaticism.[54] She was also afraid of them. These "young Chanteclercs"[55] tried to infiltrate the SSJB and were highly visible at the Fête nationale and various nationalist conventions.[56] Moreover, they personified the submissive and obedient sons that she constantly took to task. As for their mentor, Lionel Groulx, she thought *Le Devoir* should be ashamed to publish his "ridiculous theses" about the Rebellions of 1837: "This worthy soutane has no understanding of French heroism."[57] In the thirties, when the cleric put forward positions with separatist overtones, Circé-Côté, writing in *Le Monde ouvrier*, was wary, fearing that "under cover of nationalism, he would want to promote a sort of thinly veiled theocracy, whose advent he dreams of."[58] Groulx was not Circé-Côté's target of choice before his well-known lecture of 1937, but from that point on she took a stand against the man who would make "Canada independent of England and dependent on religious absolutism" and against dangerous statements that would lead to an ecclesiastical state.[59]

Aboriginal Peoples

As a patriot, Éva Circé-Côté identified, first, with her homeland and with the mother country, France, whose virtues and progress she was forever extolling. If France was the mother country, was her homeland restricted to the inhabitants of Canada of French heritage? In fact, her position was never so exclusive. From the beginning of the French colony, the colonizers had to deal with the Aboriginal Peoples, "the Red-Skins our Ancestors,"[60] and a number of Circé-Côté's columns were about them.

The Indian population of New France in the seventeenth century was estimated to be around 150,000. According to census figures, members of the First Nations during the first half of the twentieth century numbered fewer than 15,000 souls, and their proportion of the Quebec population declined from 0.65 percent in 1901 to 0.36 percent in 1951.[61] These figures most probably underestimated the presence of First Nations, but they nevertheless led ethnologists and civil servants at the federal Department of Indian Affairs to believe in the ineluctable demographic decline of the Aboriginal Peoples of Canada.

Circé-Côté's columns mentioned the Iroquois, Algonquin, and Huron, the major groups identified at the time, but she did not differentiate the various peoples within each group.[62] Montrealers generally did not live near one of Quebec's thirty-one reserves and therefore had few contacts with "Indians," except in front of hotels and in railroad stations, where Éva noticed women selling maple syrup candy bars (*palettes de sauvagesses*), or at the Marché Bonsecours, where "the Indians are reduced to selling moccasins" to passersby who look at them "like museum pieces, a sort of walking mummy that has lost its bandages."[63] Being a progressive woman, she held a benevolent view of the Indigenous Peoples and reproduced all the stereotypes of her epoch with the best of intentions.

In 1901, in her column "Caughnewaga," [now spelled Kahnawake— Trans.] written under the pen name Colombine, she lamented the slow physical and cultural demise of the inhabitants of the "desolate looking" reserve located a few kilometres from Montreal. She described the interior of the one-room houses, the cribs with babies tied up on a small board, the straw mats, and the people on the reserve still speaking Iroquois, "a strange, melodic language, full of images but limited and incomplete" and lacking abstract terms. She paid tribute to Chief John Jocks, who acted as his people's legal representative and counsellor and was "a gentleman in the full sense of the word: polite, amiable, educated, distinguished, and very popular." She attributed qualities to this community that amounted to a string of clichés: dreamy, hospitable, generous, upright, "naively simple." As for the women, they were gentle, quiet, devoted to husband and children. For Circé-Côté, the Iroquois would always remain "children of the woods."[64]

It would not do her essay justice to read it as essentially condescending and romantic in the manner of Chateaubriand. Beyond the clichés, Colombine observed "the devastating scourge" inflicted on a proud people by those claiming to "civilize" it. The "invaders'" enterprise resulted in the decline of a people, as evidenced by Caughnawaga itself: "this bald piece of land that produces just enough corn to feed the crows." Here, "the most powerful of the Indian tribes sighs out its death rattle!" Her prediction: "Within fifty years, the little bell will sound the death knell of Canada's proudest warrior tribe." She laid much of the blame on the English, who "have the infernal knack of insidiously sapping the life of a race." Because, for an anti-imperialist like Circé-Côté, the lot of the North American Indigenous Peoples was linked to the great colonial enterprise: "Yesterday, the Indians of the East, today the Red-Skins, tomorrow . . . ?"[65] The ellipsis suggests the fate of other conquered peoples, perhaps the French Canadians? Colombine considered this essay, her first on the Aboriginal Peoples, so important that she would reproduce it two years later in *Bleu, Blanc, Rouge*.

This was one of Éva Circé's very first columns, and it set the tone for her future writings on the Indigenous Peoples. The First Nations had been dispossessed, stripped of their lands, and deprived of their traditional way of life, but not without putting up resistance. In her article "Iroquois Legend," published in *L'Avenir du Nord* in 1905, the Iroquois, resisting conversion, answer the missionary in these terms: "You may have robbed our lands, destroyed our strength, and bound these arms that you fear, but you will not have our souls."[66] Then they tell the priest the legend of the creation of the world and the mystery of death. Éva must have been very fond of this legend, because many years later her daughter Ève recited it at a public reading held under the auspices of the Association des auteurs canadiens.[67]

In her biography of Papineau, Circé-Côté devotes a chapter to the "lot of the aboriginal people under English domination."[68] Twenty years after her report on Caughnawaga, her view of the situation was still pessimistic:

> Burned by alcohol, intoxicated by nicotine, ravaged by tuberculosis, our civilization has killed them like the pines and cedars of the forests. Confined to ever more remote reserves dependent on Anglo-Saxon philanthropy, they will have disappeared from British America in a hundred years, and no one will know whether they died at their dawning or at their sunset.[69]

Since the first contact between the First Nations and the invaders, it was an unfair fight and the heroes of New France "stole from the natives their forests, their rivers, their squaws,"[70] and "the Indians [*sauvages* in the original—Trans.] waited too long to rally. The sap has dried in the exhausted branches."[71] Conversions to Catholicism, one of the first explicitly stated goals of French colonization, often ended in failure: "baptism brought them under the sway of harmful influences." Indeed, "they ascribe their downfall to their betrayal of their Manitou."[72] When Quebec was hit by violent storms in the winter of 1912, she imagined what the Indigenous Peoples might make of this: "It is the dance of vexed spirits against the warriors who stripped them of their lands and their caribou."[73] Yet she did not regard these peoples, with their sometimes strange customs, as so very different from the colonizers with whom they had been thrown together.

These themes were developed as well in Circé-Côté's play *Maisonneuve*, produced in 1921, in which contacts between the French and the Iroquois prove to be far more advantageous for the former than for the conquered peoples. The Governor of Montreal is himself unsettled by the arguments of the Iroquois chief on the respective virtues of both groups. The contrast between the decadence of the French court and the nobility of Chief Antonhieiarho, the comparison between French and Indian superstitions, the denunciation of Catholic hypocrisy, and the exaltation of Iroquois frankness flew in the face of conventional thinking at the time.

On more than one occasion, Colombine or Julien Saint-Michel alluded to the blood ties between Aboriginal people and French Canadians. The day after the Saint-Jean-Baptiste holiday in 1909 she wrote:

> [...] the likes of Maisonneuve, Dollard, Chénier, Hindelang, Papineau, Parent, Cartier are not the only ones who abide within us; there are the Iroquois and the Huron and all the old, primitive races or those struck by lightning at their decline, that through their blood have passed on to you the rites of a vanished cult. You are celebrating them, too.[74]

In presenting French Canadians as a people of mixed heritage, Éva Circé, whose family tree did not include any Indian forebears, drew on the genealogical studies of Mgr Tanguay and on her husband's research.[75] Like many forward-thinking people in her circle, she believed in heredity, in the genetic transmission not only of physical features but also of traits, tastes, and behaviours now considered acquired. This social Darwinism led her to draw the following comparison between the colonized and the colonizers:

> This inclination to believe in the marvellous, this taste for endless ruminations, this passion for nicotine... this laziness that saps the wellspring of our will, this passion for metaphor, this attraction to poetry, this religiosity that leaves us more concerned with the form than the

content of belief ... the high-cheekbones, certain facial expressions, the amber-brown eyes, the curve of the eyebrows constitute a cluster of irrefutable evidence for the unbiased observer studying ethnography.[76]

There was no shame in descending from the first inhabitants, on the contrary, even if as a result the women "offer themselves and give themselves spontaneously, thus surprising and charming the stranger, because their love is not venal."[77] Nor did Circé-Côté have any scruples about idealizing a way of life.

The Aboriginal Peoples, open-handed, carefree, and generous, set numerous examples for their conquerors to follow, as the founder of Montreal does in the play *Maisonneuve*. For he envisions a future forged by the union of the conquered and the conquerors:

> [. . .] the Iroquois woman, is she not our true companion in this land that she alone knows? ... By getting closer to her, shall we not come nearer to nature, nearer to God? ... Is she not the oxygen that will invigorate our blood tainted by fifteen hundred years of debauchery? Instead of this fierce war that we wage against the natives, why not marry their daughters? ... Is that not the best way to conquer, the least dishonourable?[78]

The Indigenous Peoples maintained respect for elders, sons' veneration of their mothers; Circé-Côté was so bold as to assert that "the Indians are feminists because they are not dominated by cravings or any other secret sentiment" and because the men admit women to their celebrations while the white men exclude them from their learned societies.[79]

She wanted to see these people "rouse and react," they who were deprived of their rights, "herded inside constantly shrinking reserves, and condemned to die";[80] in order to survive they ought to shape for themselves "an ideal in keeping with the spirit of the century," in other words, give up their superstitions—advice that she repeatedly proffered to her own people—and embrace modern life. Going even further, she proposed that they throw "into the fire these clown costumes, these ignoble woollen blankets that they use to play ridiculous roles for the amusement of travellers."[81] In 1927 the folkloric aspect of the "noble savages" had become degrading for her. What they needed, according to Circé-Côté, in order to end their subjugation was patriotism, "that civilizing agent," because without it "the primitive populations, the country's natives," were unable to stand up against the aggressors.[82] For her, the Iroquois would always wear "the sad smile of declining races."[83]

Immigrants

In addition to acknowledging French Canadians' debt to the Indigenous Peoples, Éva Circé-Côté recognized the role that people who had come from abroad had played in Canada's history. But could they, like their "dyed-in-the-wool" fellow citizens, also lay claim to the title of *"Patriotes"*? In her view, all those who actively defended the interests of the homeland, its rights and traditions, and the French language were entitled to be called patriots. It was not a matter of blood and heredity. She expressed her thoughts on the subject very clearly after contemplating the monument to the *Patriotes* in front of the former Pied-du-Courant prison: "Heroes belong to all races and to all religions."[84] Charles Hindenlang, whom she brought to life on the stage, came from France but was of Swiss extraction, yet he was no less a *Patriote* for all that. He even gave his life for the cause on February 15, 1839, the date of his execution. Julien Saint-Michel pleaded, "We must not ostracize foreigners; today's foreigners will be our brothers tomorrow if we are able to assimilate them and interest them in our public affairs. Let us welcome all those of good will of all nationalities.... Let us make no false distinctions among races and beliefs."[85] What mattered to her was that all coexist under the same flag.

Éva Circé-Côté lived at a time when those called foreigners were increasingly visible in the metropolis. According to the 1911 census, Montreal, not counting suburbs like Maisonneuve, Westmount, Outremont or Verdun, had a population of 470,480 people, 6.7 percent of whom were born in Europe (excluding the British Isles), 0.41 percent in Asia, 2.2 percent in the US, and 0.06 percent in other countries.[86] By 1931, the population had grown to 818,577, of which 18 percent were immigrants (including, this time, those from the British Isles, hence skewing the comparison).[87] Many of the newcomers lived in the heart of Montreal, on both sides of Saint-Laurent Boulevard as well as to the north.

The presence of immigrants sometimes aroused fears to which nationalist groups lent their voices. In Montreal, the expansion of various associations, such as the Action catholique de la jeunesse canadienne-française and the Filles natives du Canada (Native daughters of Canada), was linked to immigration as much as it was to the economic weight of Anglophones. While perambulating through the city streets, Circé-Côté took note of the people who hailed from overseas and often discussed them in her columns, especially on the occasion of the Saint-Jean-Baptiste holiday. Imbued with the spirit of the French Jacobins, she advocated assimilation: "If we had had a national school system we would have assimilated the exotic populations whose sympathies lie with us."[88] Note that while the term "exotic" jars today, it had widespread currency at the time. In *Papineau*, published in 1924, she argued that the strength of traditions and institutions could counteract what some considered an invasion:

> Whether or not the ark containing the sacred repository of our traditions will prevail over the rising tide of immigration is entirely up to us. To this end, our institutions must not be inferior to those of other countries and we must preserve the genius of our language and of the French ideal; otherwise the foreigners will take up the torch that we will have dropped. The pace of immigration must be handled intelligently if we wish to avoid having the blood that comes to us from our ancestors replaced in our veins by exotic blood, on the pretext that it will strengthen us.[89]

At the same time, she did not hesitate to blame French Canadians for their resistance to accepting newcomers in their institutions.

> What efforts have we made to assimilate the Jews, the Slavs, the exotics in general? We have ostracized them from our schools, our national societies, our circles, our literary clubs, while the English institutions have welcomed them with open arms.

As a result, "they speak English while making up one-fifth of urban populations."[90] She articulated this harsh judgment more than once, in, among other publications, the *Jewish Daily Eagle (Kanader Adler)*: "We are the reason that, through our lack of vision, our fanaticism, our narrow outlook, all systematically maintained, we have deprived ourselves of strong and vital elements."[91] In 1934, she reminded readers that "to remain masters of our province," it would have taken a national French-language school system, "the mould where all the exotic races that have invaded us would have melded together to form a homogeneous whole. Instead of being assimilated, we would have imposed our language and traditions on the foreigners."[92]

Circé-Côté always contended that the public school was the best means to train citizens. School should also act as an agent of assimilation. But in Quebec, where the education system was confessional, all non-Catholics, whatever their first language, were sent to Protestant, English-language schools. Thus, each year, thousands of children were kept from integrating into the French-Canadian community. For a brief moment, in 1930, Montreal Jewish schools had their own school board. Other groups subsequently asked for the right to have their own educational institutions.[93] Initially, Circé-Côté was sympathetic to their demand and congratulated Louis-Athanase David, the Secretary of Quebec [a government body in charge of provincial domestic affairs that existed from 1867 to 1970—Trans.], for his bill and wrote that Premier Taschereau "showed remarkable skill and boldness" in the matter.[94] She saw this as an initiative that addressed parents' concerns about their children's education; she furthermore considered it a matter of justice, for "there is no reason to deny the eighty thousand Jews living in this city what was granted in the past to a hundred thousand French Canadians, because all men in the Dominion must be equal before the constitution."[95] Later, however, she vehemently opposed the project of separate schools: "Montreal will become a Babel, where the confusion of languages and ideas will reign."[96] What was needed was a public school open to all children, of all origins, a "Noah's Ark where everyone must find a place"; indeed, how could anyone complain that these immigrants swelled the ranks of Anglophones, since it was the Catholic schools that prevented the assimilation of immigrants.[97] Her idealized models of assimilation and integration were France and the US: "Take the example of the United States, [. . .] which, in the crucible of its tolerance and charity—which was good for its own sake—could melt diverse elements together to form a homogeneous whole."[98]

An idyllic wish for harmony was not, however, Circé-Côté's sole response to the immigration issue. In the progressive newspaper *Le Pays*, Fantasio inveighed against the government's immigration policies. In 1914, before the war put an end to the economic recession and unemployment affecting urban workers, she at times used language that was better suited to the right-wing papers than a radical weekly, as when she wrote that a "slimy stream" was flowing into the city, creating a dangerous situation because people were hungry. But, she added, one must not bear a grudge against the foreigners: "To deprive them of work on the pretext that Canadians do not have enough for themselves is an act of cruelty that could turn against us; we had better join forces to save the hapless foreigners from misery." She furthermore reminded readers that "often a sense of dignity and pride subsists among these unfortunates . . . such that they prefer to earn a dollar than accept alms." Rather than being satisfied with soup kitchens, she recommended that decision-makers shorten the workday so as to provide work for more people and pay "everyone a dollar and a half a day instead of two."[99] It was a measure rejected on every side.

The mistrust toward immigrants was also vented under Julien Saint-Michel's byline in *Le Monde ouvrier*; there, Circé-Côté took a dim view of the arrival of foreigners willing to accept wages and working conditions inferior to those prevailing in North America. The postwar depression unleashed her most disdainful xenophobic allegations:

> [. . .] like a flock of crows, a swarm of invaders, parasites that should be contained in stockades. . . . They have killed small business by taking over the main commercial arteries of the metropolis. They have discredited the workforce by offering themselves at ridiculous prices; they have defaced and stunk up our nicest neighbourhoods, and they add to the high cost of living because they increase the number of consumers without making a suitable contribution to production. If barriers were put up against Chinese immigration, why can't the same thing be done for those jamming the major urban centres and doubling the number of paupers, pariahs, and delinquents![100]

Again, Circé-Côté ascribed this situation to immigration policies that benefitted employers. As an alternative to charity, and short of closing the borders to immigration, she suggested that, at the very least, newcomers be directed to regions in need of settlers.[101] Everywhere in North America borders were being made less porous; the US enacted an immigration policy more restrictive than ever before, while in 1923 the Canadian government almost completely banned Chinese immigration.

In addition to economic issues, Circé-Côté also examined the cultural aspects of immigration; she gave voice to the concerns of French Canadians who were struggling to take their place in Montreal's cultural scene. In 1917, for example, she criticized the Société Saint-Jean-Baptiste, complaining that no French Canadian dramatist's works were being staged at the Monument-National, "where only the exotics are entitled to present their own plays."[102] She focused more on the dearth of French-Canadian playwrights than on what in her view amounted to favouritism toward the Jewish theatre. Moreover, it was, according to her, the authorities "who force on us foreigners with whom we have no affinity of race"[103] that were to blame and not the immigrants who took advantage of government policies.

While she kept her distance from the nationalist movement's alarmism in the face of the large wave of immigration in the 1920s, she feared "the danger of seeing the French element swamped by the rising tide of immigration"; nevertheless, far from restricting immigration and even further from "making life hard for these poor exiles who have come here seeking refuge from tyranny,"[104] she proposed to make French-language institutions more attractive to immigrants and to impose compulsory education so that French Canadians would not lose their "human capital," their identity, and their trades.[105] Contrary to the nationalist clerics, the issue, as she saw it, was not the survival of the race or the religion, but the economy and patriotism. "Let us cease discussing race and religion and listen only to the voice of patriotism."[106] She went so far as to compare the immigrants to "the muddy stream and the scum from the old countries" needing to be cleaned up.[107] These are unpleasant, insulting terms, though they did not apply only to people arriving from Eastern Europe.

In January 1928, when almost one out of ten unionized workers was unemployed in Quebec, Circé-Côté alias Julien Saint-Michel, addressing herself to a receptive readership, stood up against the influx of jobless British workers. Who says, she asked, that Anglo-Saxon bosses will not give the best positions "to this whole beggarly crowd, the scum of London?" The capitalist thus would get hold of a cheap workforce, "a convenient way to cut off our people's livelihood and suppress their demands."[108] And yet, in commenting on the speeches delivered at the Saint-Jean-Baptiste celebrations in 1927, she warned: "we do not need to belittle others who come to work alongside us to develop our vast riches. We will not go to get them, but seeing that they are here, we must not make their lives intolerable"; "we must not be blinded by chauvinism."[109]

As was the case with almost any issue, Circé-Côté maintained an ambiguous, even contradictory discourse dictated by circumstance. Thus, while insisting that she was not a chauvinist, let alone a xenophobe, she assailed the government for allowing immigrants to concentrate in Montreal.

> If all the Romanians, Poles, Russians, and Jews of Montreal, rather than crowding into the centre of the city, were pushed back to the North [of Quebec], if they produced fewer children and did more market gardening, farm products would be more plentiful and occasionally less expensive.[110]

Still, immigrants were not responsible for immigration policies, and they were "entitled, like us, to the sun, to roses, and to love."[111] She pointed an accusing finger at the legislators and country priests who did nothing to make the outlying regions more attractive to foreigners. The newcomers were discouraged from settling outside the large urban centres by priests who condemned their popular dances and feasts "where the devil showed his horns in the perverted imagination of these Tartuffes." Local leaders, who shunned the outside world, "give the foreigner a cool reception and do their utmost to push railroad construction as far away as possible," since this would draw immigrants away from the large cities.[112] While Circé-Côté's shocking remarks about immigrants must not be downplayed, they should be contextualized.¹¹³ Her attacks were directed primarily at the governments and not just the immigrants. When seen in perspective, her statements were very different to those made by the nationalists advocating a return to the land and the preservation of a rural population that was homogeneously French-Canadian and Catholic.

The Jews

Among the broad contingent of immigrants, one minority in particular drew the nationalists' attention: Central European Jews, who were concentrated essentially in Montreal. As of 1910, Circé-Côté was writing for newspapers whose editors could not remain indifferent to the presence of these Jews.¹¹⁴ Godfroy Langlois of Le Pays acknowledged that it was the Jews of the Saint-Louis district who had elected him to the Legislative Assembly. Accordingly, wrote Fantasio, "we have given expression to their just demands, because we could only congratulate ourselves for their intelligent cooperation in all our emancipatory undertakings."¹¹⁵ At the same time, under the pen name Julien Saint-Michel, she contributed to Le Monde ouvrier, which, speaking on behalf of the workers, made no secret of its mistrust toward immigrants, including the Jews, who entered the labour market with wages often lower than those earned by Canadian workers while unemployment persisted in Montreal.

Even though the majority of immigrants arriving each year were from Britain and the United States, far more attention was focused on those coming from Central Europe, especially the Jews, who, more than any other group, were the subject of commentary in the nationalist press. With the rise of postwar nationalism, l'Action française and nationalists of Lionel Groulx's ilk gave vent to xenophobia and even racism, but it is also worth noting the much more benevolent statements made by many progressive liberals, best exemplified by Éva Circé-Côté. At a time when few people were shocked by racist remarks about Jews, often under the guise of humour, Circé-Côté, as well as her colleagues Godfroy Langlois and T. D. Bouchard, displayed a high degree of openness toward them.¹¹⁶

In 1921, the Jewish community numbered around 50,000. Most Jews lived in an area of a few square kilometres located on either side of Saint-Laurent Street, south to north between the old port and Van Horne and east to west between de Bullion and Parc, as well as in the Papineau neighbourhood farther north. From 1910 to 1921, Éva Circé-Côté lived in the vicinity of Saint-Laurent, the proverbial Main, whose many shops sold goods from all over Eastern Europe; it was there that a high proportion of Jewish businesses could be found.[117] She daily saw these Europeans who on more than one occasion were the subject of her columns. The first time she mentioned anti-Semitism, in 1911, she described that of the Action catholique de la jeunesse canadienne-française (ACJCF) as "outmoded"; but anti-Jewish prejudice was hardly on the decline and continued to provide grist for ACJCF discourse and the pages of publications such as *L'Action française* and *La Vérité*. Circé-Côté countered by stigmatizing Bourassa's nationalism, which "declaims against the Jews in the name of patriotism and religion," she rebuked the new Catholic trade unions for excluding Jews, and she repeatedly reminded her readers that the patron saint of French Canadians, just like Jesus himself, was Jewish.[118]

We have seen in previous chapters that Circé-Côté lambasted anti-Semitism on a number of occasions. She made her position clear in *Papineau*: "We have no reason to applaud ourselves for awakening anti-Semitic prejudice. The result is that we have turned half a million inhabitants away from us."[119] Drawing on a host of clichés, she praised the qualities attributed to Jews, such as a knack for business, and debunked unfounded rumours and allegations. No, she reminded her readers, they do not control the film industry, as claimed by those accusing Hollywood and Sunday movies of immodesty and pernicious influences.[120] She furthermore insisted, "all of Israel must not be held responsible for the shortcomings of a few." The Israelites must not become "the scapegoats of Christians. Let us not re-establish the Ghettos where ignorant hate herded these beings, who were made the outcasts of the world yet have given the world celebrated writers, thinkers, playwrights, statesmen, scientists, and inventors." The Jews were associated with the Enlightenment, modern values, and scientific and cultural advances: "They pushed the wheel of progress forward, often more than others."[121] Written in 1930, this tribute to the Jews coincided with the alarming increase of anti-Semitism in nationalist discourse.

Circé-Côté was aware of the Zionist movement's presence in Montreal. Unlike the Jewish community in the United States, since the turn of the century the majority of Jews in Montreal were Zionists.[122] After the Balfour Declaration of 1917, which committed Great Britain to supporting the project of a Jewish national homeland in Palestine, Montreal Zionists, who at that time were generally social democrats, were riding high. What exactly compelled Éva Circé-Côté in 1921 to devote a column to the Zionist movement is not known. Perhaps she was familiar with the role of the Montrealer Lillian

Bilsky Freiman in Hadassah, the Women's Zionist Organization of America. At variance with the facts, Julien Saint-Michel believed that Zionism "has not recruited many followers in our city." She questions the wisdom of returning to Israel: "Is it possible for a people to swim against the current? . . . No, it must march toward its destiny. The wandering Jew cannot end his journey, not even to rest in the shade of the olive trees." He must give up the "golden seduction of a reconquered Eden." She puts forward a cosmopolitan Jew—in the positive sense of that adjective—with "homelands everywhere . . . not tied down anywhere," who must not sacrifice this universalism:

> Do you believe that they want to trade their world empire for the stagnation of a small kingdom in Palestine? . . . Will they desert the vast stage of the globe for this obscure, unknown theatre, where their talent cannot be fully deployed? . . . The Jews will never relinquish their freedom.

Whereas French Canadians ought to revel in being patriots, this is far from true for the descendants of Israel:

> Nothing is more beautiful that the Jewish ideal of being men before being patriots. Nothing is more legitimate, more rational than wanting to extend to the entire human race the benefits of the efforts made and the progress achieved, than wanting to abolish borders rather than establishing new ones, in order to strengthen the ties that should unite men and to carry out the duties of assistance, work, and pity attendant on those bonds.[123]

Éva Circé-Côté was not unknown to Jewish intellectuals. In 1932, the Yiddish-language newspaper *Kanader Adler* celebrated both the twenty-fifth anniversary of its founding and the centenary of the emancipation of the Jews in Lower Canada by publishing a commemorative edition to which French- and English-speaking notables were invited to contribute. The paper reproduced a brief excerpt from a speech made by Henri Bourassa in the House of Commons on the role of his ancestor Papineau, who was the Speaker of the Legislative Assembly that had enacted "Jewish emancipation" in Lower Canada. Olivar Asselin, then editor-in-chief of *Le Canada*, recalled his friendships with Jews and maintained that anti-Semitism did not exist among Catholics, as evidenced in Germany, Ireland, and Poland! The longest piece was that of Éva Circé-Côté, the only Francophone woman to appear in the issue.

In her article, titled "Genèse de la Pensée canadienne" (Genesis of Canadian thought), she compared the French Canadians to the Hebrews and Papineau to Moses:

> But while their arms laboured their minds slept. For a hundred years they slept, and it was not the kiss of a prince charming that drew them from their torpor but the harsh voice of the English roughneck soldier who came to conquer the lands and threatened to send them down the same road as the Acadians. Another power had arisen in the shadows and was insidiously taking hold of their souls. It was then that Papineau appeared and his saving voice rang out in the four corners of Lower Canada. Like the Hebrews, we had our law-giver, who, to lead us out of the desert, crossed a sea of blood, broke the false idols, smashed the statue of the golden calf, and wrested us from dependence on a pharaoh with powerful capital.[124]

The reaction of Jewish readers to the comparison between Papineau and Moses is not known, but Circé-Côté concluded her article by reminding them how important Papineau had been for the Jews and by expressing the wish for the emergence of a new Papineau.

One hundred years after Jews had obtained their civic rights, anti-Semitic prejudices reappeared in some Québécois circles. In 1934, a sordid incident shook Montreal's Jewish population. Doctor Samuel Rabinovitch was accepted as an intern at the Notre-Dame hospital. The ensuing outcry came not only from anti-Semitic intellectuals—this was no surprise—but also from the hospital's physicians, who went on strike in protest against their new colleague. Rabinovitch, out of concern for the patients deprived of their doctors, tendered his resignation, which was accepted immediately. Éva Circé-Côté devoted an entire column to him. She saw his withdrawal as an act of wisdom and altruism toward the patients and used it as an example, once again, of the qualities she attributed to Jews: "thrifty, sober, law-abiding and, especially, human, eager to gain the world before [gaining] heaven."[125]

Although she generously credited a group with all these positive traits on the basis of ethnicity, she was well aware of being at odds with nationalist workers and intellectuals offended by what they regarded as an invasion that would surely marginalize them. This was her response: "If we find that the Jew exploits us, let us encourage our people. If we find them bothersome in the cities, let the governments shunt them to the uncultivated lands along with all the other exotics." The burden lay with those who enticed people from abroad to settle in Quebec and Canada. Moreover, despite her criticism of government policies, she was not indifferent to the perceived threat that newcomers from different linguistic and cultural backgrounds represented to a French Canada rendered vulnerable in the North American context.

Racism and Racialism

Circé-Côté's remarks about the Jews and other "exotics" raises the question of racism in her writings. When she defended them, she did not shy away from stereotypes and attributed specific qualities and flaws to the different ethnic groups, be it the English, the French-Canadians, or the Jews. At a time when no one, not even among progressives, questioned the concept of race and differences based on ethnic origin, racialism was prevalent throughout society. Here, for example, is a comment by Circé-Côté concerning the Chinese: "these automatons of labour... pacifists... gentle and humble," and exploited in their laundries. She found discrimination against them unacceptable: "seeing as how they have been allowed to come here in accordance with international treaties, while we take over their country in the commercial sphere. Once they are here, we must treat them like other immigrants."[126]

Black people were rarely mentioned in her columns.[127] She did, however, pay tribute to the Haitians: "A valiant little people that conquered its material independence and its freedom of thought and expression at the cost of prolonged suffering!" She expressed admiration, in particular, for Dominique Hyppolite, a Haitian jurist and poet who had come to the second Congrès de la Langue française in 1937. In the same column, she denounced a delegate from Louisiana who had "refused to go up to receive his doctoral diploma awarded by the cardinal, to avoid contact with a Haitian... the blackest individual is not who one might assume, and this barbarian should not have been honoured with a distinction."[128]

Circé-Côté saw her antiracism as deriving directly from the French republican ideal dedicated to eradicating differences. All those, without distinction as to religion, ethnic origin, or race, who assimilated and spoke French were welcome in French Canada.

> We are not against the injection of foreign blood, but we should keep at bay those who will never speak our language, whom we readily adopt but who will never adopt us; those who refuse to follow our traditions and to mesh their interests with those of the land. But as soon as they have put down roots among us, we must disarm. Opinions must cease to

be banished. It is ungracious of those who defend putting souls at peace to stir up quarrels of race and religion. The homeland and religion must be benevolent toward those who have stopped being strangers. In order for everyone to try to outdo each other in emulation, in order to serve the land well, me must be able to make the atmosphere bearable for them.[129]

This last quote, drawn from the closing lines of *Papineau*, sums up her vision of the Other, one supported by Papineau's own attitude, he who "did not frown upon foreigners." As early as 1917, Circé-Côté spoke out against the concept of racial purity, and in 1933 she would be one of the rare voices in the French-language press to denounce Adolf Hitler's anti-Semitism.[130]

Éva Circé-Côté had a profound belief in a French-Canadian identity, and her writings helped to forge that identity by proposing models. Thinkers, those who define identity, generally proceed by comparing their own group—ethnic, religious, or racial—to another that is not just different but that usually serves as a foil. While Circé-Côté occasionally did this, as when she disparaged English cooking, more often than not she put forward models to be followed, qualities to be adopted, behaviours to be borrowed: the "fair play" of the British, the tolerance of the Protestants, the business acumen of the Jews, the refinement of the French were traits from which French Canadians could draw inspiration. At the same time, however, she was harsh in her assessment of the quality of the language and institutions in Quebec and admitted, quite logically, that it would be futile and even unjust to demand that others assimilate into an under-educated people. The solution, therefore, required the reform of institutions, starting with their secularization, and a modern education system able to integrate both immigrants and Indigenous Peoples, without doing them the disservice of having them share in a culture and a language that she wished to see improved.

Circé-Côté's focus on the affirmation of the French-Canadian identity and nation was not unrelated to her feminism. She viewed the social and moral regeneration of her compatriots as a women's mission, and, notwithstanding her masculine pseudonyms, devoted herself to it as a woman.[131]

* * *

The patriotism of the 1830s—secular, French, republican, and inclusive—was in Circé-Côté's view a "civilizing agent"[132] given over to progress. For her, the exploits of 1837–38 overshadowed everything that happened afterward. Confederation was pushed into the background. But when she spoke of emancipation and independence, she did not call into the question the confederal pact. "We do not wish to have the Confederation rescinded, for we support the principle of confederation. . . . Each province must have its Home Rule," she wrote in 1902.[133] Although her faith in a harmonious Canadian Confederation was shaken during the Great War and the French school crisis in Ontario, it was renewed after the armistice and fortified by the absence of a major crisis until 1942. Despite her admiration for the "modernity" of the United States, the closeness of the US and its power of cultural attraction made Canada's ties with Great Britain all the more essential. She stood united with "[French] Canadians [who] believe that the French soul has a better chance of surviving under the aegis of England than engulfed in the great American entity."[134] Her resigned loyalty to England placed her at variance with the nationalists of the interwar period. In 1937, seventy years after Confederation, she answered Groulx, who she felt was fomenting hatred, by stressing the advantages of submitting to England rather than assimilating into the United States. Great Britain conquers and subjugates, she acknowledged, but over time,

> the victor has turned into a mentor. It has given us a life as pleasant as any we could imagine, making us the envy of the entire world. It would be an anachronism to revive a hatred that can no longer be justified. Our geographic position as neighbours of the American republic, a leveller that has melted in its crucible all the tongues of its inhabitants and out of them has forged a single dialect, a uniform mentality . . . gives us a reason to be circumspect, forbearing, and logically resigned to the peaceful and tolerant regime that makes it a point of honour and generosity to protect our language and our laws, not to mention the economic arguments in favour of maintaining the status quo. Better freedom of thought than economic freedom. In choosing between two servitudes, let us choose the more humane one."[135]

Thus, in addition to the fear of a Catholic state came the fear of assimilation into the United States. On the eve of the Second World War, her attraction to the cultural advantages of belonging to the British Empire trumped the economic benefits of a North American alliance. To shield French Canada from this double jeopardy, "Great Britain owes it to itself, and to its French-Canadian subjects, to liberate them from an oppression that hampers their evolution and which, in the short term, will become a source of troubles and difficulties."[136]

CHAPTER 9

FEMINISMS: SOCIAL REFORMS AND WOMEN'S RIGHTS

The moment a woman openly declares that she is a feminist she becomes suspect.
— ÉVA CIRCÉ-CÔTÉ, 1921[1]

THE IDEAL of sexual equality, which had originated in the Enlightenment and the French Revolution, worked its way into liberalism and socialism and, closer to *Le Monde ouvrier*, Freemasonry. Éva Circé-Côté was familiar with the philosophical works on the female condition. She quoted the Marquis de Condorcet, who had defended the political equality of women at the time of the Revolution, Olympe de Gouges, author of the *Declaration of the Rights of Woman and the Female Citizen*, and John Stuart Mill, author of *The Subjection of Women*. Throughout her years as a journalist, Circé-Côté would fight injustices against women and advocate reforms aimed at improving women's lives. Early in her career, however, she did not identify herself as a feminist, and from one decade to the next her columns traced the zigzag of her thinking on the situation of women.

Feminism is both an ideology and a social movement. At the turn of the century it was easier for Circé-Côté, a young, emancipated literary woman, to embrace an ideological egalitarianism than to join a movement that she misunderstood and associated somewhat hastily with Anglo-Saxon puritanism. Feminist ideology is not monolithic; its goal can be simply equal rights or a social contribution of women based on their moral specificity or, for more utopian feminists, a new, collectivist world, where women's equality and their participation in society will exist as a matter of course. Feminists do not hold a monopoly on protesting against women's inferior status; socialists and liberals also champion equal rights, and the causes of women's subordination are central to their discourses on women. The pseudo-scientific propositions of the nineteenth century concerning nature and the effects of physiology—the size of the brain, for instance—on the intellectual abilities of each sex and the importance of protecting the female reproductive organs, were followed by sociological approaches like that of Frederick Engels, who situated women's subaltern position in the development of private property and the inequalities inherent in capitalism. Meanwhile, John Stuart Mill, like his predecessors Condorcet, Charles Fourier, and Flora Tristan, saw this question as one of environment, hence something that could be remedied through education. The words of these philosophers had a profound influence on Circé-Côté's writing.

In 1900, when, as a young journalist, she began to speak out on the women's issues, British feminists were engaged in a spectacular fight for women's right to vote. In France, feminist republicans were demanding changes to the Civil Code. In Canada, the National Council of Women demanded female suffrage and new legislation on property. In Quebec, where few Francophones laid claim to the feminist label, there were several reasons for the lack of interest in the feminist ideology and movement. In Canada, the field of social reforms offered a fertile terrain for demanding women's rights. In Quebec, however, the social reform movement was identified primarily with Anglophones, since French-language social services remained in the hands of the religious communities. Many women who might have devoted themselves to a social cause had already been recruited by religious congregations, where they could live out their altruism. Finally, the glorification of motherhood and submission to the Catholic Church left very little space, or even time, for rebellion and mobilization.

At the start of her career, Circé-Côté's alias Colombine published some articles expressing a rather crude variety of misogyny. In 1900, under the cover of "revelations of a good bachelor," she shot down feminism and women's rights as well as those who defended them, those "few sick minds, hungry for popularity." She reproduced the fashionable fears and caricatures of her day: the man, turned into a puppet, will be at home rocking the baby when the woman gets back from work in the middle of the night; the arrival of women stenographers will entail lower wages for the men.[2] When a reader jokingly named "K. Nadienne" took her to task in a letter to the editor of *La Presse*, chastising her for "poorly defending our sex," Colombine stood pat and retorted, "I wage war on feminism. So be it!"[3] At the same time, in *Les*

Débats, she feared that "vindictive society, inspired by the promoters of feminism, would levy an annual tax on bachelors in order to fatten a scholarship intended for young underprivileged girls. . . . This is truly needless cruelty."[4] In two articles dated October 1900, she assailed feminism in the name of . . . love. In keeping with the strict separation of roles, the man was the breadwinner and the woman his companion, sister, and friend. And women who did not conform to the image of the housewife would not be able to find a husband.

Colombine's goal was to amuse and to shock. For she also wrote: "And because I am an evolutionist . . . I observe with ineffable pleasure men aspiring to resemble women. . . . Man and woman will become workmates." Sharing the same tasks would lead, she hoped, to equal rights: "Sing out, supporters of feminism, the era of your triumph is dawning; greet the new day that will change the face of the world. *Et renovabis faciem terrae.*"[5] Like many of her contemporaries, Éva Circé associated turn-of-the-century feminism with puritanical Protestantism, and she did not hesitate to heap sarcasm on her Anglo-Saxon sisters. Did they not want to forbid kissing for reasons of hygiene?[6]

Éva Circé challenged the sex-based social hierarchy and, naturally, examined its roots. Inequalities were caused neither by chance nor human nature but by specific circumstances. "Woman's inferiority in centuries past and even in our society, anywhere in the world, is an accidental event brought about by the pressures of the environment in which she lived, by the pressure exerted on her intelligence, due to her lack of education, as Fourier said, due especially to this burdensome atavistic legacy."[7] Intellectual inferiority was her uppermost concern, and she made it the central topic of her campaign in favour of education for girls.[8]

But Colombine did not go so far as to regard the sexes as the same, quite the contrary. Writing in 1901, she considered the essential differences between women and men as self-evident and fixed from the moment of birth. Little girls have a characteristic passion for dolls and are destined "for their allotted role of abnegation, devotion, and love."[9] Éva Circé-Côté shared her contemporaries' belief in indisputable maternal instincts. Later, having herself become the mother of a little girl, she argued in her columns that a pension should be paid to destitute mothers, convinced as she was that there was no substitute for a child's mother. Giving money to penniless mothers was in her view preferable to nurseries, because, thanks to her instincts, "only the mother is able to perform the delicate function with her children of varying her methods, her tack in accordance with each child's personality, health, and intelligence. It is not a myth that the voice of the blood speaks through the flesh like the ocean in a conch."[10] From there it was only a small step to proclaiming women's moral superiority, which is exactly what Julien Saint-Michel did:

> On the strength of her maternal love, her conjugal tenderness, her constant devotion, and her capacity to endure the martyrdom of her fate, a woman manages to create a soul for herself that, in the opinion of psychologists, is superior in terms of sensitiveness, delicacy, prescience, intuitions, instincts, and insights, to that of a man. . . . Her essence is superior because it is drawn from the heart itself.[11]

The consequent vision of the heterosexual couple is a traditional one: the man, after a hard day's work amid figures, duplicities, and pettiness, "must find, as an antidote, the easy, gentle intimacy of the home, the continual interpenetration that makes two beings into one, the affectionate smile that brings solace for everything, even for life. Be afraid that if he does not find this in your home, he will go looking for it elsewhere. A night out can plunge a good, sensitive, but weak man into the machinery of vice; once his finger is caught in it, the rest will surely follow!"[12] A woman must seduce her husband and not regret what on their wedding day may seem like a sacrifice. "In fact, it is the start of real life because our actions have a purpose that often makes us forget how prosaic they are . . . It should be a noble ambition to strive to bind to oneself the heart of the man who, yes, swore to be faithful, but whose virtue is not always as solid as the rest of him, you know!"[13]

In 1903, she reassured the men who had come to hear her lecture on women's equality: "Gentlemen, do not think me a revolutionary because I put forward the educated woman as an ideal; the goal is your happiness."[14] That same year, in reply to one of her columns on the equality of men and women, a reader taunted Circé-Côté—an unmarried, independent woman—with this warning: "If there were many colombines in our land, it would benefit neither cooking nor the affected family, not to mention everything else." She jumped at the chance to drive home her ideas on the issue: "Just like you, sir, we have an immortal soul and an intelligence destined to the same end. . . . The envelope differs." Women's educational deficiency, she contended, not only explained their subordination but was probably "a primary cause of broken homes." For "what is required in life is that our soul sees itself mirrored in another soul, that through a slow interpenetration we come to share the same ideas on all subjects."[15] But equal intelligence and education did not imply equal functions, and Colombine made a point of reassuring her readers: a man has no more business selling corsets and lace than a woman has holding forth on

Saint Thomas Aquinas. Because a woman, after all, will fulfil herself mainly in her relationship with the man she loves: "If a woman asserts her literary knowledge, it is not to parade her learning but to hold you more tightly in her arms, gentlemen . . . to be loved for what is best and imperishable within her."[16] A meek discourse indeed. One that the readers of *Les Débats*—a broad-minded public, it should be recalled—would certainly not find alarming. It was a thoroughly diluted discourse that was inconsistent with the reality of this literary woman, who in fact was perfectly capable of discussing the church fathers.

Today, a feminism based on the specific characteristics of women, on their maternal instincts, is referred to as maternalism. A feminism grounded in the equality of human beings and their equal rights is known as egalitarianism. But these categories are theoretical, and virtually no feminists belong exclusively to one or the other. Both maternalism and egalitarianism claim to be expressions of enlightened progressivism; the former is rooted in the Enlightenment sciences, in medicine, and in writings on nature of women, while the latter includes women in the proposition that "all men are born equal."

The First World War disrupted the strict assignment of social roles; women took jobs until then reserved for men, and the flexibility achieved during the war made itself felt in postwar writing. In 1930, in *Le Monde ouvrier*, Julien Saint-Michel found it vexing that men "felt deprived of their virility" when they took part in housework.[17]

Maternity and Infant Mortality

One issue in particular highlighted the interaction of maternal and social responsibilities: infant mortality. Medical and political authorities, reformers, and nationalists were all concerned about the high proportion of mortality among very young children. In 1901, Quebec had the second highest infant mortality rate of all the Canadian provinces. Montreal and industrial cities such as Trois-Rivières were especially hard hit. The situation was slowly improving, but every new census came as a reminder of the ravages caused by this scourge. In 1931, out of the fourteen Canadian cities with infant mortality rates higher than 100 deaths of children under a year old for 1000 births, thirteen were in Quebec (see Table 1). Public health officials claimed that Montreal ranked second in the world, just after Calcutta, for the number of infant deaths. This was an idle comparison, but it hit home and raised public awareness of the scale of the catastrophe.

Éva Circé-Côté, whose mother had lost nine young children—the underprivileged classes were not the only ones affected—devoted a number of columns to the subject of infant mortality.

> Each day, the fateful procession of little coffins ascends Mount Royal. . . . The gently trotting white horses carry the light harvest to the granary of death, the green ears mowed down before yielding up the gold of their compact seeds! Following behind a vulgarly luxurious coach driven by the undertaker with his affected gravity, a humble family carriage once overflowing with laughter and shouts of joy, now transformed into a funeral car, gives the infant whose gurgling has forever gone silent its last ride around the mountain. The father, his eyes as hollow as the little coffins where the shadows of the deceased have found refuge, holds the white casket on his knees, while the mother mops her swollen face. . . . Despite the lovely weather we are having, despite the courses on infant care given so theatrically at the school hall, despite the resolutions passed at conventions, the fine speeches and ringing phrases, our little ones fall as fast as hailstones.*
>
> * Fantasio, "Attaquons le mal dans ses racines," *Le Pays*, July 26, 1913.

The problem was a moral one, she wrote, because a "social vice" was at work, which made mothers neglect their children, stoically accept their passing, and refrain from rebelling against their illnesses. Circé-Côté rarely mentioned the fathers. Religion played a part in the mothers' attitude of resignation: it inculcated the idea that children became angels in heaven. This belief—"superstition" as far as Circé-Côté was concerned—no doubt helped them endure the repeated bereavements, but it also fostered detachment and passivity: "Those who procreate for heaven, the angel-makers, do not realize that paradise must begin here below."[18] Such notions could even lead "falsely Christian, warped" mothers to be guilty of criminal negligence.

In tandem with the influence of religion, a lack of education was another cause of mothers' carelessness. Uninformed of appropriate treatments for their children, they, or "mercenary baby-sitters," continued to use opiates to quiet children down. Arthur Maheu, one of Circé-Côté's aliases, laid bare the detrimental effects of "*[la] mort fine*" (morphine) and "*l'eau d'homme*" (laudanum) and ridiculed old wives' remedies such as lice for jaundice, hot gin punch for colds, and cowpat plasters for colic.[19]

Feminisms / 255

Baptiste: "No reason to squirm, I've got the whole bunch." *Le Pays*, October 19, 1912. BAnQ.

Yet Éva Circé-Côté was aware that children died mainly of gastro-intestinal infections and communicable diseases like scarlet fever, whooping cough, and pneumonia. In 1911, Dr. Louis Laberge, a specialist with the City of Montreal's public health department, announced that three hundred and four children had died the previous year, the highest number in some thirty years. The authorities took action. Milk arriving from the countryside in non-refrigerated trains and left sitting in the stations before being distributed was inspected. It was asked that household trash be wrapped. The province's Superior Board of Public Health implored mothers to continue to breastfeed.[20] The daily *La Patrie* published a series of articles titled *"Pour contrer la grande faucheuse"* ("To fend off the Grim Reaper"), and which propagated the public health council's recommendations for mothers and babies. And Montreal's progressive mayor, James John Guerin, launched a campaign to exterminate flies. Fantasio's reaction was full of scorn. The flies are being blamed, she wrote, while "the one who is actually guilty is browsing around the shops, swapping rumours with the neighbourhood gossips, or delighting in the romantic scenes of a movie while munching on pistachios."²¹ It was up to the parents, mainly the mother, to ensure their children's health.

The heat waves of 1912 were such that the city allowed people to sleep outside on the lawns and employers gave workers time off; Circé-Côté, meanwhile, felt sorry for the child in its "filthy crib confined to a dark room and ceaselessly wailing because of the colic brought on by soured milk [...] an innocent victim of its parents' carelessness more than the heat!"²² She also noted that Jewish children had a lower mortality rate even though they were exposed to the same flies and the same climate as the others.²³ Arthur Maheu was justified in complaining that Montreal women no longer wanted to breastfeed. Indeed, bottle-feeding was a significant factor in the different infant mortality rates among the Anglos, Irish, Jews, and French-Canadians in Montreal.²⁴

Children died not only of contagious diseases but all too often in accidents as well. Almost every week, the newspapers reported on cases of children burned, fallen out of windows, poisoned, or scalded. Each time, Circé-Côté was quick to blame the mothers for the lack of supervision and demanded punishment for those who had been chattering with the neighbour or left the children alone while they were at the movie theatre.²⁵

In her columns, she asked the state to intervene so that "the police could use force to bring home these women who run around, these religious hypocrites, neighbourhood tattlers, bargain-hunters looking for a chance to spend money, or movie fans who neglect their families to go the theatre. Let them arrest the ones who scald their children or fail to instal a trellis on the balcony when they live on the third floor with a flock of kids."²⁶ Having no illusions about parents' affection for their children, she more than once denounced life insurance for children, which might induce parents to succumb to the enticement of lucre in exchange for their offspring's life: "often the damned money of corrupt insurance companies, like Judas's coins, becomes the price of blood."²⁷ It was a cynical and insulting thought, but Circé-Côté cited the example of France, where this type of insurance was forbidden so impoverished or greedy parents would not be tempted.

Because of their fatalism, the product of ignorance and piety, French-Canadian mothers as described by Circé-Côté contributed to the hecatomb evidenced by the processions of little white coffins. The relentless railing against maternal guilt and the moralizing tone are surprising coming from a progressive woman, who was nonetheless obliged to recognize the extent to which environmental factors were involved. Thus, she acknowledged elsewhere the unhealthiness of the urban environment and denounced inadequate public health measures, insalubrious, windowless flats, and polluted water and air, all of which could have been remedied through legislation and regulation. For at least the first two decades of the century, mothers, especially those who were poorly educated, remained the primary target of her columns on infantile mortality. However liberal she may have been, she went so far as to propose that the state intrude into people's homes with inspections of children's nutrition and hygiene.[28]

During those years, Éva Circé-Côté's blaming discourse was anything but original. It coincided with statements made by public health physicians, such as Séverin Lachapelle, who asserted in 1912: "The reasons for the excessive mortality in poor neighbours has more to do with the mothers' ignorance than with unhealthy living conditions."[29] That same year, Fantasio wrote that the cause lay "in our mentality, our education."[30] Education, and not just the instruction given to mothers at the Gouttes de lait (Well Baby) clinics, would make women better informed and less resigned to their fates.

In Quebec, the infant mortality rate remained above 127 deaths for 1000 births until 1930, and Circé-Côté continued to lament the "yearly harvest" manifested in "the procession of white hearses . . . containing perhaps the withered promises of our race."[31] Though she initially assailed the mothers, Circé-Côté's discourse grew more moderate, and in 1927 she enumerated the three causes of infant mortality without, this time, mentioning the mother's direct responsibility:

1. Having more children than one can feed, clothe, and educate. 2. Wages too low to allow workers and day labourers to decently provide for a large family. 3. The danger posed by some religious beliefs not supported by any sacred text let alone reason and good sense, which tend to sacrifice time for the sake of eternity and to reward death rather than life.[32]

In sum, her arguments evolved and became less focused on blaming the mothers' negligence and ignorance than on bringing to light their situation, which made unplanned births unavoidable.

Circé-Côté's voluntarism led her to consistently combat fatalism and resignation, although she had very little to say about birth control. She lambasted the nationalists for constantly demanding more children, "despite the spectre of hunger looming before us."[33] It was in a column on the United States, the "land of dreams," that she dealt with this subject most directly. Women in the US "demand the freedom to procreate" and "refuse to be automatons." While on the one hand she expressed the eugenics-influenced wish that women may refuse to marry men who were "syphilitic, alcoholic, tubercular, or simpleminded," on the other hand she concluded her column by raising questions about the excesses of Malthusianism.[34]

Not only did Circé-Côté never condemn contraception, she even advocated it, though more for economic reasons than as a component of women's emancipation. She thought that parents should not have more children than they could provide for; at the same time, her columns contained not a word in support of women's right to control their own bodies—an unfamiliar concept at the time—nor did she put forward a defence of the individual's right to plan the desired number of children. As for clandestine abortions, she referred to it only obliquely. Éva Circé-Côté's contemporaries were extremely concerned about unexpected pregnancies and anxious about the threat of opprobrium should they practise birth control, but she never examined the issue from this angle and considered only the harmful consequences of large families.

Pacifism and Social Reform

In the public arena, Éva Circé-Côté was ever more vocal about her wish to see women take an active part in bringing about the reforms needed to improve society, and she came to regard women as *naturally* inclined to promote peace. As discussed earlier, she was fiercely interventionist as to the defence of France at the start of the war, but three years on, in the face of the unjustifiable horrors of the battlefield, Circé-Côté grew increasingly disillusioned. She did not understand the English-Canadian women who were calling for conscription.[35] "Women have always been associated with the leagues for peace,"[36] she wrote, firmly convinced that "the day women write the laws . . . wars will become a thing of the past."[37] After the armistice, the women–peace dyad asserted itself. During the 1920s, Circé-Côté condemned military toys, defended disarmament, and proclaimed women's pacifist mission: "it is consistent with woman's nature to put an end to these horrific slaughters that render the long martyrdom of motherhood pointless."[38] And she went even further in 1932: "Once the voice of women predominates in politics, no more war!"[39]

It seemed obvious that, being endowed with particular qualities, women should be entrusted with huge social responsibilities. Like many female social reformers before her, Éva Circé-Côté assigned to women the mission of transforming society and making the world a better, fairer place. She took up the proposition dear to feminists during the interwar period: "Modern woman must redeem humanity, which is expiring under an iron yoke. The fate of the world is in her hands."[40] She furthermore applauded Lucien Romier's statements on "the superiority of Eve's daughters."[41] She used the grand scale of women's mission as leverage to press home the demand for better education for women and a greater role in public affairs.

Innate differences—Circé-Côté called this atavism—were not in contradiction with the ideal of equality.[42] Female particularities never served as a pretext for her to confine women to traditional types of work or to deprive them of their rights. In 1927, she exclaimed: "Take off the masks, of gallantry for men, and of condescension and passive submission for women."[43] In her writings on education and women's work, civic rights, political role, and suffrage, she explained that the potentials of both sexes are the same but that inequities were maintained by the lack of education, traditions, and ignorance: "The question of the superiority of one sex over the other is not at issue."[44] She appealed to science, which "has shown that the contributions of each sex were equivalent."[45] Already as a young woman, Éva Circé's arguments were grounded as much in the female essence as in a malleable environment that would change according to circumstances and her own intellectual evolution. Whether her subject was the role of homemaker, the right to vote, or women's work, she interwove various arguments the better to convince her readers. The number one prerequisite to overcoming inequalities, access to knowledge, was the goal of a campaign that she waged throughout her life.

Education

Because knowledge was the key to progress, Éva Circé-Côté fought tirelessly to raise French Canadians' level of education. She paid special attention to girls' education. She never doubted their intellectual potential and cited the examples of "Sappho, Semiramis, Jeanne Hachette, Saint Theresa, Jeanne d'Arc, Catherine the Great, the Countess of Noailles, de Staël, Marie Curie."[46] When she began her career in journalism, girls' education differed from that of boys when it came to access to higher learning and the contents of their respective curriculums. In 1903 she published in *L'Étincelle* a lecture she had given on "The Causes of Woman's Inferiority," which summed up her thinking on the subject and was but the first in a long series of pleas in favour of girls' education. In this essay, she based her argument, first, on the work of the utopian socialist Charles Fourier, who had stated that if men were subjected to the same education as women, "in similar circumstances of dependence, one would see what to make of their supposed moral superiority." Boys and girls did not receive the same preparation for life: the former studied science, mathematics, and rhetoric, while their sisters, in "an artificial hothouse life, all mysticism and fantasy, a perpetual irritation of their nervousness," concentrated on literature and the arts. Hence their naiveté.

What is the goal of a better education? Like other progressives, Circé-Côté saw women and education as the mainspring of social regeneration; it followed that women must be educated in order to improve their social environment and guide the next generation. As her audience included men, she made a point of reassuring them: an educated woman would know how to make them happy and keep them at home.[47] Elsewhere, she reaffirmed, "an educated woman would never ... give up her position in the home," adding, moreover, "the more education a woman has, the more inculcated she is with the sublime mission that society has devolved upon her."[48]

Éva Circé-Côté and Georgina Bélanger Gill (Gaëtane de Montreuil) demonstrated what a more comprehensive education for young middle-class women could be by founding a lycée where the physical and natural sciences were taught alongside stenography and literature.[49] The lycée existed for just two years, from 1908 to 1910, and its example was not emulated. Circé-Côté's reputation as an apostle of girls' education must have been well established, as in 1909 the *Montreal Daily Witness*, an English-language newspaper known for its social reform campaigns, published the text of Colombine's lecture at the Philanthropic Society. In it she referred to Condorcet and his four reasons why women should be educated: "1) for their children's education; 2) to be their husbands' 'worthy companions'; 3) to not dim their husbands' minds and to share their readings; 4) because it is just, because both sexes are entitled to an education."[50] This last condition would take on greater importance as her feminism grew stronger.

Over the years, as her feminism evolved, Circé-Côté placed increasing stress on education as a guarantee of economic independence. Women must earn a living, and the education they received hardly allowed them to take up any interesting occupations. She had good reason to be alarmed. Before the First World War, it was estimated that eighty-five percent of girls left school after their solemn communion, at the age of twelve, that is, after six years of schooling. A few academies offered girls courses up to the tenth grade, but enrolment was sparse beyond grade eight. Young middle-class women enrolled in boarding schools left between the ages of fifteen and seventeen.[51]

The editorial board of *Le Pays* was divided on the issue of sexual equality, for even forward-looking minds could hold utterly conventional views on women's place in society. In an article on girls' education written in 1914, the poet Jean Charbonneau, a member of the board at *Le Pays*, articulated an outlook that the clergy and traditional elites would not have rejected. He maintained that the different roles of women and men were immutable and that girls' education must be primarily practical; hence, science courses should lead to concrete applications such as hygiene. The "excessive sensitivity" of young girls requires "reasoned guidance," particularly in the teaching of literature because this field "is almost always an abyss for women." Circé-Côté certainly must have crossed swords with Charbonneau, a man leery of "disturbing the intellect" of girls, but there was no sign of disagreement in the pages of the newspaper.[52] She did not let her opinions affect her judgment and later would write laudatory reviews of her colleague's publications.

After considering the deficiencies in the education available to middle-class girls, Éva Circé soon turned to the training of those who were obliged to work and found themselves confined to traditional, low-skilled jobs in factories or the rapidly expanding service sector, where they worked as clerks or stenographer-typists. Boarding schools, convents, and academies were "hothouses" that could no longer provide adequate training for this labour force during the war. Professional, industrial, commercial, and agricultural schools "adapted to our living conditions" were needed, because, "equipped with technical instruction, which does not exclude grammar and spelling, [these young girls] could competently manage a farm, a workshop, or any business." Having justified this specialized training, she concluded that, "since they will be heads of the household . . . we must put them on notice that they must be up to the situation."[53]

The war gave women the opportunity to make their presence felt in new areas, but the education system did not reflect these social changes. In 1925, Éva took up the same plea: "instead of teaching her philosophy and belles-lettres, the little girl sews, embroiders, tinkers on the piano during the intermissions between household chores." Was it any wonder "that with such different treatments over a period of eight to ten years they should find themselves, one raised above himself, the other returned to the humility of her shell, lowered to a level beneath her nature? . . . He is an orator and a poet, while she is a little fairy capable of creating marvels with her fingers."[54] In 1930, Circé-Côté was still complaining that girls were being raised to seduce.[55] The number of boarding schools had increased, and by the end of the thirties there were a dozen high schools for girls in Quebec, but, deprived of government funding, they recruited six times fewer students than the *collèges classiques* for boys. A thirteenth high school, the lycée Marie-de-France, opened its doors in 1939. Thirty years after the Lycée des jeunes filles, Montreal finally had another girls' school independent of the religious congregations.

For the few women who finished their *cours classique*, the university door remained only half-open. Diplomas, Circé-Côté noted, are "a useless expense, one thousand dollars, if [women] cannot exercise a profession."[56] Because, while women were allowed to take university courses toward the practice of a liberal profession, for many years professional associations would be loath to accept them.

Women in the Liberal Professions

In her early years as a journalist, Éva Circé derided female doctors and lawyers: "Can you see people's rights at the mercy of 'the lady lawyer's' provocative wink[?]"[57] Only after the war of 1914 would one find columns by Circé-Côté defending women's access to the liberal professions. At first her arguments centred on the traditional female virtue of compassion.

> If the mission of lawyers is to protect widows and orphans, a woman would be playing her usual role and would be more interested than anyone else in ensuring that they not get unduly fleeced by exploiters of ignorance and obliviousness.[58]

But she continued to be deeply disdainful of the disciples of Themis and wondered if women ought not to shun this profession of parasites. She even feared that judges might be inveigled by the charms of female attorneys. Although she believed this career was doomed to disappear, as everyone would one day be able to plead his or her own case, nevertheless, "in principle all professions should be open to women, who are forced to rock a cradle while at the same time pursuing a useful career."[59] In July 1915, she unequivocally refuted one of the main arguments against admitting women to the Bar, stating that women's virtue is no more at risk when pleading all sorts of cases than that of nurses when they minister to their patients.[60] In 1925, the religious and academic authorities arrived at a compromise and Mgr Émile Chartier, Vice-Rector of the Université de Montréal, allowed Juliette Gauthier to enrol in the law faculty[61] and take the courses, but she would never be able to practise as a lawyer.

The same evolution in Éva Circé-Côté's thinking took place with respect to the medical profession. Whereas she had thought it preferable in 1903 for women to play the more discreet but no less noble role of nurse rather than that of physician, in 1931 she came to rely on female doctors to promote medical insurance.[62] In keeping with her own principles regarding individual freedom, Circé-Côté could not long continue to oppose admitting women into all the professions to which they were drawn. It should be recalled that her daughter Ève would choose not a liberal profession but a "practical" career as a librarian before going into business.

Civil Rights[63]

In jurisdictions under civil law, such as France and Quebec, feminists' first battle, even before the fight for suffrage, was against the various forms of discrimination written into the Civil Code. All women, and married women in particular, were subjected to discrimination codified and amended in the nineteenth century. For married women, such discrimination was in sum a matter of their legal incapacity and the institutions of marital and parental authority. The administration of conjugal life was assigned to the protecting husband, to whom the wife owed obedience. Obedience became "the homage paid to the power that protects her," as the jurist Toullier had put it in 1821.[64] This entailed the loss of legal capacity and the pooling of the spouses' property, which then fell under the husband's management; in other words, the wife was reduced to the position of a minor. Only a marriage contract, of which only a minority of women availed themselves, could ensure them some control over their property, but this did not entitle them to conclude a contract, hold public office, or make decisions on other matters bearing, for instance, on their children's education. While the Quebec Civil Code enshrined the attachment to French traditions and culture, it also meant that the women of Quebec, unlike their sisters elsewhere in Canada, were placed under guardianship. In a nationalist society that regarded its legal specificity as a component of its distinctive identity, a precious heritage of the French regime, and a rampart against Anglo-Saxon and Protestant influence, it was not easy to amend the Civil Code.

Marie Gérin-Lajoie carried out a pioneering study of the Civil Code in 1902 and wrote *Traité de droit usuel* (Treatise on Everyday Law), an essay aimed at women in which she popularized various articles of the Civil Code concerning the rights and obligations of the parties involved.[65] A Christian feminist caught between Catholicism, nationalism, and feminism, Gérin-Lajoie defended the Code and its organic vision of marriage while at the same time proposing amendments pertaining to the rights of married women. Circé-Côté, who had rubbed shoulders with Gérin-Lajoie at the founding of the Fédération nationale Saint-Jean-Baptiste, had kept silent on the legal issue for a long time; she first broached the subject in 1913, denouncing marital obedience, "a violation of women's dignity."[66]

The increased number of female workers during the war rendered even more egregious the articles of the Code depriving them of the management of their wages. Those who ran shops with their husbands or shared the chores around the farm started to resist their legal incapacity with respect to debts and contracts. Taking advantage of the wartime situation, then, Circé-Côté renewed her attacks against married women's legal incapacity. The very idea of marital power revolted her: "she is 'under the husband's power'; which soul that is not in thrall would not rebel against this brutal expression, more than against the fact!"[67] The pooling of property was supposed to protect her by guaranteeing her a share, among other things, of the inheritance, but Circé-Côté rejected the protection in which women were thus enveloped: if one was to protect women, it should be, rather, against their husbands' powers.[68]

Once again she resorted to *argumentum ad absurdum* to demonstrate the law's illogicality. In 1914 a court ruling absolved a husband of responsibility for his wife's "gossip" because he had not been informed of her slanders. If he had been informed he would have been found guilty of the harm done by his wife's words.[69] Digging up such anecdotes and subjecting them to a subtle and ironic analysis was typical of Fantasio's writing. She also discussed the case of a man who, accompanied by his lawyer, showed up at the munitions factory where his wife was employed to demand her wages. This sort of injustice rested on the sharing of property, which turned a woman into a perpetual minor and transformed her husband into a "little absolute monarch"; with this sharing, the wife was "strangled by the same arms that lovingly enfolded her. What appears to be solicitude is at bottom nothing but a lure, a trap, a slipknot designed to snare the slave on the fly, and feminists are right to want an overhaul of our Tables of the Law."[70] The way out of this humiliating submission was the marriage contract, and Circé-Côté recommended its use to ensure the separation of property. However, only a minority of women, often at the request of fathers wishing to protect the property their daughter would bring to the marriage, concluded such a contract.[71] This question was obviously of interest to the bourgeoisie, but it also affected female workers, who were assumed to be unfit to manage their own wages.

As of the 1920s, Circé-Côté repeatedly denounced the Civil Code. "Authority must not to be exclusively the man's privilege" and the bending of a spouse to the will of the other, "that vestige of serfdom and feudalism," was at odds with her egalitarian outlook on marriage.[72] Poorly informed, the young woman "flies hypnotized to martyrdom," and "from one day to the next [is] despoiled of her conscious freedom and the few privileges she enjoyed when she was single, like the right to manage her property, the right to vote in municipal elections and to benefit from her gainful employment."[73]

Éva Circé-Côté's conception of marriage was poles apart from the notion of joint estate. Her demands were among those put forward by the feminist movements that re-emerged in Quebec in the late 1920s. In 1927, Idola

Saint-Jean established the Alliance canadienne pour le vote des femmes (Canadian Alliance for the Women's Vote) and in 1929 the Comité provincial du suffrage féminin (Provincial Committee for Female Suffrage), successor to the Montreal Suffrage Association, became the Ligue des droits de la femme (League for Women's Rights), headed by Thérèse Casgrain. While Circé-Côté was not among the leading figures of these organizations, she shared their objectives and respected their founders.

In response to the pressure exerted by feminists, in 1929 the provincial government created a commission of inquiry on women's civil rights chaired by Justice Charles-Édouard Dorion. The commissioners, all men, had great respect for the Civil Code and the values it embodied. Five organizations submitted briefs, none of which elicited a comment from Circé-Côté: the Fédération nationale Saint-Jean-Baptiste, represented by its president Marie Gérin-Lajoie; the Alliance canadienne pour le vote des femmes, represented by Idola Saint-Jean;[74] the Ligue des droits de la femme, represented by Thérèse Casgrain;[75] the Association des femmes propriétaires (Association of Female Property Holders), represented by Irène Joly and Thaïs Lacoste-Frémont; and the Conseil local des femmes de Montreal (Montreal Local Council of Women). Once the commissioners delivered their report, Julien Saint-Michel reacted:

> Gone are the days when, on the pretext of protecting women, their will was paralyzed under the sway of their husbands, their initiative was stymied, they were bound hand and foot to masters many of whom were tyrants, and it was impossible for them to shake off an appalling yoke that violated their dignity.[76]

Any hopes that feminists may have pinned on the Dorion Commission were soon dashed. The report was exceedingly cautious. The commissioners heaped praise on the Civil Code, rejected community of acquests [that is, property acquired in common by both spouses—Trans.], and recommended the maintenance of marital and paternal authority. The husband retained the right to claim his wife's wages; she continued to be under guardianship, and her signature, no matter if her marriage was one of pooling or separation of property, had no value; the husband retained the management of his wife's property, even if she had inherited it.[77] When it was tabled at the Legislative Assembly, the report was not discussed "for lack of time." The only noteworthy gain for women, whether married or single, was a seat at the family councils.[78]

Political Rights

Throughout the year 1913, feminism, particularly in connection with the issue of women's suffrage, was headline news on a number of occasions. That year saw the founding of *La Bonne Parole*, the magazine of the Fédération nationale Saint-Jean-Baptiste. During that same year, the Montreal Suffrage Association was established by English-speaking Montrealers. Its spokeswoman, Florence Cole, managed to hurt the pride of French-Canadian women by pointing an accusing finger at the lack of education of women in rural Quebec, hence their inadequate preparation for democratic life. Her remarks prompted Henri Bourassa to write a series of articles in *Le Devoir* rejecting women's suffrage and condemning feminism.[79] He later published Florence Cole's apology but stuck to his position.[80] In *La Patrie*, it was Madeleine who replied to Cole: "We have no use for these feminist claims.... We would not lift a finger to obtain the right to vote."[81] Feminists, Anglos for the most part, nevertheless pursued their actions, and in May 1913 the Montreal Council of Women held an exhibition on suffrage, where a petition was circulated and books on the subject were put on sale.[82]

The Montreal suffragists' intervention in the public arena paled by comparison with the spectacular actions of British suffragettes described in the Canadian press. From Liverpool to Glasgow, there were reports of fires being set, physical attacks, dynamiting, and threats of kidnapping. Canadian women learned more about these events when the suffragette leader Emmeline Pankhurst came to Toronto and Montreal on a speaking tour. The militant campaign of British women received no support in French Canada. Feminist journalists at the major Montreal dailies, Fadette of *Le Devoir* and Colette of *La Presse*, lashed out at the militant British feminists. For her part, Madeleine surveyed the female readers of *La Patrie* on women's suffrage and the suffragettes' methods; while many answered that they aspired to be able to vote, all of them rejected or ridiculed the methods of Emmeline Pankhurst's followers.[83]

Before the war, Circé-Côté wrote very little on the suffrage issue. True, she did write, in 1907 in *Le Journal de Françoise*, "To oppose women's right to vote is to go back to the dark ages when the question of whether or not women had souls was taken seriously."[84] Apart from this statement, she almost never dealt with the issue again. Twice, writing in a satirical vein under the byline of Arthur Maheu, she claimed that if they were given the vote women would no longer want it. In 1912, she congratulated Prime Minister Borden for wanting to forbid British suffragettes—"those women who might open Canadian women's eyes more than men would wish"[85]—from coming to Canada. Circé-Côté alias Maheu trotted out the old refrain whereby a woman who takes an interest in politics will neglect her husband. And Maheu came back to this subject in 1913 in her "Ideas" (*Idées*) column, where she joked about the wearing of pants: "The rights they [the suffragettes] so furiously demand—what they really want are the pants!" She suggested that the British Prime Minister Asquith fling his trousers at "the mob of red chignons crowded in front of his door."[86] Under the guise of humour, hiding behind Arthur Maheu, Éva Circé-Côté sometimes rivalled the most misogynist writers of her day.

It would take almost twenty years for her to recognize the battle waged by her British colleagues. In 1931, Circé-Côté devoted a column in *Le Monde ouvrier* to nine women who recently had been elected to the British parliament, acclaiming them as "the martyrs and forerunners of feminism." Their struggle "was a magnificent act of faith, a fanatical faith in the strength of women, in their moral and intellectual equality with men, in their duty to share with men the government of their fellow citizens, to be men's allies, their companions rather than their slaves; these were the first preachings of a new religion, that of humanity."[87] What had intervened between her initial indifference and derision and this unrestrained enthusiasm was the war and the general evolution of her feminist thinking.

Owing to the social transformations engendered by the hostilities, Circé-Côté's aversion to Anglo-Saxon feminism—she made no mention of the French suffragist movement before the war—gradually gave way to her increasingly vehement demand that women be granted the right to vote. The first time she broached the subject directly was in 1915. While stating her opposition to marital power as defined in the Civil Code, she referred to the civil rights of both sexes: "While it may be necessary to refuse militant suffragettes the right to vote, the elite of women cannot be denied the possibility of working together with their companions for the common good of society."[88]

The open opposition of *L'Action sociale*, the bête noire of *Le Pays*, to women's suffrage, which supposedly was "utterly repugnant to the order established by Providence," gave Fantasio a pretext to take a clearer position in support of the vote for women and to cite the feminist positions of the revolutionary Olympe de Gouges and John Stuart Mill, a defender of nineteenth-century British feminists.[89] Like her feminist contemporaries, Circé-Côté valorized women's regenerative mission, but she also put forward egalitarian arguments. She made this explicit in 1917: "would the strong women who rub shoulders with men from seven in the morning to six at night, who toil alongside them every day, would they turn up their noses when it came time to enter the polling booth and drop their ballots into the tin box?"⁹⁰ And just like American and European suffragists, she invited the members of parliament to vote for women's suffrage because "women's role in the current war demands that they be given the same rights as those enjoyed by the representatives of the stronger sex."⁹¹

In 1917, Canadian politics made it impossible to avoid the issue of the vote for women. Or, rather, for *some* women. Prime Minister Robert Borden would be facing voters in December and asking them to endorse his war policy. To ensure his party's re-election, he was prepared to make many compromises. The vote had already been granted to women in Manitoba, Alberta, and Saskatchewan. Suffragists were pursuing their campaign for the right of women to elect their federal MPs as well. For a prime minister determined to win the election at all costs, their votes could be crucial. A private survey carried out on behalf of the government among members of the National Council of Women of Canada and the Imperial Order Daughters of the Empire showed that if nurses in the armed forces and the female relatives of soldiers could vote, they would support the governing party's conscriptionist policies and thus guarantee its re-election. With this in mind, the government passed the Military Service Act allowing conscription. In September 1917, knowing full well that the general elections could no longer be delayed, the government passed the Military Voters Act, granting the vote to female members of the armed forces, and the Wartime Elections Act, which did the same for female relatives of soldiers serving overseas, in time for the upcoming contest.⁹² Not surprisingly, Borden's Unionist Party won the election on December 17, 1917.

This electoral manoeuvre infuriated Circé-Côté. Her position was crystal clear: "we are against this government measure, although we are in favour of the vote for women."⁹³ For her, the Wartime Elections Act was a "violation of every law, every freedom, and a distortion of public opinion."⁹⁴ It was "an insult to women's honour," for how can the vote be granted to "soldiers' wives, who have no merit on their own, . . . but denied to other, equally deserving women," such as Marie Gérin-Lajoie, Rose Henderson, Joséphine Marchand-Dandurand, or Caroline Dessaulles-Béïque, all of whom would have been "a force for morality, order, and economy in the management of public affairs[?]"⁹⁵

Carried away by her indignation, Circé-Côté used whatever was to hand as grist to her mill, and she did not shy away from berating and maligning soldiers' wives, who "have no reason to be proud of this partial victory, since they are aware of the motives that inspired the country's authorities."⁹⁶ These women, she continued, were taking advantage of the generosity of the Patriotic Fund and "having a very easy time of it," to the point of "consoling themselves with others for the absence of their heroes."[97] The slur did not go unnoticed; in the face of the objections of readers outraged by such gross accusations, she tried to defend herself. But, unrepentant, she never issued an apology.[98]

Determined to "make the best of this ridiculous autocratic action by using the same weapon against those who put it in [our] hands," Circé-Côté plunged into the election campaign in support of her old idol, Wilfrid Laurier. In her view, the fate of Canada was in the hands of women, who were duty-bound to vote, because "the little white slip of paper that will be dropped into the ballot box will decide the life or death of a race."[99] In Quebec, she argued, it was incumbent on women to get Laurier elected, as he opposed conscription and still incarnated certain liberal values. This was a huge responsibility, she wrote on the eve of the election, because they must not compromise women's emancipation: "If they shirk their duty, all the blood of the victims will be on their heads. They will bear the historical burden for the crime of insulting humanity." Nevertheless, in response to Athanase David's suggestion, in the wake of Borden's victory, that women were responsible for Laurier's defeat, Circé-Côté stood up to the injustice "of making them bear the weight of this calamity," contending that the secret ballot made it impossible to know how people voted. She believed that it would take another generation for women to "vote consciously," independently of how their husbands, fathers, or sons voted.[100] Thus, she could both whip up her troops and rush to their defence when they were attacked.

While some women could elect federal MPs, none in Quebec had access to the provincial ballot box. Circé-Côté was well aware that the majority of French-Canadian women remained indifferent to electoral politics. A number of studies showed that religious organizations continued to warn their members against availing themselves of the vote, a prerogative they deemed superfluous or even degrading; nationalists went a step further, insisting on the traditional role of women, which must be confined to the domestic sphere. Starting in 1917, Fantasio and Julien Saint-Michel, in *Le Pays* and *Le Monde ouvrier* respectively, lamented this indifference toward provincial suffrage. Convinced that human beings fashion their own fates, Circé-Côté appealed to women: "If women do not demand the right to vote, it will not be given them, and we will continue to lag behind the other provinces."[101]

The passivity of women on this issue was matched by the opposition of various intellectuals and politicians in Quebec. Henri Bourassa, a champion of the established order, was indignant when in 1918 the federal government extended the vote to all Canadian women, including those in Quebec. Twice in *Le Devoir* he inveighed against "the ravages wrought by feminism in the family and society" and held forth on the female characteristics that made women unfit to vote.[102] Éva Circé-Côté hastened to reply: "The Master has lived in an ivory tower that is beyond the reach of progress." She added that his image of women is that of "the temptress of monks or the idealized fragile being"; she proceeded to refute every argument put forward in sonorous prose by this "Chrysostom": women would not forfeit their charm, mothers would not abandon the cribs to go vote; they would be no more impressionable than men and could hardly do worse than them, as women were not the ones who had "invented torpedo boats, asphyxiating gases, and all the instruments of death," nor had they caused the war; in sum, they were equal to men in soul and intelligence.[103]

In May 1918, Julien Saint-Michel devoted a column to the "Role of women in politics." The creation of a Liberal women's club provided her with the opportunity to chime in on the debates about the qualifications of female and, by the same token, of male electors. Yes, women would benefit from study sessions on economic issues, but politicians, whose carelessness she deplored, were in even greater need of lessons on civics and political economy.[104] The debate on women's suffrage put the issue of citizens' qualifications and popular democracy on the agenda. For a long time, women reproached the authorities for allowing illiterate men to vote while women could not. All the leading feminists were then in favour of instruction in civics to be offered at the Fédération nationale Saint-Jean-Baptiste or women's clubs, but they did not propose this as a requirement for voting and very much wanted to see more education for men as well as women. The discussion about electors' qualifications continued unabated in the press, including the columns of Julien Saint-Michel. Citizens' rights entailed duties, she wrote in 1927, the primary one being education; universal suffrage will prove dangerous if not accompanied by compulsory education. Demagogues must cease to manipulate voters who choose, as was the case in the city of Montreal, unworthy and incompetent representatives. "The right to vote should be the exclusive privilege of upright, hard-working, and well-informed citizens,"[105] no matter their sex.

As of 1927, Circé-Côté's plea for equal political rights grew more insistent. She used her platform in *Le Monde ouvrier* to report on a meeting held at the Windsor Hotel on November 25, 1922, by the Alliance canadienne pour le vote des femmes and chaired by Idola Saint-Jean. In addition to the provincial parliamentarian Henry Miles—who already in 1922 had introduced the first bill demanding women's suffrage—there were representatives of the Conservative Party and the Italian, Jewish, and Irish "nations." While she readily acknowledged the importance of the Alliance and the support of legislators, Julien Saint-Michel concluded her article by drawing attention to the apathy of women themselves.[106] Indeed, in every survey, most women expressed their opposition to the vote for women. The adversaries of suffrage repeated that women did not want to vote and presented this as grounds for denying them this right. Convinced that if the majority of women demanded the vote elected officials could not refuse, Circé-Côté sought the reasons for women's indifference. She took up the argument previously advanced by Marie Gérin-Lajoie: if they decline the right to vote "that is precisely why it should be granted to them."[107] Saint-Michel added: "All the more reason, if they do not revolt, to impose an instrument of liberation on them." If prejudices make women indifferent, "it is the duty of those who are enlightened to go to the aid of their inferior sisters, who are kept at the bottom of the ladder by prejudice and ignorance."[108] She later reiterated this position: "Even if women do not want the right to vote, all the more reason to impose it on them, for it is urgent to take them out of the shells, where they live a purely vegetative life."[109] Elsewhere, adopting a harsher tone, Éva Circé-Côté laid the responsibility squarely at the door of her fellow female citizens: if they did not enjoy the same rights as women in other provinces, it was because they did not demand it insistently enough.[110] Here, we recognize her intransigence and her determination to rouse her readers.

And yet, the women of Quebec were on the move. Both the Ligue des droits de la femme and the Alliance canadienne pour le vote des femmes au Québec included women's suffrage in their programs. Their leaders, respectively Thérèse Casgrain and Idola Saint-Jean, were constantly speaking out on the radio, in the press, and in public meetings. Almost every year from 1927 until 1940, the year women's suffrage was finally won, a member of the Legislative Assembly submitted a bill in favour of the vote for women. On each occasion, members of those organizations were in attendance in the gallery of the legislature. Each time, the majority of parliamentarians voted against the bill. These repeated defeats were grist for Saint-Michel's column in *Le Monde ouvrier*.[111] Her reaction, whether angry or humorous, was to denounce discrimination based on sexual difference; she laid into "these gentlemen [who] have made it perfectly clear that the supernumerary category was unneeded in politics as well," and who, "thanks to the nice variation that men enjoy through a privilege of nature without having done anything to deserve it, [. . .] possess inborn wisdom and knowledge."[112] However, Julien Saint-Michel's article on the defeat of the bill introduced by Dr. Anatole Plante, the Liberal MLA for Montreal-Mercier, was beyond the pale in the eyes of her editor-in-chief Gustave Francq. Saint-Michel's column was published, but with the following addendum signed by the editorial board:

Woman, for her part, must not spoil her cause through the misguided zeal of a few women who also go too far. One does not catch flies with vinegar. They should know this. Why, then, answer insult with threats? This only sets back a just cause instead of pushing it forward.[113]

Circé-Côté suggested that the reason men rejected women's participation in politics was that they make the mistake of attributing to women the failings of men. When she decried men's incivility and called them Bluebeards, even the most progressive ones refused to back her.

To summarize Circé-Côté's ideas on women's suffrage, during the First World War women's involvement in the war effort and the sacrifice of their sons lent weight to the arguments in favour of their right to vote. When the Pope, as of 1922, approved of women's suffrage as a rampart against Bolshevism—women were certain to vote for right-wing parties, weren't they?—and Quebec bishops refused to follow suit, Circé-Côté never failed to remind them of the papal position.[114] In all her writings on the subject, she stressed the

> What surprises me is that these gallant troubadours, these guitar players lacking serenades, these conventional worshippers of the fair sex, who burn incense under her nose and talk behind her back, are not indignant at seeing the "jewel of creation," "the angel who forgot her wings in paradise," "the incarnation of God's smile," crucified on a dirty floor or scalded in a basin of boiling water whose foul vapours drench her as though she were in a Turkish bath. These Pharisees find it proper that their spouse, mother, or sister toils at humiliating work, but they grumble on seeing her lift herself out of her condition. Oh! They are not afraid to see her spoiling her charms when she mistreats her body and her soul with abject and depressing chores that lock her in a pillory of shame and suffering, but they shed crocodile tears to see her involved in politics, which, they say, can soil her hands, debase her, diminish her character, and make her lose the charm of her adorable femininity! . . .
> This sentimentality and hypocrisy conceal an underlying selfishness and a hard-heartedness, which are typical of the male and make him cast a jealous eye on woman's emancipation. Men are afraid to lose the mechanical cleaning rag that follows behind them and wipes away their tracks, this devotion constantly swirling around them to drive away the nuisances of existence![117]

Front page of *Le Monde ouvrier*, April 6, 1929. FTQ/QFL. BAnQ.

moral superiority of women, their social responsibility, and their pacifism. In 1932, having distanced herself from communism, she too presented them as a bulwark against an imminent communist revolution.[115] It is hard to know if she insisted on the inherent qualities of women to better convince readers and authorities that she knew were susceptible to this sort of argument or because she herself felt it was of prime importance. Yet her belief in sexual equality and women's necessary contribution to the march of progress remained unwavering.[116]

Women's role in the workings of progress implied not just the election of representatives best able contribute to the evolution of humanity, but also the right to represent progressive interests in the political arena. Circé-Côté was delighted by the pacifist positions taken by Agnes Macphail, the first woman to be elected to the House of Commons in Ottawa. "Instead of a dozen children that she might have given birth to like anyone else, she will save thousands of lives, if she is lent a hand."[118]

In 1928, Canadian feminists demanded that women be appointed to the Senate. When their claim was dismissed by the court on the grounds that women were not qualified "persons" and were therefore ineligible for appointment to the Senate, Circé-Côté noted, with no small measure of irony, that "the only thing that makes the 'person' of a senator eligible ... is old age."[119] Following this initial setback, the campaign eventually ended up before the Judicial Committee of the Privy Council in London, which in 1929 decided in favour of allowing women to be appointed to the Senate. Being a good democrat, Circé-Côté regarded the Senate, appointed by the Canadian Privy Council, as less important than the Lower House, whose members were elected by the citizens; hence her sarcastic comments about sleepy senators with polished ivory skulls arriving at this "enviable stage prior to the cemetery."[120] For her, "The right to suffrage implies eligibility for the Commons and the Senate."[121]

Prostitution

While women's suffrage was for Éva Circé-Côté a matter of equal rights, it was also a guarantee of social reforms, one of which affected women especially: the trade in sexual services. Feminism brings to mind solidarity—a sisterhood in tandem with the revolutionary brotherhood—among those of the same gender. The recognition of a shared oppression results in a bias favourable to what in the late twentieth century was referred to as a gender class. When taken to the extreme, this bias dominates other political and social allegiances and leads to preferring any woman over any man in all circumstances. Circé-Côté never endorsed this bias. She wrote under several male pseudonyms while defending working women and married women, but to what extent did she identify as a woman? To what extent did she feel solidarity with all women? The prostitution issue revealed a facet of her feminism shot through with complexities and contradictions.

Late nineteenth-century feminists were very much concerned with prostitution. In Great Britain, they challenged the double standard morality that blamed prostitutes for transmitting venereal diseases while exonerating the clients who had infected them. Feminists almost everywhere campaigned against the international traffic in women and, without blaming prostitutes themselves, the regulation of the sex trade including the registration of prostitutes and their subjection to mandatory medical examinations.

Even before the First World War, Montreal was already a hub of North American prostitution; the tolerance of the authorities in conjunction with police corruption fostered the trade, while poverty and the difficulty of finding employment ensured a continual flow of women toward brothels and places of soliciting. The economic depression at the start of the war drew droves of young women into one of the only professions open to them; in 1915, prostitutes had moved out beyond the Red Light district and into bars in the city's west end as well as houses as far north as Saint-Joseph Boulevard.[122] Prostitutes were not just visible but viewed as a source of venereal disease among the general population and members of the military in particular. The city, led by Médéric Martin, who was both the Liberal Member of Parliament for Montréal-Sainte-Marie and Mayor of Montreal since 1914, had no other choice but to act. Feminists and other social reformers railed against the trade, which was thriving with total impunity. Among the reformers, a certain alderman Blumenthal's zeal was such that he carried out a field investigation and in January 1915 was lured into a trap and arrested in a brothel. The scandal prompted municipal authorities to carry out an inquiry on prostitution.

Before the war, Éva Circé-Côté had alluded a few times to "vice parading in broad daylight" and to the "flesh trade"; starting in 1915, she wrote several articles on the issue. Neither Julien Saint-Michel nor her editor-in-chief Gustave Francq condemned such activities, which they both considered a necessary evil: "Prostitution has always existed and will end only with the emancipation of women and the education of men."[123] Circé-Côté stood apart from other feminists and reformers in that, citing the example of France, she supported regulation, which involved police visits to places of prostitution, confinement of the sex trade to certain districts, and medical examinations for prostitutes. Like Francq, she opposed the inquiry, which she regarded as a pointless exercise.

Fantasio, in *Le Pays*, took up the arguments put forward since the nineteenth century by the champions of regulation: public safety and hygiene, and protection of better-off neighbourhoods against the moral contamination of the sex trade. After all, she added, why not license "'houses of commerce,' which differ from other shops only by virtue of the different nature of the goods sold there"?[124] The inquiry did not take place, but prostitution continued to be of topical interest.

When, in 1920, public health officials made known the prevalence of syphilis, thereby arousing sharp responses in the press—right-wing papers such as *La Vérité* saw it as divine punishment—Circé-Côté recommended preventive measures involving "isolating the plague-stricken women" and regulating the sex trade. Venereal diseases, she explained, were contagious and endangered people who drank from a contaminated glass or women who kissed soldiers coming home from the war or worshippers returning from Sainte-Anne-de-Beaupré![125] One wonders if she truly credited such nonsense or whether her aim, once again, was to shock her readers. An inquiry into the police was finally conducted in 1924 under the direction of Justice Louis Coderre; witnesses included recorders, public health physicians, reformers, and feminists as well as members of the police force, madams, a few prostitutes, but no clients except for the police.[126] Over some thirty columns, Circé-Côté enunciated her views on prostitution, its causes, and its remedies.

She saw ignorance and a lack of education as the basic causes of sex work. Young women naively fell into the nets of pimps and madams: "Brothel personnel is recruited among illiterate and manifestly ignorant women from the countryside."[127] "Corrupted and trampled on at an age when others are in school reciting their letters," these girls were not just illiterate but they received no sexual education from their mothers and were ready to "fall prey to debauchery" or "into the arms of the first man to come along."[128] Their mothers, whether prudish or ignorant, found themselves once again accused of causing their children's woes.

Circé-Côté also acknowledged the economic factors behind prostitution. Unemployed or poorly paid young women often resorted to selling sexual services. She admonished business owners to think it over before assigning the best-paid jobs, such as floorwalker, to men, who in many cases had come from Toronto. In defending women's work, she came back a number of times to the proposition that laying off women who had known a measure of economic independence would increase prostitution and, conversely, that guaranteeing women a basic wage would help to decrease it.[129] Since work ensured women's emancipation, it followed, she contended, that "if more women are emancipated,[130] there will be less prostitution."

Having recognized what drove women into the sex trade, Circé-Côté nevertheless agreed that it was a "natural" and universal phenomenon. Together with the church fathers, Saint Augustine, and Saint Louis, she considered prostitution a necessary evil, which should not be curbed but "cleaned up and channelled": "Just as one cannot damn up the sea or stop lava from flowing out of the mouths of craters, no power, whether divine or human, can crystallize people's vital fluids any more than one can prevent the sap from bursting the buds."[131] Hence her gibes at reformers and their futile reforms. In 1917, for example, Arthur Maheu was still mocking alderman Blumenthal and his attempts to "save some charming Sarah, Rachel, or Rebecca from vice."[132]

In most of her articles on the subject, Circé-Côté deplored prostitution as an unavoidable evil, a "sad necessity, it is the dark side, gone back into the night, of the star of love that illuminates and invigorates the world." In a 1925 column, she went so far as to consider it preferable to "the solitary passion, which addles the brain and kills"—an exclusively male passion, she believed.[133] When the Coderre inquiry was in full swing, she raised the principle of individual freedom, not in order to apply it to prostitutes—she never defended their choosing to ply the sex trade—but to defend men's freedom to obtain sexual services in a tolerant, safe environment where a medical certificate attested to the prostitutes' good health. It followed that "the unjust system of repression is tyrannical and unworthy of our civilization; to maintain it is a violation of liberty."[134] Logically, she contended, if one is to be subjected to a repressive system, justice demands that both the clients and the prostitutes be subjected to it equally. Yet, while anyone present in a bawdy house was liable to be arrested, police statistics showed that far fewer men than women were convicted after being found in such a place. Outraged by this injustice, Circé-Côté came to the defence of a prostitute accused of being in contempt of court: "How can [these women] have respect for the law if in its name they are hunted more cruelly than a wild beast and the way back to decency is forever closed off to them because they are stamped with a stigma of shame?"[135]

Prostitution, Circé-Côté insisted, was the source of material and moral corruption. Taking her cue from the French public health specialist Alexandre Parent-Duchâtelet,[136] she felt the solution resided in regulation as it had been practised for decades in "civilized" countries like France: "Let us discipline what we cannot extinguish."[137] Whereas in France this system was upheld largely by doctors hoping, in vain, to check the ravages of syphilis and other venereal diseases, regulation found little or very timid support in Quebec.[138] During the Coderre inquiry, the recorder Amédée Geoffrion was the only witness to openly espouse a regulatory system. In *Le Monde ouvrier* Gustave Francq and Julien Saint-Michel seconded his position.[139] Fully identifying with her male pseudonym, Circé-Côté praised Geoffrion's "virile language" and his "gentle hand for the horizontal [women]" by way of endorsing his plea for tolerance.[140]

Éva Circé-Côté's support for the regulation of prostitution, with all the discrimination that this system entailed—medical examinations for prostitutes but not clients, registration of prostitutes under the supervision of the authorities—contrasted with the position of feminists. Did Circé-Côté, like Gustave Francq, see regulation as a characteristic of Latin countries and a rejection of Anglo-Saxon puritanism? She made no mention of the battles waged by feminists not just in Canada, the US, and Great Britain but also in France, Belgium, and elsewhere, against the moral double standard and inspections that were of benefit to clients alone. When it came to sexual drives, she accepted the notion of the innate differences between men and women and repeatedly trotted out platitudes about the protection of the majority of women by a minority, prostitutes, who sacrificed themselves to ensure social order. Echoing an age-old contention, Fantasio concluded, "where there are no courtesans, there are precious few honest women."[141] The great principle of individual freedom, so essential to the liberalism she professed, overrode all other considerations. Yet by entrusting the state with the enactment of laws and regulations bearing on the sex trade, she was limiting the freedom of those primarily affected: the women whose role was to satisfy the demands of men in return for payment. Her columns on prostitution or some of her writings on infant mortality raise questions about the place of women's solidarity in Circé-Côté's life.

Women's Solidarity

Éva Circé-Côté almost never identified herself as a woman. She was a freethinker, a liberal, a journalist, a librarian, no different in this regard from, say, Gustave Francq, Gonzalve Desaulniers, or Frédéric Villeneuve. Not a word about her exclusion from the École littéraire de Montréal or the masonic lodge. Nor about the wage disparities between men and women at the library. One wonders if her supervisor Aegidius Fauteux would have fired a man in such an offhand manner. Not once in her writings or the few letters that have come down to us did Circé-Côté refer to any instance of discrimination against her because she was a woman. However, as we have seen, this does not indicate that she was unaware of women's unequal civic and political rights.

Circé-Côté defined herself as a feminist, at least as of the war of 1914. She defended equal rights for women, but her relationships with them were not necessarily harmonious. She wrote about them in her columns, worked side by side with them as colleagues, maintained friendships and enmities. Her representations of women prove to be as eloquent as the explicit positions she took on social and political issues.

At the turn of the century, Colombine's ideas about a woman's role in the arts could scarcely have been more conventional: woman was the muse, "the inspirer, the artist's or poet's guiding spirit."[142] And this was in spite of the fact that Circé-Côté herself was much more than the poets' muse.

In her portraits of the women of New France, her representation of women was altogether positive. She wished to restore to their rightful place the educator Marguerite Bourgeoys and Jeanne Mance, whose influence on Paul Chomedey de Maisonneuve had been neglected by chroniclers "too preoccupied with the supernatural to notice the true source of those valiant men's tenacity, energy, and stamina."[143] Her models were independent and dynamic women, who had nothing in common with "the ruminating Marie Chapdelaine," Louis Hémon's heroine.[144] In a more modern vein, she recognized Marie Curie's contribution to science.[145] But in the bulk of her writing, she paid far more attention to the heroes of the nineteenth century, whether *Patriotes* or freethinkers, than to the small number of women discussed in her columns.

In 1903, in a "Study On Women," she quoted George Sand, Germaine de Staël, and Madame Roland, and she proposed as a model of an enlightened woman Sister Marie-Anasthasie of the Sisters of Saint-Anne, where she had received her education.[146] It cannot be said that Circé-Côté contributed to the promotion of French-Canadian women writers, despite her having written a review where she analyzed the work of Madeleine, her colleague at *La Patrie*.[147] She sometimes underscored the importance of a few pioneers, such as Doctors Helen MacMurchy in Canada and Alice Hamilton in the United States, the MP Agnes Macphail, and the American pacifist Jeannette Rankin.[148] Furthermore, when she came to the defence of the Australian swimmer Annette Kellerman, who had been attacked in *L'Action catholique*, it was the right to nudity and the cult of beauty that Circé-Côté was defending rather than the athlete herself.[149] But this small group of women pales by comparison with the many men who were the subjects of her columns and her dramatic works.[150]

A number of female figures recurred in her writing, but these were negative representations. Aside from the column "Les Idées de M. Maheu," whose misogyny stood out behind the guise of humour, Circé-Côté, under her other pseudonyms, articulated opinions worthy of that old fellow, especially before the war. At the turn of the century, Colombine was hardly kinder than Maheu toward single women, who "choose to be selfish": "[the selfish old maid] is a scraggy bloom of the land of Albion! . . . Evangelist, Protector of Animals and Salvation Army orators, etc. Laugh out loud at her, you will not hurt her feelings or pride . . . she has none. . . . Put her in a comedy, a vaudeville show, etc.;

she is one of the great laughing stocks of the Anglo-Saxon race."[151] In her criticism of Anglo-Saxon mentality, the single woman was a choice target.

The caricatures abounded in her articles. Among them, unsurprisingly, were the pious women and the surly and capricious wives, those who harass their husbands as well as those "who make them say the rosary with the family before going to the movies and cannot stand to see them come home with a glass of gin or a friend; they should expect to be mercilessly cheated on at the first opportunity."[152] In 1914 she had no doubts that women lawyers could seduce the judges.[153] And in 1917, when female relatives of members of the military obtained the right to vote, no feeling of sorority restrained her from attacking soldiers' wives.

Over time, Éva Circé-Côté toned down her statements, but her feminism remained devoid of indulgence toward women. The unemployed man coming home empty-handed after a day of job-hunting was always portrayed as one dreading his bad-tempered spouse.[154] The fact that numerous columns by Circé-Côté were about women as an oppressed group dealing with injustice or ignorance must not occult her harsh views about frivolous young women, bird-brains, or unnatural mothers willing to make little angels. She was unforgiving toward vain and superficial women such as the bourgeoises who stole jobs from young women in need of work. Even women sexually harassed by their employers did not receive her unconditional support; they were also at fault because of their provocative attire, their naiveté, or their ignorant mothers.

Circé-Côté was uncompromising and never adopted a blind feminist bias that might conceal certain faults or responsibilities. If in principle she defended women's rights for the sake of equality or individual freedom, in specific situations she readily sympathized with men. Should this be seen as yet another contradiction displayed by one who could get carried away by a witty remark, was unable to resist a clever turn of phrase, and liked to shock in order to convince? She herself put her immoderate language down to humour.[155] Her malicious judgments sometimes arose from a concern for justice that outweighed all other considerations. Finally, her feminism was not complaisant toward women, and if she embraced a cause, like the campaign against infant mortality, any argument that could advance it was grist to her mill.

* * *

Circé-Côté's relationships with the men and women of her circle were not inconsistent with the impression one gets from her writings on gender relations. She was very close to her mother, with whom she lived for many years, and wrote a moving tribute to her in a letter to Marcel Dugas. During her marriage and after her husband's death, Éva was on good terms with her mother-in-law. Nothing is known about her relations with her sister Maria, the only one to have survived to adulthood. Until the age of seventeen, Éva attended a girls' school and maintained at least one lifelong friendship with a schoolmate from those years, Georgine Boucher-Normandin, who always stayed loyal to her "gentle friend."

From the moment she entered the world of letters as a young poet, Circé-Côté found herself in a male domain from which women were excluded. Yet one would be hard put to find any indictments in her writings of exclusions based on her gender. On the contrary, she wrote about such things as the pleasure of strolling around town (*flâner*) without ever mentioning the restrictions placed on women's *flânage*. By the same token, although throughout her life she put forward principles dear to the Freemasons—secularism and free education—the doors of the lodge remained closed to her. In France, the acceptance of women in the lodges owed much to the early feminists, thanks to whom the first masonic lodge open to both men and women, the Grande Loge symbolique écossaise—Droit humain, was created by Maria Deraismes and Georges Martin in 1894, prefiguring the establishment in 1901 of L'Ordre maçonnique mixte international 'le Droit humain' (The international masonic order open to both sexes and known as "Human Rights"). In Quebec, however, the presence of freethinking women evidently did not induce the brothers to accept them in the lodge, something for which Circé-Côté never once rebuked them in her writings.

In the world of journalism, she rubbed shoulders with several women and represented them in the Association des femmes journalistes (Association of women journalists) at the founding of the Fédération nationale Saint-Jean-Baptiste. But there is no evidence that she was involved in the establishment of the Canadian Women's Press Club alongside Robertine Barry and Anne-Marie Gleason.[156] As a young journalist, she was delegated in 1901 to write a series of reports on colonization in the Lac Saint-Jean region together with Georgina Bélanger (Gaëtane de Montreuil) of *La Presse* and Anne-Marie Gleason (Madeleine) of *La Patrie*. Whatever their relations were at the time, she later would excoriate them. In the 1920s, in her letters to Dugas, she expressed nothing but contempt for Georgina Bélanger; moreover, time and Circé-Côté's libertarian convictions undermined her friendship with Madeleine Huguenin, even though the latter eventually supported women's suffrage and, in 1934 and 1935, offered Circé-Côté a film review column in Huguenin's *Revue moderne*.[157] Despite everything they had in common—

both were champions of women's rights and the French language and shared the same platforms—their early friendship apparently eroded over time.

The Association des auteurs canadiens-français was one of the rare organizations in Quebec's intellectual arena that was open to men and women alike. There, Éva Circé-Côté found herself in the company of Madeleine, Marie-Claire Daveluy, Ernestine Vézina (Medjé), and Alice Pépin,[158] but none of these women shared her freethinking—not openly, at any rate—and, far from abating, her impatience with those who maintained their attachment to religion would only intensify with the passing years.

At the library, where she spent much of her time, Madame Côté, as she was called there, found herself in a female environment. Of course, a few men did work there: her supervisor as of 1909, when he was given the title of librarian that previously belonged to her, as well as a few employees, including Marcel Dugas. She had stormy relationships with her colleagues, and she would later complain about her loneliness in her letters to Dugas.[159] When Marie-Claire Daveluy was first hired, she seemed likeable to Circé-Côté. Daveluy wrote books for young people and shared Circé-Côté's interest in working women, sales clerks in particular; however, she was not just religious but quite involved in Catholic organizations.[160] Circé-Côté felt that Daveluy was wary of freethinking, while she had trouble accepting Daveluy's Catholic morals.[161]

In many ways, Éva Circé-Côté was a loner. Aside from Georgine Boucher-Normandin, she is known to have kept up only one other friendship with a woman, despite their ideological differences: Augustine Bourassa, whom she praised as "a woman of distinction by virtue of her intelligence and her heart."[162] The daughter of Napoléon Bourassa and granddaughter of Louis-Joseph Papineau, Augustine Bourassa, just like Éva Circé-Côté, venerated Papineau. Throughout her life, she endeavoured to keep alive the memory of her two great forebears by safeguarding her father's paintings and striving to convert her grandfather's Montebello manor into a museum.[163] Circé-Côté no doubt had other female friends, but no mention of them has been found.

Éva Circé-Côté stayed away from feminist organizations. After getting involved for a short time in the FNSJB when it was founded, she distanced herself from this openly Catholic association. Her name was not on the rolls of the National Council of Women of Canada, nor of the Conseil provincial des femmes (Quebec Provincial Council of Women), nor later on those of the Conseil provincial de suffrage (Provincial Committee for Women's Suffrage), the Ligue des droits de la femme, nor the Alliance canadienne pour le vote des femmes. It is not known if she was a member of the Union des femmes libérales. La Société des auteurs canadiens (the Francophone section of the Canadian Authors Association), which she cofounded, was the only organization where she left a trace. She wrote to Marcel Dugas of being ostracized, but given her refusal to compromise she probably felt uncomfortable in any association.

Nevertheless, she left us a few portraits of feminists and paid tribute to Joséphine Marchand Dandurand, stressing the "virility" of her writing. Circé-Côté wrote of both her and Robertine Barry that they were "virile, tackling social issues . . . [their] liberalism verges on anticlericalism, [they] surprise their audience and sow the seeds of scepticism while at the same time awakening the taste for beautiful things."[164] Leaving aside the use of the word "virile" as a compliment, one should take note of the qualities that stirred Éva Circé-Côté: free-spiritedness, firmness, courage. In 1932, Julien Saint-Michel saluted *La Sphère féminine* and its editor Idola Saint-Jean in these terms:

> While her strategic threats have sometimes been questioned, never have there been any doubts as to her unflagging courage and her stubborn resolve, which have not undergone the irreparable ravages of time. After years of struggle she is as vibrant, as staunch a believer in her creed as in the early days. Independent of all parties, she is unfettered.[165]

Yet this admiration was not blind. In 1936 she remarked on Saint-Jean's lack of flexibility and subtlety: "She clearly has tenacity and a firm hand, but no control. She is impulsive."[166] It is noteworthy, meanwhile, that Circé-Côté never mentioned Thérèse Casgrain despite her being very active in the public sphere following the creation in 1927 of the Ligue des droits de la femme. Circé-Côté was not impressed by notoriety.

She was without question a feminist. She made this quite clear as of the middle of the First World War. Her feminism evolved on issues such as the admission of women into the liberal professions and women's suffrage. She consistently defended women's right to work, as shall be seen in the next chapter. There were contradictions and illogicalities within this general framework, but her feminism stayed within the bounds of liberalism and never overrode her ideal of justice and equality.

CHAPTER 10

THE RIGHT TO WORK AND WOMEN'S WORK

The century of electricity glorified Work. Shame on anyone who would refuse to make a sacrifice to the god of steam and electricity.
— ÉVA CIRCÉ-CÔTÉ, 1903

Work, creator of man, that which lifts him above himself; Work, sun of Humanity, that which provides fecundity, beauty, independence, and joie de vivre.
— ÉVA CIRCÉ-CÔTÉ, 1933

IN THE DEPTHS of the economic crisis of 1921, Éva Circé-Côté reproduced the following passage from a speech made by Alphonse de Lamartine at the Assemblée nationale of France in 1848:

> The Republic must protect the citizen as regards his person, family, religion, property, and work and make available to everyone the education that is indispensable for all men; it owes assistance to needy citizens, either *by providing them with work* to the extent its resources allow or, when the family can not do so, by giving a subsistence to those out of work.[1]

Quebec was not, of course, a republic, but the duties of the state were none the less clear for Éva Circé-Côté. Work, she believed, was a fundamental right that must be guaranteed by the state.

The Right to Work

Nineteenth-century capitalism turned productivity into a virtue. Thus, the increased availability of goods and commodities, a sign of modernity, linked labour to progress. Productivity was based on work, which brought wealth to the bourgeoisie on the one hand and subsistence to workers on the other; hence, by ensuring the acquisition of material goods, "liberal" work became liberating. It enabled both workers and members of the bourgeoisie to earn money, something that Circé-Côté—in contrast to Quebec's Catholic thinkers of that period—regarded as a positive function. Far from being a punishment dating back to Genesis, work "is in the nature of our being . . . [it is the] powerful lever of our evolution."[2] For workers, material remuneration should be in line with the abilities they needed to master. In *The Protestant Ethic and the Spirit of Capitalism* (1905) Max Weber, the founder of the sociology of work, citing Benjamin Franklin, stated that earning money was an indicator of "proficiency."[3] And for Circé-Côté, workers had the right to exercise their skills, while the state was duty-bound to provide them with the opportunity to do so.

Circé-Côté admired the Protestant ethic, both as a liberal and a progressive materialist; she valorized work, whose dignity was the theme of her very first articles on the subject: "The kingdom of the world today belongs to the workers,"[4] she wrote as early as 1903. This was not true, however, of every sort of work. Productive manual labour was noble, virile, and essential both for the struggle for life and the economic future of Quebec, yet it was in her opinion too often undervalued by the middle classes and educators. She rhapsodized about the "gnarled, misshapen hands" of the artisan,[5] but when it came to office work, especially that of the "parasites" of the public service, she vented her anger about this "land where the cult of pencil pushing blossoms in all its splendour, where everyone nurtures the secret ambition of finding a position that involves 'doing nothing.'"[6] She understood parasitical work not in the Marxist sense—that of the intermediaries who interposed themselves between workers and wealth—but to denote the slackers, whom Circé-Côté held in utter contempt.

The value of work was beyond question for this woman, who spent her days in the library and her evenings at her writing desk. The lack of work had tragic consequences, and economic crises—the recessions and depressions of 1913–15, 1919–24, and 1929–40—showed how uncertain employment could be and the extent to which it was subject to the vagaries of capitalism. Progressive thinking implied that if jobs grew scarce, the state must ensure the subsistence of those who have found none and provide assistance "in the form of benefits and unemployment funds, so as to remove the element of humiliation from the financial help given to those who were in need through no fault of their own."[7] Still, Circé-Côté favoured job-creation programs such as road maintenance projects to wealth redistribution, charity, the Society of Saint-Vincent-de-Paul, the Meurling refuge, and what was referred as *secours direct* (direct aid): "Work is what should be given to those who demand it."[8] "To feed misery is to prolong it indefinitely," wrote Julien Saint-Michel.[9] Yet reliance on the state sometimes took a back seat to another fundamental value that was a recurring topic for Circé-Côté: thrift, the sure way to achieve emancipation.[10] Workers had the right to work, but they also had a duty to save to insure themselves against hard times.

Workers' Struggles

In *Le Monde ouvrier*, starting in 1916, Éva Circé-Côté passed on the values and demands of the unions. This had not always been the case. At the beginning of the century, Éva Circé bemoaned the fate of the poor, women workers, and children who worked, to the point of idealizing the working class, where, she believed, women had not perverted their instincts and mothers were more maternal.[11] The struggles waged by workers prompted Colombine to react in ways that gave no indication of the trade union columnist she would become years later.

Thus, during the long streetcar strike of 1903, Éva Circé ended up dismissing both capitalists and workers. In the streets, she wrote,

> [...] barricade orators revive the old theories of Proudhon: "Property is theft..." They stir the throng with their thundering eloquence. They chime sonorous words of liberty and fraternity out to ears of the naive, the ignorant... to catch these poor unwary souls driven toward danger by the lure of gain... The indolent, the impotent are pensioners of the state... What they await tomorrow will not be achieved for another million years.[12]

The strike dragged on during the summer of 1903; in a column that appeared in August, Éva Circé identified with the wife of a streetcar driver and lamented that it was "unfortunate that the strike is Labour's only weapon against Capital."[13] Colombine wanted to be close to the "people," but for a long time she remained aloof from their collective demands and working-class organizations. As for the exploited workers, in her view they first must acquire an education before seeking to control or, at least, influence their working conditions.

Later, no doubt because of the interaction with her trade union colleagues at *Le Monde ouvrier*, Circé-Côté's positions grew less ambiguous:

> How is it that the exploiter, the foolish, grasping millionaire, the crippled, ignorant, and stupid potentate has become the master, while the others, the producers, the workers, the inventors, those with genius and talent, stay forever exploitable at will?[14]

Notwithstanding her harsh words about capitalism and employers, she clung to an ideal of harmonious labour relations pervaded by paternalism. Her avowed interest in socialism did not keep her from brushing aside any prospect of class struggle.

The war gave rise to a dearth of manpower and consequently placed workers in a favourable negotiation position; the result was a surge in the number of labour conflicts in Canada.[15] Circé-Côté occasionally mentioned these struggles and restricted her support to those in the private sector that did not adversely affect services to the public. In 1917, she endorsed the strike in the garment industry, where the great majority of employees were women.[16] However, a strike by truck drivers in May 1919, when the moving season was at its peak, did not receive her backing. She opined that even though the workers were exploited, the strike was no solution, since the bourgeois could always get by without the strikers by hiring someone else to move their furniture.[17]

In the spring of 1919, when the economy was shaken by the termination of war contracts and the consequent reorganization of production, the return of the veterans, and the increased cost of living, Circé-Côté, from her position as columnist for *Le Monde ouvrier*, heard the people rumbling.[18] From the Atlantic to the Pacific, grass-roots frustration generated an unprecedented wave of strikes; the work stoppage in Winnipeg gave rise to the violent intervention of the police and the army. Circé-Côté, who more than once had written about the exploitation of workers unprepared to deal with the high cost of living, spoke out against the repression of the strikers. Yet a few months later, on Labour Day, she was preaching moderation for fear that higher wages would be the death of industry.[19] In Montreal, Winnipeg, and Toronto, labour militancy, which had been interrupted by the war, was rekindled and tens of thousands of workers walked out, demanding wages in line with the cost of living. At this point, Circé-Côté's columns echoed the stance of the Trades and Labor Congress of Canada (TLCC) and of Gustave Francq, who, fearing a "general strike," withdrew their support for the widening of industrial actions.[20] Ever independent-minded, Circé-Côté also criticized the strikes led by the TLCC, like that of the waterworks employees in Montreal.

When the citizens of Montreal awoke on the morning of January 1, 1920, they realized that their faucets were dry: the municipal water supply workers had gone on strike overnight. Circé-Côté reacted, but *Le Monde ouvrier* was not the best place to chastise striking workers who had been trying for months to obtain a forty-eight hour week and a pay raise.[21] Hence, it was Fantasio, in *Le Pays*, who justified the City's intransigence and denounced the strikers' "cupidity." In the name of liberalism, she went on,

> No tyranny, whether of the people or of kings, can be accepted by free spirits. It is contrary to the liberal spirit to endure the oppression of the people's brutality, having thrown off that of casts and religions. We cannot sympathize with the gnarled hands that grab us by the throat, when they owe their salvation, their deliverance, to the intellectuals.[22]

Her statement, which ignores trade union actions and attributes the workers' gains to the petit-bourgeois intelligentsia, is surprising coming from a contributor to a working-class paper. In an immediate about-face, she denied being anti-union, "since the working class owes its emancipation to them"; there is a place for labour organizations in industry, she contended, but not in the public sector. Over time, Circé-Côté increasingly defended the happy medium until she finally stopped covering labour conflicts. Already after the events of 1919, Julien Saint-Michel averred, "For we are searching for ways to reconcile capital and labour."[23] It is likely that Gustave Francq had invited Circé-Côté to join *Le Monde ouvrier* not so much for her trade-union convictions as for the quality of her writing and also, no doubt, to come to the aid of a friend, the widow of a comrade close to the Masonic lodge.

When she wrote about religion, education, the library, or journalism, she had firsthand knowledge of these subjects. But when she began discussing industrial labour, she found herself in much less familiar territory. True, she observed workingmen and women on the streetcars and read works by socialist writers, but many of her comments betrayed a social position external to the problems she was examining. She was a product of neither the union movement nor the working class, and she tended to favour political action over any mass actions. As a reformist, she placed all her hopes in an enlightened government that would enact fair labour laws. She was concerned about workers' health and safety and asked the state to follow the example of France and Germany and hold employers more accountable for the accidents and health issues that occurred in the shops and factories, "so as to protect without distinction those who fall on the field of honour of work . . . those who constitute the country's economic existence."[24] It also went without saying that the government must banish child labour by increasing the number of factory inspectors and promote pension funds and paid vacations.[25] In the face of the government's inaction, while she did not endorse a labour party, she insisted that workers must be represented in the legislature by people of their class:

> There are those among you who concern themselves with the good of the workers because they are themselves tradespeople; put them in power in preference to the briefless barristers, the failures, the exploiters who think only about growing rich.[26]

But workers were disappointed by the rare members of the legislature who came from the labour movement; elected as independents, they soon went over to the Liberal Party. On the municipal scene, where regulations directly affected their daily lives, workingmen and women were more likely to be represented by their own. The fact remains, however, that only a small proportion of Circé-Côté's total output as a writer dealt with the working class and trade unionism. Yet her writings in this area were abundant when it came to a particular aspect: women's work.

Women's Work

If there was one area where Éva Circé-Côté's feminism expressed itself unequivocally, it was in her defence of women's right to work, which was an integral part of her vision of the right to work for all. In the course of her lifetime, she witnessed an extraordinary evolution in women's work in terms of both their place in the labour market and the occupations that they followed (see Table 2 in the Appendices). The situation of working women on the eve of the Second World War was vastly different from the one that had prevailed at the turn of the century. This was especially true of Montreal women affected by the expansion of the financial and commercial services based in the metropolis.

The increased prevalence of service sector jobs, particularly those held by women, was a characteristic of the twentieth-century economy. Women's main profession since the nineteenth century had been domestic work. This part of the service sector continued to attract a significant proportion of female workers even as the sector became swollen with retail and office jobs (see Table 3 in the Appendices). Large stores such as Dupuis Frères, Eaton's, and Morgan's transformed the city's architecture, while the tall buildings housing the head offices of major corporations such as banks and insurance companies attested to Montreal's role as the financial hub of Canada. The stenographer-typist and the female shop clerk represented the iconic images of the young working women of the twentieth century's early decades. In 1939, in Quebec overall, over half of working women were in the service sector, and of this number a third did domestic work while 13 percent held office jobs; meanwhile, 22.4 percent of female employees worked in factories, plants, and workshops. The ratio of service jobs was even greater in Montreal, with 42 percent of working women in the service sector, although the concentration varied widely among the city's various districts.[27]

The presence of women in factories and offices gave rise to numerous debates, which intensified at two key moments: the war of 1914–18 and the depression of the thirties. Circé-Côté may not have experienced working-class life firsthand, but she suffered from gender-based discrimination on at least one occasion, when she had to give up her position in favour of a man subsequent to the expansion of the library. As a librarian, she encountered the division of labour along gender lines and spent her days in a largely female environment. As a journalist, she was well aware of the advantages of writing under a man's name. But always jealous of her anonymity, she never alluded to her personal situation.

Unlike other feminists—Idola Saint-Jean and Thérèse Casgrain come to mind—who began by tackling the injustices of the Civil Code and only later, during the economic crisis, dealt with the disparities inherent in women's work, Éva Circé-Côté broached this issue as of the turn of the century in order to defend women's work and dispel the prejudices surrounding it. "The strong and virile souls are those that work has poured into its mould of bronze."[28] She wrote about the journalist's profession with an intimate knowledge of the facts; she detailed the hard daily life of country schoolteachers;[29] she expressed compassion for the women going to work in the early morning: "workshop and factory, slowly and patiently, have sculpted this fragile doll for the tomb, and I am moved by the plight of these poor things."[30] She, who had never done any manual labour, valorized the toil of the laundress, the ironer, the seamstress, the factory worker, of all those who, each morning in the streetcar, reminded her of monsieur Séguin's little goat, which she so admired: "When, then, will all the world's children sit at the

"So, you claim you can't live on $1.50 a week! Very well, we'll give you a raise of thirty cents a fortnight, but keep this in mind, Miss Teacher: you'll realize soon enough that money can't buy happiness!" *Le Pays*, December 14, 1912. BAnQ.

same banquet, when will they be entitled to bread, roses, and love?"[31] Today, the tone here may seem condescending, but at the beginning of the twentieth century her words contrasted with the disparaging discourse regarding women's work.

While it brought freedom, work also constituted a twofold form of exploitation: economic, for the women who sewed through the night for the shops; and sexual, for the factory workers, the shop clerks, the law-firm stenographers coveted by their employers or colleagues, subjected to the "appalling dilemma—either give up a gainful position, the whole family's livelihood, or endure the master's attentions."[32] Still, the risks associated with employment did not prompt Circé-Côté to discourage young women from working. After the war broke out and as her collaboration with *Le Monde ouvrier* progressed, she spoke out even more often on both the advantages of paid work and the exploitation of working women, something one could not fight by withdrawing from the labour market.

The War of 1914–18

An ardent supporter of the war effort, Éva Circé-Côté approved of the measures taken by the government to fulfil Canada's military and economic obligations toward its allies. As of 1914, Fantasio applauded women's entrance into the labour market, which in her view was their duty: "I defy the most abject individual to remain unmoved before the woman who has found a way of solemnly fulfilling a twofold duty, toward herself and society, to earn her living, to work at once for herself and for others."[33]

Circé-Côté's arrival at *Le Monde ouvrier* in 1916 coincided with the first manpower shortages, after the resumption of production and voluntary enlistment had absorbed the workers left without work by the economic depression of 1913–15, and in the wake of Great Britain's appeal to the countries of the British Empire, given the continuing hostilities, to provide military materiel and foodstuffs. The demands of the war brought more and more women into the labour market, especially non-traditional occupations for which they previously had been thought unsuited; starting in 1916 this new reality set the tone for many of Julien Saint-Michel's columns in the international trade unions' newspaper. All these articles betrayed some hesitation as to the part played by woman's nature relative to the effects of the environment on the division of labour.

Was it because she considered men less open to changes in the workplace and in the sexual division of labour that Julien Saint-Michel's outlook in *Le Monde ouvrier* was at variance with Fantasio's in *Le Pays*? Representing the interests of male workers under the Saint-Michel byline, Éva Circé-Côté initially expressed serious misgivings about women's presence in the factories, particularly when they replaced men.

> By pursuing the same ambitions, the same careers as men, women, sad to say, will become bereft of poetry and grow uglier. One anticipates a perversion of their traditional role, a degeneration, such that all their charms, all the graces with which nature endowed them for the good of the species will be blunted. If women succeed in solidly establishing themselves in positions once filled by men, what will happen? We will witness the proliferation of parasitic husbands.[34]

Here, Circé-Côté, the emancipated woman, was voicing—though somewhat ambivalently—the great anxiety brought about by the presence of female industrial workers. In 1916, she still held that "those women who, without harming their health, are able to take on extra work, rent one or two rooms, do some sewing at home, raise poultry or canaries, or do laundry, should do so."[35] She had not yet gone beyond the traditional boundaries of women's work but called on them to pursue their centuries-old occupations with greater intensity. The constraints of a war economy would soon make her change her tune.

While the troops were getting bogged down in the trenches and the war dragged on, defying the worst predictions, Canada, in order to respect its military contracts, put aside the ideal of the woman-as-homemaker and asked women to replace men in the job market. Not only was the service sector increasingly dominated by women, as evidenced, for example, by the large number of female cashiers in the banks, but masses of women found work in munitions factories and heavy industry or as streetcar conductors and tractor drivers. When conscription was introduced in 1917, the term "conscription" was also used in reference to women working on the domestic front and outside the home. It was a precedent welcomed by most women, according to Circé-Côté: "They are impatient to slip into men's boots, to be in the banks, the offices, to operate streetcars and automobiles, to be barbers and carriage drivers," because if "everywhere in Europe women have replaced men, there is no reason for this not to happen in Quebec."[36] And, in spite of the traditional model of women, often referred to then as *personnes du sexe* (persons of the sex), this was indeed what took place in Quebec. Tens of thousands of women assembled munitions, sometimes for more than twelve hours a day, with many labour laws being suspended for the duration of the conflict. The presence of female workers raised not just the question of whether this was proper or that of their aptitude—innate or acquired—for this work, but it also raised the issue of wages and the exploitation of women.

Women's employment in wartime gave Circé-Côté the opportunity to express herself on the qualities specific to each sex. Regarding men, she had nothing but contempt for office work, and pencil pushing, where (male) youths withered in "this existence that atrophies a man's brain, saps his constitution, lends his complexion the sallowness of funeral candles, hollows his chest and stoops his back, and, long before he dies, turns him into a walking skeleton."[37] Yet, apparently, the same work was quite acceptable for women: "Public administration must be opened up to them, at city hall, where four-fifths of the staff could be women," for "unquestionably, bureaucratic tasks are what suit them best." Sexual differences—physical and "temperamental"—run through her egalitarian discourse, with a host of attendant consequences:

No one is challenging women's obligation to work, so long as they are given the least tiring, the least depressing jobs. Regularity in work, continuous effort—these are contrary to the female temperament. A woman is better able to make a big push than to work assiduously.[38]

She drew another example of the "natural" disparities between the sexes from her own work experience. She was happy to remind readers that female assistant-librarians had been replaced by men at the library, with regrettable results: they did not shelve the books properly and left behind a trail of ashes and matches. Julien Saint-Michel concluded that libraries, like banks, required the kind of work "essentially suited to women ... because they are methodical, precise, orderly, and direct. They are sober in their habits, a trait that serves them well when money has to be counted."[39] Yet she did not view these natural dispositions as impediments to women's ability to adapt; they apparently adjusted better to tasks considered male than the other way around.

Circé-Côté's discourse, however, did not always follow the same line. In a column about women replacing men in the service sector, Julien Saint-Michel adopted a tone worthy of her most conservative contemporaries. Starting with the observation that men, often elderly and boasting many years of service in an office or store, were being fired to make room for young women, she declared, "there is, then, no way to protect oneself against favouritism, the influence and the pretty eyes of a pretentious young thing."[40] The bantering tone befitted her alias Arthur Maheu and was reminiscent of Colombine's writing in 1900.

Circé-Côté had no doubt that women "naturally slipping into their husbands' shoes" could adapt to nontraditional jobs without "the results being any worse."[41] Her optimism was tempered, however by her thoughts on the fate of children of working mothers. In fact, very few married women and even fewer mothers of small children worked in munitions factories. But the depiction of children neglected by their absent mothers as "bundles of dirty rags" that have been "entrusted to mercenaries" provided her with arguments to support her demand that the state take measures to protect women's work."[42]

This thorny issue had given rise to divisions among late nineteenth-century feminists. In the 1890s, some of them had demanded that the state intervene to protect women by ensuring special conditions, such as a nine-hour workday or the prohibition of night work. More liberal feminists like Carrie Derrick and Julia Drummond of the Conseil local des femmes de Montréal, knowing that such measures could entail discrimination against women, invoked the principle of equality and called for reforms for both sexes.[43]

The massive entry of women into the labour force during the war put this debate back on the agenda. For Circé-Côté, women's "health [was] more frail than that of men," and they were "obliged to do a man's work with such a fragile, delicate organism" and "nerves that needed gentle care"; therefore, it made sense that they should be treated differently and that their weakness not be used as a pretext to exploit them.[44]

One aspect of wartime work was of particular concern to social commentators: night work. Honest women in those days were not supposed to go out alone after dark, so how could one justify work that required them to do so at an unreasonable time of night? The suspension of labour laws made long workdays legitimate, and night work soon became the norm in munitions factories. Circé-Côté continued to consider this unacceptable for women on the grounds of both health and morality. The night shift "always ends at a time when women and girls should not be seen in the street," and when there were no more streetcars. They were then "exposed to the bad weather ... and to assaults by vagrants and drunks." If a woman stayed at the plant, she was in peril of being sexually harassed by the "Don Juans of the factory." Circé-Côté demanded "full rights for women, except the right to be treated worse than a brute. An animal, at least, sleeps at night." The dangers were not overstated, and steps were taken to keep them under wraps so as not to discourage women from working.[45] In the summer of 1918, Saint-Michel, in a column devoted to night work, depicted the "ordeal of working women ... porters, truck drivers, brakewomen, carriage drivers, hairdressers ... old women prematurely faded."[46] Even given the best conditions, Circé-Côté remained inflexible on the prohibition of night work.

While she accepted the presence of women in male-dominated trades, she recognized the harmful effects of factory work and predicted that "fifty per cent of female workers will be casualties," pallid, emaciated, turned into wrecks. She pleaded in favour of a tea break in the afternoon at the employers' expense. And in support of her request, she pointed out that "most of them have not yet accomplished their mission as women."[47]

Maternity was always one of her concerns. Even though very few pregnant women worked outside the home, she demanded that a law be passed obliging employers to treat these women kindly: places to sit, reduced hours of work, sanitary measures, "to help them accomplish that great social duty known as maternity." In terms that someone like Henri Bourassa would not have repudiated, she described the "torment endured by these women harnessed to a thankless job, in an atmosphere of dust and fire, amid the din of the machines and the maze of trades," and whose legs could barely carry them when they left the factory, a condition that constituted "a threat to the future of the race."[48] She certainly believed what she wrote, but she was also adept at marshalling arguments capable of swaying public opinion and pressuring decision-makers to take action.

Sacrifices—for she considered work in such conditions as much a sacrifice as an obligation—must be fairly recompensed. Women's presence in a broader range of trades than ever before posed the question of their wages. Previously, they were paid between a third and half of what men earned in skilled trades or when their tasks were deemed more strenuous than those of women. The ideal was the family wage, enough to ensure the family's subsistence, therefore making it unnecessary for the wife to work. But this level of income for the breadwinning husband remained theoretical, except in rare instances among highly skilled workers. The trade unions stuck to the ideal of a sole family wage and consequently were opposed, at least in principle and especially before the war, to gainful employment for women. The unions' priority being the wages of the breadwinning husband, they showed little interest in women's wages unless this served to guarantee veterans a reasonable level of income. Not until 1919 did the Trades and Labor Congress of Canada remove its objection to women's work from its programme.

Like all those who took public positions on women's work during that period, the unions justified women's lower wages on the grounds that they would be on the labour market only temporarily. The extra income was regarded as sufficient for soon-to-be-married young women, who, in any case, had no access to the kind of technical training that would open the door to skilled trades. Circé-Côté understood very early on that women worked for economic reasons. If "most women go to the factory not out of choice but out of necessity," if they do men's work that is "equally protracted, hard, and productive," they deserve the same wages; otherwise, one would be "subordinating the weaker sex to the stronger unjustifiably."[49] Furthermore, she was aware that the hiring of lower-paid female workers would entail unfair competition for the men.

The Interwar Years

The war induced Éva Circé-Côté to adopt a discourse favourable to women's work, one that she would not abandon after the armistice. On returning to civilian life, men soon recovered their place in industry and some services, but a precedent had been set legitimizing women's work. Women had firmly established themselves in office work, demonstrated their ability to take on new occupations, and adapted their clothes and hairstyles to their new tasks;

they were determined to keep their jobs until marriage, as it was still taken for granted that a married women's place was in the home. Despite the postwar economic depression, Julien Saint-Michel persisted in defending women's right to work: "Will closing the workshops and offices to women bring them back to domestic chores? No, it will drive them to the gutter, the stream, La Maternité [a home for unwed mothers—Trans.], prison."[50] She tried to persuade husbands to accept their wives' gainful employment, which could lighten the workingmen's load. Yet in 1926 she proposed to women to go back to the same traditional occupations as in 1916, that is, those not in competition with male-dominated jobs: "garment-making, embroidery, laundering, keeping a small grocery next to the flat, a hat shop, or raising chickens, rabbits, etc.," work centred on the husband's well-being, so that he might "enjoy a few happy days before crossing the great divide."[51]

Once again, Circé-Côté showed her ability to contradict herself. Women's work was "a sad necessity of these times," she wrote in 1921, affirming that if they could, if they were respected there, most women would choose the sweetness of home. In light of the prevailing conditions in some work environments—insalubrious workshops, harassment by foremen—she no doubt was right. Why did young women work? Her answer: for the sake of independence, out of necessity, to help provide for their families, but also because they were pressured to do so by greedy parents or simply to buy themselves some trinkets. Circé-Côté returned a number of times to the case of those who "do not need to work," because "it is not fair that girls who get room and board at home should take the positions of those who are forced to earn a living and support their families." She went so far as to propose a law that would oblige parents to keep their daughters at home at least until they came of age; they could do housework and help their mothers raise their dozen children.[52]

Topping the list of those who did not work out of necessity were sales clerks, a group that was often the subject of Circé-Côté's columns. She scorned the idle young ladies who worked for frills and flounces, out of whimsy, selfishness, and vanity. They contributed to their colleagues' exploitation by accepting department store jobs that were poorly paid—three or four dollars a week—because they had no real need for money.[53] But Circé-Côté warned her readers against generalizations: not all sales clerks were frivolous; some had to earn a living, and these women deserved wages equal to those of their male colleagues.[54] In her columns she was able to conjure up the atmosphere of the large stores with her group portraits of ten girls, two clerks, and a floor walker assigned to the reception counter, "a decorative object," "a good-looking, pomaded young man, curly-haired, heart-shaped lips, fawning, and shifty," who greeted the ladies "with a string of insipid compliments," and who, "precisely because he is useless . . . enjoys immense prestige" and a good salary. Why could this "working-class Apollo" not be replaced by a woman?[55]

Circé-Côté's writing on the distinction between women who must work and those who were not obliged to was at odds with her defence of work for its own sake and for the sake of freedom. Her various articles reflected her immediate concerns: today, the right to work was beyond dispute; later, child labour must be condemned; another day, defending the most vulnerable meant setting aside universal rights such as the right to work and giving priority to the women who needed it most.

Éva Circé-Côté was not alone in combatting the exploitation of women's work. Feminists and some trade unionists like Gustave Francq pushed the government to create the Commission du salaire minimum des femmes (Commission on the minimum wage for women) in 1919. The commissioners, all men, would not hold their first meeting until 1926. Participating in that inaugural gathering, chaired by Francq, were representatives not only of unions but also of women's organizations. The Commission operated within very narrow confines: it did not set wage levels but, in response to complaints made by female workers, set up tripartite conferences among representatives of employers, workers, and "impartial persons."[56] This was a rather timid measure that would have little effect on the working conditions of women in Quebec. It is surprising, however, that Circé-Côté did not display more enthusiasm in the only column that she devoted to this matter. True, she viewed the commission as a step toward greater justice, but in 1926 she represented it as an instrument for the maintenance of the status quo and a rampart against prostitution and Bolshevism! Expressing a certain conservatism and echoing the fears of many workers, she warned that if the minimum wage were set too high employers would prefer to engage men, for "women must know that they are hired because they are paid less." Moreover, she relayed the fears of businessmen with female employees, such as shop owners, by voicing reservations about the minimum wage, which, she opined, not only would be a threat to vulnerable businesses but would also infringe on the principle of individual freedom.[57] She thus kept up, however ambiguously, her defence of petit-bourgeois interests in the name of individual liberty.

In *Le Monde ouvrier*, Circé-Côté's columns on the unionization of women were few in number, the TLCC's membership being made up of skilled workers, a category that excluded the majority of working women.

Circé-Côté herself enjoyed what could be described as a bourgeois lifestyle, and toward the end of the war she ridiculed a project to unionize domestics, still women's main line of work. Commenting on the demands of the "Union des domestiques"—eight-hour workday, six-day workweek, twelve dollars a week, fifty cents per hour of overtime—she waxed ironic about the situation of the poor bourgeois: domestics cost one hundred dollars a month in 1919, didn't they, if one took into account food and waste?[58] In reality, as indicated by the notices in the newspapers, live-in domestic workers earned no more than a few dollars a week. Yet during Éva Circé-Côté's lifetime the unionization of domestics—not to mention shop clerks and office workers—remained pie in the sky.

In the interwar period, however, her columns were focused less on the collective organization of working women than on the legitimacy of women's work itself in the context of the economic depression of the 1930s. The rise in unemployment and anxieties about the lack of work for men threw into doubt the very right of women to work. During the 1920s in Quebec, the recurring debate on women's employment, as articulated by religious, economic, and political authorities, the feminists of the Fédération nationale Saint-Jean-Baptiste, the Confédération des travailleurs catholiques du Canada (Quebec's second largest union central), and social-minded Catholics, bore on moral and economic considerations, the harm done to working women's virtue, and the competition among working women and between them and workingmen.

During the economic crisis, conservative elements, politicians, and Church representatives, who had never condoned women's economic independence, were quick to hold them responsible for unemployment among men. In spite of the sexual division of labour, which almost never placed women in direct competition with men in the labour market, the unemployment of the Great Depression fuelled the myth that working women were depriving men of jobs deemed to be rightfully theirs. In fact, in 1932, at the height of the Depression, only fifteen percent of Quebec women over the age of ten were gainfully employed.[59] Of these, a minority, most of them single women, worked in factories, while twenty-five percent worked in personal services, which, in one case out of five, was domestic work, hence no threat whatsoever to men's employment.

Wishing to subdue the public's impatience with rising unemployment, the Liberal government's Labour minister, Charles-Joseph Arcand, in a speech given in 1932 to the Cercle de l'Union des femmes libérales, proposed to raise men's wages so that women could withdraw from the labour market. This recognition of the head of the household—male, of course—satisfied the expectations of many unions and coincided with the Church's views on the respective roles of the breadwinning husband and the wife as mother and housekeeper. No doubt a trial balloon, it was well received in conservative circles and by the champions of the traditional family. Julien Saint-Michel's response was that it was unrealistic to expect women to go back to being simply housewives after so many years in the labour market. Working women would not want to give up the economic independence, however relative, derived from gainful employment. "Is it possible, once she has breathed the open air, to put her back in a cage?"[60]

In February 1933, the member of the provincial legislature J.-A. Francœur introduced a bill dealing with the problems of the Depression; among the major causes of the economic slump, he identified "the invasion of women in jobs hitherto filled by men,"[61] thereby speaking to a sentiment that was widespread among the population and relayed in newspapers like *Le Devoir*. Having pointed out that women's wages were lower than men's, Francœur concluded that fathers were being supplanted by young women who were paid less. Young men were reputedly reduced to accepting assistance from the state while their fiancées took over their positions! To protect men's jobs, Francœur proposed raising the minimum age for women in industry and commerce to twenty-one, except for those who were their families' sole breadwinners. This was put forward as not just an economic but also a moral solution, for "the return of women to the family home will restore the natural order of things."[62] He moreover asked for an inquiry on all the sectors where men were replaced by women and another on young women in the civil service. These investigations, along with his bill, were stillborn.

Year after year, the economic chaos persisted with not much relief in sight for those without work and their families. In January 1935, during the sixth winter of the crisis, Francœur was at it again, this time with another bill requiring women who did not work out of necessity to be removed from the workforce. The bill died after the Liberal government refused to support it.[63] Legislators were not alone in wishing to curb women's employment. In August 1934, Montreal's new mayor, Camilien Houde, whose election Circé-Côté had applauded a few months earlier, stated that the "return of women to the home," just like the return to the land, was a solution to unemployment. In contrast, Julien Saint-Michel could not imagine why women would give up their "honestly earned money to live in the hotel-under-the-stars, their independence and luxury to become once again an unpaid slave to the rag, the mop, and the cooking pot."[64] There was nothing unusual about the attempts to limit women's employment; they pandered to the popular belief that even in areas not considered exclusively male—banks, elevators, etc.—the inclusion of women was to blame for men's unemployment.

Le Monde ouvrier, whose readers belonged to the largest union central in Quebec and Canada, was directly concerned with this debate. Although it had moved beyond its previous position in favour of eliminating gainful employment for women, the TLCC still maintained that the husband-breadwinner's wage should be sufficient to allow his wife to stay home and attend to the children and housework.[65] In many families, it was not unusual for children, rather than the mother, to make up for the family's income shortfall due to the father's insufficient wages.[66] The union paper's editor-in-chief acknowledged this situation, and in 1934 *Le Monde ouvrier* openly supported working women, asserting that they boosted the family's capacity to buy clothing, cosmetics, and shoes, that they had proved themselves, having been obliged to work to supplement the family's inadequate income, and that they could not be ousted.[67] Among the newspaper's collaborators, it was Julien Saint-Michel more than anyone else who resisted the backlash against working women.[68]

Senseless is how Circé-Côté described the campaign against women's employment, and she reiterated all her arguments regarding women's equal or even superior qualifications.[69] As she had done during the postwar economic depression, she opposed dismissing women as a remedy for unemployment.[70] From 1930 on, she spotlighted the infringements on women's right to work. Women were threatened with exclusion in other countries and, anticipating similar attacks in Canada, Julien Saint-Michel cited the position of the Women's International Union Committee to validate her opposition to all prohibition of women's work. Such prohibition would contravene the principle of sexual equality, violate individual freedom, adversely affect family finances, and "cut short the blossoming of [woman's] personality."[71] Here, in a nutshell, were the four fundamental justifications of women's employment. She brushed aside the argument defending the wages of the head of the family, a "pretext," she affirmed, for dismissing women, and she decried the fact that during the depression "the fair sex had to pay to atone for men's misdeeds."[72] In 1936, when the country had not yet emerged from the Depression, she exclaimed: "None of God's commandments orders women to be their husbands' unpaid domestics, unremunerated factotums." She lambasted the antifeminists and "feminophobes" who "would like . . . to establish [women] as 'queen of the household,' to spare them those tasks contrary to their sex, to replace the typewriter with the basin, the pen with the wringer and the mop, to see them hang about in the kitchen among the pots and pans."[73] For Circé-Côté, the place of women in the workforce had nothing to do with the economic situation: "It is a mere coincidence that the crisis occurred just when women were turning over a new leaf."[74]

She wrote numerous articles vaunting female virtues that were assets in the workplace: women were docile, polite, sober, more methodical than their male colleagues, more deferential, more attentive, more persevering, and more punctual than them. Women were altruistic, "they rarely work for their own interests. . . . They spend money in the same way that they expend their own energy, to support poor, aging parents, for an invalid or incapacitated husband, to raise a young family. We must not ostracize women."[75] She even affirmed that employers had come to prefer women, and that men had only themselves to blame.[76] As was often the case, she illustrated her assertions with an anecdote: a major employer bitterly regretted having fired a dozen female employees after giving into patriotic considerations. "Women have won their independence through work; one cannot subject them again to the yoke of family tyranny, which they had thrown off." She went on to denounce Mussolini for wanting to force Italian women to return to their homes, and she praised Russia, where "millions of women work alongside men without conflict, friction, or any base feelings of jealousy."[77] Playing on her readers' sensibilities, she insisted that firing women who were used to being financially independent would encourage prostitution.[78]

Nevertheless, for Éva Circé-Côté, women's right to work remained conditional. She had already objected to the employment of young bourgeois women who enjoyed material comfort, the "drones" who hampered the unions. For not only did they take the place of working women obliged to earn a living or help their parents, but these coquettes held back unionization, with no consideration for the women who might benefit from it.[79] When jobs grew scarce, she again denounced the women who did not need to work. During the economic crisis, she proposed that, instead of firing women at random, employers choose those who buy themselves "fur jackets, transparent crepe negligees."[80] It was a matter of protecting the jobs of women who, or whose family, depended on this income. Similarly, she inveighed against the replacement of young women by boys paid two or three dollars for a fifty-five- or sixty-hour workweek, instead of the seven dollars earned by young women for a forty-eight-hour workweek.[81] In this case, for the sake of liberal justice, she was bringing to light an injustice; in the case of young women for whom work was an indulgence, Circé-Côté disregarded their individual freedom to hold a job to highlight what she adjudged to be prejudicial to women whose work was essential for their own or their families' subsistence.

As grist for her defence of women's employment, Circé-Côté used whatever headline, anecdote, or human-interest story was to hand. In 1934 she took advantage of the birth of the Dionne quintuplets to celebrate, somewhat tongue-in-cheek, the physiological superiority of women, deplore "male degeneration," and castigate the "persecutors of working women."[82]

The right to work, seen as a cornerstone of feminism by Marxists and an illustration of individual freedom by liberals, was the nexus of the various elements of the feminist rationale—woman's nature, sexual division, transgression of traditional roles, economic independence, personal fulfilment—all of which were discussed in Éva Circé-Côté's columns. The issue of women's work elicited angry and contradictory reactions on her part, but she consistently regarded it as crucially important and made it the subject of her writing more often than any other aspect of feminism.

CONCLUSION

The day she has nothing left to say, Colombine will break her pen.
— LA PATRIE, April 1, 1922

THROUGHOUT HER LIFE, Éva Circé-Côté championed a variety of causes, but some major constants stand out. She was a liberal and a positivist, a modern, and a lover of justice. Her ideals came directly from the *Patriotes* of 1837–38. She embraced their struggle for progress, that is to say, secularism, openness to others, women's emancipation, education, and access to books. A staunch progressive, she never lost her faith in human perfectibility and, as someone who was constantly evolving, she was able to adapt her thinking amid the rapid transformations of her epoch. While not departing from her basic principles of justice and equality, at the age of forty she espoused feminism and women's suffrage. Having received a Catholic education, she gradually distanced herself from the Church and later showed a keen interest in Protestantism. She was a devoted republican and rejected Quebec separatism the moment she saw the links between it and Catholic interests, eventually favouring even closer ties with Great Britain for the sake of safeguarding freedom of thought.

Éva Circé-Côté chose to fight with her pen. It is hard to picture her taking part in the rallies that filled the streets of Montreal, events she rarely mentioned in her columns. As far as she was concerned, progress came primarily through the written word: "a people with no literature is bound to disappear." Literature is an agent of change.[1] Aside from her poems and some thirty stories, Circé-Côté expressed herself in a genre too often deemed minor: the newspaper column. Yet such columns were particularly important in Quebec, a small nation, a French-speaking "island" far from the major centres of the French-speaking world, a colony dominated by the Catholic church, with little in the way of a modern, urban literature. With neither a Balzac nor a Zola, the dearth of realist novels, that invaluable source of social history, affected one's understanding of Quebec society. Newspaper columns made up for the lack. Éva Circé-Côté created a portrait of an entire historical period, she pondered the issues of the day and strived to make an impact on the course of events. She both reflected and interpreted her society. She was highly concerned with the didactic function of her writings, which put forward a discourse that was often at odds with or opposed to the mainstream and all the more vital for waging a tireless battle against the prevailing obscurantism. There was nothing self-evident about calling for the separation of Church and state, opposing the temporal power of the Catholic Church, standing up against censorship, demanding equality between women and men, in a word, being a freethinking woman. Éva Circé-Côté reminds us that the dominant discourse, controlled by the Church and the Catholic elites, has always had its naysayers.

In the service of her self-imposed mission to enlighten, Circé-Côté marshalled every tone, every rhetorical figure that might convince her readership—irony, sarcasm, bombast, indignation, provocation—intertwined in ways that cannot be readily unpacked. When she contradicted herself or let her pen outstrip her ideas, was it to shock her readers? To cajole them? Or perhaps she did not always properly gauge the effect of her statements. Elsewhere she was all caution and ambiguity; was she then bowing to her editor's demands and her readers' expectations? This is hardly likely, given how proud she was to have remained independent and how often she rebuked those who had not.

Circé-Côté never defined herself as an intellectual and this may have shielded her from having to conform to the expectations of an identifiable social group. The use of the word "intellectual" in Quebec was out of step with the situation in France after the Dreyfus affair, when the term, originally confined to continental France, was made known abroad. In Quebec, the intellectual—always male—had a bad reputation, and it was considered in good taste to refer to *pseudo*-intellectuals, as if the genuine ones could only be found somewhere else.[2] Still, there were writers in Quebec who met the established criteria justifying that epithet and Éva Circé-Côté was among them, though one reservation should be noted: her anonymity. She was known as a librarian, poet, dramatist, and speaker, but the bulk of her written work was not associated with her person; this may have limited the impact of both the articles published under her name and the anonymous ones, though had the latter been attributed to a woman they probably would have been devalued. Many politically committed individuals paid a heavy price for their intellectual independence; Circé-Côté, too, had paid and, what's more, often anonymously, hence without recognition. Her comrades of the early days, Madeleine, Louvigny de Montigny, Arsène Bessette, wrote for the major dailies; her columns, meanwhile, were published—but not even under an identifiable name—in weeklies, which, though certainly of a high calibre, were not as widely distributed.

Éva Circé-Côté considered herself modern and, indeed, she embodied Montreal's modernity throughout nearly half a century. She optimistically greeted the upheavals of her epoch: the reign of electricity, the expansion of the city's boundaries, streetcars, the magic of film, the omnipresence of the radio, realism in novels, non-traditional jobs for women. Her ideas on the separation of church and state or compulsory education may have appeared modern in Quebec, but despite her exhortations to look to the future, Circé-Côté arguably belonged to 1795—the year Condorcet published his *Outlines of an Historical View of the Progress of the Human Mind*—and 1837–38—the apogee of liberal ideas in Canada—or even to the century of Zola and Spencer, more than to that of Freud, Picasso, Colette, and Ravel. Her philosophical references stopped on the threshold of the twentieth century and were no longer avant-garde. In literature, she admired Romain Rolland, Maxim Gorki, and Anatole France, but aside from them, she cited very few twentieth-century European authors, except for minor ones like André Thérive. Undeniably, Quebec lagged behind France, and this was a major reason for the gap in her readings. What had become passé in Europe swept like a fresh wind of freedom over Quebec, corseted as it was in intellectual and religious conservatism, though in reality, this wind emanated from the previous century. The exceptions were secularism and feminism, which actually blossomed in the twentieth century.

The Montreal that she travelled through morning and night on her way to and from the library has changed. The houses where she lived have given way to new buildings; her library is being used for other purposes, and the Gagnon collection and the other books she had acquired and shelved are now in the Grande Bibliothèque. The streets have been widened to accommodate more cars, and the occasional rails sticking out through the asphalt are the only reminders of the old streetcar routes; except for Saturdays in the spring, fewer people crowd the streets, while the metro and underground shops are full. Yet the throng is as disparate as ever. Today, those whom Circé-Côté called exotics hail from countries farther away than Central Europe, but, like their predecessors, they will speak their languages and keep their customs for one or two generations before blending into a perpetually changing Quebec.

Exploring such a singular life raises an endless series of questions. How was Éva Circé-Côté seen by those who knew her? The few individuals who have left a written record of their observations—from Louvigny de Montigny at the start of her career in journalism to Georgine Boucher-Normandin at the end of her life—all spoke of her gentleness, her generosity, and her sense of justice. By 1949 she had already been forgotten in the cultural milieu. When she died, there was no funeral oration, no tribute by friends, as is customary at the death of a public figure. Nor did the City of Montreal commemorate her contribution to the development of its libraries.

Éva Circé-Côté was an original, a rebel, an avant-garde woman, but this did not make her unique; her critiques and proposals were among those advanced by a whole current, which she helped to enrich. In Quebec, intellectuals, especially historians, have constructed a past that leaves little room for entire generations of progressives. Marie Gérin-Lajoie, Godfroy Langlois, and Gustave Francq may have their biographers, but a complete cohort still awaits recognition; Robertine Barry, Arsène Bessette, Anne-Marie Gleason-Huguenin, Gonzalve Desaulniers, Louvigny de Montigny, Idola Saint-Jean, and many others are still largely unknown. They are all part of a Quebec that is less bleak than the usual representations of it, less submissive, less monolithic, more complex and more open to influences from abroad. Circé-Côté added her voice to a current of progressive intellectuals who prepared what would come to be known a few decades on as the Quiet Revolution.

Her battles bore fruit, some of them even during her lifetime. She worked in the monumental library that she had so ardently wished for. In the final years of her life, women won the right to vote and access to a university education and to the professions, and education became compulsory for all children. Circé-Côte had been dead twenty years when social services became secular. Tolerance, openness toward the outside world, the end of censorship are now taken for granted. Other struggles continue: wage disparities between men and women persist, and women are still confronted with what is referred to as the glass ceiling; the integration of immigrants is still a matter of debate as are the protection of the French language and the political future of Quebec; social inequalities are greater now than they were in her day. And the fight for freedom of thought is as intense as ever.

NOTES

Chapter 1

1 Saint-Jean-Baptiste de Montréal parish certificate of baptism B 493. All the genealogical information was provided to me by Charles-Eugène Labbé, Andrée Michaud, the great-niece of Éva Circé, and Danaé Michaud-Mastoras. Hubert Charbonneau clarified certain obscure genealogical points.
2 Madeleine, "Nos canadiennes-françaises," *La Patrie*, May 16, 1903, 22. In this article of praise published in the woman's page, "Le royaume des femmes," Madeleine writes that Éva Circé was born of a French mother and father, which is incorrect.
3 The spelling, Circé or Sircé, varies from one document to another. Today Saint-Philippe is part of the regional municipality of Roussillon County.
4 The testimony of a magistrate cited in Allan Greer, *The Patriots and the People: The Rebellion of 1837 in Rural Lower Canada* (Toronto: University of Toronto Press, 1993), 239.
5 Jules Verne, *Famille-Sans-Nom* [1889] (Montréal: Réédition Québec, 1970). In the tenth chapter, Verne provides a quasi-ethnographic description of the Chipogan farm as being located seven leagues from La Prairie. Regarding the war of 1812, see Jean-Pierre Wallot, *Un Québec qui bougeait: trame socio-politique au tournant du XIXe siècle* (Montreal: Boréal Express, 1973), 111–31.
6 The spelling of Descarries was not yet standardized and Marie-Philomène signed herself as Descary. Louis Kingsley married Marie-Louise, another sister of Marie-Azélie. Genealogical tree of Jean-Baptiste Descarries and Louise Lanthier, Charles-Eugène Labbé and Andrée Michaud.
7 *Lovell's Montreal Directory 1888–1889* (Montréal), 352.
8 The church was destroyed by fire in 1904, but by this date the Circés had left Sainte-Cunégonde.
9 The journalist and filmmaker J.-Arthur Hommier wrote an eloquent description of the rat hunts at the Saint-Laurent market which, in 1885, was situated in front of the future Monument-National. "Montréal il y a quarante ans," *La Revue de Manon*, April 1925, 4.
10 Marie-Philomène Descarries entered into the Carmelite monastery at the time it was founded, some four years before the birth of Éva Circé.
11 Circé-Côté to Dugas, Montréal, July 1924. Fonds Courteau, série Marcel Dugas. Centre d'archives régionales de Lanaudière (CARDL).

12 Colombine, "Souvenirs champêtres," *Les Débats*, June 7, 1903.
13 Archives des Sœurs de Sainte-Anne (ASSA), LQ/11/104/1r. Rapports annuels faits au surintendant de l'Instruction publique, 1882–1888; Circé-Côté à Dugas, July 1924, CARDL.
14 ASSA, LQ11/139.1.
15 ASSA, LQ/11/100,5, bulletins des élèves (student report cards), 1885–1888.
16 H. Harrison, *National Reference Book of Canadian Men and Women with Other General Information*, 5th ed. (Montreal: Canadian Newspaper Service, 1936), 847.
17 Colombine, "Étude sur la femme," *L'Avenir du Nord*, August 13, 1903.
18 Fantasio, "Autour d'un conventum," *Le Pays*, June 5, 1915.
19 Fantasio, "Si nous avions une critique littéraire," *Le Pays*, May 12, 1917.
20 Clara Lanctôt (1886–1958) was blind and published *Visions d'aveugle* in 1912 and *Visions encloses* in 1930. *La Vie littéraire au Québec*, ed. Denis Saint-Jacques and Maurice Lemire, vol. 1, *1895–1918: Sois fidèle à ta Laurentie* (Quebec: Presses de l'Université Laval, 2005), 326.
21 *Le Passe-Temps*, May 11, 1901. My thanks to Marie-Thérèse Lefebvre for this information about Clara Lanctôt and Charles Labelle.
22 Three of these paintings are part of the collection of Anne Michaud, the great-niece of Éva Circé.
23 Canada, *Census of 1901*; *Lovell's Montreal Directory*, 1902.
24 Denis Saint-Jacques, "De Québec à Montréal: Essai de géographie historique," in *La Vie culturelle à Montréal vers 1900*, ed. Micheline Cambron (Montréal: Fides/Bibliothèque nationale du Québec, 2005), 34; Pierre Rajotte, "Cercles et autonomie littéraires au tournant du XXe siècle," in Cambron, *La Vie culturelle*, 39.
25 Charles Gill, "Un mot au lecteur," in *Les Soirées du Château Ramezay par l'École littéraire de Montréal* (Montreal: Eusèbe Senécal, 1900), vii.
26 Julien Saint-Michel, "Autres temps! Autres mœurs," *Le Monde ouvrier*, October 15, 1927.
27 *L'Arche* was located in the attic of 22 Notre-Dame Street, which is today 26–28 Notre-Dame East, in front of the former Montreal Court House. The *Café Ayotte* was situated at 1744 St. Catherine East, between Saint-Denis and Sanguinet Streets, the site today of the De-Sève Building of the Université du Québec à Montréal. Richard Foisy, *L'Arche: Un atelier d'artistes dans le Vieux-Montréal* (Montreal: VLB, 2009), 9.
28 Victor Barbeau, a habitué de *L'Arche*, writes: "We immediately came to the mutual agreement not to admit women ... with an exception for La Ferrière, who was studying painting." Foisy, *L'Arche*, 88. The journalist Georgina Bélanger would have liked to become a member de *l'École littéraire de Montréal*, but was refused access. It was not until the third reincarnation of *l'École*, in 1921, that a woman, Marie Nantais, was admitted. Paul Wyczynski, "L'École littéraire de Montréal: Origine, évolution, mouvement," in *Archives des lettres canadiennes*, ed. Paul Wyczynski, vol. 2, *L'École littéraire de Montréal* (Ottawa: CRCCF de l'Université d'Ottawa, 1961), 28.
29 Micheline Cambron affirms that "a woman could not visit the loft of a bachelor, or join in a discussion in a restaurant, without being considered 'fallen.'" Micheline Cambron, "Mondanité et vie culturelle," in Cambron, *La Vie culturelle*, 129.

30 Olivar Asselin to Edmond de Nevers, Montreal, November 20, 1902. Fonds Olivar Asselin, AVM, BM55, 2, 11.
31 Colombine, "Confessions," *Les Débats*, September 16, 1900.
32 Colombine, "Nouvelle Canadienne: La voix de la raison," *Les Débats*, August 11, 1901; "Nouvelle vécue: La voix de la raison," in *Bleu, Blanc, Rouge. Poésie, paysages, causeries* (Montreal: Déom Frères, 1903), 174–81.
33 Colombine, "Parlons du féminisme," *L'Avenir*, October 28, 1900.
34 Musette, "Fusain: Le Havre," *Les Débats*, May 26, 1901.
35 Musette, "Chronique," *Les Débats*, March 3, 1901.
36 Colombine, "Napierville," *Les Débats*, September 8, 1901.
37 Colombine, "Québec," *Le Monde illustré*, November 30, 1901.
38 Louvigny de Montigny, "Silhouette," *Le Monde illustré*, September 7, 1901.
39 de Montigny, "Silhouette."
40 This situation was also common in Europe where, as Nathalie Heinich writes, "independence as a writer demands the adoption of a literary pseudonym, affirming that, prior to family affiliation—whether paternal or by marriage—the subject exists first through her practice as a writer, as signified by an invented name." Nathalie Heinich, "Femmes écrivains: écriture et indépendance," in *Intellectuelles: Du genre en histoire des intellectuels*, ed. Nicole Racine and Michel Trebitsch (Paris: Complexe, 2004), 150.
41 Colombine, "Parlons-en encore," *L'Avenir*, November 4, 1900. Marie-Pier Luneau considers the pseudonym to be a transparent mask. Marie-Pier Luneau, "L'auteur en quête de sa figure: Évolution de la pratique du pseudonyme au Québec, des origines à 1979," *Voix et Images* 88 (Autumn 2004), 7.
42 Hélène Pelletier-Baillargeon, *Olivar Asselin et son temps*, vol. 1, *Le Militant* (Montreal: Fides, 1996), 175.
43 Pelletier-Baillargeon, *Olivar Asselin et son temps*, vol. 1, 192, 197.
44 The buckboard was a year-round, all-purpose means of transport drawn by horses and used to travel over difficult terrain. Designed to transport materials, it was very uncomfortable for passengers.
45 *Le Soleil*, October 21, 22, 24, and 25, 1901; Gaëtane de Montreuil, *La Presse*, October 26, 1901.
46 Colombine, "Le Lac Saint-Jean à vol d'oiseau." *Le Pionnier*, October 27, 1901.
47 *L'Événement*, October 26, 1901. See the photograph in *La Patrie*, October 26, 1901.
48 Gaston and Louvigny de Montigny, *Le Passe-Temps*, May 11, 1901, 1.
49 Gaston and Louvigny de Montigny, *Le Passe-Temps*, May 11, 1901, 1.
50 Albert Lozeau, "Silhouette," *Le Monde illustré*, August 24, 1901, 259.
51 de Montigny, "Silhouette."
52 Interview with Gustave Labbé, 2005.
53 Charles Aupin, "La Rédaction du 'Pionnier,'" *Le Monde illustré*, November 23, 1901.
54 Asselin to Louvigny de Montigny, October 13, 1901. Archives de la Ville de Montréal (AVM), BM55/2,8. The circulation of the *Pionnier* climbed from 1,500 to 18,000 copies. Charles Aupin, "La Rédaction du *Pionnier*," *Le Monde illustré*, November 23, 1901.

55 The full staff was composed of Olivar Asselin, A. Beauchesne, Germain Beaulieu, Louis-Charles Bélanger, H. Bernard, Thomas-Alfred Bernier, J.-G. Boissonneault, M. Bourdon, Rodolphe Brunet, Cécilia, Jérôme Adolphe Chicoyne, Colombine, Gustave Comte, Stanislas Côté, Gaston De Montigny, Joseph-Marie-Amédée Denault, A. Dorais, Georges Dugas, Raoul Dumouchel, Évangéline, Wilfrid Gascon, Jean-Eugène, A.-A. Gingras, David Gosselin, A. Guilmet, E. Guimont, Omer Héroux, Paul Hyssons (J.-Étienne Gauthier), Sir Pierre-Amand Landry, Laurentienne, J.-W. Lévesque, E. de Lorimier, Albert Lozeau, Margot (Marguerite de Louvigny), Édouard-Zotique Massicotte, Louvigny de Montigny, Myrto, Antonio Pelletier, F. Pelletier, Pascal Poirier, Adjutor Rivard, L.-G. Robillard, Joseph Royal, Télesphore Saint-Pierre, R. Sainte-Foye, Arthur Sauvé, Suavita, Charles Thibault, and U. Tremblay. *Le Monde illustré*, November 23, 1901, 480–81.

56 Musette, "Bravo!" *Le Monde illustré*, September 22, 1901; November 23, 1901.

57 Joseph-Jérôme Grignon (1864–1930), a lawyer and prothonotary, was the father of the novelist Germaine Guèvremont.

58 *L'Avenir du Nord*, March 6, 1902.

59 Arthur Buies, *Chroniques II* (Montreal: Presses de l'Université de Montréal, 1991), 429, cited by Francis Parmentier, "Formes, contenu et évolution du libéralisme d'Arthur Buies," in *Combats libéraux au tournant du XXe siècle*, ed. Yvan Lamonde (Montreal: Fides, 1995), 88.

60 Musette, "Chronique," *Les Débats*, February 17, 1901. Reprinted in "Le mal d'écrire," *Bleu, Blanc, Rouge*, 329.

61 *Census of Canada*, 1911, vol. 4, Table 5, 222–23.

62 At the time, this organization was referred to as either the Société or Association Saint-Jean-Baptiste.

63 Colombine, "Lumen en Coelo," *L'Avenir du Nord*, July 30, 1903.

64 Colombine, "Réponse: Au personnage anonyme qui écrit dans *L'Étoile du Nord*," *L'Avenir du Nord*, September 10, 1903.

65 Musette, "Chronique," *Les Débats*, February 10, 1901.

66 Harrison, *National Reference Book*, 848. Beaulieu and Hamelin named Claire Ethel Prad as the director of *L'Étincelle*. It was impossible to solve this enigma even though all other references to the newspaper cite Éva Circé as its director. André Beaulieu and Jean Hamelin, *La Presse québécoise des origines à nos jours*, vol. 4, *1896–1910* (Quebec: Presses de l'Université Laval, 1979), 157.

67 Cazeneuve, *L'Étincelle*, January 31, 1903. His son, Paul Cazeneuve, artistic director of the Théâtre Français, would later act in her play *Hindelang et Delorimier*.

68 Musette, "La Revue des livres," *L'Étincelle*, January 10, 1903.

69 Colombine, "Comment se fait un journal," *L'Étincelle*, January 24, 1903.

70 Colombine, "Comment se fait un journal," *L'Avenir du Nord*, June 4, 1903.

71 Jean Ney, "La bourse," *L'Étincelle*, January 10, 1903.

72 Éva Circé, *L'Étincelle*, January 31, 1903. See Chapter 10.

73 *La Patrie*, October 5, 1903.

74 *Les Débats*, October 4, 1903.

75 Colombine, "La femme et la médecine," November 1, 1903; "Conte turc: 'La coquille de noix,'" November 8, 1903; "A la tombe de Papineau," November 15, 1903; "La

taxe sur les chiens," November 22, 1903; "Les conducteurs de tramway," *Le Combat*, November 29, 1903.

76 Beaulieu and Hamelin, *La Presse québécoise*, 175.

77 Fernande Roy, *Histoire de la librairie au Québec* (Montreal: Leméac, 2000), 151.

78 Léonise Valois, known under the pseudonym of Atala, published her first collection of poetry, *Fleurs sauvages*, in 1919. Louise Warren, *Léonise Valois, femme de lettres (1868–1939)* (Montreal: L'Hexagone, 1993).

79 Louis Fréchette, *Satires et polémiques II* (Montreal: Presses de l'Université de Montreal, Collection Bibliothèque du Nouveau Monde, 1993), 1259. A contemporary of Éva Circé, who was also an anti-clerical liberal and a journalist, Télesphore-Damien Bouchard, described the conflict between clerics and liberals over the question of the flag. *Mémoires de T. D. Bouchard, vol. 2* (Montreal: Beauchemin, 1960), 36, 100, 212.

80 *Le Soleil*, May 2, 1903.

81 *La Patrie*, April 20, 1903.

82 *L'Album universel*, May 2, 1903.

83 *Le Soleil*, December 21, 1903.

84 The same was true of *Denis le patriote* by Louis Guyon in September 1902, *Familles sans nom* by Germain Beaulieu, and *Madeleine* by Ernest Choquette. Lucie Robert, "Patriots-on-Broadway: *Denis le patriote* de Louis Guyon," *Études françaises* 32, no. 3 (1996), 81. In this article, Robert demonstrates how the French theatre aesthetic enters Quebec at the turn of the century by way of the United States, while the production methods of stage plays in Quebec remained distinctly North American. These plays about the rebellions contributed to the Canadianization of these two influences (79).

85 Colombine, "Napierville," *Les Débats*, September 8, 1901.

86 *La Patrie*, May 19, 1903.

87 Jos Labrèche, *Les Débats*, May 17, 1903.

88 *La Patrie*, May 19, 1903.

89 Jean-Marc Larrue, *Le Monument inattendu. Le Monument national 1893–1993* (Montreal, HMH, 1993), 179; *La Patrie*, May 16, 1903; John E. Hare, "Sablonnière, Blanche de la," in *The Oxford Companion to Canadian Theatre*, ed. Eugene Benson and L. W. Conolly (Toronto: Oxford University Press, 1989), 481–82. "It's at the 'National' that the theatrical careers of J. P. Filion, Elzéar Hamel and Palmieri (Joseph Sergius Archambault) truly begin and for years after they were known in Montreal as the French-Canadian Triumverate. At the time, they were called 'The Three Musketeers in stovepipe hats (*tuyaux de castor*) from the Faubourg de Québec.'" Gilles W. Filion, "Joseph Philias Filion: Comédien, Censeur (1841–1940)," *La Feuillée*, January 1989, 12.

90 *Le Canada*, May 19, 1903.

91 Filion, "Joseph Philias Filion: Comédien."

92 "A *public* library, open to everyone without distinction, run by men who are incompetent, negligent, or without scruples, becomes, in short order and unfailingly, a source of appalling corruption." *La Vérité*, June 21, 1902.

93 Fantasio, "Ce que sera notre bibliothèque. Un mot de réponse de Mgr Gauthier qui voudrait la limiter aux livres techniques. La bibliothèque municipale, et neutre forcément, doit avoir autant de droits qu'une bibliothèque religieuse comme Saint-Sulpice,"

["What our library will be. A word in response to Monseignor Gauthier who would like to limit it to technical books. The Municipal Library, which must be neutral, must also have as many rights as a religious library such as the Saint-Sulpice]," *Le Pays*, November 27, 1915; "Une question vitale," *Le Pays*, April 18, 1914.

94 Françoise, *Le Journal de Françoise*, October 25, 1902.

95 The Library Commission, composed of nine members chosen by the Municipal Council, was created in 1902 to manage the Free Public Library of Montreal (Bibliothèque Publique et Gratuite de Montréal). Michèle Dagenais, "Vie culturelle et pouvoirs publics locaux: La fondation de la bibliothèque municipale de Montréal," *Urban History Review / Revue d'histoire urbaine* 25, no. 2 (March 1996), 45–46.

96 *La Patrie*, January 26, 1903.

97 Pierre Savard, *Jules-Paul Tardivel, la France et les États-Unis 1851–1905* (Quebec: Presses de l'Université Laval, 1967), 382–83.

98 *Les Débats*, May 31, 1903; Dagenais, "Vie culturelle et pouvoirs publics locaux," 46.

99 *La Patrie*, January 26 and 27, 1903.

100 *La Patrie*, January 30, 1903.

101 Dagenais, "Vie culturelle et pouvoirs publics locaux," 46.

102 Fantasio, "Ce que sera notre bibliothèque," *Le Pays*, November 27, 1915.

103 Les dames patronnesses of the Association Saint-Jean-Baptiste, including mainly but not exclusively the wives of members of the administrative council of the Association Saint-Jean-Baptiste, constituted the female section. They founded the Fédération nationale Saint-Jean-Baptiste in 1907. Colombine, "Pour vous mes dames!" *Le Pionnier*, May 4, 1902. Reprinted as "Les dames patronnesses de la St-Jean-Baptiste," in *Bleu, Blanc, Rouge*. See Chapter 2.

104 AVM, VN1. Excerpted from the minutes of a meeting of the Sous-Commission de la Bibliothèque Publique, Montreal, August 1, 1903. *La Patrie*, August 12, 1903.

105 *La Presse*, July 12, 1903.

106 *Les Débats*, October 4, 1903.

Chapter 2

1 Louvigny de Montigny, *Étoffe du pays* (Montreal: Beauchemin, 1951), 30.

2 Paroisse Saint-Jean-Baptiste, marriage certificate, 40, April 29, 1905.

3 *Le Nationaliste*, April 30, 1905.

4 Pelletier-Baillargeon, *Olivar Asselin et son temps*, 360; *Le Nationaliste*, May 22, 1904.

5 The Côté family resembles the Saint-Laurents, a family of merchants of Quai Rimouski, as depicted by Maude-Emmanuelle Lambert: "A household of petit bourgeois who embodied typical values, cultural practices, and consumer habits of a Francophone family during Québec's *Belle Époque*." *Revue d'histoire de l'Amérique française* 51, no. 1 (Summer 2007): 37–65.

Joseph Salomon grew up in the family home, adjacent to his father's general store. The origins of his mother, Ann Jane Haney, are shrouded in mystery. She claimed to be the daughter of a high-ranking Irish military man who supposedly had emigrated from Ireland when she was seven, a crossing that her mother had not survived. According to her, she and her brother were taken in by a Quebec City family. Yet, according to the marriage certificate of Ann Jane and Elzéar Côté, her father, James Haney, was born in Ireland in 1811 and was a store clerk in the Faubourg Saint-Louis in Quebec City. It was there that he had been jailed for vagrancy in 1847. His children, Ann Jane, Elizabeth, and James were reportedly born in Canada and their mother died giving birth to James, when Ann Jane was three years old. Paul Blouin, *De Jean Côté à Isabelle Côté*. Manuscript. Interview with Paul Blouin, October 22, 2014.

6 Thanks to Charles-Eugène Labbé, Andrée Michaud, and the demographer Hubert Charbonneau for the genealogical information, and to my colleague Marcel Bellavance, whose grandmother, Omerile Danjou, married Elzéar Zabulon Côté, the brother of Pierre-Salomon Côté.

7 Colombine, "Bas les armes!," *Les Débats*, July 12, 1903. La Société de la protection des malades, one of the first mutual aid societies, would become the Union franco-canadienne d'assurance-vie. Martin Petitclerc, "Une forme d'entraide populaire: histoire des sociétés québécoises de secours mutuels au 19e siècle" (PhD diss., Université du Québec à Montréal, 2004), 298. Magloire Auclair (1846–1911) was the curé of the Saint-Jean-Baptiste parish from 1880 to 1911. Élie Auclair, *Saint-Jean-Baptiste de Montréal. Monographie paroissiale, 1874–1924*, Québec, 1924.

8 *Le Canada*, December 23, 1909.

9 Circé-Côté to Dugas, September 17, 1924, CARDL.

10 Circé-Côté to Dugas, July 14, 1924, CARDL.

11 Joseph Salomon Maurice Michaud was baptized March 4, 1906, at the Saint-Pierre church in Sorel. Document drafted by Emma Michaud.

12 Raymond Douville, *La Vie aventureuse d'Arthur Buies* (Montreal: Albert Lévesque, 1933), 177.

13 Auguste Côté later stood as a candidate for the Conservative Party. In 1920 he defended a Law dissertation on "La puissance paternelle" (paternal power).

14 Parmentier, "Formes, contenu et évolution du libéralisme d'Arthur Buies," 79, 92.

15 Pelletier-Baillargeon, *Olivar Asselin et son temps*, 40.

16 Jean Nay, "Rimouski," *Le Pays*, May 28, 1910.

17 Roger Le Moine, "Le Grand Orient de France dans le contexte québécois (1896–1923)," in Lamonde, *Combats libéraux*, 147.

18 Antoine de Baeque and Françoise Mélonio, *Lumières et liberté. Les dix-huitième et dix-neuvième siècles* (Paris: Seuil, 2005), 64–65.

19 Roger Le Moine, *Deux loges montréalaises du Grand Orient de France* (Ottawa: Presses de l'Université d'Ottawa, 1991), 11–12; Patrice Dutil, *L'Avocat du diable. Godfroy Langlois et le libéralisme progressiste dans le Québec de Wilfrid Laurier* (Montreal: Robert Davies, 1995), 60.

20 Le Moine, "Le Grand Orient," 152.

21 "Acta Apostolicae sedis. Constitution of Pope Pie IX," October 12, 1869; "Humanum genus, Encyclical of Pope Leo XIII on Freemasonry," April 20, 1884; "Dell' alto del' apostolico Seggio, Encyclical of Pope Leo XIII on Freemasonry in Italy," October 15, 1890.

22 Héroux mentions fifty Jewish names associated with English Lodges in Montreal and adds: "I conclude that there is currently an attempt by Jews to infiltrate the Lodges." *Le Nationaliste*, January 24, 1908.

23 Claude Roland and G. Leprince, *Francs-Maçons, vaudeville en trois actes* (Paris, C. Joubert, 1905); "Chronique théâtrale," *Le Nationaliste*, October 10, 1909; *La Presse*, October 2, 1909, and October 5 1909. The play was staged five more times, between 1912 and 1932. Thanks to Lucie Robert for this information.

24 Le Moine, "Le Grand Orient," 152.

25 Albert-J. Lemieux, *La Loge L'Émancipation* (Montreal: La Croix, 1910).

26 Bouchard, *Mémoires*, 217–19; Le Moine, *Deux loges*, 50–52. In spite of his secular convictions, Larose (1868–1915) decorated several churches, including the chapel of Sacré-Cœur de Notre-Dame in Montreal. He appealed against his expulsion from the Commission scolaire des écoles catholiques (Catholic School Commission), but after being dismissed from the École du Plateau, where he had taught Marc-Aurèle Fortin, amongst others, he continued to teach in Westmount from 1912 to 1915. Alison Longstaff, "Vie intellectuelle et libre-pensée au tournant du XXe siècle: le cas de Ludger Larose" (master's thesis, Université du Québec à Trois-Rivières, 1999). Upon his death in 1915, Éva Circé-Côté wrote a beautiful eulogy for "this righteous person who suffered persecution in the pursuit of justice." Paul S. Bédard, "Feu Ludger Larose," *Le Pays*, November 20, 1915.

27 Colombine, "Réformons le code," *L'Avenir du Nord*, May 5, 1904.

28 "L'enseignement qu'on donne au peuple," *La Vérité*, June 1, 1904.

29 Guy de Maupassant (pseudonym), "Méli-mélo," *L'Avenir du Nord*, June 2, 1904.

30 "Ça et là," *La Vérité*, June 15, 1904; "Méli-mélo," *L'Avenir du Nord*, June 30, 1904; JEP (Jules-Édouard Prévost), "Les erreurs de *La Vérité*," *L'Avenir du Nord*, July 21, 1904; "Naïveté de Jules-Ed.," *La Nation*, July 30, 1904; JEP, "*La Nation* vs Bon sens et vérité," *L'Avenir du Nord*, August 4, 1904; "Mensonges et erreurs," *La Nation*, August 13, 1904; "Méli-mélo," *L'Avenir du Nord*, August 18, 1904; "Erreurs et mensonges," *La Nation*, August 27, 1904; "Naïveté," *La Nation*, August 27, 1904; "Platitudes," *La Vérité*, September 10, 1904; "Un vieux de la vieille, 'Pour clore une discussion,'" *L'Avenir du Nord*, September 1, 1904.

31 Colombine, "Du bec et de l'aile," *L'Avenir du Nord*, August 18, 1904.

32 Camille, "Femmes de lettres. Canadiennes-Françaises," *La Patrie*, June 24, 1905, 22.

33 Colombine, "Impressions de Pierrot sur la ville," *La Patrie*, June 24, 1905, 23.

34 Colombine to Olivar Asselin, Montreal, February 26, 1904. AVM, BM55, S2, D14.

35 *Le Nationaliste*, March 6, 1904.

36 Éva Circé, "Mensonge," *Le Nationaliste*, March 13, 1904.

37 Until that point in time newspapers used Société and Association interchangeably. Asselin officially changed the organization's name to Société Saint-Jean-Baptiste.

38 *Bulletin de la Caisse d'économie* 1, no. 1 (June 1904): 6–9; 1, no. 3 (August 1904): 4–5. See Chapter 8.

39 "L'avenir des Canadiens-Français. Les Femmes de Lettres," *Le Nationaliste*, November 19, 1905.

40 "L'avenir des Canadiens-Français. Les Femmes de Lettres."

41 Anne Carrier, "Barry, Robertine, dite Françoise," in *Dictionnaire biographique du Canada, 1901–1910*, 13, ed. Ramsay Cook and Jean Hamelin (Quebec: Presses de l'Université Laval), 47.

42 Carrier, "Barry, Robertine, dite Françoise."

43 Carrier, "Barry, Robertine, dite Françoise."
44 Robert Rumilly, *Histoire de la Société Saint-Jean-Baptiste de Montréal, des patriotes au fleurdelysé, 1834–1948* (Montreal: L'Aurore, 1975), 20, 21, and 53.
45 Rumilly, *Histoire de la Société Saint-Jean-Baptiste de Montréal*, 184–85; Larrue, *Le Monument inattendu*, 111–19.
46 Colombine, "Pour vous mes dames!," *Le Pionnier*, May 4, 1902. Reproduced in *Bleu, Blanc, Rouge* under the title, "Les dames patronnesses de la St-Jean-Baptiste," 339–40. She lists thirty-eight members of the steering committee, followed by "etc."
47 Marie Gérin-Lajoie to W. Lebon, September 18, 1908. BNQ, Montréal, fonds de l'Institut Notre-Dame-du-Bon-Conseil (FINDBC), P783, P2/D10, 02.
48 Colombine, *Bleu, Blanc, Rouge*, 339–40.
49 Anne-Marie Sicotte, *Marie Gérin-Lajoie: Conquérante de la liberté* (Montreal: Éditions du remue-ménage, 2005), 149.
50 Requête des dames de la Saint-Jean-Baptiste à sa Grandeur Mgr Bruchési, Montreal, October 30, 1906. FINDBC, P 783, P2/D10, 02.
51 Paul Bruchési aux dames de la Saint-Jean-Baptiste, November 2, 1906. FINDBC, P783, P2/D10, 02.
52 Fonds de la Fédération nationale Saint-Jean-Baptiste (FFNSJB), BNQ.
53 *Le Canada*, May 27, 1907.
54 *La Patrie*, May 31, 1907, 5.
55 *La Patrie*, May 27, 1907, 8.
56 Éva Circé-Côté to Marie Gérin-Lajoie, Montreal, June 10, 1907. FINDBP, P783, P2/D10, 01.
57 Marie Gérin-Lajoie to W. Lebon, September 18, 1908. FINDBC, P783, P2/D10, 02.
58 Archives de la paroisse Saint-Jean-Baptiste de Montréal, extrait de baptême B 493.
59 Line Gosselin, *Les Journalistes québécoises, 1880–1930* (Montreal: Regroupement des chercheurs-chercheures en histoire des travailleurs et travailleuses du Québec, Collection RCHTQ Études et documents, 7, 1995), 68. Gaëtane de Montreuil would take up her pen again in 1913 after her separation from Gill.
60 Éva Circé-Côté was nevertheless sought after on the cultural scene. The first issue of *La Vie artistique* in November 1905 announced the collaboration of stylists like Colombine, yet none of her writings appeared in this journal, which put out just five issues.
61 Colombine, "Une réponse," *Le Nationaliste*, August 29, 1909.
62 Colombine, "La Vie est dans le Sang," *L'Avenir du Nord*, July 30, 1909.
63 Colombine, "La Vie est dans le Sang" ; Colombine, "La Vie est dans le Sang," *La Vigie*, August 4, 1909; "Jeune séminariste," *Le Nationaliste*, August 22, 1909.
64 Colombine, "Une réponse," *Le Nationaliste*, August 29, 1909.
65 Other notables include the liberal senators Raoul Dandurand and Louis-Antoine Dessaulles, the speaker of the Legislative Assembly, L.-P. Brodeur, and the city clerk, Louis-Olivier David. Ruby Heaps, "La Ligue de l'enseignement (1902–1904): héritage du passé et nouveau défis," *Revue d'histoire de l'Amérique française* 36, no. 3 (December 1982), 346.
66 *La Patrie*, April 25, 1908. 286 later became 1592 St. Denis Street. It was located just south of today's Théâtre Saint-Denis.

67 *La Patrie*, April 25, 1908; *Le Journal de Françoise*, June 20, 1908; *La Patrie*, August 7, 1909.
68 *La Patrie*, August 10, 1909.
69 *La Patrie*, June 16, 1909.
70 *Le Nationaliste*, August 8, 1909.
71 Marcelle Brisson and Suzanne Côté-Gauthier, *Montréal de vive mémoire, 1900–1939* (Montreal: Triptyque, 1994), 23.
72 Although no generalizations can be made from the social profile of one student, it is worth noting the case of Albina Sanguinet, who lived in the Faubourg Québec, whose parents were separated because of her father's alcoholism, and who was able to attend the Lycée thanks to the generosity of her maternal uncle. Her family "went to mass on Sunday, but that was all." Albina Sanguinet never married; she worked for forty years as the manager of Le Petit Versailles, a luxury items store on Saint-Denis Street. Interview with Albina Sanguinet conducted by Suzanne Côté-Gauthier. My thanks to Suzanne Côté-Gauthier for kindly sharing the typed copy of the interview with me.
73 Archives des sœurs de la Congrégation de Notre-Dame (ACND), Sr. Sainte-Euphrosyne to Msgr. Bernard and to Msgr. Bégin, June 8, 1908. Female solidarity did not always play in favour of Éva Circé-Côté's Lycée; Marie Gérin-Lajoie reportedly pressured the Sisters of the Notre-Dame Congregation to demand the establishment of a *collège classique*, and that is where she eventually sent her daughter, Marie. Lucienne Plante, *La fondation de l'enseignement classique féminin au Québec, 1908–1926* (Diplôme d'Études supérieures (histoire), licence en lettres, Université Laval, 1967), 54.
74 ACND, Sr. Stéphane-Marie, "La Fondation," 6.
75 ACND, Lomer Gouin to Sr. Sainte-Anne-Marie, Quebec, September 28, 1908.
76 Jacques-Antoine-Hippolyte, comte de Guibert, *Le Connétable de Bourbon, tragédie en 5 actes* (Paris : Didot, 1785), quoted in ACND, Msgr Bruchési to Sr. Sainte-Euphrosyne, June 16, 1908; Archives de l'archevêché de Montréal, correspondance de Mgr Bruchési, t. 5.
77 Collectif Clio, *L'Histoire des femmes au Québec depuis quatre siècles* (Montreal: Quinze, 1982), 321–22.
78 Le Moine, *Deux loges*, 79.
79 Oscar Normandin, a shoemaker and fur merchant, would be apprenticed to the Force et Courage lodge in 1913. Le Moine, *Deux loges*, 135.
80 *La Vérité*, June 25, 1910.
81 AVM, FBM, BM60, S2, SS3, D2, 2/49.
82 Fantasio, "Ce que sera notre bibliothèque."
83 Fantasio, "Opinions. Marchons plutôt vers le Levant. Au lieu de n'acheter que des vieilleries que ne songe-t-on pas à moderniser l'embryon de bibliothèque que nous avons," *Le Pays*, April 12, 1913.
84 Pelletier-Baillargeon, *Olivar Asselin et son temps*, 429.
85 Fantasio, "Opinions. Marchons plutôt vers le Levant."
86 Thomas Côté to Éva Circé-Côté, Montreal, October 27, 1915.
87 Le Moine, *Deux loges*, 61.
88 "La version de Colombine," *La Vérité*, March 26, 1910.
89 "La version de Colombine."

90 *Le Canada*, December 23, 1909.
91 "Lettre de Mme Côté," *Le Pays*, January 29, 1910.
92 No information exists about the Ligue pour l'instruction. It may have been an emulator of the defunct Ligue de l'enseignement or simply the result of a journalistic error.
93 *La Presse*, December 27, 1909.
94 "La version de Colombine"; "Les impies et libres penseurs de Montréal à l'oeuvre," *La Vérité*, February 26, 1910. These numbers were called into question by "a Catholic," who claimed to have counted only 160 people. "Grosse exagération," *La Vérité*, April 2, 1910.
95 "Affligeant scandale," *L'Action sociale*, December 28, 1909.
96 "Affligeant scandale."
97 *Le Soleil*, December 29, 1909.
98 "Calmez-vous *Soleil*" and "Faisceau de preuves," *L'Action sociale*, December 30, 1909.
99 The newspaper's retraction was as follows: "We do not balk at recognizing that the remarks made in an article last Wednesday in our editorial page under the title 'Affligeant scandale,' remarks directed against the article that had appeared the day before in the *L'Action sociale* under the headline 'Affligeant scandale,' were misplaced and unjustified.... We readily acknowledge that our collaborator was wrong to take offense and we were wrong to publish his remarks." Éditorial, "Un Blanc et un Noir," *Le Soleil*, December 31, 1909.
100 "Pour mourir en chien," *La Vérité*, January 1, 1910. "Cet affligeant scandale," *L'Action sociale*, January 1, 1910.
101 "Un scandale," *L'Action sociale*, January 1, 1910.
102 "Un Scandale," *La Croix*, January 1, 1910.
103 "Vers l'abîme," *La Croix*, January 8, 1910; "Le maçon Charbonneau nous écrit," *La Croix*, January 22, 1910; "En passant," *La Vérité*, January 22, 1910; "La mort sans Dieu et la crémation," *La Croix*, February 12, 1910.
104 "Une lettre du Sénateur David," *La Patrie*, December 30, 1909.
105 "La version de Colombine."
106 Le Moine, *Deux loges*, 87.
107 Asselin compared Côté's funeral to the Guibord affair, the nineteenth-century sorry incident around Joseph Guibord's funerals, by way of insisting on greater tolerance in 1909. Olivar Asselin, "Deux mots," *Le Nationaliste*, January 2, 1910. Gonzalve Desaulniers also deserted. "La version de Colombine."
108 Olivar Asselin, "Au four, les gars!," *Le Nationaliste*, January 20, 1910.
109 "Le respect de la vérité," *La Patrie*, January 4, 1910.
110 "Une lettre du Sénateur David," *L'Action sociale*, December 30, 1909.
111 *L'Aurore*, January 14, 1910.
112 *L'Aurore*, January 14, 1910.
113 Polignac, "Un incident," *Le Pays*, January 15, 1910.
114 "Est-ce un scandale?," *Le Pays*, February 5, 1910.
115 "A Bas les Masques," *Le Devoir*, January 21, 1910.
116 "Une lettre de Mme Côté," *Le Devoir*, January 26, 1910. *Le Pays* reprinted the letter on January 29, 1910.

320 / Freethinker

117 "Cette Lettre," *La Vérité*, February 12, 1910.
118 "Cette lettre d'Eva Circé-Côté," *La Croix*, January 29, 1910.
119 André Chauveau, "Cette 'respectable confrérie,'" *La Croix*, February 9, 1910.
120 "Les impies et libres penseurs de Montréal à l'oeuvre," *La Vérité*, February 26, 1910.
121 "La version de Colombine."
122 "Deux réponses à Colombine," *La Vérité*, April 23, 1910.
123 Elzéar-Auguste Côté, *La puissance paternelle* (Rimouski: Imprimerie générale S. Vachon, 1926). Thanks to Marcel Bellavance for providing me with a copy of this thesis.
124 J. J. Côté, *La Vérité*, April 23, 1910.
125 Circé-Côté to Dugas, 1921, CARDL.
126 "La crémation," *L'Avenir*, April 14, 1901; "La crémation. Ses progrès à travers le monde," *Le Pays*, June 18, 1910.
127 According to the historian Brian Young, "cremation was perceived by its advocates as clean, efficient, and technologically attractive, and it responded to public health concerns about air and water pollution emanating from burial grounds. Symbolically, the crematorium represented the superiority of modern science and industrial furnaces over nature's slow putrefaction process." Brian Young, *Respectable Burial. Montreal's Mount Royal Cemetery* (Montreal/Kingston: McGill-Queen's University Press, 2003), 125.
128 Fantasio, "Testament outragé. Comment on respecte les dernières volontés d'un mourant dans notre pays. Une protestation," *Le Pays*, January 16, 1915, 2.
129 Fantasio, "Le pape reste figé dans sa neutralité. Il n'a aucune interdiction pour les Allemands qui font la réduction chimique de leurs cadavres. La crémation est défendue sous peine d'excommunication chez nous," *Le Pays*, April 28, 1917.
130 Jean Nay, "Le Devoir," *Le Pays*, January 15, 1910.
131 *Le Pays*, January 10, 1910.
132 Langlois, who had been the managing editor of *Le Canada* since its founding seven years earlier, was fired on January 7, 1910. He launched the first issue of *Le Pays* on January 15, 1910. *La Presse*, January 7, 1910; *Le Canada*, January 7, 1910; *Le Pays*, January 15, 1910. He served as an MLA for Montréal-Saint-Louis from 1904 to 1914. In August 1910, Dr Louis Laberge, who had been caught up in the "scandale de l'Émancipation," stepped down as chair of the Canadian section of the Alliance scientifique universelle de Paris, a renowned ethnographic institution, which he did not want to see tarnished by his presence. *La Patrie*, August 1, 1910.
133 AVM, fonds de la Commission spéciale d'enquête Milette vs Grandchamps et Laberge, 1910, VM71; Bouchard, *Mémoires*, 50.
134 Bouchard, *Mémoires*, 228.
135 Bouchard, *Mémoires*, 239.
136 *La Patrie*, August 1, 1910.
137 *Le Devoir*, January 24, 1910.
138 "Claims her young son is being brought up to practise strange ceremonies," *Standard*, November 14, 1908.
139 *Eva Circé et vir vs Geo. Murray Publishing*, P. of Quebec, Superior Court, District of Montreal, no 323, November 20, 1908.

140 *Eva Circé et vir vs Geo. Murray Publishing*, November 30, 1908. Thanks to Eric Reiter for sharing his research on this case.
141 *Eva Circé et vir vs Geo. Murray Publishing*, October 26, 1911. Jean-Martin Charcot (1825–93) was known for his experimental use of hypnosis to treat patients for hysteria.
142 *Eva Circé et vir vs Geo. Murray Publishing*, Justice Bruneau, December 28, 1911.
143 Circé-Côté to Dugas, July 14, 1924, CARDL.
144 AVM, FBM, BM60, S2, SS3, D1.
145 When Circé-Côté was hired at the Bibliothèque technique, her annual salary was set at $400 and was subsequently increased to $500 and then $600 in 1908. However, in January 1910, she became the assistant to Prince's successor, Frédéric Villeneuve, who set her salary at $350.
146 *Le Devoir*, January 17, 1910; *La Patrie*, January 21, 1910; Dagenais, "Vie culturelle et pouvoirs publics locaux," 48–49.
147 *Le Pays*, January 15, 1910.
148 Ève Circé-Côté, *Papineau. Son influence sur la pensée canadienne. Essai de psychologie historique* (Montreal: R. A. Regnault, 1924), 240.
149 *Le Pays*, January 15, 1910. Msgr. Bruchési was not wrong, because as of 1914 Éva Circé-Côté had published no fewer than 163 columns on the subject of religion or the clergy.
150 *Le Pays* had drawn the ire of Msgr. Bourget due to its radical positions, including support for the Institut canadien, which had been condemned by the Bishop in 1869. Dessaulles was the managing editor of *Le Pays* and president of the Institut canadien. Yvan Lamonde, *Louis-Antoine Dessaulles. Un seigneur libéral et anticlerical* (Montreal: Fides, 1994), 117, 354.
151 Archives de l'archevêché de Montréal, Mgr Bruchési to Fernand Rinfret, January 17, 1910.
152 Olivar Asselin, preface to Jules Fournier, *Mon encrier* (Montreal: Mme Jules Fournier), xvi.
153 Jean Nay, "Histoire d'une âme," *Le Pays*, January 29, 1910.
154 Nay, "Histoire d'une âme."
155 Is this the first incarnation of Éva Circé as Fantasio? Between 1898 and 1899 a Fantasio had written a column on Parisian theatre for *La Revue des Deux Frances*. The *Revue* was aimed at French "*canadophiles*" and Canadians staying in France. In it, there were pieces by Victor Hugo, Alexandre Dumas, or Tristan Bernard next to articles by Benjamin Sulte, de Pamphile Lemay, and Arthur Buies. *La Revue des Deux Frances* was directed by Achille Steens, the pseudonym of Ernest La Jeunesse, an anarchist, a Dreyfus supporter, a friend of Octave Mirbeau and Oscar Wilde, and whose wife was Québécoise. If this Fantasio *was* Éva Circé, she would have known the Dreyfus support circles, which would be consistent with her numerous denunciations of anti-Semitism. Fantasio, "Les Théâtres," *La Revue des Deux Frances*, January 1898, 85–87; October 1898, 278–79; July 1899, 86; "Richard Ellmann Revisited: The Funeral of Oscar Wilde (2)," *The Scholars, An Electronic Journal for the Exchange of Information on Current Research, Publications and Productions concerning Oscar Wilde and His Circles* 3, no. 4 (April 2003): 549–50.

156 The heteronym, a term made famous by Fernando Pessoa, posits a real writer with a well-developed biography. Here, Fantasio is an androgynous figure and Arthur Maheu is a *habitant*.

157 Gosselin, *Les Journalistes québécoises, 1880–1930*, 57, 104–5.

158 Dutil, *L'Avocat du diable*, 244. Arthur Maheu is clearly identified as a pseudonym of Éva Circé-Côté in Bernard Vinet, *Pseudonymes québécois*, a book based on the one by Francis-J. Audet and Gérard Malchelosse, *Pseudonymes canadiens* (Quebec: Garneau, 1974).

159 Maheu complains that his father made him leave school too soon to work the land. *Le Pays*, February 1, 1913.

160 Gosselin, *Les Journalistes québécoises, 1880–1930*, 101. See Marie-Pier Luneau's study of this phenomenon, "L'auteur en quête de sa figure," 1–18.

161 *La Patrie*, July 2, 1910, 11.

162 Jean Nay, "Le patriotisme explosif," *Le Pays*, July 2, 1910.

163 Virginia Woolf, *Mr Bennett and Mrs Brown*, 1924. The quotation alludes to the Post-Impressionist exhibition, which, for Woolf, made manifest the beginning of modernism and of modernity.

164 Robert de Roquebrune, *Testament de mon enfance* (Montreal: Fides, 1958), 15; *Quartier Saint-Louis* (Montreal: Fides, 1966), 34.

Chapter 3

1 Fantasio, "Une mise au point," *Le Pays*, August 20, 1921.

2 Colombine, "La Pensionnaire. Causerie d'une montréalaise," *L'Avenir du Nord*, August 3, 1906. The bronze statue of the patriot Jean-Olivier Chénie, erected in 1895, was the work of Alfonso Pelzer.

3 Fantasio, "Etudes de mœurs canadiennes. En vacance," *Le Pays*, August 1, 1914.

4 Julien Saint-Michel, "Un Coup de balai," *Le Monde ouvrier*, April 14, 1917.

5 Fantasio, "Le problème des sans-travail. Il ne faut pas revenir au régime du ghetto. Nous payons aujourd'hui pour l'immigration à outrance de ces dernières années," *Le Pays*, October 31, 1914.

6 Fantasio, "Chambly," *Le Pays*, August 30, 1913.

7 Fantasio, "Retour de vacances," *Les Débats*, September 4, 1915.

8 Julien Saint-Michel, "Par un jour de pluie. Étude de mœurs," *Le Monde ouvrier*, December 9, 1916.

9 Fantasio, "Le bilan d'un pays. L'agonie d'une race," *Le Pays*, August 19, 1911.

10 Fantasio, "Le bilan d'un pays. L'agonie d'une race"; "Rendez à César. . . . L'action de l'Angleterre dans les circonstances—La haute capacité de ses hommes d'état. L'Anglais est un homme libre. A qui faut-il s'en prendre si nous avons été écrasés?," *Le Pays*, October 24, 1914.

11 Fantasio, "Rendez à César."

12 Fantasio, "Rendez à César."

13 Arthur Maheu, "Les Idées de M. Maheu," *Le Pays*, January 3, 1914.

14 Julien Saint-Michel, "Volons les gens de la ville," *Le Monde ouvrier*, August 9, 1919; "Conscience élastique," *Le Monde ouvrier*, April 17, 1920.
15 Saint-Michel, "Volons les gens de la ville."
16 Fantasio, "Retour de vacances."
17 Fantasio, "Retour de vacances."
18 Fantasio, "Chambly," *Le Pays*, August 30, 1913.
19 Paul S. Bédard, "Nos arrières," *Le Pays*, February 20, 1920.
20 Julien Saint-Michel, "Vers un autre idéal," *Le Monde ouvrier*, November 4, 1916. This article continues in such a misogynistic vein ("Where is the eternal feminine headed? In the course of pursuing the same ambitions and the same careers as men we think, sadly, that women will de-poeticize themselves and make themselves ugly") that one wonders if it was written by the same person who, during the same period, defended non-traditional employment for women. It gives the impression of a trial balloon meant to sound out the electorate.
21 Julien Saint-Michel, "La dépopulation rurale," *Le Monde ouvrier*, October 5, 1918.
22 Joseph-Arthur D'Amours (1865–1929), a doctor of theology, was the vicar of the Saint-Mathieu parish of Central Falls, Rhode Island, before being named head of the seminary in Rimouski from 1902 to 1905. In 1909, he became the editor-in-chief of *L'Action catholique* and continued as a journalist until 1918. Joanne D'Amours, "Un 'D'Amours' vicaire aux Etats-Unis," *Le Sanglier* 1, no. 4 (May 1, 2002): 49–52.
23 Fantasio, "A propos de la peine de mort. La thèse de l' 'Action catholique,'" *Le Pays*, January 22, 1916. It was easy for her to mock Quebec City, as several of her contemporaries did it shamelessly. Jules Fournier, for example, published a scathing column about the smugness and laziness of Québécquois [sic] in *L'Action*, May 13, 1913. Jules Fournier, *Mon encrier*, 109–13.
24 Fantasio, "Le Pont de Québec. Et le génie de l'homme," *Le Pays*, September 16, 1916.
25 Fantasio, "Les divagations de l'"Action catholique,'" *Le Pays*, April 17, 1920.
26 Fantasio, "Les divagations de l'"Action catholique'"; Julien Saint-Michel, "Qui donne aux pauvres," *Le Monde ouvrier*, June 27, 1925.
27 Ottawa, *Census of Canada*, 1911, vol. 2, Table 14.
28 Julien Saint-Michel, "A propos de bilinguisme," *Le Monde ouvrier*, October 13, 1917.
29 Fantasio, "Ayons des vertus viriles. Notre infériorité est accidentelle," *Le Pays*, December 9, 1911.
30 Jean Nay, "Pour cinq sous d'illusions," *Le Pays*, June 11, 1910; Fantasio, "La crème à la glace. Étude de mœurs," *Le Pays*, July 22, 1911; Fantasio, "Pensées printanières," May 1, 1915; Arthur Maheu, "Les Idées de M. Maheu," *Le Pays*, July 21, 1917.
31 Arthur Maheu, "Les Idées de M. Maheu," *Le Pays*, September 2, 1916; Fantasio, "L'inutile création," *Le Pays*, July 15, 1911.
32 Paul S. Bédard, "Les écorchés vifs. Les prix des loyers augmentera-t-il encore cette année? Le pauvre peuple qu'on pressure commence à se lasser," *Le Pays*, February 7, 1914.
33 Fantasio, "Opinion. A propos de nos cimetières," *Le Pays*, August 24, 1912.
34 Fantasio, "Scènes de la vie montréalaise. Le Square Lafontaine," *Le Pays*, July 11, 1914.

35 Fantasio, "Le problème des sans-travail."
36 Fantasio, "Visions du Jour de l'An," *Le Pays*, January 1, 1916.
37 Julien Saint-Michel, "L'exposition de l'École technique. Le mécanisme est destiné à accomplir des merveilles, il représente l'avenir et la prospérité du pays," *Le Monde ouvrier*, July 1, 1916.
38 Musette, "Fusain. Le Havre," *Les Débats*, May 26, 1901; Colombine, "Au Jardin Sohmer," *Les Débats*, September 15, 1901; Julien Saint-Michel, "La terreur de nos villes," *Le Monde ouvrier*, March 24, 1917.
39 Fantasio, "Etudes de mœurs canadiennes. En vacance," *Le Pays*, August 1, 1914.
40 Julien Saint-Michel, "La baisse des salaires," *Le Monde ouvrier*, July 23, 1921.
41 Julien Saint-Michel, "La vie chère," *Le Monde ouvrier*, August 26, 1916.
42 Musette, "Chronique," *Les Débats*, February 24, 1901; Colombine, "Royaume de Dieu," *L'Avenir du Nord*, June 7, 1906; Arthur Maheu, "Les Idées de M. Maheu," *Le Pays*, February 19, 1916; Fantasio, "Le droit au silence," *Le Pays*, April 11, 1914; "Joffre, l'homme a fait le miracle," *Le Pays*, May 19, 1917.
43 Fantasio, "Propos de Sainte-Catherine. La transformation de la vieille fille," *Le Pays*, November 29, 1913.
44 Fantasio, "La Poudrerie," *Le Pays*, February 25, 1911; "La pluie," *Le Pays*, October 12, 1912; Paul S. Bédard, "La Question des tramways. Le point de vue du gros public," *Le Pays*, November 21, 1914.
45 Arthur Maheu, "Les Idées de M. Maheu," *Le Pays*, May 2, 1914; Julien Saint-Michel, "À propos de bilinguisme."
46 Fantasio, "Ignorance n'est pas vertu," *Le Pays*, November 12, 1910.
47 Fantasio, "Réflexions estivales," *Le Pays*, July 13, 1912; Arthur Maheu, "Les Idées de M. Maheu," *Le Pays*, January 16, 1915.
48 Arthur Maheu, "Les Idées de M. Maheu," *Le Pays*, November 18, 1916; Julien Saint-Michel, "La co-éducation des sexes. Les écoles mixtes tendent à adoucir la brutalité des garçons et à viriliser les filles," *Le Monde ouvrier*, November 18, 1916.
49 Colombine, "Les deux sons de cloche," *Les Débats*, July 19, 1903.
50 Fantasio, "Le problème des sans-travail."
51 Fantasio, "Le courage de notre maire. M. Martin regarde froidement le mal que la prostitution fait à Montréal et il se prononce pour la réglementation," *Le Pays*, August 19, 1916.
52 Arthur Maheu, "Les Idées de M. Maheu," *Le Pays*, May 6, 1916.
53 Musette, "Chronique," *Les Débats*, April 14, 1901.
54 Arthur Maheu, "Les Idées de M. Maheu," *Le Pays*, May 6, 1916; Julien Saint-Michel, "Potins de déménagement," *Le Monde ouvrier*, May 7, 1932. As an example of the extent of the phenomenon, in 1913, in three days, 30,000 families moved house. *La Patrie*, May 2, 1913.
55 *La Presse*, May 11, 1904.
56 Avi Santo, "Film Chronicles in Montreal's *La Presse*, 1906–1908," *Canadian Journal of Film Studies* (Spring 2003): 69–91; *Le Panorama* 1, no. 1 (October 1919), 60.
57 Jean Nay, "Le rire s'en va," *Le Pays*, August 6, 1910.
58 *La Patrie*, August 31, 1927. Justice Louis Boyer headed a commission of inquiry estab-

lished after seventy-eight children died in the Laurier Palace cinema fire of 1927. See Chapter 4.
59 Arthur Maheu, "Les Idées de M. Maheu," *Le Pays*, May 31, 1913.
60 Julien Saint-Michel, "Le cinéma et les enfants," *Le Monde ouvrier*, May 25, 1918.
61 Saint-Michel, "Le cinéma et les enfants."
62 Nay, "Le rire s'en va."
63 Saint-Michel, "Le cinéma et les enfants."
64 Colombine, "Mortalité infantile," *L'Avenir du Nord*, August 6, 1903; Fantasio, "Dialectique des mouches," *Le Pays*, June 10, 1911; "L'inutile création," *Le Pays*, July 15, 1911; "Les chaleurs s'en viennent," *Le Pays*, May 23, 1914; Julien Saint-Michel, "Ayons soin des petits," *Le Monde ouvrier*, May 16, 1916.
65 Arthur Maheu, "Les Idées de M. Maheu," *Le Pays*, January 18, 1913.
66 Fantasio, "Nous sommes une race prolifique! Mais où la négligence des parents conduit-elle?" *Le Pays*, December 19, 1914.
67 Two of several examples are Arthur Maheu, "Les Idées de M. Maheu," October 28, 1916, and Julien Saint-Michel, "La routine ennemie du talent et de l'initiative," *Le Monde ouvrier*, June 16, 1917.
68 Arthur Maheu, "Les Idées de M. Maheu," *Le Pays*, April 11, 1914; Fantasio, "Une question vitale," *Le Pays*, April 18, 1914.
69 Arthur Maheu, "Les Idées de M. Maheu," July 15, 1916.
70 Julien Saint-Michel, "Un coup de balai s.v.p.," *Le Monde ouvrier*, April 14, 1917; "Pour sauver la barque municipale," *Le Monde ouvrier*, May 5, 1917.
71 Julien Saint-Michel, "Montréal en tutelle. Les bons et les mauvais côtés du projet de réforme municipale," *Le Monde ouvrier*, February 2, 1918; "Le 'barda' à l'Hôtel-de-Ville," *Le Monde ouvrier*, February 27, 1918.
72 Julien Saint-Michel, "Emparons-nous de l'industrie," *Le Monde ouvrier*, August 12, 1917.
73 That is, $47.75 per fortnight. Fonds de la Bibliothèque municipale de Montréal (FBM), Archives de la Ville de Montréal (AVM), FBM, BM60, S2, SS2, D1 (3/3).
74 F. Villeneuve to Messieurs les Commissaires de la Cité, February 5, 1914, AVM, FBM, BM60, S2, SS2, D1.
75 AVM, BM60, S2, SS2; BM60; S2, SS1, D1, 3/3.
76 Paul S. Bédard, "Feu Fred Villeneuve," *Le Pays*, May 1, 1915.
77 Marie Baboyant, "La Bibliothèque de la Ville de Montréal, la collection Gagnon et son fondateur Philéas Gagnon," *Les Cahiers d'histoire du Québec au XXe siècle*, vol. 6 (Autumn 1996), 73.
78 Thomas Côté to Madame Côté, October 27 and November 2, 1915, AVM, BM60 SO48, 99-04-2-2.
89 Madame Côté to M. L. Giroux, December 21, 1915, BM60, SO49, 99-04-2-2. When Circé-Côté requested a residential telephone, she was quickly turned down. L. H. Senécal to E. C. Côté, June 19, 1915.
80 The collection included twenty-three volumes of the Canadian Census, the *Récits de voyage* of Alexandre Dumas, and twelve volumes of the works of Victor Hugo, all of which were on the Catholic Church's Index of banned books. Thomas Côté to

Madame Côté, October 27, 1915, BM60, SO48, 99-04-2-2; "Doit à l'honorable Juge Bruneau," June 29,1916.
81 Paul S. Bédard, "Bibliothèque roulette," *Le Pays*, April 22, 1911.
82 AVM, FBM, BM60, S1, SS2, D1.
83 Fantasio, "L'apothéose du verbe. Nous sommes entraînés dans le remous," *Le Pays*, July 6, 1912.
84 AVM, FBM, BM60, S1, SS2, D1.
85 AVM, FBM, BM60, S3, SS2, D2. Dagenais, "Vie culturelle et pouvoirs publics locaux."
86 Fantasio, "Enfin, nous allons l'avoir!" *Le Pays*, June 27, 1914. It is ironic that years later Martin would be one of the last to oppose women's suffrage.
87 Fantasio, "A propos de bibliothèques. Si les membres de l'Institut canadien furent excommuniés, c'est qu'ils étaient en avance de cinquante ans. On retrouve à Saint-Sulpice les mêmes livres qu'ils avaient. Le geste des Sulpiciens," *Le Pays*, Supplement, November 13, 1915.
88 Paul S. Bédard, "M. Hector Garneau," *Le Pays*, April 10, 1915; Julien Saint-Michel, "La Bibliothèque municipale. L'ouvrier est appelé à en bénéficier dans un avenir peu lointain," *Le Monde ouvrier*, June 24, 1916; Fantasio, "La Genèse d'une idée. La bibliothèque municipale," *Le Pays*, September 8, 1917.
89 AVM, FBM, BM60, S12, SS3, D1.
90 At the time, Dugas wrote under the names Turc, Marcel Dac, Persan, and Marcel Henry.
91 Annette Hayward, "Marcel Dugas, défenseur du modernisme," *Voix et Images* 17, no. 2 (Winter 1992): 184–202.
92 Interview with Gustave Labbé, June 1905.
93 Marcel Valois (Jean Dufresne) to Gustave Labbé, May 6, 1971; interview with G. Labbé, January 2, 2006.
94 Arthur Maheu, "Les Idées de M. Maheu," *Le Pays*, August 12, 1916. Years later, in *Le Monde ouvrier*, Circé-Côté expressed the typical prejudices of the period according to which homosexuals were inverts and mama's boys, whose bearing was effeminate and who swayed their hips like young ladies, etc. The article denounced the fact children were being kept out of school by their mothers and made to do chores at home, and was aimed at workers who prided themselves on their virility. Her goal was to convince the electorate that education played an important role in making boys manlier. Julien Saint-Michel, "L'exploitation de l'enfance," *Le Monde ouvrier*, May 5, 1928.
95 J. B., "A la bibliothèque. Simple justice," *Le Pays*, November 4, 1916.
96 Julien Saint-Michel, "L'influence indue," *Le Monde ouvrier*, October 21, 1916.
97 AVM, BM60, S2, SS1, D1, 3/3.
98 AVM, BM60, S1, D5, unsigned letter to Joseph Aisney, October 28, 1916.
99 Julien Saint-Michel, "L'influence indue." Garneau also opposed patronage that compromised the hiring of competent personnel. Garneau to the members of the administrative commission (*Commission administrative*) of the City of Montreal, May 25, 1920. AVM, BM60, S1, SS1, D2.
100 AVM, FBM, BM60, S3, SS1, DF1.
101 Marie-Claire Daveluy, "Les conditions morales à l'usine," *La Bonne Parole* 10, no. 10 (October 1922): 9–10.

102 Julien Saint-Michel, "La Bibliothèque municipale. L'ouvrier est appelé à en bénéficier dans un avenir peu lointain," *Le Monde ouvrier*, June 24, 1916.
103 Fantasio, "Joffre, l'homme a fait le miracle," *Le Pays*, May 19, 1917.
104 Fantasio, "La Genèse d'une Idée. La Bibliothèque municipale," *Le Pays*, September 8, 1917.
105 Julien Saint-Michel, "La Bibliothèque municipale. Qu'on la dote de livres immédiatement au lieu de perdre son temps à faire mousser des candidatures à des postes inutiles," *Le Monde ouvrier*, September 29, 1917.
106 Fantasio, "La genèse d'une bibliothèque," *Le Pays*, July 9, 1921.
107 In 1917, the Saint-Sulpice Library had 100,000 titles, of which it loaned 60,900, and employed fourteen people. Aegidius Fauteux to the Commissioners, October 8, 1917. Aegidius Fauteux to the Commissioners, October 8, 1917. Meanwhile, the Fraser Institute employed seven people, had 80,266 titles and 144 journals and newspapers, and loaned 102,163. AVM, FBM, BM60, S1, SS1, D3.
108 Fantasio, "La Genèse d'une idée"; Julien Saint-Michel, "Chinoiserie de là-bas et d'ici," *Le Monde ouvrier*, May 28, 1927.
109 Fantasio, "La genèse d'une bibliothèque."
110 "Procès-verbal de la séance de la Commission de la Bibliothèque de la Ville de Montréal," May 31, 1917, AVM, FBM, BM60, S1, SS1, D2.
111 Julien Saint-Michel, "La Bibliothèque municipale. Qu'on la dote de livres . . ."
112 E. R. Décary to Hector Garneau, November 1918, AVM, FBM, BM60, S1, SS1, D2.
113 The Index of banned books was maintained until reforms were implemented by the Second Vatican Council in 1966.
114 Julien Saint-Michel, "La routine ennemie du talent et de l'initiative," *Le Monde ouvrier*, June 16, 1917; Fantasio, "Choses municipales," *Le Pays*, March 6, 1920.
115 AVM, FBM, BM60, S1, SS1, D3.
116 AVM, FBM, BM60, S2, SS1, D1, 3/3.
117 Beaulieu and Hamelin, *La Presse québécoise*, vol. 4; André LeBlanc, "The Labour Movement Seen through the Pages of Montreal's *Le Monde ouvrier/Labor World* (1916–1926)," (Diplôme d'Études supérieures thesis, Université de Montréal, 1971).
118 Curiously, in 1901, a science column in *Les Debats* dealing with graphology, among other subjects, was signed Julien Saint-Michel. It may have been written by Éva Circé, but the *Dictionnaire des pseudonymes* also attributes the name Saint-Michel to Olivar Asselin. "Chronique scientifique," *Les Débats*, August 4, 1901.
119 Julien Saint-Michel, "Les voleurs d'inventions," *Le Monde ouvrier*, December 18, 1920.
120 Julien Saint-Michel, "La journée indivisée," *Le Monde ouvrier*, November 26, 1927.
121 Julien Saint-Michel, "Fausse conception," *Le Monde ouvrier*, November 6, 1920.
122 Julien Saint-Michel, "À farceur, farceur et demi," *Le Monde ouvrier*, July 9, 1927.
123 Julien Saint-Michel, "Notre fête nationale," *Le Monde ouvrier*, July 15, 1916; Fantasio, "La meilleure part"; Arthur Maheu, "Les Idées de M. Maheu"; Paul S. Bédard, "Psyché au cinéma," *Le Pays*, July 15, 1916.
124 Julien Saint-Michel, "La manie de fumer," *Le Monde ouvrier*, January 26, 1929.
125 Saint-Michel, "La manie de fumer."

126 Éva Circé-Côté to Marcel Dugas, August 20, 1920. The letter was given to the author by Gustave Labbé.

127 Fantasio, "'Les Blessures' par Jean Charbonneau," *Le Pays*, January 18, 1913.

128 Fantasio, "Les influences françaises au Canada par M. Jean Charbonneau. Il y a plusieurs moyens de servir la France, le premier et le plus beau est la culture de la langue et de l'idéal français. En sommes-nous rendus à la Renaissance?," *Le Pays*, February 17, 1917.

129 Fantasio, "Les influences françaises au Canada par M. Jean Charbonneau."

130 Fantasio, "L'apothéose du verbe français. Echos du banquet de l'Alliance Française," *Le Pays*, March 17, 1917.

131 Fantasio, "Le Livre de M. de Montigny. Que vont faire les jeunes écrivains canadiens-français dans le cimetière de la Société royale? 'La Langue française au Canada,'" *Le Pays*, January 6, 1917; "Si nous avions une critique littéraire. Il y aurait plus de modération dans les louanges, et on tomberait moins brutalement sur ceux qui nous déplaisent. Encore un mot sur le livre de M. de Montigny," *Le Pays*, May 12, 1917.

132 Paul S. Bédard, "Feux de Bengale à Verlaine glorieux, de M. Marcel Dugas," *Le Pays*, January 22, 1916.

133 Paul S. Bédard, "Psyché au cinéma," *Le Pays*, July 15, 1916.

134 Jean Ney, "Bibliographie. 'Versions' par M. Marcel Dugas. Études sur les poètes Le Cardonnel et Charles Péguy," *Le Pays*, November 3, 1917.

135 Fantasio, "L'humanité fait marche en arrière. Le spectre de la guerre s'est matérialisé. Si, au moins, l'on pouvait espérer que de ce conflit sortira une paix durable," *Le Pays*, August 8, 1914.

136 Fantasio, "Notre caste militaire. Nos gars prennent goût au métier des armes. Les lendemains de cette guerre atroce," *Le Pays*, August 5, 1916.

137 Fantasio, "L'humanité fait marche en arrière."

138 Arthur Maheu, "Les Idées de M. Maheu," *Le Pays*, May 20, 1916.

139 Julien Saint-Michel, "A propos de recrutement. La protestation des ouvriers contre la conscription qui s'annonce. Où nous mène-t-on?" *Le Monde ouvrier*, August 26, 1916.

140 Fantasio, "Visions du Jour de l'An. A propos de jouets—Tout nous ramène à la guerre," *Le Pays*, January 1, 1916.

141 Fantasio, "L'attitude des États-Unis. Mentalité de neutres," *Le Pays*, May 15, 1915.

142 Fantasio, "La maladie à la mode. Une violente attaque de lâcheté. 'Ils ne mouraient pas tous, mais tous étaient frappés,'" *Le Pays*, November 18, 1916.

143 Arthur Maheu, "Les Idées de M. Maheu," *Le Pays*, February 10, 1917.

144 Fantasio, "L'attitude de Melle Rankin. La présence des femmes dans les corps législatifs ne peut qu'adoucir les mœurs et mettre un terme aux guerres," *Le Pays*, April 14, 1917. Rankin, a social worker, suffragist, and pacifist, was the first woman elected to the House of Representatives of the United States.

145 Fantasio, "La sainte ritournelle. (Dieu bénit la France). M. Bourassa s'en sert sur mandat et presque sans rire," *Le Pays*, July 7, 1917.

146 Fantasio, "Toujours comme des petits garçons. C'est ainsi que nous traitent nos évêques en venant benoitement nous montrer la route à suivre. Le cardinal Bégin, Mgr Bruchési et la question du Service," *Le Pays*, January 13, 1917; Julien Saint-Michel, "Autour de l'enregistrement," *Le Monde ouvrier*, June 22, 1918.

147 Fantasio, "Sur Sir Wilfrid Laurier," *Le Pays*, September 1, 1917.
148 Fantasio, "A propos de recrutement. La protestation des ouvriers contre la conscription qui s'annonce. Où nous mène-t-on?" *Le Pays*, August 26, 1916.
149 Fantasio, "Venant après le volontariat la conscription est injuste. Le britishisme n'est pas une affaire de religion, n'en déplaise à l'abbé D'Amour. On tient à sa peau avant sa chemise," *Le Pays*, March 17, 1917.
150 Fantasio, "Vers la paix," *Le Pays*, July 9, 1921.
151 *La Patrie*, September 13, 1915.
152 Fantasio, "Les larmes d'un crocodile royal," *Le Pays*, September 18, 1915.
153 Julien Saint-Michel, "Des ouvriers mal payés. Quand nos gouvernants prendront-ils des mesures pour protéger les travailleurs?" *Le Monde ouvrier*, July 18, 1917.
154 Desmond Morton, *Fight or Pay. Soldiers' Families in the Great War* (Vancouver: University of British Columbia Press, 2004), 23.
155 Fantasio, "Mœurs barbares," *Le Pays*, January 30, 1915.
156 Garneau was particularly attached to his indispensable employees, such as Marcel Dugas, a classifier of whom he said "we would never see the likes of his competence and literary value again," Estelle Lemire, E. Z. Massicotte of the Sainte-Cunégonde branch of the library, and the branch's security guard and messenger boy (*petit chasseur*).
157 E. Z. Massicotte, "Rapport de la Bibliothèque Sainte-Cunégonde," 1916, AVM, ABM, BM60, S1, D5.
158 Julien Saint-Michel, "Notre fête nationale," *Le Monde ouvrier*, July 15, 1916.
159 Desmond Morton, "Entente cordiale? La section montréalaise du Fonds patriotique canadien, 1914–1923: le bénévolat de guerre à Montréal," *Revue d'histoire de l'Amérique française* 8, no. 2 (Fall 1999), 233.
160 Arthur Maheu, "Les Idées de M. Maheu," *Le Pays*, October 24, 1914.
161 AVM, FBM, BM60, S1, SS1, D3.
162 Fantasio, "Mœurs barbares."
163 Arthur Maheu, "Les Idées de M. Maheu," *Le Pays*, August 14, 1915.
164 Julien Saint-Michel, "Visions d'enfer. Hommes et femmes se tuent pour récolter la manne qui passe. La vie dans les usines. Les profits des trustards," *Le Monde ouvrier*, December 2, 1916.
165 Saint-Michel, "A propos de recrutement."
166 Julien Saint-Michel, "Les éternelles victimes," *Le Monde ouvrier*, August 11, 1917.
167 Jean Ney, "La Force des Choses," *L'Étincelle*, December 20, 1902.
168 Julien Saint-Michel, "Le contrôle des vivres," *Le Monde ouvrier*, September 15, 1917.
169 Julien Saint-Michel, "Des ouvriers mal payés," *Le Monde ouvrier*, August 18, 1917; "Les accidents de travail et le surmenage," *Le Monde ouvrier*, July 27, 1918.
170 Julien Saint-Michel, "Les mauvais prophètes," *Le Monde ouvrier*, January 20, 1917.
171 Fantasio, "L'impôt sur le revenu. N'est-il pas temps de songer à alléger le poids des taxes qui porte exclusivement sur le propriétaire?," *Le Pays*, November 7, 1914.
172 Paul S. Bédard, "Les écorchés vifs. Les prix des loyers augmentera-t-il encore cette année? Le pauvre peuple qu'on pressure commence à se lasser," *Le Pays*, February 7, 1914.

330 / Freethinker

173 Saint-Michel, "Les éternelles victimes"; Arthur Maheu, "Les Idées de M. Maheu," *Le Pays*, April 3, 1915.
174 Julien Saint-Michel, "Sauvons les enfants et leurs mamans. Les bébés sont privés de lait parce qu'il coûte trop cher. Le sort des femmes travaillant à l'usine et l'avenir de la race," *Le Monde ouvrier*, October 20, 1917; "La crise des vivres. A propos des petits enfants qui vont à l'école le ventre creux," *Le Monde ouvrier*, October 27, 1917.
175 Fantasio, "Le fétichisme des bouts de rubans. Pourquoi verser des larmes de crocodile sur l'absence de décorations qui nous laissent plus qu'indifférents? Les parchemins ne changent pas la couleur du sang," *Le Pays*, February 24, 1917.
176 Fantasio, "Le beau mérite d'avoir exploité la grande tuerie. Les profiteurs de guerre sont décorés; les pauvres éclopés seront éclaboussés. Qu'avons-nous fait de ces oripeaux des vieilles cours européennes?" *Le Pays*, June 9, 1917.
177 Julien Saint-Michel, "Ceux que l'on décore," *Le Monde ouvrier*, July 21, 1917.
178 Fantasio, "Le beau mérite d'avoir exploité la grande tuerie."
179 For a sympathetic biography of Flavelle, see Michael Bliss, *A Canadian Millionaire: The Life and Business Times of Sir Joseph Flavelle, Bart., 1858–1939* (Toronto: University of Toronto Press, 1992).
180 Julien Saint-Michel, "L'émancipation de la femme," *Le Monde ouvrier*, March 10, 1917.
181 Arthur Maheu, "Les Idées de M. Maheu," *Le Pays*, December 1, 1917.
182 Arthur Maheu, "Les Idées de M. Maheu," *Le Pays*, Supplement no. 3, April 15, 1916.
183 Julien Saint-Michel, "Le prix du sang," *Le Monde ouvrier*, January 6, 1917. Criticism of the zeal and intrusiveness of visiting volunteers was often justified, but the allowances provided by the Foundation enabled some families to emerge from poverty. See Morton, *Fight or Pay*, 112, 122, 130–31.
184 Fantasio, "Le parlement qui disparaît," *Le Pays*, September 22, 1917.
185 Fantasio and Paul S. Bédard, "Un dernier mot. De Fantasio et de Paul S. Bédard sur une légère actualité," *Le Pays*, October 27, 1917.
186 Fantasio and Bédard, "Un dernier mot." This time, Éva Circé-Côté's penchant for using anything as grist to her mill at the expense of logic or accuracy drew protests from readers.
187 Julien Saint-Michel, "Le sort des vieux commis de magasins," *Le Monde ouvrier*, June 29, 1918.
188 Fantasio, "Pensées d'automne," *Le Pays*, September 26, 1914.
189 Fantasio, "En marge de la Semaine sociale," *Le Pays*, July 24, 1920.
190 Julien Saint-Michel, "Les profiteurs de guerre," *Le Monde ouvrier*, March 13, 1920.
191 Fantasio, "Quatrième Épître à Théodore," *Le Pays*, March 13, 1920.
192 Julien Saint-Michel, "Le bien-être futur des travailleurs," *Le Monde ouvrier*, October 16, 1920.
193 Julien Saint-Michel, "Sauvons les enfants et leurs mamans"; Fantasio and Bédard, "Un dernier mot."
194 All information about Rose Henderson is drawn from the biography by Peter Campbell, *Rose Henderson: A Woman for the People* (Montreal-Kingston: McGill-Queen's University Press, 2010).
195 Mont-Royal Cemetery, Burial division, no 1040, section L.

Chapter 4

1 Julien Saint-Michel, "Luttons pour la vie, non pour la mort," *Le Monde ouvrier*, November 19, 1927.
2 Fantasio, "La critique de nos historiens," *Le Pays*, January 22, 1921.
3 Fantasio, "La sainte ritournelle. (Dieu bénit la France). M. Bourassa s'en sert sur mandat et presque sans rire," *Le Pays*, July 7, 1917.
4 Fantasio, "Quatrième Épître à Théodore," *Le Pays*, March 13, 1920.
5 Julien Saint-Michel, "La monarchie agonise," *Le Monde ouvrier*, July 23, 1917.
6 Fantasio, "Les influences françaises au Canada," *Le Pays*, October 30, 1920.
7 Fantasio, "La critique de nos historiens."
8 *La Patrie*, April 4, 1911.
9 Circé-Côté to Dugas, December 26, 1921, CARDL.
10 During the 1920s, Éva Circé-Côté wrote several columns about pedagogy in which she advocated respect for children and spoke out against corporal punishment and cramming.
11 Réginald Hamel, "Gaëtane de Montreuil, sa vie, son oeuvre" (PhD diss., Université Laval, 1971), 59.
12 AVM, BM60, S2, SS1, D1, 3/3.
13 In July 1914, Langlois left to assume the post of Quebec's Agent-General in Belgium. He would stay there until his death in 1928.
14 Circé-Côté to Dugas, August 20, 1920.
15 Between 1917 and 1920, some columns were signed Paul G. Bédard. The style and the themes are so similar to those of Paul S. Bédard that I have conflated the two pseudonyms.
16 These figures are from the summer of 1920.
17 Fantasio, "Vers la paix," *Le Pays*, July 18, 1921, 1 and 3.
18 Colombine, "L'érable," *Le Passe-Temps*, 661, July 24, 1920, 350. Gustave Comte's *Le Passe-Temps* had Gaëtane de Montreuil as its editor-in-chief.
19 Julien Saint-Michel, "La baisse des salaires," *Le Monde ouvrier*, July 23, 1921.
20 Julien Saint-Michel, "Le résultat de l'exploitation du peuple," *Le Monde ouvrier*, April 26, 1919; "La cause de nos maux," May 3, 1919; "Le Droit de grève," June 26, 1920.
21 Julien Saint-Michel, "Les Profiteurs," *Le Monde ouvrier*, August 30, 1919.
22 Julien Saint-Michel, "Les sans-travail," *Le Monde ouvrier*, February 22, 1919; "Guerre aux trusts," *Le Monde ouvrier*, February 14, 1920; "Qui doit gouverner?" *Le Monde ouvrier*, February 28, 1920.
23 Paul-André Linteau, *Histoire de Montréal depuis la Confédération* (Montreal: Boréal, 1992), 311.
24 Julien Saint-Michel, "Souvenirs de 'By-town,'" *Le Monde ouvrier*, September 1, 1928.
25 Julien Saint-Michel, "Une mentalité faussée," *Le Monde ouvrier*, March 12, 1932.
26 Linteau, *Histoire de Montréal depuis la Confédération*, 415.
27 Julien Saint-Michel, "Protégeons la jeunesse," *Le Monde ouvrier*, February 19, 1927; "La fréquentation scolaire obligatoire," *Le Monde ouvrier*, January 25, 1930.

28 Julien Saint-Michel, "Comment endiguer le flot montant de la corruption," *Le Monde ouvrier*, January 3, 1925; "L''enquête' et la théologie," *Le Monde ouvrier*, January 17, 1925.
29 Fantasio, "Le fanatisme religieux," *Le Pays*, December 4, 1920.
30 Fantasio, "Le fanatisme religieux." See Chapter 8.
31 Saint-Michel, "Les sans-travail."
32 Julien Saint-Michel, "Le socialisme est-il anti-chrétien?" *Le Monde ouvrier*, December 6, 1919.
33 Fantasio, "Bolchevisme et soumission," *Le Pays*, October 9, 1920.
34 Julien Saint-Michel, "Le problème de l'heure," *Le Monde ouvrier*, August 27, 1921.
35 Olivar Asselin to Roger Maillet, Montréal, April 25, 1922, fonds Olivar Asselin, AVM, BM55 S2, D40.
36 Fantasio, "Ignorance n'est pas vertu," *Le Pays*, November 12, 1910.
37 Julien Saint-Michel, "La Sainte-Catherine," *Le Monde ouvrier*, November 27, 1926.
38 Julien Saint-Michel, "Il faut des preuves substantielles," *Le Monde ouvrier*, November 12, 1927.
39 Paul S. Bédard, "Reliquats de préjugé. L'arrêt du Concile de Trente n'est pas aboli. Serions-nous en retard des autres pays?" *Le Pays*, May 12, 1917; Saint-Michel, "La Sainte-Catherine."
40 Paul G. [sic] Bédard, "Pudeur intempestive," *Le Pays*, March 27, 1920.
41 Julien Saint-Michel, "Décence et hypocrisie," *Le Monde ouvrier*, April 30, 1921.
42 Julien Saint-Michel, "La Sainte Catherine d'antan," *Le Monde ouvrier*, November 29, 1919.
43 *La Patrie*, February 18, 1922, 1. This photograph was reproduced in Raphaël Ouimet's *Biographies canadiennes-françaises* (Montreal: n.p., 1924).
44 Julien Saint-Michel, "Y a-t-il une raison de s'alarmer . . . !" *Le Monde ouvrier*, December 15, 1928.
45 Fantasio, "Sixième Épître à Théodore," *Le Pays*, March 27, 1920.
46 In 1937 she would write to her friend Georgine, "May the sea be gentle for you—as gentle as you are. For one thing, it is familiar to you—not me. I am still waiting for my 'maiden trip' [in English in the original—Trans.], provided it is not the final voyage." Éva Circé-Côté to Georgine Boucher-Normandin, May 1, 1937.
47 Fantasio, "Cinquième Épître à Théodore," *Le Pays*, March 20, 1920.
48 Danaé Michaud-Mastoras, Éva Circé-Côté's great-niece, applied a sociocritical approach to *Maisonneuve* for her master's thesis, "Étude sociocritique de la pièce *Maisonneuve* d'Éva Circé-Côté" (Université de Montréal, 2006).
49 For information on other stage plays inspired by the founder of Montreal, see Michaud-Mastoras, "Étude sociocritique de la pièce *Maisonneuve* d'Éva Circé-Côté," 57–59.
50 Colombine, *Maisonneuve* (Montreal, 1921).
51 *La Patrie*, April 4, 1921; *Le Canada*, April 4 and 9, 1921; *La Presse*, April 4 and May 7, 1921.
52 *La Presse*, March 26, 1921.
53 *Maisonneuve*, Archives Lionel Groulx, fonds de l'Imprimerie populaire, P56/C3, 6., n.d.

54 Fantasio, "La critique de nos historiens."
55 François-Xavier Garneau, *Histoire du Canada*, 5th edition, revised, annotated and published with an introduction and appendices by his grandson, Hector Garneau, and a preface by M. Gabriel Hanotaux (Paris: Librairie Félix Alcan, 1913).
56 Fantasio, "Marguerite Bourgeoys," *Le Pays*, May 8, 1920.
57 Fantasio, "Les influences françaises au Canada."
58 Fantasio, "Méditation sur Jeanne Mance," *Le Pays*, May 22, 1920.
59 Arthur Lebel, "Il a su mourir comme il avait vécu," *Le Pays*, July 9, 1921.
60 Musette, "Erin Go Bragh!" *Les Débats*, March 17, 1901. It was reprinted in *Bleu, Blanc, Rouge*, 331, but with the simple dedication, "To Madame Elz. Côté."
61 Circé-Côté to Dugas, December 26, 1921, CARDL. Charles-Eugène Labbé was kind enough to provide me with the Côté family's genealogy.
62 Interview with Marcel Bellavance, great-grandson of Elzéar Côté, Longueuil, August 2005.
63 Circé-Côté to Dugas, December 26, 1921, CARDL.
64 Circé-Côté to Dugas, December 26, 1921, CARDL.
65 Georges Bellerive, *Brèves apologies de nos auteurs féminins* (Quebec: Garneau, 1920), 77.
66 Bellerive, *Brèves apologies de nos auteurs féminins*, 79.
67 Fantasio, "Nos femmes de lettres," *Le Pays*, December 11, 1920.
68 Pierre Hébert, in collaboration with Patrick Nicol, *Censure et littérature au Québec: le livre crucifié, 1625–1919* (Montreal: Fides, 1997); Pierre Hébert and Élise Salaün, *Censure et littérature au Québec: des vieux couvents au plaisir de vivre (1920–1959)* (Montreal: Fides, 2004).
69 Fantasio, "Nos femmes de lettres."
70 Years later, Francq's nephew, who had inherited the newspaper, could not recall who Julien Saint-Michel might have been. Testimony of André LeBlanc, 1990.
71 To a reader identifying himself as Cyrano, she replied: "My sex, or sex in general perhaps, is a matter of concern for you. Know that I am a conscience, a thought. Can it inhabit this creature 'whose hair is long and who is short on ideas?' Believe me, Mr. Cyrano, this is an unimportant detail." Fantasio, "Si nous avions une critique littéraire," *Le Pays*, May 12, 1917.
72 Fantasio, "Nos femmes de lettres."
73 Camille Roy, *Érables en fleurs* (Quebec: L'Action sociale, 1923), 180, cited in Aurélien Boivin and Kenneth Landry, "Françoise et Madeleine, pionnières du journalism féminin au Québec," *Voix et Images* 4, no. 2 (December 1978): 238. Camille Roy (1870–1943) founded the faculty of literature at Université Laval and was the rector of the university when *Érables en fleurs* was published. In 1939, he published *Manuel d'histoire de la littérature canadienne de langue française* (Montreal: Beauchemin), in which no mention is made of Éva Circé-Côté. In the 1920s, Éva Circé-Côté broke off her relations with Madeleine. As she wrote to Dugas, "Madeleine, who had filled the province with her loquaciousness, suddenly tumbled from the fragile pedestal where she had perched her stupidity and ignorance." Circé-Côté to Dugas, December 20, 1926, CARDL.
74 Circé-Côté to Dugas, July 1924, CARDL.

75 Was Dugas's dedication in *Flacons à la mer*, "La nuit me regarde. À C...," addressed to Circé-Côté? Perhaps it refers to another person, such as his sister, Corinne, as was suggested to me by Gustave Labbé Dugas. Marcel Dugas, *Flacons à la mer: proses* (Paris: Les Gémaux, 1923), 76–79.
76 Circé-Côté to Dugas, September 17, 1924, CARDL.
77 Circé-Côté to Dugas, December 26, 1921, CARDL.
78 Circé-Côté to Dugas, December 20, 1926, CARDL.
79 Interview with Gustave Labbé, June 2006.
80 Circé-Côté to Dugas, September 17, 1924, CARDL.
81 Circé-Côté to Dugas, September 17, 1924, CARDL.
82 Circé-Côté to Dugas, September 17, 1924, CARDL.
83 Circé-Côté to Dugas, September 17, 1924, CARDL.
84 Circé-Côté to Dugas, August 20, 1920.
85 Marcel Dugas, Tristan Choiseul [pseud.], *Confins* (Paris: 1921).
86 B. Brunet, *Mercure de France*, July 1, 1922. I thank Gustave Labbé for having drawn my attention to this critique.
87 Circé-Côté to Dugas, August 20, 1920.
88 *L'Action française* 4, no. 4 (April 1920), 178.
89 R. Lemoine, "Les Anglomanes," *Le Combat*, November 1, 1903. This is a recurring subject in French Canada. At the beginning of the nineteenth century, Joseph Quesnel played in *L'Anglomanie ou Le Dîner à l'anglaise* (1802), a one-act comedy in verse.
90 Magali Michelet, who signed her columns as Magali, had been responsible for the "Coin féminin" (women's page) of Edmonton's *Courrier de l'Ouest*.
91 *L'Action française* 6, no. 5 (November 1921), 686.
92 Circé-Côté to Dugas, December 26, 1921, CARDL.
93 *La Presse*, March 14, 1922, 6.
94 *Le Canada*, March 6, 1922, 5; *La Patrie*, March 7, 1922.
95 *La Presse*, March 14, 1922, 8.
96 The rest of the crew included W. Boissonnière, who was also the manager, Paul Gérard, the artistic director, Raymond de Marcy of the Odéon de Paris, the director, and the actors Jeanne Laviolette, Paul Gérardi, Ph. Rhesels, M. de Verbois (who plays the transvestite, Mme Bennington), Juliette Reyna, Fernand Hicquet, Mme Boissonière, and Rosette Langlais. *La Presse*, March 14, 1922, 6.
97 *La Presse*, March 14, 1922, 6.
98 *La Presse*, March 14, 1922, 8; *Le Canada*, March 6, 1922, 5; *La Patrie*, March 18, 1922, 20.
99 Jean-Marc Larrue, *Le Monument inattendu. Le Monument national 1893–1993* (Montreal: HMH, 1993), 79.
100 *La Patrie*, March 22, 1922, 9.
101 *La Patrie*, March 25, 1922, 22.
102 *Le Paquebot ténacité* was the first modern theatre in Montreal. Larrue, *Le Monument inattendu*, 195.
103 Julien Saint-Michel, "Une question que rien n'étouffe," *Le Monde ouvrier*, August 7, 1920.

104 The Association gave itself the following objectives: 1. To act on behalf of the mutual benefit and protection of Canadian authors and the maintenance of the ideals and best practices of the literary profession; 2. to achieve adequate copyright for authors; 3. to assist in the protection of the literary property of its members, in the dissemination of information concerning the rights and interests of its members, as well as of other authors; 4. to promote the professional interests of all creators whose works should be protected by the law; and 5. to encourage cordial relations between members and the authors of other countries. Lyn Harrington, *Syllables of Recorded Time* (Toronto: Simon & Pierre, 1981), 16–23.

105 *La Patrie*, November 7, 1921.

106 National Library, Collection of the Canadian Authors Association, MSS-061. Luc Aubry, "Les Échos," *La Revue moderne*, April 15, 1921, 26.

107 Already in 1918, Julien Saint-Michel decried the antifeminism of Madeleine as follows: "this friend of the established order, preaches the passive submission of women to their saviour and master, this enemy of feminism . . . " Saint-Michel, "La femme et la politique," *Le Monde ouvrier*, November 30, 1918.

108 Minutes of the meeting of the Canadian Authors Association, April 17, 1921, ANQ, Collection of the Canadian Authors Association, and MSS-061, box 22.

109 Fantasio, "Du choc des idées naissent les . . . ténèbres," *Le Pays*, April 23, 1921. Josée Vincent, "Un premier regroupement 'professionnel' d'écrivains au Québec: la section française de la Canadian Authors Association (1921–1936)," in *Lieux et réseaux de sociabilité littéraire au Québec*, ed. Pierre Rajotte (Quebec: Nota bene, 2001), 286–89.

110 Harrington, *Syllables of Recorded Time*, 46. The Association created branches in most major cities, but none was as autonomous as the French-Canadian section. Morin had presided over the Library Commission at City Hall as of 1910 and played a central role in the establishment of a real public library. See Dagenais, "Vie culturelle et pouvoirs publics locaux," 49.

111 *La Patrie*, November 19, 1921. To write about the history of French-Canadian literature, the newspaper called upon Aegidius Fauteux, while Éva Circé-Côté wrote in *Le Pays*.

112 *La Patrie*, November 7, 1921.

113 *La Patrie*, November 21, 1921.

114 Fantasio, "Exhumation de "l'auteur inconnu,'" *Le Pays*, December 3, 1921; *La Patrie*, November 21, 22, 23, 25, 26, and 28, 1921.

115 BNQ, Collection of the Canadian Authors Association, MSS-061, box 23, p.-v. AGA February 25, 1922; *La Patrie*, February 27, 1922. In his book about L'Arche, Robert Foisy insists upon the role of Victor Barbeau in the Canadian Authors Association and stresses the importance of its network at the beginning of the twentieth century. Out of thirty-three authors in the new association, eight had frequented L'Arche. Foisy, *L'Arche*, 171. Many of the author-founders were associated with the École littéraire de Montréal. No women officially belonged to such networks, but in their roles as journalists they gravitated to the all-male societies.

116 *La Presse*, February 27, 1922; *Le Canada*, February 28, 1922; *Le Nationaliste*, March 12, 1922.

117 *La Presse*, April 22, May 8 and 11, 1922.

118 *Le Devoir*, October 28, 1922; *La Presse*, October 30, 1922. Of this stay in Canada, Cécile Sorel would only recall the delirious reception that she received from the students, who pushed their enthusiasm to the point of blocking the tracks to prevent her train from leaving before the president of the student association had finished singing Sorel's praises. Cécile Sorel, *Les Belles heures de ma vie* (Monaco: Du Rocher, 1946), 256–57.

119 Information provided by the musicologist, Marie-Thérèse Lefebvre. The journal, founded by Émiliano Renaud and the critic and librettist Gustave Comte, put out only three issues.

120 Yves Roby, *Les Franco-Américains de la Nouvelle-Angleterre 1776–1930* (Quebec: Septentrion, 1990), 273–78.

121 Jean Nay, "Restons chez nous. L'exode des Canadiens aux États-Unis," *Le Passe-Temps* 724, January 20, 1923, 20.

122 Olivar Asselin, Montreal, to Marcel de Verneuil, Paris, April 23, 1922, AVM, BM55, S2, D40. Asselin was severe because Maillet had had a long career in journalism. Roger and Roland Maillet named their newspaper *Le Mâtin* to distinguish it from the one published by their father, Gaston Maillet, *Le Matin*.

123 In Alphonse Daudet's popular story, Mr Séguin's goat longs to be free, a recurrent theme in Circé-Côté's writings.

124 "Les Cahiers de Polémarque," *Le Mâtin*, July 21, 1923; Fantasio, "L'avenir est à Dieu," *Le Pays*, January 17, 1914.

125 Circé-Côté to Dugas, September 17, 1924, CARDL.

126 Circé-Côté to Dugas, July 1924, CARDL.

127 Medical report, November 8, 1922, AVM, BM60, S2, SS1, D1, 3/3.

128 BM60, S2, SS1, D1, 2/3.

129 Julien Saint-Michel, "Uniformité de salaire pour les deux Sexes," *Le Monde ouvrier*, April 12, 1924.

130 Julien Saint-Michel, "En marge des élections," *Le Monde ouvrier*, April 12, 1924; "Les Enfants trouvés. Quel est leur sort? Les statistiques sont muettes sur ce sujet et sur bien d'autres," May 3, 1924; "L'Exploitation de l'enfance," June 14, 1924; "Quand abolira-t-on la peine capitale?" July 18, 1924; "Herriot et les Congrégations," October 18, 1924; "Pour enrayer la Plaie sociale," October 25, 1924; "Une lettre discutable," December 13, 1924; "La Hantise des Pendus," November 1, 1924.

131 Circé-Côté to Dugas, July 1924, CARDL.

132 Circé-Côté to Dugas, September 17, 1924, CARDL. The lake is actually Saint-Aimé-du-Lac-des-Îles, located eighteen kilometres south of Mont-Laurier.

133 Circé-Côté to Dugas, July 1924, CARDL.

134 Interview with Gustave Labbé, January 2, 2006.

135 Circé-Côté to Dugas, July 1924, CARDL.

136 Circé-Côté to Dugas, July 1924, CARDL.

137 Circé-Côté to Dugas, July 1924, CARDL.

138 Circé-Côté to Dugas, September 17, 1924, CARDL.

139 Circé-Côté to Dugas, September 17, 1924, CARDL.

140 Circé-Côté to Dugas, September 17, 1924, CARDL.

141 Circé-Côté to Dugas, September 17, 1924, CARDL.
142 Circé-Côté to Dugas, July 1924, CARDL.
143 Circé-Côté to Dugas, September 17, 1924, CARDL.
144 Circé-Côté to Dugas, September 17, 1924, CARDL.
145 Circé-Côté to Dugas, December 20, 1926, CARDL.
146 Circé-Côté to Dugas, December 20, 1926, CARDL. For more on the friendship between the two men, see Chantale Gingras, *Victor Barbeau: Un réseau d'influences littéraires* (Montreal: L'Hexagone, 2000), 56–57, 70, 98–102.
147 Circé-Côté to Dugas, December 20, 1926, CARDL. In her book *Papineau*, published two years earlier, she portrayed Barbeau, whom she compared with the historian Michel Bibaud, as someone "hypnotized by the Herculean stature of the Anglo-Saxon and disdainful of local productions." Circé-Côté, *Papineau*, 59.
148 Circé-Côté to Dugas, December 26, 1921, CARDL. Thérive (1891–1967), a right-wing writer and critic, would compromise himself several years later during the Vichy regime when he accompanied Pierre Drieu la Rochelle, Paul Morand, Marcel Jouhandeau, Jacques Chardonne (Boutelleau) and several others to the Congress of European Writers convened by Goebbels in Weimar in 1942. François Dufay, *Le Soufre et le Moisi. La Droite littéraire après 1945: Chardonne, Morand et les Hussards* (Paris: Perrin, 2006). After the war, he was associated with a coterie of former collaborators who were against *la littérature engagée*. Michel Winock, *Le Siècle des intellectuels* (Paris: Seuil, 1997), 471.
149 Georgine Boucher-Normandin to André Thérive, Paris, October 20, 1925.
150 Colombine, "A la tombe de Papineau," *Le Combat*, November 15, 1903.
151 Fantasio, "Tableau vivant: Dollard mort!," *Le Pays*, July 8, 1911.
152 Circé-Côté, *Papineau*, Chapter 2, 2–3.
153 Circé-Côté, *Papineau*, Chapter 2, 3.
154 Circé-Côté to Dugas, July 1924, Montreal, CARDL.
155 Circé-Côté to Dugas, September 17, 1924, CARDL.
156 Fantasio, "Marguerite Bourgeoys."
157 Boucher-Normandin to Thérive, Paris, October 20, 1925.
158 Archives of the Sisters of Sainte-Anne (ASSA), LQ/11/40.
159 It was to Lucienne Boucher that the *Lettres à Lucienne* by Alain Grandbois were addressed. Interview with Gustave Labbé, January 2, 2006, April 25, 2007. See also, "La musique en Europe," *Le Canada Musical* 4, no. 8, Saturday, August 21, 1920, 3.
160 Hodent was the author of several texts about Canada. Maurice Guénard-Hodent, "La vérité sur le Canada," *La Canadienne*, 1909, vii; Guénard-Hodent, *La tradition renouée.—Les Relations entre la France et le Canada depuis soixante années* (Paris: Éditions Paris-Canada, 1930).
161 E. Armand, Gérard de Lacaze-Duthiers, and Abel Léger, *L'Homosexualité, l'Onanisme et les Individualistes*, prefaced by Gérard de Lacaze-Duthiers, "Des préjugés en matières sexuelles," and followed by Abel Léger, "La Honteuse Hypocrisie" (Paris/Orléans: Éditions de l'En-dehors, 1931). On French-Canadian networks in Paris, see Michel Lacroix, "Lien social, idéologie et cercles d'appartenance: le réseau 'latin' des Québécois en France, 1923–1939," *Études littéraires* 36, no. 2 (2004): 51–70.
162 *Paris-Canada*, November 1, 1925.

163 Éva Circé-Côté to Gaëtane de Montreuil, December 28, 1925, cited in Réginald Hamel, "Gaëtane de Montreuil," 122–24.
164 Fantasio, "Nos Femmes de lettres," *Le Pays*, December 11, 1920. Writing in *Brèves apologies de nos auteurs féminins*, Éva Circé-Côté deplored it that Bellerive did not look beyond Colombine, unaware that she was pursuing her career under other pseudonyms.
165 "[...] la escritora canadiense que figura entre las primeras de la generacion actual [...]." Anonymous, "Salones literarios," *Universitario*, July 1926, 33–34.
166 Circé-Côté to Dugas, December 20, 1926, CARDL.
167 Circé-Côté to Dugas, December 20, 1926, CARDL
168 AVM, BM60, S2, SS1, D1, 3/3. She lived at 634 Plessis Street.
169 Circé-Côté to Dugas, December 20, 1926, CARDL.
170 Circé-Côté to Dugas, December 20, 1926, CARDL.
171 Circé-Côté to Dugas, December 20, 1926, CARDL.
172 Éva Circé-Côté to Georgine Boucher-Normandin, May 1, 1937.
173 *La Presse*, September 8, 1925.
174 Circé-Côté to Dugas, September 17, 1924, CARDL.
175 Circé-Côté to Dugas, August 20,1920, CARDL.
176 Circé-Côté to Dugas, July 1924, CARDL.
177 Circé-Côté to Dugas, December 20, 1926, CARDL; Fantasio, "Les arts au Canada. M. Philippe Hébert. M. Napoléon Bourassa," *Le Pays*, June 23, 1917.
178 Circé-Côté to Gaëtane de Montreuil, December 28, 1925, cited in Hamel, "Gaëtane de Montreuil," 122–24.
179 Circé-Côté to Dugas, December 26, 1921, CARDL.
180 Circé-Côté to Dugas, September 17, 1924, CARDL.
181 Circé-Côté to Dugas, December 20, 1926, CARDL.
182 Circé-Côté to Dugas, December 20, 1926, CARDL.
183 *La Presse*, October 21, 1927, 15.
184 "La soirée de nos auteurs à S.-Sulpice. M. Louis Francœur y lut une causerie intitulée 'Auteur, Critique, Public.' Une soirée réussie," *La Patrie*, October 21, 1927, 14; "L'Association des Auteurs canadiens, Section française," *La Revue moderne*, June 1928, 16.
185 *Le Petit journal*, June 24, July 1, and September 23, 1928.
186 Julien Saint-Michel, "Le culte du souvenir," *Le Monde ouvrier*, June 14, 1930.
187 Julien Saint-Michel, "À la mémoire de Papineau," *Le Monde ouvrier*, April 19, 1930. The construction of the Seigniory Club in Montebello was one of the last large real estate projects before Quebec became mired in the economic depression for the next decade.
188 Julien Saint-Michel, "Réformons au lieu de détruire," *Le Monde ouvrier*, July 30, 1927; "L'ambition perd son maître," September 24, 1927.
189 Antonin Dupont, "Louis-Alexandre Taschereau et la législation sociale au Québec, 1920–1936," *Revue d'histoire de l'Amérique française* 26, no. 3 (December 1972), 410.
190 The Commission of Enquiry sat from April 28 to June 30, 1927. The report by Justice Boyer would be endorsed by the National Assembly in 1928. *La Patrie*, August 31, 1927, 8 and 15; Magda Fahrni, "Children and Risk in the Modern City: The Laurier

Palace Fire of 1927," unpublished paper, Cordoue, May 2006; Farhni, "Glimpsing Working-Class Childhood through the Laurier Palace Fire of 1927: The Ordinary, the Tragic, and the Historian's Gaze," *Journal of the History of Childhood and Youth* 8, no. 3 (Fall 2015): 426–50.

191 Julien Saint-Michel, "Protégeons la jeunesse," *Le Monde ouvrier*, February 19, 1927.
192 Julien Saint-Michel, *Le Monde ouvrier*, May 7, 1927.
193 Julien Saint-Michel, *Le Monde ouvrier*, February 19, May 7, July 30, and August 6, 1927. The report of Justice Boyer showed that priests in industrial villages like Valleyfield and Saint-Jerome were much more tolerant than their superiors and did not object to their parishioners going to the movies on Sunday.
194 Julien Saint-Michel, "Ne prenons pas nos désirs pour des réalités," *Le Monde ouvrier*, May 7, 1927.
195 Saint-Michel, "Une mentalité faussée."
196 Saint-Michel, "Réformons au lieu de détruire."
197 Julien Saint-Michel, "Une loi de pharisiens," *Le Monde ouvrier*, April 14, 1928; "Du grand air pour les petits," *Le Monde ouvrier*, June 2, 1928.
198 *Le Devoir*, January 16 and February 6, 1932.
199 *La Patrie*, January 16, 1932; *Le Petit Journal*, January 24, 1932.
200 *La Patrie*, January 16, 1932.
201 *La Presse*, February 9, 1932. *La Patrie*, where Madeleine was still a contributor, completely ignored the event.
202 Julien Saint-Michel, "Comment remédier au chômage?," *Le Monde ouvrier*, May 9, 1931.
203 Julien Saint-Michel, "'Sauvez la France' . . . C'est fait," *Le Monde ouvrier*, October 17, 1931.
204 Saint-Michel, "'Sauvez la France' . . . C'est fait."
205 Julien Saint-Michel, "Renvoyer la femme au foyer, est-ce possible?" *Le Monde ouvrier*, December 1, 1934.
206 *La Patrie*, January 23 and 24, 1935; *La Presse*, January 23, 1935.
207 Julien Saint-Michel, "S'habitue-t-on à avoir faim?" *Le Monde ouvrier*, September 9, 1933.
208 Julien Saint-Michel, "Quelques 'à côté' de la crise," *Le Monde ouvrier*, July 21, 1934.
209 Fantasio, "Juste répartition de l'impôt," *Le Monde ouvrier*, August 6, 1921.
210 Circé-Côté to Dugas, December 26, 1921, CARDL.
211 Circé-Côté to Dugas, December 26, 1921, CARDL.
212 Circé-Côté to Dugas, August 20, 1920, CARDL.
213 Circé-Côté to Dugas, July 1924, CARDL.
214 Circé-Côté to Dugas, September 17, 1924, CARDL.
215 Lettre du bibliothécaire en chef au personnel (Letter from the Chief Librarian to the Staff), January 5, 1923, BM60, S2, SS1, D1, 3/32, May 1924.
216 Circé-Côté to Dugas, September 17, 1924, CARDL.
217 Circé-Côté to Dugas, July 1924, CARDL.
218 Ross Gordon, "Félix Desrochers, bibliothécaire général 1933–1956," *La Revue parlementaire canadienne* 23, no. 3 (2000).

219 *La Presse*, December 21, 1901, cited in Michèle Dagenais, "Autour de la Bibliothèque municipale de Montréal. Lecture des enjeux culturels et politiques," in *La Vie culturelle à Montréal vers 1900*, ed. Micheline Cambron (Montreal: Fides/Bibliothèque nationale du Québec, 2005), 108.
220 Olivar Asselin to Marcel Dugas, Montreal, December 28, 1925, in *Études françaises* 7 (1971), 294.
221 Julien Saint-Michel, "Le suffrage féminin," *Le Monde ouvrier*, March 24, 1928.
222 Rapport Fauteux, July 3, 1932, AVM, VM1, 3rd series.
223 Aegidius Fauteux to the clerk of the City of Montreal, July 13, 1933, AVM, VM1, 2324.
224 Fantasio, "A propos de bibliothèques. Si les membres de l'Institut canadien furent excommuniés, c'est qu'ils étaient en avance de cinquante ans. On retrouve à Saint-Sulpice les mêmes livres qu'ils avaient. Le geste des Sulpiciens," *Le Pays*, November 13, 1915; Julien Saint-Michel, "La Bibliothèque municipale. L'ouvrier est appelé à en bénéficier dans un avenir peu lointain," *Le Monde ouvrier*, June 24, 1916. In 1930, she demanded that all libraries in Quebec have a children's section, as was the case in the City of Westmount, the Fraser-Hickson Institute, and libraries in the United States. "Le goût de la lecture," *Le Monde ouvrier*, November 1, 1930.
225 Aegidius Fauteux to J.-Étienne Gauthier, September 22, 1932, AVM, VM1, 3rd series, 2423.
226 S. Dugas-Audiot to E. Achard, Montreal, 1932, AVM, VM2423 AVM, an extract from the minutes of the assembly of the Executive Committee of the City of Montreal, September 13, 1932, 3rd series, 2Y23.
227 Clerk of the City of Montreal to Éva Circé-Côté, September 15, 1932, AVM, VM1, 3rd series, 2423.
228 Clerk of the City of Montreal to Éva Circé-Côté, September 15, 1932.
229 Clerk of the City of Montreal to Éva Circé-Côté, September 15, 1932.
230 In addition to her work and her writing, she also had to deal with everyday problems, such as a claim for compensation from the City of Montreal after her home was flooded. AVM, VM1, 3rd series, 45156.

Chapter 5

1 Colombine, "Automne! Hiver!" *L'Avenir*, November 11, 1900.
2 Julien Saint-Michel, "Les trépassés," *Le Monde ouvrier*, November 3, 1928.
3 *La Presse*, September 8, 1933.
4 W. Stewart Wallace, ed., *The Encyclopedia of Canada*, vol. 4 (Toronto: University Associates of Canada, 1948), 384.
5 Réginald Hamel, Gaëtane de Montreuil's biographer, attributes the founding of the Filles natives du Canada and its "campaign against undesirable foreigners" to her animosity towards the journalist Laure Hurteau. Hamel, "Gaëtane de Montreuil," 71–72. She also pursued her nationalist objectives in creating the Union des Gens de chez nous, which Éva Circé-Côté does not seem to have been associated with.
6 See Hamel, 74–75, regarding Gaëtane de Montreuil's xenophobia.
7 Julien Saint-Michel, "La retour à la terre et le chômage," *Le Monde ouvrier*, May 30, 1931.

8   Colombine, "Un Rêve," *L'Avenir du Nord*, May 21, 1903.
9   Julien Saint-Michel, "Retournons à la terre," *Le Monde ouvrier*, May 28, 1932.
10 Julien Saint-Michel, "Le sens-pratique nous manque," *Le Monde ouvrier*, October 20, 1934.
11 For a summary of this "affair," see Pierre Anctil, *Le Rendez-vous manqué. Les Juifs de Montréal face au Québec de l'entre-deux-guerres* (Quebec: Institut québécois de recherche sur la culture, 1988), 131-34. See also Olivar Asselin, *Pensée française. Pages choisies* (Montreal: Édition de l'Action canadienne-française, 1937), 206.
12 Julien Saint-Michel, "Question de race," *Le Monde ouvrier*, July 7, 1934. See Chapter 8, 244.
13 Georgina Bélanger Gill to Éva Circé-Côté, April 8, 1934, cited in Hamel, 10-12, 76, 80, 82. Hamel ascribes this dispute to Georgina Bélanger's bitterness, intransigence, and lack of a sense of democracy. The Rosalie-Papineau committee was disbanded in 1936.
14 "Un deuil pour nos lettres," *La Revue moderne*, vol. 15 (May 1934), 10. In his portrait of Desaulniers, Germain Beaulieu, a fellow member of the École littéraire de Montréal, praises him for his distinctive erudition and refined spirit. Germain Beaulieu, *Les Immortels* (Montreal: Éditions Albert Lévesque, 1931), 60-69; *Canadian Jewish Chronicle*, July 22, 1932.
15 Fantasio, "Les influences françaises au Canada par M. Jean Charbonneau," *Le Pays*, February 7, 1917; Fantasio, "Le beau mérite d'avoir exploité la grande tuerie. Les profiteurs de guerre sont décorés; les pauvres éclopés seront éclaboussés. Qu'avons nous fait de ces oripeaux des vieilles cours européennes?" *Le Pays*, June 9, 1917; Circé-Côté to Dugas, July 1924, CARDL.
16 Harrison, *National Reference Book*, 849.
17 Georgine Boucher-Normandin to Marcel Dugas, Montreal, January 23, 1938. Archives of Gustave Labbé.
18 Éva Circé-Côté to Georgine Boucher-Normandin, May 1, 1937. My thanks to Danile Laprès for providing me with a photocopy of this letter.
19 Georgine Boucher-Normandin to Marcel Dugas, Montreal, January 23, 1938.
20 Fantasio, "Faisons le point," *La Revue moderne*, December 1935.
21 There were twenty-eight articles all told. *L'Aurore*, 1938-1939. It's thanks to Jean-Louis Lalonde that I was able to find this journal in the Faculté de théologie évangélique.
22 Fernande Roy, "Le journal *L'Autorité* dans le cadre de la presse libérale montréalaise," in Lamonde, *Combats libéraux*, 231; Yvan Lamonde, "Le libéralisme et le passage dans le XXe siècle," in Lamonde, *Combats libéraux*, 234-45.
23 Harrison, *National Reference Book*, 849. The Soirée des auteurs canadiens, organized by Édouard Garant, was held in the Saint-Sulpice hall on October 20, 1927.
24 Harrison, *National Reference Book*, 849.
25 Two other works that were banned were the 1868 and 1869 editions of the Annuaire de l'Institut canadien. *Annuaire de l'Institut-Canadien pour 1868. Célébration du 24e anniversaire de la fondation de l'Institut-Canadien le 17 décembre 1868* (Montreal: Le Pays, 1868). Pierre Hébert, 15. Regarding David, see Jean Landry, "Laurent Olivier David (1840-1926)," *Dictionary of Canadian Biography*, vol. 15.

26 Paul S. Bédard, "Le Rapport de M. David. Sur les bibliothèques de Montréal. Voudrait-on faire avorter le projet de bibliothèque municipale?" *Le Pays*, February 14, 1914.

27 A dozen columns make reference to L. O. David. Among others: Paul S. Bédard, "L'hon. M. David. Ses réquisitoires contre nos collèges classiques et contre notre système scolaire," *Le Pays*, January 25, 1913; Fantasio, "Le sénateur David et l'impérialisme. Un régime qui limiterait davantage nos libertés civiles porterait en soi le germe de la désagrégation. Ne lâchons pas la proie pour l'ombre—Pour un speech nos politiciens vendraient leur âme," *Le Pays*, March 3, 1917; Fantasio, "Nouvelle frasque de Mgr Fallon. Insultes aux Canadiens-Français," *Le Pays*, December 22, 1917.

28 Circé-Côté to Dugas, December 20, 1926, CARDL.

29 Colombine, "La Pensionnaire. Causerie d'une montréalaise," *L'Avenir du Nord*, August 3, 1906.

30 Fantasio, "Le 'Flat,'" *Le Pays*, July 1, 1911.

31 Fantasio, "L'impôt sur le revenu. N'est-il pas temps de songer à alléger le poids des taxes qui porte exclusivement sur le propriétaire?" *Le Pays*, November 7, 1914; Paul S. Bédard, "Les écorchés vifs. Les prix des loyers augmentera-t-il encore cette année? Le pauvre peuple qu'on pressure commence à se lasser," *Le Pays*, February 7, 1914.

32 Julien Saint-Michel, "Les éternelles victimes. Les propriétaires auraient-ils l'intention de faire payer par les salaires la taxe que le gouvernement vient d'imposer le pauvre contre la voracité des riches," *Le Monde ouvrier*, August 11, 1917.

33 Julien Saint-Michel, "Lisez votre bail avant de le signer," *Le Monde ouvrier*, February 18, 1928.

34 Interview about these two properties with Gustave Labbé, who had spoken to Lucienne Boucher-Dumas, 2006; Julien Saint-Michel, "La visite des logements," *Le Monde ouvrier*, February 20, 1932; "Le bien d'autrui," *Le Monde ouvrier*, May 14, 1932; "Potins de déménagement," *Le Monde ouvrier*, May 7, 1932.

35 Julien Saint-Michel, "L'infériorité économique," *Le Monde ouvrier*, May 9, 1936; "La joie d'être propriétaire," *Le Canada*, May 26, 1936.

36 Julien Saint-Michel, "Remettre l'ordre dans l'état social," *Le Monde ouvrier*, October 1, 1936.

37 Julien Saint-Michel, "Les frères siamois et la désunion," *Le Monde ouvrier*, July 11, 1936.

38 Saint-Michel, "Les frères siamois et la désunion."

39 Julien Saint-Michel, "Le nouveau régime," *Le Monde ouvrier*, April 22, 1936.

40 Saint-Michel, "Le nouveau régime."

41 Ève Circé-Côté, "Les fugues du Cardinal Villeneuve," *L'Aurore*, June 7, 1940.

42 Julien Saint-Michel, "Les deux fléaux de l'humanité," *Le Monde ouvrier*, March 28, 1936; "Un raffinement de cruautés," April 26, 1936.

43 Julien Saint-Michel, "Qui sème le vent, récolte la tempête," *Le Monde ouvrier*, July 31, 1937.

44 Julien Saint-Michel, "Le Travail de la femme," *Le Monde ouvrier*, February 8, 1936; "Pourquoi déplacer le secours direct?" *Le Monde ouvrier*, February 15, 1936; "Le vote des femmes," *Le Monde ouvrier*, June 20, 1936.

45 Julien Saint-Michel, "Qu'arrivera-t-il de demain?" *Le Monde ouvrier*, February 8, 1936; "Tant va la cruche à l'eau," *Le Monde ouvrier*, March 7, 1936.
46 Harrison, *National Reference Book*, 648–49.
47 Marcel Martel, *Le Deuil d'un pays imaginé. Rêves, luttes et déroute du Canada français. Les rapports entre le Québec et la francophonie canadienne (1867–1975)* (Ottawa: University of Ottawa Press, Collection Amérique française, 1997), 36; Congrès de la langue française au Canada, *Deuxième congrès de la langue française au Canada, Québec, 27 juin–1er juillet 1937: compte rendu* (Quebec: Imprimerie de l'Action catholique, 1938).
48 Julien Saint-Michel, "Les secrets de la nature," *Le Monde ouvrier*, August 14, 1937.
49 Julien Saint-Michel, "La persécution n'a jamais tué l'idée," *Le Monde ouvrier*, October 30, 1937.
50 Fantasio, "Si nous avions une critique littéraire. Il y aurait plus de modération dans les louanges, et on tomberait moins brutalement sur ceux qui nous déplaisent. Encore un mot sur le livre de M. de Montigny," *Le Pays*, May 12, 1917. Meanwhile, in 1915, Fantasio adopted a very masculine tone in an article titled "A Propos de recrutement. Nous sommes des hommes et voulons être traités comme des hommes," *Le Pays*, July 31, 1915.
51 Fernand Ouellet, "Bédard, Pierre-Stanislas," *Dictionary of Canadian Biography*, vol. 6.
52 Julien Circé, aka Saint-Michel, was born in 1818, but the date of his death is not known; however, he was a witness at an interment in Saint-Philippe in 1878. Hence, it is certain that Éva knew him, at least until she was seven-and-a-half years old.
53 Fantasio, "Si nous avions une critique littéraire." *Le Pays*, May 12, 1917.
54 Minutes of the monthly meeting of the Association des auteurs canadiens, October 30, 1924, BANQ, Fonds de la Société des écrivains canadiens, MSS-61, box 22.
55 Julien Saint-Michel, "L'envoûtement de nos pèlerins humanitaires," *Le Monde ouvrier*, July 2, 1921; "Éperons nos mœurs," *Le Monde ouvrier*, May 11, 1929; "L'Attitude de l'Allemagne," *Le Monde ouvrier*, May 27, 1933; "La paix par la volonté du peuple," *Le Monde ouvrier*, March 3, 1934; "Il faut faire régner la paix," November 2, 1935; "Les deux fléaux de l'humanité," *Le Monde ouvrier*, March 28, 1936.
56 Julien Saint-Michel, "L'éducation qui compte," *Le Monde ouvrier*, September 7, 1935.
57 Julien Saint-Michel, "Les profiteurs de guerres," *Le Monde ouvrier*, October 6, 1934.
58 Ève Circé-Côté, "Les fugues du Cardinal Villeneuve," *L'Aurore*, June 7, 1940.
59 In her rush to leave Paris, Georgine Boucher-Normandin had abandoned her possessions, including her portrait and her sculpted bust, as well as suitcases of documents that would drift from one closet to another until her daughter, Lucienne, retrieved what was left after the Armistice. Lucienne nevertheless left behind two or three suitcases that may have contained the correspondence of the two friends. Boucher-Normandin to Thérive, Montreal, n.d., letter in the possession of Gustave Labbé. Interview with G. Labbé, January 2, 2006.
60 Ruth Roach Pierson, *"They're Still Women After All": The Second World War and Canadian Womanhood* (Toronto: McClelland and Stewart, 1986).
61 Lucienne Boucher, Georgine Boucher-Normandin's daughter, made the churlish remark that Circé-Côté was no longer "presentable," that her cat did its business behind her piano yet she did not smell it, and that she was "dressed in an absurd getup." Though this statement should be taken with a grain of salt, it was corroborated

by an equally unsparing journalist, Marcel Valois (Jean Dufresne), who also found that Circé-Côté was letting herself go. Valois, the literary and music critic for *La Patrie* and *La Presse*, had met her at the Société des auteurs canadiens; he described her as unkempt and dirty, in a dress fastened with safety pins: "Her soft, murmuring voice uttered terrible things, spiteful things rather than profanities." Gustave Labbé's interview with Marcel Valois, May 6, 1971, as related to me by G. Labbé, September 25, 2006. Gustave Labbé interviewed Lucienne Boucher on June 10, 1970.

62 See Brian Young, *Respectable Burial. Montreal's Mount Royal Cemetery* (Montreal/Kingston: McGill-Queen's University Press, 2003).

63 Fantasio, "Le pape reste figé dans sa neutralité. Il n'a aucune interdiction pour les Allemands qui font la réduction chimique de leurs cadavres. La crémation est défendue sous peine d'excommunication chez nous," *Le Pays*, April 28, 1917.

64 Colombine, "Automne! Hiver!" *L'Avenir*, November 11, 1900.

65 Julien Saint-Michel, "Pensons aux disparus," *Le Monde ouvrier*, November 15, 1919.

66 Fantasio, "Théâtre de rue," *Le Pays*, May 22, 1915.

67 Colombine, "Le mois des morts," *Le Pionnier*, November 10, 1901; Julien Saint-Michel, "Propos macabres," *Le Monde ouvrier*, March 10, 1934.

68 Fantasio, "Le pape reste figé dans sa neutralité," *Le Pays*, April 28, 1917.

69 Colombine, "Boucherville," *Les Débats*, July 28, 1901. Pierre-Aimable Boucher of Boucherville (1780–1857) was perhaps excommunicated for his sympathies towards the 1838 *Patriotes*. Website of the Quebec National Assembly, assnat.qc.ca.

70 Colombine, "Sainte-Luce," *Le Journal de Françoise*, September 7, 1907.

71 Jean Nay, "L'aumône d'une poignée de terre," *Le Pays*, May 14, 1910.

72 Colombine, "Autour de l'échafaud," *Les Débats*, March 1, 1903. See also Julien Saint-Michel, "Mise en scène moyenageuse," *Le Monde ouvrier*, November 12, 1910.

73 Julien Saint-Michel, "La sécurité dans le travail," *Le Monde ouvrier*, February 5, 1921; "La mortalité infantile," *Le Monde ouvrier*, February 16, 1929.

74 Circé-Côté to Dugas, July 1924, CARDL.

75 Fantasio, "Le pape reste figé dans sa neutralité," *Le Pays*, April 28, 1917.

76 *La Presse*, April 20, 1927; Young, *Respectable Burial*, 102.

77 Fantasio, "On enterre les morts de l'hiver," *Le Pays*, May 6, 1916.

78 Circé-Côté to Dugas, December 20, 1926, CARDL.

79 *La Patrie*, January 8, 1947.

80 Julien Saint-Michel, "Les bienfaits de l'économie," *Le Monde ouvrier*, July 8, 1916. She lived at 3512 Vendôme Avenue, between Sherbrooke and Côte-Saint-Antoine streets in the Notre-Dame-de-Grâce district.

81 *Winnipeg Free Press*, July 4, 1947. In 1949, she took over her mother's house and used it for two years as the head office of her company, Côté et compagnie. No trace of her has been found after 1951. *Lovell's Montreal Directory*, 1947–1952. Lucienne Boucher-Laliberté, when interviewed by Gustave Labbé on January 6, 1970, affirmed that Ève Côté had moved to Florida. Interview with G. Labbé, November 2, 2006.

82 Parmentier, "Formes, contenu et évolution du libéralisme d'Arthur Buies," 89.

83 Fantasio, "Sixième Épître à Théodore," *Le Pays*, March 27, 1920.

84 The Église unie Saint-Jean has existed as a French-speaking Protestant community

since 1841. It has been at its current address on Sainte-Catherine Street since the church was built in 1896. The Saint-Jean parish has been part of the United Church of Canada since its establishment in 1925. Information provided by Pastor Thierry Delay of the Saint-Jean parish.

Regarding Circé-Côté's possible conversion, Jean-Louis Lalonde, the historian of Francophone Québécois Protestantism, has said: "I believe that, having escaped the fetters of Catholicism, she did not want to officially affiliate herself with another denomination." March 24, 2010.

85 Gustave Labbé's interview with Lucienne Boucher, June 10, 1970, related to me by G. Labbé on September 25, 2006.
86 Mrs. Roger Maillet to Gustave Labbé, Autumn 1970. Interview with G. Labbé, January 2, 2006.
87 Julien Saint-Michel, "Les trépassés," *Le Monde ouvrier*, November 3, 1928. This passage was inspired by a visit to the military cemetery on Papineau Street.
88 Christophe Charle, *Naissance des intellectuels 1880–1900* (Paris: Minuit, 1990); Delphine Naudier, "La reconnaissance sociale et littéraire des femmes écrivains depuis les années 1950," in *Intellectuelles. Du genre en histoire des intellectuels*, ed. Nicole Racine and Michel Trebisch (Paris: IHTP/CNRS, Complexe, 2004), 126; see also Michel Winock, *Le Siècle des intellectuels* (Paris: Seuil, Collection Essais, 1997; rev. ed., Seuil, Collection Points, 1999).

Chapter 6

1 Altogether, Circé-Côté quoted Voltaire at least forty times and Rousseau twenty times, Adam Smith and Goldwin Smith each only once, and John Locke never. Pascal was cited six times, Plato five times, while Aristotle and Socrates were entitled to two quotes each.
2 Fantasio, "Rendez à César."
3 Paul G. Bédard, "Les vérités de l'abbé Levé," *Le Pays*, June 5, 1920.
4 Jean-Antoine-Nicolas de Caritat, Marquis de Condorcet, *Outlines of an Historical View of the Progress of the Human Mind* (Baltimore: J. Frank, 1802), 9.
5 On the Whig interpretation of history, see Herbert Butterfield, *The Whig Interpretation of History* (1931; repr., New York: W. W. Norton, 1965).
6 Circé-Côté, *Papineau*, 16, 133.
7 Circé-Côté, *Papineau*, 141.
8 Parmentier, "Formes, contenu et évolution du libéralisme d'Arthur Buies," 82.
9 Colombine, "Sainte-Luce," *Le Journal de Françoise*, September 7, 1907.
10 Fantasio, "Opinions. Marchons plutôt vers le Levant. Au lieu de n'acheter que des vieilleries que ne songe-t-on pas à moderniser l'embryon de bibliothèque que nous avons," *Le Pays*, April 12, 1913; "Autour d'un conventum," *Le Pays*, June 5, 1915.
11 Fantasio, "L'action des morts est dans le geste des vivants. Roger Valois, le fustigateur des gens du banc d'oeuvre, a réveillé l'idéal qui s'éteignait. La randonnée au milieu des dévots," *Le Pays*, May 5, 1917; "La genèse d'une bibliothèque," *Le Pays*, July 9, 1921.
12 Fantasio, "Le cas de Stephen Conroy," *Le Pays*, October 13, 1917; "Nous bougeons," *Le Pays*, September 3, 1921.

13 Fantasio, "La fin du monde," *Le Pays*, August 18, 1917.
14 Julien Saint-Michel, "Une fumisterie," *Le Monde ouvrier*, January 23, 1926.
15 *La Patrie*, January 3 and 8, 1901.
16 Julien Saint-Michel, "Profitons de l'avenir," *Le Monde ouvrier*, January 6, 1934. Éva Circé-Côté denounced the belief in luck, games of chance, and fortune-tellers.
17 Fantasio, "Honneur à la Province de Québec. L'assiduité aux écoles," *Le Pays*, January 13, 1912.
18 Julien Saint-Michel, "Les droits des mères," *Le Monde ouvrier*, February 14, 1925. Circé-Côté, however, did not call for the ties with the British Empire to be rejected.
19 Julien Saint-Michel, "C'est notre faute, notre propre faute," *Le Monde ouvrier*, June 2, 1917; "L'instruction obligatoire," *Le Monde ouvrier*, January 11, 1919; "L'obligation scolaire," *Le Monde ouvrier*, August 10, 1929.
20 Circé-Côté, *Papineau*, 262–63.
21 Julien Saint-Michel, "Y a-t-il une opinion publique?" *Le Monde ouvrier*, May 11, 1927.
22 Paul S. Bédard, "Nos arrières," *Le Pays*, February 20, 1920.
23 Julien Saint-Michel, "L'instruction obligatoire," *Le Monde ouvrier*, January 11, 1919.
24 See Quebec, *Debates of the Legislative Assembly*, 13th Legislature, 1st session, November 12, 26–28, 1912, 160–209.
25 Julien Saint-Michel, "La femme instruite est une valeur," *Le Monde ouvrier*, September 17, 1927.
26 Julien Saint-Michel, "Emparons-nous de l'industrie," *Le Monde ouvrier*, August 12, 1917.
27 Julien Saint-Michel, "Un cinéma en plein air," *Le Monde ouvrier*, October 26, 1929.
28 Fantasio, "Le sourire de Guillaume," *Le Pays*, August 15, 1914.
29 Arthur Maheu, "Les Idées de M. Maheu," *Le Pays*, September 26, 1916.
30 Fantasio, "La Belgique glorieuse," *Le Pays*, July 29, 1916.
31 She was responding to the Methodist minister, Harold Young. Fantasio, "Le clergé et la conscription. Les craintes du R. P. Villeneuve sont vaines," *Le Pays*, July 14, 1917.
32 Fantasio, "Le suprême attentat. On veut bâillonner la presse de ce pays. Pourquoi les journaux ne protestent pas," *Le Pays*, July 28, 1917.
33 France was "the herald of a new era born of chaos and blood." Fantasio, "L'aide à la France. Un appel à tous ceux qui s'honorent du titre de français. Le cadeau que la France fait en ce moment à l'univers," *Le Pays*, November 14, 1914; "Les faiseurs de chaos ont leur prédestination puisque la lumière surgit des ténèbres et que l'ordre naît de la confusion," "Les gloires anormales—Napoléon," *Le Pays*, July 23, 1921.
34 Fantasio, "L'envoûtement de nos pèlerins humanitaires," *Le Pays*, July 2, 1921.
35 Julien Saint-Michel, "Les affres du chômage," *Le Monde ouvrier*, July 7, 1928.
36 On the liberal order in Canada, see Ian McKay, "The Liberal Order Framework: A Prospectus for a Reconnaissance of Canadian History," *Canadian Historical Review* 81, no. 4 (December 2000): 617–45.
37 Julien Saint-Michel, "Un problème angoissant," *Le Monde ouvrier*, June 11, 1932; however, her optimism was toned down in "La société se transforme-t-elle?" *Le Monde ouvrier*, October 8, 1932.
38 Julien Saint-Michel, "La justice miséricordieuse," *Le Monde ouvrier*, May 19, 1934.
39 Circé-Côté, *Papineau*, 175.

40 See, among other writings, Fantasio, "Souffle de liberté," *Le Pays*, September 19, 1914.
41 Voltaire, *Traité sur la tolérance* (Paris, 1763), ed. Jan Van den Heuvel (Paris: Poche, 2003).
42 Circé-Côté, *Papineau*, 264.
43 Quanta Cura, Encyclical of Pope Pius IX, December 8, 1864, *Syllabus errorum. Condemning Current Errors* (Syllabus complectens præciuos nostræ ætatis errores . . .).
44 Georges Burdeau ascribes the opposition between freedom and the state, "this turnaround in liberal thought," to the second generation of French liberals and orthodox economists; he contends "that the antagonism between the individual and the State is a deviation from liberalism, not its essence." Georges Burdeau, *Le Libéralisme* (Paris: Seuil, 1979), 45–46.
45 Voltaire, *Traité sur la tolérance*, 102.
46 "The only purpose for which power can be rightfully exercised over any member of a civilized community, against his will, is to prevent harm to others." John Stuart Mill, *On Liberty* (1860; repr., London: Oxford University Press, 1966), 15.
47 Paul S. Bédard, "Simplement des libéraux," *Le Monde ouvrier*, December 10, 1910.
48 Julien Saint-Michel, "La prison comme refuge," *Le Monde ouvrier*, November 1, 1919.
49 Julien Saint-Michel, "L'instruction gratuite et obligatoire," *Le Monde ouvrier*, September 25, 1926; "L'obligation scolaire."
50 Julien Saint-Michel, "La race de l'avenir," *Le Monde ouvrier*, July 6, 1929.
51 Saint-Michel, "La race de l'avenir."
52 Angus McLaren, *Our Own Master Race. Eugenics in Canada, 1885–1945* (Toronto: McClelland & Stewart, 1990), 82.
53 Fantasio, "Échos de la Semaine sociale," *Le Pays*, July 3, 1920.
54 Jean Nay, "Rimouski," *Le Pays*, May 28, 1910.
55 Julien Saint-Michel, "Pourquoi déplacer le secours direct?" *Le Monde ouvrier*, February 15, 1936.
56 Saint-Michel, "Les affres du chômage."
57 Julien Saint-Michel, "Le salaire minimum des femmes," *Le Monde ouvrier*, May 22, 1926.
58 Julien Saint-Michel, "Le travail des enfants," *Le Monde ouvrier*, March 24, 1934.
59 Julien Saint-Michel, "Une loi de l'épargne," *Le Monde ouvrier*, August 5, 1916; "Les sans-travail," February 22, 1919. See also Saint-Michel, "Le salut est dans l'épargne," April 22, 1921; "Avarice n'est pas économie," March 5, 1927; "Qui paie ses dettes s'enrichit," June 18, 1927; "Epargnons pour les mauvais jours," July 21, 1928.
60 Fantasio, "Soyons les plus forts. C'est-à-dire soyons les plus riches. C'est la seule façon de sauver l'influence française en notre pays. Le vil métal," *Le Pays*, May 23, 1914.
61 Julien Saint-Michel, "L'enquête parlementaire," *Le Monde ouvrier*, November 14, 1934.
62 Julien Saint-Michel, "Le problème de l'heure," *Le Monde ouvrier*, August 27, 1921; "Migration et Atavisme," *Le Monde ouvrier*, October 31, 1925.

63 Julien Saint-Michel, "Le suffrage féminin," *Le Monde ouvrier*, October 24, 1925.
64 Julien Saint-Michel, "La Conférence impériale," *Le Monde ouvrier*, July 23, 1932.
65 Julien Saint-Michel, "La Guerre aux trusts," *Le Monde ouvrier*, February 14, 1920.
66 Fantasio, "Haines de races. Toujours l'antisémitisme. La victoire de M. Bercovitch. Les Juifs et la Commission scolaire protestante," *Le Pays*, May 27, 1916; Julien Saint-Michel, "Les pensions maternelles," *Le Monde ouvrier*, April 29, 1916; Saint-Michel, "Emparons-nous de l'industrie"; Fantasio, "La Lettre de Lord Landsdowne," *Le Pays*, December 8, 1917; Paul S. Bédard, "Fausse doctrine," *Le Pays*, July 31, 1920.
67 Colombine, "Réponse au personnage anonyme qui écrit dans *L'Étoile du Nord*," *L'Avenir du Nord*, September 10, 1903.
68 Julien Saint-Michel, "Les Jérémiades de l'*Action catholique*," *Le Monde ouvrier*, October 18, 1919.
69 Julien Saint-Michel, "C'est notre faute, notre propre faute"; "L'obligation scolaire"; "Sachons nous exprimer," July 24, 1920. This "we" includes belonging to the working class, as evidenced by this lament: "as if we were beasts of burden . . . our life is a perpetual Lent." Julien Saint-Michel "Propos de carême," *Le Monde ouvrier*, April 2, 1927.
70 Colombine, "Chronique," *Les Débats*, June 30, 1901.
71 Julien Saint-Michel, "Le contrôle des vivres," *Le Monde ouvrier*, September 15, 1915; "Ceux que l'on décore," July 21, 1917; "Des ouvriers mal payés. Quand nos gouvernants prendront-ils des mesures pour protéger les travailleurs?," August 18, 1917.
72 Julien Saint-Michel, "Travaillons à notre Avenir," *Le Monde ouvrier*, September 12, 1925.
73 Ian McKay, *Reasoning Otherwise: Leftists and the People's Enlightenment in Canada, 1890–1920* (Toronto: Between the Lines, 2008).
74 Fantasio, "La Révolution en Russie. La philosophie des événements. Leçon à ceux qui nous privent d'un ministère de l'instruction publique," *Le Pays*, March 24, 1917.
75 Julien Saint-Michel, "Vers l'évolution sociale," *Le Monde ouvrier*, May 12, 1917.
76 Julien Saint-Michel, "Le socialisme est-il anti-chrétien?" *Le Monde ouvrier*, December 6, 1919.
77 Fantasio, "Bolchevisme et soumission," *Le Pays*, October 9, 1920; "Parlons moins, agissons davantage," *Le Pays*, September 10, 1921. In 1929, she expressed her appreciation of the revolution for having eliminated the parasitic middlemen between producers and consumers. Julien Saint-Michel, "Une injustice sociale," *Le Monde ouvrier*, September 14, 1929.
78 Fantasio, "Le Vatican et la Démocratie," *Le Pays*, September 27, 1919; Saint-Michel, "Le socialisme est-il anti-chrétien?"
79 "Charity is illogical, because it does nothing but legitimize a false principle and sanction the reign of tyranny." Fantasio, "Chômage et charité," *Le Pays*, January 29, 1921.
80 Julien Saint-Michel, "Un juste milieu," *Le Monde ouvrier*, June 7, 1919.
81 Julien Saint-Michel, "La dégringolade est-elle commencée?" *Le Monde ouvrier*, October 25, 1919.
82 Julien Saint-Michel, "On ne connaît pas les gens par la verge," *Le Monde ouvrier*, September 20, 1919.
83 Éric Leroux, *Gustave Francq. Figure marquante du syndicalisme et précurseur de la FTQ* (Montreal: VLB, 2001), 199–204).

84 Julien Saint-Michel, "Le salaire minimum des femmes"; "Ne soyons pas 'grippe-sous,'" *Le Monde ouvrier*, September 10, 1917.
85 Julien Saint-Michel, "La peine de mort," *Le Monde ouvrier*, August 27, 1927. The Italian-American anarchists, Sacco and Vanzetti, were accused of murder and subsequently electrocuted on August 22, 1927.
86 W. L. Mackenzie King, *Industry and Humanity. A Study in the Principles Under-Lying Industrial Reconstruction* (Toronto: T. Allen / Boston: Houghton Mifflin, 1918); published in French as *La Question sociale et le Canada: industrie et humanité*, tr. Altiar, prefaced by Gabriel Hanotaux (Paris: Félix Alcan, 1925).
87 Julien Saint-Michel, "'*Industrie et humanité*.' Réflexions sur ce livre de l'hon. Mackenzie King," *Le Monde ouvrier*, January 28, 1928.
88 Thanks to Ian McKay for pointing out the connection with the concept of liberal revolution developed in Italy.
89 Julien Saint-Michel, "Le communisme russe," *Le Monde ouvrier*, May 3, 1930.
90 Julien Saint-Michel, "Le vrai remède au mal social," *Le Monde ouvrier*, September 26, 1931; "Tant va la cruche à l'eau," *Le Monde ouvrier*, October 10, 1931.
91 Julien Saint-Michel, "Le vote de la femme à l'avenir," *Le Monde ouvrier*, November 5, 1932.
92 Julien Saint-Michel, "Remettre l'ordre dans l'état social," *Le Monde ouvrier*, October 31, 1936.
93 Julien Saint-Michel, "La persécution n'a jamais tué l'idée," *Le Monde ouvrier*, October 30, 1937.
94 Saint-Michel, "La persécution n'a jamais tué l'idée."
95 Julien Saint-Michel, "L'aide aux sans-travail," *Le Monde ouvrier*, July 2, 1932.
96 Saint-Michel, "La Guerre aux trusts."
97 Julien Saint-Michel, "Devenons propriétaire," *Le Monde ouvrier*, June 22, 1929.
98 Fantasio, "Débauche du verbe. Le mal d'une race. Les assauts de M. Bourassa," *Le Pays*, August 5, 1911.
99 Fantasio, "Une loi uniforme s'impose," *Le Pays*, October 23, 1920.
100 Circé-Côté, *Papineau*, i-ii.
101 *Divini Illius Magistri*, Encyclical of Pope Pius XI On Christian Education, December 31, 1929. w2.vatican.va.
102 Godfroy Langlois, *Débats de l'Assemblée législative*, 11th Legislature, 4th Session, April 6, 1908, 310.
103 J. T. Finnie, *Débats de l'Assemblée législative*, 13th Legislature, 1st Session, 36; November 27, 1912, 180–84; November 28, 1912, 209.
104 Paul S. Bédard, "Varus, rends-moi mes légions!," *Le Pays*, November 22, 1913.
105 Lamonde, *Histoire sociale des idées*, vol. 2, 201. The successive Liberal governments between 1905 and 1920 increased subsidies to school commissions and established many new technical schools, teacher training schools, domestic science (home economics) schools, and kindergartens. In 1910, free education was introduced at the Montreal Catholic School Commission. Two years later, it was enacted throughout Quebec. The reformers associated with *Le Pays* won their first victory in 1914, when about twenty school commissions distributed free textbooks.

106 Fantasio, "Pygmalion fait défaut!" *Le Pays*, November 28, 1914.
107 Julien Saint-Michel, "Le devoir des parents envers leurs enfants," *Le Monde ouvrier*, April 28, 1918.
108 Gouin was already a Knight of the Legion of Honour of France (1907) when he was knighted by King Edward VII in 1908; he was made a Grand Officer of the Order of Leopold of Belgium in 1912, a Commander of the Order of Saint Michael and Saint George in 1913, and a Commander of the Order of the Crown of Belgium in 1920.
109 Julien Saint-Michel, "Titres et décorations," *Le Monde ouvrier*, June 20, 1931.
110 Julien Saint-Michel, "A propos de décorations," *Le Monde ouvrier*, October 13, 1934.
111 Julien Saint-Michel, "Le renversement des valeurs," *Le Monde ouvrier*, November 19, 1921.
112 Fantasio, "Le renversement des valeurs. Alliance fatale de la politique et de l'autel," *Le Pays*, November 26, 1921.
113 Paul Dutil, "The Politics of Progressivism in Quebec: The Gouin 'Coup' Revisited," *Canadian Historical Review* 69, no. 4 (December, 1988), 452–56.
114 Bouchard, *Mémoires*, 250.
115 Réal Bélanger, *Wilfrid Laurier. Quand la politique devient passion* (Quebec/Montreal: Presses de l'Université Laval/Entreprises Radio-Canada, 1986); "Le libéralisme de Wilfrid Laurier: évolution et contenu (1841–1919)," in Lamonde, *Combats libéraux*, 49–52, 55–58.
116 Fantasio, "Libéralisme épuré," *Le Pays*, October 11, 1913.
117 Fantasio, "Le suprême attentat. On veut bâillonner la presse de ce pays. Pourquoi les journaux ne protestent pas," *Le Pays*, July 28, 1917.
118 Fantasio, "Elle portait le bonnet phrygien," *Le Pays*, November 18, 1911.
119 In 1916, Laurier put forward a new kind of liberalism that was prepared to accept government involvement in social affairs. Bélanger, *Wilfrid Laurier*, 69.
120 Fantasio, "Il faut ramasser le flambeau," *Le Pays*, October 29, 1921.
121 Fantasio, "Personnalité qui domine," *Le Pays*, December 18, 1920.
122 Fantasio, "Personnalité qui domine."
123 The phrase "stayed too old in a world too young" plays on a line from a poem by Alfred de Musset: "Je suis venu trop tard dans un monde trop vieux." Julien Saint-Michel, "Le nouveau régime," *Le Monde ouvrier*, August 22, 1936.
124 Circé-Côté, *Papineau*, 258–59.
125 Roy, "Le journal *L'Autorité*," 13.

Chapter 7

1 Herbert Spencer, *The Study of Sociology* (New York: D. Appleton & Co., 1896), 284. Consulted online at archive.org.
2 Fantasio, "Sixième et dernière épître à Théodore," *Le Pays*, March 27, 1920.
3 I learned this from the historian Micheline Dumont, who graciously offered me the copy of *Bleu, Blanc, Rouge* that her grandmother, Blanche Castonguay, had received as a prize in 1904.

4   Musette, "Chronique," *Les Débats*, February 10, 1901.
5   Musette, "Mysticisme," *Les Débats*, February 17, 1901.
6   Musette, "Mysticisme."
7   Musette, "Chroniquette," *Les Débats*, April 7, 1901; "Chronique," *Les Débats*, May 5, 1901.
8   Colombine, "Le petit St. Jean-Baptiste," *L'Avenir du Nord*, July 16, 1903.
9   Musette, "Chroniquette."
10 Fantasio, "La mort du Christ. Aujourd'hui ceux qui se disent ses disciples ne ménagent guère le vent et la tempête à la pauvre agnette tondue," *Le Pays*, April 7, 1917.
11 Colombine, "Le mois des morts," *Le Pionnier*, November 10, 1901.
12 Musette, "Chronique," *Les Débats*, March 17, 1901.
13 Colombine, "Québec," *Le Monde illustré* 218, November 30, 1901, 491.
14 Colombine, "Bas les armes!" *Les Débats*, July 12, 1903.
15 Éva Circé-Côté to Marcel Dugas, July 1924, CARDL.
16 Colombine, "Royaume de Dieu," *L'Avenir du Nord*, June 7, 1906.
17 Fantasio, "Pygmalion fait défaut!," *Le Pays*, February 28, 1914.
18 Fantasio, "Autour d'une conférence de Mgr Lenfant. La véritable physionomie d'Ernest Renan. La critique française et catholique ne le voit pas comme l'évêque de Digne," *Le Pays*, April 15, 1915.
19 Arthur Maheu, "Les Idées de M. Maheu," *Le Pays*, April 21, 1917.
20 Fantasio, "Gott mit uns! Le Kaiser a-t-il voulu rendre Dieu solidaire de sespropres crimes?" *Le Pays*, December 12, 1914.
21 Fantasio, "Charles Péguy et la guerre. A propos de militarism," *Le Pays*, March 11, 1916.
22 Fantasio, "Joffre, l'homme a fait le miracle. Le passage rapide du héros de la Marne laissera un souvenir ineffaçable. On ne diminuera pas sa gloire en en attribuant une partie à la divinité," *Le Pays*, May 19, 1917.
23 Fantasio, "Gott mit uns!"-
24 Fantasio, "La mort du Christ."
25 Fantasio, "Gott mit uns!"
26 Fantasio, "La Mort du Christ."
27 Fantasio, "Les convertis de la dernière heure," *Le Pays*, November 24, 1917.
28 Circé-Côté to Dugas, December 26, 1921, CARDL.
29 Fantasio, "Sixième et dernière Épître à Théodore."
30 Circé-Côté to Dugas, December 26, 1921, CARDL.
31 Circé-Côté to Dugas, July 14, 1924, CARDL.
32 Circé-Côté to Dugas, September 17, 1924, CARDL.
33 Circé-Côté to Dugas, July 1924, CARDL.
34 Fantasio, "Quatrième Épître à Théodore," *Le Pays*, March 13, 1920.
35 Fantasio, "Autour d'une conférence de Mgr Lenfant."
36 Julien Saint-Michel, "La foi aveugle," *Le Monde ouvrier*, January 20, 1934.
37 See Chapter 4.

38 Circé-Côté to Dugas, July 1924, CARDL.
39 Circé-Côté to Dugas, July 1924, CARDL.
40 Circé-Côté to Dugas, July 1924, CARDL.
41 Julien Saint-Michel, "Variations sur le Thème pascal," *Le Monde ouvrier*, April 11, 1925.
42 Circé-Côté to Dugas, July 1924, CARDL.
43 Circé-Côté to Dugas, July 1924, CARDL.
44 Fantasio, "Incohérences sociales," *Le Pays*, July 17, 1920.
45 Fantasio, "Les influences françaises au Canada," *Le Pays*, October 30, 1920.
46 Fantasio, "L'autre son de la cloche," *Le Pays*, January 24, 1920.
47 Fantasio, "La Révolution en Russie. La philosophie des événements. Leçon à ceux qui nous privent d'un ministère de l'instruction publique. Leçon à l'abbé Damour," *Le Pays*, March 24, 1917.
48 Fantasio, "Les mariages annulés," *Le Pays*, July 31, 1920.
49 Julien Saint-Michel, "Herriot et les Congrégations," *Le Monde ouvrier*, October 18, 1924.
50 Fantasio, "Venant après le volontariat la conscription est injuste. Le britishisme n'est pas une affaire de religion, n'en déplaise à l'abbé D'Amours. On tient à sa peaavant sa chemise," *Le Pays*, March 17, 1917.
51 Fantasio, "L'A.C.J.C. et la politique. Un de ses membres déclare que, lorsque le curé ne peut pas dire à ses paroissiens comment voter, il se sert de cette association. Etrange doctrine qui laisserait soupçonner une infinité d'intrigues," *Le Pays*, April 1, 1916; Fantasio, "Le Clergé et la politique. Après avoir déchaîné une campagne nationaliste dans notre province 'L'Action sociale' déclare maintenant que le principe des nationalités est révolutionnaire. Et elle voudrait 'catholiciser' l'impérialisme," *Le Pays*, September 25, 1915; Fantasio, "Bas les pattes César!!" *Le Pays*, November 20, 1920.
52 Fantasio, "Riel, De Wet, Bourassa et Taché. Hautes trahisons et punitions. L'intervention de Mgr Taché dans l'affaire Riel. Les deux poids et deux mesures du chef nationaliste," *Le Pays*, July 3, 1915.
53 Fantasio, "Le péril de l'honnêteté. Les honnêtes gens sont devenus des gens dangereux dans notre province. Saint-Ambroise collaborateur du 'Pays,'" *Le Pays*, October 30, 1915; "Une loi uniforme s'impose," *Le Pays*, October 23, 1920, in which Circé-Côté alludes to "The Theological Bias," the title of Chapter 12 of *The Study of Sociology* by Spencer, published in 1873.
54 L'Action catholique de la jeunesse canadienne-française (ACJC), founded in 1904 by Father Lionel Groulx and Father Émile Chartier, defined itself as a community service organization and championed the values of the Church and of Catholic, French-speaking, Quebec. The ACJC fought against both liberalism and socialism. See Jean-Philippe Warren, "La découverte de la 'question sociale': Sociologie et mouvements de jeunesse canadiens-français," *Revue d'histoire de l'Amérique française* 4, no. 4 (Spring 2002): 545–57. The periodical *L'Action sociale*, founded by Msgr Bégin of Quebec in 1907, identified itself as the organ of the archdiocese.
55 "Ignorance persistante," *L'Action catholique*, September 15, 1915; Fantasio, "Le Clergé et la politique."

56 Fantasio, "Propos de la St-Jean-Baptiste," *Le Pays*, June 26, 1915.
57 Fantasio, "Le Clergé et la politique"; "Notre loyauté mise en doute. Les Canadiens-français et l'Angleterre. L'incident Papineau-Bourassa. La loyauté du clergé. Que le 'Spectator' calme ses appréhensions," *Le Pays*, September 2, 1916.
58 See Chapter 3 on the war and Chapter 8 on nationalism.
59 Fantasio, "Le Clergé et la politique."
60 Robert Craig Brown, *Robert Laird Borden: A Biography*, vol. 2 (Toronto: Macmillan, 1980), 64; J. L. Granatstein and J. M. Hitsman, *Broken Promises: A History of Conscription in Canada* (Toronto: Oxford University Press, 1977), 45.
61 Brown, *Borden*, 91; Robert Craig Brown and Ramsay Cook, *Canada 1896–1921* (Toronto: University of Toronto Press, 1974), 270.
62 Fantasio, "La thèse impérialiste de l'abbé Damour," *Le Pays*, March 31, 1917; Fantasio, "Et autour d'un chapeau rouge qui persiste à se dérober. Autour d'un article de la Gazette," *Le Pays*, August 4, 1917.
63 Fantasio, "Toujours comme des petits garçons. C'est ainsi que nous traitent nos évêques en venant benoietement nous montrer la route à suivre. Le cardinal Bégin, Mgr Bruchési et la question du Service," *Le Pays*, January 13, 1917.
64 Fantasio, "Heures d'anxiété," *Le Pays*, May 8, 1915; Fantasio, "M. Bourassa, le pape et la guerre. Contre les évêques peut-être, mais avec le Pape. L'histoire de la France à laquelle croit le chef nationaliste," *Le Pays*, September 30, 1916.
65 Fantasio, "La maladie à la mode. Une violente attaque de lâcheté. 'Ils ne mouraient pas tous, mais tous étaient frappés,'" *Le Pays*, November 18, 1916.
66 Fantasio, "Le pacifisme de M. Bourassa. La guerre n'est plus sainte comme autrefois? Le retour aux idées chrétiennes entraîne-t-il la suppression de la guerre? Les véritables pères du pacifisme. Pourquoi bat-on avec des fleurs cet orgueilleux pécheur?" *Le Pays*, August 21, 1915.
67 Fantasio, "Le Vatican et la paix," *Le Pays*, August 25, 1916.
68 Fantasio, "La querelle française en Ontario et l'usage de la chaire à ce sujet par les prêtres," *Le Pays*, January 15, 1916; Fantasio, "Le silence de M. Bourassa. Le chef nationaliste n'a donc rien à dire en marge de la lettre du Pape. Après avoir été durant des années, le plus vaillant défenseur des droits de la langue française, un mot du Pape suffit-il pour le faire rentrer sous terre?" *Le Pays*, November 25, 1916.
69 Fantasio, "La Provenance de nos maux," *Le Pays*, December 1, 1917.
70 Paul S. Bédard, "Théâtre de la vie," *Le Pays*, June 19, 1920.
71 The subtitles of these columns are all equally eloquent: Fantasio, "Et autour d'un chapeau rouge qui persiste à se dérober. Autour d'un article de la 'Gazette,'" *Le Pays*, August 4, 1917; Fantasio, "Nouvelle frasque de Mgr Fallon. Insultes aux Canadiens-Français," *Le Pays*, December 22, 1917; Paul S. Bédard, "Le papillon aux ailes brûlées. À la recherche de la gloire," *Le Pays*, March 24, 1917; Fantasio, "Vendus et trahis par les nôtres. Dans leur course au chapeau, nos évêques oublient la couronne d'épines et ressemblent à des écuyers de cirque. Une casuistique échauffourée sur des pointes de baïonnettes," *Le Pays*, June 2, 1917.
72 Fantasio, "Le péril de l'honnêteté. Les honnêtes gens sont devenus des gens dangereux dans notre province," *Le Pays*, October 30, 1915.
73 Fantasio, "Et autour d'un chapeau rouge."

74 Fantasio, "La sainte ritournelle. (Dieu bénit la France). M. Bourassa s'en sert sur mandat et presque sans rire," *Le Pays*, July 7, 1917; Fantasio, "Juste répartition de l'impôt," *Le Pays*, August 6, 1921; Fantasio, "Prévoir, c'est régner," *Le Pays*, October 8, 1921.

75 Julien Saint-Michel, "Un Coup de balai," *Le Monde ouvrier*, April 14, 1917.

76 Jean Nay, "Rimouski," *Le Pays*, May 28, 1910; Julien Saint-Michel, "A propos d'un 'léger déficit,'" *Le Monde ouvrier*, May 24, 1924; Julien Saint-Michel, "Pour sauver Concordia," *Le Monde ouvrier*, January 12, 1935.

77 Fantasio, "Et autour d'un chapeau rouge."

78 Fantasio, "Quatrième Épître à Théodore."

79 Fantasio, "La Provenance de nos maux."

80 Fantasio, "Autour d'une conférence de Mgr Lenfant."

81 Arthur Maheu, "Les idées de M. Maheu," *Le Pays*, January 22, 1916.

82 Julien Saint-Michel, "Autour d'une grève," *Le Monde ouvrier*, January 29, 1938. This commentary was prompted by the activism of the striking students of the École.

83 Robert de Roquebrune, *Testament de mon enfance* (Montreal: Fides, 1958), 87.

84 Abbot Louis Bethléem, *Romans à lire, Romans à proscrire, essai de classification au point de vue moral des principaux romans et romanciers depuis l'an 1500* (Paris: n.p. 1905). This book, published by the Éditions de la revue des lectures, went through twelve editions between 1908 and 1932, reaching a total print run of 140,000 copies.

85 Circé-Côté, *Papineau*, 133, 139–52.

86 Heaps, "La Ligue de l'enseignement (1902–1904)," 339–73.

87 Annette Hayward, "Modernité et liberalisme," in Lamonde, *Combats libéraux*, 179.

88 Fantasio, "Ce que sera notre bibliothèque. Un mot de réponse de Mgr Gauthier qui voudrait la limiter aux livres techniques. La bibliothèque municipale, et neutre forcément, doit avoir autant de droits qu'une bibliothèque religieuse comme Saint-Sulpice," *Le Pays*, November 27, 1915.

89 Fantasio, "Le droit du plus fort," *Le Pays*, October 11, 1919; Fantasio, "A Bas l'absolutisme," *Le Pays*, February 14, 1920.

90 Fantasio, "Le droit du plus fort."

91 Fantasio, "L'A.C.J.C. et la politique."

92 Julien Saint-Michel, "Les Jérémiades de l'*Action catholique*," *Le Monde ouvrier*, October 19, 1919.

93 Fantasio, "Les retraites fermées," *Le Pays*, October 23, 1915.

94 Fantasio, "Un fusil que l'on change d'épaule," *Le Pays*, November 12, 1921.

95 Fantasio, "Les femmes doivent-elles voter? C'est contre l'ordre établi par la Providence, décrète l'*Action catholique*. La femme et ses égaux politiques. Une réforme qui s'en vient," *Le Pays*, November 20, 1915; Susan Mann Trofimenkoff, "Henri Bourassa et la question des femmes," in *Travailleuses et féministes. Les femmes dans la société québécoise*, ed. Marie Lavigne and Yolande Pinard (Montreal: Boréal, 1983), 293–306.

96 In July 1919, exactly two months after the canonization of Jeanne D'Arc, Pope Benedict XV, during an audience with British suffragists of the League of Catholic Women, openly declared himself in favour of female suffrage: "Yes, we approve! We would like to see female voters everywhere." S. Hause and A. R. Kenney, *Women's Suffrage and*

Social Politics in the French Third Republic (Princeton: Princeton University Press, 1984), 232.
97 Paul S. Bédard, "Fausse doctrine," *Le Pays*, July 31, 1920.
98 Luigi Trifiro, "Une intervention à Rome dans la lutte pour le suffrage féminin," *Revue d'histoire de l'Amérique française* 32, no. 1 (June 1978), 10, 14, and 15. On women's suffrage, see Chapter 9.
99 This was a Superior Court ruling by Justice Allard. The marriage was dissolved because the man's first wife was the first cousin of his second wife. Fantasio, "Petite cause, grands effets. Un cas civil intéressant," *Le Pays*, December 29, 1917; *La Presse*, December 20, 1917.
100 Musette, "Respect de la femme," *Les Débats*, February 3, 1901. A Catholic marriage could also be annulled in Rome on various grounds such as mental incapacity, abduction, antecedent and perpetual impotence, etc. This procedure was costly and reserved to very few.
101 Fantasio, "La fin d'une cause célèbre," *Le Pays*, February 19, 1921; Fantasio, "Les mariages annulés," *Le Pays*, July 31, 1920; Fantasio, "Le mensonge matrimonial," *Le Pays*, March 19, 1921.
102 *La Patrie*, November 15, 1917, 3. De Martigny was in a coma for several days before his brother summoned Msgr Bruchési. See Roger Le Moine, "Martigny (Le Moyne de Martigny), Adelstan de," *Dictionary of Canadian Biography*, vol. 14 (Toronto/Quebec: University of Toronto Press/Presses de l'Université Laval, 2000).
103 Fantasio, "Les convertis de la dernière heure," *Le Pays*, November 24, 1917
104 Fantasio, "La Provenance de nos maux."
105 Fantasio, "Marguerite Bourgeois," *Le Pays*, May 8, 1920.
106 Circe-Côté to Dugas, July 1924, CARDL.
107 Boucher-Normandin to Dugas, August 15, 1933, Collection Gustave Labbé. Boucher-Normandin was very close to Dugas and sent him "an elder sister's fraternal kisses."
108 Circé-Côté to Dugas, July 1924, CARDL.
109 Colombine, "Bas les armes!" *Les Débats*, July 12, 1903; "La version de Colombine."
110 Fantasio, "La Provenance de nos maux."
111 Arthur Curotte supported women's suffrage; Philippe Perrier was a humanist priest; Louis-Adélard Desrosiers was an educator and historian; Joseph Nazaire Dubois, as inspector of Catholic schools in Montreal, recommended compulsory education in his 1914 report; he later became the principal of the École normale and was a supporter of the Municipal Library and of standard textbooks; Étienne Blanchard was a lexicographer who defended the French language.
112 Colombine, "Boucherville."
113 Colombine, "Lumen in Coelo," *L'Avenir du Nord*, 1903.
114 Statement of Thierry Delay and Jean-Louis Lalonde, March 2010.
115 Circé-Côté, *Papineau*, 177.
116 Fantasio, "Méditation sur Jeanne Mance," *Le Pays*, May 22, 1920.
117 Fantasio, "Cinquième centenaire de Luther," *Le Pays*, April 30, 1921.
118 Circé-Côté, *Papineau*, 63.

119 Fantasio, "Incohérences sociales"; Fantasio, "Les mariages annulés"; Fantasio, "La fin d'une cause célèbre"; Julien Saint-Michel, "Autres temps, autres mœurs," *Le Monde ouvrier*, November 26, 1932. During the Great Depression, the United Church campaigned for unemployment insurance, old age pensions, and the improvement of labour laws, and it provided assistance to the unemployed, soup kitchens, and employment offices. Jean-Louis Lalonde, *Des loups dans la bergerie. Les Protestants de langue française au Québec* (Montreal: Fides, 2002), 243.

120 Alphonse Primeau-Robert, *La Place des protestants dans la nationalité canadienne-française: conférence donnée à l'église du Rédempteur le 23 décembre 1923* (Montreal: 1924), 4.

121 Saint-Michel, "Les Jérémiades de *l'Action catholique*."

122 Fantasio, "La danse est-elle immorale?" *Le Pays*, November 27, 1920.

123 Fantasio, "Intervention intempestive," *Le Pays*, April 3, 1920.

124 Julien Saint-Michel, "Réformons au lieu de détruire," *Le Monde ouvrier*, July 30, 1927.

125 Fantasio, "La Provenance de nos maux."

126 Circé-Côté to Dugas, September 17, 1924, CARDL.

127 Circé-Côté to Dugas, September 17, 1924, CARDL.

128 Circé-Côté to Dugas, September 17, 1924, CARDL.

129 Bédard, "Théâtre de la vie."

130 Bédard, "Théâtre de la vie."

131 Ève Circé-Côté, "Préface," Primeau-Robert, *La Place des protestants*, 6.

132 Circé-Côté to Dugas, August 20, 1920, CARDL.

133 Colombine, "Chronique," *L'Avenir*, December 23, 1900; *Bleu, Blanc, Rouge*, 279.

Chapter 8

1 Julie Boivin, "Le monument à Octave Crémazie," in *Louis-Philippe Hébert 1850–1917*, ed. Daniel Drouin (Quebec: Musée du Québec, 2001), 210–13. Louis Fréchette organized a public subscription for the erection of a monument to the author of the "Drapeau de Carillon." In 1902, Anne-Marie Gleason-Huguenin (Madeleine) devoted several of her columns to the monument and donated the royalties from her play, *L'adieu au poète*, to it. The monument was unveiled in Saint-Louis Square on June 24, 1906.

2 *Bulletin de la Caisse d'économie* 1, no. 1 (June 1904), 6–9; 3 (August 1904), 4–5. This monthly was the official organ of the Caisse d'économie (credit union) founded in 1899 by the Association Saint-Jean-Baptiste in order "to inculcate in our compatriots the habits of thrift, and to encourage them to save for themselves and their children." Its main office was located at the Monument-National. *La Patrie*, July 8, 1904.

3 Circé-Côté, *Papineau*, 3.

4 "[. . .] the large rock that impedes their development. The question of race and religion." Julien Saint-Michel, "L'esprit des bêtes," *Le Monde ouvrier*, November 8, 1918. The historian Fernand Ouellet highlighted the contrast between Papineau's social conservatism and his religious liberalism: "a deist, he nevertheless remained a prisoner of that social institution, the Church." See Fernand Ouellet, "Papineau, Louis-Joseph," in *Dictionary of Canadian Biography*, vol. 10, ed. Marc La Terreur (Quebec: Presses de l'Université Laval, 1972), 625.

5 Julien Saint-Michel, "Rendons hommage à nos patriotes," *Le Monde ouvrier*, August 28, 1937.
6 Julien Saint-Michel, "A la mémoire de Papineau," *Le Monde ouvrier*, April 19, 1930.
7 Ève Circé-Côté, "Les fugues du Cardinal Villeneuve," *L'Aurore*, June 7, 1940.
8 Fantasio, "La conférence de l'abbé Groulx. Des patriotes de 37 à Dollard et ses compagnons. De Mgr Lartigue à Pierre Cauchon," *Le Pays*, Deecember 23, 1916.
9 Saint-Michel, "Rendons hommage à nos patriotes"; *Papineau*, 35.
10 Circé-Côté, *Papineau*, 67; Saint-Michel, "Emparons-nous de l'industrie"; Fantasio, "La Provenance de nos maux"; Saint-Michel, "Migration et atavisme."
11 Fantasio, "La fin du monde," *Le Pays*, August 18, 1917; Fantasio, "Les bienfaits de la petite école," *Le Pays*, June 5, 1920; Circé-Côté, *Papineau*, 27.
12 Fantasio, "Tableau vivant: Dollard mort!," *Le Pays*, July 8, 1913.
13 Fantasio, "Mal avoué est à moitié guéri! Laissons de côté les vieux clichés. Notre dessein providentiel! La pluie de roses d'un ancien tyran," *Le Pays*, November 2, 1912.
14 Langlois was responding to the MLA from Kamouraska, who had said: "It is our strict duty to preserve our beautiful province's superiority, of which we are justly proud." Godfroy Langlois, *Les débats de l'Assemblée législative*, 13th Legislature, 1st session, March 21, 1910, 60.
15 Fantasio, "Le gavage," *Le Pays*, February 17, 1912; Arthur Maheu, "Les idées de M. Maheu. Ce qu'il dit de la mortalité infantile. Sa théorie sur les mères," *Le Pays*, September 7, 1912.
16 Fantasio, "La Pluie," *Le Pays*, October 12, 1912.
17 Fantasio, "Une Leçon d'énergie," *Le Pays*, March 2, 1912.
18 Fantasio, "Pudibonderic," *Le Pays*, December 20, 1913. See also Colombine, "À bon entendeur, salut!" *L'Avenir du Nord*, February 23, 1905.
19 Jean Nay, "Le patriotisme explosif," *Le Pays*, July 2, 1910.
20 Great Britain declared war on Germany the day after Germany's declaration of war against France. Fantasio, "Rendez à César . . . L'action de l'Angleterre dans les circonstances—La haute capacité de ses hommes d'état. L'Anglais est un homme libre. A qui faut-il s'en prendre si nous avons été écrasés?" *Le Pays*, October 24, 1914.
21 Fantasio, "Rendez à César."
22 Julien Saint-Michel, "Qui donne aux pauvres," *Le Monde ouvrier*, June 27, 1925; "Catholiques vs protestants," *Le Monde ouvrier*, April 24, 1926.
23 Fantasio, "L'Université McGill," *Le Pays*, July 12, 1913.
24 Fantasio, "La liberté de parole. Autour de l'incident Bourassa à Ottawa," *Le Pays*, November 28, 1914.
25 Fantasio, "Rendez à César."
26 Fantasio, "Notre loyauté mise en doute. Les Canadiens-français et l'Angleterre. L'incident Papineau-Bourassa. La loyauté du clergé. Que le "Spectator" calme ses appréhensions," *Le Pays*, September 2, 1916.
27 Circé-Côté felt that Lord Lansdowne was speaking on behalf of her country when in November 1917 he publicly called for a revision of the objectives of the war with a view to expediting a negotiated peace. Fantasio, "La Lettre de Lord Lansdowne," *Le Pays*, December 8, 1917.

28 Julien Saint-Michel, "Un grand homme d'État," *Le Monde ouvrier*, August 11, 1928.
29 Julien Saint-Michel, "Variations sur le Thème pascal," *Le Monde ouvrier*, April 11, 1925.
30 Fantasio, "Tableau vivant: Dollard mort!"; Fantasio, "La révolution irlandaise. La sévérité du gouvernement anglais Les conquêtes du libéralisme mise [sic] en danger par le césarisme. Le sentiment religieux des Irlandais. Catholiques et orangistes irrémédiablement divisés," *Le Pays*, May 13, 1916; Fantasio, "Simples réflexions. En marge de l'exécution de Sir Roger Casement," *Le Pays*, August 12, 1916; Arthur Maheu, "Les Idées de M. Maheu," *Le Pays*, February 17, 1917; Julien Saint-Michel, "Ceux que l'on décore," *Le Monde ouvrier*, July 21, 1917.
31 Fantasio, "Rendez à César."
32 Jean Nay, "Ils présentent l'autre joue," *Le Pays*, February 12, 1910; Paul S. Bédard, "Aurons-nous un cardinal? Le Canada à Rome," *Le Pays*, November 18, 1911; Fantasio, "La maladie à la mode. Une violente attaque de lâcheté," *Le Pays*, November 18, 1916; Julien Saint-Michel, "A propos de bilinguisme," *Le Monde ouvrier*, October 13, 1917; Fantasio, "L'affaire de Ford City. Celui qui en est responsable," *Le Pays*, September 15, 1917; Paul S. Bédard, "Fallon le menteur," *Le Pays*, July 3, 1920; Fantasio, "Rome et les Y.M.C.A.," *Le Pays*, January 1, 1921.
33 Julien Saint-Michel, "Le sentiment national," *Le Pays*, November 25, 1916.
34 Ève Circé-Côté, "La Vérité, pupille du Cardinal et du Clergé canadien," *L'Aurore*, April 1, 1938.
35 Ève Circé-Côté, "Mariages annulés," *L'Aurore*, December 10, 1937. See also "Le Mouvement séparatiste," October 1, 1937.
36 Fantasio, "La scène et l'écran. Le film parlant français," *La Revue moderne* 16, July 9, 1935, 6.
37 Fantasio, "La scène et l'écran. La nouvelle saison," *La Revue moderne* 16, October 16, 1935.
38 Julien Saint-Michel, "Une école nationale vraiment française," *Le Monde ouvrier*, November 3, 1934.
39 Karim Larose, "'Les fous d'espoir.' Autour du Deuxième Congrès de la langue française au Canada," in *1937: un tournant culturel*, ed. Yvan Lamonde and Denis Saint-Jacques, (Québec: Presses de l'Université Laval, 2009), 20–25. Circé-Côté had already taken the literary critic Camille Roy to task for his interpretation of the roles played by Fleury Mesplet and Papineau. Circé-Côté, *Papineau*, 96–98.
40 Ève Circé-Côté, "Rayonnement de la pourpre cardinalice," *L'Aurore*, May 20, 1938.
41 Julien Saint-Michel, "La langue française," *Le Monde ouvrier*, July 17, 1937.
42 Julien Saint-Michel, "Les Unions internationales," *Le Monde ouvrier*, May 19, 1919.
43 Julien Saint-Michel, "Parons la crise économique," *Le Monde ouvrier*, March 8, 1919.
44 Fantasio, "La révolution irlandaise. La sévérité du gouvernement anglais"; Circé-Côté, *Papineau*, 41.
45 Fantasio, "Pour fonder un parti catholique on commence par séparer le bas clergé du nationalisme," *Le Pays*, September 23, 1916.
46 Fantasio, "Honneur à la Province de Québec. L'assiduité aux écoles," *Le Pays*, January 13, 1912.
47 *Le Devoir*, January 10, 1910.

48 In a series of articles written upon his return from Europe at the end of August 1914, Bourassa came out in support of conscription and declared that he saw the war as a punishment. Robert Rumilly, *Henri Bourassa. La vie publique d'un grand Canadien* (Montreal: Chanteclerc, 1953), 505.

49 However, Bourassa's position on this subject evolved. See Pierre Anctil, *Le Devoir, les Juifs et l'immigration* (Quebec: IQRC, 1988), 50–61.

50 Julien Saint-Michel, "Profiteurs de guerre," *Le Monde ouvrier*, March 13, 1920.

51 Fantasio, "L'avenir est à Dieu," *Le Pays*, January 17, 1914. Asselin made no secret of his contempt for the suffragettes, which he expressed in a letter to a Parisian friend: "Miss St-Jean does not want to see me anymore since I wrote that we should scold and spank our suffragettes." Olivar Asselin, Montreal, to Marcel de Verneuil, Paris, April 23, 1922, AVM, BM55, S2, D40.

52 Fantasio, "Le sous de la pensée française," *Le Pays*, June 21, 1913; Madeleine, "La Pensée Française," *La Patrie*, June 21, 1913.

53 Fantasio, "Le sous de la pensée française." On the debate about *la Saint-Jean* (Feast Day of St. John), see Pelletier-Baillargeon, *Olivar Asselin et son temps*, 579–607. Several parishes nevertheless held religious processions.

54 Fantasio, "Plutôt la tolérance. Les jeunes de l'A.C.J.C. en ont plus besoin que de l'apologétique. La guerre religieuse et ses réaction," *Le Pays*, December 4, 1915; Arthur Maheu, "Les idées de M. Maheu," *Le Pays*, December 4, 1915; Fantasio, "L'A.C.J.C. et la politique. Un de ses membres déclare que, lorsque le curé ne peut pas dire à ses paroissiens comment voter, il se sert de cette association. Etrange doctrine qui laisserait soupçonner une infinité d'intrigues," *Le Pays*, April 1, 1916.

55 This is both an allusion to Chantecler, the rooster in the tale by Renart, and a sophisticated pun: *chante* + *clercs* = singers of the clerics. Chantecler, like cocorico today, means nationalist (i.e., the French coq gaulois).

56 "La Société Saint-Jean-Baptiste, ce qu'elle fait, ce qu'elle ne fait pas," *Le Pays*, October 6, 1917.

57 Fantasio, "La conférence de l'abbé Groulx. Des patriotes de 37 à Dollard et ses compagnons. De Mgr Lartigue à Pierre Cauchon," *Le Pays*, December 23, 1916.

58 Julien Saint-Michel, "La langue française," *Le Monde ouvrier*, July 17, 1937.

59 Ève Circé-Côté, "Le Mouvement séparatiste," *L'Aurore*, October 1, 1937; "M. H. Bourassa veut-il nous faire reculer au moyen-âge?" *L'Autorité*, December 18, 1937; "Les droits de l'homme," *L'Aurore*, February 7, 1941.

60 Julien Saint-Michel, "Véritable snobisme," *Le Monde ouvrier*, June 27, 1931.

61 Canada, *Annuaire du Canada 1936* (Ottawa: Imprimeur du Roi, 1936), 1086; *Annuaire du Canada 1956* (Ottawa: Imprimeur de la Reine, 1937), 174.

62 That is to say the Abenaki, Atikamekw, Cree, Wendat, Maliseet, Mi'kmaq, Mohawk, and Innu (Montagnais-Naskapi).

63 Colombine, "Caughnawaga," *Les Débats*, July 21, 1901; *Bleu, Blanc, Rouge*, 109; Circé-Côté, *Papineau*, 72.

64 Colombine, "Caughnawaga"; *Bleu, Blanc, Rouge*, 106–9.

65 Colombine, "Caughnawaga"; *Bleu, Blanc, Rouge*, 106–9.

66 Colombine, "Légende iroquoise. Les deux rives," *L'Avenir du Nord*, June 29, 1905.

67 *La Presse*, February 28, 1922.
68 Circé-Côté, *Papineau*, 67.
69 Circé-Côté, *Papineau*, 72.
70 Julien Saint-Michel, "Le problème de la criminalité," *Le Monde ouvrier*, July 16, 1932.
71 Julien Saint-Michel, "Une Race intéressante qui se meurt," *Le Monde ouvrier*, December 6, 1924.
72 Saint-Michel, "Une Race intéressante qui se meurt."
73 Fantasio, "Une Leçon d'énergie."
74 Colombine, "La Vie est dans le Sang," *L'Avenir du Nord*, July 30, 1909.
75 To quote the reference to Pierre-Salomon Côté: "Dr. Côté, after comparative brain studies, came to the conclusion that the skulls of whites had distinctive features, such as the protruding cheekbones, the flattened foreheads of Indian skulls," Circé-Côté, *Papineau*, 67. Cyprien Tanguay, *Dictionnaire généalogique des familles canadiennes depuis la fondation de la colonie jusqu'à nos jours* (Montreal: E. Sénécal, 1871–1890).
76 Fantasio, "Quatrième Épître à Théodore," *Le Pays*, March 13, 1920. Here, Circé-Côté echoes the observations of the explorer and botanist, Peter Kalm, who had visited Quebec in the middle of the 18th century. *Voyage de Kalm en Amérique, 1753–1761*, trans. L. W. Marchand, 2 vols., Mémoires de la Société historique de Montréal (Montreal: T. Berthiaume, 1880) 136, 208.
77 Fantasio, "Quatrième Épître à Théodore."
78 Colombine, *Maisonneuve*, 1921.
79 In October 1927, the pow-wow organized at Caughnawaga by Chief Dominique Tékani hoken (Two-Axes) provided Éva Circé-Côté with the opportunity to deplore the persistent ignorance of those of European descent regarding the "legitimate masters" of the country. She revisited the fate of "this generous and gentle race that required so little to be happy," lamenting that it was "a dying race, unless this is its dawning." Julien Saint-Michel, "Autres temps! Autres mœurs," *Le Monde ouvrier*, October 15, 1927.
80 Saint-Michel, "Le sentiment national."
81 Saint-Michel, "Autres temps! Autres mœurs."
82 Saint-Michel, "Le sentiment national."
83 Circé-Côté, *Papineau*, 67.
84 Julien Saint-Michel, "Rendons hommage à nos patriotes." Reflecting on the same monument eleven years earlier, Éva Circé-Côté wrote, with respect to Hindenlang: "We must not ostracize foreigners.... Today's foreigners are our brothers tomorrow." See also "Soyons dignes de notre race," *Le Monde ouvrier*, June 26, 1926.
85 Saint-Michel, "Soyons dignes de notre race."
86 Canada, *Bulletin 14, 5th Census of Canada*, Ottawa, 1911, Table F, "Percentage of the population by birthplace in cities with 20,000 inhabitants or more."
87 Canada, *7th Census of Canada*, 1931, vol. 2, Table 52, "Immigrant Population," 788; "Population of Cities," Table 16, 144. The arrival of Europeans who would spread out across Canada was brought home to the Québécois when the port of Quebec, after the spring thaw, received seven steamships carrying some 4,590 immigrants in the space of two days. *La Presse*, May 1, 1924.

88 Ève Circé-Côté, *Edition-souvenir du Jewish Eagle* (Kanader Adler), 1932, 65.
89 Circé-Côté, *Papineau*, 36.
90 This proportion is clearly overstated. Julien Saint-Michel, "Variations sur le Thème pascal," *Le Monde ouvrier*, April 11, 1925.
91 Circé-Côté, *Edition-souvenir du Jewish Eagle*, 1932, 65.
92 Julien Saint-Michel, "Une école nationale vraiment française," *Le Monde ouvrier*, November 3, 1934. See also Ève Circé-Côté, *Edition-souvenir du Jewish Eagle*, 1932, 64–65.
93 *La Loi concernant l'éducation des enfants de croyance judaïque dans l'Ile de Montréal*, April 4, 1930. The Jewish community was split over this question and the Jewish school board was shortlived. An agreement was soon reached between the Jewish community and the Protestant School Board.
94 Julien Saint-Michel, "Silhouettes politiques," *Le Monde ouvrier*, April 5, 1930.
95 Julien Saint-Michel, "Le 'fair play' britannique," *Le Monde ouvrier*, April 13, 1930.
96 Saint-Michel, "Le 'fair play' britannique."
97 Julien Saint-Michel, "Le 'fair play' britannique"; "Notre système d'éducation," *Le Monde ouvrier*, November 14, 1925; "Les écoles juives," *Le Monde ouvrier*, April 26, 1930. Note that in 1930 Bourassa supported Jewish confessional schools on grounds of giving priority to a religious education.
98 Julien Saint-Michel, "Notre fête nationale," *Le Monde ouvrier*, June 25, 1927.
99 Fantasio, "Le problème des sans-travail. Il ne faut pas revenir au régime du ghetto. Nous payons aujourd'hui pour l'immigration à outrance de ces dernières années," *Le Pays*, October 31, 1914.
100 Fantasio, "Chômage et charité," *Le Pays*, January 29, 1921.
101 Her position here was at variance with that of her colleague Madeleine Huguenin, who, in 1903, proposed to found a women's league that would provide aid exclusively to French-Canadians and not "deliver our beautiful country to the Doukhobors and Finns." Madeleine, "Chronique," *La Patrie*, January 5, 1903, 4.
102 The remark was part of a broadside against the Saint-Jean-Baptiste Society, which, according to Circé-Côté, by not actively supporting the movement against conscription, failed to fulfil its role. Fantasio, "La Société Saint-Jean-Baptiste. Ce qu'elle fait, ce qu'elle ne fait pas," *Le Pays*, October 6, 1917. The Monument-National had been hosting Yiddish theatre since 1897 and was home to a permanent company as of 1913, yet French-language playwrights had their own halls where their works were staged. Larrue, *Le Monument inattendu*, 187–95.
103 Saint-Michel, "Notre fête nationale."
104 Fantasio, "Chômage et charité," *Le Pays*, January 29, 1921.
105 Julien Saint-Michel, "Notre fête nationale"; "L'instruction gratuite et obligatoire"; "L'immigration intense," *Le Monde ouvrier*, March 19, 1927.
106 Saint-Michel, "L'instruction gratuite et obligatoire."
107 Saint-Michel, "Notre fête nationale."
108 Julien Saint-Michel, "Nous d'abord, les autres ensuite," *Le Monde ouvrier*, January 19, 1928.
109 Saint-Michel, "Notre fête nationale."
110 Fantasio, "En marge de la Semaine sociale," *Le Pays*, July 24, 1920.

111 Fantasio, "En marge de la Semaine sociale."
112 Fantasio, "En marge de la Semaine sociale." We cannot help but note that she added, "let them have fewer children."
113 To be fair, it should be stressed that these words represented less than a paragraph in a column of 29,000 words, which was mostly a diatribe against la Semaine sociale of 1920, in which Circé-Côté laid out the economic difficulties of the postwar period, deplored the exodus from the countryside, and assailed liberals and conservatives alike both in Quebec and Ottawa.
114 Éva Circé's circle in the early years of her career was not free of anti-Semitism. After Colombine's departure, the new director of *Le Pionnier*, the Luxembourger, Firmin Picard, had "La juiverie, voila l'ennemi" ["Jewry, that's the enemy"] printed in the header of the paper's front page. France was in the middle of the Dreyfus Affair. See F. Picard to O. Asselin, Montreal, March 10, 1903. ABM, BM55, S2, D12. One can hardly imagine Éva being associated with such a paper. Picard moved to Moncton in 1907. To learn more about his career in Acadia, see Michelle Savoie, "Firmin Picard et la Rencontre de trois cultures littéraires" (master's thesis, University of Moncton, 2001).
115 Fantasio, "Le fanatisme religieux," *Le Pays*, December 4, 1920.
116 Bouchard, *Mémoires*, vol. 2, 100–1.
117 Ignace Olazabal, Khaverim. *Les Juifs Ashkenazes de Montréal au début du XXe siècle* (Quebec: Nota bene, 2006), 205.
118 Fantasio, "Tableau vivant: Dollard mort!"; "Plutôt la tolérance."; "Haines de races"; Julien Saint-Michel, "Pourquoi nous les combattons," *Le Monde ouvrier*, October 23, 1920; "Réminiscences de la St-Jean-Baptiste," July 4, 1931. Although Bourassa, nurtured by Drumont and the anti-Dreyfusard literature of his youth, had subscribed to a form of anti-Semitism before the Great War, his thinking evolved, especially through his contact with Samuel Jacob. Anctil, *Le Devoir, les Juifs et l'Immigration*, 54–57.
119 Circé-Côté, *Papineau*, 245–46.
120 Julien Saint-Michel, "Réformons au lieu de détruire," *Le Monde ouvrier*, July 30, 1927. Circé-Côté reminded her readers that movie theatres were owned by people with unmistakably French-Canadian names such as Ouimet, Cardinal, and de Roche. Julien Saint- Michel, "Cinémas et journaux dénoncés," *Le Monde ouvrier*, May 19, 1928.
121 Saint-Michel. "Notre fête nationale"; "by temperament they are in favour of progress and the ideas of tomorrow," "Le 'fair play' britannique," *Le Monde ouvrier*, April 13, 1930.
122 Olazabal, *Khaverim*, 187.
123 Julien Saint-Michel, "La marche du destin," *Le Monde ouvrier*, February 12, 1921.
124 Circé-Côté, *Edition-souvenir du Jewish Eagle*, 1932, 64.
125 Julien Saint-Michel, "Question de race," *Le Monde ouvrier*, July 7, 1934.
126 Julien Saint-Michel, "Mentalité de Chinois," *Le Monde ouvrier*, February 6, 1926. It would be wrong to conclude that there was a significant Chinese population in Montreal during the first half of the twentieth century: between 1911 and 1931 the Chinese community represented a tiny percentage of the city's population.
127 These figures probably minimize the number of black people in Montreal. *Census of Canada*, 1921; Dorothy W. Williams, *Blacks in Montreal: An Urban Demography* (Montreal: Yvon Blais, 1989), 40 and 116.

128 The census identified 862 black people In Montreal in 1921, and more than a thousand in 1930. They were concentrated in the Saint-Antoine district. Julien Saint-Michel, "La langue française," *Le Monde ouvrier*, July 17, 1937. See Wikipedia, "Dominique Hyppolite," https://fr.wikipedia.org/wiki/Dominique_Hippolyte.
129 Circé-Côté, *Papineau*, 245.
130 Julien Saint-Michel, "A propos de races. La lignée héroïque dont nous descendons permet de nous enorgueillir du sang qui coule dans nos veines," *Le Monde ouvrier*, December 15, 1917; "L'Attitude de l'Allemagne," *Le Monde ouvrier*, May 27, 1933.
131 Jenne MacLean, who has studied Julien Saint-Michel's feminist ideas, states: "Circé-Côté offered what can be described as a modern 'feminist cure' to those longstanding concerned [sic] about the 'weakened' and 'ailing condition' of the French Canadian identity/race." Jenne MacLean, "Parrots, Picnics and Psychic Phenomena: The Feminism, Nationalism and Social Reform of Eva Circé-Côté in *Le Monde ouvrier*'s Montreal, 1900–1940" (master's thesis, Queen's University, 2000), 93.
132 Saint-Michel, "Le sentiment national."
133 Julien Saint-Michel, "La Confédération," *Le Monde ouvrier*, July 3, 1902.
134 Julien Saint-Michel, "À propos du vote des femmes," *Le Monde ouvrier*, March 3, 1928.
135 Julien Saint-Michel, "La langue française," *Le Monde ouvrier*, July 17, 1937.
136 Ève Circé-Côté, "La Vérité, pupille du Cardinal et du Clergé canadien."

Chapter 9

1 Julien Saint-Michel, "Notre société se transforme," *Le Monde ouvrier*, January 12, 1929.
2 Colombine, "Parlons du féminisme," *L'Avenir*, October 28, 1900.
3 K. Nadienne, "Le féminisme au palais," *La Presse*, October 30, 1900. This correspondent criticized her in particular for running down female stenographers though there was only one at the courthouse.
4 Colombine, "Songeries d'octobre," *Les Débats*, October 7, 1900. The idea of such a tax was not completely outlandish. From 1919 to 1923, the City of Montreal levied a tax on single men, which brought in about $70,000 a year. There were apparently never more than 11,000 men who paid it. *Le Canada*, June 5, 1923, 10.
5 Colombine, "Coups de plume," *Bleu, Blanc, Rouge*, 128; "Chronique," July 7, 1901.
6 Colombine, "Le Microbe sympathique," *Les Débats*, December 30, 1900.
7 Colombine, "Réponse. Au personnage anonyme de *L'Étoile du Nord*," *L'Avenir du Nord*, September 24, 1903.
8 Colombine, "Étude sur la femme," *L'Avenir du Nord*, August 13, 1903.
9 Musette, "Chronique," *Les Débats*, May 5, 1901.
10 Julien Saint-Michel, "Les pensions maternelles," *Le Monde ouvrier*, April 29, 1916.
11 Julien Saint-Michel, "L'émancipation de la femme," *Le Monde ouvrier*, January 10, 1920.
12 Musette, "Chronique," *Les Débats*, March 31, 1901.
13 Colombine, "Parlons du féminisme," *L'Avenir*, October 28, 1900.

14 Éva Circé, "Etude sur les causes de l'infériorité de la femme," *L'Étincelle*, January 31, 1903.
15 Colombine, "Réponse au personnage anonyme qui écrit dans *L'Étoile de Nord*," *L'Avenir du Nord*, September 10, 1903.
16 Colombine, "Réponse. Au personnage anonyme de *L'Étoile du Nord*."
17 Julien Saint-Michel, "La dignité masculine," *Le Monde ouvrier*, May 17, 1930.
18 Julien Saint-Michel, "La mortalité infantile," *Le Monde ouvrier*, June 21, 1930. The expression "faiseuse d'anges" (angel maker) was usually applied to female abortionists, but Circé-Côté is using it here to designate mothers responsible for the deaths of their children.
19 Arthur Maheu, "Les idées de M. Maheu," *Le Pays*, September 7, 1912; *Le Pays*, February 5, 1916.
20 *La Patrie*, June 8, July 12–14, 1911.
21 Fantasio, "Dialectique des mouches," *Le Pays*, June 10, 1911; Fantasio, "L'inutile création," July 15, 1911.
22 Fantasio, "Réflexions estivales," *Le Pays*, July 13, 1912.
23 Fantasio, "L'inutile création"; Fantasio, "Ces pauvres petites bêtes," *Le Pays*, August 31, 1912.
24 Patricia A. Thornton and Sherry Olson, "Infant Vulnerability in Three Cultural Settings in Montreal 1880," in *Infant and Child Mortality in the Past*, ed. Alain Bideau, Bertrand Desjardins, and Hector Pérez Brignoli (Oxford: Clarendon, Collection of International Studies in Demography, 1997), 216–41.
25 Fantasio, "Nous sommes une race prolifique! Mais où la négligence des parents conduit-elle?" *Le Pays*, December 19, 1914; Julien Saint-Michel, "Les mères imprévoyantes," *Le Monde ouvrier*, October 13, 1928; "Veillons sur l'enfance," June 15, 1929; "Le respect de la vie d'autrui," June 19, 1932.
26 Julien Saint-Michel, "La sécurité avant tout," *Le Monde ouvrier*, May 12, 1928.
27 Jean Nay, "La mortalité infantile. L'assurance des enfants. Le pessimisme maternel," *Le Pays*, July 30, 1910; Colombine, "Mortalité infantile," *L'Avenir du Nord*, August 6, 1903; Paul S. Bédard, "Les chaleurs s'en viennent," *Le Monde ouvrier*, May 23, 1914; Julien Saint-Michel, "La mortalité infantile," *Le Monde ouvrier*, June 30, 1917; "L'exploitation de l'enfance," May 5, 1928.
28 Paul S. Bédard, "Les chaleurs s'en viennent," *Le Pays*, May 23, 1914; Julien Saint-Michel, "La mortalité infantile," *Le Monde ouvrier*, June 30, 1917.
29 Lachapelle, 1912, cited in Denyse Baillargeon, *Un Québec en mal d'enfants. La médicalisation de la maternité* (Montreal: Éditions du remue-ménage, 2004), 94–95.
30 Fantasio, "Ces pauvres petites bêtes," *Le Pays*, August 31, 1912.
31 Saint-Michel, "L'instruction gratuite et obligatoire."
32 Julien Saint-Michel, "La mortalité infantile," *Le Monde ouvrier*, July 23, 1927. Two years later, she returned to the subject: "Infant mortality is caused by poverty and the physiological weakness of women who, being hospital cases themselves, bring into the world defective, frail beings unable to fight for life.... Female workers are poor precisely because they have many children in their care." "La mortalité infantile," *Le Monde ouvrier*, February 16, 1929.
33 Fantasio, "Cinquième Épître à Théodore," *Le Pays*, March 20, 1920.

34 Julien Saint-Michel, "Au Pays des Rêves," *Le Monde ouvrier*, April 18, 1925.
35 Arthur Maheu, "Les Idées de M. Maheu," *Le Pays*, March 17, 1917.
36 Paul S. Bédard, "Reliquats de préjugé. L'arrêt du Concile de Trente n'est pas aboli. Serions-nous en retard des autres pays?" *Le Pays*, May 12, 1917; Julien Saint-Michel, "Le rôle de la femme en politique," *Le Monde ouvrier*, May 11, 1918.
37 Julien Saint-Michel, "Le suffrage féminin," *Le Monde ouvrier*, July 14, 1917; Fantasio, "La Lettre de Lord Landsdowne," *Le Pays*, December 8, 1917.
38 Julien Saint-Michel, "Les droits des mères," *Le Monde ouvrier*, February 14, 1925.
39 Julien Saint-Michel, "Le suffrage féminin," *Le Monde ouvrier*, February 27, 1932.
40 Saint-Michel, "Le suffrage féminin," February 27, 1932.
41 Julien Saint-Michel, "L'évolution féminine," *Le Monde ouvrier*, October 22, 1932. From September 29 to October 25, 1932, Romier gave a series of conferences at the Écoles des Hautes Études commerciales of Montreal on the "Problèmes économiques de l'heure présente" (current economic issues).
42 See Jenne MacLean: "she challenged Montreal's classical liberal models while confirming the parameters of new liberal gender ideals. This seeming contradiction was not a sign of Circé-Côté's puzzlement but, rather, signalled the extraordinary complex and paradoxical effect both the classical and new liberal frameworks caused when applied to women's lives." MacLean, "Parrots, Picnics and Psychic Phenomena," 1–2.
43 Julien Saint-Michel, "L'évolution de la femme," *Le Monde ouvrier*, October 8, 1927.
44 Saint-Michel, "L'évolution de la femme."
45 Julien Saint-Michel, "Le droit de vote aux femmes," *Le Monde ouvrier*, February 5, 1927.
46 Julien Saint-Michel, "Le véritable aspect du problème féministe," *Le Monde ouvrier*, April 4, 1925.
47 Éva Circé, "Etude sur les causes de l'infériorité de la femme," *L'Étincelle*, January 31, 1903.
48 Colombine, "Réponse au personnage anonyme qui écrit dans *L'Étoile du Nord*," *L'Avenir du Nord*, September 10, 1903.
49 *La Patrie*, June 16, 1909.
50 Colombine, "Resurrexit," *Montreal Daily Witness*, May 15, 1909.
51 Interview with Micheline Dumont, who made a detailed study of this matter.
52 Jean Charbonneau, "L'éducation des filles," *Le Pays*, February 7, 1914.
53 Julien Saint-Michel, "L'éducation de nos filles. Elles doivent être protégées pour les luttes de la vie," *Le Monde ouvrier*, April 22, 1916.
54 Julien Saint-Michel, "Le véritable aspect du problème féministe."
55 Julien Saint-Michel, "Le féminisme intégral," *Le Monde ouvrier*, July 19, 1930.
56 Fantasio, "Les femmes avocates. Faisons changer la loi, s'il le faut. L'honorabilité d'une femme et la profession d'avocat," *Le Pays*, February 20, 1920.
57 Colombine, "Parlons du féminisme," *L'Avenir*, October 28, 1900.
58 Fantasio, "Profession ingrate. Les femmes devraient-elles être admises au Barreau de la province de Québec?" *Le Pays*, July 25, 1914.
59 Fantasio, "Profession ingrate."
60 Fantasio, "Les femmes avocates. Faisons changer la loi, s'il le faut."

61 *La Patrie*, September 9, 1925.
62 Julien Saint-Michel, "Le rôle moderne de la femme," *Le Monde ouvrier*, September 19, 1931.
63 This section is drawn in part from "Le Code civil au Québec. Femmes mineure et féministes," in *Résistance et transgression. Études en histoir des femmes au Québec*, Andrée Lévesque (Montreal: Éditions du remue-ménage, 1995), 19–46.
64 C. B. M. Toullier, *Le Droit civil français sur l'ordre du Code* (Paris, 1821).
65 Marie Gérin-Lajoie, *Traité de Droit usuel* (Montreal: C.O. Beauchemin & Fils, 1902).
66 Fantasio, "Mouvement de recul. Les fantaisies de Melle Wilson," *Le Pays*, December 6, 1913.
67 Fantasio, "Les femmes avocates. Faisons changer la loi, s'il le faut."
68 Julien Saint-Michel, "Autres temps, autres mœurs. Le nouveau rôle de la femme. Les maris despotes et la communautés de biens," *Le Monde ouvrier*, October 28, 1916.
69 Fantasio, "Vers le féminisme. Quelques chinoiseries de la loi canadienne. Les maris sont responsables des torts causés par les bavardages de leurs femmes, s'ils en sont avertis," *Le Pays*, July 18, 1914.
70 Fantasio, "Vers le féminisme."
71 Jennifer Stoddart, "Quand des gens de robe se penchent sur les droits des femmes: le cas de la commission Dorion, 1919–1931," in Lavigne and Pinard, *Travailleuses et féministes*, 308.
72 Julien Saint-Michel, "Le suffrage féminin," *Le Monde ouvrier*, March 24, 1928.
73 Fantasio, "Les merveilles du radium," *Le Pays*, June 4, 1921.
74 Idola Saint-Jean devoted a series of articles in the *Montreal Herald* to the injustices of the Civil Code. At the Dorion Commission, she recommended the elimination of laws inimical to women and the adoption of the measures demanded by the l'Alliance canadienne pour le vote des femmes (Canadian alliance for women's vote), as follows: amendment of articles 115 and 119 pertaining to marital authority so as to require both parents' consent for the marriage of minors; raising the legal age for marriage from twelve to sixteen; reduction of separation costs; amendment of article 280 to abolish liability for debts contracted before a marriage; access to insurance policies for married women; imposition on business women of the same legal regulations as those imposed on men; amendment of articles 187 and 188 pertaining to the unequal criteria for obtaining a legal separation on grounds of adultery. Thus, with no prospect of eliminating all discriminatory articles from the Code, Saint-Jean restricted herself to demanding specific reforms. *Montreal Herald*, December 5, 1929, and May 29, 1930.
75 Thérèse Casgrain, on behalf of the Ligue des droits de la femme (League for the rights of women), demanded that article 298 be amended so as to empower a married woman estranged from her husband to manage her private property without interference from, and without the authorization of, her husband or a judge.
76 Julien Saint-Michel, "Autres temps, autres mœurs," *Le Monde ouvrier*, November 30, 1929.
77 Idola Saint-Jean, *Montreal Herald*, April 10, 1930.
78 Stoddart, "Quand des gens de robe se penchent sur les droits des femmes," 308.
79 Henri Bourassa, "Déplorable ignorance des Canadiennes-Françaises," *Le Devoir*, March 31, 1913; "Éducation et instruction," *Le Devoir*, April 5, 1913; "Rôle social de

la femme," *Le Devoir*, April 24, 1913. See Susan Mann Trofimenkoff, "Henri Bourassa and the Woman Question," *Journal of Canadian Studies* 10, no. 4 (November 1975): 3–11. Over time, Bourassa tempered his opinions; on February 7, 1937, at the invitation of the Alliance canadienne pour le vote des femmes, he addressed a meeting on the subject of peace organized by the Alliance to celebrate its tenth anniversary. The topic of his speech was "Women and Peace," a theme consistent with Bourassa's views on women. *La Patrie*, February 4, 1937, 16. Idola Saint-Jean was capable of forgiving.

80 "À propos de suffragisme. Une lettre de Mme Cole," *Le Devoir*, April 5, 1913.
81 Madeleine, *La Patrie*, April 14, 1913, 4.
82 The exhibition was held at 622, Saint-Catherine Street, West.
83 *La Patrie*, August 30, and 6, 13, 20 and 27 September, 1913. Pankhurst and militant suffragettes resorted to illegal methods in their call for the right to vote, while other suffragists confined themselves to pressure tactics, campaigns to educate the public, and the media, to convince politicians to give women the suffrage.
84 *Le Journal de Françoise*, January 1907, 297.
85 Arthur Maheu, "Les idées de M. Maheu. M. Borden a raison de ne pas laisser entrer les suffragettes au Canada," *Le Pays*, October 12, 1912.
86 Arthur Maheu, " Les Idées de M. Maheu," *Le Pays*, September 27, 1913.
87 Julien Saint-Michel, "Le succès des suffragettes," *Le Monde ouvrier*, October 31, 1931.
88 Fantasio, "Les femmes avocates. Faisons changer la loi, s'il le faut."
89 Fantasio, "Les femmes doivent-elles voter? C'est contre l'ordre établi par la Providence, décrète *L'Action catholique*. La femme et ses égaux politiques. Une réforme qui s'en vient," *Le Pays*, November 20, 1915.
90 Paul S. Bédard, "Reliquats de préjugé. L'arrêt du Concile de Trente n'est pas aboli. Serions-nous en retard des autres pays?" *Le Pays*, May 12, 1917.
91 Julien Saint-Michel, "Le suffrage féminin," *Le Monde ouvrier*, July 14, 1917.
92 Meanwhile, the Wartime Elections Act also withdrew the right to vote from conscientious objectors and from Canadian citizens born in an enemy country and naturalized after 1902.
93 Julien Saint-Michel, "Le vote des femmes. Les femmes doivent-elles se prévaloir du droit qui leur a été donné? Le devoir de la nouvelle citoyenne," *Le Monde ouvrier*, December 8, 1917.
94 Fantasio, "Le parlement qui disparaît," *Le Pays*, September 22, 1917.
95 Fantasio and Paul S. Bédard, "Un dernier mot. De Fantasio et de Paul S. Bédard sur une légère actualité," *Le Pays*, October 27, 1917.
96 Fantasio, "Vous voterez donc, Mesdames!" *Le Pays*, December 15, 1917.
97 Fantasio, "Le parlement qui disparaît."
98 Fantasio and Bédard, "Un dernier mot."
99 Saint-Michel, "Le vote des femmes. Les femmes doivent-elles se prévaloir du droit qui leur a été donné?"; Fantasio, "Vous voterez donc, Mesdames!"
100 Julien Saint-Michel, "Ces dames aux 'pools'. A propos du vote des femmes dans la dernière élection générale," *Le Monde ouvrier*, December 22, 1917.
101 Julien Saint-Michel, "L'émancipation de la femme. Pourquoi refuse-t-on le droit de vote aux Canadiennes de la Province de Québec? Serions-nous toujours en arrière des

provinces sœurs? On n'est jamais si bien servi que par soi-même," *Le Monde ouvrier*, March 10, 1917; "Le suffrage féminin," *Le Monde ouvrier*, July 14, 1917; "Le droit de vote aux femmes."

102 Henri Bourassa, "Désarroi des cerveaux—triomphe de la démocratie," *Le Devoir*, March 28, 1918; "L'influence politique des femmes—pays avancés—femmes enculottées," *Le Devoir*, April 1, 1918. Bourassa would reoffend years later in *Femmes-hommes ou hommes-femmes? Études à bâtons rompus sur le féminisme* (Montreal: Le Devoir, 1925). See also Mann Trofimenkoff, "Henri Bourassa and 'the Woman Question,'" 104–15.

103 Julien Saint-Michel, "M. Bourassa et le vote des femmes," *Le Monde ouvrier*, April 6, 1918.

104 Julien Saint-Michel, "Le rôle de la femme en politique," *Le Monde ouvrier*, May 11, 1918.

105 Julien Saint-Michel, "Le droit de vote aux femmes"; "Y a-t-il une opinion publique?" *Le Monde ouvrier*, May 15, 1927; "Le suffrage féminin," *Le Monde ouvrier*, November 5, 1927; "La lutte pour le vote des femmes," *Le Monde ouvrier*, December 3, 1927; "À propos du vote des femmes," March 3, 1928; "Le suffrage féminin," *Le Monde ouvrier*, March 24, 1928.

106 Julien Saint-Michel, "Le droit de vote aux femmes."

107 Marie Gérin-Lajoie, "Le vote féminin et la question familiale," *La Bonne Parole*, February 1922. Gérin-Lajoie quoted Gladstone, who had made the same argument concerning the voting rights of Britain's farmers.

108 Saint-Michel, "Le droit de vote aux femmes."

109 Julien Saint-Michel, "Qui donnera le vote aux femmes," *Le Monde ouvrier*, October 22, 1927.

110 Saint-Michel, "La lutte pour le vote des femmes."

111 On the so-called Tremblay bill, see Julien Saint-Michel, "A propos du vote des femmes," *Le Monde ouvrier*, March 3, 1927.

112 Julien Saint-Michel, "Le droit de chacun à la vie," *Le Monde ouvrier*, March 17, 1928.

113 Julien Saint-Michel, "Le vote des femmes," *Le Monde ouvrier*, January 30, 1932.

114 Saint-Michel, "L'évolution de la femme."

115 Julien Saint-Michel, "Le vote de la femme à l'avenir," *Le Monde ouvrier*, November 5, 1932.

116 Saint-Michel, "Le droit de vote aux femmes."

117 Saint-Michel, "L'évolution de la femme."

118 Julien Saint-Michel, "L'entraînement militaire en chambre," *Le Monde ouvrier*, June 8, 1929.

119 Julien Saint-Michel, "Exclusion des femmes au Sénat," *Le Monde ouvrier*, April 28, 1928; "Le Sénat fermé aux femmes," *Le Monde ouvrier*, August 25, 1928.

120 Saint-Michel, "Exclusion des femmes au Sénat." In 1930 Carine Wilson became the first female Canadian Senator, but Éva Circé-Côté did not live to see the fruits of her efforts to open such positions to Quebec women; in 1953, Mariana Beauchamp-Jodoin became the first French-speaking woman named to the Senate. Agnes MacPhail held a seat in the House of Commons as of 1921, but Claire Kirkland-Casgrain, in 1961, was the first Québécoise elected to the National Assembly of Quebec,

and it took another ten years for Monique Bégin, Albanie Morin, and Jeanne Sauvé to become the first Québécoises elected to the House of Commons.
121 Julien Saint-Michel, "Le suffrage féminin," *Le Monde ouvrier*, November 5, 1927.
122 AVM, *Enquête sur la police (Enquête Coderre) Procès-verbaux*, 1924–1925, vol. 3, p. 2316; vol. 8, p. 6229.
123 Julien Saint-Michel, "La prostitution à Montréal," *Le Monde ouvrier*, March 16, 1918.
124 Fantasio, "Rengainons l'enquête. Si on n'a pas l'intention d'extirper la racine du mal, à quoi servirait une enquête sur la police? Comprendra-t-on jamais que dans une grande ville il faut réglementer la prostitution?" *Le Pays*, February 6, 1915.
125 Julien Saint-Michel, "Où nous mène notre hypocrisie," *Le Monde ouvrier*, February 21, 1920.
126 Andrée Lévesque, "L'Enquête Coderre," in *De la Belle époque à la CriseCrise. Chroniques de la vie culturelle à Montréal* (Montreal: Nota Bene, 2015), 271–86.
127 Julien Saint-Michel, "'L'enquête' et la théologie," *Le Monde ouvrier*, January 17, 1925.
128 Fantasio, "Ignorance n'est pas vertu," *Le Pays*, November 12, 1910; Fantasio, "L'éternelle comédie! On parle d'une nouvelle enquête, mais à propos de mœurs cette fois. Montréal serait le centre d'une organisation pour la traite des blanches. La corruption de notre ville," *Le Pays*, September 9, 1916; "L'instruction obligatoire," April 24, 1920; Julien Saint-Michel, "La co-éducation des sexes. Les écoles mixtes tendent à adoucir la brutalité des garçons et à viriliser les filles," *Le Monde ouvrier*, November 18, 1916; "Que doit-on apprendre à nos jeunes filles," January 25, 1919; "L'enquête et la théologie," January 17, 1925; "La femme instruite est une valeur," September 17, 1927.
129 Julien Saint-Michel, "Le salaire minimum des femmes," *Le Monde ouvrier*, May 22, 1926; "Le travail de la femme," *Le Monde ouvrier*, February 8, 1936.
130 Julien Saint-Michel, "Le travail des femmes," *Le Monde ouvrier*, May 12, 1934.
131 Julien Saint-Michel, "Pour enrayer le vice," *Le Monde ouvrier*, December 7, 1918; "Comment endiguer le flot montant de la corruption," *Le Monde ouvrier*, January 3, 1925.
132 Arthur Maheu, "Les Idées de M. Maheu," *Le Pays*, June 9, 1917.
133 This is followed by a description of effeminate men and their "abnormal" passion. Julien Saint-Michel, "Une verte réplique," *Le Monde ouvrier*, March 21, 1925. This description echoes nineteenth-century anxieties about the subject of male masturbation. See B. Barker-Benfield, *The Horror of the Unknown Life: Male Attitudes Toward Women and Sexuality in Nineteenth-Century America* (New York: Harper & Row, 1976), 163–74, 234–35.
134 Julien Saint-Michel, "Comment endiguer le flot montant de la corruption"; "Pour enrayer la plaie sociale"; "Une Emotion . . . un peu tardive," November 22, 1924.
135 Julien Saint-Michel, "Le respect au prétoire," *Le Monde ouvrier*, November 14, 1931.
136 Alexandre Parent-Duchâtelet, *De la prostitution dans la ville de Paris considérée sous le rapport de l'hygiène publique, de la morale et de l'administration*, 2 vols. (Paris: J. Baillière, 1836).
137 Fantasio, "Le courage de notre maire. M. Martin regarde froidement le mal que la prostitution fait à Montréal et il se prononce pour la réglementation," *Le Pays*, August 19, 1919.

138 For almost a year, in 1907–1908, prostitution was regulated in Montreal, but in response to the commission of enquiry into the police headed by Mr. Justice Cannon and the objections of social reformers, regulation advocates backed down. Lévesque, *Résistance et transgression*, 93–102, 110.
139 Julien Saint-Michel, "Pour enrayer le vice"; Gustave Francq, "Nos policiers sont défendus," *Le Monde ouvrier*, March 21, 1925.
140 Saint-Michel, "Comment endiguer le flot montant de la corruption."
141 Fantasio, "Le courage de notre maire."
142 Colombine, "Réponse dernière. Au personnage anonyme de *L'Étoile du Nord*," *L'Avenir du Nord*, October 22, 1903.
143 Fantasio, "Vous voterez donc, Mesdames!"
144 Circé-Côté, *Papineau*, 51.
145 Fantasio, "Les merveilles du radium."
146 Colombine, "Etude sur la femme," *L'Avenir du Nord*, August 13, 1903.
147 Musette, "La revue des livres," *L'Étincelle*, January 10, 1903.
148 Saint-Michel, "Le rôle moderne de la femme"; Fantasio, "L'attitude de Melle Rankin. La présence des femmes dans les corps législatifs ne peut qu'adoucir les mœurs et mettre un terme aux guerres," *Le Pays*, April 14, 1917.
149 Paul G. [sic] Bédard, "Pudeur intempestive," *Le Pays*, March 27, 1920.
150 Colombine, "L'Inconnu," *Le Pionnier*, November 17, 1901; Éva Circé-Côté dedicated an article to the memory of her uncle, F.-X. Beauchamp; she paid homage to the journalist Stanislas Côté; she wrote laudatory reviews of poems by Jean Charbonneau, Marcel Dugas, and Français Berthaud, and she warmly congratulated Louvigny de Montigny on the occasion of his admission to the Royal Society, but few women were similarly honoured by her. Colombine, "M. Stanislas Côté," *Le Pionnier*, December 1, 1901; Fantasio, "'Les Blessures' par Jean Charbonneau," *Le Pays*, January 18, 1913; Paul S. Bédard, "Feux de Bengale à Verlaine glorieux de M. Marcel Dugas," *Le Pays*, January 22, 1916; Paul S. Bédard, "Psyché au cinéma," *Le Pays*, July 15, 1916; Musette, "La France et le Poète," *Les Débats*, August 4, 1901; Fantasio, "Le livre de M. de Montigny," *Le Pays*, January 6, 1917.
151 Colombine, "La Sainte-Catherine," *L'Avenir*, November 25, 1900.
152 Julien Saint-Michel, "Les Jérémiades de l'*Action catholique*," *Le Monde ouvrier*, October 18, 1919; Fantasio, "Invention de Satan," *Le Pays*, November 22, 1913.
153 Fantasio, "Profession ingrate."
154 Julien Saint-Michel, "Les affres du chômage," *Le Monde ouvrier*, July 7, 1928.
155 Fantasio and Bédard, "Un dernier mot."
156 Gosselin, *Les Journalistes québécoises, 1880–1930*, 108–9.
157 To learn more about Madeleine, see Aurélien Boivin and Kenneth Landry, "Françoise et Madeleine, pionnières du journalisme féminin au Québec," *Voix et Images* 4, no. 2 (December 1978), 237–40.
158 Luc Aubry, "Notes et Échos," *La Revue moderne*, May 1926.
159 Éva Circé-Côté to Marcel Dugas, July 1924, CARDL.
160 Marie-Claire Daveluy, "Les conditions morales à l'usine," *La Bonne Parole* 10, no. 10 (October 1922), 9.

161 Circé-Côté to Dugas, December 20, 1926, CARDL.
162 Circé-Côté to Dugas, December 20, 1926, CARDL; Circé-Côté, *Papineau*, 241. She may have maintained other friendships, but because her correspondence was destroyed it is impossible to retrace her circle of intimates.
163 Julien Saint-Michel, "A la mémoire de Papineau," *Le Monde ouvrier*, April 19, 1930; "Le culte du souvenir," June 14, 1930.
164 Fantasio, "Vive la Canadienne!" *Le Pays*, July 8, 1916; Circé-Côté, *Papineau*, 240.
165 Julien Saint-Michel, "L'émancipation de la femme," *Le Monde ouvrier*, November 19, 1932.
166 Julien Saint-Michel, "Le vote des femmes," *Le Monde ouvrier*, June 20, 1936. The remark was not disinterested, given that Saint-Jean opposed Mackenzie King's intention of naming Louis-Alexandre Taschereau to the Senate, whereas Circé-Côté, ever the liberal, apparently welcomed this nomination.

Chapter 10

1 Julien Saint-Michel, "Le Droit au travail et à la vie," *Le Monde ouvrier*, October 1, 1921. Italics added.
2 Julien Saint-Michel, "Le travail régénérateur," *Le Monde ouvrier*, April 9, 1932.
3 Max Weber, *The Protestant Ethic and the Spirit of Capitalism*, trans. Stephen Kalberg (Chicago: Fitzroy Dearborn, 2001).
4 Colombine, "Le Travail," *L'Avenir du Nord*, July 9, 1903.
5 Fantasio, "Cinquième Épître à Théodore," *Le Pays*, March 20, 1920.
6 Fantasio, "Un si beau sort," *Le Pays*, February 1, 1913.
7 Julien Saint-Michel, "Le Droit au travail et à la vie," *Le Monde ouvrier*, October 1, 1921. This article was written in the wake of the *Semaine sociale*, whose conventional positions on workers' duties prompted Circé-Côté to insist on the duties of the State.
8 Julien Saint-Michel, "Parons la crise économique," *Le Monde ouvrier*, March 8, 1919.
9 Julien Saint-Michel, "Du travail au lieu d'aumônes," *Le Monde ouvrier*, January 5, 1929.
10 She cited the French economist Émile de Girardin in an epigraph as evidence that, "It was through saving that the people gradually emancipated itself." Fantasio, "Revenons au bas de laine de nos grand mères," *Le Pays*, October 1, 1910.
11 Colombine, "Chronique," *L'Avenir*, December 23, 1900; "Deux sous!" *L'Avenir du Nord*, October 1, 1903; Julien Saint-Michel, "L'enlèvement d'un enfant," *Le Monde ouvrier*, March 19, 1932.
12 Colombine, "La Grève," *L'Avenir du Nord*, May 28, 1903. She added, condescendingly: "Nobody believes more than me in the people's sovereignty, but their hour has not yet come. It would be dangerous to hand them the reins of government at this time. They would abuse their power, because our people are like children and do not have the maturity that education brings; they have barely emerged from their puerile childhood. A rattle, not a sceptre, should be placed in their hands."
13 Colombine, "Echos de la grève," *Les Débats*, August 9, 1903.
14 Paul G. [sic] Bédard, "Après la fête. Derniers échos et commentaires. Quelques rapprochements d'ordre élevé," *Le Pays*, September 15, 1917.

15 Julien Saint-Michel, "La crise des chemineaux," *Le Monde ouvrier*, September 9, 1916.
16 Julien Saint-Michel, "Le Droit du faible. Les ouvriers n'ont qu'un seul moyen de se protéger contre la cupidité des patrons c'est de s'unir et personne ne pourra les en empêcher. Les moutons ne sont plus si facile à tondre," *Le Monde ouvrier*, February 24, 1917.
17 Julien Saint-Michel, "Le chambardement annuel," *Le Monde ouvrier*, May 10, 1919.
18 Julien Saint-Michel, "Le résultat de l'exploitation du peuple," *Le Monde ouvrier*, April 26, 1919.
19 Julien Saint-Michel, "La fête du travail," *Le Monde ouvrier*, September 6, 1919.
20 Éric Leroux, *Gustave Francq. Figure marquante du syndicalisme et précurseur de la FTQ* (Montreal: VLB, 2001), 173–75. On the labour strife in Montreal in 1919, see Geoffrey Ewen, "Quebec: Class and Ethnicity," in *The Workers' Revolt in Canada*, ed. Craig Heron (Toronto: University of Toronto Press, 1998), 99–116.
21 *La Patrie*, January 2, 3, 5, and 7, 1920.
22 Fantasio, "Une dure leçon," *Le Pays*, January 10, 1920. Italics added.
23 Julien Saint-Michel, "Patrons et caisses de retraite," *Le Monde ouvrier*, October 11, 1919.
24 Julien Saint-Michel, "Les accidents du travail," February 1, 1919.
25 Julien Saint-Michel, "Protégeons nos apprentis," *Le Monde ouvrier*, June 12, 1920; "L'apprentissage forcé," *Le Monde ouvrier*, January 31, 1920; "L'exploitation de nos propres enfants," *Le Monde ouvrier*, July 20, 1929; "Patrons et caisses de retraite," *Le Monde ouvrier*, October 11, 1919; "La nécessité des vacances," *Le Monde ouvrier*, July 16, 1921.
26 Julien Saint-Michel, "Le choix des administrateurs," *Le Monde ouvrier*, March 17, 1934.
27 *Canada Year Book* (Ottawa: 1939), 777–78; *Census of Canada*, 1941, vol. 7, Table 7.
28 Colombine, "Le Travail," *L'Avenir du Nord*, July 9, 1903.
29 Fantasio, "Etude de mœurs," *Le Pays*, March 9, 1912.
30 Colombine, "L'Ouvrière," *Les Débats*, April 5, 1903.
31 Colombine, "L'Ouvrière."
32 Fantasio, "A brebis tondue épargnons le vent," *Le Pays*, December 17, 1910; Julien Saint-Michel, "Précoce émancipation," *Le Monde ouvrier*, March 20, 1920.
33 Fantasio, "Les femmes avocates. Faisons changer la loi, s'il le faut. L'honorabilité d'une femme et la profession d'avocat," *Le Pays*, February 20, 1915.
34 Julien Saint-Michel, "Vers un autre idéal," *Le Monde ouvrier*, November 4, 1916.
35 Julien Saint-Michel, "Les bienfaits de l'économie," *Le Monde ouvrier*, July 8, 1916.
36 Julien Saint-Michel, "Le sort du sexe féminin," *Le Monde ouvrier*, March 9, 1918.
37 Julien Saint-Michel, "Prévenons le danger," *Le Monde ouvrier*, September 8, 1917.
38 Julien Saint-Michel, "Prévenons le danger"; "Les dangers du travail de nuit pour les femmes," *Le Monde ouvrier*, August 3, 1918.
39 Julien Saint-Michel, "Ostracisme du sexe féminin," *Le Monde ouvrier*, October 8, 1921.
40 Julien Saint-Michel, "Que vont devenir les hommes?" *Le Monde ouvrier*, September 28, 1918.

41 Julien Saint-Michel, "Un beau jour naît pour les femmes," *Le Monde ouvrier*, March 25, 1916; "Prévenons le danger."
42 Julien Saint-Michel, "Sauvons les enfants et leurs mamans. Les bébés sont privés de lait parce qu'il coûte trop cher. Le sort des femmes travaillant à l'usine et l'avenir de la race," *Le Monde ouvrier*, October 20, 1917.
43 Julia Drummond, "Contre une législation ouvrière protectionniste pour les femmes (1896)," cited in Micheline Dumont and Louise Toupin, *La Pensée féministe au Québec. Anthologie 1900–1985* (Montreal: Éditions du remue-ménage, 2003), 82–84.
44 Julien Saint-Michel, "Les dangers du travail de nuit pour les femmes," *Le Monde ouvrier*, August 3, 1918; Julien Saint-Michel, "Sauvons les enfants et leurs mamans," *Le Monde ouvrier*, October 23, 1917; "La femme à l'atelier," April 27, 1918; "Les dangers du travail de nuit pour les femmes," *Le Monde ouvrier*, August 3, 1918.
45 Mark H. Irish to Colonel E. J. Chambers, chief censor of the press, October 27, 1916, Library and Archives Canada, RG6, vol. 529, dossier 178-B-5, in Jeanne Lespérance, *Vers des horizons nouveaux: la femme canadienne de 1870 à 1940* (Ottawa: National Library and Archives Canada, 1982), 52.
46 Saint-Michel, "Les dangers du travail de nuit pour les femmes."
47 Julien Saint-Michel, "La femme à l'atelier," *Le Monde ouvrier*, April 27, 1918.
48 Saint-Michel, "Sauvons les enfants et leurs mamans."
49 Julien Saint-Michel, "Travail égal, salaire égal. Pourquoi les femmes qui font un travail aussi pénible que les hommes ne seraient pas aussi bien rémunérées?" *Le Monde ouvrier*, August 25, 1917.
50 Julien Saint-Michel, "Les femmes dans l'industrie," *Le Monde ouvrier*, January 31, 1920.
51 Julien Saint-Michel, "Comment comprendre l'économie," *Le Monde ouvrier*, March 12, 1927.
52 Julien Saint-Michel, "Le travail des femmes," *Le Monde ouvrier*, June 18, 1921.
53 Julien Saint-Michel, "Chacun à sa place," *Le Monde ouvrier*, June 21, 1919; "Trop de luxe," May 29, 1920; "Ostracisme du sexe féminin," October 8, 1921.
54 Julien Saint-Michel, "Uniformité de salaire pour les deux sexes," *Le Monde ouvrier*, April 26, 1924.
55 Saint-Michel, "Travail égal, salaire égal."
56 Julien Saint-Michel, "Le salaire minimum des femmes," *Le Monde ouvrier*, May 1, 1926.
57 Julien Saint-Michel, "Le salaire minimum des femmes," *Le Monde ouvrier*, May 22, 1926.
58 Julien Saint-Michel, "Au tour des domestiques," *Le Monde ouvrier*, November 22, 1919.
59 Quebec, *Annuaire statistique 1932* (Quebec: 1932), 91.
60 Julien Saint-Michel, "Le retour au foyer," *Le Monde ouvrier*, November 12, 1932.
61 *La Presse*, February 3, 1933, 15.
62 *La Presse*, February 3, 1933, 15.
63 The Liberal Premier, Alexandre Taschereau, invited Francœur to withdraw his bill, but the MLA refused. The discussion only lasted a half-hour, during which time three

members of the Liberal Party, Athanase David, Peter Bercovitch, and Gontran Saint-Onge, refuted his arguments and defended women's right to work. The bill would be defeated by forty-seven votes to sixteen, indicating a change if not in public opinion, then at least amongst politicians. *La Patrie*, January 23 and 24, 1935; *La Presse*, January 23, 1935.

64 Julien Saint-Michel, "Le retour à la terre," *Le Monde ouvrier*, August 11, 1934.

65 Julien Saint-Michel, "Le travail des femmes mariées," *Le Monde ouvrier*, March 13, 1930; "La femme mariée dans l'industrie," June 14, 1930.

66 For many households of unskilled or semi-skilled workers, the situation had barely changed since the nineteenth century. See Bettina Bradbury, *Working Families: Age, Gender, and Daily Survival in Industrializing Montreal* (Toronto: University of Toronto Press, 1993); Terry Copp, *The Anatomy of Poverty. The Condition of the Working Class in Montreal, 1897–1929* (Toronto: McClelland and Stewart, 1974), 45, 55–56.

67 Anon, "Le travail des femmes," *Le Monde ouvrier*, October 20, 1934, 3. This came in response to a speech by T.-A. Russell, president of Massey-Harris, to the Chamber of Commerce of Winnipeg, in which he said that working women were the third cause of the Great Depression and recommended that society adapt to this new situation.

68 Éva Circé-Côté and *Le Monde ouvrier* were not totally isolated in their defence of working women. While *Le Devoir* praised deputy Francœur for his courage, liberal newspapers like *La Patrie* generally agreed with the trade union newspaper. Julien Saint-Michel quoted Jean-Charles Harvey who, writing in *Le Jour*, denounced the illusion of being able to resolve unemployment by targeting working women. *Le Monde ouvrier* reprinted the article by Harvey, prompting Gustave Francq to exclaim: "Bravo Harvey." *Le Devoir*, February 2, 1933; *La Patrie*, February 2, 1933; Julien Saint-Michel, "Le Travail de la femme," *Le Monde ouvrier*, February 8, 1936; Editorial, *Le Monde ouvrier*, February 8, 1936.

69 Julien Saint-Michel, "Le travail des femmes," *Le Monde ouvrier*, May 12, 1934.

70 Julien Saint-Michel, "Les femmes dans l'industrie," *Le Monde ouvrier*, January 31, 1920.

71 Julien Saint-Michel, "Le travail des femmes mariées," *Le Monde ouvrier*, March 13, 1930. She reiterated these arguments in 1934: "It allows women to acquire independence and emancipation; they make positive contributions to the economy by increasing productivity, as well as the buying power of households." "Le travail des femmes."

72 Julien Saint-Michel, "N'ostracisons pas les femmes," *Le Monde ouvrier*, December 5, 1931. See also "La femme mariée dans l'industrie," *Le Monde ouvrier*, June 14, 1930.

73 Julien Saint-Michel, "Pourquoi déplacer le secours direct?" *Le Monde ouvrier*, February 15, 1936.

74 Julien Saint-Michel, "Renvoyer la femme au foyer, est-ce possible?" *Le Monde ouvrier*, December 1, 1934.

75 Julien Saint-Michel, "N'ostracisons pas les femmes," *Le Monde ouvrier*, December 5, 1931; "Le travail des femmes."

76 Julien Saint-Michel, "Vengeance infâme," *Le Monde ouvrier*, March 14, 1931; "Letravail féminin est-il préféré?" February 17, 1934; "Le travail des femmes."

77 Julien Saint-Michel, "Renvoyer la femme au foyer, est-ce possible?" *Le Monde ouvrier*, December 1, 1934.

78 Julien Saint-Michel, "Le travail de la femme," *Le Monde ouvrier*, February 8, 1936.

79 Julien Saint-Michel, "Esclavage moderne," *Le Monde ouvrier*, February 7, 1925.
80 Julien Saint-Michel, "N'ostracisons pas les femmes," *Le Monde ouvrier*, December 5, 1931. She added: "We must make a distinction and not employ women who have no one in their care and who squander most of their income on silk dresses, fur coats, jewelry, toiletries, cigarettes, candies, and trivial things." "Le travail de la femme," *Le Monde ouvrier*, June 4, 1932.
81 Julien Saint-Michel, "Le travail de la femme," *Le Monde ouvrier*, February 8, 1936.
82 Julien Saint-Michel, "L'utilité de la gent féminine," *Le Monde ouvrier*, June 23, 1934.

Conclusion

1 Julien Saint-Michel, "Une question que rien n'étouffe," *Le Monde ouvrier*, August 7, 1920; Ève Circé-Côté, "Rayonnement de la pourpre cardinalice, suite," *L'Aurore*, May 13, 1938.
2 Jean-François Sirinelli, *Les Intellectuels en France. De l'affaire Dreyfus à nos jours* (Paris: Armand Colin, 2002). Christophe Charle, *Les Intellectuels en Europe au XIXe siècle: essai d'histoire comparée* (Paris: Seuil, 1996). No women are discussed in Catherine Pomeyrols's thesis, *Les Intellectuels québécois: formation et engagements, 1919–1939* (Paris/Montreal: L'Harmattan, 1996), nor in the proceedings of the conference (Actes du colloque) devoted to the subject that was organized in Trois-Rivières by the Centre interuniversitaire d'études québécoises de l'Université du Québec à Trois-Rivières and Université Laval in 1997: *L'Inscription sociale de l'intellectuel*, ed. Manon Brunet and Pierre Lanthier (Sainte-Foy: Presses de l'Université Laval, 2000). The historian Yvan Lamonde blames the strong influence of the Catholic Church in Quebec for the scarcity, even absence, of intellectuals. Yvan Lamonde, "L'époque des francs-tireurs: les intellectuels au Québec, 1900–1930," in Brunet and Lanthier, *L'Inscription sociale de l'intellectuel*. It is telling that, unlike France, Canada never included the category "intellectuals" in its census.

APPENDICES

Éva Circé-Côté's Pseudonyms
(in chronological order)

Colombine
Musette
Fantasio
Jean Nay
Jean Ney
Paul S. Bédard
Arthur Maheu
Julien Saint-Michel
Loup de velours
Polémarque (?)

Publications to Which Éva Circé-Côté Contributed
(number of columns or articles in parentheses)

L'*Album universel*, 1903 (1)
L'*Aurore*, 1910, 1937–1941 (26)
L'*Autorité*, 1937 (3)
L'*Avenir*, 1900–1901 (13)
L'*Avenir du Nord*, 1900–1909 (39)
Le *Bulletin de la Caisse nationale* (2)
d'*économie*, 1904 (2)
Le *Combat*
Les *Débats*, 1900–1903 (62)
L'*Étincelle*
Jewish Daily Eagle/Kanader Adler (1)
Le *Journal de Françoise*, 1902–1909 (4)

Le *Mâtin*, 1922–1923 (?)
Le *Monde illustré*, 1901–1902 (14)
Le *Monde ouvrier*, 1916–1942 (767)
Le *Nationaliste*, 1904, 1909 (4)
Le *Passe-Temps*, 1920, 1923 (2)
La *Patrie*, 1905 (1)
Le *Pays*, 1910–1921 (803)
Le *Pionnier*, 1901–1902 (21)
La *Revue moderne*, 1935 (12)
La *Vigie*, 1909 (3)
The *Daily Witness* (1)

Columns by Éva Circé-Côté (Number Published Each Year)
(divided according to the respective periods covered in the chapters of Part One)

1900–1913		1914–1918		1919–1932		1933–1942	
1900	14	1914	91	1919	58	1933	16
1901	67	1915	91	1920	139	1934	30
1902	12	1916	131	1921	137	1935	34
1903	61	1917	149	1922	1	1936	16
1904	10	1918	49	1923	1	1937	24
1905	5	total	511	1924	28	1938	16
1906	3			1925	46	1939	5
1907	2			1926	39	1940	2
1908	1			1927	51	1941	3
1909	9			1928	50	1942	1
1910	49			1929	44	total	147
1911	47			1930	47		
1912	50			1931	45		
1913	86			1932	46		
total	416			total	432		

Total : 1506 (columns, cards, poems, and reviews)

TABLE 1
Infant Mortality
Province of Quebec
Number of Deaths Per Thousand Live Births
1910–1939

1911–1915	165.6
1916–1920	148.8
1921–1925	124
1926–1930	127
1931–1935	98
1936–1940	83

Source: *Annuaire de la Province de Québec* (Yearbook), *1922*, p. 46; *1931*, p 70; *1939*, p. 94; *1958*, p. 122.

TABLE 2
Labour Force Participation Rate (%) of Women
Quebec, 1891–1941*

1891	11
1901	12
1911	14.31
1921	16
1931	18.8
1941	22.3

* The participation rates of men during this period were between 57% and 60%. From 1891 to 1931, the statistics include women over ten years old, but women over fourteen years old in 1941.
Source: *Census of Canada, 1921*, vol. IV, Table 3, p. xxxvii; *1931*, vol. VII, Table 3, p. 5; *1941*, vol. VII, Table 3, p. 18.

TABLE 3
Top Five Gainful Occupations of Women in Quebec
1911–1941

	1911	1921	1931	1941
Domestics	20,184	35,440	44,371	52,375
Clothing workers*	18,680	18,339	20,298	36,729
Teachers**	11,560	16,236	21,372	23,891
Sales clerks	5,562	7,543	11,645	14,088
Office workers***	2,178	2,545		37,716
Gainfully employed women over 10 years old	101,101	139,151	202,423	260,372

*Employed in factories or workshops in any of the tailoring operations.
**Includes only secular positions.
*** This category varies from one census to the next. In 1921, it covered public administration workers and officer workers, stenographers, and typists.
Source: *Census of Canada, 1911*, vol. VI, Table C, p. 206-227; *1921*, vol. IV, Table 4, p. 188–214; *1931*, vol. VII, Table 41, p. 108–120; *1941*, vol. VII, Table 5, 106–111.

BIBLIOGRAPHY

Archives

Archives de la Paroisse Saint-Jean-Baptiste de Montréal
Registre des baptêmes
Registre des mariages

Archives de l'archevêché de Montréal
Registre des lettres de Mgr Bruchési, Vol. 2 (January 18, 1901–May 2, 1904); Vol. 4, 1906–1908; Vol. 5, 1908–1911

Archives de la Ville de Montréal
Enquête sur la police (Enquête Coderre), procès-verbaux, 1924–1925, Vol. 3; Vol. 8
Fonds de la Bibliothèque de la Ville de Montréal, BM60
Fonds de la Commission spéciale d'enquête Milette vs Grandchamps et Laberge, 1910, VM71
Fonds du Conseil de Ville de la Ville de Montréal, VM1
Fonds Olivar Asselin, BM55 S2, D6
Rapport de l'honorable juge Louis Boyer sur les théâtres de la province de Québec à la suite de l'enquête sur les causes du Cinéma Laurier Palace, August 25, 1927

Archives de l'Université de Montreal
Fonds Louvigny de Montigny, P75
Fonds Réginald Hamel, P382

Archives des soeurs de la Congrégation de Notre-Dame (ACND)
Correspondance
Soeur Sainte-Euphrosine, *La Fondation*

Archives des Soeurs de Sainte-Anne (ASSA)
Bulletins des élèves, 1885–1888, LQ/11, LQ/10
Rapports annuels faits au surintendant de l'Instruction publique, 1882–1888, LQ11/40

Archives Lionel Groulx
Fonds de l'Imprimerie populaire, P56/C3, 6

Bibliothèque et archives nationales du Québec (BANQ)
Centre d'archives de Montreal

Fonds de l'Association des auteurs canadiens-français (Société des auteurs canadiens-français) MSS-061

Fonds de l'Institut Notre-Dame du Bon Conseil (FINDBC), Fonds Marie-Gérin Lajoie, P783

Fonds de la Fédération nationale Saint-Jean-Baptiste, M-P120/06

Fonds Gabriel Nadeau (MSS177), archives de Louis Dantin (Eugène Seers)

Fonds Marie Gérin-Lajoie, P578

Centre de recherche en civilisation canadienne-française (CRCCF), Université d'Ottawa

Centre régional d'archives de Lanaudière (CARDL), Collège L'Assomption
Collection Réginald Hamel, P109
Fonds Albert Laberge, P6
Fonds Arthur de Bussières (Joseph-Marie-Arthur), P83
Fonds Charles Gill, P192
Fonds École littéraire de Montréal, C1
Fonds Guy Courteau, série Marcel Dugas
Fonds Jean Charbonneau (1875–1960), P2
Fonds Louvigny de Montigny

Newspapers

L'Action/Le Combat, 1900–1902; 1903–1904
L'Action (Jules Fournier), 1911–1916
L'Action française, 1920–1921
L'Action sociale, 1909
L'Album universel, 1903
L'Aurore, 1910, 1937–1941
L'Autorité, 1937
L'Avenir, 1899–1900
L'Avenir du Nord, 1900–1909
La Bonne Parole, 1922
Le Bulletin de la Caisse nationale d'économie, 1904
Le Canada, 1903, 1907, 1909–1910, 1922, 1936, 1949
Le Canada français, 1909–1910
La Croix, 1910
The Daily Witness, 1909
Les Débats, 1899–1903
Le Devoir, 1910, 1913, 1918, 1922, 1925, 1932, 1933
L'Étincelle, 1902–1903
L'Illustration, 1932
Jewish Daily Eagle/Kanader Adler, édition souvenir 1932
Le Journal, 1900
Le Journal de Françoise, 1902–1909
Le Mâtin, 1922–1923
Le Monde illustré, 1901–1902

Le Monde ouvrier, 1916–1942
Montreal Daily Star, 1921
Montreal Herald, 1929–1930
La Nation, 1904
Le Nationaliste, 1904, 1905, 1909, 1910
Le Panorama, 1919
Paris-Canada, 1925
Le Passe-Temps, 1901, 1920, 1922, 1923
La Patrie, 1901–1905, 1907–1920, 1927, 1932–1935, 1937, 1947
Le Pays, 1910–1921
Le Petit Journal, 1932
Le Pionnier, 1901–1902
La Presse, 1900, 1909–1910, 1922, 1932, 1935, 1949
La Revue canadienne, vol. 44, 1903
La Revue de Manon, April 1925
La Revue des Deux Frances, 1898–1899
La Revue moderne, 1923, 1924, 1927, 1928, 1935, 1940
Le Saint-Laurent, 1923
Le Soleil, 1901, 1909–1910, 1922
The Standard, 1909–1911
La Vérité, 1902–1904
La Vie artistique, 1903, 1905
La Vigie, 1909
Winnipeg Free Press, 1947

Published Works by Éva Circé-Côté

Circé-Côté, Ève. "Préface." *Alphonse Primeau-Robert, La Place des protestants: conférence donnée à l'église du Rédempteur le 23 décembre 1923*, 6–13. Montreal: 1924.
Circé-Côté, Ève. *Papineau. Son influence sur la pensée canadienne. Essai de psychologie historique*. Montreal: Regnault, 1924. Montreal: Lux, 2002.
Colombine. *Bleu, Blanc, Rouge. Poésie, paysages, causeries*. Montreal: Déom Frères, 1903.

Letterpress Printed Work by Éva Circé-Côté

Maisonneuve. Fonds de l'Imprimerie populaire, Archives Lionel-Groulx, P56/C3, 6., s.d.

Reference Works

Audet, Francis-J., and Gérard Malchelosse. *Pseudonymes canadiens*. Québec: Garneau, 1974.
Beaulieu, André, and Jean Hamelin. *La Presse québécoise des origines à nos jours. Vol. 4, 1896–1910*. Quebec: Les Presses de l'Université Laval, 1979.
Dictionary of Canadian Biography. Vols. 13, 14, 15. Toronto/Quebec: University of Toronto Press/Les Presses de l'Université Laval, 2000.
Dominion Bureau of Statistics. *Canada Yearbook*. Ottawa: King's Printer, 1936, 1939.

Dominion Bureau of Statistics. *Census of Canada*. Ottawa: King's Printer, 1901, 1911, 1921, 1931, 1941.
Harrison, H., ed. *National Reference Book on Canadian Men and Women with other General Information for Library, Newspaper, Educational and Individual Use*. 5th ed. Montreal: Canadian Newspaper Service Registered, 1936.
Lovell's Montreal Directory, 1888–1889; 1902; 1947–1952. Montreal: John Lovell.
Ouimet, Raphaël. *Biographies canadiennes-françaises*. Montreal: 1924.
Québec. *Annuaire Statistique 1932*. Quebec: 1932.
Québec. *Débats de l'Assemblée législative*. 1908–1912.

Books

Alpern, Sara, et al., eds. *The Challenge of Feminist Biography*. Chicago: University of Illinois Press, 1992.
Anctil, Pierre. *"Le Devoir," les Juifs et l'Immigration*. Quebec: IQRC, 1988.
Anctil, Pierre. *Le Rendez-vous manqué. Les Juifs de Montréal face au Québec de l'entre-deux-guerres*. Québec: IQRC, 1988.
Armand, E., Gérard de Lacaze-Duthiers, and Abel Léger. *L'Homosexualité, l'Onanisme et les Individualistes*. Preceded by Gérard de Lacaze-Duthiers, "Des préjugés en matières sexuelles," and Abel Léger, "La Honteuse Hypocrisie." Paris/Orléans: Édition de l'En-dehors, 1931.
Asselin, Olivar. *Pensée française. Pages choisies*. Édition de l'Association canadienne-française, 1937.
Auclair, Élie. *Saint-Jean-Baptiste de Montréal, Monographie paroissiale 1874–1924*. Quebec: 1924.
Baillargeon, à Denyse. *Un Québec en mal d'enfants, La médicalisation de la maternité 1910–1970*. Montreal: Éditions du remue-ménage, 2004.
Barbeau, Victor. *La Société des Écrivains canadiens*. Montreal: Société des Écrivains canadiens, 1944.
Barker-Benfield, G. J. *The Horror of the Unknown Life: Male Attitudes Toward Women and Sexuality in Nineteenth-Century America*. New York, Harper & Row, 1976.
Beaulieu, Germain, avec Albéric Bourgeois. *Nos Immortels: Caricatures de Bourgeois*. Montreal: Albert Lévesque, 1931.
Bélanger, Réal. *Wilfrid Laurier: Quand la politique devient passion*. Quebec/Montreal: Presses de l'Université Laval/Entreprises Radio-Canada, 1986.
Bellerive, Georges. *Brèves apologies de nos auteurs féminins*. Quebec: Garneau, 1920.
Bellerive, Georges. *Nos auteurs dramatiques anciens et contemporains*: répertoire analytique, Québec (Québec): Librairie Garneau, 1933.
Bernard, Henri. *La Ligue de l'enseignement: histoire d'une conspiration maçonnique à Montréal*. Montreal: Notre-Dame des Neiges-Ouest: n.p., 1903.
Bessette, Arsène. *Le Débutant*. Montreal: 1914.
Bethléem, Louis, Abbé. *Romans à lire, Romans à proscrire. Essai de classification au point de vue moral des principaux romans et romanciers depuis l'an 1500*. Paris: n.p., 1905.
Biographies canadiennes-françaises. Montreal: Ouimet, 1922; 1923; 1924; 1925.
Bliss, Michael. *A Canadian Millionaire: The Life and Business Times of Sir Joseph Flavelle, 1858–1939*. Toronto: Macmillan of Canada, 1978.
Bouchard, Télesphore Damien. *Mémoires de T. D. Bouchard*. Vol. 2, *Gravissant la colline*. Montreal: Beauchemin, 1960.

Bourassa, Henri. *Femmes-Hommes ou hommes-femmes? Études à bâtons rompus sur le féminisme*. Montreal: Le Devoir, 1925.
Bradbury, Bettina. *Working Families: Age, Gender, and Daily Survival in Industrializing Montreal*. Toronto: University of Toronto Press, 1993.
Brisson, Marcelle, and Suzanne Côté-Gauthier. *Montréal de vive mémoire, 1900–1939*. Montreal: Triptyque, 1994.
Brown, Robert Craig. *Robert Laird Borden. A Biography*. Vol. 2. Toronto: Macmillan of Canada, 1980.
Brown, Robert Craig, and Ramsay Cook. *Canada, 1896–1921: A Nation Transformed*. Toronto: McClelland & Stewart, 1974.
Brunet, Manon, and Pierre Lanthier, eds. *L'Inscription sociale de l'intellectuel*. Sainte-Foy: Presses de l'Université Laval, 2000.
Buis, Arthur. *Chroniques II*. Montreal: Presses de l'Université de Montréal, 1991.
Burdeau, Georges. *Le Libéralisme*. Paris: Seuil, 1979.
Butterfield, Herbert. *The Whig Interpretation of History*. 1931. New York: W. W. Norton, 1965.
Cambron, Micheline, ed. *La Vie culturelle à Montréal vers 1900*. Montreal: Fides/Bibliothèque nationale du Québec, 2005.
Chabot, Juliette. *Montréal et le Rayonnement des bibliothèques publiques*. Montreal: Fides, 1963.
Charle, Christophe. *Naissance des intellectuels, 1880–1900*. Paris: Minuit, 1990.
Collectif Clio. *L'Histoire des femmes au Québec depuis quatre siècles*. Montreal: Quinze, 1982.
Condorcet, Jean-Antoine-Nicolas de Caritat, Marquis de. *Outlines of an Historical View of the Progress of the Human Mind*. Baltimore: J. Frank, 1802.
Congrès de la langue française au Canada. *Deuxième congrès de la langue française au Canada, Québec, 27 juin–1er juillet 1937: compte rendu*. Québec: Imprimerie de l'Action catholique, 1938.
Copp, Terry. *The Anatomy of Poverty: The Condition of the Working Class in Montreal, 1897–1929*. Montreal: McClelland & Stewart, 1974.
Côté, Elzéar-Auguste. *La Puissance paternelle*. Rimouski: Imprimerie générale S. Vachon, 1926.
CSN-CEQ. *Histoire du mouvement ouvrier au Québec (1825–1976): 150 ans de luttes*. Montreal: CSN/CEQ, 1979.
Dandurand, Raoul. *Mémoires*, ed. Marcel Hamelin. Québec: Presses de l'Université Laval, 1967.
De Baeque, Antoine, and Françoise Mélonio. *Lumières et liberté: Les dix-huitième et dix-neuvième siècles*. Paris: Seuil, 2005.
De Montigny, Louvigny. *Étoffe du pays*. Montreal: Beauchemin, 1951.
De Roquebrune, Robert. *Testament de mon enfance*. Paris, Palatine/Plon, 1951.
De Roquebrune, Robert. *Testament de mon enfance*. Montreal: Fides, 1958.
De Roquebrune, Robert. *Quartier Saint-Louis*. Montreal: Fides, 1966.
Desmond, Adrian, and James Moore. *Darwin: The Life of a Tormented Evolutionist*. New York: Warner Books, 1991.
Douville, Raymond. *La Vie aventureuse d'Arthur Buies*. Montreal: Albert Lévesque, 1933.
Drouin, Daniel, ed. *Louis-Philippe Hébert, 1850–1917*. Québec, Musée du Québec, 2001.
Dugas, Marcel. *Flacons à la mer: proses*. Paris: Les Gémaux, 1923.
Dumont, Micheline, and Louise Toupin. *La Pensée féministe au Québec: Anthologie 1900–1985*. Montreal: Éditions du remue-ménage, 2003.
Dutil, Patrice. *Devil's Advocate: Godfroy Langlois and the Politics of Liberal Progressivism in Laurier's Quebec*. Montreal: Robert Davies, 1994. Translated by the author as *L'Avocat du*

diable: Godfroy Langlois et le libéralisme progressiste dans le Québec de Wilfrid Laurier. Montreal: Robert Davies, 1995.
Fahmy-Eid, Nadia, ed. *Maîtresses de maison, maîtresses d'école: femmes, famille et éducation dans l'histoire du Québec.* Montreal: Boréal, 1983.
Foisy, Richard. *L'Arche: Un atelier d'artistes dans le Vieux-Montréal.* Montreal: VLB, 2009.
Fournier, Jules. *Mon encrier.* Montreal: Madame Jules Fournier, 1922.
Fréchette, Louis. *Satires et polémiques II.* Montreal: Presses de l'Université de Montreal: Collection BNM, 1993.
Gagnon, Marcel-A. *La Vie orageuse d'Olivar Asselin.* 2 vols. Montreal: Édition de l'Homme, 1962.
Garneau, François-Xavier. *Histoire du Canada.* 5th edition. Revised, annotated and published with an introduction and appendices by his grandson, Hector Garneau. Preface by M. Gabriel Hanotaux. Paris: Félix Alcan, 1913.
Gérin-Lajoie, Marie. *Traité de Droit usuel.* Montreal: C.O., Beauchemin & Fils, 1902.
Gill, Charles. *Correspondance*, ed. Réginald Hamel. Montreal: Partis-pris, 1969.
Gosselin, Line. *Les journalistes québécoises, 1880–1930.* Montreal: Regroupement des chercheurs-chercheures en histoire des travailleurs et travailleuses du Québec, Collection RCHTQ: Études et documents, no. 7, 1995.
Granatstein, J. L., and J. M. Hitsman. *Broken Promises: A History of Conscription in Canada.* Toronto: Oxford University Press, 1977.
Greer, Allan. *The Patriots and the People: The Rebellion of 1837 in Rural Lower Canada.* Toronto: University of Toronto Press, 1993.
Guénard-Hodent, Maurice. *La tradition renouée. Les Relations entre la France et le Canada depuis soixante années.* Paris: Édition Paris-Canada, 1930.
Hamel, Réginald. *Gaëtane de Montreuil: journaliste québécoise (1867–1951).* Montreal: L'Aurore, 1976.
Kalm, Peter. *Voyage de Kalm en Amérique, 1753–1761.* 2 Vols. Translated by L.-W. Marchand. Montreal: T. Berthiaume (Mémoires de la Société historique de Montreal), 1880.
Harrington, Lyn. *Syllables of Recorded Time.* Toronto: Simon & Pierre, 1981.
Hause, Steven C., and Anne R. Kenney. *Women's Suffrage and Social Politics in the French Third Republic.* Princeton: Princeton University Press, 1984.
Hébert, Pierre, with Patrick Nicol. *Censure et littérature au Québec.* Vol. 1, *Le livre crucifié (1625–1919).* Montreal: Fides, 1997.
Hébert, Pierre, and Élise Salaün. *Censure et littérature au Québec, Tome 2, Des vieux couvents au plaisir de vivre (1920–1959).* Montreal: Fides, 2004.
King, William Lyon Mackenzie. *Industry and Humanity. A Study in the Principles Under-Lying Industrial Reconstruction.* Toronto & Boston: T. Allen & Houghton Mifflin, 1918. Translated by Altair, under the title *La question sociale et le Canada: industrie et humanité.* Preface by Gabriel Hanotaux. Paris: Félix Alcan, 1925.
Laberge, Albert. *Peintres et écrivains d'hier et d'aujourd'hui.* Montreal: n.p., 1938.
Laberge, Albert. *Journalistes, écrivains et artistes.* Montreal: n.p., 1945.
Lalonde, Jean-Louis. *Des loups dans la bergerie: Les Protestants de langue française au Québec.* Montreal: Fides, 2002.
Lamonde, Yvan. *Les bibliothèques de collectivités à Montreal (17e–19e siècles).* Montreal: Bibliothèque nationale du Québec, 1979.
Lamonde, Yvan. *Louis-Antoine Dessaulles, un seigneur libéral et anticlerical.* Montreal: Fides, 1994.
Lamonde, Yvan, ed. *Combats libéraux au tournant du XXe siècle.* Montreal: Fides, 1995.
Lamonde, Yvan. *Histoire sociale des idées au Québec, 1896–1929.* Montreal: Fides, 2004.

Lamonde, Yvan and Denis Saint-Jacques. *1937: un tournant culturel*. Quebec: Presses de l'Université Laval, 2009.
Lamontagne, Léopold. *Arthur Buies: Homme de lettres*. Quebec: Presses universitaires Laval, 1967.
Larrue, Jean-Marc. *Le Monument inattendu: Le Monument national 1893–1993*. Montreal: HMH, 1993.
Lassonde, Jean-René. *La Bibliothèque Saint-Sulpice, 1910–1931*. Montreal: Bibliothèque nationale du Québec, 1986.
Lemieux, Albert-J. *La Loge l'Émancipation*. Montreal: La Croix, 1910.
Le Moine, Roger. *Deux loges montréalaises du Grand Orient de France*. Ottawa: Presses de l'Université d'Ottawa, 1991.
Leroux, Éric. *Gustave Francq, figure marquante du syndicalisme et précurseur de la FTQ*. Montreal: VLB, 2001.
L'Espérance, Jeanne. *Vers des horizons nouveaux: la femme canadienne de 1870 à 1940*. Ottawa: Archives publiques et Bibliothèque nationale du Canada, 1982.
Lévesque, Andrée. *Résistance et transgression: Études en histoire des femmes au Québec*. Montreal: Remue-ménage, 1995.
Linteau, Paul-André. *Histoire de Montréal depuis la Confédération*. Montreal: Boréal, 1992.
Martel, Marcel. *Le Deuil d'un pays imaginé: Rêves, luttes et déroute du Canada français. Les rapports entre le Québec et la francophonie canadienne (1867–1975)*. Ottawa: Presses de l'Université d'Ottawa, Collection Amérique française, 1997.
McKay, Ian. *Reasoning Otherwise: Leftists and the People's Enlightenment in Canada, 1890–1920*. Toronto: Between the Lines, 2008.
McLaren, Angus. *Our Own Master Race: Eugenics in Canada, 1885–1945*. Toronto, McClelland & Stewart, 1990.
Mill, John Stuart. *On Liberty*. 1860. London: Oxford University Press, 1966.
Morton, Desmond. *Fight or Pay: Soldiers' Families in the Great War*. Vancouver: University of British Columbia Press, 2004.
Olazabal, Ignace. *Khaverim: Les Juifs Ashkénazes de Montréal au début du XXe siècle*. Québec: Nota bene, 2006.
Parent-Duchâtelet, Alexandre. *De la prostitution dans la ville de Paris considérée sous le rapport de l'hygiène publique, de la morale et de l'administration*. 2 Vols. Paris: J. Baillière, 1836.
Pelletier-Baillargeon, Hélène. *Olivar Asselin et son temps*. Vol. 1, *Le Militant*. Montreal: Fides, 1996.
Pierson, Ruth Roach. *"They're Still Women After All": The Second World War and Canadian Womanhood*. Toronto: McClelland & Stewart, 1986.
Primeau-Robert, Alphonse. *La Place des protestants dans la nationalité canadienne-française: conférence donnée à l'église du Rédempteur le 23 décembre 1923*. Montreal: n.p., 1924.
Quanta Cura. Lettre encyclique de SS Pie IX, 8 décembre 1984, *Syllabus errorum, Recueil (*) renfermant les principales erreurs de notre temps qui sont notées dans les allocutions consistoriales, encycliques et autres lettres apostoliques de Notre Très Saint-Père le pape Pie IX (Syllabus complectens præciuos nostræ* ætatis errores.
Racine, Nicole, and Michel Trebisch. *Intellectuelles, Du genre en histoire des intellectuels*. Paris: IHTP/CNRS, Complexe, 2004.
Rajotte, Pierre, ed. *Lieux et réseaux de sociabilité littéraire au Québec*. Quebec: Nota bene, Collection Séminaires, 2001.
Ricoeur, Paul. *Du texte à l'action: Essais d'herméneutique*. Paris: Seuil, 1986.
Ricoeur, Paul. *Soi-même comme un autre*. Paris: Seuil, 1990.

Roby, Yves. *Les Franco-Américains de la Nouvelle-Angleterre, 1776–1930.* Quebec: Septentrion, 1990.
Roy, Fernande. *Progrès, harmonie, liberté: Le libéralisme des milieux d'affaires francophones à Montréal au tournant du siècle.* Montreal: Boréal, 1988.
Roy, Fernande. *Histoire de la librairie au Québec.* Montreal: Leméac, 2000.
Rumilly, Robert. *Henri Bourassa: La vie publique d'un grand Canadien.* Montreal: Chanteclerc, 1953.
Rumilly, Robert. *Histoire de la Société Saint-Jean-Baptiste de Montréal: des patriotes au fleurdelysé, 1834–1948.* Montreal: L'Aurore, 1975.
Rumilly, Robert. *Histoire de la province de Québec.* Vol. 11. Montreal: Bernard Valiquette.
Saint-Jacques, Denis. *L'Artiste et ses Lieux: Les régionalismes de l'entre-deux guerres face à la modernité.* Quebec: Nota bene, 2007.
Saint-Jacques, Denis, and Maurice Lemire, eds. *La Vie littéraire au Québec, tome V, (1895–1918): Sois fidèle à ta Laurentie.* Québec: Presses de l'Université Laval, 2005.
Savard, Pierre. *Jules-Paul Tardivel, la France et les États-Unis, 1851–1905.* Quebec: Presses de l'Université Laval, 1967.
Sicotte, Anne-Marie. *Marie Gérin-Lajoie: conquérante de la liberté.* Montreal: Éditions du remue-ménage, 2005.
Spencer, Herbert. *The Study of Sociology.* New York: D. Appleton & Co., 1896. [Consulted online at archive.org.]
Tanguay, Cyprien. *Dictionnaire généalogique des familles canadiennes depuis la fondation de la colonie jusqu'à nos jours.* Montreal: E. Sénécal, Imprimeur-éditeur, 1871–1890.
Toullier, C.B.M. *Le Droit civil français sur l'ordre du Code.* Paris: 1821.
Vanderpelen-Diagre, Cécile. *Mémoire d'y croire. Le monde catholique et la littérature au Québec (1920–1960).* Quebec: Nota bene, 2007.
Van Slyck, Abigail A. *Carnegie Libraries & American Culture, 1890–1920.* Chicago: University of Chicago Press, 1995.
Verne, Jules. *Famille-Sans-Nom.* Montreal: Stanké, 1999. First published 1889 by Éditions Hetzel, Paris.
Vinet, Bernard. *Pseudonymes québécois.* Quebec: Garneau, 1974.
Voltaire, François-Marie Arouet. *Traité sur la tolerance.* 1763. Edited by Jacques Van den Heuvel. Paris, Poche, 2003.
Wallace, W. Stewart, ed. *The Encyclopedia of Canada.* Vol. 4. Toronto: University Associates of Canada, 1948.
Wallot, Jean-Pierre. *Un Québec qui bougeait: trame socio-politique au tournant du XIXe siècle.* Montreal: Boréal Express, 1973.
Warren, Louise. *Léonise Valois, femme de lettres (1868–1939).* Montreal: L'Hexagone, 1993.
Weber, Max. *The Protestant Ethic and the Spirit of Capitalism.* Tr. Stephen Kalberg. Chicago: Fitzroy Dearborn, 2001.
Williams, Dorothy W. *Blacks in Montreal: An Urban Demography.* Montreal: Yvon Blais, 1989.
Wilson, Edmund. *O Canada: An American's Notes on Canadian Culture.* New York: Farrar, Straus & Giroux, 1964.
Winock, Michel. *Le Siècle des intellectuels.* Rev. ed. Seuil, Collection Points, 1999.
Woolf, Virginia. *Mr. Bennett and Mrs. Brown,* London: Hogarth Press, 1924.
Wyczynski, Paul et al. eds., *Archives des lettres canadiennes.* Vol. 2, *L'École littéraire de Montreal.* Montreal: Fides, 1972.
Young, Brian. *Respectable Burial: Montreal's Mount Royal Cemetery.* Montreal & Kingston: McGill-Queen's University Press, 2003.

Articles

Auclair, Élie J. "Le Congrès des Canadiennes Françaises." *La Revue canadienne* 6, no. 2 (August 1910): 135–47.
Baboyant, Marie. "La bibliothèque de la Ville de Montréal, la collection Gagnon et son fondateur Philéas Gagnon." *Les Cahiers d'histoire du Québec au XXe siècle* 6 (Autumn 1996): 67–82.
Bélanger, Réal. "Le libéralisme de Wilfrid Laurier: évolution et contenu (1841–1919)." In *Combats libéraux au tournant du XXe siècle*, ed. Yvan Lamonde, 39–72. Montreal: Fides, 1995.
Boivin, Aurélien, and Kenneth Landry. "Françoise et Madeleine, pionnières du journalisme féminin au Québec." *Voix et Images* 4, no. 2 (December 1978): 63–74.
Boivin, Julie. "Le monument à Octave Crémazie." In *Louis-Philippe Hébert 1850–1917*, ed. Daniel Drouin, 210–13. Quebec: Musée du Québec, 2001.
Cambron, Micheline. "Mondanité et vie culturelle." In *La Vie culturelle à Montréal vers 1900*, ed. Micheline Cambron, 121–34. Montreal: Fides/Bibliothèque nationale du Québec, 2005.
Carrier, Anne. "Barry, Robertine, dite Françoise." In *Dictionnaire biographique du Canada, 1901–1910*. Vol. 13, ed. Ramsay Cook and Jean Hamelin, 47. Québec: Presses de l'Université Laval, 1994.
Couture, François. "Le réseau associatif de l'École littéraire de Montréal." In *La Vie culturelle à Montréal vers 1900*, ed. Micheline Cambron, 289–303. Montreal: Fides/Bibliothèque nationale du Québec, 2005.
Dagenais, Michèle. "Vie culturelle et pouvoirs publics locaux: La fondation de la bibliothèque municipale de Montréal," *Urban History Review/Revue d'histoire urbaine* 24, no. 2 (March 1996): 40–56.
Dagenais, Michèle. "Autour de la Bibliothèque municipale de Montréal, Lecture des enjeux culturels et politiques." In *La Vie culturelle à Montréal vers 1900*, ed. Micheline Cambron, 103–20. Montreal: Fides/Bibliothèque nationale du Québec, 2005.
D'Amours, Joanne, "Un 'D'Amours' vicaire aux États-Unis." *Le Sanglier* 1, no. 4 (May 1, 2002): 49–52.
Demers, Jeanne. "Entre chien et loup: Prolégomènes à une étude du conte écrit québécois." In *La Vie culturelle à Montréal vers 1900*, ed. Micheline Cambron, 175–89. Montreal: Fides/Bibliothèque nationale du Québec, 2005.
Dupont, Antonin. "Louis-Alexandre Taschereau et la législation sociale au Québec, 1920–1936." *Revue d'histoire de l'Amérique française* 26, no. 3 (December 1972): 397–426.
Dutil, Patrice. "'Adieu demeure chaste et pure': Godfroy Langlois et le virage vers le progressisme libéral." In *Combats libéraux au tournant du XXe siècle*, ed. Yvan Lamonde, 247–76. Montreal: Fides, 1995.
Dutil, Paul. "The Politics of Progressivism in Quebec: the Gouin 'Coup' Revisited." *Canadian Historical Review* 69, no. 4 (December 1988): 441–65.
Ewen, Geoffrey. "Québec: Class and Ethnicity." In *The Workers' Revolt in Canada*, ed. Craig Heron, 99–116. Toronto: University of Toronto Press, 1998.
Farhni, Magda. "Glimpsing Working-Class Childhood through the Laurier Palace Fire of 1927: The Ordinary, the Tragic, and the Historian's Gaze," *Journal of the History of Childhood and Youth* 8, no. 3 (Fall 2015): 426–50.
Filion, Gilles W. "Joseph Phillias Filion: Comédien, Censeur (1841–1940)." *La Feuillée*, 1989.
Gill, Charles. "Un mot au lecteur." In *Les Soirées du Château Ramezay*, v–ix. Montreal: Eusèbe Senécal, 1900.

Girouard, Lisette. "Reconnaissances. Éva, Colombine, Julien." *Arcade* 23 (Winter 1992): 61–65.
Gordon, Ross. "Félix Desrochers, bibliothécaire général 1933–1956." *La Revue parlementaire canadienne* 23, no. 3 (2000): 14–20.
Guénard-Hodent, Maurice. "La vérité sur le Canada." *La Canadienne* 7 (1909).
Hamel, Thérèse. "Obligation scolaire et travail des enfants au Québec: 1900–1950." *Revue d'histoire de l'Amérique française* 38, no. 1 (Summer 1984): 39–58.
Hare, John E. "Sablonnière, Blanche de la." In *The Oxford Companion to Canadian Theatre*, ed. E. Benson and L. W. Conolly. Toronto: Oxford University Press, 1989.
Hayward, Annette. "Marcel Dugas, défenseur du modernisme." *Voix et Images* 17, no. 2 (Winter 1992): 184–202.
Hayward, Annette. "La littérature de la modernité et le libéralisme nationaliste au Québec entre 1899 et 1916." In *Combats libéraux au tournant du XXe siècle*, ed. Yvan Lamonde, 159–84. Montreal: Fides, 1995.
Hayward, Annette. "Marcel Dugas et l'habitus de l'art pour l'art." In *L'Artiste et ses Lieux: Les régionalismes de l'entre-deux-guerres face à la modernité*, ed. Denis Saint-Jacques, 127–50. Quebec: Nota bene, 2007.
Heap, Ruby. "La Ligue de l'enseignement (1902–1904): héritage du passé et nouveaux défis." *Revue d'histoire de l'Amérique française* 36, no. 3 (December 1982): 339–73.
Heap, Ruby. "Libéralisme et éducation au Québec à la fin du XIXe et au début du XXe siècle." In *Combats libéraux au tournant du XXe siècle*, ed. Yvan Lamonde, 99–118. Montreal: Fides, 1995.
Heinich, Nathalie. "Femmes écrivains: écriture et indépendance." In *Intellectuelles. Du genre en histoire des intellectuels*, eds. Nicole Racine and Michel Trebisch, 137–67. Paris: IHTP/CNRS, Complexe, 2004.
Homier, J.-Arthur. "Montréal il y a quarante ans." *La Revue de Manon* (April 1925): 4.
Lacroix, Laurier. "L'art au service de 'l'utile et du patriotique.'" In *La Vie culturelle à Montréal vers 1900*, ed. Micheline Cambron, 55–70. Montreal: Fides/Bibliothèque nationale du Québec, 2005.
Lacroix, Michel. "De Montesquiou à Montréal: Le *Nigog* et la mondanité." *Voix et Images* 29, no. 1 (Autumn 2003): 105–14.
Lacroix, Michel. "Lien social, idéologie et cercles d'appartenance: le réseau "latin" des Québécois en France, 1923–1939." *Études littéraires* 36, no. 2 (2004): 51–70.
Lajeunesse, Marcel. "Les bibliothèques québécoises: les avatars de leur rôle social à travers les âges." In *L'Évolution du rôle social des imprimés et de ses agents au Québec*, 46–76. Montreal: Conférences Aegidius-Fauteux, 1980.
Lambert, Maude-Emmanuelle. "Un ménage de petit bourgeois du Québec de la Belle Époque: valeurs, pratiques culturelles et consommation d'une famille francophone." *Revue d'histoire de l'Amérique française* 51, no. 1 (Summer 2007): 37–65.
Lamond, Yvan. "Le libéralisme et le passage dans le XXe siècle." In *Combats libéraux au tournant du XXe siècle*, ed. Yvan Lamonde, 9–38. Montreal: Fides, 1995.
Landry, Jean. "David, Laurent Olivier (1840–1926)." In *Dictionnaire biographique du Canada*. Vol. 15. www.biographi.ca.
Landry, Kenneth. "'Bleu, Blanc, Rouge,' chroniques et poèmes de Colombine." In *Dictionnaire des oeuvres littéraires du Québec, 1900–1939*. Vol. 2, ed. Maurice Lemire, 149–51. Montreal: Fides, 1987.
Larose, Karim. "'Les fous d'espoir.' Autour du Deuxième Congrès de la langue française au Canada." In *1937: un tournant culturel*, ed. Yvan Lamonde and Denis Saint-Jacques, 15–25. Québec: Presses de l'Université Laval, 2009.

Lefebvre, Marie-Thérèse. "L'École littéraire de Montréal et la vie musicale." In *La Vie culturelle à Montréal vers 1900*, ed. Micheline Cambron, 87–102. Montreal: Fides/Bibliothèque nationale du Québec, 2005.

Le Moine, Roger. "Le Grand Orient de France dans le contexte québécois (1896–1923)." In *Combats libéraux au tournant du XXe siècle*, ed. Yvan Lamonde, 145–57. Montreal: Fides, 1995.

Le Moine, Roger. "Martigny (Le Moyne de Martigny), Adelstan de." In *Dictionnaire biographique du Canada*. Vol. 15, 811–12. Toronto/Québec: University of Toronto Press/Presses de l'Université Laval, 2000.

"Lettres adressées à Marcel Dugas (1912–1944)." *Études françaises* 7, no. 3 (August 1971): 294.

Linteau, Paul-André. "Le personnel politique de Montréal 1880–1914: évolution d'une élite municipale." *Revue d'histoire de l'Amérique française* 52, no. 2 (Autumn 1998): 189–215.

Longstaff, Alison. "The Price of Passion." *The Beaver* (October 2005): 37–40.

Luneau, Marie-Pier. "L'auteur en quête de sa figure. Évolution de la pratique du pseudonyme au Québec, des origines à 1979." *Voix et Images* 88 (Autumn 2004): 13–30.

Luneau, Marie-Pier. "Le nom supposé comme outil de transgression, d'"Un Illuminé' au 'Frère Untel,' De l'usage de la fausse signature chez les prêtres au Québec (1809–1979), SCHEC." *Études d'histoire religieuse* 70 (2004): 41–57.

Mann Trofimenkoff, Susan. "Henri Bourassa et la question des femmes." In *Travailleuses et féministes. Les femmes dans la société québécoise*, ed. Marie Lavigne and Yolande Pinard, 293–306. Montreal: Boréal, 1983. Originally published as "Henri Bourassa and the Woman Question." *Journal of Canadian Studies* 10, no. 4 (November 1975): 3–11.

McKay, Ian. "The Liberal Order Framework: A Prospectus for a Reconnaissance of Canadian history." *Canadian Historical Review* 81, no. 4 (December 2000): 617–45.

Mizare, Adam. "Les disparus." *Bulletin de recherches historiques* 31, no. 4 (April 1925): 124.

Morton, Desmond. "Entente cordiale? La section montréalaise du Fonds patriotique canadien, 1914–1923: le bénévolat de guerre à Montréal." *Revue d'histoire de l'Amérique française* 8, no. 2 (Autumn 1999): 207–46.

Naudier, Delphine. "La reconnaissance sociale et littéraire des femmes écrivains depuis les années 1950." In *Intellectuelles: Du genre en histoire des intellectuels*, ed. Nicole Racine and Michel Trebisch. Paris: IHTP/CNRS, Complexe, 2004.

Ouellet, Fernand. "Bédard, Pierre-Stanislas." In *Dictionnaire biographique du Canada*. Vol. 6. www.biographi.ca.

Ouellet, Fernand. "Papineau, Louis-Joseph." In *Dictionnaire biographique du Canada*. Vol. 10, ed. Marc La Terreur, 624–27. Quebec: Presses de l'Université Laval, 1972.

Parmentier, Francis. "Formes, contenu et évolution du libéralisme d'Arthur Buies." In *Combats libéraux au tournant du XXe siècle*, ed. Yvan Lamonde, 73–98. Montreal: Fides, 1995.

Rajotte, Pierre. "Cercles et autonomie littéraire au tournant du XXe siècle." In *La Vie culturelle à Montréal vers 1900*, ed. Micheline Cambron, 39–54. Montreal: Fides/Bibliothèque nationale du Québec, 2005.

Robert, Lucie. "Patriots-on-Broadway: Denis le patriote de Louis Guyon." *Études françaises* 33, no. 3 (1996): 77–93.

Robert, Lucie. "Chronique de la vie théâtrale." In *La Vie culturelle à Montréal vers 1900*, ed. Micheline Cambron, 71–86. Montreal: Fides/Bibliothèque nationale du Québec, 2005.

Roy, Fernande. "Le journal *L'Autorité* dans le cadre de la presse libérale montréalaise." In *Combats libéraux au tournant du XXe siècle*, ed. Yvan Lamonde. 231–46. Montreal: Fides, 1995.

Saint-Jacques, Denis. "De Québec à Montréal: Essai de géographie historique." In *La Vie culturelle à Montréal vers 1900*, ed. Micheline Cambron, 27–37. Montreal: Fides/ Bibliothèque nationale du Québec, 2005.

Santo, Avi. "Film Chronicles in Montreal's *La Presse*, 1906–1908." *Canadian Journal of Film Studies* (Spring 2003): 69.

Savoie, Chantal. "Des salons aux annales: les réseaux et associations des femmes de lettres à Montréal au tournant du XXe siècle." *Voix et Images* 27, no. 2 (Winter 2002): 238–53.

Savoie, Chantal. "L'Exposition universelle de Paris (1900) et son influence sur les réseaux des femmes de lettres canadiennes." In the Special Issue *Les réseaux littéraires France-Québec au début du XXe siècle*, ed. Gérard Fabre and Denis Saint-Jacques. Études littéraires 36, no. 2 (Autumn 2004): 17–30.

Savoie, Chantal. "Persister et signer: Les signatures et l'évolution de la reconnaissance sociale de l'écrivaine (1893–1929)." *Voix et Images* 18 (Autumn 2004): 67–79.

Stoddart, Jennifer. "Quand des gens de robe se penchent sur les droits des femmes: le cas de la commission Dorion, 1919–1931." In *Travailleuses et féministes, Les femmes dans la société québécoise*, ed. Marie Lavigne et Yolande Pinard. Montreal: Boréal, 1983.

Stoddart, Jennifer, Marie Lavigne, and Yolande Pinard. "La Fédération nationale Saint-Jean-Baptiste et les revendications féministes au début du 20e siècle." *Revue d'histoire de l'Amérique française* 29, no. 3 (December 1975): 353–73.

Thornton, Patricia A., and Sherry Oslon. "Infant Vulnerability in Three Cultural Settings in Montreal 1880." In *Infant and Child Mortality in the Past*, ed. Alain Bideau, Bertrand Desjardins, and Hector Pérez Brignoli, 216–41. Oxford/Toronto: Clarendon Press, International Studies in Demography, 1997.

Trépanier, Esther. "Un Nigog lancé de la mare des arts plastiques." In *Archives des Lettres canadiennes*. Vol. 7, *Le Nigog*, ed. Paul Wyczynski, 238–67. Montreal: Fides, 1987.

Trifiro, Luigi. "Une intervention à Rome dans la lutte pour le suffrage féminin." *Revue d'histoire de l'Amérique française* 32, no. 1 (June 1978): 3–18.

Vincent, Josée. "Un premier regroupement 'professionnel' d'écrivains au Québec: La section française de la Canadian Authors' Association (1921–1936)." In *Lieux et réseaux de sociabilité littéraire au Québec*, ed. Pierre Rajotte, 275–333. Quebec: Nota bene, 2001.

Warren, Jean-Philippe. "La découverte de la 'question sociale': Sociologie et mouvements de jeunesse canadiens-français." *Revue d'histoire de l'Amérique française* 55, no. 4 (Spring 2002): 545–57.

Wyczynski, Paul. "L'École littéraire de Montréal: origine-évolution-rayonnement." In *Archives des lettres canadiennes*. Vol 2, *L'École littéraire de Montréal*, ed. Paul Wyczynski et al. Ottawa: CRCCF, Université d'Ottawa, 1961.

Theses & Dissertations

Goulet, Micheline. "Une littérature de la contrainte et de l'obédience: analyse des oeuvres des écrivains féminins du Canada français de 1900 à 1919." PhD diss., Université de Sherbrooke, 2001.

Hamel, Réginald. "Gaëtane de Montreuil, sa vie, son oeuvre." PhD Diss., Université de Montreal, 1971.

Hébert, Raymonde. "Notes bio-bibliographiques sur Éva Circé-Côté." Master's thesis, Université de Montréal, 1952.

LeBlanc, André. "The Labour Movement Seen Through the Pages of Montreal's *Le Monde ouvrier/Labor World* (1916–1926)." Diplôme d'Études supérieures thesis, Université de Montréal, 1971.

Longstaff, Alison. "Vie intellectuelle et libre-pensée au tournant du XXe siècle: le cas de Ludger Larose." Master's thesis, Université du Québec à Trois-Rivières, 1999.

MacLean, Jenne. "Parrots, Picnics and Psychic Phenomena: The Feminism, Nationalism and Social Reform of Eva Circé-Côté in *Le Monde ouvrier's* Montreal, 1900–1940." Master's thesis, Queen's University, 2000.

Michaud-Mastoras, Danaé. "Maisonneuve." Master's thesis, Université de Montreal, 2006.

Petitclerc, Martin. "Une forme d'entraide populaire: histoire des sociétés québécoises de secours mutuels au 19e siècle." PhD diss., Université du Québec à Montreal, 2004.

Plante, Lucienne. "La Fondation de l'enseignement classique féminin au Québec, 1908–1926." Diplôme d'Études supérieures, Licence en lettres, Université Laval, 1967.

Savoie, Michelle. "Firmin Picard et la Rencontre de trois cultures littéraires." Master's thesis, Université de Moncton, 2001.

Unpublished Texts

Fahrni, Magda. "Parents, Children, and Commercial Leisure in Working-Class Montreal: The Laurier Palace Fire of 1927." Paper presented at the conference *Labouring Feminism* Toronto, September 2005.

Fahrni, Magda. "Children and Risk in the Modern City: The Laurier Palace Fire of 1927." Unpublished paper. Cordoue, May 2006.

Interviews

Micheline Dumont, 2006.

Gustave Labbé, May 5, 2005; June 5, 2005; June 22, 2006; November 2, 2006; April 25, 2007.

INDEX

Note: page numbers in italics refer to illustrations

Abord-à-Plouffe, 189
Aboriginal Peoples. *See* Indigenous Peoples
abortion, 258
accidents, 80, 85, 162, 166, 290; and children, 89, 256
Action catholique de la jeunesse canadienne française (ACJC), 42, 131, 206, 212, 230, 236, 242
Action catholique, L', 80, 129, 164, 188, 279
Action française, 127, 128, 241, 242
Action libérale nationale, 162–63, 196
Action sociale, L', 41, 56, 188, 206–7, 230; anticommunist, 117, 188; and Pierre-Salomon Côté's funeral, 60–61; and women, 213, 267
agriculture, 88, 117, 134, 156–57, 180, 222, 244
Album universel, L', 29, 46, 57
alcohol, 15, 102, 147, 161, 183, 233, 257
Algonquins, 232
Alliance canadienne pour le vote des femmes, 265, 270, 271, 282
Alliance française, 54, 98, 102, 157
Alliance scientifique universelle, 59
Alpha Oméga, 41, 59
American Federation of Labor, 99, 105, 184
Angers, Félicité (Laure Conan), 50, 120–21, 123, 132
Anglomanie, L', 127, 129, 228
Anglophones, 77, 98, 130, 131, 185, 208, 211, 219, 224–28, 236–38, 258; economic position, 5, 80, 240; Montreal, 80, 81; Quebec City, 80; social reforms, 250; suffragists, 48, 251, 266, 267; women, 24
Angus, factories, 85
anti-imperialism, Circé-Côté, 44, 118, 161, 227, 229, 230, 233; *Les Débats*, 13
anti-Semitism, 82, 146, 157, 181, 206, 231, 242–46
anticlericalism, 4, 10, 40, 41, 66, 200, 216, 283
anticommunism, 117, 157, 162, 188, 189, 244
Arcand, Charles-Joseph, 149, 300
Archambault, Joseph (Palmieri), 59
Arche, L', 12, 94, 152
architecture, 93, 96, 116, 291
archives, 57, 111, 122, 123
archivists, 7, 11
armament. *See* war
armistice, 113, 196, 247, 258, 297
Artus, Michelle, 4
Asselin, Olivar, 17, 18, 40, 47, 71, 134, 151, 243; journalist, 13, 21, 22, 24, 38, 42, 45, 52, 118; public library, 57; nationalist, 44, 131, 211, 229–31; and Pierre-Salomon Côté's funeral, 59, 61
Association des dames patronnesses, 48
Association des femmes journalistes, 24, 49, 50, 281
Association des femmes propriétaires, 265
Association Saint-Jean-Baptiste. *See* Société nationale Saint-Jean-Baptiste
atheism, 39, 41, 68, 195, 202, 204
Atonhieiarho, 121, 122
Auclair, Magloire, 37–39, 58, 63, 64, 216
Augustine, Saint, 7, 134, 200, 276

Aurore, L', 62, 159, *160*, 165, 217
automobiles, 76, 83, 153, 162, 180, 294
autonomy, 44, 45, 229, 230
Autorité, L', 159
Avenir du Nord, L', 23–25, *25*, 27, 42–44, 51, 52, 198, 233
Avenir, L', 17, 65, 176, 196, 205
aviation, 73, 105, 166

Balzac, Honoré, 21, 142, 169, 306
Barbeau, Victor, 132, 137
Barbusse, Henri, 75, 104, 138, 180
Bariteau, Lorenzo, 147
Barry, Robertine (Françoise), 54, 62, 72, 308; feminist, 50; journalist, 13, 24, 26, 32, 45, 46, 48, 71, 281, 283
Barthe, J.-G., 139
Bayard, Pierre, 61
Beaugrand, Honoré, 40, 46, 123, 205
Beaulieu, Germain, 7, 12, 13, 31, 132
beauty, 116, 118–19, 135, 158, 179, 230, 279, 285
Bédard, Pierre-Stanislas, 193
Bégin, Mgr Louis-Nazaire, 41, 190, 206, 213
Béïque, Caroline Dessaulles, 48, 49, 268
Béïque, Frédéric-Ligori, 48
Bélanger, Georgina (Gaëtane de Montreuil Gill), 12, *20*, 48, 50, 95, 111, 114, 281; correspondence with Éva Circé-Côté, 143–44; journalist, 13, 18–20, 26; and the Lycée des jeunes filles, 53, 54, 260; nationalist, 156, 157
Belgium, 78, 104, 207, 278
Bellerive, Georges, 124–26, 142
Benedict XV, 208, 213
Bernard, Henri, 22, 68
Berthelot, Marie-Madeleine, 4
Bessette, Arsène, 31, 307, 308; death of, 123; freemason, 40, 123; journalist, 13, 26, 114, 307; *Le Débutant*, 91, 123
Bibaud, Michel, 138
biography, 4, 138, 146, 159, 164, 170, 233
Birth Control League, 183
Black people, 245
Bleu, Blanc, Rouge, 3, 15, 28–30, 36, 38, 48, 79, 120, 142, 164, 198, 233
Bloy, Léon, 208
Blumenthal, Abraham, 275, 277
bohemians, 11, 39, 164
Bolshevism. *See* communism
Bonne Parole, La, 96, 266

Bonsecours hall, 10
Bonsecours market, 29, *30*, 44, 232
Bonsecours Street, 75–76
Borden, Robert, 103, 105, 186, 207, 266, 268, 269
bosses, 83, 100, 106, 149, 187, 188, 239, 290; Anglo-Saxon, 240; paternalism, 288 Patriotic Fund, 107; and women, 280, 292, 296, 299, 303
Bouchard, Télesphore-Damien, 66, 67, 192, 194, 241
Boucher-Normandin, Georgine, 10, 166, 167, 215, 281, 282, 308; correspondence with Éva Circé-Côté, 142, 158, 159, 216; salon, 140–44, *140*, *141*
Boucher, Lucienne (Boucher-Laliberté, Boucher Dumas), 169
Boucher, Urgel-P., 141
Boucherville, 16, 167
Boucherville, P. A. Boucher de, 123
Bouchette, Errol, 18
Bourassa, Augustine, 143, 145, 216, 282
Bourassa, Henri, 100, 296; anti-imperialist, 44, 229; Catholic, 190, 206, 208, 213, 214, 217, 223; and the First World War, 109, 113; journalist, 66; misogynist, 230, 266, 269; nationalist, 115, 159, 217, 229, 230, 242; politician, 145, 175, 243
Bourassa, Napoléon, 282
bourgeoisie, 11, 149, 170, 213, 264, 286
Bourgeoys, Marguerite, 55, 123, 141, 216, 279
Bourget, Mgr. Ignace, 32, 71
Bourget, Paul, 201
Boyd, John, 98
Boyer, Louis, Justice, 87, 146
Brèves apologie de nos auteurs féminins, 124
Briand, Aristide, 41
Brisebois, Napoléon, 211
Brisson, Marcelle, 55
British Columbia, 156, 183
Brodeur, Henriette, 145
Brodeur, Louise Marmette (Louyse de Bienville), 50, 132, 145
brothel. *See* prostitution
Bruchési, Mgr Paul, 100, 200, 209, 215, 226; and censorship, 28, 71, 99, 161, 181, 194, 211; and cinema, 146; and Pierre-Salomon Côté's funeral, 59, 62; and the Fédération nationale Saint-Jean-Baptiste, 48, 49; and the First World War, 206–10;

and the library, 33, 35, 58; and the Lycée des jeunes filles, 55
Bruneau, Justice, 69, 92
Buies, Arthur, 18, 23, 39, 156, 169, 177
Buissonneau, Mrs., 145
Bulletin de la Caisse nationale d'Économie, Le, 44, 221
Bureau de censure, 87
Bussières, Arthur, 17

Café Ayotte, 12
Cahier de Turc, 132
Cahiers des Droits de l'Homme, Les, 41
Calvin, Jean, 217, 218
Canada, 18, 19, 88, 130, 186, 194, 227; and the First World War, 103–7, 109, 293, 294; and Great Britain, 30, 45, 231, 247; and liberalism, 185, 190, 191, 269; and Indigenous Peoples, 232–33
Canada, Le, 49, 66, 68, 70, 122, 128, 141, 243; and Pierre-Salomon Côté's funeral, 58, 59; liberal, 42, 93, 190; women's page, 31
Canadian Authors Association, 32, 129–32, 137, 283
Canadian Book Week 1921, 131, 132
Canadian Bookman, The, 130
Canadian Women's Press Club, 281
Canadien, Le, 165, 176
capitalism, 33, 77, 180, 185, 186, 250, 286, 288
Carillon, 83
Carnegie, Andrew, 33, 97
carnival, 84
Carreau, Casimir, 95
Casement, Robert, 227
Casgrain, Thérèse, 265, 271, 283, 291
castor. *See* ultramontane
Catholic Church: and censorship, 17, 41, 98, 152, 181, 211; and Circé-Côté, 199, 200, 202–5, 305, 306; and education, 210–12; and the First World War, 104, 207–8; and French Canada, 208–11, 223–24, 227; and politics, 205–7; and women, 213–16
Catholicism. *See* religion
Caughnawaga. *See* Kahnawake
Cazeneuve, Paul, (Georges Alba), 26, 30, 31
cemeteries, 167; Côte-des-Neiges, 7, 59, 64–66, 83, 89, 166, 167; Montebello, 28; Montreal Memorial Park, 169; Mount-Royal, 28, 59, 61, 65, 112
censorship, 41, 43, 115, 118, 161, 306, 308; of books, 32, 33, 91–93, 98, 200, 205, 210–11; of cinema, 87, 146, 147, 205; of the press, 72, 109, 125, 181, 194
Central Europe, 80, 117, 141, 241, 307
Chambly, 76
Champfort, Nicolas de, 41
Chapais, Thomas, 80
Chapleau, Joseph-Adolphe, 7
Charbonneau, Hélène, 145
Charbonneau, Jean, 12, 13, 101, 145, 169, 260, 261
Charlier, Édouard, 27
Charrier, Stanislas, 56, 62
Chartier, Mgr Émile, 211, 262
Chartier, Victor, 66
Chassé, Honoré, 18
Château Ramezay, 12
Chateaubriand, François-René de, 232
Chauveau, André, 64
Chénier, Jean-Olivier, 23, 75, 190, 234
childhood, of Éva Circé-Côté, 4, 5, 7, 37
children, 39, 83, 86–89, 116, 135, 150–52, 274, 295; and accidents, 116, 146, 256; and cinema, 88, 147; and education, 62, 162, 183, 186, 191–92, 237–38, 260, 263; girls, 276; health of, 89, 108, 111, 166–68, 169, 237, 253–58; and work, 111, 287, 290, 299, 302, 308. *See also* infant mortality
Chinese, 46, 167, 239, 245
Choquet, François-Xavier, 111
Choquette, Ernest, 31
Choquette, Philippe-Auguste, 61
Christmas, 15, 51, 69, 104, 124, 164, 200
church fathers, 36, 200, 253, 276
cinema, 79, 87, 146, 159, 205, 228, 242, 256; censorship of, 87, 146, 147, 205; Circé-Côté's views on, 88, 112, 146, 147, 159, 218
Circé, Arthur, 7, *9*, 37
Circé, Maria, 7–9, *8*, *9*, 39, 166, 168, 281
Circé, Marie-Thérèse, 4, 7
Circé, Narcisse, 3–5, 7, *9*, 37, 39, 114
Civil Code, 214, 230, 250, 263–65, 267, 291, 366n74
Civil Service Commission, 156
Clemenceau, Georges, 208
Clement XII, 41
Clergé canadien: sa mission et son œuvre, Le, 160, 205
clergy, 28, 41, 42, 60, 102, 146, 160, 205–15, 218, 227; influence, 4, 12, 50, 191–94, 205; and women, 49, 50, 149

Clermont, Louise, 147
Coderre Commission, 117, 135, 277
Coderre, Louis, 276
Cœurs-Unis, Lodge, 40
Cole, Florence, 266
Colombine, 38, 70, 72
colonization, 18–20, 44, 156, 157, 239, 244
Combe, Émile, 41, 43
comedy, 31, 42, 128, 129, 148, 228, 279
communism, 117, 118, 157, 162, 180–82, 187–89, 272, 273, 299, 303
Comte, Gustave, 22, 59
Conan, Laure. *See* Félicité Angers
Condorcet, Jean-Antoine-Nicolas de Caritat, Marquis de, 175, 176, 249, 250, 260, 307
Confédération des travailleurs catholiques du Canada (CTCC), 212, 300
Confederation, 160, 194, 246, 247
Confins, 127
Congrégation de Notre-Dame, 55, 56, 192, 216
Congrès de la langue française 1937, 164, 228, 245
Congrès du film français (1935), 228
Congrès du parler français (1911), 92
conscription, 161, 180, 193, 195, 207, 208, 226, 230, 258, 268, 269, 294
Conservative Party, 162, 194, 222, 270
consumption, 75, 80, 104, 242, 286, 291, 298
contraception, 215, 218, 258
conversion, religious, 202, 203, 215, 217, 233, 234
Corday, Michel, 138
corporal punishment, 111
Corpus Christi, 84
correspondence, 61, 63–65, 152; with Georgina Bélanger-Gill, 143–44; with Georgine Boucher-Normandin, 142, 158, 159, 216; with Marcel Dugas, 65, 69, 114, 124–28, 134–40, 142, 143, 144, 150–51, 168, 202–4
corruption, 53, 72, 73, 89, 90, 115, 116, 162, 179, 192, 197, 275, 277
Côté-Gauthier, Suzanne, 55
Côté, Ann Jane Haney, 38, 65, 124
Côté, Elzéar-Auguste, 64, 65
Côté, Elzéar, 38
Côté, Ève, 50, 69, 73, 75, 112, 114, 139, 145, 157–59, 166, 168, 169, 233, 262
Côté, Jean-Joachim, 65
Côté, Pierre-Salomon, 37–40, 67, 72, 86, 112, 123, 136, 168, 204, 216; funeral of, 58–68, 59, 124, 125, 157
Côté, Stanislas, 22
Côté, Thomas, 91
Côté, Yvonne Buies, 39
Cotret, René de. *See* René Detertoc
countryside, 19, 76, 79, 156–57, 276
cremation, 60, 62, 64–66
Crémazie, Octave, 222
criminality, 43, 53, 167, 254
criticism, literary, 12, 35, 100, 102, 122, 144
Croix, La, 23, 41, 61, 62, 64
Curie, Marie, 259, 279

D'Amours, Joseph-Arthur, 80, 206, 207
D'Arc, Jeanne, 102, 201, 216, 259
D'estrée, Paul. *See* Fernand Rinfret
Dagneau, Georges-Henri, 164
Daily Witness, The, 260,
Dames patronnesses, 35, 48–49, 314n103
dance, 54, 55, 121, 218, 240
Dandurand Commission on education, 83
Dandurand, Joséphine Marchand (Françoise), 50, 191, 196, 222, 268, 283
Dandurand, Raoul, 50, 59, 67, 102, 191
Daoust, Charles, 70
Daoust, Émilien, 131
Daoust, Julien, 47
Darwin, Charles, 47, 175, 176, 183, 234
Daveluy, Marie-Claire, 95, 96, 111, 150, 152, 282
Daviault, P.-Alfred, 129, 132
David Award, 119
David-Rainville, Élisa (Lisette), 45, 46
David, Laurent-Olivier, 29, 48, 59, 61, 139, 160–61, 191, 196, 205, 221
David, Louis Athanase, 238, 269
De La Chaux, Mrs., 54, 69
De La Sablonnière, Blanche, 31
De Lorimier, Chevalier, 3, 30, 31, 222
De Martigny, Adelstan Le Moyne, 40, 215
De Martigny, Paul Le Moyne, 13, 54
De Montigny, Gaston, 17, 20–21, 28, 59
De Montigny, Louvigny, 11–13, *16*, 27, 28, 37, 38, 102; author, 31, 222; Canadian Authors Association, 130, 131; journalist, 16–18, 20–22, 59
De Montigny, Marguerite (Margot), 22, 45, 46
De Nevers, Edmond, 18
De Roquebrune, Robert, 21, 73, 169, 210

De Verchères, Madeleine, 223
death penalty, 43, 51, 73, 89, 111, 188
death, 104, 142, 166–68, 170, 201, 202, 308; of Bessette, 123; Catholic, 215–16; children's, 7; 168, 253–56; of Ézilda Descarries Circé, 124, 142, 143, 168; Freemasons and, 63, 215; of Jane Haney Côté, 65, 124; of Pierre-Salomon Côté, 58, 60–67, 69, 142, 216. *See also* infant mortality
Débats, Les, 11, 13–18, *14*, 21, 27–28, 39, 83, 91, 98, 194, 211, 229, 253
Débutant, Le, 91, 123
Décarrie, Julie-Ézilda Circé (Exilda), 3, 4, 7, 9, 39, 142
Decary, E. R., 98
Déclaration des droits de la femme, 249
deism, 201, 203
Delacourt, André, 142
Delpit Affair, 214
demography. *See* population
Denault, Amédée, 21, 23
Déom Frères, 28, 150
Department of Public Education, 192
Deraisme, Marie, 41, 281
Derick, Carrie, 295
Des Ormeaux, Dollard, 97, 138, 223
Desaulniers, Gonzalve, 12, 23, 40, 114, 145, 211, 222, 278, 308; author, 32, 101, 102, 143; and Pierre-Salomon Côté's funeral, 59, 61; death of, 157; lawyer, 68, 171; and Lycée des jeunes filles, 54, 56
Descarries dit Le Houx, Jean (1620–1687), 4
Descarries, Marie-Philomène, 5
Despatie-Tremblay Affair, 214, 215
Desrochers, Félix, 130, 151, 164
Dessaulles-Béïque, Caroline, 268
Dessaulles, Henriette (Fadette), 266
Dessaulles, Louis-Antoine, 70, 123, 176, 177, 193, 211
Detertoc, René (de Cotret), 7, 171
Devoir, Le, 61, 63, 66, 67, 120, *133*, 208, 213, 229–31, 266, 269
disarmament, 115, 258
disease, 39, 124, 135; contagious, 88, 89, 255, 256, 275–77; Pierre-Salomon Côté's, 58
divorce, 194, 214, 215, 218
doctors, 37, 40, 59, 135, 183, 244, 257, 276; Freemasons, 67, 215; women, 28, 262, 277, 279
domestic, 149, 291, 299, 300

Dorion Commission, 265, 366n74
Dorion, Charles-Édouard, 265
Doutre, Gonzalve, 211
Doutre, Joseph, 62, 176, 193
Dreyfus Affair, 102, 306
Droit, Le, 117, 219, 231
Drolet, Mrs., 59
Drummond, George Alexander, 62
Drummond, Julia Grace Parker, 295
Dubeau, Eudore, 98
Duclos, Alexandre, 17
Dugas, Marcel, 12, 145, 159; correspondence with Éva Circé-Côté, 65, 69, 114, 124–28, 134–40, 142, 143, 144, 150–51, 168, 202–4; library, 93, 94, 98, 282; in Paris, 141, 150, 158; poet, 94, 100, 102, 118, 132, 135
Dumas, Alexandre, 57
Dumouchel, Jos, 5
Duplessis, Maurice, 162, 163, 169, 196
Dupuis-Saint-Michel, Catherine, 6

Easter, 15, 200
École d'enseignement supérieur, 56
École des Hautes Études commerciales, 192
École littéraire de Montréal, 11–13, 32, 59, 215, 278
economy, 77, 89, 148, 176–81, 226, 236, 240, 247, 290; depressions, 148–49, 285, 286, 288, 291, 293, 298, 300; liberalism, 185–87, 194, 196, 276; saving, 163; wartime, 106, 275, 294, 300–3
ecumenism, 219
Edgar, Pelham, 130
education, 26, 28, 47, 53, 67, 73, 77, 111, 157, 177, 183, 186, 188, 221, 250, 285; Catholic, 205, 208, 211, 212, 227, 237; Circé-Côté's, 7–10, 36, 53, 200, 279; compulsory, 28, 73, 89, 92, 177, 178, 191, 192, 195, 239, 307, 308; curriculum, 54, 161, 227, 229, 259; democracy, 79, 192, 27; free, 177, 192; Freemasons, 32, 41, 281; men's, 275; secular, 41, *193*, 205, 211, 246; women's, 10, 21, 47, 49, 50, 53–56, 61, 114, 168, 170, 251–54, 257–62, 266, 276, 308; workers', 192, 288
egalitarianism, 118, 149, 177, 249–53, 259, 264, 267, 270, 278, 295, 299
elections, 53, 182; federal, 195, 268, 269; municipal, 63, 135, 264; provincial, 162, 163, 189, 196
electricity, 73, 83, 92, 180, 285, 307

elite, 13, 33, 42, 62, 67, 117, 126, 221, 267, 306
Émancipation Lodge, 40, 41, 58, 63, 66, 67, 99, 123, 157, 205
emigration, 134, 185
empire. *See* imperialism
employers. *See* bosses
encyclical letter, 187; *Quanta Cura*, 181, 182
Engels, Frederik, 250
England, 40, 46, 183, 195, 208, 219, 222, 226–28, 231, 247
English, 127, 128, 139, 185, 193, 211, 224–28, 233
Enlightenment, 21, 41, 51, 103, 121, 152, 175, 176, 197, 205, 249, 253; Freemasons, 40; Jews, 242
epidemic, 7, 46, 59, 89, 255
"Épistles to Théodore," 119, 202, 203
"Erin Go Bragh," 38, 124
Esquisse d'un tableau historique des progrès de l'esprit humain, 176
essay, 12, 15, 23, 28, 71, 73, 115, 118, 135, 138, 259
Ethiopia, 163
ethnicity, 223, 229, 244–46
Étincelle, L', 26, 27, 71, 107, 123, 259
Eucharistic Congress (1910), 42, 66, 67
eugenics, 43, 183, 257
Événement, L', 19
evolution, 108, 109, 130, 178, 180, 186, 197, 251, 274, 286; French Canadian, 228, 247; theory of, 47, 58, 176; women's, 213, 259, 290
exploitation, 186; of women, 292, 294, 298, 299; of workers, 106, 189, 288

Fabre-Surveyer, Édouard, 114
factory, 106, 107, 264, 290–92, 296, 297
Fadette. *See* Henriette Dessaulles
Fallon, Mgr Michael Francis, 227
family, 83, 161, 166, 184, 257, 265, 270, 297, 301, 302; of Éva Circé, 3–9, 11, 39, 89, 165, 217, 234; of Pierre-Salomon Côté, 38–40, 60, 64–66; of women, 213, 270, 301–3
farmers, 78, 79, 134, 157, 219, 222
fashion, 50, 85, 118
Fauteux, Aegedius, 131, 151, 152, 278
Fédération nationale Saint-Jean-Baptiste (FNSJB), 47–50, 92, 96, 230, 263, 265, 266, 270, 281, 300

femininity, 250, 272, 303
feminism, 230, 246, 249–83, 304; Catholic, 49, 213; and Circé-Côté, 32, 89, 290, 305
Feu du couchant, Le, 138
Feu, Le, 75, 104
Feux de Bengale à Verlaine glorieux, 102
Filion, Joseph-Philéas, 31
finance, 27, 33, 77, 185
Finnie, Joseph Thomas, 191
First Nations. *See* Indigenous Peoples
First World War, 106, 179, 180, 201, 207–8, 226; and women's work, 107, 109. *See also* conscription
flag, 28, 29, 156
Flavelle, Joseph, 109
Force et Courage, lodge, 40, 56, 58, 62, 205
Ford, John, 159
Fourier, Charles, 250, 251, 259
Fournier, Jules, 229, 230
France, 4, 28, 29, 40, 41, 51, 78, 97, 117, 120, 121, 143, 148, 175–77, 189, 200, 223, 285; culture, 87, 238, 306; education, 51, 55; and First World War, 103, 104, 106, 109, 110, 113, 207, 208, 226, 258; prostitution, 275, 277, 278; women, 250, 281
France, Anatole, 21, 138, 165, 206, 307
Franco-Ontarians, 227, 230
Francœur, Joseph-Achille, 149, 301
Francœur, Louis, 144
Francophiles, 52, 94, 103, 139, 157, 200
Francq, Gustave: freemason, 66; journalist, 90, 99, 196, 271; politician, 188; and prostitution, 275, 277, 278; trade unionist, 40, 184, 289, 299
Fraser Institute, 32, 41, 97, 131, 158, 161
Frazer, James George, 41
Fréchette, Louis, 29, 31, 62
freedom, 41, 72, 101, 111, 118, 142, 193; individual, 103, 110, 117, 118, 120, 181–85, 193, 214; political, 46, 187, 222, 245; of the press, 17, 28, 109, 181; Protestant, 217–19; religious, 181, 217; sexual, 127, 277, 278; of thought, 17, 127, 177, 194–97, 200, 205, 210, 215, 227, 247, 305, 307, 308; women's, 12, 119, 143, 257, 262, 264, 280, 292, 299–304
Freemasonry, 39, 40, 41, 58–60, 63, 65
French Canadians, 51, 58, 77, 81, 83, 104, 128, 141, 145, 195, 217; mentality, 176, 177, 208, 210, 224, 256; First World War, 207; literature, 29 130, 131, 137;

nationalism, 29, 46, 47, 51, 221–48; women, 49, 55, 185
Frères des Écoles chrétiennes (Brothers of Christian Schools, Christian Brothers), 139
friendship, 12, 28, 50, 58, 63, 136, 137, 141, 144, 216, 282; Boucher-Normandin, 10, 141, 158, 281; Dugas, 94, 102, 126, 136; Desaulniers, 68, 143
Fumeur endiablé, 31, 32, 132, 147, 148
funerals, 166, 167; children's, 254, Chinese, 167; Circé-Côté, 169, 308; George V, 163; L.-J. Papineau, 139; of Pierre-Salomon Côté, 58–67, 70, 122, 123, 125, 157, 229

Gadbois, Dr. Jean-Pierre, 63
Gagnon collection, 70, 144, 150, 152, 307
Gagnon, Philéas, 70, 91
Garant, Édouard, 144
Garneau, François-Xavier, 122, 138, 211
Garneau, Hector, 93, 95, 96, 98, 106, 122, 130, 135, 150, 151
Gaspésie, 79, 156
Gauthier, Conrad, 147
Gauthier, J.-Étienne (Paul Hyssons), 17
Gauthier, Juliette, 262
Gauthier, Mgr Georges, 117, 187
Gauvreau, Georges, 31
genealogy, 4–6, 150, 234
Geoffrion, Amédée, 117, 177
Georges Martin, 281
Gérin-Lajoie, Marie Lacoste, 26, 48–50, 55, 214, 263, 265, 268, 271
Germans, 46, 66, 103, 105, 202
Germany, 104, 109, 207, 208, 226, 243, 290
Gervais, Honoré, 59, 62
Gibbons, John Murray, 130
Gill, Charles, 12, 13, 23, 26, 50
Gionnel, Suzanne, 142
Giroux, Germaine, 129, 132
Gleason-Huguenin, Anne-Marie (Madeleine), 20, 27, 40, 50, 126, 130–32, 145; journalism, 4, 13, 18–20, 29, 45, 46, 48, 124, 159, 222, 231, 266, 279, 281, 282; *Le Baiser*, 132; *Premier péché*, 26
Godbout, Adélard, 165, 190, 191
Goldman, Emma, 84
Gorki, Maxim, 307
gospel, 43, 62, 147, 188, 199, 200–4
Gouges, Olympe de, 249, 267
Gouin, Lomer, 7, 18, 72, 175, 190–96

Gouin, Paul, 145, 162
Grand Lodge of Quebec, 40
Grand Orient, lodge, 40
Grandchamp, 59, 67
Great Britain, 177, 275; Canada's relations with, 45, 247; democracy; First World War, 103, 180, 226; immigrants, 80, 224, 240; imperialism, 13, 44, 51, 226, 229, 293; women, 250, 266, 267
Greek, 46, 81; language, 161
Grenier, Victor, 7
Grignon, J.-J., 23
Groulx, Lionel, 88, 122; historian, 146, 164, 223, 231, 247; and nationalism, 138, 157, 206, 223, 228, 231, 241
Guénard-Hodent, Maurice, 141
Guerin, James John, 255

Haiti, 245
Haney, Ann Jane. *See* Ann Haney Côté
harassment: of women, 280, 292, 296; of workers, 298
Hébert, Louis-Philippe, 222
Hébert, Louis, 222
Helbronner, Jules, 59
Hémon, Louis, 270
Henderson, Rose, 108, 111, 112, 268
heredity, 43, 51, 58, 178, 223, 234, 236
Héroux, Omer, 22, 23, 42, 230
Herriot, Édouard, 135
heteronym. *See* pseudonym
heterosexuality, 134, 252
Hindelang et Delorimier, 30, 31, 45, 122
Hindenlang, Charles, 30, 31, 222, 234, 236
Histoire biologique des Canadiens-Français, 58
historiography, 122
Hitler, Adolf, 246
homosexuality, 94, 95, 127, 142, 277, 326n94
homosociability, 12, 13
Houde, Camilien, 301
House of Commons, 243, 274
housing, 88–90, 108, 116, 161, 162, 168, 232
Huette, Joseph, 67
Hugo, Victor, 23, 53
Hugues, Samuel, 107
Humanité, L', 41
humour, 86, 128, 130, 225, 241, 267, 279, 280
Huron, 51, 232, 234
hygiene. *See* public health
Hyppolite, Dominique, 150, 245
Hyssons, Paul. *See* J.-Étienne Gauthier

Île-Jésus, 189
Île-Sainte-Hélène, 83, 84
immigrants, 5, 46, 83, 117, 186, 236–46, 308; Belgian, 104, British, 80; Eastern and Central European, 80; European, 80; French 52, 78, 104; Irish, 227; Jewish, 117
immigration, policies regarding, 77, 78, 117, 156
Imperial Munitions Board, 109
Imperial Order Daughters of the Empire, 268
imperialism, 206, 207, 233; British, 44, 195, 277, 229
incineration. *See* cremation
Indian. *See* Indigenous Peoples
Indigenous Peoples, 77, 120, 121, 139, 163, 209, 210, 223, 232–35, 246
industrial workers, women, 117
industrialization, 37, 77–80, 89, 106, 116, 179, 180, 194, 289
Industry and Humanity (William Lyon Mackenzie King), 188
industry, war industry and munitions, 78, 79, 107, 109, 264; women and, 264, 288, 291–97, 301
infant mortality, 38, 89, 111, 167, 168, 215, 253–58, *255*, 278
inflation, 78, 91, 106, 108
Institut canadien, 18, 32, 41, 177, 194, 205, 210, 211
insurance, 116, 162, 182, 256, 262, 291
intellectuals, 10, 45, 103, 130, 148, 170, 221, 289, 306, 308; Catholic, 269; Circé-Côté, 306; Jewish, 259; women, 375n2
International Eucharistic Congress, 66, 67
internationalism, 115, 119
Irish people, 38, 46, 80, 124, 138, 227, 256, 270
Irlande, 104, 111, 124, 159, 219, 227
irony, 16, 119, 134, 203, 274, 306
Iroquois, 232–35
Israel, 221, 242, 243
Italians, 46, 81, 303
Italy, 26, 80, 208, 270

Jansenism, 210
Jaurès, Jean, 103, 117, 118, 182, 186, 187, 189
jazz, 117, 153, 229
Jesuits, 29, 121, 192, 206, 211
Jewish Daily Eagle/Kanader Adler, 237
Jews, 42, 80–84, 117, 186, 202, 221, 237, 240–46; children, 83, 256; schools, 237, 238. *See also* anti-Semitism
Jocks, John, 232
Joffre, Joseph Maréchal, 96, 97
Joly, Irène, 265
Journal de Françoise, Le
journalism, 24, 27, 60, 71, 90, 91, 123; Circé-Côté, 15, 17, 21, 23, 36, 56–59, 71, 89, 99–101, 165, 214, 281; women, 18–21, 23, 24, 26, 27, 46, 48, 71, 145, 222, 281

Kahnawake (Caughnawaga), 16, 232, 233
Kellerman, Annette, 119, 279
Keynes, John Maynard, 117, 182
King, William Lyon Mackenzie, 188, 190
Kingsley, Louis, 5
Kodarh, 141

L.-O. David et les hommes proéminents de son temps, 159
L'Espérance, Zotique, 98
La Prairie-de-la-Madeleine, 4
La Prairie, 5, 108
Labelle, Charles, 10
Labelle, François-Xavier-Antoine curé, 18, 23, 156
Laberge, Albert, 59
Laberge, Dr. Louis, 59, 66, 67, 255
labour conflict. *See* strike
Labour Day, 149, 288
Labour Party, 32
labour. *See* work
Lac Bouchette, 19
Lac Saint-Jean, 19, 20, 27, 130, 156, 281
Lachine, convent, 7, 10, 53
Lacoste-Frémont, Thaïs, 265
Lafontaine, Louise-Hippolyte, 62
Lafontaine, Park, 11, 85, 88, 93, 96, 97, 151, 153
Lamartine, Alphonse de, 285
Lambert, Albert, 132
Lanctôt, Clara, 10
landladies, 161
landlords, 83, 108, 161, 162, 184
Langlois, Godfroy, 48, 53, 59, 63, 114; freemason, 63; journalist, 40, 42, 62, 66, 68, 70; politics, 42, 63, 83, 191, 192, 194, 224, 241
language, 128, 188, 213, 246; English, 114, 127, 227; French, 19, 62, 77, 164, 190, 211, 215, 227–31, 236–39, 308; Iroquois, 232

Lanthier, Marie-Louise, 4, 20
Larose, Ludger, 42, 54, 316n26
Laurier Palace, 146, 147, 218
Laurier, Wilfrid, 66, 115, 175, 193, 229; election of 1917, 105, 269; prime minister, 190; Rouge, 191, 194, 195
Laval, University, 38, 64, 192, 211
lawyer, 40, 59, 68, 93; women, 262, 264, 280
Le Dantec, Félix, 41
Le Normand, Michelle, 132
Leacock, Stephen, 130
League of Nations, 115, 165
Lebel, Arthur, 123
Léger, Abel, 142
Legislative Assembly, 147, 149, 163, 179, 186, 191, 192, 224, 243, 271, 290
leisure, 146, 147, 183, 218
Lemaire, Georgine, 132
Lemieux, Albert-J., 42
Lenin, Vladimir Ilich, 118
Leo XIII, 216
Lesage, Édouardine (Colette), 46, 48
Lesseps, Jacques de, 73
Lévis, 209
Liberal Party: federal, 17, 32, 35, 66, 71, 162, 182, 190, 195; provincial, 162, 190, 194, 300, 301
Liberal Women's Club, 270
liberalism, 70, 139, 307; Circé-Côté and, 117, 175–96, 197, 210, 222, 227, 229, 278, 305; and feminism, 249, 250, 262, 283, 304; workers', 290
librarians, 3, 32, 35, 58, 69, 70, 90–98, 150, 152
libraries: City of Montreal, 33, 57, 70, 92, 93, 96–98, 120, 131, 151; McGill University, 226; Sainte-Cunégonde, 106; Saint-Sulpice, 151; Technical, 2, 32, 33, 35, 58, 92
Library Commission. See City of Montreal
Libre Parole, La, 42
Ligue de l'enseignement, 39, 53, 59, 60, 67, 191, 211
Ligue des droits des femmes, 265, 271, 282, 283
Ligue des filles natives canadiennes, 155
Les Filles natives du Canada. See Native Daughters of Canada
Ligue féminine pour la décence (Women's League for Decency), 119
Ligue nationaliste, 44, 229

Ligue pour l'instruction, 59
Loiselle, Ernest, 147
Longue-Pointe, 16
Loranger, Jean-Aubert, 132
Lorrain, Léon, 128
Loti, Pierre, 165
Louis, saint, 276
Loup de velours, 128
Lozeau, Albert, 21, 22
Luther, Martin, 217, 218
Lycée des jeunes filles, 53–56, 59, 61, 68, 69, 157, 260

MacDonald, John A., 190
MacDonald, Ramsay, 227
Machiavelli, Niccolò, 119
Mackay, Ian, 186
Macphail, Agnes, 274, 279
Madeleine. See Gleason-Huguenin, Anne-Marie
Maillet, Roger, 118, 134
Maisonneuve, 120–22, 130, 234, 235
Maisonneuve, Paul Chomedey de, 121, 144, 206, 234, 235, 279
Maisonneuve, city of, 76, 108, 146, 236
Mance, Jeanne, 121, 123, 216, 222, 279
Manitoba, 268
Marchand, Félix-Gabriel, 190, 191
Marcil, Dr. Alfred, 40, 58, 59
Marie-Anasthasie, Sister, 10, 279
marital authority, 263–65, 267, 366n74
market, 78; Bonsecours, 29, 30, 44; Saint-Laurent, 34–35, 75; stock market, 27, 111
marriage, 4, 15, 50, 101, 134, 183, 298; Catholic, 214; Circé's, 37–39, 50, 94; Civil Code, 214, 263–65; Protestant, 214, 215, 218, 219
Martin, Albertine, 148
Martin, Médéric, 90, 93, 100, 116, 135, 275
Marx, Karl, 187, 203
Marxism, 184, 286, 304
Massicotte, Édouard-Zotique, 7, 22, 106
materialism, 40, 169, 177, 200, 201, 217, 228, 286
maternalism, 112, 151, 252, 253, 258, 259
Mâtin, Le, 101, 118, 134
Maurault, Olivier, 128, 229
May Day, 84
McGill University, 55, 81, 95, 98, 130, 211, 212, 226
medicine, 38, 171, 253

mentality, 51, 163, 218; Anglo-Saxon, 185, 224, 226, 280; French-Canadian, 208, 219; women, 155
Mercier, Honoré, 32, 62, 190, 191
Mercure de France, 120, 127
Merry del Val, Rafael, 214
Merry-Girard theatre troupe, 129
Michaud, J. S. H., 39
Michelet, Jules, 51
Michelet, Magali, 128
Michelet, Victor-Émile, 142
Miles, Henry, 270
militarism, 104, 163, 165, 180, 258, 294
Military Service Act, 105, 207, 268
Military Service Act, 105, 207, 268, 294
military service, 105, 108, 166, 268
Mill, John Stuart, 178, 182, 249, 250, 267, 279
misogyny, 250, 266, 267, 279
modernity, 44, 87, 106, 116, 175–78, 181, 200, 227; American, 247; Circé-Côté, 73, 83, 307, 308; literature, 12, 94; women, 29, 54, 84, 119, 258
Monde illustré, Le, 17, 18, *19*, 21, 22, *24*, 71
Monde ouvrier, Le, 82, 83, 90, 96, 99, 103, 105, 135, 164; and labour, 90, 96, 105, 108, 287–89, 293, 302; and women, *273*, 302
Monk, Frédérick-Debartzch, 222
Montebello, 28, 145, 167, 282
Montet, Edmond, 132
Montpetit, Édouard, 101, 102, 128
Montreal Daily Star, 67
Montreal Daily Witness, 269
Montreal Local Council of Women, 48, 265, 266
Montreal Memorial Park, 169
Montreal Suffrage Association, 265, 266
Montreal, City of, 37, 89, 92, 107, 116, 209, 270, 308; City Council, 32, 33, 67, 70, 73, 89, 97, 129; Civil Service Commission, 156; Control Commission, 90; Library Commission, 32–35, 57, 63, 90, 90–93, 95, 98, 106, 150–52, 314n95; Pension Commission, 152; public health service, 67, 255
Monument National, 48, 85, 88, 92, 125, 160; library, 34, 35; theatre, 120, 129, 147, 179, 239
Morin, Paul, 101
Morin, Victor, 98, 131, 132, 144
motherhood, 183, 250, 253–58, 296
Mount Royal, 83, 88, 144, 167, 179

moving, 5, 84, 86–87, *86*, 192
Murray, George, 68
music, 8, 10 19, 31, 52, 54, 83, 92, 141; Circé-Côté and, 9, 115, 130, 146, 164
MusiCanada, 134
Musset, Alfred de, 71
Mussolini, Benito, 202, 364
mysticism, 43, 44, 102, 115, 198

Nantais, Isaïe, 12
Nantel, Guillaume-Alphonse, 43
Nation, La, 43
National Council of Women of Canada, 250, 268, 282
National Reference Book, 163, 217
nationalism, 71, 227, 241; Catholic, 29, 128, 146, 149, 164, 206, 212, 215, 223; Circé-Côté, 127, 217, 222, 228, 236, 239, 247; economic, 18, 115, 240; French-Canadian, 44, 155–57, 164, 212, 217, 229–31, 236, 242; liberal, 93, 138, 139, 162, 223; women, 155, 215, 253, 257, 263, 269. *See also* immigration; Jews
Nationaliste, Le, 38, 42, 44, 45, 52, 57, 61, 62, 68
Native Daughters of Canada, 156, 157, 236
Native Peoples. *See* Indigenous Peoples
Native Sons of Canada, 155–57
Nelligan, Émile, 17, 26, 28
nepotism, 89, 95, 163, 192
New England, 13, 134
New France, 4, 20, 51, 96, 120, 121, 222, 233, 279
Normandin, Georgine Boucher, 10, 140–43, 158, 166, 215, 216, 281, 308
Normandin, Oscar, 56
Notre-Dame Hospital, 153, 157, 244
Notre-Dame-de-Grâce, 153
Notre-Dame Street, 27, 36, 40, 81, 81, 94
novels, 4, 49, 56, 57, 91, 104, 138, 144, 161, 306, 307; Circé-Côté, 137, 145, 159

old age, 157, 158, 163–66, 168, 274
Ontario, 53, 183, 227; French schools, 208, 228, 230, 231, 247
Ottawa, 33, 117, 219
Ouimet, Léo-Ernest, 87
Ouimetoscope, 87

painting, 10, *11*, 42, 54, 58, 83, 164, 179, 282
Palmieri. *See* Joseph Archambault

Pankhurst, Emmeline, 266
Papineau: Son influence sur la pensée canadienne (Éva Circé-Côté), 142, 191, 196, 205, 211, 233, 237; Protestants, 217, 242; publication of, 138, 139
Papineau, Louis-Joseph, 138, 139, 223, 243, 244; liberal, 70, 176, 193, 222, 223; Montebello, 28, 145, 282
Parent-Duchâtelet, Alexandre, 277
Parent, Honoré, 12, 152
Parent, Simon-Napoléon, 18, 190, 194, 234
Paris, 4, 20, 49, 50, 64, 69, 120, 143; Georgine Boucher-Normandin in, 140, 141, 215; Marcel Dugas in, 94, 126, 135, 150; Universal Exhibition (1900), 46
Passe-Temps, Le, 20, 115, 134
Pasteur, Louis, 201
Patenaude, N., 38
Patrie, La, 4, 19, 31, 33, 35, 44, 53; critics, 122, 129, 145, 148; Godfroy Langlois, 190, 191; women's page, 13, 46, 266
Patriotes, 17, 138, 165, 194, 199, 222, 313; monument, 236; Rebellions, 30, 70, 159, 223
Patriotic Fund, 107, 110, 207, 268
patriotism, 26, 88, 129, 171, 221, 236, 246; Circé-Côté and, 171, 198, 235; women and, 222
Payette, Eugène, 93, 96
Payette, Louis, 54
Payment, Miss, 70
Pays, Le, 62, 65, 66, 70–72, 124, 230; and Freemasons, 57; and the Catholic Church, 91, 99, 194, 211, 215; Circé-Côté and, 103, 114, 115; women and, 84, 100, 260, 267
Péguy, Charles, 102
Pépin, Alice (Monique), 145, 282
Petit Journal, Le, 145, 148
petite bourgeoisie, 5, 162, 189
Philanthropic Society, 260
philanthropy, 33, 88, 118, 226, 233
Philosophers, 40, 41, 110, 182, 250
philosophy, 35, 51, 55, 57, 88, 176, 261
picnic, 48, 83, 166
Pionnier, Le, 21, 24, 56, 211; Circé-Côté, 18, 19, 46
Pius VII, 64
Pius IX, 181, 182
Plamondon, Rodolphe, 143
Plante, Anatole, 271
Plateau, School, 42

poets: Éva Circé-Côté, 28; Gonzalve Desaulniers, 101; Marcel Dugas, 100, 127; Paul Morin, 101; Victor Morin, 98
poetry, 138, 234, 293
Poincaré, Henri, 41
Polémarque, 101, 134
Poles, 46, 83, 117, 240
police, 40, 86, 117, 135, 187, 256, 275, 276, 288
pollution, 89
population, 117
poverty, 15, 39, 135, 157, 180, 185, 257; Circé-Côté on, 59; women, 273, 303
Préfontaine, Raymond, 33
press, 33, 109, 270, 271; Catholic, 32, 33, 41, 56, 61, 62, 208, 213; freedom of the, 28, 181; right-wing, 43, 62, 276; liberal, 32, 46, 63, 122, 157
Presse, La, 13, 23, 46, 59, 60, 122, 148, 250
Prévost, Jules-Édouard, 23, 43, 52
Prince de Galle, 101
Prince, Lorenzo, 42, 70, 91, 93, 145
profiteers, 78, 107, 109, 115, 186
progress, 24, 103, 111, 171, 187, 305; Catholic, 197, 199, 201, 205, 208, 210, 216; education and, 53, 259, 260; France and, 175, 226, 231; Jews and, 242; liberalism and, 175–81, 186; Protestant, 218, 224, 286
progressives, 31, 33, 65, 308; and the Enlightenment, 41, Freemasons, 40–42, 196; and politics, 117, 119, 162, 191, 194–96, 274; and the press, 3, 135, 159, 196; and reform, 89, 111, 179, 183
prohibition, 116, 183, 218
prostitution, 274–78; abolition, 179, 183; brothels, 42, 218; prostitutes, 85, 303; regulation, 117, 184; tolerance, 117
Protestantism. *See* religion
Proudhon, Pierre-Joseph, 187, 287
Provincial Committee for Female Suffrage, 265, 282
Provincial Committee for Women's Suffrage, 265, 282
pseudonyms, 17, 45, 71, 72, 165; Arthur Maheu, 72; Colombine, 26; Fantasio, 51, 71, 165; Jean Nay, 71; Jean Ney, 27; Julien Saint-Michel, 78, 99, 165, 277, 293; Musette, 16; Paul S. Bédard, 71; Polémarque, 134
Psyché au cinéma, 100, 102

psychology, 138, 176, 185
public health, 182, 253, 255, 257; prostitution, 184, 276, 277
puritanism, 146, 218, 249, 278
Puthoste, Roger (André Thérive), 138, 307

Quanta Cura, encyclical, *181*
Quatre Demoiselles Lépine, Les, 159
Quebec City, 17, 40, 66, 80
Quotidien, Le, 41

Rabinovitch, Samuel, 157, 244
racism, 46, 83, 241, 245–46
radio, 143, 155, 180, 271, 307
Rankin, Jeannette, 104, 279
Rebellions of 1837–1839, 4, 45, 138, 139, 159, 223, 231; in theatre, 30, 31
Reclus, Élisée, 41
religion, 41, 193, 197–220; Catholicism, 28, 29, 60, 135, 306; and education, 53, 177, 191; Protestantism, 169, 224; and women, 54, 61, 183, 254, 263, 267
Renan, Ernest, 201, 216
republic, 46, 103, 178, 305; American, 104; French, 29, 41, 120, 285
Revanche, La, 138, 159, 228, 281
revolution, 188; French, 249; Russian, 118, 187
Revue moderne, La, 132
Ribot, Théodule, 120
Rimouski, 40, 61, 134, 209
Rinfret, Fernand (Paul d'Estrée), 71
Rivard, Adjutor, 22
Roberval, 18, 19
Roland, Manon, 279
Rolland, Romain, 138, 180, 307
Romier, Lucien, 258
Rondeau, S., 62
Rouges, 40, 177, 194, 195, 205
Rousseau, Jean-Jacques, 51
Roy, Camille, 126, 228
Royal Canadian Air Force, 166
Royal Society of Canada, 93, 102
Russia. *See* Union of Soviet Social Republics

Sacco, Nicola, 188
Saint Lawrence River, 79
Saint-Aimé-du-Lac-des-Îles, 156
Saint-Antoine, 5
Saint-Henri, 76
Saint-Hyacinthe, 66, 67, 209

Saint-Jean-Baptiste Association, Society, 24, 192; dames patronesses, 35, 48; foundation, 48; library, 34, 35, 92; Monument national, 48, 92, 239; nationalism, 131, 217, 221
Saint-Jean-Baptiste (National Day), 44, 51, *84*, 106, 138, 206, *225*, 240
Saint-Jean-Baptiste (parish), 37, 153, 216
Saint-Jean-sur-Richelieu, 4
Saint-Jean, Idola, 35, 130, 145, 308; and women's suffrage, 265, 270, 271, 283, 291, 366n74
Saint-Jean, Lac, 18–20, 27, 130, 156, 281
Saint-Jean, United Church, 169
Saint-Joseph, Collège, 38
Saint-Laurent, market, 34
Saint-Laurent Street/Boulevard, *81*, *82*, 83, 85, 87, 236, 241, 242
Saint-Louis Square, 86
Saint-Louis Ward, 63, 82, 83, 241
Saint-Martin, Albert, 53, 59, 118
Saint-Michel, François Sircé de, 4
Saint-Michel, Julien, *6*, 78, 99, 165
Saint-Philippe de Laprairie, 4
Saint-Sulpice Library, 57, 93, 95, 132, 152, 327n107
Sainte-Anne-Marie, Mother, 55
Sainte-Cunégonde, 5, 7, 106
Sainte-Euphrosyne, Sister, 56
Sainte-Flavie, 40, 61
Sainte-Luce, 38, 39, 61, 64, 65, 124
Sainte-Sophorine, Sister, 55
salary: Éva Circé-Côté, 36, 63, 69, 91, 114, 135, 143, 152; librarians, 91, 98; teachers salon, literary, 141–43
Sand, George, 26, 169, 279
Sandwell, B. K., 130
Sanger, Margaret, 183
Saskatchewan, 268
Sauvalle, Mrs. Marc, 13
Schopenhauer, Arthur, 57, 167
science, 65, 69, 73, 185, 200, 279; education, 88, 161, 259, 260; library, 93, 139, 157; psychic, 67; and women, 259
Seers, Eugène (Louis Dantin), 17
Semaines sociales, 96, 206
Semeur canadien, Le, 217
Senate, 156, 214, 274
separatism, 228, 305
Séverine (Caroline Rémy Guebhard), 21, 26, 169

shop assistants, 84, 291, 298
shopkeepers, 263, 299
shops, 5, 37, 242; bookshop, 7, 131; department store, 84, 291, 298; Greek, 81
Sisters of Saint Anne, 7, 192, 279
Six Éponges, 12
smoking, 12, 31, 101, 147, 233, 234
social democracy, 180, 182
social reforms, 163, 179, 260; women, 250, 258, 274, 275
socialism, 103, 175, 181, 184, 186; Catholic condemnation, 181, 182, 188, Circé-Côté, 118, 184, 187, 288; women, 250
Société de colonisation du Lac Saint-Jean, 18
Société des Gens et des Lettres, 46
Société nationale Saint-Jean-Baptiste, 45, 48, 92, 192, 221, 239; foundation, 48; library, 33, 35; nationalism, 131, 157, 217; presidents, 48, 132, 230, women, 24, 48
Sohmer, Park, 75, 83, 87, 153
Soleil, Le, 19, 20, 29, 60, 190
Sorel, Cécile, 132
Sou de la pensée française, 230
sounds, 17, 44, 75, 83, 84
South Africa, 13
Spain, 163, 216
speculation, financial, 27, 108, 111, 115, 116, 178
Spencer, Herbert, 47, 176, 183, 185, 197, 206
spiritualism, 67, 69, 81
Staël, Germaine Necker de, 169, 259, 279
Standard, 67–70
state, the, 109, 182; education, 53, 56; labour, 184, 286; liberal, 182, 278; religion, 182, 204, 215, 231, 247; social, 89, 135, 257, 286, 287, 290; and women, 257, 278, 295
stenographers, 23, 106, 250, 261, 291, 292
stenography, 54, 260
strikes, 49, 117, 187; 1919, 187, 288–89; medical interns, 244; garment industry, 288 streetcar, 287; truck drivers, 288
"struggle for life," 54, 114, 185, 186, 224, 286
style: Circé-Côté's, 71, 100, 102, 148, 166, 228; Papineau's, 139; Saint-Michel's, 100
Subjection of Women, The (John Stuart Mill), 249
suburb, 37, 8
suffrage: Bills, 163; Bourassa and, 230; and the Catholic Church, 213, 214; and Éva Circé-Côté, 110, 112, 189, 266, 268, 305; opposition to, 151, 213, 214, 230, 266,

269; universal, 110, 178; women's, 112, 159, 163, 180, 189, 263–73, 273, 305
suffragettes, 134, 266, 267
suffragists. *See* suffrage
Sunday observance, 28, 88, 146, 147, 183, 218
superstition, 176, 181, 203, 234
Surveyer, L. J. A., 48, 144
Switzerland, 46, 104
Syllabus errorum (Pius IX), 181, 182
Syrians, 46, 83

Taine, Hyppolite, 150
tales, 201; Christmas, 51, 69, 164
Tanguay, Cyprien, 150, 234
Tardivel, Jules-Paul, 19, 32, 33, 43, 80, 190
tariff, 185, 194
Tarte, Israël, 17
Taschereau, Alexandre, 190, 194, 196, 238
Tassé, Henriette, 95
taxation, 88; on bachelors, 251; on Church property, 193, 209; on dogs, 28; property, 116, 161, 162
teachers, 10, 42, 211, 379; college, 191, 192; women, 91, 291, 292
Technical School, 77, 92, 186, 349n105
temperance. *See* alcohol
tenants, 116, 143, 162, 189; rights of, 67, 161
Théâtre National Français, 3, 30, 31, 44
theatre, 31, 77, 87, 92, 224, 239, Circé-Côté, 30, 129, 147, 148; criticism, 31, 71, 98, 122
theocracy, 231
Thérive, André. *See* Roger Puthoste
tolerance, 181, 238; of prostitution, 117, 217, 275, 277; religious, 181, 216, 246
Tolstoy, Léon, 118, 187, 188
Toronto, 131, 266, 288
tourism, 116
trade unions, 189, 299; Catholic, 205, 242; women and, 149, 297
Trades and Labor Congress of Canada, 32, 105, 187, 188, 192, 205, 212, 289; and *Le Monde ouvrier*, 90, 99; and women, 297
Traité de droit usuel (Marie Gérin-Lajoie), 26, 263
tramway, 28, 73, 75, 83–85, 89, 96, 108; strike, 287; and women, 294, 291
Trèves, Jacques 142
Tribu des casoars, 12, 118, 152
Tristan, Flora, 250
Trois-Rivières, 253

trusts, 107, 115, 178, 185, 186, 194, 230
tuberculosis, 58, 117, 183, 233
Tytgat, Louis, 29

ultramontanism, 121, 190, 191, 206, 229
unemployment insurance, 117, 133
unemployment, 104, 106, 107, 240; post-First World War, 115; 1930s, 148, 149, 156, 180, 286, 288, 300; women and, 276, 300–2
Union des femmes libérales, 300
Union nationale, 162, 163, 196
Union of Soviet Social Republics, 118, 187, 189, 303
United Church, 169
United States, 33, 77, 247; culture, 87, 247, 186, 228, 303n84; education, 54, 177; and the First World War, 104; immigration, 238, 241; women, 257, 279
Universitario, 142
University of Montreal, 262
University of Toronto, 55
university, 12, 211, 212, 226; women and, 55, 71, 261, 262, 308

Valois, Marcel, (Jean Dufresne) 94
Valois, Roger, 177
Van Loo, Esther, 142
Vanzetti, Bartolomeo, 188
Vatican, 104, 207, 208, 213, 230
Veillées du Bon Vieux Temps, 147
Vérité, La, 60, 63, 64
Verne, Jules, 21
Vézina, Ernestine (Medjé), 282
Viger, Louis Labrèche, 70
Viger, Square, 35, 75, 104
Vigie, La, 51, 71
Villa Anna boarding school, 7–9
Ville-Marie, 1915, 121, 123
Villeneuve, cardinal Rodrigue, 163, 166, 229
Villeneuve, Frédéric, 42, 59, 91, 92–94, 278

Villeray, 76
Vimy, 105
virility, 21, 101, 253, 277, 283, 286, 291
Voltaire, François-Marie Arouet, 41

wages, 84, 98, 148, 188, 250, 288; Circé-Côté, 278; depression and, 149; equal pay, 109, 135, 298; family, 149, 297, 300, 302; immigrants, 238, 241; wartime, 106, 107; women, 184, 263–65, 276, 291–92, *292*, 294, 297, 299
War of 1812, 4
Wartime Elections Act, 268
Webb, Beatrice, 183
Webb, Sidney, 183
Weber, Max, 286
Westmount, 32, 152, 153, 158, 236
Whig interpretation, 176
widows, 109; Circé-Côté, 69, 111, 152, 161
Wilhelm II, 180
Wilson, Woodrow, 104
Winnipeg, 187, 288
Women's Minimum Wage Commission, 184, 299
women's suffrage, 110, 112, 180, 189, 263–73, 305; Bills, 163; Bourassa and, 230; and the Catholic Church, 213, 214
Woolf, Virginia, 73
work, 285–91; civil service, 89, 301; clerical, 286, 294; domestic, 300; industrial, 293; manual, 157, 286; night, 295, 296; sexual division of labour, 293, 300; wartime, 107, 109; women's, 49, 96, 106, 109, 290–304, *292*, 379
working class, 28, 37, 88

xenophobia, 128, 156, 239–41

Zionism, 242, 243
Zola, Émile, 29, 51, 75, 306, 307